A Scottish Family Tale 1650-1950

- voyages in uncharted waters

Fay N. Simmonds-Peters

A Scottish Family Tale 1650-1950
voyages in uncharted waters

First published in Australia by Planarm Services Pty. Ltd 2020
www.scottishfamilytale1650-1950.com

Copyright © Fay Peters 2020
All Rights Reserved

 A catalogue record for this book is available from the National Library of Australia

ISBN: 978-0-9925686-2-7 (pbk)

Typesetting and design by Publicious Book Publishing
Published with the assistance of Publicious Book Publishing
www.publicious.com.au

No part of this book may be reproduced in any form, by photocopying or by any electronic or mechanical means, including information storage or retrieval systems, without permission in writing from both the copyright owner and the publisher of this book.

Dedication

It has been my privilege to tell this story
On behalf of all the brave sailors
Past, Present and Future.

Acknowledgements

Projects of this magnitude do not come together without the assistance and support of a great many people. Firstly, I would like to acknowledge the work of Emeritus Professor Chesley W. Sanger, University of Newfoundland, Dr. Eric Graham, University of Edinburgh, Scottish Historian Sue Mowat of Edinburgh and record my formal appreciation to them, and to the dedicated staff of the Universities, Archives, Libraries, Museums and historical sites visited in order to ensure that this story was as complete as records allow. Special mention needs to be made of the extraordinary work undertaken by Colin Walker and Colin Robertson for their tireless dedication to information gathering. Over the decades, several family members have contributed vast amounts of material with my most grateful thanks being extended to Madge Nickerson. In making this project a reality I acknowledge the considerable contributions made by Marilyn Astle, Janet Aisbett, Elaine Hamilton, Ailsa Doig, Mary Petrie and Jean Ffrench. Down the decades, the generosity of people has been outstanding, and so to all who have offered information, material items, direction or assistance - my most grateful thanks to each and every one of you. Lastly, to my long suffering and supportive friends and family – Thank You.

Table of Contents

Foreword i

Preamble iii

Historical Overview x

Introduction to the First Century - 1650-1750 1

Chapter 1 3
    Burgess & Freeman of Canongate
    Merchants & Craftsmen in Edinburgh
    Mastering Social & Religious Mores
    Surviving Disease Famine & Civil War

Chapter 2 29
    The Port of Leith • Privateering in the
    North Sea • Impressing - Smuggling
    Riots • The Darien Scheme & Wars
    Raging in International Waters

Chapter 3 86
    Prenuptial Agreements & Marrying
    Into the Business • Sailors Mariners
    Sea Captains Ship Owners • &
    Establishing a Maritime Legacy

Chapter 4 124
    The Arctic Whale Fishing Industry
    The Origins • The History • The Species
    The Seasons • The Grounds • The Skirmishes
    Scotland's Role & Government Incentives

Introduction to the Second Century - 1750 - 1850 159

Chapter 5 161
    The Men • The Ships • The Trade Routes
    Baltic & Archangel • Jamaica & West Indies
    Whaling • Spitzbergen Greenland Davis Straits
    The Montrose Whale Fishing Company

Chapter 6 250
    The Pre-Napoleonic French Connection
    Unarmed Arctic Whalers Vs Mighty French Navy
    A Courageous Tale of Capture Imprisonment
    Détente and Daring

Chapter 7 276
    Proceedings in the Admiralty Courts
    The Ransoming of the Eliza Swan
    America Vs Britain • Rodgers Vs Young
    It's a Whale of a Tale!

Chapter 8 322
    The End of Sail and the Beginning of Steam
    A New Family Paradigm Emerges
    Sons take Voyages to New Frontiers
    Maritime Adventure • Mercantile Plans

Introduction to the Third Century - 1850 – 1950 416

Chapter 9 419
    The Pirate Son • Rogue & Scoundrel
    Trail of Destruction Across the Oceans
    Scotland New Zealand and Australia
    Bigamy • Prison • Bankruptcy and More ....

Chapter 10 452
    The Model Son • Exemplar of Victorian Success
    Scotland England Siam Ceylon
    Enmeshed with Exotic Kings & Oxford Dons
    With Links to the Famous Physic Gardens

Chapter 11 491
    Transition • Sea Captain to Silk Manufacturer
    Darwin's Commandment & Religious Fervour
    Enduring Friendship & Business Partnership
    Son Husband Father Lay Preacher • Believer!

Chapter 12 550
    Seafaring Legacy • Six Generations & Going Strong
    Father & Son • Marine Engineers with Global Reach
    Ww2 Liberty Ships & Sinking of the Andrea Doria
    Pinnacle • Chairman American Bureau of Shipping

Conclusion 607
    Threads, Loose Ends and dispelling Myths

The following Addenda can be accessed on our website at:
www.scottishfamilytale1650-1950.com

1. Reading List
2. Glossary of Terminology
3. Young Family Charts
4. Regal Timeline for England & Scotland
5. People in this Story
6. Ships & Shipping Company Logos
7. Personal Items in Family Collections
8. Locations, Maps & Residences

Foreword

Fay Simmonds-Peters and I first became acquainted in the early days of internet genealogy when we connected online about a family we were both researching. We later collaborated on an article about our research. Although a few face-to-face meetings have occurred over the years, most of our contact has been by email, most recently when Fay sought volunteer beta readers for this, her second book.

I have thoroughly enjoyed reading about the lives and achievements of the Youngs and their kin in the chapters of *A Scottish Family Tale 1650-1950*. It is a pleasure to work with a fellow genealogist and family historian whose research and writing are of such a high calibre. Fay's curiosity about this Young family has persisted for decades as she searched for the pertinent elements of their lives. She also travelling to various locations in order to consult with experts in diverse fields. So, whether describing marine technology or the social and political conditions of their lives, Fay shows that she has prepared herself by immersion in these wide-ranging topics.

Whether you are drawn to this book because it is about your relatives or your community or because you have an interest in maritime history, the Arctic Whaling, Scottish history or Australian history or maybe because you too are a family historian looking for inspiration in telling your own family stories, an adventure awaits you in these pages. You will learn of the Young family characteristics that led to their success over a span of three centuries, first as land-based craftsmen and merchants then as seafarers, initially by sail then by steam, and finally in related 20th century occupations.

The author's flair for storytelling and passionate interest in the lives of her subjects reveals high drama at sea, ranging from international incidents to naval impressment to acts of out and out piracy. Individual personalities shine forth, notably in one generation where the model son and his rogue brother are contrasted. As a result, that combination of exhaustive research and narrative skill means that Fay Simmonds-Peters has managed to produce a work that will be consulted for generations to come.

Marilyn M. Astle, Ph.D.
Genealogist & Family Historian
Lethbridge, Alberta, Canada
15 January 2020

Preamble

It was 1980 when I first embarked on a journey to explore my own family's history. It all began quite innocently as an interest I could share with my elderly widowed mother, but little did I realise then that I would soon find myself seduced by the chase and what it could reveal. I quickly learned there were conversations never had with those who had already passed, and that my mother was now the keeper of the keys when it came to unlocking stories about her family and to some extent my father's family as well. I would soon learn this was true for all families, and that this incidental involvement heralded my metamorphosis into an enthusiastic self-designated family historian for my extended clan.

In terms of this particular book I must confess that over the last forty years, I have willingly whiled away many hours, days and even weeks - bunkered down in libraries and archives across the world, visiting significant places of interest or meeting up with close and distant family folk in an attempt to tease out those elusive and more intriguing details which are truly the essence of anyone's life story. For me the chase remains intoxicating and what's more I have come to the realisation that my personality and dogged determination are a perfect fit for such activity.

Often when I arrived at what seemed the end point, there was an unexpected twist, a richer bounty as it were; where somehow the truth revealed itself to be so much more than I ever could have imagined. In several instances I also found myself confronted with unpleasant detail surrounding dire outcomes. So, although it was not always a positive and pleasing discovery and life for some folks seemed harsh and cruel, it was, after all, their reality.

What my curiosity has taught me is that those people who leave a mark in this world appear determined to do so. They choose to stand a little taller, speak a little louder and definitely prefer to be noticed rather than slide through life under the radar. Whether their legacy is large or small; whether social, political, communal or familial; whether it came about because of their escapades or accomplishments, their business acumen or selfless contributions to their communities or cultures; or a combination of some or all of the above - leave a mark they most certainly did.

These marks, when discovered by any family historian, go a long way toward enriching the researcher's overall understanding of the true person and definitely enables the painting of a far more detailed, colourful and, dare I say, more realistic picture of the lives of these hitherto unknowns. Sadly, I feel far too many family researchers embark on their quest of discovery in the one-dimensional, colourless environment of names, dates and places. In fact, they are almost compelled to do so by the very format of how genealogy data is presented in today's technological world.

The advent of the Internet has widened avenues for discovery and numerous dedicated search engines support the burgeoning multi-billion-dollar industry that genealogy has become. More and more information is becoming available via the output of government initiatives to digitise their holdings for financial gain. The growth and evolution in this newly created 'pay to view' world over the past two decades, in particular, has been nothing short of astonishing. However, I would genuinely encourage everyone to seek out the hidden truths, to put more 'flesh on the bones' as it were, because then, and only then, can anyone fully experience the thrill of gaining a more expansive insight into the authentic life of any ancestor.

When I first contemplated telling the story of the Young Family whose origins are so very deeply rooted in Scotland, it was not the unique and famous Scottish aspect of Clan Culture that was the stand-out feature of their lives. Rather, it was my appreciation that this family had survived the blood-thirsty history which had pervaded every corner of Scotland, and I recognised the wit and tenacity they needed to possess in order to prevail economically and socially in a country whose history had run red with the blood of war and treachery for centuries. Despite this legacy, vestigial records show that they emerged victorious and they went on to prosper globally.

I have chosen to begin their story around 1650 and follow their memorable, often meteoric and sometimes dangerous journey all the way from 'Auld Reekie' – Edinburgh - to every point of the compass. Even before 1650 they are known to be active community members, working and giving back, God fearing to a man and all the signs are there that they functioned as a tight family unit. Their seafaring adventures came later and are predicated on a lingering and divergent association with all things maritime. It began in the harsh and challenging era of canvas and wood and ultimately carried generation after generation all the way through steam and steel to the modern era of WWII warships and beyond.

But there is so much more to tell.

In my hunt for clues I scoured a number of international repositories that offered up documentary evidence of some death defying adventures, risk-taking, legal fights all the way to the highest court in the land, great hardship, sad and sudden loss interposed with some well-deserved successes. Some of these Youngs proved themselves to be opportunistic, strategic, steely and even wily when circumstances dictated. My research told me that their survival during those very early days in Edinburgh demanded astuteness, conformity, integrity and honesty. From the outset, their seafaring days of plying trade routes to foreign lands called upon all these characteristics plus a whole new skill set focused on navigation, astronomy, meteorology and an understanding of international law, both maritime and general.

The fact that they succeeded at all in those fledgling years of the Merchant Navy bears witness to their seamanship, leadership and the empathy they showed for their men and their ships. It also stands as testament to their intellect in showing considered respect for their operating environment. Later, when exploring the social and commercial aspects of people's lives I came face to face with just how formidable their times were. Where this story starts around 1650, day-to-day life was a constant struggle and their mere survival depended on walking a very narrow tightrope controlled by others. They had to compete for burgess and brethren status as well as wrestle with conditional employment law designed and superintended by that inextricable power base of Church and State. They had to survive deplorably unsanitary living conditions and were obliged to carry arms in order to defend their city.

By 1700 they had embarked on a life at sea. After centuries as landlubbers, more recently as Baxter's and Tailors in Edinburgh, suddenly the oceans became their business arena, their ships became their offices, workplaces and part-time homes, and global ports were their new marketplaces. They had to learn how to withstand the unpredictability and torment of Mother Nature, as well as face up to the massive economic pressures arising from the growing and fierce international competition in the Whaling and Mercantile sectors. Overlay these hardships and challenges with the menace of Impressment and Privateering and we will soon see that mere survival became problematic for so very many.

Notwithstanding these erratic and hazardous times, the maritime seductress lured countless Young menfolk into the Merchant Navy and the Royal Navy. Many are known to have been sacrificed to the depths and one Captain Young is known to have fallen victim to a nefarious foreign Navy in the North Sea, but there are many more whose fates will forever remain a mystery.

For this Young Family, the end of the era of sail was a pivotal point not only in this family's maritime history but also in world history. It came with the dawn of the Industrial Age, completely without precedent, arriving as a storm set to turn the Young's world upside down and create a new family paradigm. It sounded the death knell to the Youngs' hitherto enduring careers under canvas and forced the closure of several family businesses. It was unquestionably a resounding low for the senior generation and would prove to be the family's greatest challenge yet.

But was it all doom and gloom?

The phenomenon that was the Industrial Revolution saw Merchant Shipping increase in importance as the distribution of manufactured goods and the movement of people took a dramatic upswing. Correspondingly, this generated a need for more ships and saw opportunities abound for the design and construction of new vessels. With this came an upswing in business for all shipwrights, both in the construction of new ships and the repair of damaged ones. Soon came the introduction of steam power and the use of iron and steel in shipbuilding, with associated advances in hull design. All of these factors combined to make sea travel faster and more reliable.

The upshot was that by 1819 steam powered vessels were no longer restricted to the rivers of Britain and Europe but could be seen undertaking longer ocean voyages. Exports and Shipping were underscoring manufacturing growth globally, and with trade routes expanding, the vastly up-scaled Maritime Industry became paramount to not only the growth of the British Economy, but to Scotland in particular, and was the catalyst for great prosperity for several enterprising individuals in this Young Family.

These all-encompassing changes in the maritime sector worldwide would have raised vexing questions for many. Likewise, I too began to wonder about its impact on the 'victim generation' financially, socially and personally. Also, what did it mean employment-wise for later generations who would have traditionally been assured of a job for life in the family's sailing business. Were the enduring seafaring escapades of their forefathers destined to linger only as the subject of dinner table conversation for a generation or two before being lost forever? Whatever the outcome, these Youngs would need to call upon all their reserves of every kind plus their undoubted skills, courage, nous and leadership ability to ride out this storm of change. Luckily for them, so far in their history all these qualities had remained unflagging.

As I delved deeper and deeper into the lives of certain individuals, an intriguing common thread emerged. The life choices they made were fine examples of a great sense of self, of confidence and pride, and in part were made possible by the respect the family had earned backed up by the level of education achieved. These defining life choices also extended to their selection of marital partners, the ships they sailed and the far-flung ports they visited. Not content to rest on their laurels, many individuals pursued achievement and self-improvement throughout their lives, and at the same time remained active in the social and commercial arenas within their communities.

Regardless of the global changes thrust upon countries and peoples, for these Youngs, the strongest single thread remained their evolving history in association with the sea. It began with Sealing and Whaling and later advanced to Mercantile, Brokerage and Marine Engineering. Their seafaring history alone is somewhat extraordinary and most certainly rare in today's world of change and diversity, where children are not so persuaded to 'follow in their father's footsteps'. Perpetuated generational family values and traditions are now less commonplace because families seem to have become far more transient, fractured and disparate.

When contemplating the Young's maritime activities, it was necessary to do so in the context of their times. For instance, today's enlightened world has quite a different view of Whaling and Sealing, and rightly so. Most modern day societies fully recognise the senselessness and pointlessness and, dare it be said, the utter stupidity of slaughtering these incredible mammals. But this family's deeds must be considered in the context of yesterday's world order: after all, Whale Fishing was government sanctioned, and at times vigorously encouraged by the payment of a substantial bounty. Whale by-products were seen as vital to the economies and lifestyles of countries right across the globe back then, much like coal mining and coal-fired power stations are a dilemma for today's societies.

Therefore, it was unequivocal that I should retain the simple phrase *'yesterday's world order'* front of mind as I pursued the last shreds of finer detail viewed as essential in order to answer the many outstanding questions. I understood that these changing times would be an appropriate backdrop to describing events that appear, on more than one occasion, to have resulted from governmental and environmental influences. Ironically, in so doing I realised that the changes in individual's profiles were more germane and understandable when taken in the context of their lives and times.

Over these past decades, apart from scouring the archives, it has been my good fortune to correspond with numerous academics and subject experts who are highly qualified and widely read on these topics and annals of history. On other occasions, I have had the pleasure to meet with some of these experts and enjoy the privilege of open discussion on historical seafaring, specific mercantile events and the exploits that have contributed to shaping the lives of several Young family members. To all these academics and experts, let me say I am most grateful for your generous contribution of time and knowledge.

In compiling this document, I have done my damnedest to sieve reality from fiction, actuality from assumption, and apply certitude to the earmarked events by only drawing on the most trusted material. Clearly, not every family member can be represented, but rather I intend to focus on the key players, the 'marker' men and women who were the game-breakers in their day. The one's who undeniably left their mark. In so doing, I hope to open a window into their lives which gives an appreciation of how they influenced or contributed to their times, their families, their industry, their communities and, in some cases, world history itself because, after all, life does not exist in a vacuum.

Finally, Science in the twenty-first century has offered the world new ways of exploring human origins and individual difference, and one hypothesis gaining momentum and acceptance is - what people are and who they become is all 'in their DNA'. Whilst I am keen to join in this conversation and to see for myself if this could truly be how traits and characteristics are handed down generation upon generation, I am not yet convinced. Is the answer really that simple? Are we totally pre-programmed and therefore compelled to completely cast off the notion of *'nature vs nurture'* in favour of that singular concept that it is 'in our DNA'?

Historical Overview

Before I even began to write their story I felt an imperative to put their lives into a spatial context politically, geographically and archaeologically. Having defined precisely what I needed to learn from the history books about the age leading up to where I could confidently begin, then the question became - how far back in history do I need to go? The absolute year was difficult to define; however, it seemed appropriate to delve until such time as a contextual framework for their life in Edinburgh could adequately be established. I was convinced that this precursor period was unequivocally important to consider since mankind as a whole had been in a constant state of transition for centuries, evolving socially and politically and those who did survive would wear the scars of those who went before. After all, to some extent we are all products of our environments as it were.

While it was not considered necessary to labour this point, it was considered essential to glean a greater insight into those historical events that had shaped the men and women of this family and determined the family's status, community situation, family values and to some extent their occupations. In arriving at this appreciation, experience told me two things – one, that life decisions are made more often in the context of past experience than in isolation; and two, by delving into the past one gains a fuller understanding of what truly constituted life for these citizens, because they were far more disenfranchised and enjoyed few of the freedoms we take for granted today. Therefore, in contemplation of their lives and the paths they chose, it became imperative to put ourselves in their shoes for a while. Only then can any one of us come to a full and frighteningly realistic

Historical Overview

understanding of the power of the Monarchy, Church and in more recent times, the Parliament, and the paralysing effect all of these entities had on the everyday lives of ordinary Scots – which includes these Youngs.

For the non-history buffs, here is a broad overview of English, Scottish and European history -

The Medieval Period across Europe covers those years from the Fifth to the Fifteenth Century when treachery, bloodshed and land grabbing proliferated. The fall of the Roman Empire and the rise of Christianity were the catalysts for some of the most barbaric man-on-man warfare ever recorded. Great wealth and power was seen to rest, on occasions, in the hands of a few, who established clans and kingdoms. Powerful family dynasties were born but many were short-lived as a new phenomenon called 'civil unrest' began to pervade. In mainland Europe, the chief perpetrators were the Saracens from the south, Hungarians from the East and the Vikings from the North. Scotland's history, in particular, is full of spine tingling tales of Viking led invasions.

While these battles were principally about land and power for the overlords, it was also a period when many with aspirations recognised the value of distinguishing themselves on the field of battle, and consequently set about to do so and win favour with their liege or chieftain. In recognition of their successes often they were awarded land and/or titles. In the case of Scotland, this gave rise to the likes of Clan Lands. For a while these ever-changing imaginary lines across the Scottish countryside determined the dynamic geography of that country, as it did for many other countries in Europe. Then, by the mid-point of the Medieval Period in Europe we begin to see the organisation of mankind take a new direction. This has often been referred to as the Medieval Warm Period, a time of the earliest known episode of climate change. Records clearly show that the seasons became warmer, rains more reliable, crops more successful and plentiful, which gave rise to the phenomena of Manorialism and

Feudalism; or the organisation of people into village life for the very first time in human history.

For Scotland, however, a slightly different picture emerged; one where competing Clans remained on a bloody war footing. Adding to this unrest, from the time of the death of Domnall II in 900 AD until the death of King Alexander III in 1286, invasion in Scotland was commonplace as disparate factions, namely the Anglo-Saxons and Gaels together with the Scandinavians, remained relentless in their quest for Scottish land. Eventually, the Gaelic Lords firmed their foothold in the east of Scotland then moved south and finally west and north. Meanwhile, across mainland Europe, the Gaels had already proved themselves dominant strategically and economically, thanks to their highly developed skills in organised agriculture together with their successful exploits in trade and money dealing.

Understandably, the Gaelic language too had become dominant across Europe, and this would prove an important factor for the Scots when future maritime trade routes were being established. However, the previously mentioned death of King Alexander III in 1286 put an end to any kind of hope for peace for the poor Scots for well over a century to come. On the contrary, it signalled the outbreak of hostilities in what we now know as the First Scottish Wars of Independence, and cuts to the heart of Scottish Culture. This was a protracted event but can be encapsulated this way:

Skirmishes persisted between the Scots and the English. Scot William Wallace was seen as the rising hope for leadership and achievement of independence for Scotland. He scores a spirit-lifting victory over the English at Stirling Bridge, but shortly afterwards was captured and tossed into the Tower of London. While a ransom was still in negotiation, the King of England issued a decree for him to be hung, drawn and quartered - an act that rightly outraged and greatly incited the Scots.

Next the Scots looked toward Robert the Bruce as their potential Saviour and for a time their prayers were answered. He scored several well-strategized and well-fought victories including the legendary events at Bannockburn; however, the Scots had underestimated the antagonistic Edward I who, without notice, granted the Scottish throne to one John Balliol. Needless to say, the Scots became increasingly irascible at the interference of England in Scotland's affairs and in order to regain control they appointed The Council of Twelve to rule Scotland. Then, in an attempt designed to outmanoeuvre the English King, the Scots set in train actions whereby The Council of Twelve negotiated and signed a Treaty with France who was at that time an arch-enemy of England. In retaliation Edward declared war on Scotland. Checkmate!

Ancestors of these Youngs and their fellow citizens would have suffered through the savagery that pervaded at these times. Then came yet another period of renewed instability. The death from dysentery of Edward I in 1307 saw his son, Edward II take the throne at the age of 23. His twenty-year reign came to an abrupt and somewhat mysterious and probably murderous end; and, whilst stories abound, the only certainty is that the truth will forever remain shrouded in conjecture. Thus, begins the reign of Edward III who was just 15 years of age when crowned and clearly at the mercy of a manipulative and powerful Royal Court.

Little did the Scots realise that for them it would be third time lucky. Edward III is regarded as one of the most successful Kings of Medieval Britain. Ruling for fifty years he oversaw developments in law and governance that would prove vital to the creation of the strong parliamentary system existing in the United Kingdom today and indeed has been adopted across much of the Commonwealth - commonly referred to as the Westminster System. However, even a cavalier King such as Edward III was found wanting when it came to abuse of power. At one point, Edward found himself in major disputation with the omnipotent Archbishop of Canterbury, in an environment where Church and State were still intrinsically intertwined. This put Edward in direct conflict with not only the Church, but also his own Parliament, whereupon he was forced to capitulate and strike an agreement in order to retain his sovereignty.

Towards the end of the Fourteenth Century in Scotland, Robert II takes over the Scottish throne as the first Stuart King, and once again there was an air of renewed optimism throughout the entire populace. Initially, these hopes appeared well founded as Scotland moved toward building stronger foundations for the future. Then, in 1390 Robert II died and his son John took the throne at the age of 50 as King Robert III of Scotland. The new century begins inauspiciously with a King who, in his memoir penned by Abbot Walter Bower, proclaimed himself to be 'the worst of kings and the most miserable of men'. Subsequently, modern day Historians too have described him as a failure like his father. And so, England and Scotland remained on a war footing and during the reign of Henry IV [1399-1413] there were significant Scottish battle losses to England at Nesbit Muir and Homildon Hill in 1402.

The most positive news coming from this period seems to be that Scotland regained ownership of the Orkneys from Denmark and the Shetlands from Norway. There was another light on the horizon, and this related to Education. In fact, throughout history, Scotland has led the way in Britain in terms of Education and some of the most impressive early milestones in Scottish Education relate to the creation of Universities in St Andrews and Glasgow. Shortly afterwards, in 1495, came the establishment of the University of Aberdeen. This Education Century, as I call it, concluded with the Scottish Parliament legislating the Education Act of 1496. This vanguard legislation was designed to compel Barons and Landowners to have their sons and heirs educated to set achievement levels primarily in Latin, Art and Law. The real intent was to improve legal process and devolve some of these responsibilities to a local level, thereby lessening the call by the Poor on the 'King's Purse'. So strident was it intended for this Act to be enforced, that a £20 fine (a very substantial sum for the time), was imposed on those Barons and Landowners who did not comply.

Just like the Scots of the time no doubt, I was beginning to feel all warm and positive about the future, but, like so many generations before them, the Youngs of the day were about to ride yet another roller-coaster of uncertainty. The dawn of the next Century brought with it yet another period of sustained and bitter conflict that would see England and Scotland locked in fierce battle once again. Beginning in 1513 James IV was killed at Flodden. His infant son James V inherited the throne, but he died of a nervous breakdown following the defeat of his forces at the Battle of Solway Moss in 1542. Next, Mary returned from France to take the throne in December 1542 under the law of 'cognatic primogeniture'. In 1548 Mary Queen of Scots travelled back to France and married Dauphin, a young French Prince, in order to secure a Catholic alliance against England.

Alas, in 1560 the Scottish Parliament legislated for Protestant Reformation and Scotsman John Knox is credited with the formation of the Church of Scotland. In 1561 the French Prince Dauphin died while still in his teens and Queen Mary once again returned to Scotland. She attempted to impose Catholicism, but this proved grossly unpopular with the majority of Scots and, in the face of strident and physical opposition she fled to England whereupon she found herself amid scandal and yet another royal family struggle for power. Queen Elizabeth I felt her monarchy was under threat since she and Mary were both Grand-daughters of Mary of Tudor. Firstly, Queen Mary was forced to abdicate the Scottish throne then shortly afterward Mary found herself arrested and incarcerated in the Tower of London.

Meanwhile, her 13-month-old son James VI was declared King of the Scots. As he grew to adulthood, educated and mentored by one Sir Peter Young, Scots in general were beginning to feel they finally had a liege who was demonstrating political intelligence and diplomacy in order to control the government. Eventually, it was he who united the crowns of Scotland and England when he was crowned James I of England in 1603 following the death of Elizabeth I. Elizabeth was the last of the Tudor Monarchs, and also James' Godmother and one in the same person responsible for having his mother, Mary, beheaded in the Tower of London.

A sidebar to Scotland's Religious Proclamation of 1560 is that Christendom had been at war with itself virtually since the beginning. The centuries-old Catholic versus Protestant antagonism had remained centre stage across England, Scotland and Ireland but it needs to be understood that since the reign of Henry VIII [1507-1547] the predominant religion to be embraced by the population at any point in Britain's history was always that decreed and followed by the monarch of the day. This de facto religious authority of the Crown, often with the support of

Papal good will and benefit when Catholicism prevailed, was not harmonious and was frequently the subject of scandalous gossip.

More relevant to this story, is that period of religious ebb and flow which coincided with the incidence of new religious thinking flowing out of Europe, bringing with it wider dialogue on Calvinism, Lutheranism, Judaism and Islam along with Catholicism and Protestantism. Scotland meanwhile was exploring, and in parts, embracing its own form of Celtic Christianity despite the risks to any person holding a view contrary to that of the ruling monarch. In this, the Young Family, like their neighbours, would have had to be fully mindful and cautious, as many a religious zealot and lay-preacher was beheaded or burned at the stake for openly voicing contrary beliefs. One very high profile example is Queen Mary who had been tried and convicted on two counts. One - treason, for supposedly plotting against Elizabeth, and two - for holding Catholic beliefs at a time when Elizabeth was directing her subjects to embrace Protestantism. Mary Stuart defied her cousin Queen on both fronts and paid the ultimate price of losing her head in the cause of the Pope and the Crown of England.

How does any of this relate to the Youngs, if at all?

It is relevant to point out that everyday citizens were not immune to the effects of such events; in fact, they suffered socially, religiously and personally because their survival and livelihood could turn on the whim of any one of these prognostic Monarchs. Those Young ancestors alive in that period would have been forced to ride this ebb and flow of life throughout this tumultuous period. Their story will demonstrate that families who became established and survived these treacherous periods of the Middle Ages and beyond, would have done so on their wits, wisdom and a fair degree of good fortune.

The long and sordid tale for these ancestors' experiences culminated in The National Covenant of the Church of Scotland drawn up and signed in Greyfriars Kirk, Edinburgh, in February 1638, and later adopted by the Scottish Parliament. This heralded a period of savage conflict where Charles I of England, who believed in the Divine Right of Kings, raised an army in protest and once again civil war erupted in England, Scotland and Ireland. It is estimated that over 127,000 non-combatants [Citizens - Burgesses - who were required to bear arms and are found cited in the Burgess Registers with various hand-guns to their names], including over 40,000 others [non-burgess citizens who were unarmed], were listed as casualties. But this time, not even the King was safe. Charles was arrested and tried for treason and under the authority of a death warrant signed by Oliver Cromwell, King Charles I was beheaded in the Tower of London in January 1649. Cromwell was proclaimed Lord Protector of the Commonwealth of England, Scotland and Ireland.

For a time in the early half of the 1600s The Covenanters were the *de facto* government in Scotland, which meant Presbyterianism was meant to prevail. However, this did not occur, nor did it quell the fighting between the Covenanter Presbyterian faction and the Royalists who were mostly Catholics and Episcopalians like the Youngs of the day. Overlaying this religious fighting was a legacy of cultural division in Scotland existing between the people of the Highlands and those of the Lowlands where respective Clan Leaders mostly determined religious preferences. The Lowland fighters proved no match for the fierce Highlanders who were much later described by Daniel Defoe as - 'inhumane and barbarous'.

After two decades of fierce and bloody fighting, 1652 saw the absolute defeat of the Covenanters. Images of these 'Killing Times' would have been indelibly etched into the memories of those who were there including members of this subject family. Today, there is a lasting memorial to this bloodshed - The Martyrs Monument Tablet in Greyfriars Kirkyard, Edinburgh. It survives for all to see and reads in part -

'Halt passenger,
take heed what you do see.
This tomb doth shew for
what some men did die'.

Few statistics exist for these wars but most scribes, including Daniel Defoe, estimate that over 18,000 Scots, comprising Covenanters and their supporters, died as a result of these bloody religion-based Civil Wars that continued until 1680. Many thousands more were transported to the colonies or elected to depart their homeland for a new life of religious freedom in the Americas. Were there Young forebears caught up in this? Definitely! Throughout these years there is evidence that these Youngs and their related families were residing as Burgesses in Edinburgh before relocating to the nearby Port of Leith.

Now it is time to take up their story ....

Introduction -
In the Beginning 1650-1750

'We look to Scotland for all our ideas of civilisation ...'
Voltaire [1694-1778]

*'Of all the small nations of this earth,
perhaps only the ancient Greeks surpass the Scots
in their contribution to mankind'*
Winston Churchill [1874-1965]

As you can see from the above quotations, many non-Scots have acknowledged that this relatively small country has enjoyed an enviable position in the global community from a time well before the Middle Ages. Her people have been admired for their wit, their sagacity, their fighting prowess as well as their providential outlook on life. The question is – do these core national characteristics shine through in this Young Family?

Given scant personal family records survive from this 1650-1750 period for the majority of non-titled citizens of Scotland, we have to rely on the annals of Scotland's history to provide the framework to position these ancestors in their rightful places. Various relevant events have been chosen to showcase aspects of society, politics, religion and employment in this century, and to thus open a window into their reality and their world. After all, we can only appreciate the end game when we know the starting point.

Clearly, this was a time when life was very different from what we can relate to in our own daily lives. More importantly, for those of us who are neither students of Scottish History nor raised in Scotland, these lessons are critical to our absolute appreciation and understanding of not only the lives of these early generations but more importantly the generations who followed.

A Scot and fellow resident of Edinburgh around this time, David Hume [1711-1776], once wrote *'Nothing is more surprising than the easiness with which the many are governed by the few.'* This gives a poignant summation to life in this century for these Youngs and their fellow Scots.

In the beginning 1650-1750

Chapter 1

**Burgess & Freeman of Canongate
Merchants & Craftsmen in Edinburgh
Mastering Social & Religious Mores
Surviving Disease, Famine & Civil War**

Today Edinburgh is a vibrant sophisticated City moving to a pulse largely determined by its trade, commerce and politics; in fact, much as it has done down the centuries. Its history and architecture have had a pervasive effect on its cityscape. Prevailing against the elements, Edinburgh stands proud, forcing an awareness of yesterday which is impossible to ignore. Modern day visitors experience a consciousness of a city which is both cruelly historic and at the same time beautiful and enduring. This dichotomy creates a need to stop and take it in, to retrogress to its more tempestuous past regardless of how uncomfortable or confronting that place and sight may be.

The crumbling Kirk on the Brae that once stood guard over the City is now charged with the youthful energy of those who flock to revel in its history, marvel at its relics and embrace its educational offerings. Whilst Edinburgh is one of the most conducive and spiritually enriching environments anywhere in Britain, intrinsically we also know that this City is, as it has been for centuries, the political powerhouse of Scotland. There are also several shrouded images lurking to arrest and surprise the visitor; they are the old and weather worn plaques and seemingly obscure monuments strategically located which bear testament to a bygone era and survive as reminders of some poignant moments in that City's turbulent past. There are ragged remnants outlining the skyline, some as large classic fragments protruding from hilltops while others are found boldly embellishing new builds, standing resplendent and tastefully integrated into these new constructs in celebration of the City's past wealth and current sophistication. But Edinburgh has not always been such a grand and incontestably plenary City.

Down the centuries this staunchly matriarchal Royal Burgh of Edinburgh has endured considerable scorn not only from its own inhabitants but from fellow Scots right across Caledonia. Much blood has been shed and much pain and suffering inflicted by this City on its own inhabitants, its neighbours and indeed the rest of Scotland. To have been alive in this most bloody period in Scottish history and to have survived to witness the evolution of Edinburgh in particular, would have been challenging on many fronts. But survive and remain this Young Family did for well over three centuries, and no event in Edinburgh would have been more arresting than that of the notorious 'Black Dinner'. This sordid tale sees the powerful Douglas Clan of the Lowlands taking centre stage in a story of treachery and bloodshed as barbaric as any Polanski movie. This incident occurred in 1440 and involved Sir William Crichton, the then Lord Chancellor of Scotland.

Acting on behalf of his Stewart King, ten-year old James II, Crichton invited sixteen-year old William Douglas, 6th Earl of Douglas, and his younger brother to dine with the child King. The blood-curdling script for that evening unfolds like this – Earl William Douglas and his brother were partaking of a luxurious dinner when a severed and bloody black bull's head, a symbol of death, was presented on the table before them. At this point their imminent danger would have become very apparent to the young Douglas boys and their sense of tension and fear would have sent their pulses racing in disbelief at the peril they were facing. They were subsequently dragged out of Edinburgh Castle and, on Castle Hill, after a mock trial, the young boys were callously beheaded. All this because of the perceived threat their family may have presented to the Stewart Liege on account of the significant power and popularity the Douglas Clan enjoyed.

In 1452 a similar murder was perpetrated on another William Douglas, this time the 8th Earl of Douglas, and again after a promise of safe passage. Culpability for these cruel and duplicitous misdeeds by a few, were blanketed on the entire Edinburgh population. This villainous event has been immortalised in explicit lyrics that record for all time the disdain the Scottish countryside held for the murderous City of Edinburgh which, by default, would have included our Young family. The lyrics read in part -

> *Edinburgh Castle, towne and tower,*
> *God grant thou sinke for sinne;*
> *An' that even for the black dinner*
> *Earle Douglas gat theirin.*

There are scant surviving written records from which to unequivocally reconstruct a detailed dossier of the very earliest families of Scotland (except for those of the nobility) however what has become clear is that this Young Family inhabited Edinburgh well before 1650, but this is approximately the year where we can confidently begin their ancestral story. Thus, some members of the family had, with craft and good fortune, survived the numerous events of war and pestilence, including the 1645 outbreak of the 'Black Death' or Bubonic Plague that reportedly claimed up to half of the population of Britain, including a third of greater Edinburgh. Undoubtedly, this would have touched every family in some way and wreaked untold personal and financial hardship on all of that City's inhabitants. Combine this with the well-chronicled religious struggles courtesy of The Covenanters plus the political struggle for realm and regal power once Scotland's own James VI was residing in Westminster; and Edinburgh's citizens, including the Youngs, would have been innocent bystanders to many a calamity.

1650, it seems, was quite a momentous year. Edinburgh's inhabitants of the day firstly witnessed the execution by hanging of James Graham, 1st Marquis of Montrose; then they were consumed with dread and uncertainty as Oliver Cromwell and his troops scored that lamentable victory at the Battle of Dunbar in the September of that year. The aftermath of this would see the Scots forced to surrender Edinburgh, its port of Leith as well as Edinburgh Castle. Such actions no doubt engendered fear in the local community and visited financial hardship on local businesses, merchants and shipowners which had a flow-on effect for the entire populace.

Cromwell wasted no time in asserting his military dominance, exercising regal power by imposing and collecting taxes and resorting to thinly veiled extortion, in order to accommodate and provision his war wearied Army. Then there was a very frightening event, a terrific blaze which threatened both the life and livelihood of those inhabitants living in and around Holyrood Palace. In the day, many of the commercial and farm buildings were extremely fire prone; some were byre-houses constructed of hand-hewn timber, other dwellings were cruck-framed houses of wattle, turf, clay and stone. But more significantly, Holyrood Palace had been the centrepiece of regal life in Scotland for centuries and once again the citizens of Edinburgh were confronted with a scene of black horror. They were forced to watch as the Palace was set aflame. It sustained substantial damage which was directly attributed to Cromwell's soldiers garrisoned within.

Around this time, there were some particularly arresting political and parliamentary events unfolding which would have impacted the lives and businesses of people right across Britain. The period 1649-1660 is termed The Interregnum or Commonwealth of England, and because Ireland and Scotland were currently both in the possession of England thanks to Cromwell and his military successes, it encompassed them as well. Liegeless Cromwell, the self-proclaimed 1st Lord Protector of the Commonwealth, was firmly entrenched at its head and wielding immense power. In fact, Oliver Cromwell is probably the only man in history to have refused to accept the Crown of England. Instead, Cromwell's preference was to use his omnipotent license to manage affairs of state more along the lines of a Republic, a foreign concept to Commonwealth citizens. Given his autocratic behaviour and without a successor designate, it is therefore understandable that Cromwell's untimely death in 1658 heralded yet another period of great instability and uncertainty. Despite ructions in the Royal Court and in the Parliament in London, curiously, the administration of Edinburgh remained firmly in the grip of the Edinburgh Town Council which in turn was managed by the Burgesses of that City.

This brings us to the curious and complicated circumstances surrounding the title of Burgess, which appears to have had its origins way back in the eleventh century. In the case of Edinburgh, the Burgess Class were constituted of Merchants and Craftsmen with the Merchants being larger in number of prime appointees; that is to say, the Merchants held all the strategic positions of power within the local administration such as Magistrates, Provosts and Town Councillors. And, with subsequent positions being elected by the outgoing office-bearers, records indicate that success in appointment was largely restricted to the descendants of the wealthier merchant families, their in-laws and their apprentices. This inclusion of apprentices may seem at odds with modern day intuition, but in this era, apprenticeship was far more valued and important strategically and socially, especially when explained in the context of marriage.

For these generations of Youngs, marriage and indeed the choosing of a spouse became a social and economic imperative for two reasons. One, it was written in law that no man could become a Burgess without being married. Two, it was written that by marrying the master's daughter an apprentice could ensure a 'fast track' entry to Burgess and Guild Brethren status. These conditions applied equally to both Merchants and Craftsmen alike; however, Craftsmen were required to walk a longer and more complicated road than Merchants. First, craftsmen served either a five or seven-year apprenticeship depending on their chosen 'trade'. They were subsequently required to work at their trade or craft for an additional three years before achieving Burgess status; with a further three years to be served before achieving Guild Brethren status or Deacon. With apprenticeships commencing at around age twelve years and with life expectancy being around thirty-five to forty years, marrying the master's daughter was most assuredly an attractive option.

It is interesting here to note three further unique and equally important factors in relation to becoming a Burgess. Firstly, a person's religion was not a determining factor in achieving Burgess status, which is most unusual in this era of religious zeal; secondly, almost three-quarters of the men so designated inherited burgess status from their father or father-in-law, and lastly, and perhaps the most important factor of all, a Burgess had to reside within the City Walls. In fact, there are numerous records demonstrating where direct threats were made to revoke the Burgess status of anyone who tried to flout this third rule. At a time when it was quite common to be living in one place and working in another; and, given that the distances involved were only a couple of miles at most, it seems grossly controlling and somewhat unfair. Evidence of this Rule being threateningly applied is plentiful. The following example can be found in the Burgess Register for 1674. It reads -

> '22 July 1674. The which day compeared Alexr. Mathieson and John Steuart, wrights, burgesses in Edinburgh, indwellers in Leith, who hes been fyned this day be the Toum councell for buying bargans of Timber and Retaining the same at Leith albeit they be not Residenters in Edr...unless they have their actuall Residence at Edr. and that under the Tincell of their liberty as burgesses and payt. of the respective penaltys contained in the acts of councell ....'.

As Edinburgh merchants and craftsmen looked to grow their business opportunities, it is natural to presume that this economic expansion would push these acceptable geographical boundaries wider. It took quite a long time, decades in fact, but sanity eventually prevailed as later records of the Edinburgh Commissary Court reveal that this rule was eventually relaxed and thankfully for some Young forebears, it became less relevant towards the end of the seventeenth century. This would have been especially important for those Youngs who are known to have latterly married into merchant and seafaring families from Leith. And, given their occupational changes the obvious next move for several of the Youngs, especially those embarking on a maritime career, was to permanently decamp from Edinburgh. It appears the first family member to do so was probably Robert Young [1723-1797].

Precisely how long the Young Family had been resident in Edinburgh is not proven conclusively. What is proved, is that these Young ancestors and their related families were Burgesses in Edinburgh and Leith pre 1650, and that they maintained this status for several generations to come. As far as the genealogy is concerned, it will be incredibly difficult for any researcher to identify precisely who was the first man of this family to attain this status or how it was achieved, because sadly, Burgess Records are not sufficiently definitive, nor do they survive far enough back in history for any researcher to be 'certain beyond reasonable doubt' of any person listed in the records.

This is so because of the Scottish Naming Protocol. Whilst this is helpful in identifying one Young Family from another, it makes identification within any one family more fraught. Also, had the family practice been to include a second christian name, that would have been a helpful identifier; but alas this was not a common practice in Scotland in this century. To complicate matters further, the Youngs adherence to the Naming Protocol gives rise to the situation where the same christian name was perpetuated by several lines in each generation which means it is quite common to unearth records for multiple people with the same christian and surname and the same occupation alive in the same parish in the same time-period. The upside to this behaviour; is that it is thanks to these naming rituals the one person we can be certain of is Robert's grandfather, David Young [1650-1706]. Why so? Well, bearing in mind this Scottish naming tradition can present both a challenge and a benefit at different times, it certainly remained a strong consideration when endeavouring to accurately identify that the nominated David Young, Baxter [Baker], is in fact the bona fide ancestor and grandfather of our Robert Young.

On exploring the Canongate Parish Marriage Records, it was discovered that a David Young, Baxter, had married one Margaret Thomson. Then, in attempting to apply the child naming test as a means of verification, the next step was to turn to the Baptismal Register for the same parish and establish a family group. In this case, the names were as expected plus the names of both parents were included in full for all seven children. This is not always the case and is dependent on the whim of the Parish Clerk who is the person responsible for such record keeping. Frequently, parish records are found to be lacking in detail, others grossly inaccurate; but, in this instance one could rightly surmise that these two parents were well known to the Parish Clerk, as their names are also spelt correctly and identical in every instance. This is a luxury not always enjoyed by researchers, especially in this era when spelling was approached phonetically.

The vital connection came with a previous discovery relating to a John Young christened on the 22 February 1680, son of David Young, Baxter and Margaret Thomson. Could this be the same John Young, Baxter, father to Robert baptised 26 May 1723? Another vital clue was contained in the Marriage Register for this John Young and Margaret Dick wherein John Young was identified as 'Baxter Burgess and Freeman of the Canongate'. It had previously been established that several generations later, another John Young, Captain John Young [1811-1871] had decided to take the family naming tradition of his father and grandfather one step further wherein he would immortalise some of his earlier ancestors by incorporating both their christian and surname into the names of his children. This proved to be the final piece in the puzzle - that third piece of evidence I always advocate. In this case, Captain John Young and his wife Mary Donaclift had named nine of their ten children after ancestors from both sides- Alexander Donaclift Young, Francis Spittal Young, Liston Wilcox Young, Joshua Richmond Young and of course their first-born daughter was Margaret Thomson Young in memory of John's third great grandmother.

What else has been learned about this David Young [1650-1706]?

Records show that he began his apprenticeship on 3 June 1663 and served his time as a Baxter with John Anderson.

This record identifies him as David Young son of George Young. David serves out his time and marries at the end of his apprenticeship whereupon he is then listed in The Register of Marriages 1595-1700 for Edinburgh as David Young, Baxter, marrying Margaret Thomson on 26 Jun 1673. One further entry of interest in the Register of Apprentices 1666-1700 shows that David Young subsequently took on a young apprentice in 1678.

Are there other records which can tell us more about David Young's parents especially in terms of perhaps their character, social position or life prospects?

Turning to the Parish Records, we see he was christened on the 11th day of January 1650 at Canongate Parish Church and his parents are identified in the register as George Young and Anna Watson. But what connects these families, if anything? Well, Anna's father, John Watson, was a tailor by profession, as was George's father. Anna's parents were married in the Holyrood Palace Church, as were David's parents, George Young and Anna Watson. From this evidence it is fair to suggest these families were quite well known to each other. Holyrood Palace Church in their day was what would later be known as the Parish of Canongate. This parish is strategic, central, and very significant to several generations of the Young family and happens to include the precincts of Holyrood Palace and the Scottish Parliament. Therefore, there is evidence that at one point in history these families both resided and plied their crafts in the beating heart of Edinburgh. Further information in respect of their status came to light in The Commissariot Records of Edinburgh, Register of Testaments for the period 1601-1700 where the entry in respect of the Will of Anna's mother reads 'Walkinschaw, Katherine, sometime spouse to John Watson, tailor, burgess of Edinburgh 10 Jan 1629'. [This entry also highlights a peculiarity of Scottish Marriage Law by which women retain their maiden names after marriage.]

A full transcript of Katherine Walkingschaw's [sic] Will has been made. This document speaks volumes when considered in the context of 1629; a time when women, married or single, were without status and not entitled to hold or own property. It is also extremely enlightening for other reasons. One, it boasts Lords and Ladies as debtors; and two, the sum owed is the princely amount of £784.3s.4d. The Cautioner in this instance was James Stewart, Tailor, Burgess in Edinburgh and no doubt a contemporary of Katherine Walkinschaw's husband John Watson. Now, to put this 1629 sum in the context of income value in 2017 it would be equivalent to a staggering £4.23 million; or stated as the sum equivalent to the economic power value of that income it would extend to some £44.09 million. By any definition this was a family of substantial means.

It is opportune here to discuss the actual title of Burgess and the importance for anyone to strive to achieve this level of skill and social recognition. Burgess was a title that designated a certain status and carried privileges within a Burgh community. As previously stated, it applied to both Merchants and Craftsman. Baxter's at that time were considered as 'craftsmen' not as 'merchants'. They could attain Burgess status via the previously described methods and/or as decreed under an Act of Parliament as set out in the legislation of 1583. However, what this earlier legislation makes very clear is the strong social, commercial and political divide between Merchants and Craftsmen in Scotland. This law goes to the heart of any family's status, repute and dare it be concluded - opportunity. Extracts of this law are referenced in an article entitled *'Ratification of the decreet arbital between the merchants and craftsmen of Edinburgh'*. While in total it is a difficult and laboured document this small excerpt cuts to the heart of the implications.

It reads inter alia -

> 'At Edinburgh on 19 June 1583, in the presence of the lords in council .... [who] have ordained and ordain the said act and decreet arbital to be inserted and registered in the said books .... Here follows the tenor of the said decreet arbitral: At Hollyroodhouse on 22 April 1582, we, ... indwellers of the said burgh, on that other part, and the right, potent and illustrious prince, James, by the grace of God, king of Scots, our sovereign lord,

arbitrator and oversman communally chosen by advice and consent of both the said parties, concerning the removing of all questions, differences and controversies which are or have been between the said merchants and craftsmen ..... have all in one voice accorded and agreed upon the heads and articles following: first, to take away all differences which have been heretofore concerning the persons who had the government of the town, their number, power or authority and manner of election, it is finally concorded, decreed and concluded thereupon as follows: the magistrates and office men, such as provost, bailies, dean of guild and treasurer, to be in all time coming of the estate and calling of merchants, according to the acts of parliament; and if any craftsmen exercising merchandise shall for his good qualities be promoted thereto, in that case he shall leave his craft and not occupy the same by himself nor his servants during the time of his office, and shall not return thereto at any time thereafter until he obtain special licence of the provost, bailies and council to that effect. The council to consist of ten merchants, to wit, the old provost, four old bailies, dean of guild and treasurer of the next year preceding and the other merchants to be chosen yearly to them, and also to consist of eight craftsmen thereof, six deacons and two other craftsmen, making in the whole the said council eighteen persons; and this by the office men of that year, to wit, the provost, bailies, dean of guild and treasurer. And as to the manner of the election, it is first generally accorded and concluded that no manner of persons be chosen provost, bailies, dean of guild or treasurer, suppose they be burgesses of the burgh and able thereof, unless they have been a year or two upon the council of before; and concerning the council, the old manner of giving in of tickets by the deacons out of the which the two craftsmen were yearly chosen to be abrogated, discharged, cease and expire in all time coming, so that the said two craftsmen shall be chosen yearly without any giving in of tickets indifferently of the best and worthiest of the crafts by the said provost, bailies and council only; and none to be of the council above two years together, unless they be office men or by virtue of their offices be on the council.'

This extract underscores the curious circumstance for all craftsmen like the Youngs who, in fact, were subject to even more restrictions than their fellow Merchants. Firstly, Guild Deacons could only be elected from the various Craft Guilds and from those nominees who had served a minimum of two years as Masters of their craft. This implies that the taking of apprentices was one step on the ladder to becoming a Guild Deacon. Secondly, one could only take on the office of Deacon for a maximum period of two years. A craftsman was designated as anyone pursuing one of fourteen nominated occupations, the constitution of which appears, in part, somewhat at odds with today's occupational values. These occupations are - surgeons, goldsmiths, skinners, furriers, hammer men [blacksmith], wrights [shipwrights], masons, tailors, bakers, butchers, shoemakers, weavers, fullers [those using fuller's earth to remove the oil and lanolin from wool ahead of the spinning and weaving process] and bonnet-makers.

Curiously, Baxters at one point were considered the highest ranked of the crafts and their motto was 'Floreant Pistores' or 'May the Bakers Flourish'. In *The History of Edinburgh*, Book IV and the Chapter headed *'Of Arts and Companies'*, it seems Baxter's had organised themselves into a Company prior to 21 March 1522 when a grant came from the Common Council of the City which shows them as a Society being empowered to grind their corn at the Town's Mills. While we may consider a Baxter or Baker not a high status trade today, in their day Baxters such as these early Young ancestors obviously carried far more status and respectability than other craftsmen. For the earlier generations of Youngs who were working as Tailors, their craft origins are traceable to an altar in the Church of St Giles pre 1500. A history of their craft states in part 'contenandt certane Statutis and Rewles devisit be thame, to be affirmit be us, for the loving of God Almichty, the Honour of the Realme, and Worschip and Profit of this gude Toune, and the Profit of all our soverame Lordis,

Lieges, and utheris...'. [Best read with a Scottish twang!]. David's son John Young was not only a Baxter and Burgess, but his Will identifies him as 'sometime Deacon of the Baxter's of Edinburgh', so he achieved the highest level of status and respectability available to his craft and class in his lifetime.

Notwithstanding all of that, there was one further restriction that makes the value to craftsmen aspiring to Burgess status a little difficult to comprehend. This restriction provides that craftsmen who are nominated and voted to Burgess status do not and will not have either leet or voting rights in the selection of the higher office positions within the Burgh such as Provost, Baillie, Councillor, Deacon, Dean of Guild or Treasurer. As a point of clarification, 'leet' in the Scottish language has a unique meaning and refers to an entitlement to nominate a person as a candidate for higher office. It would therefore follow that those craftsmen who do achieve such Deacon or Dean status required the endorsement of local merchants in order to be nominated and voted to the positions of Deacon or Dean of Guild. From this, it could be further inferred that those such as John Young abovementioned, who achieved Deacon status, were deemed not only to be leaders in their craft but leaders in their communities and of better character and social standing; at least in the eyes of the Merchants of the day who nominated them.

The over-riding benefit to these craftsmen, for becoming a Burgess in a Burgh such as Edinburgh, was it gave them the entitlement to trade free of taxes in that Burgh. All those non-Burgess merchants and craftsmen resident in Edinburgh, along with those who were Burgess of another Burgh but wished to trade in Edinburgh on Market Day, were all required to pay a tax for the privilege of doing business. Whilst it might be contended that these circumstances were draconian, this Act remained in force until 1834 when it was finally reformed.

Another financial benefit and market advantage for this David Young and his fellow Burgess in Edinburgh would most certainly be that Edinburgh was a Royal Burgh and one of the wealthiest in Scotland. This Royal status afforded two things; one, that on Market Day the Burgh of Edinburgh could impose hefty tolls and taxes on traders coming into the City from outlying settlements including Leith; and two, that Edinburgh Burgesses had the exclusive right to trade with foreign countries. For those who attempted to be 'too entrepreneurial' there were severe penalties and even direct threats. The Scottish Record Society Roll of Edinburgh, Burgesses and Guildbrethren 1406-1841 gives clear indications of the rigour with which this rule was enforced. Turning to the year of 1705, there is a notation on the 9 Jan which states 'Patrick Wilkie and Archibald Hamilton, merchants in Leith, be thir presents binds and oblidges them and each of them while they live or reseid in Leith that they shall not hereafter deall in forraigne trade under the penalty of five hundred merks Scots to be payde be each of them, in caise of failyie attour being oblidged imediately thereafter to come and reseid at Edr'.

Thanks to the successful lobbying by Edinburgh's elite and powerful Merchants, Leith was not only illegally deprived of its Royal Burgh status, but Leith's merchants and craftsmen were precluded from doing business with foreign traders. This for a port town, and indeed <u>the</u> port for Edinburgh, was a ludicrous situation. In the end, that rule was flouted by many and is one prime example of the extreme and punitive impediments Edinburgh would impose on Leith down the centuries. As this Young Family tale progresses, family members move from Edinburgh to Leith, and that is when this deprivation becomes relevant and personal. Meanwhile, there is much more to be told about the overlording of Edinburgh on its near neighbour and primary port town of Leith. For the longest time Leithers would be faced with this persecution and adversity as a day-to-day struggle. On the other hand, for Edinburgh's ruling class, it was all about power and greed!

For good or ill, we find David Young firmly entrenched as part of the Burgess and Guild fabric of Edinburgh, albeit without 'leet'. What is certain is that serving an apprenticeship and then establishing a business in any craft or trade, remaining buoyant and maintaining a family would have been as difficult then as it is today. History books describe the decades of the mid to late seventeenth century as being overshadowed by famine and disease, interspersed with bad seasons and poor harvests. Add to this the Cromwellian factor and it is fair to say the Merchants and Craftsmen had to carefully manage their businesses in a constantly fluctuating market, overshadowed by periods of severe economic depression and stress. These occurrences of famines and plagues would have not only seen Burgesses fall victim, these deaths would have the flow-on effect of restricting the availability of places for future apprentices. The extreme impact of just one of these adverse seasonal events is attested to in a quote in the 1675 Burgess Register for Edinburgh wherein it highlights the dire predicament for all the citizens of Edinburgh on this occasion. It reads '28 July 1675 No council this day in respect of the fast for the great drouth.'

This indicates that conditions in Edinburgh were very grim indeed and demanded extreme action. It is incredible to comprehend that all the citizens of a major trading city would be compelled to fast for an entire day and that commerce was forced to be abandoned in order to attempt to deal with catastrophic food shortages brought about by a prolonged drought. Modern visitors to Edinburgh would be glad for a day without rain and drizzle in a City which charts a monthly average of +50mm and whose residents frequently use the word drear to describe Edinburgh skies and precipitation. I wonder what our Climate Change Scientists would make of this point in climate history.

It is now time to turn our thoughts to life on the street for the Youngs and their fellow residents of Edinburgh. We need to learn something of what Edinburgh looked, smelt and sounded like as a City way back then. What were everyday living conditions like for David Young and his neighbours? What issues and conditions would they have faced in going about their daily lives?

Some of the answers can be found in an interesting article entitled *'Life and Death in Old Edinburgh'* which provides a citizen's vivid insight into life on the street in Old Town. At the time of Union in 1707 it says that Edinburgh was reputed to be one of the largest cities in population terms anywhere in Britain, but it was known by the unflattering nickname of 'Auld Reekie' or 'Old Smelly!'. In another very unflattering article Edinburgh is described as a very dirty place. But why was this so?

Well, theories abound but perhaps the most disgusting of all concerns the disposal of human waste. It was common practice to throw such matter out of the windows of the upper levels of the tenements with a warning cry of 'gardy loo!' ("gardez-l'eau", or 'watch out for the water'). Presumably this was done to alert unsuspecting pedestrians walking on the 'ladder' stairs or along the street below. This *'Life and Death in Old Edinburgh'* article goes on to state that although some residents built closets (toilets), these jutted out over the streets, which simply meant that excrement fell directly below, presumably without the benefit of a warning cry. In conjuring up an image of the sight and smell on those streets one would have to concede that Edinburgh's seemingly cruel nickname was probably justly deserved.

Knowing what we do today about hygiene, this scenario as a way of everyday life just seems too unsanitary to contemplate and could account for the numerous episodes of disease and plague which ravaged the population on and off for decades. These incredible conditions become even more incongruous when it is realised that for the most part the residents relied on the rain to wash the streets clean. What then in times of drought, one wonders? It is further written that 'When dealt with at all this waste was deposited in Nor Loch the current site of the Princes Street Gardens'. It is frightening to imagine that this cesspool also served as a water resource for many. The more fortunate citizens drew their water from public wells located up and down the Royal Mile. Meanwhile the rich folk paid 'caddies' to fetch barrels of water which were delivered to their homes.

In the beginning 1650-1750

Those familiar with Edinburgh will recall it as a hilly City in parts and those who ventured wider would have trudged her steep ladder/stairways and cobblestone streets. The question then arises as to what role did her rugged topography play in the social and commercial development of Edinburgh?

In geographical terms, the earliest surviving map of Edinburgh City defines it as constituting some 140 acres of quite undulating land, which by the beginning of the Seventeenth Century had become totally enclosed by defensive fortifications known as the Flodden and Telfer Walls. The flatter portions of this 'enclosure land', as it was termed, were given over to basic agriculture such as the growing of crops for both humans and animals with some areas reserved for natural pasture upon which livestock were grazed. For those who are not familiar with this City, Edinburgh is often described as having been built on seven hills, as perhaps a vague comparison to Rome. The best-known remnant outcrop is the jagged and steep sided Castle Rock, which to this day remains one of Edinburgh's best-known landmarks. Once that early agrarian settlement began to mature into a more modern town, a road system for horse and cart traffic became established. This necessitated the building of several bridges to accommodate the massive and frequent height changes in the local topography. For the twenty-first century pedestrian remnants of those very steep staircases or 'ladders', which join certain streets, can still be traversed in Old Town.

As Edinburgh's population grew its walled confines placed incredible demands on the land footprint available for residential housing. As a result, it became imperative to utilise some of the steeper slopes for housing, which in turn created the necessity to design buildings of a multi-storcy construct way in advance of modern architecture. Dwellings of eleven and up to fifteen stories were built in such a way that they have been described as clinging to the sides of some of the very steepest hillsides. One foreign visitor wrote that Edinburgh was an uninviting city with a 'maze of narrow, squalid side streets, flanked by high stone tenements, which plummeted down the hillsides ...'. Today, most of the historic city walls have been lost to time and almost all the very early tenements have been lost too; replaced in the Nineteenth Century by much grander Victorian buildings.

An obvious downside to this concentrated living was that Edinburgh's 'very densely populated environment provided perfect conditions for the spread of disease, and epidemics of infectious and contagious illnesses periodically swept through the city. Known at the time as the plague or the pest, diseases included typhus (carried by lice), typhoid (spread in water), bubonic plague (spread by fleas on rats) or simply diarrhoea, known as flux.' The worst of these outbreaks is known to have lasted for several years. One such prolonged event began in 1644 and while actual mortality figures are unknown, best estimates suggest the number could be as high as one-quarter of the population of Edinburgh perishing. Given the peaks and valleys of life, it seems even a catastrophe can create industry, as this further excerpt from that time testifies 'The extent of the epidemic is revealed in the city's financial records, which document the cost of dealing with the sick and paying people to carry out plague duties, such as removing bodies, digging graves, cleansing the homes of plague victims and constructing isolation 'booths' on the outskirts of the city – on the Burgh Muir, Leith Links and by Salisbury Crags.'

We know at least some of the Youngs did survive; however, these aforesaid events could provide one possible explanation for why George Young and Anna Watson appear to have had only three surviving children. The over-riding point here is that all these events are not just someone else's history, it was their history. These events are not just a part of someone else's life story, they are also a part of this family's story and the mere fact that some Young ancestors rode out the storm is marvellous given the circumstances; because, unfortunately many family lines are known to have been completely wiped out.

There is one further by-product of Edinburgh's topography which is relevant to its sociology. It developed as a result of Edinburgh's unique multi-story architecture of the day and its consequential living conditions. It seemingly gave rise to a class behavioural model which was endemic to Edinburgh. Back then Edinburgh's citizens were the subject of quiet consternation on behalf of English and European visitors alike who observed a peculiar social model which they ascribed to the topography and architecture unique to that city.

Citizens living in those clinging tenements were said to be not only residing in close proximity to one another; but, that this cheek by jowl living gave rise to what was for Edinburghers, a natural social interaction between the social classes. Most foreign observers believed this to be quite a phenomenon. Most international visitors were aghast to find Tradesmen and Professionals could be found sharing residence in the same 'lofty houses', all living in flats built in the wynds. Access to their various lodgings was via the steep and narrow staircases which did the job of a vertical street and as such naturally gave rise to conversation. One particular article states that 'In the same building lived families of all grades and classes, each in its flat entered off the same steep staircase - the sweep and caddie in the cellars, poor mechanics in the garrets, while in the intermediate stories might live a noble, a lord of session, a doctor or city minister, a dowager countess, or writer [lawyer]; higher up, over their heads, lived shopkeepers, dancing masters or clerks' and all the time 'rubbing shoulders with each other on the common stair'. What a shock that would have been for the extremely class-conscious English!

Social Demographers have suggested that these egalitarian living arrangements in Edinburgh could be responsible for engendering the broad spirit of inquiry noted among its citizens which they associate positively with the period of the Scottish Enlightenment. This social example prevailed until around 1752 when the Convention of Royal Burghs concluded that 'improvements to the capital for the benefit of commerce' should be undertaken. This initiative was to provide for residential construction in areas outside the Wall to the north and south of Old Town. Hence, it was the building of what was termed New Town which was cited as a catalyst for change to the social order for the good citizens of Edinburgh.

This development outside the City Walls not only changed living conditions in Edinburgh, it was ultimately responsible for disentangling the populace in a manner which changed that city's social culture forever. Well credentialed phrenologist, author and publisher, Robert Chambers, wrote in the 1820s, that the 'new order' in Edinburgh was now reflecting 'a kind of double city - first, an ancient and picturesque hill-built one, occupied chiefly by the humbler classes; and second, an elegant modern one, of much regularity of aspect, and possessed almost as exclusively by the more refined portion of society'. To gain a fuller appreciation of what this dislocation and relocation meant for Edinburgh society as a whole we need look no further than a report some decades after the establishment of New Town, wherein Scottish Historian, A.J. Youngson reported that the 'Unity of social feeling was one of the most valuable heritages of old Edinburgh, and its disappearance was widely and properly lamented.'

David Young for one can be placed residing without the Wall prior to 1723 as a member of the more socially refined sector of the community. His daughter Margaret was married in that year and the record of her marriage reads 'Miller/Millar, John, merchant, in N.N.K. p., Mary Young, d. of the late David Y., baker, burgess, now in N.K. p. 01 Dec 1723'. [N.N.K. p. = New North Kirk Parish, and N.K. p. = is the original Greyfriars]. New North Kirk is a part of Greyfriars parish, which is in fact the oldest surviving church in Edinburgh, and one whose history is shared by this family. Also, daughter Margaret is marrying up as it were, not into the ranks of craftsmen but into the merchant class so it is assumed that David left a reasonable legacy to ensure daughter Margaret had a suitable dowry.

Greyfriars Church is pivotal to Edinburgh's history as well as to the history of some of these Young ancestors. While Queen Mary granted the land by charter back in 1562, unfortunately it was 1602 before construction of the Church began and it was Christmas Day 1620 before the first Church Service was held. Greyfriars was founded on the pre-Reformation site of a Franciscan Order of Grey Friars from whence it gets its name. It stands today as one of the oldest surviving buildings constructed outside the Old Town. Outwardly it is a church of simple design: six bays, following the gothic architectural style with side aisles and pillars where worshippers like the Youngs would have either stood or come along to Services with their own stools.

Greyfriars has also been the scene of some of Scotland's most momentous events. 1638 saw the National Covenant signed in the Churchyard, 1650-53 Cromwell used the building as barracks, and come 1679, 1200 Covenanters were imprisoned in Greyfriars Kirkyard pending trial. Then in 1718 the unthinkable, a small squat tower beyond the west arch, which was being used as a gunpowder store by the Town Council, exploded destroying several bays of the church. A new section was built on the north side which became known as New North Kirk Parish. The church then had two separate areas of worship - north and south. These shared a common wall but were not, for reasons of parish domain, interconnected. From the records, we can place family member's residing in New North Parish and witnessing all these events.

The words parish and community are quite often used interchangeably these days; however, their meaning had a much wider and different implication in earlier centuries.

From early times the word 'parish' basically defined a geographical area located around a church; however, at various points in history its meaning, powers and implications were far more wide ranging than simply relating to geography and worship. For instance, although Social Security Payments as we know them today did not exist way back then, there was a payment termed Poor Relief, and the administration of this was one of the responsibilities of the Parish Council. In Scotland it worked like this: Heritor Tax was collected and managed by the Kirk Session or Parish Court. These taxes were used to finance the expenses of the Parish in terms of maintaining the church, the manse [the minister's house], the minister's stipend and the school. Other funds were set aside to provide support to the less fortunate in the parish by way of payments of Poor Relief.

The details for payments of Poor Relief exist in all Kirk Session Records. These can provide a wealth of family, parish and social information about a point in time in which an ancestor lived, regardless of whether they were rich or poor. These Registers hold details of the names of every feudal landowner, the value of his property, the taxes collected, a list of parish inhabitants and more specifically the names of those in receipt of Poor Relief, including children. Entitlement was restricted to those who were registered parishioners of the said parish; that is, those baptised into that specific parish church as well as those who were accepted as relocations. All those so entitled have had their names duly entered in the Parish Register. Subsequently, under the terms of an Act of Parliament of 1649 the King no longer saw his funds set aside for Poor Relief, rather the responsibility for this payment fell on the respective parish and its landowners.

Furthermore, the scope of the Kirk Sessions via the Parish Court was far more pervasive than might first appear. Kirk Sessions were also empowered to impose kirk discipline by way of religious sanctions such as excommunication or denial of baptism. These measures were designed to ensure more godlike behaviour and obedience. Activities such as well-dressing [a long standing pagan tradition of placing flowers and petals around wells, springs and the like to give thanks for the water], bonfires, guising [a Celtic terms for a 'Trick or Treat' style event held on 1 November which was All Saints Day and purely meant as a welcome to the forthcoming winter season], penny weddings [a wedding where the guests pay part of the charge], and dancing were all banned at various times by order of the Parish Court as they were all considered to be unchristian.

Kirk Sessions were also used as a means of persecuting people, especially women, when the church sought to extinguish those thought to be involved in witchcraft. The Parish Court used every means at their disposal to stamp out superstitious and Catholic practices in Scottish society and the Witch Hunts in Scotland alone saw over 1500 executions of which 75% were women. The last execution was in 1706, the last trial in 1727. Amazingly, the Witchcraft Act of 1563 was not finally repealed until 1736. Incontrovertibly, these were treacherous times for even ordinary Scots folk. To find oneself on the wrong side of a neighbour or business associate could see a person accused and blasphemed where the ultimate revenge of an adversary was to have the accused reported to the Parish Court.

The County of Midlothian is recognised as the epicenter of witchcraft persecution in Scotland. These Young ancestors lived in Edinburgh, County of Midlothian, during the period of

In the beginning 1650-1750

The Great Scottish Witch Hunt of 1661-62. Indeed, right across Scotland there had been several witch hunts prior to this; the first one on record was 1590-91 and then more latterly in 1649-50. In fact, there is a landmark known as Witches Well on the western end of Castle Hill in Edinburgh where in the sixteenth century more witches were burned at the stake on that part of Castle Hill than anywhere else in Scotland. Today, a small plaque on the west wall of what is now The Tartan Weaving Mill marks the spot where many of these three hundred plus women of Edinburgh lost their lives.

One of the most notable victims was a woman of title by the name of Dame Euphane MacCalzean. She was accused of using cantrip [the casting of a spell] to sink a vessel off Leith and for attempting to sink the ship of King James VI as it sailed into Berwick. Clearly these were outrageous accusations and these events only go to shows just how deep superstition ran and how easy it was for absolutely anyone, regardless of class, to find themselves on the wrong side of community thinking. Many of the accused witches were tortured and almost as many were drowned by being 'douked' in the contaminated cesspool of Nor Loch before being tied to the stake and burned - alive or dead. It is difficult to see how this could possibly be sanctioned as Christian behaviour, but history is there as the everlasting proof of that famous Robert Burns quote 'man's inhumanity to man'.

In today's world, if we are looking to determine Standards of Living, we have a number of economic indicators to draw upon to compare and contrast countries and cities. In most instances, food is invariably considered one of the primary categories and since it has long been contended that 'Bread is the staff of life', it does make sense that an economist could conduct such a study based on bread alone. Since our David Young and his son John were both Baxter's [Bakers], such research findings could offer a valuable insight into their business activity and potential earning capacity which could be extrapolated to reflect something of their standard of living. Well, as luck would have it, such a study does exist. The premise of the study is that bread is considered paramount to assessing the overall economic health of a Burgh, and in the case of the study uncovered, very conveniently the Burgh is Edinburgh.

The data used was extracted from Privy Council Records, and at its core it shows that the weight of a loaf of bread fluctuated considerably within and between the decades of 1650 and 1680 in particular. All indications are that the price per loaf was set by the Baxter Burgess and remained unchanged at one Scottish Shilling. What is not clear is who was responsible for determining what the standard weight of a loaf of bread should be at any given point in time. What we can infer from the data is that Baxter's were varying the weight of a loaf of bread to enable them to cover their costs and maintain their profit margins. This would have been even more extreme in those periods of drought and/or when imported grain was more expensive. We see that over these three decades the weight of a loaf bounced around between 8 ounces and 14.5 ounces. This is a considerable weight variation, and one would have to believe that many a mother trying to feed a household of hungry children would have surely gone without herself when the weight of a loaf was reduced to almost half the normal size.

There is one further very important life asset to this family in this century which has not been fully explored as yet, and it relates to Education. As previously stated, Scotland has long enjoyed a reputation for being one of the best educated societies in the world. The Reformation played a major role in changing how education was delivered in that country. The Church of Scotland strongly held the view that everyone, male and female, should be independently capable of reading the Bible and reading and learning the Catechism. It was, however, not until the full ambit of the Education Act of 1646 was restored half a century later in 1696, that education for the masses was comprehensively legislated. From that point forward, the cities and towns had Burgh Schools or Parish Schools. In the more remote and rural parts of Scotland education was required to be offered by the landowners, who were compelled by Law to provide a schoolhouse and a schoolmaster known colloquially in Scotland as a 'dominie' school. The local church minister and the local presbytery were responsible for oversighting the quality of education offered and to ensure that it aligned to the prescribed subjects set down in the Act. Of course, these were different for boys and girls.

London born Daniel Defoe is known to have remarked that while England was a land 'full of ignorance', in Scotland even the 'poorest people have their children taught and instructed'. Some others of the early schools were called 'Inglis' Schools and were said to offer tuition 'in the vernacular' to enrolled children up to the age 7 years, and later the grammar schools instructed boys to 12 years of age. Subjects for boys included Catechism, Latin, French, Classic Literature and Sport.

Despite the edict of the Church of Scotland there is evidence to suggest that girls were only accepted if there were insufficient boys enrolled to cover any stipend paid by the parish. At that time there was a widely held belief that the female gender possessed limited intellectual and moral capacity. Basically, girls were considered inferior, incapable, and not entitled to the same level of academic instruction as boys. Even when girls were accepted, they were subjected to segregation, and for many girls their education was left lacking in that many were taught to read but not write. After all, the primary aim was to be able to read the Bible and Catechism. The girls also spent time on handicraft activities like sewing and knitting rather than the traditional male subjects related to the Arts.

Finally, what do we know about Law and Order and Religious Freedom in Edinburgh in this century?

One excellent reference is contained in the *'Records of The Kirk of Scotland containing the Acts and Proceedings of the General Assemblies ....'*. This book deals with matters of religion and religious observance, issues that were paramount in the day. The insistence by James VI that the Church of Scotland observe the Liturgy and Canons caused such a raucous outcry it was described as 'one of the most formidable and best constructed oppositions to which any government ever was exposed'. 1680-1688 was another period of bloodshed, often referred to as the Killing Time, heralded by the assassination of the Archbishop of St. Andrews. This upheaval was in response to The Sanquhar Declaration of 1680 announcing that the people of Scotland could not accept the authority of a King who would not recognise their religion. Read out loud by a group of Covenanters, it amounted to sedition whereupon the Scottish Privy Council authorised field execution of anyone caught with arms and who failed to not only swear loyalty and fealty to the King but who also refused to denounce the Covenant. These were landmark historical events that affected everyday people just like the Youngs.

With tensions rising in both Scotland and England, and the House of Stewart descending into chaos, an impasse was only reached after the Glorious Revolution of 1688 which brought an end to the reign of James II of England, alias James VII of Scotland, who fled to France in exile. This made way for the Scottish Parliament to enact the Claim of Right Act that established Scots Law. This coincided with the accession of William of Orange as King William II of Scotland and the acceptance of Presbyterianism by the Act of Settlement shortly afterwards in 1690. James Renwick was the last Covenanter martyr executed on the Young's doorstep. He was hung at Grassmarket, Edinburgh on 17 February 1688 at the age of 26. He was born the son of a weaver from Dumfries, and following his father's death in 1675, Renwick decided to study religion at St Andrews University. He was very proudly Scottish and a devout Presbyterian and for this he was captured and upon refusing to swear allegiance to the King or to renounce his religion, his fate was sealed. After his execution James Renwick's head and hands were severed from his body and affixed to the gates of the city.

One would seriously have to question what kind of authority or religion behaves in this way? Furthermore, it would be interesting to know how such events were viewed by the Youngs and their fellow citizens in the day and what influence it had on their future behaviour, if any.

In the beginning 1650-1750

Chapter 2

The Port of Leith • Privateering in the North Sea • Impressing • Smuggling Riots • The Darien Scheme & Wars Raging in International Waters

To date these Young ancestors have been land-lubbers, living and working in Edinburgh and successfully plying their trades as bakers and tailors for over a century, but a wind of change has blown some of them out to sea. Yes, the current generation has decided it is time to join with their relatives, embrace the new world and take their careers in a different direction. So begins a maritime love affair set to last for over two and a half centuries. It cannot be overstated what a massive step this was. For Robert Young it would have felt like stepping into a totally foreign world where he would have been confronted with a very steep learning curve. There's a vast difference between navigating the streets of Edinburgh by lamplight and navigating the oceans of the world by the stars. And, there is just no comparing a baker's oven or tailor's needle and shears to a sailing ship as a tool of trade. However, summoning up the courage to face the unpredictability and cruelty of Mother Nature as she dispassionately and ruthlessly imposes her will on all who venture onto the oceans, would have been their harshest lesson of all.

This career change also caused Robert to relocate from the warm safe matriarchal heart of the Royal Burgh of Edinburgh to join the struggling overlorded and downtrodden folk in the port Burgh of Leith. At first glance this radical change of occupation from baker to mariner looked like a big step, but his relocation to Leith, clearly crucial to his success, would have required a significant change of mindset too given the confrontational relationship Edinburghers and Leithers had endured down the ages. Any modern study of human nature tells us that generally speaking people are uncomfortable with change with some avoiding change at all cost, so to take such a monumental decision speaks volumes about the person who took it, about his sense of self and strength of character.

This is not normally the kind of decision one takes independently or lightly, certainly not without a strong belief in one's own ability to be able to face up to the obstacles and to do so clear in the knowledge that there was a very strong chance of success. And then, there was a requirement for Robert to seek and secure Parish Consent for the move. In England anyone moving between parishes simply obtained a Relocation Certificate, but in Scotland such moves were arbitrated in the Kirk Sessions and not even marrying into a parish family meant consent was a given. However, there were two strong factors in Robert's favour; one, his mother was from Leith and, two, he was about to marry into a very well established Leith family. Understanding that the parish would become responsible for him and his family henceforward, these factors would have most assuredly aided his cause. Notwithstanding his undoubted familial support, such a brave move also demonstrates his commitment, his strong belief in the future of the seafaring industry plus the conviction that seizing this opportunity would improve his life in the short term as well as be the best opportunity for him to provide a solid future for his own children and future generations.

So, just what was life going to be like for him once he moved to Leith?

Robert knew Leith was geographically resting at the entrance to the Firth of Forth and had been the busy seaboard gateway to Edinburgh for centuries. He was probably privy to conversations around how it had witnessed many pivotal historical events pre and post the period in question, some of which have been discussed here already in either an historical or political context. When considering the Leith family connections Robert had recently married into, it is clear their genealogy discloses generation after generation for centuries living and working in and out of Leith, with a prized history in maritime pursuits - principally fishing and the merchant trade. We already know that Robert's father, John Young had married into the Dick family, and that this Dick family had been long-time residents in Leith. As an example of their position in the Leith community, prior to Union in 1707 Sir William Dick was cited as being the richest citizen in Leith. Frankly, it is not unreasonable to assert that it was probably the shared tales of life on the high seas recounted to Robert Young [1723-1797] by his grandfather, Captain Gilbert Dick, which were so intoxicating and enticing that Robert was persuaded to cast himself adrift with the likes of the Dicks and Thomsons rather than follow in his own father's and grandfathers' footsteps and become a Baker.

Robert Young would have started out as a 'boy' on a ship at around age ten to twelve. For him, it would have been on the job learning and a circumstance where the quality of his prior education would have supported his new vocational training, the success of which rested entirely in the hands of his instructors, his shipboard comrades – because there were no text books; learning was principally by osmosis. Whilst we will never know how it actually was for Robert Young what we do know from historical records is how basic those very early wooden sailing ships were, how tough the life was for sailors, and how ever-present the dangers were that these intrepid men faced. Add to this the frequency of wars being fought in international waters and one wonders why anyone took to the sea. Whatever seduced Robert into taking up this seafaring life, it was a very strong pull.

Logically, there would have been the usual family gatherings; occasions when the Dicks, Youngs and others would have sat huddled together around a warming fire on a cold and blustery evening when conversation would have naturally strayed to times past. The perfect occasion for Gilbert Dick to recount a maritime tale or two. Gilbert had a long association with the sea and it is not impossible to imagine him as the quintessential tar with a craggy weather-beaten face, bushy beard, pipe comfortably nested in the corner of his mouth, cap shadowing his brow in the soft glow of the evening firelight and a far-away look on his face as he recalled the many experiences of his life or better still the stories told to him by his father and grandfather. Stories so intoxicating and riveting that his audience was stilled and silenced as Gilbert, speaking in slow motion so he too could savour every moment, recounted his treasured family reminiscences of Leith, the sea and of life as a mariner.

Surely, one romantic family favourite story would be that of his great-great-grandfather Gilbert Dick the Elder who would have witnessed the historic return of Queen Mary to Scotland's shores. This would have been a story many generations of these old knights of the tarbrush would have told and retold with pride while pondering the majesty of those awesome Spanish galleons as they drifted into Leith Harbour on that misty morn. Being mariners proud and true, this family tale would most assuredly have focused on the ships. Maybe, Robert even detected a touch of envy in his grandfather's voice, for what skipper of his ilk would not wish that he too had seen those statuesque galleons under full sail.

Much has been written about that historic day, about how those giants of the waves emerged out of the mist. It would certainly have been a sight to behold and a keen eyed old sea dog like Gilbert Dick the Elder would have relished such a moment, taking in every detail as if eyeing a good woman. He would have recounted how proudly and safely those vessels entered the Roads of Leith at 6 a.m. on that auspicious day in August 1561. It goes without saying that he knew the best vantage point from which to observe their beauty. With a light breeze they would have had sheets to the wind and then with guns polished, crew in uniform, soldiers standing to attention with colourful plumes fluttering, polished brass glistening and flags flying high it would have been a most regal spectacle indeed. No other ship afloat could overshadow the majesty of those Titanics of their time. On such a memorable day it is also fair to assume that all the citizens of Leith rose before the cock crowed in order to take their place on the quayside or to crowd the Royal Mile.

As testament to Leith's long and proud maritime history Alexander Campbell described these events in his *'The History of Leith, from the Earliest Accounts to the Present Period; with a Sketch of the Antiquities of the Town'* as a time when 'The sound of cannon from the gallies which accompanied Mary from France, mingled with the shouts of the multitude.' Leith harbour would have been alive with activity, resplendent in colour, and joyous at the opportunity to welcome home their new Scottish Queen. Her square-rigged galleons would soon crowd the piffling docks. Surely there would be nothing on that day which could stop Leithers from smiling, and bravely whispering behind hand as they gossiped about the Lords and Ladies in their finery, the Prior in his religious regalia all paying homage and pledging loyalty in the hopes of winning favour with the young Queen. The simple townsfolk too would be out in their 'Sunday Best', conscious they were witnessing history in the making.

The depth of feeling for all Scots as these momentous events unfolded are best summed up in a legendary poem by James Hogg, a contemporary of Sir Walter Scott. It is entitled *'Queen's Wake'*, and excerpts read in part [best read with a Scottish burr] -

> 'Each harp was strung in woodland bower,
> In Praise of beauty's bonniest flower.
> The chiefs forsook their ladies fair;
> The priest his beads and books of prayer;
> The farmer left his harvest day,
> The shepherd all his flocks to stray;
> The forester forsook the wood,
> And hastened on to Holyrood.
>
> The lovely Mary once again
> Set foot upon her native plain;
> Kneeled on the pier with modest grace,
> And turned to heaven her beauteous face.
> 'Twas them the caps in air were blended,

A thousand thousand shouts ascended;
Shivered the breeze around the throng;
Gray barrier cliffs the peals prolong;
And every tongue gave thanks to Heaven,
That Mary to their hopes was given.

Light on her airy steed she sprung,
Around with golden tassels hung;
No chieftain there rode half so free,
Or half so light and gracefully.

How sweet to see her ringlets pale
Wide waving in the southland gale,
Which through the broom-wood blossoms flew,
To fan her cheeks of rosy hue.

And when her courser's mane it swung,
A thousand silver bells were rung.
A sight so fair, on Scottish plain,
A Scot shall never see again.

Slowly she ambled on her way,
Amid her lords and ladies gay'
Priest, abbot, layman, all were there,
And Presbyter, with look severe.
There rode the lords of France and Spain,
of England, Flanders, and Lorraine;
While serried thousands round them stood,
From Shore of Leith to Holyrood.'

These were proud days for Scotland but even more so for the Port of Leith, and it would have been events such as this that were so precious to those who had dedicated their lives to the sea. It is what inspired their antecedents and it was the retelling that would certainly seduce future generations.

Then there was an occurrence that would have exaggerated the divide between Edinburgh and Leith. It was an occasion where the parents and grandparents on both sides would have recalled the aftermath differently. Nevertheless, it was to impact the lives of all Scottish citizens when in 1603, James VI, after attending divine service at St Giles Church, Edinburgh, made his farewell speech to his homeland as he prepared to journey to London to take the throne of England as James I following the death of the Queen and his aunt Elizabeth I. It was reported in some quarters that 'The people, who were very numerous, cryed in most bitter lamentations, that they should never again have a king to reside amongst them as they had in times past.'

It is fair to say that whilst Edinburghers may have felt great sadness it was probably much less so for the poor wretches in the vassal town of Leith. As an unfree town outside the Edinburgh wall, their diminution in the eyes of those in the Royal Burgh although more exaggerated in Queen Mary's time when the Edinburgh leaders strongly protested against the French soldiers occupying Leith, sadly the situation for Leithers did not improve one iota after her son James became King. Leith remained a vassal town, it had no Town Council; rather, affairs were managed by the Kirk Sessions. In fact, the trade and craft Incorporations and Guilds set up centuries prior, had done more for the ordinary people.

Relevant to this story, it needs to be said that the Masters and Mariners of Trinity House in the Kirkgate became the wealthiest of all those Guilds because for time immemorial they had been in receipt of port dues known historically as 'prime gilt'. This accrued wealth was not held for the exclusive use of Masters and Mariners, moreover it was put to community projects such as the building of the first hospital in Leith which was made available to all citizens. Over time that hospital has been replaced; however, the remnants of the original can still be seen in the basement of Trinity House. These Guilds and Incorporations wielded great power in their day and played a vital role in the social and industrial life of Leith. Their varied significance is demonstrated by this handful of examples from the Kirk Session Records of South Leith -

'25th Febrii 1669. The which day James Auchterlony for the Trafficquers, Johne Watsone for the Seamen, John Valantyne for Maltmen and Hugh Mossman for the trades compeirand before the Sessione declared that by trew information Mr. John Corsaur late second minister of this Kirk was transported from hence to Dalgetie and ordained minister there, And they desired the Moderator to declair his judgement therein who ….'. [John Watson is related to Anna Watson wife of George Young 1616-1664].

Then there is yet another example in 1681 -

'10th November 1681. Captain John Watson and David Gillies for the Seamen, James Dalgame and William Aitken for the Maltmen, John Stewart and John Cleugh for the Trades and for ye Traffecquers, John Dudgeon and James Louden are to get in money for their several corporation for payt. of the clock and horologe boards and guilding yr of.'. [The Dudgeon family too will come in for mention at another time and are related to these Youngs by marriage.]

Extracts from the Register of the Meeting House which replaced Kirk Sessions after 'Libertie was proclaimed' [post Oliver Cromwell] and relate to the social administration of the town -

'17 Nov. 1692 - This day Wm. Lamb gardiner was rebuiked for cutting of cabbage on ye Sabbath day and promised to do so no more.'.

'Janr. 23 1690 - Appoints James Meikle and Patrick Glass to speak to the Magistrats to punish cursers swearers drunkards especially these upon the Sabbath day'.

The social welfare side of the Parish in 1689 is best explained by these entries -

In the beginning 1650-1750

'May 23 - To Andro Oliver a cripple to help to buy a tree leg to him - 3s.0d.'

'Novr 21 - For the Scots prisoners in France - £71 15s 0d.'

[Were these prisoners mariners perhaps? If so, their capture and incarceration is probably as a consequence of the Nine Years War [1688-1697] where France was joined by Irish and Scots Jacobites in a war against the Dutch, English, Spanish, Scots and other armies.]

Apart from day to day conditions of shipboard life, what is known of the extraneous maritime conditions Robert Young, as a mariner, would have had to contend with?

First up, Gilbert Dick and others would have acquainted him with the impact of Privateering on the maritime community. It was a serious issue in their day: real, frequent, costly, dangerous and also the subject of several entries in the Kirk Sessions records of the era. One example from 14 August 1690 reads 'To John Hay and Wm. Frazer who were taken by a French privateer as they were coming from the West Indies whose goods were all taken from them to the value of £700 Starling [sic] ....'. The extent of the danger and brutality of Privateering is best explained in the context of one case in particular, which would directly impact the Port of Leith and because of its far-reaching ramifications, change the course of history for all Scots; and more especially, the mariner community of Leith. It occurred shortly before Robert's parents married and would have been a cause of great concern for all parents of existing and future mariners in Leith. It was also a landmark event in Scots-Anglo maritime history and a story deeply imprinted on the memory of seafaring families such as Dick, Lundie, Thomson, Liston and Waddell – in fact all Leithers.

We are about to learn how Scotland was to ride a tidal wave of insult and innuendo as England launched a broadside in its direction in retaliation for Leith's treatment of a young English

Privateer by the name of Captain Thomas Green. Green was reputed to be in possession of a Letter of Marque from the English Admiralty which should have given him immunity to capture and prosecution. But so heinous were his alleged crimes that all such privileges were voided in the judgement of the Scottish Admiralty. In the aftermath of Captain Green's trial, England vigorously denounced Leith as the port of Scottish Privateers and Scots as warlike and undisciplined. Frankly, it is incredible to think that this one single act of presumed piracy could spark outrage at the level this one event did, especially considering that piracy was commonplace at the time. In fact, it had received Royal sanction decades prior by England's own Queen Elizabeth I.

Indeed, the annals of the Court of the Admiralty in England have volume after volume describing similar claims and counter-claims made by Englishmen against Englishmen, which only goes to make their extreme reaction in this instance appear somewhat farcical and smacks of political bias. Why were these accusations by the Scots classified as grossly unwarranted by the English Parliament? From the Scots perspective the attitude taken by the English was yet another show of political brinksmanship. Regardless of the politics, feelings were running very high and the opinion held in many quarters in England insinuated that this trial and its aftermath were events solely responsible for the English Parliament's determination to bring about the Act of Union when it did. Whether it was retaliatory action by the English against the Scots because of the way the trial was handled, or for the Scot's audacious Darien Scheme, or as a cover-up for the blatant favouritism England enjoyed in International Trade is all a matter of opinion; however, what is clear is that this trial and the decisions made by the Court of the Admiralty in Scotland left scars on the English which refused to heal.

The trial of Privateer Captain Thomas Green and his subsequent hanging became such a politically sensitive story it created substantial public interest right across Britain and beyond.

Numerous accounts have been written, some at the time and others down the centuries, and from the seven or so located thus far it is bewildering to note a baffling lack of agreement on many of the most salient points including the name of the ship pirated and the name of the ship's Captain. Even modern day Historians, with the benefit of access to a vast array of archival material, have published works at odds with each other, including the lingering disagreement on the name of the ship - was it the *Rising Sun* or the *Speedy Return*. The *Rising Sun* conjecture could be a Freudian slip as this vessel was one of the fleet of four Scots vessels that the English later learned had set out from Leith as part of the third Darien Scheme expedition. When the *Rising Sun* arrived at Caledonia, the new Scottish settlement in Panama, it is recorded that a Captain Thomas Drummond, or was it Captain Robert Drummond, was already at anchor in the harbour? His ship was the *Speedy Return*.

Other accounts avoid naming the ship altogether and simply refer to it as Drummond's Sloop or the Scottish Sloop. It is interesting to note that these numerous and diametrically opposed views on what occurred on this occasion are reminiscent of the accounts written about another maritime disaster over two centuries later which involved the collision and sinking of the *Andrea Doria* which occurred off New York in 1956. Whilst the *Andrea Doria* event will be dealt with in far greater detail much later on in this family's story, in both instances it seems that the views expressed have in some way been influenced by the nationality of the expresser.

Notwithstanding the above, so contentious was the case of Captain Green that it is almost impossible to distil facts from fiction. Some accounts reek of pure propaganda, one of these being the so-called '*Last speeches and dying-words of Captain Thomas Green .... And Captain John Madder...*'. This essay is a very lengthy account indeed and would infer they endured an extremely long and painfully slow death. In fact, they were hanged - quick and decisive. Another account published in 1705 in London bears the provocative and presumptive titles '*The Innocency of Captain Green ...*' that included affidavits by an Israel Phipeny and a Peter Freeland who is purported to be one of the crew members supposedly murdered by Green. Virtually a dead man talking! Another version which was dismissed is the *'Information for Captain Thomas Green commander of the Worcester, Captain John Madder his chief mate, and others, against Mr Alexander Higgins Advocat prosecutor-fiscal of the High Court of Admiralty'* which simply does not appear genuine.

There is only one item discovered which explains the depth of reprisal action in the day and it is found in *'Publications of the Navy Records Society Vol. XLVI - The Old Scots Navy From 1689-1710'* edited by James Grant, L.L.B. It adds another layer of political intrigue to this Thomas Green story by introducing matters involving yet another ship, its Scottish Letters of Marque and their impact on prisoner exchange arrangements with the English. The crux of this Scots Navy story is that on 3rd January 1704 the Scots government issued Letters of Marque to the *Annandale*, Captain Ap Rice. The article reads 'The Annandale belonging to the African Company of Scotland, was fitted out in an expiring effort to prosecute the East Indian trade. On her maiden voyage to the East she was detained in the Downs by the East India Company of England and was condemned as prize. This was the cause of the capture in reprisal by the African Company in Leith roads in February; 1705, of the English ship the Worcester, commanded by Captain Green. On 5th March Green and others of this crew were condemned to death by the Scottish Court of Admiralty for piracy and for murdering Captain Drummond of the Speedy Return, belonging to the African Company; and he and two others were hanged. This incident gave rise to such extraordinary bitterness of feeling between England and Scotland that it became an important compelling cause of the Union of 1707.' The serious aftermath for all merchant navy seamen was that 'In 1705, owing to the strained relations existing between England and Scotland, arising out of Captain Green's affair, the old method of exchanging prisoners through the English Admiralty received a check.'

There are other stories by notables like Sir Walter Scott and Daniel Defoe; however, since these men were fiction writers and their prose composed in hindsight these were dismissed as well. The Naval Chronicle Vol. 33 for 1815 contains a critical appraisal which illustrates the long-running interest in this particular convoluted story. This brings us to the last few versions perused,

Hugo Arnot's publication of *'A Collection and Abridgement of Celebrated Criminal Trials in Scotland From A.D. 1536-1784 ....'* and T.B. Howell's version entitled *'Complete Collection of State Trials and Proceedings for High Treason and Other Crimes and Misdemeanors 1700-1708'*. Renowned modern day Scottish Historian Eric Graham also mentions this incident among others in his book *'Seawolves Pirates & the Scots'* published in 2013.

What is evident, from the profusion of opinion regarding this 1702 episode, is that for over three centuries this story has challenged professional historians, baffled pirate aficionados, made compelling reading and today it is still worthy of the re-telling because this episode would have definitely been fresh in the mind of John Young and Margaret Dick as they supported and prepared their son Robert for his life as a mariner. Furthermore, it was not an isolated event and its long term impact on Leith and Scotland should never be underestimated!

For the purposes of this Young story and to gain a better understanding of the seafaring life these Youngs were about to embark on, it is the original J. Briggs transcript of 1705 which is being quoted. Briggs composed his transcript at the time of the trial, and it carries the laboured title of *'The Tyral [sic], Examination and Condemnation, of Captain Green of the Worcester, and His Whole Ships Crew: For the Murther [Murder] of Captain Drummond, and All His Scots Ships Crew, Near Malaba; Before the High Court of the Admiralty in Scotland on the 14th of March 1705'*. It has also been chosen because it draws on the first-hand encounters of Leithers with Green's crew as well as reports from those who boarded Green's ship. Above all, what needs to be remembered is that the Admiralty Court of Scotland gave due credence to the evidence given by several local folk described as respectable local citizens. The prime witnesses who gave evidence were listed as a Gunner in Her Majesty's Artillery [the trial was during the reign of Queen Anne], an Edinburgh Goldsmith and the Master of the Ships and Seamen Incorporation of

Leith who actually went on board Captain Green's ship the *Worcester* when it came into Leith Harbour in the July of 1702. The last two citizens of Edinburgh who would offer themselves as witnesses are a Writer to the Signet [Solicitor] and a Tailor both of whom had a chance encounter with a *Worcester* crewmember at an Inn one evening when they just happened to sit together at the same table. All of these witnesses offered first-hand intelligence regarding the events leading up to the loss of the sloop and her Leith crew.

The Writer and Tailor of Edinburgh advised the court that they later shared their story with the daughter of the Innkeeper who was known to the family of one of Drummond's crew. On a subsequent evening, she engaged said crewmember in conversation to make further enquiries on behalf of the Wilky/Wilkie family [a name which also appears prominently on the Young Family Tree] and then alerted the family concerned to a probable disastrous end for their son. She later gave sworn testimony about said conversation before the Court of the Admiralty of Scotland. All these first-hand witness conversations were had when the *Worcester* put into Leith on the first occasion. However, when Green was forced to put into Leith on the second occasion, fate played into the hands of the Leithers who had already had their suspicions raised, and were on the lookout for the *Worcester*. Ironically, Captain Green only put into Leith to escape French Pirates. Green had been advised they were marauding in the waters between Leith and London, so he planned to take safe harbour until his signal for a British Navy escort was answered. Ultimately, this would prove a fatal decision for Green and his men.

If there is any truth in the evidence given at the trial, it is clear that the attack on Drummond and his crew was treacherously contrived and extremely swift and violent. It has been said that the *Worcester* lured the *Speedy Return* to her fate by showing a flag of being a friendly vessel but after the *Worcester* got alongside, her crew attacked. The *Worcester*'s reported rampage of murder and mayhem was so swift that they failed to learn anything of the Captain or his crew. Clearly, they were focused on capturing their prize, for had they taken the time to question the Captain, or any of his men for that matter, they would have learned they were Scots, predominantly Leithers, and thereafter the *Worcester* could have avoided that fateful port.

The Court of the Admiralty of Scotland's case notes reveal that when Green dropped anchor in Leith Harbour on 3 July 1704 it was also unbeknown to him that he had sailed into a hornets' nest for yet another reason. He was in a 'Scotland seething with anti-English feeling'. But this sentiment would have been superficially subdued by the local folk in order that they could begin to cautiously question the crew of the *Worcester*. Paramount for them would have been their desire to learn what news they could of their kith and kin. It should be pointed out here that such action would not have raised any suspicions for it was common practice in the day to seek information of ships encountered from the Captain and crewmembers of visiting ships. Often the only opportunity a family had to learn about their absent marine family members came from visiting ships. What would happen is that when a ship entered a port the locals would purposely go down to the quay and enquire for intelligence of the places that vessel had visited and the ships they had encountered on their voyage.

Briggs recounted evidence to the effect that 'George Hayns; Stward [sic] in the Ship, being ask'd at Burnt-island by James Wilks, a Citizen of Edinburgh, if ever he had seen Andrew Wilks his Brother, who went Surgon in Captain Drummond's Ship' quickly 'fell out in Passion, and ask'd what Devil was his Concern with Captain Drumond'. It seems that James Wilkes, whose brother was surgeon on Drummond's sloop, had heard the *Worcester* was back in port and he too took himself down to the Inn to chat to any crew who may be drinking there. Not satisfied with Hayns' responses, and sensing Hayns was upset about something and not telling all he knew, but at the same time acknowledging he was inebriated, James Wilkie pressed Haynes once again and it was then that the steward is reputed to have admitted 'That when they were upon the Coast of Malabar, a Dutch ship inform'd them, that Captain Drummond, with a Scots Ship and Sloop, was turn'd Pirates'. At the trial further evidence was heard that Hayns had later confessed that he knew where Drummond's Logbook was hidden but it was not likely to be discovered unless the *Worcester* was pulled apart plank by plank.

Next, came the evidence of Ann Seaton of Burntisland, the Innkeeper's daughter, and Kenneth Mackenzie an indweller of Canongate, declaring that Hayns had admitted 'That he knew more of Captain Drummond than he would tell at that time, and that if Andrew Wilky was with Drummond he would never be seen again'. When questioned further Ann Seaton told the court that she had heard Hayns own up to and declare their wickedness at a time when she was in company with the sworn William Wood, a Gunner in Her Majesty's Artillery and John Henderson a Writer in Edinburgh. Henderson of all people would surely not vouch untruths in an Admiralty Court or any other Court otherwise he would be struck off.

Ann Seaton told how they were all at her mother's Inn in September last, and that 'after a Health or two', the said Hayns fell into a melancholy fit, and expressed himself thus 'That it's a Wonder, since we did not sink at Sea, God does not make the Ground to swallow us up for the Wickedness that has been committed during the last Voyage, on Board of that old Bitch Bess, pointing to Captain Green's Ship'. He had gone on to incriminate John Madder, the First Mate, by suggesting that for his part he deserved to be boiled in oil, just like his Uncle had been at the hands of the Dutch when he had attempted to set fire to a Dutch ship.

In the Naval Chronicle:Vol 33 it is stated 'Haines further confessed, that he would have acknowledged the truth sooner, had not Captain Green's agents made him believe that the defences for the crew would certainly bring them off, and if they all agreed in one mind, and kept close mouths, there would be no fear, as nothing could otherwise be proved against them.' Then, 'John Bruckley, cooper of the Worcester, confessed, that after coming on the coast of Malabar, the ship and sloop chased ... and ... the supercargo, Callent, Captain Madden [et al] said that the vessel was Captain Drummond's ship, belonging to the Scots African Company.' Antonio Ferdinando, cook's mate of the *Worcester*, stated 'that Captain Green, Captain Madden, and others, were on board the sloop .... that the crew of the latter were taken up from below decks, killed with hatchets, and thrown overboard.' Finally, Charles May, surgeon of the *Worcester* gave evidence, that while ashore at Malabar, he heard firing, and was informed that the Worcester was engaged. When he later attended to the wounded and enquired of them regarding their wounds 'Mr Madden, who overheard what he said, bid him ask no questions, and likewise charged the patients not to answer any questions, on their peril.' The respondent described the previous English view of events as chimerical - a figment of imagination.

Returning to Briggs version of events, there was further damning evidence contained in two letters offered to the Court. The first was written by John Reynolds, Second Mate on the *Worcester*, to his wife, and the second was dated January past being the reply he received from his sister-in-law. The one to his wife confessed his guilt, and the one from his sister-in-law acknowledged his confessed wickedness and voiced her concern that he may 'bring himself to the gallows' for his crime. It is further entered into the records of the Admiralty Court trial that a Committee of the Council had been despatched to Burntisland in order to search and unload the *Worcester*. Those men appointed to the task, the Master and others of the Skippers and Mariners Incorporation of Trinity House, reported that the goods were not stowed or labelled in a manner consistent with Merchant cargo. They observed that there was 'confusion in the Hold as if taken by Piracy'. The delegation stated they had also encountered John Madder who surprised them when he took from his own pocket the 'Seal of the African Company' that they knew he had not come by legally. [The *Speedy Return* was reported to be a ship of the Indian and African Company of Scotland].

On the weight of evidence, the Captain and his crew were called to face two separate indictments and on Wednesday 14 March 1705 Captain Thomas Green of the *Worcester* and all his ship's crew were duly brought before the High Court of the Admiralty of Scotland where they were charged that somewhere between February and May of 1703, off the Coast of Malaba, near Calcutta, the *Worcester* had met a vessel sailing under a red flag, [indicating it had an English/Scottish crew], and that without just cause they attacked said vessel with guns and arms [swords and knives]. When the sloop was run down, Captain Green and his men boarded, seized all hands, and coldly set about slaughtering everyone before tossing their bodies overboard. Green's men then seized their prized cargo, transferring it to the hold of the *Worcester*. They then sailed the sloop a short distance south to the Keilon River where they sold it to a local merchant.

Now the English on the other hand, chose to seize upon the convenient truth that the *Speedy Return* had some 5 or 6 years prior been associated with the Darien Scheme. In reality, on the subject voyage in 1703 this sloop *Speedy Return* was indeed sailing as a vessel of the Indian and African Company of Scotland. To bolster their position, the English even went so far as to coerce two alleged seamen into swearing that they were part of the crew of the *Speedy Return* and of course their joint statement gave a far different account of that Scottish sloop's fate. Strangely enough, after this particular document came to light, the two seamen conveniently vanished from Plymouth altogether, never to be seen or heard of again. A more challenging question which remains unanswered is - were the English also endeavouring to protect their British East India Company's monopoly on trade with India and in the Far East? In order to sway the Court of the Admiralty in Scotland it followed that there was claim and counter-claim and some seizures of Scot's vessels by the English, but nothing would prevent the Scots and Leith from dealing out justice to the crew of the *Worcester*.

Briggs' final comment on the matter is that 'The Court sum'd up the Evidence, and gave Charge to the Jury, they soon return'd and brought the Persons abovementioned in Guilty of Piracy and Murther, and they receiv'd Sentence of Death for the same'. Now there have been some outrageous figures quoted for the number of people witnessing these executions but what is crystal clear is that every-day folk, like these Youngs and their related families living in Leith, were caught up in these mesmerising events. Leith had lost so many young sons, brave mariners, and it is fair to say Leithers would most certainly have been high in numbers among the onlookers that fateful day. The final sentencing is written in the Admiralty Court Criminal Records stating that The Court did 'Adjudge the said Captain Thomas Green [and others ...] .... to be taken to the Sands of Leith within the floodmark upon the first wednesday of Apryle next, being the fourth day of the said moneth Betwix the hours of Elevin o'clock in the forenoon and four o'clock in the afternoon and there to be hanged upon a gibbet till they be dead' .

In the aftermath of the executions, Leith's shipping industry was heavily targeted by English Merchants as they continued to lobby Westminster for absolute control over British Trade. Scotland's mercantile sector began to struggle in the face of this concerted opposition, and it was about to get worse once the King, their own James VI now James I of England, decided to take a broadside at his homeland and Leith in particular. Knowing that the lion's share of Scottish exports at that time passed through the Port of Leith, and not always on Scottish vessels, King James issued a Royal decree citing that henceforth all Scottish exports could only be carried by Scottish ships. This was an attempt to hit back at Leithers and more specifically members of the Skippers and Mariners Incorporation of Trinity House for their role in the Thomas Green Affair.

Naturally, this would have certainly had an effect on all the Skippers and Merchants in Leith and more particularly those involved in the lucrative and important Herring Trade. The English lobbyists advising the King would have realised that three-quarters of Scotland's Herring Exports were being shipped through the Port of Leith, and that a large proportion of these herrings were not carried on Scottish vessels. Also, after this legislation was implemented, it would severely restrict all cargo movements in and out of Leith, which in turn would restrict revenue for Leith Skippers and Merchants and the local economy as a whole would suffer. Undoubtedly this was the intent of the King.

Notwithstanding the effrontery of this restriction, Scots Merchants took up the fight and decided to go head to head with the Crown by calling their bluff by announcing that they ' ... will be compelled to leave our trade of herrings which we transport to the East Countries (Baltic), because the best occasion of the transport thereof is offered only in the months of September and October, in the which season we have the commodity of some Dutch ...ships here, which have imported timber within this realm and will be content to transport our goods for a third of the freight which Scottish ships may serve for, because if they lack this employment they will return empty'. This action by the Herring Traders would directly affect revenue flowing into the coffers of the Crown. Their decision seemed reasonable in the circumstances, when it is considered that many of these voyages were undertaken on the cusp of winter, when it was logical to assume that if Scottish vessels were pressed into service and met adverse weather conditions some could be forced to over-winter in foreign ports or worse it could see both ships and crews lost. All in all, the current practice of utilising the facility of empty foreign ships returning to homeport made sound strategic and economic sense.

Alas, Leithers didn't realise the King was actually attempting to achieve a three-fold purpose. The first was to placate the greedy English Merchants and Skippers who wanted an even larger share of the British Merchant Trade, assuming they had the capacity. Their second aim was to restrict the market expansion of Scottish vessels sailing from Leith and lastly, to punish Leith Merchants and Skippers for trading with England's old archenemy France. It is written that the King had received intelligence advising Leith Skippers in particular had been quite entrepreneurial and would carry cargo for any merchant from any country as and when the opportunity presented itself. This Scottish entrepreneurship extended to merchants from enemy countries of the Crown such as France. The King took umbrage at this and eventually showed his true colours when he declared his displeasure that 'the greatest number of the best ships of Scotland .... [were being] ... continually employed in the service of Frenchmen, not only within the dominions of France, but also within the bounds of Spain, Italy and Barbary [Coast] ....'.

In truth, it was not uncommon for Leith Skippers to undertake to carry cargo between foreign countries after completing their initial voyage from Scotland to ports in the Baltic or Flanders. It was also a well-known fact that Scottish Captains enjoyed cordial relations with foreign merchants, the French in particular, who were at this time quite actively trading with Spain and ports along the Barbary Coast, where the new highly profitable cargo was tobacco. Such voyages were so commonplace that many Leith seamen are known to have been buried in these foreign lands, some as a result of disease and others from encounters with privateers. These events occurred in the early decades of our Youngs taking to the sea and would have been a sobering lesson to all sailors including Robert Young.

Worse still, in years past, captive Scottish seamen are known to have been sold to slave traders. In 1621 a church collection was taken up in Leith for the relief of Scots prisoners in Tunis and Algiers, then again in 1636 for the Captain and crew of the *John* of Leith. From 1615 comes the story of how the Captain and crew of the vessel *Unicorn* of Leith fell victim to Turkish pirates. Fortunately for this crew a fellow Scot, John Fraser, happened to be resident in Algiers at the time. Upon seeing his countrymen being offered for sale in the local marketplace he stepped in and convinced the trader to free them in exchange for a payment of £140. In today's money that 'ransom' is equivalent to a figure in excess of £7 million; so a very generous and patriotic act on behalf of this ex-pat and serves as an example of the money some canny Scots were making in foreign countries.

Despite these treacherous events and the harshness of life at sea, Robert Young was not dissuaded from his new ambition.

As the seventeenth century drew to a close there was a notable downturn in shipping movements in and out of the Port of Leith because of the embargo imposed by King James; however, the port precinct remained a hub of activity as Leithers diversified into shipbuilding. This industry remained strong with a significant number of shipwrights and ships carpenters engaged in all facets of the business from the design and construction of new ships to the refit and repair of aged and crippled vessels. More specifically, it was the Newhaven area in North Leith which had established itself as the shipbuilding hub of Scotland in the day and there were Young family members and friends involved as well.

For those Youngs involved in the very early days of shipbuilding, working conditions were quite primitive. Shipwrights could be seen hard at work clambering over the stocks built on the mudflats on the side of the Forth. Later, came the 'grease way' method of hauling vessels up but this proved both dangerous and time consuming. Whilst these early shipwrights were resourceful and persevering folk, little did they know it would be a century or so before the first of a new generation of improved slipways would be built. It took until 1818 for Thomas Morton, a local Leith shipbuilder, to perfect his slipway design which he built and patent in 1819. It was, in fact, the first worldwide patent for a slipway. It would have greatly benefited shipwright families like Liston, Menzies, Strachan, Dryburgh, Cunynghame [sic], Woods and Young many of whom were well known in the Newhaven area of North Leith. Many of whom were connected to the Young family by either marriage or business.

In the absence of official historical records to quantify or indeed learn about any known shipwright family business, or the Leith shipbuilding industry for that matter, Historian Sue Mowat for one contends that Testaments offer one of the best insights. Curiously, these documents often contain information regarding the dimensions of ships under construction, the number of ships being built, how the wrights went about their business and more. She cites one Testament of a Shipbuilder by the name of John Lowrie, dated 1603, which paints an informative picture of his business at the time of his death. His Will states Lowrie had two keels of 87 ribs under construction and his other business assets included new and old oak and pine deals [a stock quantity measure of timber], two tree trunks, some 1,364 nails which are listed as reclaimed from wrecks, plus 68 old iron bolts weighting 31 stone [approx. 200 kg]. In another instance, the Edinburgh Council Records mention an Abraham Turnbull, Sailmaker,

In the beginning 1650-1750

where in '1626 he owed for 80 ells [91 metres] of sail canvas and another entry for the following year for a cable weighing 756 Flemish lb'. From these and many more records like them it can be seen that Leith's Shipbuilding Industry was alive and well way back then and by the time the likes of later Youngs and others took up shipbuilding or related occupations, they were entering an established and growing industry and should have made a reasonable living.

One very surprising element which contributed to their success and profitability no doubt, was the pursuit of reclamation and recycling which was important even way back in the early seventeenth century. The dangers faced by sailing ships were many and it was not an uncommon sight for the skeletons of wrecks to be seen lying where they floundered on the shoreline. Alternatively, those who had managed to hobble back into harbour often found a final resting place on the mud flats of the Forth where the earliest wrights could purchase them for reclamation. The solid commercial value of the timber alone can be directly attributed to the relative cost of imported timber and the recognised diminution of Scottish and English forests by the beginning of the 1600s. Several of the fittings found on these early sailing ships such as deadeyes, fids and bees were fashioned from timber and were, more often than not, recovered and recycled.

To better understand recycling in shipbuilding in the day there is a story surviving from 1607 involving the wreck of the vessel *Pelican* which was apparently left languishing on the banks of Leith Harbour. The relevance if this story is the twist in the tale. It appears that the *Pelican's* ex-master, Andrew Ochiltree, first bought the wreck in partnership with a Frenchman, then on-sold her for the princely sum of 400 merks [Scottish money] to a North Leith skipper by the name of Hugh Somerville and a Baker in Leith by the name of John Anderson [the one and the same Baxter with whom David Young had served his apprenticeship]. Andrew Ochiltree died a decade later and his Testament contains an Inventory of items he still owned, included 'anchors, sails, cables, tows, munition and whole apparelling' and whilst it is not known for certain that these belonged to the *Pelican* per se it is clear that such second-hand items with an estimated value for the purposes of probate was assessed to be some 1000 Merks it certainly made them quite valuable assets indeed. What is even more important is the fact that the scrap timber from these wrecks was a major windfall for at least one Baker in Leith as it was a known fact that although peat and coal were being utilised as fuel for forges and kilns, such fuels were entirely unsuitable for burning in a baker's oven.

It seems that for Leithers, fortune was favouring the tide. December 1651 sees free trade reinstated with great fanfare and literally the beating of drums in the streets; but, come October 1653 their fortunes and hopes would be dashed yet again when Parliament in Westminster reversed this decision. Edinburgh's right of control over Leith was reinstated and once again we see Leithers developing a strategy to counter their misfortune. Hoping to capitalise on their recent cordial relationship with Cromwell and his local military leader General Monck, the Burgh leaders of Leith strategized to take their case directly to Cromwell highlighting their long years of oppression and subjugation endured at the hands of the dictatorial Edinburgh Council. Unbeknown to the Burgesses of Leith and probably Cromwell too, Monck was formulating his own plans for the Port.

In line with Cromwell's expressed desire to improve fortifications, Monck was considering two options. One involved the building of an Enclosure Wall and the other option was the building of a Citadel. When word of Monck's plans reached the ears of those on the Edinburgh Council they responded quickly and decisively. Monck was offered £5000 sterling to settle for the Citadel option. Their justification for offering this 'bribe' was that it was desperate times for Edinburgh's Merchants who were already suffering economic stress, but the counterpoint to this is that Leithers had experienced even greater economic woes, more

In the beginning 1650-1750

political interference and more domination. To call it a 'bribe' is not a harsh judgement call at all when one considers that the final bill for the construction of the said Citadel was a staggering £100,000. Therefore, it becomes obvious to any casual observer that the £5000 was personal and designed to influence Monck's decision on what to build rather than be an insultingly meagre contribution to the overall building cost.

The next pressing matter for Leithers would have been the swift completion of the Citadel. It appears that the South Kirk of their parish church had been commandeered by Cromwell to be utilised as an Army magazine, or storage facility for provisions, guns, ammunition and it has also been written that horses were stabled there as well. Now, despite the protestations of the parishioners it was decreed by Monck that the Kirk would continue to be so utilised until the Citadel was completed. Meanwhile, Cromwell had instructed that all parishioners in Leith should utilise the North Kirk. The South Leith Kirk Session Records for the 26th June 1656 state that 'Anthoine Rosewell, James Cutler and John Young Tailer are desyred to goe to the North Kirk Session of Leith to intimat unto them that ye Counsell of State in Scotland efter ye sight of ane reference (from his heighness The Lord Protector) haith appoynted the south congregation of Leith to have the use of the north kirk to preach in for a tyme until the Magasin be removit from ye south paroch unto ye Citidal, at which tym the south congregatioun are to be restored to yr owne south kirk again, God willing.' This would imply that this John Young, tailor, quite possibly related to or one in the same as our John Young [1597-1648] tailor, was a parish leader, in South Kirk and that he in company with two other empowered parishioners were ordered by Cromwell to pass on his instructions in relation to the annexation of South Kirk to be used as a magazine store for his garrison.

Gen. George Monck as Commander-in-Chief of the Leith Garrison has quickly gained a first-hand appreciation of the importance of Leith as a commercial centre and at one point extended invitations to English merchants to travel north. His inducement was the opportunities that abounded to supply his men and the town. Those English who made the move to Leith were already wealthy merchants and arrived fully expecting that the free trade arrangements they had enjoyed in England for so many years were also available to them north of the border. They were in for quite a shock. It was not long before they realised the full extent of the restrictions placed on Leith merchants by the Edinburgh Council and thereupon metamorphosed from interloping English merchant enemy of Leithers to allies and collaborators in the fight with the Edinburgh Council. They initially approached General Monck with their grievances and although Monck wrote sympathetic correspondence to Protector Cromwell, Monck received a reply ordering that he and two Scottish judges should redress the matters locally.

In the face of Monck's inaction, and without any formal resolution, a number of English Traders decided to stand strong against Edinburgh and simply refused absolutely to pay the 'Merk per Tun Tax' Edinburgh was levying on Leith merchants only. It was not long before there was a change of heart and it should be stated that this is one of the rare occasions when Edinburgh can be seen to buckle under the concerted pressure of opposition from any Incorporation or group. The November 1654 Edinburgh Council Records show that they voted to exempt only English goods from this tax. Despite this blatant prejudice and discrimination, all in all these were good times for most merchants in Leith and several English chancers did manage to establish substantial businesses.

Recurrently, Testaments are the most reliable source of data to gain an insight into what business opportunity prevailed in any decade. Again, Scottish Historian Sue Mowat, in her publication *'The Port of Leith - Its History & Its People'*, regales the story of one such English Merchant by the name of Barnaby Darroch, who hailed from Yarmouth in Norfolk. His Testament Dative includes an Inventory that serves as a case in point. It itemises products like sugar, copper, alum, rosin, tobacco, wood, paper, books and wine with a value of £3,924 Scots. It also lists his shares in two Leith vessels and one Yarmouth vessel plus he had on hand £1,000 sterling in ready cash money. He was living pretty well too it seems because at a time when a well-to-do local Leith Merchant's Will would list £100-200 Scots as the value of his 'personal chamber possessions' Darroch's was valued at £300 with a staggering £46,107 owed to him by debtors. Make no mistake, this trader had done extremely well indeed as this debtors ledger equivalent today would be in the order of £136.4 million.

But there was still more to contend with! Those Merchants and Skippers wishing to turn a profit had yet another obstacle placed in their way. Come 1653 the Edinburgh Council decided to appoint a Quaymaster in Leith and needless to say the appointee was an Edinburgh Merchant not a Leither. He was accordingly charged with a range of responsibilities, including organising berths for ships, collecting shore dues, arranging ballast and overseeing Law and Order in the port. These were certainly important tasks in terms of keeping the port functioning and safe for merchants, skippers and crews, but it came at a cost. And 'cost' remained one of the major lingering difficulties for anyone trying to do business in the Port of Leith; but that was Edinburgh's plan. In fact, it has been said that it was these extraordinarily high charges that drove down business and forced mariners to desert in droves in favour of other ports on the Forth. Whilst the Council took the drastic action of doing away with the Merk per Tun Tax on English imports sadly this only went part way to finding a solution to the downturn in port activity. The major remaining impediment was the range and cost of service charges imposed on those wishing to do business in Leith.

Records exist detailing the type and range of the imposts Merchants and Skippers were required to pay. Again, Mowat gives a fine example from 1688 outlining what one Edinburgh Merchant by the name of George Clarke was required to pay for his cargo arriving into Leith from Danzig -

	£	s.	d.
The May Light	19	10	00
Primegilt	13	00	00
Beaconage and Anchorage	7	8	4
Shoremaster	3	18	00
Flag money	1	10	00
A boat to help the ship in	0	14	00
Shore dues	33	11	8
Plank mail (paid to the porters for use of their gangplank)	2	16	00
To the rowers	12	00	00
To the seamen to drink	2	16	00
Custom of lint, knapholt, deals, planks and entry to the Waiters	186	2	06
To the workmen (porters) for carrying the whole lading	80	00	00
Bush mail (timber bush)	18	00	00'

Quite substantial overheads!

With the growing importance of merchant shipping worldwide it seems appropriate here to acknowledge the legion of workers on land - the coopers, wrights, porters, carters, metters, clerks and others who the likes of Gilbert Dick and Robert Young relied on to keep ships and goods moving. Many of these jobs are unfamiliar to us today but in that era they played a vital role and several of these jobs were taken up by members of the Young family. Most of these maritime workers as we know were originally forcibly organised into quasi unions called Incorporations or Guilds. As new occupations emerged, these workers too formed themselves into Incorporations. All members paid fees and as the Incorporations grew in membership numbers, as a collective they began to flex their muscle, much as unions do today whereby they attempted restricting employment to only those persons who were financial members. At one time a further restriction was instigated whereby only those who were also 'resident in Leith' would qualify for membership and hence be entitled to work on the Leith docks. This was done to ensure preferential treatment for bona fide residents of the Port Burgh ahead of any interlopers.

Of all the various groups, it was the Skippers and Mariners who appear to have remained the strongest fraternity and ancestral family members of Youngs, Dicks, Lundies, Spittals, Thomsons, Listons, Waddells and Watsons were definitely among their ranks. Early on, the Incorporation of Masters & Mariners had established headquarters in what was known as Trinity House and to this day it remains the Incorporation's ancestral home, although now its major function is as a well-appointed Maritime Museum. Down the centuries Trinity House has been the sight of many and varied activities. We already know it was the site of the first hospital, later The Grammar School held classes there and in fact this continued right up until 1710. Although the rent was small a search of the Session Records reveals the whole history. One such example is this record of 19 December 1664 which states 'The wich [sic] day Mr. Johne Hamiltoune Modr. Mr. John Corsaur ministers ... elders appoyntit be the session to meitt with Wm. Johnstoune bailie James Kerse Johne Watsone Skippers to setill and aggrie with them, both for yr feu dutie of the fraternitie house (ie. Trinity House) yei are awand to the session as also for the School rent ...'.

There is no denying that these Incorporations played an important role in the port and the local community. As their functions evolved, the Masters of Trinity House down the years carried out varied responsibilities ranging from providing pilots for ships coming into port, acting as arbitrators in certain maritime disputes to setting the standards for and conducting examinations of would-be skippers and pilots. The significance of Trinity House to the close-knit maritime community of Leith cannot be overstated. One of its very important benevolent functions was offering financial assistance to seamen and their families who were not receiving any or sufficient parish relief. In 1731 it was these Leith Incorporations who finally determined to take their Burgh fight to Edinburgh.

They took their grievances to the Court of Session where in Edinburgh in 1734 Edinburgh was forced to admit that the

Charters granted to Leith by Lord Logan of Restalrig were valid and all the Incorporations and their members should be designated as Freemen. All those centuries of struggles, all the lives lost, all the heavy taxes paid - were now wiped away. This was very significant for our Masters and Merchants at the time because Unfreemen were required to pay twice the tax of Freemen when importing and weighing goods at the harbour of Leith. In fact, there was a time when no Leith Merchants could sell their imported goods in Leith at all, without having first been forced to sell them to Edinburgh Merchants and then buy the goods back again. Tax by stealth, market manipulation, call it what you may it is just another reason why Leithers felt nothing but disdain and distrust for their neighbours.

Perhaps one of the lesser-known functions these Incorporations performed relates to the provision of a Mort Cloth. Up until the early sixteenth century in Scotland it was customary for the common people to be buried in an unmarked grave without a coffin. Nobility burials often had the body sheathed in a shroud cloth of some kind. This latterly led to the practice of covering a body as it was carried to the grave site. The use and availability of such a cloth was largely determined by what the deceased person's family could afford. Originally, the Mort Cloth was instituted to cover an uncoffined body and then later to shroud a simple coffin as it was carried from the deceased's home to the church and then on to the graveyard. Then, in order to curtail the ever-growing desire for more and more elaborate funerals, the use of a Mort Cloth was proclaimed into Law by the Privy Council in 1684.

The Mort Cloth has a very long history in both Scotland and England. In Scotland the Mort Cloth was either owned by the Kirk Sessions, the Burghs or in rural areas by the Parish. Whilst the purchase price was mostly around £12 Scots money they would be hired out to families for a few shillings a time. It is not uncommon to find entries in Scottish Kirk Session Records for church revenue derived from the provision of a Mort Cloth.

A lesser known fact is that many of the Guilds had their own Mort Cloth for the exclusive use of their members. Trinity House and the Masters and Mariners Incorporation [their name was changed over time] of Leith was one such Guild, and their records demonstrate just how extraordinarily grand their Mort Cloth was by comparison. Once again Sue Mowat's book gives a stunning example of how highly valued this Mort Cloth was to the Mariners in North Leith in particular. It reads -

'9 ells of velvet at £16 13s 4d per ell	£150 05s
for lining, and the poke thereto	£10 16s
for a fringe weighing 3lb 31/3oz	£56 13s
for sewing silk and fringes for the poke	£1 09s
for the workmanship thereof	£6 13s
for extraordinary charges about the business	£3 00s
	£279 08s'

This is not only an astonishing amount of money compared to the norm but it speaks volumes about the financial standing of this Incorporation and the strength of kinship these mariners and their families enjoyed and also stands as proof of the depth of the camaraderie enjoyed by those who put their life on the line every voyage. To gauge the value placed on life, death and an appropriate funeral, by contrast, it is written that the same fraternity of Leith mariners only had about £50 cash money in their Guild Box to deal with 'contingencies'. It seems Robert Young was about to embark on a career that came with a built in extended family born out of a fraternity of daring and caring souls.

From these few stories we can glean something of what life was like for David Young's youngest son and Robert's father, John Young, when he married into this Leith history in 1709. What John would have known when he decided to hitch his star to that of his spouse Margaret Dick, is that her family had a long association with the sea; however, what would have come as a surprise to him, had he been told, is their name is attached to events deeply etched in the English Parliamentary Record. He would have known that the Dick family were 'well fixed' as the saying goes and one indication of this is when on the occasion of Margaret's parents' marriage in July 1682 the newly-weds gave a 3/- (three shilling) donation to the poor of the parish. This may not sound like a huge sum of money; however, its 'economic power value' [base on GDP] would be equivalent to something like £4852 in 2018, so not such a pittance after all, and clearly the expected amount given the Dick family's status in the community.

Yet another way to gauge a person's or a family's status in such times relates to the allocation of seats in the parish church. These were God fearing days, there was no separation of church and State, church attendance, belief and worship were compulsory features of everyday life as this entry in the South Kirk Session Records of Leith attests. 'October 6, 1687 It was aggried that intimation should be made that all within the toun and parish of South Leith who intended to take seatts in the meeting house would be pleased to come tomorrow at two afternoon because att that tyme the desks and seattes are to be divided'. That particular record goes on to explain that there is an accompanying drawing which clearly lays out the plan for seat allocations. In the northwest quarter the first pew was reserved for those who have children to be baptised and those who are presenting for marriage, affording them easy access to the pulpit. The second row plus the following five were reserved for the sole use of the Laird of Dreghorn and his family. On the corresponding south-side the first row was reserved for the 'precentor' as he was termed; the person who assisted with worship and led the congregation in song and so on, and the second pew was designated for the minister and his family.

The remainder of the reserved seating was to be allocated to the long list of those who have already put forward their names, notables such as Lady Caldwell, Lady Boighall, and there on the list was the name of Captain Gilbert Dick. The Watson family also attended the same parish church, and there was an entry for John Watson the Younger, David Young's uncle. John Watson was also mentioned on the 29 October 1657 as one of those charged with the responsibility of meeting with the Glazier to assess and report on the cost of repairs to the church post its occupation by Cromwell's troops. Come 17 January 1661 both John Young [1620-1680] and John Watson [C1620 -] in the company of three others, James Seatone, John Gray and James Bell were appointed 'to be at the up-putting of my Lord Balmerinoch his seats in the Kirke never they shall be put up at any tym heirafter'. One would have to say that only the most respected in the parish community would be charged with such responsibilities.

There is so much more to the background of Gilbert Dick. Banns records of 1682 describe Gilbert Dick as a Ships Captain - quite a well-respected profession at the time, but what has also been learned from the genealogy is that the Christian name of Gilbert, although uncommon in Scotland, is a perpetuated family Christian name in the Dick family for several generations with several men bearing the name of Gilbert Dick known to have left their mark. Margaret's father for one is well documented, however, it is another Captain Gilbert Dick, who appears to be the first in the family to warrant a personal mention in the Scottish Calendar of State Papers. Scottish Historian and Academic Steve Murdoch has extracted several articles from these Papers and published them in a book he entitled *The Terror of the Seas? : Scottish Maritime Warfare 1513-1713'*. One such account regales the capture of a Scottish ship on 30 November 1582, and it reads in part -

> 'James VI ... became involved in cases of piracy between Scotland and several other countries, including England.....a particularly brutal attack occurred in 1582 when the 'James' of Pittenweem (William Stevenson master) was attacked by Captain Vaughan Gower off the Isle of Wight and the crew suffered some fatalities when resisting the attack. The survivors were robbed, stripped and some put ashore and told to return with £200 sterling to redeem, the ship and goods. To the usual complaints of piracy and unnecessary brutality were added that this assault on the Godly aboard, particularly Gilbert Dick, could not go unpunished, particularly

not by such a leading protestant power as England.' Sadly, all efforts to follow this story have failed to find any further details as to what actually happened to that Captain Gilbert Dick on this occasion.

There is one further historical mention of the Dick family member in the Parliamentary Records and this relates to the matter of reparations. This time it is a brother to Margaret by the name of William Dick. But first a little background - we know that James VI, at one point, wrote to Elizabeth I requesting or was it demanding reparations for those Scots who sustained losses at the hands of English Privateers. Needless to say his requests were ignored and no funds were ever forthcoming, and, despite his numerous formal protests the English attacks continued. This prompted the Commissioners in the Royal Burgh of Edinburgh to levy a 'war' tax designed to raise the funds needed to build and fit-out Scottish warships in an attempt to protect Scottish merchant vessels.

Residents of ports like Leith, Aberdeen and Kirkcaldy all witnessed Scottish warships setting sail in pursuit of foreign pirates to wit Scotland ultimately raised a fleet of some six vessels in all. This Scotch Guard naval squadron included Lewis Dick on *James* of Wemyss, Alexander Campbell on *Marigold* and Andrew Heatley on *David*. Later, 'The Scotch Guard was bolstered by the deployment of three further warships readied by the Covenanters in March 1647, of which two were commissioned to carry 18 guns and 60 personnel and supported by a 10 gun pinnace with 30 men.'

'Despite these patrols there were still occasional losses such as Janet of Leith, which had been bound for Stornoway in the Western Isles with 40 tons of salt and other goods in 1647.' We know that privateering was an activity instigated and sanctioned by the English Queen and on more than one occasion the English Admiralty

In the beginning 1650-1750

> Court records show where it was called upon to settle cases arising from the disputed ownership of prizes or to pass determination on the sharing of prizes on behalf of English privateer crews and ships of the Crown with one classic case in point involving 'the entire crew of HMS *Lyon* complaining en masse against Archibald Douglas.' It was quite a bizarre circumstance really - Theft and murder by Royal assent.

Anyhow, the abovementioned William Dick, was the son of Gilbert Dick and Alisone Foreman and is cited in the Marriage Register in 1640 as Servitor to Sir Alexander Clerk, Provost of Edinburgh and an Indweller in Leith. When considered in the context of Edinburgh Leith antagonism this is difficult to reconcile except to conclude that family status clearly overrides inter-Burgh infighting. This William Dick is presumed to be the same William Dick mentioned as one of the first to have his case for reparations discussed in Parliament as cited in a Charles I manuscript relating to the 17 August 1641 sitting of the Edinburgh Parliament. This item [1641/8/238] reads 'Reference in favoures of Williame Dicke, James Ferquhar and others - The quhilk day the supplication givine in to the parliament be Williame Dicke of Braid, James Ferquhar and certain otheres, craveing recommendacione from the king and parliament to the parliament of England for the supplicantes there reparatione for ane shipe and loadining thereof, takine from them be the Englishe, being this day moved in parliament to his majestie and estates of parliament, his majestie and estates foirsaidis hes remitted and remitts the same to his hienes secreet counsell.'

There is yet another mention of William Dick in Alan R. MacDonald's *'The Burghs and Parliament in Scotland, c.1550-1651'* wherein he cites incidents relating to raising an army and armaments against Charles I. 'In the desperate preparations for war in 1638, specie flooded out of Scotland and in 1638, burghs were asked to gather coin and plate from their inhabitants and send it to Edinburgh ..... Individual merchants also lent huge sume: by 1644, William Dick of Braid was already owed 840,000 merks (£560,000) but he never received more than a fraction of it. Taxes of all sorts were levied....'. Indeed, the King and his Privy Council under correspondence dated 17 November 1641 did refer the initial matter but sadly it probably suffered the same fate as the reparations correspondence. There is no doubt that various members of the Dick family held positions of influence and it could be construed that these Youngs appear to have married well.

However, before getting too far ahead of ourselves there is a little piece of genealogy which demands inclusion as it goes to the relevance of this Dick family in the life of these generations of Youngs. It concerns the 1645 Testament Dative of Alisone Foreman [C1577-1645] the wife of Gilbert Dick [C1575-Pre1653] and mother of Margaret who became the wife of John Young. This Will is extremely informative because it positively links this Young/Dick family to that of Sir William Dick, the man Historians cited as so wealthy at one point prior to the Cromwell invasion that they excluded him from their statistics because his wealth would skew their averaging.

Later that same year, on the 10 July 1645, there is another source entry in the Kirk Session Records for South Leith which more directly sheds light on at least one of Sir William's business activities. It reads 'Recommended to ye Bailies to wryt to Sir Wm Dick to try if he will let his brewarie brew aill for ye publicke heir.' The Session Clerk who recompiled these records centuries later in 1911 added his own footnote to the margin, and it reads [Note - This was the Sir Wm Dick of Grange House referred to in the 'Heart of Midlothian' as the Scottish millionaire. He was ruined by Cromwell. His house and business premises still stand in the Advocate's Close.] At least from this time forward these Youngs are known to be moving in the upper echelon of Leith society.

Furthermore, the genealogy of Alisone Foreman [1578-1645] gave up another historic link to Scotland's past of even greater interest and importance. For those family members and readers who are passionate Scots it is fair to say that to have a link to Sir William Wallace, regardless of how tenuous, would be a far more coveted prize than a link to Sir William Dick; and it is thanks to Alisone Foreman's Will that such a link exists via a James Tinto [1616-]. This James Tinto is the son-in-law of Alisone Foreman and Gilbert Dick C1575-Pre1653], Merchant and Episcopalian

Bookseller and is cited in the Burgess Register as 'Tinto (Tynto), James, B. and G., writer, by r. of w. Catheren dr. of umq. Gilbert Dick, mt., B. and G. 7 Sept 1653.'

When translated this states that James Tinto (Tynto) is a Writer [lawyer/solicitor] and was admitted Burgess and Guild on 7 Sept 1653 by rite of his wife Catheren [sic], daughter of the deceased Gilbert Dick, Merchant in Edinburgh. That directory has a secondary note which reads 'From Tinto in Lanarkshire. There was a family of Tynto of Crymcramp in the barony of Crawford-Douglas in 1528.' The barony of Crawford is thought to be Norman in origin and is documented widely in Lanarkshire and will no doubt be a study for another day. This James Tinto [1616-1655] is the son of James Tinto [C1580-1642], and his grandfather is Robert Tynto/Tinto of Crympcrampt whose Will was probated at Edinburgh on 30 November 1570.

Meanwhile, the lineage of James Tinto has been traced all the way to Sir John Tinto of Lanarkshire who was a knight who rode into battle with Sir William Wallace. There is a publication entitled *'The Life and Acts of the most Famous and Valiant Champion, Sir William Wallace, Knight of Ellerslie; Maintainer of the Liberty of Scotland....'*. Published in Glasgow in 1712 which contains several references to this Sir John Tinto/Tynto as present at the Battle at Bigger [Spelt Biggar in current Bartholomew's Gazetteer] in 1297. Page 133 of the above publication confirms events as -

> 'Of Cunningham and Kyle came Men of vail,
> To Lanark fought on Horse a thousand hail.
> Sir John the Graham, and his good chevalry,
> Sir John of Tinto with Men that he might hy:
> Good Auchleck that Wallace Uncle was:'

Reading on, page 136 recounts the actual deeds of Sir John Tinto, Knight, at the Battle at Bigger -

> 'Forth from his Men them Wallace raiked right,
> To hi, he called Sir John Tinto the Knight,
> And let him woe to vissy he would go
> The English Host, and bade him tell no no

What ever he spiered, till that he come again.
Wallace disguised, thus bowned he over plain,
Betwixt Cutler and Bigger as he past.'

The background to these events reads like a blood curdling Polanski sequel and relate to the life of William Wallace and his family. The whole story is very convoluted indeed, but there are certain key events that influenced John Tinto and others to collaborate with William Wallace on this occasion and they unfold this way.

Firstly, the English murdered William Wallace's father in 1291 and then persecuted his mother to her demise. In May 1297 the Sheriff of Lanark, Englishman Sir William Heselrig, murdered William Wallace's wife and baby then torched their house in retaliation for her detaining Heselrig in conversation while Wallace made good his escape. This was a major tactical error on Heselrig's part because on hearing this news Wallace became deeply enraged and consumed with grief. This proved to be the turning point in Wallace's battle hardened life where rather than Wallace's fight being about freedom for Scotland, it escalated into a personal vendetta, which Wallace and his knight comrades executed with determination.

They took their revenge by proceeding to Heselrig's house in the dead of night whereupon they beheaded Heselrig, disembowelled his son and torched Heselrig's house. This final excerpt explains the prose above in the context of these events and Sir John Tinto's role in the affair. 'The news of William Wallace's lastest attack on the English would have rippled through out Scotland, and it had the effect of rallying like-minded men from all over Scotland flocking to join him. Before long William Wallace found himself in command of three thousand wellarmed men, all rallying under the banner of freedom. From Kyel and Cunningham alone a thousand men on horseback were raised, old friends like Adam Wallace and Robert Boyd and new ones like Sir John Tinto, also joined, together with their vassals.'

Now that is a story worth the re-telling. Surely it would have been well known within the wider family and been the source of much family pride I would have thought. So, when Captain

John Young [1789-1836] and his wife Jean Lamb named their son William Wallace Young in 1828 one can only speculate as to whether or not they had any knowledge of this ancient family connection? Probably not, it is more likely the child was so named out of Scottish passion and pride.

From treachery on land we now segue to treachery at sea. Dodging the piranha on top of the water was a reality for all Mariners way back then and today too it seems with modern day pirates operating out of Somalia in East Africa. It is probably fair to say that there are few people alive currently who would ever dream that their ancestors were mixed up in pirate skirmishes because it all seems too far-fetched; but, rest assured, these Youngs have more than one encounter dotted through their maritime past. Now while stories, myths and legends about Pirates, Privateers, Corsairs and Buccaneers abound, all too often these names are seen as synonyms and used interchangeably.

For the record, Pirates are classified as those persons who use the sea to break the Law, i.e. they use ships to attack other ships, ships crews, mainland towns, peoples and seaports, and among their ranks one could include the likes of Slave Traders. On the other hand, a Privateer, or as the French would say 'Corsair', is a person who does legally what pirates do illegally. Privateers are sometimes described as 'Pirate Contractors' since they enjoy immunity to prosecution under a Government Licence called a Letter of Marque.

This Letter of Marque was issued to the Captain of a vessel by his National Admiralty. Supposedly Privateers raided only enemy vessels in times of war but there is ample documented evidence to shows that this was not always the case. A Letter of Marque was designed to be used in the event of capture and designed to save the Captain and his crew from the gallows. A Privateer or Corsair taken by an enemy Navy would receive Prisoner of War status by the Captain presenting his Letter of Marque. This was considered far preferable to being arrested, imprisoned and forced to face the courts as a Pirate where those found guilty would most likely be sentenced to death.

England, France and Spain in particular participated in this scheme. The line of distinction between Naval vessels attacking enemy shipping and Privateers attacking enemy shipping is that the Navy vessels were Government owned, crewed and provisioned and were considered warships, whereas the Privateers undertook such activity totally at their own risk and expense; that is to say they owned their own ships, hired their own crews, shared the 'prizes' as wages and acted pretty much autonomously. Corsairs were generally those Privateers of France who sailed and plundered mostly along the Barbery Coast. The word Buccaneer is also derived from the French and was applied to those Pirates or Privateers who operated exclusively in the waters of the Caribbean. From around 1620 onwards the 'Boucaniers' or Buccaneers became quite highly skilled in navigation and sharpshooting with many achieving notoriety for their combat prowess. However, these descriptions are open to interpretation, especially when we see the blurring of the lines in respect of men such as Sir Henry Morgan who was classified as a pirate by the Spanish, a privateer by the English but qualified as a Buccaneer because of his geographical area of activity.

Whilst Hollywood movies have glorified the swashbuckling lives of several of the more dashing pirates, the point needs to be made that they presented a real threat in their day. The most famous privateer of all has to be that well lauded mariner, Sir Francis Drake [1540-1595]. He has been variably described as Sea Captain, Privateer, Navigator, Slaver and Politician of the Elizabethan Era. Drake was so successful that Queen Elizabeth I bestowed a knighthood upon him in 1581 in recognition of his piratical accomplishments achieved in that famous ship the *Golden Hind*. He considered Spain his arrant foe, as did she, and often under her instruction he would lay siege to Spanish ships and Spanish settlements globally but more especially along the Florida coastline. There is no disputing Drake's sailing ability and as a tribute to his accomplishments he is credited with being only the second man in his lifetime to have circumnavigated the globe. He was later given the title Vice Admiral by his Queen.

In the beginning 1650-1750

What is not so well known is that Scotland too was not without her own home-grown examples of pirates and privateers. Perhaps one of the most famous Scottish pirates of all time was Captain William Kidd [1645-1701], a stylish native of Scotland and afterwards citizen of New York City who was given a Royal Warrant by William III in 1695 to hunt down the likes of Captain Thomas Wake and Captain Thomas Tew. Curiously, he is also credited with contributing financially to the building of Trinity House in Leith; so it seems family connections with such events were never far away. Other notable pirates and privateers include the dashing Bristol born Englishman nicknamed 'Blackbeard', aka Edward Teach [1680-1718] who also used aliases of Thatch and Drummond. 'Blackbeard' was renowned for charging into battle with a cutlass in both hands and several knives and pistols at the ready in his belt. Widely feared, he reputedly captured over forty merchant ships in the Caribbean and is known to have murdered countless prisoners.

Next there is Welshman Bartholomew Roberts [1682-1722] affectionately known as 'Black Bart'. Roberts, who has been described as enterprising and imaginative, was widely admired for his sense of adventure, his courage, his competency at navigation, his charisma and bravado, and above all, those who knew him well all agreed that he was venerated by his crew. Black Bart is credited with plundering over 400 ships, and achieved great fame in his lifetime, renowned for captaining a well-armoured ship. It cannot be stressed too strongly, that all these savage opportunists posed real and deadly threats to all sailors in the day including those family members sailing to distant ports.

However, the biggest surprise in the pages of pirate history is that women were also prominent. Several proved themselves to be formidable, successful, surprisingly ruthless and incredibly courageous. Anne Bonny [1700-1782] was an Irish lass born in County Cork and daughter of an Attorney-at-Law. She disguised herself as a man for most of her pirate days and was not afraid to drink and fight as a man either. Anne and fellow female pirate Mary Read at one time were known to be working in company with pirate John 'Calico Jack' Rackham. However, these women also achieved notoriety for their own feats and for encouraging their fellow crewmates to greater bloodshed and violence. What is clear is that all these scoundrels posed prodigious danger to all forms of shipping. They killed thousands of people on land and sea, and in the Golden Age of Piracy, which was basically 1650-1730, the oceans, seas and rivers of the world were infested with this menace and Young family ancestors were not immune to the disease.

Curiously, the person, male or female, who posed the greatest danger to shipping and who takes the prize in the pirate stakes is a Chinese woman. Although she came on the scene in the Far East much later than her Atlantic counterparts, she is an unequivocal stand out for the sheer size of her operation. Ching Shih [1785-1844] also known as Ching I Sao lived a long and fascinating life dominated by her pirate exploits. Her entré to the business came via her marriage to a Chinese pirate. By all reports she quickly became his equal and competently took over his empire following his death. This beautiful former prostitute had a personal armada consisting of some 300 junks and upwards of 40,000 men, women and children. However, her entire fleet, part of which was under the control of her subordinates, is recorded to have been in the realm of 1500 ships and 80,000 men. The immeasurable value of the 'prizes' taken was shared on the basis that the seizing vessel retained twenty per cent and the remaining eighty per cent was placed in a 'community chest' and shared amongst the whole 'pirate crew family'. Insubordination was not tolerated at all and everyone was required to abide by 'The Code'. Those who did not were beheaded.

She terrorised and robbed towns and plundered ships up and down the entire coastline of the South China Sea, which would have involved those ships sailing to the Far East from England and Scotland. Later she married her adopted son who she had previously appointed as her second-in-command. In the end, the Chinese Government were so frustrated in their unsuccessful attempts to arrest her activity that they eventually offered her a 'Pirate Amnesty' in exchange for peace. She accepted their offer and lived out the remainder of her 69 years managing a brothel and casino in Guangzhou, Guangdong Province in China. Ching

Shih lived a colourful and long life at a time when life expectancy for pirates was less than 40 years. Ching Shih would have posed a real threat to all those sailing to the East Indies and China in that 1801-1810 period including Scots.

Why did this whole era of Privateering and Piracy happen when it did?

There are several factors really – governments wished to expand their reach, colonise new lands and expand trade opportunities. Most experts agree the evolution in hull design made such daring exploits even more possible because vessels became stronger, faster and more manoeuvrable at a time when there was a corresponding innovation in munitions. Impetus for the hull design changes came from the English who had resolved that their best defence as an island nation was via a strong Navy not a large Army. This shifted the focus of innovation onto English shipwrights. Progress was slow at first and eventually they were forced to collaborate with their Italian counterparts so that by the end of the reign of Elizabeth I, England's new look Navy was ready for action. Eventually these innovations in hull design filtered through to merchant ships as well.

Evolution in the design and understanding of cannon and handheld firearms had added to the knowledge base as the world headed into the seventeenth century. Cannon were built with longer barrels to enable the latest design of more spherical balls to be projected further which proved a distinct advantage for those engaging in sea battles. Once upon a time, cannon balls were fashioned from stone; but by the seventeenth century, iron was the most common material used. There was also a growing understanding of the intricacies of the behaviour of gunpowder, whereby the fine powder was eventually replaced by a coarser grain with its corresponding pockets of air. This allowed the fire to travel through the mass of gunpowder more efficiently and in turn would ignite the entire charge more uniformly and thus produce more projectile velocity. Again, the relevance of this information is that since many merchantmen like our Youngs sailed with hand arms and cannon these innovations would have added to their safety also.

With this Young family finally taking their place on the high seas, all these historical events and evolutions would most certainly have given them cause to think long and hard about the veracity of such a move. As for Robert Young's immediate descendants, a great many of those Young boys took to the sea at between ten and twelve years of age, with several making Captains before the age of twenty-five. Only a handful are known to have joined the Royal Navy. The majority of Youngs joined the Merchant Navy and some became whalers and fishermen, but they all would have been conversant with cannon and handheld firearms at different times. To get a better understanding of their actual work environment we need to turn to one of the leading authorities in this field, Michael Morris Oppenheim, a pioneering historian of English Naval Administration. He made this research and reporting his life's work.

Oppenheim's credentials are that he completed his medical training at University College Hospital, London and after a year at Middlesex Hospital he sat his Royal College of Surgeons examinations in 1879. He then went to sea as a Ships Surgeon in the days when Surgeons were properly trained and fully qualified medical graduates (unlike Andrew Wilkie in the days of the *Speedy Return in 1702*). It was only after Oppenheim inherited a sizeable sum of money that he could indulged his passion and become a self-supporting independent researcher of maritime history. By all accounts he had all things nautical in his blood and after a solid career in the Royal Navy he went on to receive universal acknowledgment for this research work and was latterly awarded the title of Master of Maritime History.

He published many articles and books, but it is his massive publication *'A History of the Administration of the Royal Navy and of Merchant Shipping - 1509-1660'* published 1896 which will provide the most elucidating and interesting input to our story. Oppenheim gives a wonderful insight into the life of mariners like our Gilbert Dick, but it is Oppenheim's expert views on Impressing which are about to take centre stage in this story. He contends that Impressing was one of the most pervasive, destructive and vexatious issues confronting Skippers and mariners in their day.

Impressing is a word with which most modern day landlubbers will be totally unfamiliar. Impressing, Impressment or Press Ganging, the most common phrase, basically alludes to recruitment by force. Although press-ganging for the purpose of recruiting soldiers for the English Army had been a common practice since at least the thirteenth century, it was not until Queen Elizabeth I decided to establish a sizeable Navy that it was extended to include seamen. In 1563 she passed the first Act of Parliament designed to ensure that her Navy was fully manned to the level of its fleet capability. The Royal Navy had already been routinely dealing with manpower shortages due in the most part to the harsh conditions onboard ship, the prolonged absences from home and the poor pay being offered.

Citizens in coastal areas in particular lived in fear of having their men and boys pressed into service. This was especially the case for those living in seaport towns such as Leith as it was presumed by the authorities that those citizens would have a greater understanding of the sea and possess some maritime skills. Leithers lived in constant fear of the 'Press Gangs' who would patrol their waterfront, raid taverns, and there are even reports of vigilante press gangs kidnapping men from their bedchambers. Mostly, pressing took place at sea when a Navy vessel would pull alongside a merchant ship and ransack it of its most able seamen, frequently taking all and only the very best of men. The Press Gangs felt no compunction about leaving the poor merchantman short of enough hands to safely make the next port.

The Impressment situation was exacerbated by the fact that the Navy was building ships faster than they could recruit seamen. The situation became so desperate that the Admiralty, as far back as 1597, had pushed through legislation tagged *'The Vagrancy Act'* in order to help resolve the urgent need for large numbers of sailors. This Act permitted 'men of disrepute' to be 'press-ganged' into the service of the Royal Navy. Whilst many viewed this distasteful business of Impressing as unconstitutional and inhumane, the Law as it stood remained in force until well into the eighteenth century.

Another legislative attempt to redress negative public opinion came much later in 1740 when a new Act of Parliament declared that all men under 18 and over 55, including foreigners, who had served on British ships were now exempted from being pressed into service. But as usual, this was largely ignored by the Navy Press Gangs who simply carried on as usual. There is evidence to suggest that they simply refocused their activity more onto foreigners. Come 1780 and the British Admiralty had successfully lobbied to have the Exemption Legislation withdrawn. To understand the sheer scale of the threat to merchant sailors and to appreciate the dire manpower shortages facing the Royal Navy, it needs to be understood that the British Parliament had agreed to increase the size of its British Naval Fleet from 135 to 584 vessels with a corresponding need to massively increase its navy personnel count from a very low base of 36,000 to a staggering 114,000 seamen. By contrast, Merchant Marine numbers at the that time, which included the Youngs and their relatives, was estimated to be in the vicinity of 118,000 hands.

At one point, in utter frustration and in a desperate attempt to fulfil their quotas, the Royal Navy Press Gangs made a major tactical error; they turned their attention to raiding American merchant vessels. It is estimated that between 1793 and 1812, the Royal Navy impressed as many as 15,000 sailors from American vessels in order to meet their immediate quotas of seamen to crew those vessels of the British Fleet involved in the Napoleonic Wars. Although Impressing was not a solely British activity, the scale of the British affront on the Americans angered them so greatly that they retaliated by declaring war on Britain on the 18th June 1812. Impressment was cited as a major bone of contention.

In the beginning 1650-1750

To this time, it is not known for certain if any family members were ever impressed into service, but these truths are not readily available because the names of those so recruited were not separately recorded. There are records in The National Archives in Kew entitled *'Registers of Applications for the Release of Impressed Seamen, 1793-1802'* which cover certain British and foreign seamen. Although this list is far from complete, no related persons have been identified so far. If evidence to the contrary did come to light perhaps it would tell a story not unlike that of Englishman Charles Davis. His story is not unique, according to Author and American Naval Genealogist John P. Deeben who gives a wonderful account of how Charles Davis came to find himself impressed. This is an abridged extract from *'The War of 1812 - Stoking the Fires: The Impressment of Seaman Charles Davis by the U.S. Navy'* by John P. Deeben -

Charles Davis was born in the parish of St Mary's in Dublin, Ireland, about 1789. In 1795 at the age of nine, he was apprenticed to a Dublin mariner named Edward Murphy, the master of a merchant vessel called the Valentine. Murphy taught the young lad the basic aspects of the seafaring trade for two years and then sent David to sea on several merchant vessels for practical experience. One voyage even drew Davis into the nefarious world of the Atlantic slave trade, when he sailed on the slave ship 'Princess Amelia' from Liverpool to the coast of Africa and them to Santo Domingo and Grenada in the West Indies. While docked at the port of Antigua [a port visited by several of our family from time to time during this same period] with the merchant brig Ann in February 1807, Davis experienced impressment for the first time when he was abducted by the HMS St. Lucia. That ordeal ended after two French privateers captured the British schooner. Davis finally returned to Liverpool in August 1807, where he worked in the dockyards as a rigger for about three years.

> 'On August 5, 1810 Davis went back to sea on the merchant ship 'Margaret' for what would prove to be his final civilian voyage. The 'Margaret' brought Davis to America for the first time on October 2, landing at the port of Charleston, South Carolina. After four days

aboard ship Davis and three shipmates went ashore to a local tavern. By his own admission, Davis imbibed too much and could not recall what happened next, except that on the following morning he found himself on board the American sloop of war 'Wasp'. ... finding himself addressed as seaman Thomas Holland, Davis immediately applied to First Lieutenant Ingles of the Wasp to be returned to the Margaret, pointing out that he was British rather than an American citizen. Inglis bluntly refused, stating that he would see Davis "drowned first, 'for the English keep the Americans and I will keep you".

'Thus began 13 months of forced labour in the American Navy under an assumed name. The Wasp cruised for a time along the coast of Georgia and South Carolina, during which Ingles put Davis in irons on several occasions for refusing to work and threatening to jump ship at the first opportunity. On November 20, 1810 he finally succeeded in slipping his chains after the Wasp returned to Charleston harbor. Swimming to shore, Davis walked 124 miles to Savannah where, unfortunately, another Charleston tavern keeper recognised him and caused Davis to be arrested. After Davis returned to the Wasp, the captain placed him in double, irons for 72 days. For attempting to desert, Davis was also court-martialled and sentenced to 78 lashes with a cat-o-nine tails, with the punishment to be administered on board the USS John Adams in Hampton Roads, Virginia.

Around the time of his trial and punishment the USS Constitution arrived at Hampton Roads in July 1811 to seek a draft of new men for her crew. Capt. Isaac Hull of the Constitution boarded the John Adams twice to requisition crewmembers while Davis was still on board. At first, Hull rejected Davis because of his nationality, which suggested there was indeed some validity to the latter's claim of being held illicitly on the naval ship. After returning for a second look, however, Hull decided to take Davis, reportedly commenting: 'I don't care a damn lest you be English or what you will. I will run the risk of taking you.' With Capt. Hull's pronouncement, Charles Davis boarded the Constitution on July 27 and began the voyage that finally ended with his dramatic escape at Spithead on November 12, 1811'.

It would be interesting to know if any Young family members were impressed by the Americans or the English for that matter. These were real life events effecting ordinary folk, and there is no reason to believe that the Youngs would have escaped completely. Life at sea was not always clear sailing!

As far as the Royal Navy is concerned, the official line is that post Cromwell's victory in the North of Britain the Scottish Navy was splintered and absorbed into what was tagged for a while as the Commonwealth Navy. It is also written that Scottish seamen were later given some protection against arbitrary impressment by the Royal Navy on the understanding that a fixed quota of conscripts would be levied on nominated Scottish seacoast burghs. This policy appears to have remained in place right through the second half of the seventeenth century. There is anecdotal evidence within the Young family, and written up by Doreen Young in 1964, that later generations of Youngs were successful in devising a cunning plan to avert the loss of their Arctic hardened seamen. Doreen was led to believe that the Youngs firstly formed alliances with local Navy Commanders, but what has been learned subsequently is that, for a period at least, all Greenland whale fishermen were excluded by Government Decree on account of Britain's greater need for the whale oil in particular. Later this was curtailed to relate to Officers only, but more on that later.

What is proved is that it was common practice for whaler crewmembers to join a vessel in ports in the far north of Scotland such as the Orkneys and Shetlands. Similarly, these same Scottish Captains would routinely disembark the bulk of their crew ahead of arriving at their mainland homeports such as Leith, Aberdeen and Montrose. For the Youngs and others the dangers of impressment were more apparent closer to these homeports, especially Leith which had accommodated a Naval Base since the outbreak of the Napoleonic Wars.

Taken on balance though, some mariners are known to have actually benefited from their impressment and Scot John Campbell is a classic example of how those of humble origins could rise through the ranks and achieve greatness. Born the son of a minister in Kirkcudbright, Scotland, he was serving as an apprentice on a coastal coal vessel when a British Press Gang struck. He was not initially selected but volunteered to take the place of The Mate who had a wife and young children. Campbell did not return to Scotland for almost twelve years whereupon he sat his Lieutenants Exams and two years later took his first command at age 27. This seems young but was not unusual because we know Captain John Young [1789-1836] was commanding a Greenlandman at age 24. Campbell moved swiftly up the ranks on the back of numerous battle successes and eventually made Vice-Admiral. After forty years of illustrious service in the Royal Navy John Campbell was handsomely rewarded with his appointment as Commander-in-Chief and Governor of Newfoundland. Along the way, he became an accomplished navigator and astronomer and his name has also been linked to that of inventor Thomas Mudge and the first chronometer. Quite a different outcome for this impressed apprentice seaman compared to the aforementioned Charles Davis.

Apart from the Impress Gangs and Pirates, smuggling had become endemic in Scotland and Leith is reputed to have been a breeding ground for smugglers. While Scots in the highlands were notorious for illegally distilling whisky in their secret Bothies hidden in the glens, this whiskey was not the only commodity on the smugglers' minds. They dealt in spirits of all kinds as well as cattle, tea, salt, silk items and tobacco. These smuggling activities involved goods coming in and going out of the country. Most of the smuggled goods arrived and left Scotland by sea, and there was a time when the Isle of Man became a major storehouse for smugglers in general and some Scottish smugglers too are known to have taken advantage of its isolation. It is said that at one time the smuggling trade was so lucrative that people relocated to the border areas to cash in on this 'new industry'.

John Russell, in his book *'The Story of Leith'* writes that after the Union in 1707, Scotland was suffering under great disadvantage from higher and new taxes and new customs duties. The Scots, in general, were equally affronted by the legion of English officials who invaded from across the border and by the manner in which they employed strong-arm tactics in order to collect revenue. The Scots raison d'être, especially among the Jacobite segment of the merchant community, was that any opportunity to defraud this alien English government was fair play. Meanwhile, the more daring and cunning Scottish merchants seized the opportunity to trade their illegal foreign imports across the border in England for even greater profits.

Oddly enough it was the religious oppression of the general population that in turn saw them unite behind the smugglers. This meant that, in the unusual circumstance that someone was actually arrested, the jury would rarely convict, and, even where a conviction was secured the fines imposed were mostly of a paltry nature. Russell says that 'smuggling had always been a paying occupation in Leith' and his opinion seems to be upheld by others who identified that, while rural precincts in the inland may have had up to three officers to deal with the smugglers, the seaport of Leith had fourteen. Chris Cooney, in his book *'Smuggling on the South Coast'* asserts that 'Many Scots were not averse to the open smuggling of goods both in and out of their country'; in fact, one author wrote that smuggling was their 'national besetting sin'. Smuggling seems to have been permitted to flourish with the aid of the Precinct Officials who simply turned a blind eye, made false entries in their logbooks and in some cases were found guilty of taking bribes. The smugglers were a tough and often brutal bunch and it has been written that those officials who were not complicit in the smuggler's activities often came to a violent end.

But smuggling was an international activity and these 'free traders' as they were labelled, were proliferating not only in England but also in Denmark, Norway, Sweden, the Americas and the Mediterranean. Pirating and smuggling seemed to fit hand in glove for many. By far the most shamefully violent and infamous smuggling story in Edinburgh's history, and indeed Scottish history, is that associated with the Porteous Riots that took place in Edinburgh and Leith in 1736 following the arrest of three smugglers - Wilson, Hall and Robertson. They were arrested, tried and condemned to death. Robertson made good his escape, enabled by Wilson. It happened while they were both attending a church service at the Tolbooth Church. Then, Robertson, with the added help of some sympathetic supporters among the parishioners, successfully made his way to the Netherlands.

Hall had his sentence commuted to exile and that left the remaining prisoner Wilson who was sentenced to be publicly hanged in Grassmarket on 14 April. When his body was cut down against the wishes of the mob, a riot broke out. An alarmed Lord Provost instructed Captain Porteous, the Captain of the Edinburgh Guard, to call out the entire guard and arm them with powder and shot. Now, it needs to be remembered that this scene was playing out on the streets where these Youngs lived and whilst accounts of events are often at counterpoint, what is known is the angry mob began to throw stones at the Guards. Porteous instructs his men to fire above the heads of the rioters. They did so without realising that they were firing directly into the upper windows of the tenements where they indiscriminately wounded innocent people. The mob became irascible and confronted with this ugly scene Porteous issued a second directive to fire into the mob and several rioters were slain. This turned the situation on its head!

Porteous found himself arrested that very afternoon, charged with murder, and subsequently tried in the High Court. Given the testimony of the majority of witnesses verified that Porteous had personally fired into the mob, the prisoner was found guilty of murder. Porteous did appeal his conviction. Meanwhile, word of these riotous events and their aftermath had finally reached London and Sir Robert Walpole, the first *de facto* Prime Minister of Great Britain, interceded amidst rumours of a conspiracy on the part of Edinburgh City Magistrates. On hearing of Walpole's actions and fearing Porteous may be successful in his appeal Edinburghers hatched a plot.

It is said a crowd in excess of four thousand assembled at Portsburgh in the west of Edinburgh, whereupon they advanced en masse across Grassmarket to Cowgate and up High Street to the Tolbooth. They dragged Porteous from his cell, proceeded back down to Grassmarket where Porteous was lynched using a rope taken from a nearby draper's shop. Matters as this point went horribly wrong when the mob realised in their haste they had failed to place a hood over Porteous' head. They lowered him down to strip off his shirt and nightgown to wrap around his head but as they attempted to haul him up for the second time Porteous managed to struggle free because they had also failed to tie his hands. Determined that he should not escape he was then beaten, and attempts were made to set fire to his foot before he was strung up for the third and final time. His body was buried in Greyfriars Churchyard the very next day.

In the aftermath of this vigilante activity there was an English Parliamentary Inquiry and Edinburgh as a whole was punished. A £2000 fine was imposed on the City with the proviso that a portion of the funds be set aside as financial support for Porteous' widow. This was followed by the disbarment of the Lord Provost, Alexander Wilson, and despite a substantial reward of £200 being offered for information leading to the conviction of anyone responsible for the murder of Captain Porteous, no one ever faced court, although strong rumours abounded. A plaque to honour Porteous was later erected but the citizens chose to spit on it when passing, and it is said that even today those who know the sordid history of this event will spit on the Porteous Memorial Plaque in the Grassmarket. This spitting tradition became so deeply etched into Edinburgh psyche that decades later Sir Walter Scott would regale the event in stirring and compelling prose in his novel 'The Heart of Midlothian'.

But the riotous behaviour didn't end there. Scotland's citizens were regularly confronted with the outbreak of riots. One such event followed the ratification of the Acts of Union by the Parliaments of England and Scotland. Although this Act was purportedly designed to settle such unrest and harmoniously and permanently join the Parliaments of Scotland and England, it remained a diabolically unstable time in Scot's history. Scotland had been walking a political tightrope for the last 50 years where from the time the first steps were taken to quell unrest. For instance, in 1651 there was the Tender of Union Declaration to the drawing up of the first Act of Union in June 1657, the Glorious Revolution of 1688 was followed by a hiatus with the enthronement of William and Mary followed by another abortive attempt in 1670. By the 1690s Scotland's economy was in rapid decline, they were suffering from a seriously unequal balance of foreign trade already mentioned; wherein the English were given the lion's share. Relations were further soured over the Captain Green Affair and it was during the latter years of the reign of Queen Anne [1702-1714] that negotiations were re-ignited by the appointment of 31 Commissioners.

In the interim, in an attempt to resolve their economic woes, the wealthier Scots merchants were hatching a secret scheme of their own which we know today as the Darien Scheme in Panama. In 2016 the World witnessed the Panama Papers Scandal which exposed the financial affairs of wealthy citizens prominent in public and political life. In 1690 there was a much more outrageous Panama Scandal being concocted by some of the wealthiest investors in the Kingdom of Scotland. The Darien Scheme in a nutshell was an audacious plan to establish a Scottish colony in Central America. They planned to call it 'Caledonia' the Latin name given by the Romans to the land that is now Scotland. Part of their master plan was to build a road joining the Atlantic and Pacific coastlines.

In July 1698 the first expeditionary fleet of five ships left Leith with some 1200 brave souls on board. Their voyage was made all the more uncomfortable given these passengers were often forced to cower below decks for hours so as not to raise the interest of any English vessels in their path. They made landfall on 2 November 1698 when it quickly became apparent there were serious problems due to poor planning, inadequate provisioning, divided leadership and lack of demand for trade goods. This was followed by devastating epidemics from tropical diseases and a complete under-estimation of the climatic and environmental challenges of establishing such a remote tropical settlement.

This incited great unrest amongst the settlers and the militia alike. Sadly, none of these negative reports reached Scotland in time to prevent the second wave of 1000 souls from departing from the Clyde. Led by the Company's new expeditionary flagship, *The Rising Sun*, which arrived in Caledonia Bay on 30 November 1699. Conditions in 'Caledonia' continued to deteriorate but above all else the planners had grossly misjudged the reaction of the Spanish who had, for some considerable time past, established themselves in the region and naturally became fearful for their lucrative silver trade. The Spaniards saw the Scots as posing a potential threat to the alliances they had formed with the local Indian tribes and to settle the matter once and for all the 'Caledonia' settlement was besieged by Spanish forces who attacked from land and sea. Spanish ships blockaded the harbour - game over! The settlement was abandoned in the March of 1700 with only a few hundred of the 2500 settlers surviving.

How did this affect the ordinary citizens of Scotland? And, how was Queen Anne complicit? Well, that explanation is simple. Since the Scottish Darien Company was largely made up of the wealthiest and most influential people in Scotland, who reputedly were in control of as much as 50% of all the money circulating in that country at the time, it goes without saying that several of the said newly appointed '31 Commissioners' were among their ranks. These merchants had invested heavily and what's more were expecting to recoup their losses through compensation via The Equivalent. The Equivalent was a very large sum of money, some £398,000 English, or almost £600,000 in Scottish money, which England agreed to pay to Scotland following the Act of Union. It was actually intended for the benefit of all Scots citizens as a hedge against Scottish taxpayers propping up future English debt and to offset future higher taxes which the English were about to levy on the Scottish economy. Unfortunately, an estimated 60% of The Equivalent is said to have landed in the hands of those wealthy merchants involved in the failed Darien Scheme. Amidst continuing allegations of bribery and corruption pervading Scottish folklore, many years later Robert Burns expressed his feelings thus -

> *'We're bought and sold for English Gold,*
> *Such a Parcel of Rogues in a Nation'.*

The aftermath of this fiasco reads like a modern day espionage thriller. It seems trust was at a premium in those days pre and post Union, so much so that England hired spies to infiltrate Scottish ranks and report back to Westminster. One notable was none other than Daniel Defoe the renowned English author of *'Robinson Crusoe'*. His first reports were vivid descriptions of violent demonstrations against the Union. He further believed that 'A Scots rabble is the worst of its kind,' and he went on to report 'for every Scot in favour there is 99 against'. Years later Sir John Clerk 2nd Baronet of Penicuik and a Commissioner for the Union of Parliaments for the Whig Party, wrote in his memoirs that Defoe had been sent as a 'Godolphin' and unbeknown to everyone '(Defoe) was a spy among us, but not known as such, otherwise the Mob of Edinburgh would pull him to pieces'. Today's reader could liken this level of disenchantment to the voter backlash after the Scottish Vote for Independence or the recent fallout over the Brexit result. So strong was Scottish opposition that it is further written that not one petition in favour of the union was received by parliament in London and, on the very day the Treaty was signed into Law, the carillonneur at St Giles Cathedral in Edinburgh rang the bells to the tune of *'Why should I be so sad on my wedding day'*. In the face of growing agitation north of the border and the perceived threat of widespread civil unrest erupting right across the land, Parliament in Westminster imposed Martial Law on Scotland.

In the beginning 1650-1750

There were also Wars raging in International waters and safe passage on the high seas was as much about luck as seamanship. Between 1650 and 1750 there is a litany of incidents where Royal Naval ships engaged in long running battles. First there was the Anglo-Dutch War, then the Anglo Spanish War, the Second Anglo-Dutch War, the Franco-Dutch War, the Third Anglo-Dutch War and the list goes on. All these countries had significant Navy Fleets and at one point, when unrest escalated, Scottish merchantmen were being afforded Royal Navy escorts. The Merchant Fleet were then facing a new danger - the misdeeds of some unscrupulous Royal Navy Captains. It is said these underpaid, overworked Royal Navy Captains would frequently demand a personal financial reward for their escort services. As a consequence, many a Scots merchantman decided to arm themselves with guns and canon rather than fall in with miscreant Navy Captains who would firstly make a demand and later abscond under cover of darkness. Skippers, like these Youngs, and their crews would have been constantly on the alert and their very survival would demand being able to identify rogue Navy vessels from any number of European and Mediterranean nations who were, from time to time, at war with England and in the aftermath of Cromwell and his British Commonwealth Alliance that included Scotland as well. Before the Union, Scottish shipping had enjoyed an easy relationship with their trading partners, but after the Union of the Parliaments there was disquiet amongst Scottish Skippers as they became embroiled in English politics and their ships therefore became open to attack from those foreign countries that were enemies of England.

Gilbert Dick, John Watson, John Waddell, Robert Young and thousands more Scots like them were all traversing these International waters, following their dream of life on the high sea and clearly it was only their courage, sound seamanship, bravery and good fortune that kept them alive and enabled them to protect their crews and bring their ships safely to port.

Chapter 3

Prenuptial Agreements & Marrying Into the Business • Sailors Mariners Sea Captains • Ship Owners • & Establishing a Maritime Legacy

In a time when Church and State were intrinsically entwined in cruel and bizarre ways, life within families too was interwoven; but fortunately for most families it proved advantageous rather than destructive. Also, Marriage in Scotland in this century for the most part was viewed very differently. We have already learned that marriage was an imperative, a work and societal necessity for any tradesman or merchant who wished to become a Burgess or who aspired to any higher office for that matter. These conditions most certainly applied to all Young ancestors who wished to advance themselves and hold a respected social position within their community. We also know that the roles for men and women were vastly different from what we know today. So how can we come to understand more about what their lives were like? Some of the best social demographers down the centuries have been essayists and poets and some of their selected works can offer a descriptive insight into life and society in a particular timeframe and have proved a very useful tool for looking behind closed doors for this century of our Young Story.

To try to understand what marriage and society was for them it is necessary to also come to some appreciation of the extreme stratification of society in Scotland in this 1650-1750 century. For instance, rural Scotland had its own hierarchy where at the apex were the Lairds, who were the major Estate landholders, then came the Yeomen, who were often referred to as Bonnet Lairds. These individuals also held title to land but of smaller holdings. Next in the hierarchy were the Husbandmen who were the minor landholders and/or free tenants and at the bottom of the social scale were the Crofters, Cottars and Grassmen which various names were given to the field workers and farm labourers. In urban Scotland, where we find the majority of Youngs, the hierarchy was somewhat different, and from what we have learned so far control of land ownership there was vested in the hands of the wealthy merchants. These men held the highest official positions of Advocates, Councillors, and Bailies; they presided over the Kirk Sessions and handed down judgements in the various Courts. Below these men came the craftsmen, Burgess and non-Burgess, and lastly the urban labourer or general workforce. These last two categories of craftsmen and general labourers were in the greatest number in any urban population across Scotland. All the remaining citizens in both rural and urban areas were classified as 'Masterless Men'. They were the vagrants and beggars who through illness, injury or age constituted the unemployed sector of society.

Unlike their English cousins whose kinship was basically cognate or where equal importance was placed on the male and female ancestry of a person, in Scotland it was agnatic or where only the father's lineage was of importance. A descriptor more commonly used today would be primogeniture. In rural Scotland agnatic kinship and feudal land obligation gave rise to the Highland Clan system we are so familiar with in Scottish culture where leadership of these Clans went to the eldest son of the eldest son. These conditions remained in place until the Jacobite Uprising in 1745 at which time Highland dress was banned, there was enforced disarming of clansmen and the compulsory purchase of heritable lands. Clan Chiefs were exiled, and some clansmen were transported to the colonies as indentured labour. The ultimate plan was to downgrade the status of Lairds to simple landholders and this was pretty much achieved within one generation.

Although Scottish society was known to be moving to two different sets of rules depending on whether one lived in rural and urban areas, Marriage appears to have been one facet of society where the laws were common across the rural urban divide. Marriage in Scotland took basically two forms - civil unions including irregular marriages, and religious unions. Marriage Law in Scotland was subject to Scots Law and the Law of the Church of Scotland. The two hallmarks were Sacrament and Consent. In fact, there was a time in Scotland, not so long before this 1650-1750 century, when a woman could be imprisoned for not consenting to a marriage. One case in point was that of Marion Campbell, the daughter of Donnchadh Campbell of Glen Lyon, who in the late 1560s refused to acquiesce to an arranged marriage initiated by her father and was consequently imprisoned. This occurred at the height of the Campbell and MacGregor feuds, and while she was imprisoned MÒr [the Gaelic equivalent of Marion], shared her experiences in a poem so powerful it survived in folklore until 1813 when it was finally written down. Mòr then wrote another poem after her MacGregor husband and child were executed in 1570. Her poems, about marriage, love and societal law including 'Grioghal Cridhe', are sung within the oral tradition of the Campbell Clan to this very day.

Marriage in the day was not always a church affair. Irregular marriages were commonplace and basically took three forms - firstly, there was the signing of a contract by the consenting parties and the witnessing of same, secondly by mutual agreement without a contract, or thirdly by making a public promise followed by consummation, cohabitation and repute. Curiously, these arrangements were not reformed until the Marriage (Scotland) Act 1939 and in fact Scotland was the last European nation to abolish common-law marriage by a further Act of Parliament in 2006. And, although Scotland was basically a patriarchal society one major difference in that country was that women - 'retained their own surname after marriage and were not forced to sacrifice their family for that of their husband's kin group'. For a genealogist this is extremely helpful when attempting to identify one 'Mrs Young' from another. It was written into Law that all married women would be described in the various ecclesiastical registers as, - Helen Liston spouse of Alexander Young.

In the beginning 1650-1750

As for the wedding ceremony itself, it was mostly celebrated in a similar manner across all levels of society. It was a feasting occasion shared with family and friends with the only difference being the level of expense and fanfare. Obviously the wealthy would host a grand affair befitting their status while the less wealthy came to embrace the tradition of 'penny weddings'. Here guests contributed to the cost of the ceremony and the meal and later joined in the music and dancing. After their nuptials a wife's role has been broadly defined as one of chastity, obedience and duty to her husband indicating a subservient position for wives in Scottish society; however, there is ample evidence to the contrary. In fact, one foreign visitor has described Scottish wives as forthright individuals who were 'absolute mistresses of their houses and even their husbands'. This underscores the known contributions made by many women in both marriage and business despite their frequently inferred frailty, incapacity and disenfranchisement.

In fact, many women throughout Scottish history have proven themselves entirely capable of meeting the different challenges of coping with major social changes. On occasion, circumstances arose which had their genesis in necessity when women were forced to cope during the prolonged absences of their menfolk. The groundswell for this new status quo began way back in the time of Cromwell's invasion of Scotland. Once womenfolk attained a position of mastership they strived to maintain their position and their voice. One such example is Margaret Fell [1614-1670], designated the Mother of Quakerism. She gave a voice to women inside the Church and in the face of God where no female voice had been heard before. Another is Scottish born Royalist Anne Halkett [1623-1699] who took the lead role in orchestrating the successful escape of the Duke of York from Parliamentary custody. Sometime later the Duke returned from exile and was crowned James II of England and James VII of Scotland and it was during his reign that he would learn, in 1676, that Anne Halkett had been widowed following the death of her husband Sir James. A grateful King James, in a rare show of regal appreciation, personally decreed to provide Anne with a pension for life in acknowledgement of her selfless actions and incredible daring and bravery when she dressed the Duke as a woman in order to facilitate his safe passage to exile in Europe.

But it didn't stop there, later came the esteemed and formidable Margaret Cavendish [1661-1717], Duchess of Newcastle-Upon-Tyne and poet, philosopher, writer, essayist and playwright. She had the audacity to publish under her own name, openly addressing such contentious issues as gender, power, manners, scientific methods and philosophy in a time when it was considered such thinking and opinion to be beyond the capacity of the female mind. The male establishment found her unstoppable and irrepressible. In 1667 she was the first woman to attend a meeting of the Royal Society of London, which until then had remained a totally male bastion - 'a Boys Club'. Interestingly, the Society's motto is - 'Nullius in Verba' - Take Nobody's Word for It. This was certainly a philosophy close to the heart of Lady Cavendish as she went in search of her own truths. Renowned for her eccentricity in all things related to society and fashion, she was nicknamed 'Mad Madge'.

Returning to the subject of Scottish Marriage, there is a modern poem written by Sir Hugh Roberton that tells the story of irregular marriages. Roberton is a Glaswegian described as a strident political activist and committed socialist and was once banned by the BBC. He was clearly a complex individual as this bright tale of Mhàiri's Wedding clearly exemplifies. Again, it is best read with a Scottish twang. [N.B. Mhàiri is Gaelic for Mary and a 'shieling' is a hut in the hills used when out hunting animals].

> Over hillways up and down
> Myrtle green and bracken brown,
> Past the shieling through the town
> All for sake of Mhàiri
>
> Step me gaily, off we go
> Heel for heel and toe for toe,
> Arm in arm and off we go
> All for Mhàiri's wedding

Plenty herring, plenty meal
Plenty peat to fill her creel,
Plenty bonny bairns as weel
That's the toast for Mhàiri

Cheeks as bright as rowans are
Brighter far than any star,
Fairest o' them all by far
Is my darlin' Mhàiri

So, just how did these social constraints translate into the lives of ordinary folk the likes of the Youngs?

Well, in general terms history recounts a very similar story for many. Understandably, there is little written specifically on this subject which relates directly to the lives of ordinary women in society, but what has been learned is that Scottish Law is more reflective of European attitudes to women and women's rights. In Scotland, the position for women in general and wives in particular was definitely more favourable than in England say, and although in theory wives needed their husband's permission for certain activities such as the making of a Will, it was generally a permission which was forthcoming. There are numerous examples of early Wills held within The National Records of Scotland, and the mere existence of these documents provides an invaluable source of information about the roles of women, the nature of their relationships to their kin, their husband's family, friends and often where property and business are concerned, demonstrates their astuteness in managing economic affairs. We have already witnessed an example of same within this Young family with the Will of Alisone Foreman and there is yet Will relating to Katrien/Katherene Walkingschaw from C1628 that is equally as elucidating.

Also, given the higher mortality rates for men in this 1650-1750 century due to disease and warring, it has been suggested by some Historians that one in five households in Scotland in this era at one time was headed by a woman who, despite being offered lesser opportunities in education, proved themselves quite competent in dealing with household and business management responsibilities. Another positive for Scottish women at this time as defined by law was that they did not face gender impediments to inheritance excepting where it was defined in a Will or Contract of Marriage. As far back as 1635 the twice widowed Margaret Ker, dowager Lady Yester, was described as having - 'the greatest conjunct fie [fiefdom] that any lady has in Scotland'. In an essay on Burgess Wealth in Edinburgh, where one William Dick is excluded because his extreme wealth would distort the figures, Lady Yester is frequently mentioned as an affluent owner of property equivalent to that of the said Sir William Dick.

Following the Reformation in 1648, all the old neo-pagan customs surrounding marriage gave way to a new four-stage process involving betrothal, proclamation of banns, and the receiving of a clerical blessing in a church, which then permitted legal cohabitation. The actual choosing of a partner, however, becomes a more ambiguous question. For families of wealth, marriage was often more political in nature and founded in a desire to strengthen a family's social position, and perhaps their financial fortune. In such circumstances it became more of a transaction of convenience rather than of affection or emotion and there is a Young family example of just this situation. It follows that the richer and more ambitious the father of the bride, the more complex and drawn out were the negotiations over her 'tocher' or dowry.

Even amongst the trade classes, it seems that parents desired their sons and daughters should marry well. One very useful source of evidence for this claim can be found in the Apprenticeship Records and Burgess Registers, where so many an apprentice can be found marrying the Masters' daughters. This fulfilled two immediate needs: firstly, the necessity for taking a wife in order to achieve Burgess status and secondly, the immediate acquiring of Burgess status via such a union. So commonplace were such marital arrangements that a special phrase was coined and appears on every page in the Burgess Register. It is - 'by r. of w.' which means: 'achieved by right of wife'.

Another interesting aspect of marriage at this time relates to Ante-Nuptial Agreements or Contracts of Marriage. Most modern day readers would believe the 'Pre-Nup' to be a recent phenomenon of the Hollywood A-Lister generation, but in fact it has been documented to Egyptian times, and the term 'pre-nuptial agreement' could have its genesis in 'The Ketubah', the Hebrew marriage contract which is over 2000 years old and is thought to be the oldest document ever discovered, which gives financial and legal rights to women. In the Scottish example, a prenuptial agreement is generally referred to as the Contract of Marriage' or 'Ante-nuptial Contract'. It is drawn up prior to the marriage and cited in the Will of the husband. Such documents are legally binding on all parties and for added legal security and voracity they are entered into the Books of Session of the Commissary Court of Scotland.

So, whether marrying into the business or marrying into wealth, this Contract of Marriage was more widely utilised than might be first thought. As for these Young ancestors, the oldest example discovered to date appears to belong to the first Young to achieve Captain status, Alexander Young [1750-1817]. Given the contents of his 1817 Will, it is easy to understand why he found it necessary to protect his assets. Later examples of documents termed 'Ante-nuptial Agreements' also exist within this family. In the case of Captain Alexander Young his 'Ante-nuptial Contract' was drawn up on the 25 Nov 1802 in advance of his second marriage in an attempt to preserve his wealth and assets for his children. His second spouse, Susan Pattinson, was left under no misapprehension as to what her position would be should she find herself his widow. The substance of that particular Ante-nuptial Agreements is contained in a Contract of Marriage. It provides that Susan Pattinson is entitled to receive a cash allowance and retain certain furniture so long as she remained a widow; but, should she decide to re-marry she would cease to receive any allowance and be required to surrender the furniture and any and all items inherited by her. This seemingly unfair and dispassionate arrangement demonstrates neither empathy nor recognition for the fifteen years of faithful caring and support she gave to her husband.

> Alexander's Will words it this way - 'Secondly in the event of my wife surviving me I direct and appoint my said Trustees to lay out and employ out of the first and readiest of my means and Estate above conveyed the sum of £1000 upon heritable security, taking the bond therefore payable to Mrs Susan Pattinson, my wife in liferent for her liferent use only on which she shall remain my widow and to my said Trustee or Trustees acceptors or survivors of them in the fee for the end uses and purposes of this Trust and further to deliver over to her one rooms furniture or in her option to pay to her in heir and place thereof, the sum of £50 for purchasing furniture at the first term, of which Sunday or Martinmas that shall happen after my decease all in terms of an ante-nuptial contract of marriage entered into between her and me dated the 25 day of November Eighteen Hundred and Two years'.

What do we know of this Alexander Young [1750-1817]?

Well, he was born the eldest grandson of John Young and Margaret Dick, and eldest son of Robert Young [1723-1797] and Janet Lundie [1731-1794]. Father Robert was a Seaman and his mother Janet Lundie came from a long line of seafaring folk, mostly fishermen during centuries prior. Janet Lundie's parents were Walter Lundie and Janet Carnie/Carnay. The Carnies/Carnays were also seafarers. Alexander's first wife was Helen Liston. The Liston family were already a well-established and propertied family in Newhaven, an ancient fishing port on the waterfront of North Leith. For centuries the Newhaven fishing fleet had been renowned and numerous members of the Liston, Lundie and Carnie/Carnay families are known to have been part of the local fishing fleet. It should not be underestimated what a significant contribution these families would have made to Alexander's career and future wealth outcome.

Fishing had been the lifeblood of the port and a solid industry in the day and had contributed greatly to making Newhaven an ancient and wealthy settlement. Historically it was known as 'Our Lady's Port of Grace' when it was originally founded around 1488. The settlement boasts a long and proud history and although Newhaven was but a small cluster of simple houses, it prevailed. Later a small chapel was built in 1513 and the prosperous port was set to enjoy a bright future, but the actions of James IV, illegally granting feudal overlordship to Edinburgh sealed the fate of not only Newhaven but the whole of the Burgh of Leith for centuries to come. For a time, the entire area went into decline, or rather, in Newhaven's case, it just ceased to prosper although it did remain an active fishing port. The original fishermen to settle in Newhaven were mostly from the Netherlands, Belgium and France, especially from around Normandy and Brittany. There were many skilled craftsmen and notables amongst its very early settlers, including one Jacques Terrell, a Frenchman by birth, who later became King James' master wright [shipwright] and Chief Naval Designer.

These fishing immigrants included Listons, Lundies and Canays, were among the founders of The Society of Free Fishermen in 1572 and this Society remains in existence with its nominated head carrying the ancient title of Preses [President]. The Preses is supported by the Boxmaster, or Treasurer. The role of Boxmaster was a very important one indeed because the Society managed revenue from the Oyster Fishery, membership fees as well as 'fues' from the Society's grounds in Newhaven and rents from various properties. While it began as a charitable institution to help families in times of trouble, it is written - 'that every member was expected to take turns to stand at the foot of the Whale Brae with a large pewter plate in front of him, and a notice beside the plate - Please remember the poor of Newhaven'. The Society gained status within and without the fishing community and with the support of its membership later expanded its portfolio of responsibility to include the issuance of fishing licences.

There is documented evidence indicating this long-standing function was maintained for over 250 years. Today, any such Society would be crucified for being engaged in restricted trade practice but its *raison d'etre* was always about protecting livelihoods through sustainable fishing. As recently as 1821, overfishing had been flagged as an issue and made worse by so many from outside Newhaven applying for membership and licences. It was at that time the Society resolved to take the unprecedented step of restricting membership to - 'the lawful sons of fishermen whose names were clear on the Society books'. So not only did an applicant have to be the son of a member fisherman but he had to be clear of debt as well. This is the background to the family stability and status Alexander married into and goes to the core of how he got his start!

As for the seafaring community and seafaring traditions in Newhaven, it is fair to say these Newhaven fishermen and more especially their womenfolk became legendary in Scotland and indeed across Britain. During the 250 years that generations of local men and boys appear to have been engaged in fishing, their womenfolk were walking the streets of Edinburgh and Leith, selling the fish and oysters for which the area became so very famous. These women were acclaimed for their physical strength and their ability to carry the heavy cane baskets of seafood by means of a leather head-strap. They further distinguished themselves by their individually designed aprons and the special songs they sang as they walked the hilly streets hail, rain or shine. There are several lines from a poem by William E Henley very aptly entitled 'In Fisherrow' which describe these women and their condition -

> A hard north-easter fifty winters long
> Has bronzed and shrivelled sere her face and neck
> Her locks are wild and grey, her teeth a wreck;
> Her foot is vast her bowed leg spare and strong.
> A wide blue cloak, a squat and sturdy throng
> Of curt blue coats, a mutch without a speck,

> A white vest broidered black, her person deck,
> Nor seems their picked, stern, old-world quaintness wrong.
> Her great creel forehead-slung, she wanders nigh,
> Easing the heavy strap with gnarled, brown fingers
> The spirit of traffic watchful in her eye,
> Ever and anon imploring you to buy,
> As looking down the street she onward lingers,
> Reproachful, with a strange and doleful cry.

Newhaven women have been immortalised in a series of old prints housed in The Newhaven Heritage Centre, as well as numerous postcard series down the years depicting Newhaven fisherwomen wearing their distinctive frilled caps so indicative of their connection to Flanders, Normandy and the coast of Brittany. As their fame spread throughout the land, some English communities were so taken with their stories that on numerous occasions groups of these 'fisher-wives' found themselves invited to participate in concerts in English towns, particularly around Fayre times. On one occasion, in 1883, a dozen or so received an Official Invitation to London to attend the Great London Fisheries Exhibition. Greeted in a way which belied their class it is further written that they were 'hospitably entertained by Queen Victoria at Windsor Castle' no less, and afterwards by the Prince and Princess of Wales at Marlborough House.

Newhaven fishermen in particular and Scottish fishermen in general, had much to be proud of. They were given honourable mention in The Fisheries Exhibition Literature published in London in 1884 wherein the Scottish industry was sized as 15,049 fishing vessels manned by 48,100 fishermen. To put this into some perspective and to vouch for the importance of the Fishing Industry to the Scottish economy, when these figures are compared to that for the whole of Britain, their numbers constitute 46% of all vessels and 44% of the total manpower employed. Their skill levels were the envy of many, with loss of life in Scotland registered as 11.83 casualties per 1000 boats compared to 42.35 for Ireland and 19.06 for England's principal fishing port of Weymouth.

Newhaven was where Alexander had settled originally and it remained a proud, hardworking, closely knit hamlet of fisher families well supported by its own kinfolk. In fact, they were such a closely knit community females rarely married anyone from outside the locale. Weddings therefore were very much a community affair, as vouched for by this passage - 'The bride in her braws, accompanied by her sweetheart, went round some time before and invited the guests personally. On the wedding day they walked in couples from the bride's house to the 'Peacock', the 'Marine' or other hotel, where the marriage was to be celebrated.' Eve Blantyre Simpson records in her publication of 'Folk Lore in Lowland Scotland', an old ballad about a Newhaven wedding. The lyrics read in part -

> 'Weel Friday cam', the growing moon
> 'Shone beautifully clear,
> An' a' the boats wi' flags were drest
> Frae Annfield to the pier.
> An' Doctor Johnston, worthy man,
> 'Had twa-three hours to spare,
> Sae he toddled to Newhaven
> An' spliced the happy pair.'

Simpson has certainly done her homework because at one time there was a greatly loved cleric at St Ninian's Church in Ferry Road, North Leith, by the name of Dr. David Johnston. He ministered to the local Newhaven parish for almost sixty years, from 12 June 1765 to his death at Leith on the 4 July 1824 at the ripe old age of 90 years. He was definitely one of 'them', a Newhavener through and through! His biographer wrote that the fishwives of Newhaven always called him the 'Bonnie Doctor'. Johnston had married the daughter of a South Leith shipwright and his only son became a Lieutenant in the H.E.I.C.S. [Honourable East India Company Service]. Sadly, his son died at Bombay at the very young age of 24. The 'Bonnie Doctor' officiated at an incredible number of marriages in Newhaven and Leith including several members of the extended Young family.

In the beginning 1650-1750

Sir Walter Scott too was very familiar with the uniqueness of the Newhaven community, and went to great lengths to record various notable facets of life there in his publication 'The Antiquary'. In relation to family life and the role of women, Scott says 'The Newhaven fishwife is indeed the head of the household, ruling her husband along with the other members of the family. Scott maintains 'Them that sell the goods guide the purse; them that guide the purse rule the house.' And so, despite their deficits in educational opportunities and their asserted inabilities it seems that the Newhaven fishwives proficiency at money management is well noted by Scott and others, who cite it as - 'borne out by the fact that Newhaven is reckoned to have the wealthiest fishing community on the Forth, many of the houses being owned by their thrifty occupants'.

Often, local Newhaven marriages were aptly described as a 'union of talents' and this is a description that could well apply to these early Young ancestors. The Liston, Carnie and Lundie families, into which Robert [1723-1797] and Alexander Young [1750-1817] married, were among Newhaven's most successful and highly regarded founding seafarers. To dwell on the importance of Newhaven and its community is not to overstate the importance this place, and these people were to Robert and his son Alexander. These historical reminiscences highlight their good fortune in being accepted and ultimately welcomed into this closed community. To my mind it says quite a deal about the men, how they conducted themselves, their talents and their probity.

By the end of the eighteenth century, Newhaven could vaunt over 300 households, mostly inter-married, owning well over one hundred fishing boats capable of putting to sea. Newhaven and Leith became pivotal to this generation of Youngs, and although it is but a tiny enclave, to this day it maintains some very proud traditions. Many poems, stories and anecdotes survive which stand witness to its history. A more recent piece, written by Ian Sinclair in 2005, is entitled 'Newhaven's Pier Parliament'. Two of the three families mentioned, the Listons and Wilsons, soon become very relevant to our own story. Sinclair's poem reads in part

> 'I'd walk doon the pier where ma face wis weel kent
> By the auld men sitting there doon at Pier Parliament.
> There were nae fancy benches, or ony such like -
> They jist sat on a fish box in the lee o' the dyke,
> As I listened tae tales a' wis aye sae inspired,
> Aboot their days going tae sea afore they retired.
> They were Listons and Rutherfords, Wilsons and all,'

[Again, best read with a Scottish twang!]

The seafaring segment of this first century of the Young Story began in earnest on 22 May 1709 when John Young married Margaret Dick. Although John was not the eldest son he followed into his father's profession of Baxter. John and Margaret's sons Alexander and Robert were the first to break away from family tradition. Alexander became a shipwright and Robert a seaman. As time went by, their related families of Liston, Wilson, Carnie, Spittal, Richmond, Strachan, Waddell and Thomson contributed to the rich fabric of their seafaring journey. These families came into the lives of the Youngs brandishing their own individual chronicles of maritime exploits. The call of the sea quickly got into Robert's blood and his passion was passed on to his eldest son Alexander. They persevered with a great sense of belonging; embracing the realisation that this is where their future lay. In the case of Alexander, he took matters one giant step forward and set about creating a substantial legacy for his sons and daughters. These actions of Robert and Alexander were supported by the Industrial Revolution, advancements in shipping and they were simply in the right place at the right time. They also arrived and set up business during a period of positive change in the history of Edinburgh and Leith. This father and son would set the tone for so many sons and grandsons who would aspire to become sailors, captains, ship owners and more.

In the beginning 1650-1750

As I delved deeper and deeper into the maritime records the waters became a little murky as these official documents are scattered with a variety of terms like: Sailor, Mariner, Skipper, Captain and Master. Now I was most definitely a maritime novice and began to wonder what these words meant in their day and what can such terms tell us about the people and their roles?

The 1627 book of *'Sea-Mans Grammar'* compiled by Captain John Smith states that a Sailor is - 'the older man who hoists the sails'. The word mariner is not mentioned at all in that 1627 publication but in a later publication entitled *'The British Seaman 1200-1860: A Social Survey'*, there are chapters headed - *'The Medieval Mariner'* and *'The Tudor Mariner'* - where the writer Christopher Lloyd contends that the word 'Seaman' is the oldest in use, then comes Mariner and latterly Sailor. Christopher Lloyd's research shows that the esteemed Navy Commander Sir Richard Hawkins [C1560-1622] Vice-Admiral of Devon, maintained that the term Mariner - 'ought not to be given but to the man who is able to build his ship, to fit and provide her of all things necessary, and after to carry her about the world the residue to be but sailors'. Amidst this conjecture, it would seem that entry level was as a Sailor or Seaman, and as skills are acquired and experience and seamanship are gained so their title changes to Mariner.

Christopher Lloyd also gives a set of definitions for Skipper, Captain and Master. The general consensus of opinion seems to be that the Skipper is the person who steers and manages the running of a vessel, and he may or may not have been required to achieve a licence or qualification, whereas a Master or Captain is the person on board with formal qualifications and a government licence. Also, the Captain or Master is in complete overall charge of the vessel. In certain circumstances the Captain will be described as Shipmaster in some historical documents. For instance, Captain Alexander Young [1750-1817] is described as Shipmaster and Shipowner in his Will, which is a true reflection of his particular achievements.

How were these nametags applied to those families into whom the Youngs married? And, can they be relied upon as a true guide to their relevant occupations?

This is debateable as we see that Walter Lundie [C1678 -] is described as 'Seaman' in his marriage Banns in 1703 and we know from other records that he was a fisherman. Regarding the Thomsons, there are several men named John Thomson listed as Skipper, Seaman and Mariner in the period 1634-1662 and although we do not know which is our John Thomson, it is safe to say he too was a seafarer like Helen Liston's father, John Liston [1716 - +1761], and his father William Liston [1680-1739]. The lineage of this Liston line shows that they intermarried with the Carnie/Carnay clan of Newhaven over several generations and perusal, of the wealth of information discovered about both these families, will show many listed as 'seaman' who were known to be 'fisherman'. Alexander's sons and daughters also married into families associated with the sea. Of his surviving children, his first-born daughter Anne married Merchant Navy man, Captain William Dick, his second daughter Helen married Captain Joshua Richmond, an Irish born Naval Commander who retired from the Royal Navy to join the Merchant Navy ranks for a decade or more before he is found Deputy Master of Trinity House in Leith, son Alexander married the daughter of a ship owner and son John married into the Lamb family whose lineage vouches both Navy and Army heritage.

As far as establishing a maritime legacy goes, it is the Will of Captain Alexander Young [1750-1817] that provides the best documentary evidence of the foundation of this family's wealth. His Will is very illuminating with respect to his level of professional and financial success and stands testament to his belief in the long term viability of Merchant Shipping Industry which, in his lifetime, was experiencing unprecedented growth and morphing into a very professional economic contributor to the Scottish Economy. In the absence of a Will for his father Robert, it is fair to say that Alexander's

Will is the primary record for explaining from where and how he made his fortune and shows that his legacy provided a grand inheritance for his children.

The cash component of Alexander's estate is extracted as follows -

Inventory of the Personal Estate of Capt Alexander Young, ship owner in Leith, who died on the 13th day of January 1817 years, with interest due on principle sums at that date: –

'Impremise cash in the house	£18.18 .0
2nd Principle sum contained in Bank Receipt by Messrs Ramsay Bonars & Co Bankers in Edinburgh dated 22 July 1816 -	£735.0.0.
Interest due there on at three percent 175 days	£10.11.5.
	£745.11.5.

[Note - Mansfield, Ramsay and Co was a private firm doing banking business in Edinburgh from around 1746. It later became known as Ramsay, Bonars and Co. The principals were Sir John Marjoribanks of Lees, Bart., and Sir James Stirling of Lambert, Bart., both of whom were at one time known to hold the Office of Lord Provosts of Edinburgh.]

3rd Principal sum in Promisory Note by John Young to the Deceased dated 15 March 1814 & payable 12 months after date £280.0.0. Deduct paid to account on 6 April 1814 £100.0.0. Remains £190.0.0.
Note - There was an agreement betwixt the said John Young and the Deceased that no interest was to be charged on this Promisory Note

4th Principal sum in Bond by the Lord Provost Magistrates and Council in Edinburgh to the Deceased, containing an assignment in security to the respective

dock duties & other Annual revenue therein mentioned
which Bond is No. 426, and dated 6 Feb 1811 - £100
Interest thereon at 5 percent since 22 July 1816
175 days   £2.7.11 3/
                 £102.7.11 3/

5th Principal sum in Bond by the Lord Provost Magistrates
And Council in Edinburgh to the Deceased, containing an
Assignment in security to the respective dock duties & other
Annual revenue therein mentioned which Bond is No. 427,
and dated 6 Feb 1811 - £100
Interest thereon at 5 percent since 22 July 1816
175 days   £2.7.11 3/
                 £102.7.11 3/

6th Principal sum in Bond by the Lord Provost
And Council in Edinburgh to the Deceased, containing
a similar Assignment in security which Bond is No. 575,
and dated 27 Apr 1814 - £100
Interest thereon at 5 percent since 14 Oct 1816
91 days   £1.4.11 2/
                 £101.4.11 2/

7th Principal sum in Bond by the said Lord Provost
And Council of Edinburgh to the Deceased containing on
Assignment similar to the above in security which Bond is
No. 576 and is dated the said 27 April 1814 £100
Interest thereon at 5% cents since 14 October 1816
91 days   .£1.4.11 2/
                 £101.4.11 2/

8th Shares of the capital stock of the Whale Fishing
Company of Montrose comprehending inter alia 7/54 part
of the ship or vessel called the 'Eliza Swan' of Montrose
with her pertinence and 3/32 parts or shares of the ship or
vessel called the 'Monarch'
In all valued at £1000.0.0.

9th Share or stock in the Leith & Hamburg Shipping Company valued at £ 50.0.0.

10th Share or stock in the London & Edinburgh Shipping Company valued at £120.0.0.

11th Arrears of rent falling under executery £ 3.0.0.

12th The deceased Household Furniture, Bed and Table linen, plates in his house in Leith, of which the deceased widow claims the life-rent valued by William Bruce Jr conformed to Inventory & Appraisement dated 27 March 1817 £130.19.4.

13th The deceased watch, gold and silver buckles and certain other articles bequeathed to various members of the deceased family valued at £ 30.0.0.
Value of the deceased estate in Scotland £2695.14.5 [2/]

Exclusive of certain funds and effects which the deceased was possessed of or entitled to as Trustee for others, but not beneficially. The deceased also died possessed of £500 3% consolidated annuities valued at 63 1/8% being the highest selling price on 13 January 1817 £315.12.6.

Value of said stock £315.12 .6.'

On the face of it, this first set of figures appears to be not a large sum of money, but when extrapolated to a current day equivalent value the position becomes much more interesting indeed. To do this I have used the services of 'Measuring Worth'. This is an Association formed by over twenty Universities world-wide which have collaborated to develop an algorithm for calculating a 'point in time' value for historical money. Alexander's approximately £3010 Estate in 1817 has an Economic Status Value in 2017 in the order of £3.0 Million. 'Economic Status Value measures the relative 'prestige value' of an amount of income or wealth between two periods using the income index of the per-capita GDP.' Therefore, it follows that the nomination of Executors in this case would have been a matter for very serious consideration for Alexander. His Will declares four Trustees, firstly his two sons Alexander and John who are now Shipmasters in Montrose, together with a local Leith boat-builder by the name of Peter Latta Wilson and a Leith Merchant, Walter Bruce.

Who were these two new people, his Executors Peter Latta Wilson and Walter Bruce? What role did they play in Alexander's life? And, lastly, what qualifications or personal qualities did they possess which made their selection ideal for such an important role?

The revelations of this research are quite intriguing and stand as a good illustration of the status Alexander Young managed to achieve in a short space of time in a somewhat closed community. Firstly, in the case of Peter Latta Wilson, his father Alexander Wilson was a Mariner who had married an Ann Latta in Lady Yester's Parish in Dec 1771. To have been aligned with Lady Yester's parish was quite prestigious, as it is written up as being one of the foremost churches in the Burgh of Edinburgh. This Alexander Wilson was born around 1750, therefore he was about the same age as Alexander Young give or take a year. Combine this with the fact that both gentlemen lived in Leith and both took to the sea, it is not unreasonable to conclude that Alexander Young chose Peter Latta Wilson as Trustee on the grounds that he had known the man and his family for many years, had watched Peter grow up and was aware that his ethics and honesty could not be called into question: prime requisites for any Executor.

What then were the credentials Walter Bruce Jr brought to his role as Executor? The first piece of information which came to light brought Walter's life and social position into clear focus, for he is listed in several editions of The Post Office Directory for Edinburgh as a Merchant in Leith, and we have already established that Merchants are in the top echelon of Burgh society. His business was located in Sugar House Close, Tolbooth Wynd, but more importantly he lived at No. 40 Constitution

Street, Leith. Alexander Young lived at No. 104 Constitution Street, so these two men were near neighbours. Even more interesting was the entry above Walter Bruce Jr which cites Walter Bruce & Sons, wrights, located at 19 Charlotte Street. Sea Captains like Alexander and Shipwrights like Walter Bruce Jnr and Snr worked and lived hand in glove in the days of the wooden sailing ship.

Walter Bruce Jnr. was identified as the son of Walter Bruce Snr and Katharine Heriot. Young Walter was born in 1780 in Leith, and had four brothers James, William, Charles and John. Then on the same page in the 1814-15 P.O. Directory for Edinburgh, which includes Leith, is a Major James Bruce of Naval Yard, with his personal residence listed as 'Jessfield', Newhaven; a John Bruce, Clerk in the said Naval Yard, with a home on Elbe Street and lastly Robert Bruce, Manager, London and Edinburgh Shipping Company, Ferry Road, Leith. That last entry explained everything - Alexander Young is known to have been a shareholder in the London and Edinburgh Shipping Company; therefore, would have been well acquainted with Robert Bruce, who was cousin to his Executor, Walter Bruce Jnr.

In piecing together the lives of the Bruce Family, my attention turned to a map of Leith and Newhaven from the 1790s. At this point in history there were no property numbers as we know them today, rather houses were identified by their given names and land was identified by its original owner as a means of creating a line of ownership and geography. This map identifies, firstly, land belonging to Walter's mother, Katharine Heriot and her family, which denotes them as one of the major landholders and a founding family of Leith. The Heriots not only have their heritage indelibly emblazoned into the original maps of the Burgh, they also had property holdings on both sides of Queensferry Road where on one substantial block of land is located the Heriot Hospital. Obviously the Heriots were a very prominent and wealthy family within the community pre-1790.

In the Scottish Post Office Directory for 1817-1818, the year of Alexander's death, there is a listing for P.L. [Peter Latta] Wilson as a boat-builder, living at 24 Shirra Brae, and for Alexander Young, shipmaster, 104 Constitution Street. Whilst these are but fragments of these people's lives, they do position them in a place and time and give insights which demonstrate that Alexander had not only woven himself into the seafaring fabric of Newhaven and Leith but into that of those families who were prominent socially and financially, and dare I say cornerstones of a Burgh community which we know were cautious where newcomers were concerned. This can be taken as further proof that Alexander was welcomed, accepted and to my mind supports the many character assumptions made about the man himself.

But what else is there to learn about Alexander Young that could finally cement him as the key person who created the business and wealth opportunities responsible for setting up this family's seafaring legacy?

Further on in Alexander's Will mention is made of three Merchant Shipping companies in which he held shares 'in [the] Ships, Stock and Premises belonging to the Whale Shipping Company of Montrose and likewise my shares in the London & Edinburgh Shipping Company and in the Hamburg Shipping Company of Leith'. The Whale Fishing Company of Montrose was the company set up by Alexander and now operated by his sons Alexander and John who had, some time ago, decamped from Leith. They had married Montrose girls and settled in that town where they were successfully carving out seafaring careers whaling in the Arctic. The bigger story of The Montrose Whale Fishing Company will be expanded later.

As for The London & Edinburgh Shipping Company - it was formed by a group of Leith Merchants in 1809 and would go on to trade for 150 years. Along with Alexander perhaps members of the Wilson and Bruce families were also investors? That company's initial fleet was made up of six smacks purchased from the Berwick Union Company. Then, The London & Edinburgh Shipping Company immediately set about ordering a further five smacks of 160 tons each from shipbuilder William Good of Bridport, Devon. The business of passenger transportation on the Leith to London route continued to thrive. Just a few years later the fleet was augmented by a further five vessels. These were ordered from a local Leith Shipbuilding Company whose owner Robert Menzies was a known friend of Alexander Young. One of the Robert Menzie & Sons built smacks was launched in 1823 and named *Robert Bruce* after the long-time Manager of the London & Edinburgh Shipping Company.

In considering these friendships and close business relationships there is no doubt that Alexander would have enjoyed an intimate knowledge of the Company and its business operations. The 1820/21 Post Office Directory has a notation for this Company that reads -

> 'The London and Edinburgh Shipping Company's Smacks sail from Leith on Tuesdays and Fridays; and from Miller's Wharf, London on Sundays and Thursdays.
> - Office 72 Shore Street - Robert Bruce, Manager.

SMACKS	MASTERS
Favourite	Mark Sanderson
Superb	William Ballingall
Pilot	William Anderson
Comet	Thomas Marshall
Prompt	George Marshall
Trusty	Robert Fussey
Fifeshire	David Millar'

As luck would have it, The Director's Minute Books, Register of Documents, Books of Account and Wharfage and Shipping Records of this wonderful old company have survived and are currently held in the collection of historical documents within the National Records of Scotland (formerly known as the National Archives of Scotland). The London & Edinburgh Shipping Company later established a Head Office at 8-9 Commercial Street, Leith. There are advertisements from more recent times touting comfortable, safe, swift passage between Leith and London. [See Website]

This brings us to Alexander's shareholding in a company styled The Hamburg Shipping Company of Leith. This proved a little more challenging to explore as no company with that specific name could be identified; however, there are records pertaining to a Leith & Hamburg Shipping Company in Leith which appears to have come into being in 1816 with a fleet of sailing brigs. Once again, the Post Office Directory for 1820-21 has an entry - 'Leith and Hamburgh Shipping Company, 7 Dock Street, Leith'. Nick Robins, through his book - *'Scotland and the Sea: The Scottish Dimension in Maritime History'* - shines a faint light on the operations of this company. His work discloses that the establishment of steamer services along the east coast of Scotland to destinations across the North Sea were slow to develop, which presented opportunities for those sailing vessels otherwise unemployed. This would certainly have pleased our Captain Alexander Young whose own sailing days were on wooden vessels under canvas. The Leith & Hamburg Shipping Company appears to have persevered with sailing ships until 1848. Eventually it was forced to move with the times and embrace steam. In fact, the company remained in operation until at least the mid-1870s, as Lloyds Register contains a reference to an SS Prague, built in 1872 which was owned and operated by the Leith & Hamburg Shipping Company. Well done Alexander - that embryonic business venture you supported, prevailed against the competition, moved with times and eventually embraced steam. It certainly proved a very wise investment.

Since both The London & Edinburgh Shipping Company and The Hamburg Shipping Company of Leith were merchant shipping businesses, it was relevant to look at what was happening in that industry sector in his time to prompt Alexander to invest. Professor Robert Lee edited a publication entitled - *'Commerce and Culture: Nineteenth Century Business Elites'* – and in it he includes an essay written by Michael Nix. This essay devotes a segment to ship ownership, based on documents of a Scottish merchant shipping company by the name of Michael Henley and Son, which, Nix contends, demonstrates that more professional ship ownership was emerging in the 1800s.

In the beginning 1650-1750

The London & Edinburgh Shipping Company would prove to be another example. Established around 1809 as the Thames and Forth, it was later caused to change its name because the original name was considered too ambiguous. Nix's report also states that by 1812 58% of the shares in this company were held by persons or entities involved in the maritime sector, which was typical of what we know for whaling fleet ownership around that time. As evidence of the developing professionalism, it seems the Directors of The London & Edinburgh Shipping Company came with impeccable business credentials and proved themselves innovative as well. One of their tenets of operation provided that the Company should set aside 5% of the original cost of its ships out of its operating net profit each year. This constituted a type of 'sinking fund', an in-house insurance fund as it were, which was subsequently and securely invested in Government Bonds. Surely on that basis alone Alexander would have been satisfied that he was making a sound investment in a well-managed and soundly operated Company.

It is now time to turn attention to the property portfolio segment of Alexander's Will. This segment itemises various properties as - 'half of the ground story of the Tenement of land lying on the north side of the village of Newhaven near the east end thereof erected by the deceased John Liston Fisherman in Newhaven on all and hail that piece of ground lying in the Town of Newhaven' .... 'together with the pertinents of the said subjects all as presently possessed by Alexander Liston Fisherman there, as also my upper and higher houses lying on the north side of the said village of Newhaven and my upper house lying east from the two houses above his deponed with the whole parts and pertinents of the subjects as presently possessed by Philip Young, George Johnston and Jean Thornton, my tenants and also all the whole the third and attic storeys of a Tenement of Land in Constitution Street, Leith erected by Charles Murray builder there on a piece of ground fenced by him from John Thomson Blockmaster in Leith and which Tenement is bounded on the west by Constitution Street on the South by the mutual wall and gable which separates them from the house and property of John Thomson Wright [107 Constitution Street] now deceased, on the east by the background deponed by the said Charles Murray to Charles May Shipmaster in Leith, and on the north by mutual gable of another Tenement built by the said Charles Murray [101 Constitution Street] all as marked on a ground plan with the right to a pump well behind the said Tenements in common with the other inhabitants of the said two tenements Together with the two cellars belonging to the said two storeys above deponed' ....' described in my rights and Infeftment thereof '....'and all rights title and interest which I have'.

An historic map of Leith and Newhaven from 1822 shows all the properties as described in this Will, with the names Charles Murray, John Thomson and others imprinted on properties on Constitution Street. As for Philip Young, he was unmarried at the time his name appeared in Alexander's Will, but later in the 1851 Census for Newhaven, Philip Young and his wife Catherine Hamilton can be found residing in Lambs Court, Newhaven. Philip was then aged 60 years, with his occupation listed as Fisherman, as was his father, another Alexander Young. It is not proved whether or not this Philip Young is in any way related to our Alexander's branch of the Youngs. What is known is that Philip Young's family had been in Leith for several generations, and his son Philip married an Ann Liston in 1852 in North Leith; so, the inter-marriage in Newhaven continued and it does make genealogy research in this enclave quite a challenge.

After Alexander had resolved all the money and property matters in his Will relating to banks, bonds, shares, sasines, warrendices and infeftments, he finally turns to personal family matters. He settles all instructions related to Susan Pattison first, then details bequests to his children, in which he is strident, fair and explicit. At a time when it was generally accepted that the eldest son received the lion's share of the family estate and other children received but a pittance, if anything at all, Alexander shows himself to be uncommonly egalitarian. He would have been aware that Death Duties Legislation had been ratified by Parliament in 1796 wherein close relatives and immediate family were exempt from the payment of such Duty. A shrewd Scot would take this into account, and that is exactly what Alexander did.

At the time of his death he had six surviving children, two daughters - Anne who was married to Captain William Dick and Helen who was married to Captain Joshua Richmond - and four sons, Alexander, John, Robert and George. He declared that they each should receive an equal one-sixth share and in the case of the daughters it was in 'jus mariti'. This is a curious Scottish legal term, now obsolete, but in 1817 provided for the husband to administer his wife's goods, rents and moveable estate whether he became vested in these at the time of marriage or if they were acquired afterwards. However, the exception to this rule was when the wife received property as a bequest, and although it was bequeathed to her at a time during her marriage, the husband had no such right over the paraphernalia component (i.e. any clothes or jewellery and their receptacles).

Now, it seems every family has a 'black sheep' and this family is no exception. For this generation of Youngs it is Alexander's son, Robert, who gets singled out for special mention and harsh comment and treatment. In his Will Alexander stipulates that 'the remaining sixth part or share at interest to Robert Young, my son. But it is provided and declared that he shall be entitled to uplift the principal sum, so employed in the event of his marrying any decent woman or on the event of his conduct meeting the approbation of the Trustees'. From this instruction, it is clear that Robert was to receive only the interest on the principal unless he 'mended his ways'. One can only ruminate on what he may have done to so raise the ire of a father who has so far demonstrated himself to be quite a fair and even-handed person. Was it purely the fact that Robert was 30 years old and unmarried? It was pre-Victorian times, so was poor Robert the victim of some rising morality or anxiety over-riding religious and social norms?

This discrimination against Robert was not confined to the financial portion of his father's estate, as Alexander's instructions to his Trustees regarding the distribution of his personal belongings shows that Robert was not kindly endowed. This section of the Will reads 'deliver over to Alexander Young my eldest son on my death one pair of knee buckles set in gold, one stock silver buckle and a gold headed cane. <u>To Robert Young my second son one plane stock buckle and a pair of silver knee buckles and my silver watch with his own gold seal and key and also my silver headed cane</u>. To John Young my third son, a large pair of silver shoe buckles and one pair of silver knee buckles and a gold headed cane marked with the letter 'Y' To George Young my fourth son, my gold watch and chain with my gold seal and one pair of set silver buttons and to divide equally among my said sons, my whole wearing apparel and linens and my gold sleeve buttons ...'. The seafaring items listed in this inventory were definitely not the personal possessions of an impoverished man!

For some logical reason Alexander chose to cite his sons in their chronological order of birth but makes his feelings clear as to his opinion of each person by the description of their heritables. He then displays a touch of vanity wherein he declares that his image is to be handed down in perpetuity. He instructs his Trustees to ensure that - 'after the death of my said wife to deliver my miniature picture to the said Ann Young my eldest daughter and failing her to deliver the same to Helen Young my second daughter'. Why to his daughters and not the eldest son? Was it a given that these images were more valued by the females than the males? Sadly, the whereabouts of this image miniature is unknown; however, there are several portraits surviving from this early time. One is a portrait of Alexander Young Jnr and the other is a fourth generation Young Family image collection which is greatly prized. It has his eldest son Alexander and wife Jean Strachan at the head followed by their eldest son John and wife Mary Donaclift, then their eldest son Alexander Donaclift Young with Jane Donald and lastly their first-born son James Buckland Young along with his wife Elizabeth Dawes. [See Website]

The value of a Will as a means of discovery is sometimes chancy and other times boundless. This dissection of Alexander Young's Will of 1817 adds greatly to our understanding and image of the man, his place in the community, the respect he had earned, the wealth he had acquired and built. It highlights his legacy to his family, his opinion as to the character of each of his children, as well as vouching for his executors. All of these findings emanate from a time when documents were more likely to be discarded, scarce or simply non-existent.

Taking all this into account, several observations can be made on behalf of these early Young Ancestors.

Firstly, looking back to the beginning of this 1650-1750 century it is clear that just as the wives of the Revolutionary fighters were forced to take the reins of home affairs so too the wives of these early Young Mariners, Skippers and Shipmasters were required to be resourceful and self-reliant. We have learned the fishwives of Newhaven were renowned for their strong bodies, jovial natures and heritage songs, but no doubt they were strong of spirit and resourceful too, as all too often their menfolk were absent for extended periods and, as we are about to learn, many of the Youngs met with untimely ends at sea, never to return at all. Marrying into this culture was about to set this family on a completely different path. Alexander is the first of a line who became competent and confident seafarers and astute businessmen. Above all, there is no doubt that Alexander earned the respect and friendship of many in high places. Curiously, he actually mentions the word '<u>friendship</u>' in his Will when alluding to his Executors.

From what we have learned so far, it is fair to conclude that Captain Alexander Young Snr lived a long, fulfilled and wonderful life.

Now we have a quaint and quirky sidebar to Alexander Young's Will.

Every now and then when exploring this wonderful world of historical material, a story will pop up which grabs the attention, challenges the imagination and simply demands to be put on the page. At first, I was delighted to have discovered what appeared to be an interesting profile for one of Alexander's tenants, but then I began to question the veracity of the story - was the magazine article fact or fiction, or does it hold a modicum of truth somewhere in the telling? The story uncovered relates to a vessel by the name of *Camperdown* of Leith, which could be one and that sailed by Alexander. The story relates to Alexander's tenant Captain Charles May, Shipmaster in Leith, and involves a Danish pirate by the name of Lars Vonved, all wrapped up in an intriguing essay on the self-styled Count of Elisnore and one of his most trusted men, Marmaduke Dunraven. The essay was published under the title Vonved the Dane: Count of Elsinore in Two Volumes by Richard Bentley of London in 1861. The Publisher writes a disclaimer that the English Author sojourned in Denmark and his work originally appeared in the Dublin University Magazine, which is where I found this tale.

Here is the Charles May story -

The Writer, Richard Bentley, actually begins his tale with a preamble designed to set the scene for the final extraordinary tale. It reads in part - 'In 1849 I resided for a few months near the famous fishing village of Newhaven ...'. At the same time, it transpired that a mysterious man was a boarder with a Mrs Macrae in a cottage close to the Firth of Forth. This Writer and the stranger would regularly take a stroll along the shoreline, but each reserved their acquaintance. The Writer expressed his curiosity about the man who he says possessed a - 'mien that stamped him a gentleman born.' When the Writer challenged the landlady Mrs Macrae for information to satisfy his curiosity about this stranger, she gladly offered that his name was Marmaduke Dunraven, that he received but three letters in the past year, paid his board on time, wrote a lot but kept to himself in conversation and society. Several days after this exchange Mrs Macrae accosted the Writer whilst he was on his seaboard stroll. She said that the stranger had become drastically ill upon reading his latest letter. She explained that - 'after reading the fatal letter over and over again, he thrust it in the fire, and in a state of frightful agitation opened his drawers and cast heap after heap of papers and documents on the floor, all of which he successively thrust between the bars of the grate, muttering to himself like a maniac all the while.'

She further related, that sometime later she heard a thud and, having engaged the assistance of a local fisherman who was passing by, they both proceeded upstairs to investigate. After forcing open his door they found him lying insensible in a pool of blood with his books and small possessions scattered in every direction. The doctor was summoned and pronounced the stranger terminally ill, having burst a blood vessel from mental excitement. Mrs Macrae suggested to the Writer, that if he was still curious, he should visit upon her boarder before it was too late as he was dying. The Writer was so taken with his inquisitiveness that he decided to oblige himself of the opportunity, being determined to quietly satisfy his curiosity. Upon entering the room, the two men exchanged initial pleasantries. A short time later, Dunraven requested the Writer to open the bottom drawer of his cabinet and bring the box therein to him. Dunraven, upon receiving the box, pressed a secret spring; the lid came open and he emptied the contents onto his bed. 'There was a locket or two, a small French Testament, a pocket compass, a silver snuff-box, a finely embroidered muslin handkerchief, a curious gold seal, a bookmark of green silk, and a miniature portrait in a plain ebony case, with a long black ribbon looped to it.' Dunraven clasped the handkerchief to his face, inhaling its perfume then took up the miniature. The Writer got only a fleeting glance at the face of a beautiful woman who seems to have signed her name at the bottom. Dunraven placed the handkerchief on his chest and the miniature around his neck so as the two items could rest together close to his heart. He instructed his new advocate that upon his death no man was to view the image and extracted a solemn promise to that effect.

Dunraven then proceeded to dictate his Will to the Writer, including details of where he was to be buried. He had chosen Cramond Cemetery, which does exist by the way, as it had a wonderful view to the Firth, but he demanded no stone, only the planting of a red rose at his head and a cypress at his feet. He contended he had no family to mourn for him and that he was happy to die as he was not so in love with life anymore. He left his books, manuscripts and little souvenirs to the Writer and the rest and residue of his estate to Mrs Macrae for her kindness in caring for him. He then begged that the window of his room be thrown open to afford him the opportunity to take the sea air and gaze upon the vessels in the Firth for one last time. Dunraven then shared a hushed personal thought with the Writer 'Never more shall I feel the bounding motion of a buoyant bark! Many's the cruise that I have made on nearly every ocean and sea of this world, but my voyage of life is ended, and I shall soon anchor in the ocean of eternity.'

The Writer enquired if he had been a sailor. Dunraven's reply was very forthright indeed 'A sailor! Ay, and what is more than a sailor, a thorough seaman', and then he added that 'There are countries, sir where the name and fame of the Count of Elsinore will be remembered generations hence; and when they speak of the noble Rover of the Baltic, they will not forget his faithful friend and officer, whose last moments you, an unknown stranger, have generously come to soothe.' Dunraven made one final comment on this matter - 'I shared the fortunes of my noble and dearly-loved friend, the Count of Elsinore!'; 'I have bequeathed you all my papers, and you will learn from them whatever you wish to know of the career of us both.'

Dunraven made one final request. He implored Mrs Macrae to open the sea chest in his room and take out his old sea cloak, but to be careful as it contains a flask of wine and a precious goblet. She carefully did as she was instructed; first taking the goblet in hand and then pouring some of the wine. Dunraven drank it and told them it was a Cyprus Red, his father's favourite wine. He went on to explain that the cloak was a gift from his mother, and he wished it to be spread over him as a pall. The jewel encrusted antique goblet was a family heirloom which his father had only used on high festival occasions, and, when Dunraven had drunk of his wine, he told the Writer it was now his to keep. This was all too much for the Writer who was so dumb struck he could only nod an acceptance. Then in a final loving gesture Dunraven calmly kissed the goblet before handing it to the Writer. Marmaduke Dunraven then sank backwards into his last long sleep.

Now, the Writer asserts that he kept all his solemn oaths to Dunraven, and then a short time after the burial he set to exploring the papers and books he had been bequeathed. There were letters by different hands, sheets of notes and memoranda. Piece by piece they began to come together like 'link[s] of a chain' of events where each one was a 'Wild and romantic adventures - deeds of daring - the most powerful passions of human nature - the worst and the best demotions of the soul - these formed the groundwork of the canvas, so to speak; and in the foreground stood forth a few pre-eminent actors in the drama. Dunraven himself was a prominent character, yet a subordinate one.'

The challenge for the Writer was to decide just what he should do with his heritables. Certain items felt familiar, it seemed that - 'these papers had from time to time been made public - but the bare facts only - and other portions which alone could elucidate the mystery enveloping the main incidents, - had hitherto remained profoundly secret.' He deduced that, since Dunraven had bequeathed them to him without restriction or covenant, he was free to use them as he chose. His first thought was to write a narrative of fact but he decided that the facts were so absurd as to be unbelievable and, fearing repercussions that it would appear completely fabricated, he determined that he should 'weave the narrative into a fictitious shape - to give Reality the outward garb of Romance -[so] no possible harm could accrue.' 'So have I done' - he wrote.

This brings us to the passage in Dunraven's papers involving Charles May, Captain of the *Camperdown* of Leith. It is for the reader to decide whether it is coincidence or a case of stolen identity or dare it be said - truth! We will never know the answer, but a man by the same name and occupation in the same time as that person was mentioned in the Will of Alexander

Young as a tenant of one of his properties in Leith. Life imitating Art? Or Art imitating Life?

Dunraven's story begins - The British barque, *Camperdown*, under the command of one Captain Charles May was sailing homeward from St. Petersburg. It was a stormy night on the Baltic Sea, the Mate was on watch, the *Camperdown* was sailing east of the large Danish Island of Bornholm, under a close-reefed topsail in clear moonlight when the Mate espied something in the water that kept disappearing and re-appearing in the swell. Then through a night-telescope he discerned a human clinging to a spar. He informed the Captain who promptly ordered a change of course and the crew made ready to lower a boat. The sea was choppy but the ship heaved-to, the crew lowered a boat and retrieved the castaway and returned to the barque. The man was weak and cold, but after a good night's sleep in a warm berth he seemed well recovered. He was described as clothed with seaman's trousers of fine blue cloth, wearing a richly embroidered crimson silk belt, a white linen shirt of extraordinary fineness, thick Icelandic stockings and light shoes with unusual silver buckles. His apparel was set out to dry while he slept. In his belt was an ornate dagger in a leather sheath, and in his pocket was a silver snuffbox. His garb declared him a mariner, probably Scandinavian or Russian it was thought, and he looked to be of around thirty years of age, yet he was a man of - 'no common stamp'.

Next morning Captain May and the rescued stranger exchanged pleasantries and with a smile the Captain assured him he had fallen into safe hands. Captain May established the stranger could understand English, albeit a little, and so he attempted to engage him in conversation. First they discussed the rescue and then in the course of conversation the Captain declared that his name was Charles May, the barque was the *Camperdown* of Leith and they were homeward bound from St. Petersburg. After the stranger had finished his meal Captain May enquired if he had been shipwrecked? The stranger's response was that not two of her timbers hang together. When pressed for information for his Captain's log the stranger admitted that it was a Danish ship, it had struck Jomfru Reef in the storm with all hands lost save his fortunate soul. Were you the skipper

In the beginning 1650-1750

Captain May probed further? The stranger almost gave a nod then lowered his head whereupon Captain May assumed that he was rightly upset about the outcome and settled the conversation by suggesting even the best of ships are lost however well they are officered.

Captain May moved on to enquire again of the stranger's name. The man declared himself to be Lars Vonved. Captain May was aware that this declaration came with expression and attitude as if he was a Lord High Admiral! May declared he was not an accomplished man at spelling, especially not foreign words, so passed over pen and paper for the castaway to write his name first so May could copy it into his Log. The castaway wrote - 'Enighteens Minde - For Charles May, Captain of the Camperdown, of Leith. June 28th, 18__ Lars Vonved'. His script was gothic and bold, and Vonved then attached his seal. When May enquired as to the meaning of the insignia on his seal Vonved obliged with 'The ship must sail swiftly lest the eagle drop the sword on her deck!'. The stranger handed the paper back to May with the odd comment - 'Keep this carefully, the day may come when it will prove of service to you'. In order to continue in polite conversation Captain May shared his own ideas for a personal seal and what it might contain. Vonved enquired as to May's motto. Captain May thought for a moment and then declared - 'The three L's': Latitude Lead and Lookout - no ship can navigate safely without them.' Captain May then placed the paper in his Logbook and declared he was heading out on deck.

Two unrelated but equally baffling events then took place. Firstly, Vonved had followed May up on deck and enquired as to the whereabouts of the Mate who had been so observant while on watch. When they came face-to-face Vonved passed to the Mate all the gold coins in his pocket. The Mate initially refused them but a grateful Vonved insisted. Then, scanning the horizon Vonved espied a vessel he recognised, a Danish joegt. He untied his red sash and held it aloft as if to signal the ship, and when Captain May raised his telescope, to his astonishment, he saw men on the quarter-deck readying a craft. Shortly after there was a flash of a gun whereupon the Danish joegt 'put forth every stitch of canvas and stood towards the barque.' Then things just got curiouser and curiouser - when the craft came alongside, Vonved greeted the men with a foreign sounding command and they in turn doffed their caps and made a respectful salute. In response to Vonved's enquiry they replied - 'Redt godt, Capitain Vonved! (All is right, Captain Vonved!).' The grateful Vonved reiterated his words to May about the note he had written, and also expressed his thanks once again to the Captain and the Mate. He then moved quickly on board the joegt the vessel fired a farewell gun salute to the *Camperdown* and sailed off until it was but 'a mere speck on the horizon.'

Captain May continued on his planned voyage and, as scheduled, put into Copenhagen to load cargo. He met with the British Consul who enquired if he had sailed near Bornholm Island as an appalling story of a renowned fredlos Lars Vonved had come to his notice in the local newspaper. The Consul went on to say that it was thought that Vonved had gone to terrorise another ocean but had apparently been on the island. It seems he was betrayed by one of his own men, taken captive and was being conveyed on board the *Falk*, a brig-of-war, when it suddenly exploded. Only one man escaped and after he was rescued by another unknown boat he reported that Vonved was not searched for hidden daggers when taken on board but rather he was thrust straight into the hold, where he must have cut his way into the powder magazine and, preferring not to meet his fate in Copenhagen, decided to blow himself up.

The Consul enquired if Captain May had seen or heard an explosion, to which May replied in the negative. May was astonished and enquired further as to the deeds of this man Vonved and was he really a Rover? The Consul was equally as perplexed that May had never heard of Lars Vonved the notorious Baltic Pirate. After more discussion, the Captain decided to show the Consul the piece of paper from his Log to adjudge whether the castaway's signature compared to that circulated by the Danish authorities. The Consul could confirm the lavish scrolling signature to be genuine and was obviously eager to learn under what circumstances Captain May had obtained such a paper. On returning the autograph, the Consul commented that it would be May's safe passage in the Baltic as Vonved never harmed or broke his word to friend or foe. He went on to say that should May have recognised this Dane and put him in irons and brought him to Copenhagen, the King would have lavished money and honour on him as a reward.

May needed no time to consider this before responding that, whilst like any God-fearing mariner he abhors Rovers and wished them all a short life and a hempen necklace, the man he rescued could not be half as miscreant as they say, and he believed that it was God's will that he should be saved. The Consul implored May to keep his rescue actions a 'profound secret' as it could bode very badly for him in the future especially with the Danish Government. Unfortunately, the scuttle of these recent events had already been spread by members of the crew of the *Camperdown* who, upon hearing about the explosion and rescue story, went on to relate their own version of the events of that night.

Once their encounter was exposed the authorities issued a Proclamation denouncing Vonved and his daring escape and placed a price on his head for capture and a free pardon to anyone who betrayed him.

Chapter 4

The Arctic Whale Fishing Industry
The History • The Origins • The Species
The Season • The Grounds • The Skirmishes
Scotland's Role & Government Incentives

Mid 2016, news broke of a whale jawbone unearthed at an Iron Age archaeological dig on the Orkney island of South Ronaldsay. It was discovered buried together with human bones and the results of radiocarbon dating showed that the human bones were of a male person who died sometime between CE120 and CE240. This project, being undertaken by the University of the Highlands and Islands, has been instrumental in establishing that whales and humans, in Scotland at least, have been interacting far longer than was previously assumed. Similarly, in 2008 the University of Alaska published findings of a joint Russia America Project focused on prehistoric whaling and their study showed that Inuit interaction with whales probably occurred around 1000 BC, or over 3000 years ago. Clearly, these very early encounters would have been land based, that is they occurred when whales beached themselves and humans took advantage of the resource.

Determining at what point in time humans actually took to the sea in order to fish for whales is quite a different matter. It is academically conceded that the Basques were probably the first and would have done so around 1059. Basque fishermen are geographically associated with that part of Europe bordering what is known as the Atlantic north coast of Spain and the south coast of France, in the region charted as the Bay of Biscay.

In the beginning 1650-1750

More particularly, these fishermen were natives of the town of Bayonne on the Ardour River. In the centuries prior to 1059, humans were largely opportunistic, taking advantage of those whales discovered stranded on the shoreline. The value to early man of the oil, meat and bone, particularly in prehistoric times, when humankind were largely hunter gatherers, cannot be overestimated. As mankind evolved the value of the whale to humans ebbed and flowed as new uses were found for various whale parts and as other products and materials came to be used. Notwithstanding all that, it is clear that the whale had always been considered a 'rich prize'.

What do we know of the earliest British involvement with whales and whaling?

Professor Chesley W. Sanger, in his paper entitled - *'The Origins of British Whaling: Pre-1750 English and Scottish Involvement in the Northern Whale Fishery'* – states the earliest known English notation of the whale is in a Charter granted in 1148 by Pope Eugenius III to Hilary, Bishop of Chichester, confirming that the latter was entitled to - 'any whale found on the land of the church of Chichester, except the tongue, which is the King's'. Moving forward almost two centuries and the value of the whale has gone to another level as Sanger explains that in 1315 - 'Edward II reserved to himself the right of all whales cast by chance upon the shore', and likewise it would appear that successive Scottish monarchs claimed the same or similar privileges down the ages.

The earliest and most notable English commercial attempt at whale fishing is attributed to a London-based merchant organisation, the Muscovy Company, sometimes referred to in very early documents as the Russia Company. The Muscovy Company was charted in 1555, born out of a plan hatched during the reign of Edward VI, when a group of entrepreneurial London merchants were inspired by reports that Italian explorer Sebastian Cabot had attempted to discover a North-West Passage over North America. Since trade with the Far East was a burgeoning market, these English merchants conceived their own plan whereby they would send a fleet of ships to search for a North-East Passage to China and the East Indies. One of their fleet reached Russia and began what was termed 'amicable intercourse and profitable commerce'. This established a trade route and a trade relationship that has persisted down the centuries. Other discoveries made during these explorations inspired the Muscovy Company to become involved in whale fishing and this Company has been credited with being the enterprise which launched the English Whale Fishing Industry.

These far northern regions were still largely unexplored in the late 1500s. Some segments of shoreline had been charted; however, there was a great deal more work still to be done. With this in mind, some British ships set sail for these far northern latitudes purely on missions of exploration and navigation. Captain John Davis [C1550-1605] was a remarkable pioneering Explorer, Navigator and Sea Captain of the Elizabethan era who distinguished himself as Pilot and Captain for both Dutch and English voyages to the East Indies. He discovered the Falkland Islands and commanded *Black Dog* against the Spanish Armada. He also received Letters Patent from his Queen before sailing to the Arctic from London on the 17 June 1585 in the 50 ton, 23 man barque *Sunshine*. Accompanying him on that first voyage was Captain Bruton sailing the Dartmouth Sloop *Moonshine* which was a mere 35 tons and manned by a crew of just 19 men. Heading deep into the Arctic north, Davis and Bruton would have sailed in largely uncharted waters in unfamiliar environments where they would have often experienced dire weather conditions as they optimistically pushed further and further towards Latitude 70°N.

Evidence from this expedition would show that these vessels were far too light for the sea conditions encountered. Also, given the dangerous mist and fog which shrouds the deadly pack-ice and driven on by the gales, it cannot be overstated the seriousness of their many unprecedented navigational concerns. They were lucky to survive at all. Make no mistake, these intrepid explorers who finally reached what is now known as the southern tip of Greenland were incredibly brave hearted souls. Davis' expedition pushed on and discovered the passage

In the beginning 1650-1750

to the west of Greenland which now bears his name - the Davis Straits. That place will receive greater mention later as one of the most fruitful whale fishing grounds in history; however, in achieving such acclaim it became infamous as the burial ground for countless ships and men. Given what is about to be learnt about the unpredictability and extreme challenges of these northern waters, it is astonishing to realise that those two tiny vessels of Davis and Bruton persisted for seven weeks, exploring and charting the region before making a safe return journey to London.

Davis considered his Arctic exploration unfinished business, and immediately went looking for financial backing in order to undertake another voyage. By 19 April 1586, Davis had received some £1175, largely from Exeter merchants in his home County of Devon, with whose support he assembled and provisioned a new fleet of ships for a much longer and more arduous voyage. He hastily put an exploration party together and sailed out of Dartmouth on May 7, 1586. On this second voyage Davis was commanding the 120 ton flagship *Mermaid* while the *Sunshine* of 60 tons, *Moonshine* 35 tons and the *North Star*, a 10 ton pinnace, acted as his consorts. Sadly, the *North Star* was lost quite early into the voyage as a result of a severe storm; however, *Mermaid*, *Sunshine* and *Moonshine* completed their six months voyage and returned home to a great reception. Davis made a third and final voyage where he charted Davis Inlet and the coast of Labrador. It has been written that Davis's Log of this third voyage became - 'the model for later Captains for centuries.'

Another decade would pass before Dutch explorer Willem Barents would make his discovery of Bear Island in 1596. This revived interest in the north and many believe it took the joint reports of Davis and Barents, of - 'armies of whales to be seen blowing and playing amongst the ice floes' – to generate a call to action. Barents' news came as a well-timed reminder to the whale fishing community to rethink their future given the Bay of Biscay had been fished to a point of non-viability. So, enticed by the prospect of enormous numbers of whales in the vicinity of Bear Island, the Basques and others were determined to set sail in pursuit of the whale. Bear Island for the modern reader is a 178 square kilometre island in the waters north of Norway at the junction of the Greenland Sea and the Barents Sea, approximately midway to the Svalbard Archipelago.

Before long the English, Dutch and Basques were jostling for a share of the seasonal catch. The Dutch and Basques proved themselves vastly superior fishermen to the English. The Muscovy Company's skippers lacked the skills and know-how of the Dutch in particular and proved so unsuccessful in fishing for whale they concentrated their efforts on the capture of walrus and seal. Basil Lubbock writes a wonderful history of these early days sourced from ship's logs. One descriptive entry states that 'On March 9, 1610, the Amitie of 70 tons (master, Jonas Poole, crew 14 men and a boy), and the still smaller Lionesse (master, Thomas Edge), weighed from London, and on May 16 reached East Greenland. The sight which met the eyes of these first Greenlandmen must have been a wonderful one. The whole length of the Spitzbergen west coast with its deep fiords was teeming with whales disporting themselves and quite indifferent to their approaching human enemies. The great fish had yet to learn that the curious creatures with their many legs, the shallops of the Amitie and Lionesse, held any danger for them.'

By 1611 we see 'the Muskovy Company send the *Mary Margaret* of 150 tons (Steven Bennet, master; Thomas Edge, factor and commander) and the Elizabeth of 50 tons (Jonas Poole, master and grand pilot).' What is most interesting is that - 'Beside her English crew, six skilled harpooners from the Basque port of St. Jean de Luz were put aboard the *Mary Margaret*, in order to show the English seamen how to kill whales.' Edge was also under instruction from the Muscovy Company to treat the Basques kindly and be sure that his men learned 'the better sorts of whale from the worse, whereby in their striking they may choose the good and leave the bad.' This last comment is particularly pertinent and is perhaps the earliest acknowledgement that species differentiation was acknowledged as critical to success. Sadly, no one was really listening!

In the beginning 1650-1750

The potential for these voyages to encounter fatal danger was acute, and it was that very season that the *Mary Margaret* and the *Elizabeth* were both lost in separate incidents. Initially, sailing in convoy en route to Spitzbergen, they were forced to part company with the rest of the fleet, due to bad weather, even before they had reached Cherie Island. In the case of the *Mary Margaret*, she continued sailing along the west coast and, after finding all the sounds full of pack ice, changed course for Crosse Road where she finally anchored for a time before proceeding to Sir Thomas Smyth's Bay. It was whilst most of her hands were ashore boiling out the oil from sea-horses [walruses] that the *Mary Margaret* was cast ashore, forced up by the drifting pack-ice. Captain Thomas Edge was held wholly responsible for the loss. Thankfully, the ten men who had remained aboard made it to the ice, but all their supplies were either lost or spoiled. The fifty men took to the four sloops (whaleboats) and the ship's long-boats. After sailing south for about forty leagues, they too became separated. As if this would not have been frightening enough, there was worse to come.

Ship's logs further reveal that - ' .... one sloop and the ship's boat fell in with the *Hopewell* of Hull, which sailed back to Foule Sound with them in order to salve what had been landed from the wreck, which was valued at £1500.' The others reached - 'Cherie Island on July 29 in a great storm of wind.' Having made land on the south side of the island, they discovered the *Elizabeth* about to weigh anchor for England. It is here the Logs expose a series of events which speak volumes about the knowledge and skills required of Captains in grasping the physics of keeling, centre of gravity and cargo placement and movement.

Their experience played out like this - Captain Poole of the *Elizabeth* realised that he needed to lighten his cargo load in order to take the shipwrecked men on board, so he discarded moose hinds and empty casks. Then the *Elizabeth* set sail for Foule Sound and 14 days later arrived in time to see the *Hopewell* at work salvaging what remained of the *Mary Margaret's* stores. Anxious to also take aboard the oil from *Mary Margaret's* 500 sea-horse catch, it was then that Poole made his fatal miscalculation. In shifting his cargo in the manner that he did he unbalanced the *Elizabeth* to the point where she capsized and sank. Although Poole was still on board he did manage to escape. He and his men were forced to take to the surviving small boats and row for the *Hopewell*. It was at this point that matters escalated and became violent and downright ugly.

Captain Marmaduke of the *Hopewell* had his men arm themselves with pikes and lances in order to ward off the boarding party. Thankfully Edge managed to talk the Hull Captain around, so Poole and his men could finally scramble aboard although not without a seriously bloody skirmish. Poole described his wounds as 'having mine head broke to the skull and my brow that one might see the bare bones; and by mine eare [sic] I had a sore sound, likewise the ribs of my right side were all broken and sore bruised, and the collarbone of my left shoulder is broken, besides my back so sore that I could not suffer any man to touch it'. Perhaps the inducement for Marmaduke was the £5 per ton he contracted with Edge to transport the salvaged goods. It may seem callous and somewhat harsh; however, these were incredibly perilous times when danger was ever-present, costs were high and profits hard to come by and seemingly life was cheap.

It is important for this story to put Scots in the mix of these events and once again it is thanks to Sanger's 'Notes to Chapter 2' of his publication *'Scottish Arctic Whaling'* that we can confidently say that - 'individual Scotsmen had served on the earliest Muscovy Company and foreign whaling voyages to Spitsbergen'. But when it comes to historical references, it is Henry Elking's original 1722 publication 'A *View to the Greenland Trade and Whale-Fishery with the National and Private Advantages thereof...*' that provides the oldest written reference and acknowledgement of Scots participation. Elking's work shows that the very successful Dutch fleet relied heavily on manpower from countries such as Jutland, Holstein, Scotland, Norway and Bremen for the strategic and highly skilled roles of Commander, Harpooner and Steersman. Interestingly, way back then the men were paid on results, they did not receive a regular wage rather they received a 'per Punchion on the oil they bring Home.' Elking's publication and British Government records are also a source of evidence that Dutch seamen were more highly valued and therefore paid more than their English counterparts; considerably more in fact, 16-20 Guilders per month or 30-40 Shillings Sterling for the Dutch compared to 24-26 Shillings for English seamen. This occurred at a time when Scottish seamen experienced no impediments to working on foreign ships or in foreign lands. However, it goes without saying that had the King been made aware of their involvement with the Dutch there is no doubt he would have been disapproving. Fortunately for these 'ordinary unknowns' they managed to successfully work abroad without drawing attention to themselves at home.

As for the Muscovy Company, it had powerful backers and can trace its roots to the likes of Sir Hugh Willoughby an English Arctic Explorer and Captain of the *Bona Esperanza*; to Sebastian Cabot, an Italian born pioneering seafarer on behalf of England and Spain, and Richard Chancellor, a little-known English Explorer who in his ship *Edward Bonaventure* explored the northern coast of Norway. Chancellor once reported he met with Scottish fishermen at Vardo [70°N 29°E] who warned him of the hazards on the Arctic coast of polar Russia. He decided to ignore their warnings and sailed on towards the White Sea and finally dropped anchor in the port of Archangel. There lingers a fanciful story that Chancellor's arrival was such a novelty for the Russians that the reigning Tsar, Ivan the Terrible, sent a horse drawn sleigh to convey Chancellor an unbelievable 600 miles [1000 klms] through the snow to Moscow to dine at the Royal Court as the Tsar's 'exotic guest'. Notwithstanding these tall tales, there is no doubt that these early voyages are credited with setting the foundation for the lucrative and long surviving Baltic Trade. These men called themselves the Company of Merchant Adventurers to New Lands - a very apt description indeed.

Powerful and hell-bent on success, the Muscovy Company was known to have the ear of the King of England and to this end manoeuvred to shore up their monopoly on the whale fishing grounds in Greenland. Where there is competition invariably there is a catalyst for conflict and it was not too long before the three major players - England, Denmark and Holland - were caught up in a bit of a fracas, not as you would presume as a result of the highly prized whales; rather it was regarding land ownership. The status hungry London Merchants backing the Muscovy Company had fallen victim to the fashionable and selfish desire to win favour with their liege and decided to lay claim to these new lands more in the name of 'Ego' than 'Empire'. The initial regal land grab was made by J. Fotherby of the Muscovy Company in 1613. He laid claim to Spitsbergen, the largest island in the Svalbard Archipelago in the name of King James I of England [James VI of Scotland].

Subsequently, the Muscovy Company proceeded to erect several outposts in the north-west region of the island. When their actions came to the attention of the Dutch, they were naturally and rightly incensed. The next season saw the Dutch send an even bigger fleet of fishing vessels to Spitzbergen along with what was termed 'protective vessels', which can only mean some type of men-of-war ships equipped with canon and armed soldiers. This was not the end of it: when this territorial infringement came to the notice of the King of Denmark in 1618 [I guess news travelled slowly in those days] the King made a counter-claim that Spitsbergen was in fact a part of Greenland, a long time Danish possession. He told them all - 'hands off'. Historical records indicate that neither the English nor the Dutch took the Danish King's assertion seriously.

There was another phenomenon occurring around that same time which has been ascribed to the fact that more and more foreign captains and harpooners were being hired onboard ships not of their native nation. As a result, these men became international peacemakers who took it upon themselves to divvy up the landscape according to terms set and agreed between themselves. They also devised and agreed a Code of Behaviour as it were. Evidence of this first occurrence exists to this day on the maps of the region showing landmarks such as English Bay and English Harbour, Hollanders Bay and Amsterdam Island, Danes Island and Danes Bay, Hamburghers Bay and Biscayners Point and so on.

For a time, life in these waters continued quite harmoniously. Those who did venture to the grounds sailed and fished in accordance with the Code of Behaviour whereby each nation fished their own inlet areas exclusively on the understanding that the seacoast was a free zone. There was also a Captain's Agreement where any ship could take refuge in a non-geographic zone when threatened by storms or other emergencies or when forced to wait for favourable winds. The final and most important stipulation was that should any vessel lower one of its whaleboats in a non-geographic or foreign harbour their harpoon was to be removed from its rest as a signal that the whaleboat was not in pursuit of prey.

As word of fishing success spread, the number of countries wishing to participate grew and soon there were several hundred vessels taking to the fishing grounds each year. The result was severe and dangerous overcrowding overlaid with intense competition. It was at this point the English decided to sail further to the north and east in search of new grounds. Meanwhile, the Dutch maintained their hierarchical position as the most successful whalers and as they became more and more solidly entrenched they decided to establish seasonal villages for processing and overwintering. These took the form of mini tent cities housing as many as 2,000 men. Eventually these tent cities spread out right across Amsterdam Island. Today, the only evidence that remains of these settlements is some scant brick foundations here and there in the graveyards; lasting monuments to the acute danger these intrepid seafarers faced. Once upon a time, whale skeletons littered the beaches, but they too are gone without a trace.

By the middle of the seventeenth century the monopoly imposed by the Dutch Noordsche Compagnie and the English

Muscovy Company had run its course and new 'interlopers' were entering the industry. The Dutch were undaunted and persisted, shored up by their well-deserved success and the unwavering support of their investors which saw Dutch fleet numbers increase from 70 ships in 1654 to 246 by 1684. The English fleet on the other hand was depleted to a mere handful of ships. Chesley Sanger explains the virtual cessation of English whaling during the third quarter of the seventeenth century as attributable to internal discordance on two levels. One, the Muscovy Company Londoners and the Hull & York Investors and Masters were fighting among themselves in the fishing grounds. This resulted in short seasons and massive losses for both sides. And two, from around 1640 to 1675 there was a redeployment of manpower and financial resources in order to shore up England's position in Civil Wars at home and International Wars abroad.

For instance - 1642 marked the outbreak of The First English Civil War, then in 1646 King Charles I is forced to surrender to the Scots and The First Civil War ends. 1648 saw a purge in Westminster, the First Rump Parliament and Civil War flared up again. All the while, Cromwell had been leading his army of Roundheads to victory after victory across England, Scotland and Ireland and then in 1649 Cromwell signs the warrant for Charles I to be beheaded. 1652-54 marked the first Anglo-Dutch War, 1653 Cromwell declares himself Lord Protector of England; however, in 1658 Cromwell dies unexpectedly which gives rise to the second Rump Parliament. Later, in 1660 Charles II takes the throne. 1665 is the year of the Great Plague of London, 1665-67 also marked The Second Anglo-Dutch War, and 1666 was the year of the Great Fire of London. 1672-74 is when The Third Anglo-Dutch War was fought. So, it is not hard to imagine that these events were consuming vital manpower and financial resources and when combined with a disjointed Parliament and regal instability, it is a given that whaling would have been very low on the agenda of priorities for either the authorities or investors.

There remained lingering difficulties for England - 1685 Charles II dies and James II takes the throne. He was an unpopular Roman Catholic King whose reign lasted for less than four years. Then by late 1688 England was in the grip of the infamous - 'Glorious, Bloodless Revolution' which sees James II flee abroad and William and Mary assume the throne. This meant that the London Merchants and Investors who once upon a time had the ear of the King and Parliament were now more focused on keeping their heads than investing in a pursuit which to date had proved largely unprofitable. England's departure from the whale fishery at this time left the way clear for the Germans to enter the fishing grounds. Notwithstanding the obvious lack of success for the English, the British Parliament remained keen to see participation reinvigorated in order to help curb their growing trade deficit with the Dutch. This was brought about as a result of ever-increasing prices for whale oil and whale fin, which in turn was being fuelled by rising demand for these products right across Britain and Europe.

Westminster was influenced by two other very important factors. Firstly, they came to recognise the importance of these northern whale fishing grounds as a nursery for blooding hardy seamen; and secondly, they acknowledged that the fishing provided valuable employment for a large number of ships and men. For England, there was only one way forward and Parliament's priority was to re-establish a whaling fleet. As far back as 1672 Parliament had passed an Act essentially aimed at three things - redressing the deficit, re-establishing an English fleet, and acknowledging that prior success was impeded because of a lack of adequately skilled men, especially harpooners and linesmen. This demanded a number of serious compromises.

The new Act determined that whilst future fleets would still have to be English built vessels with English Captains, now only half the crew were required to be English and the other half could be made up of 'natives of Holland or other expert fishers'. The Act included other sweeteners too which were clearly intended to placate the profit-focused English merchants whereby English whale products would henceforth be exempt of all duties while imported whale products would attract a tax of £9 per ton for oil and £18 per ton for fins. Initially, the English investors and merchants were sceptical; they were dithering and remained unconvinced until such time as Dutch supply was diminished, and prices rose sufficiently to encourage them to get back in the game; to risk their money to send ships and men to the high northern latitudes.

Success was not a given, the seasons remained variable, losses of ships and men remained high yet despite these negatives the overall number of vessels heading north kept increasing. Records for the 1683 season, for instance, indicate that there were 204 Dutch and 50 Hamburg ships fishing for whale that year. As catch numbers continued to dwindle in the waters of Jan Mayen [north of Iceland] and in the Greenland Sea, the Dutch began to push further west into the waters of the Davis Strait on the western side of Greenland. This remained the status quo for almost forty years during which time there were innovations to ships and harpoons that began pushing catch numbers higher once again. By 1721, the Dutch had an expanded fleet of over 250 ships and the Germans 79 ships.

With this as the backdrop, it is now time to focus on our Young family whalers, and more specifically on the origins of the Scottish Whaling Industry; however, given this pre-history one would have to wonder why any of the Youngs got involved at all.

From Sanger and Elking we have already learned that Scots were part of the crew of some of the very early Muscovy Company's voyages to Spitsbergen. Sanger has devoted his life to exploring the trials and tribulations of Scottish Arctic Whaling and in his latest publication entitled *'Scottish Arctic Whaling'* he commits an entire chapter to *'Origins: Pre 1750 British Arctic Whaling'*. In this part of his work he singles out Scotland's attempts to get in the game and their several unsuccessful endeavours prior to 1750 as indicative of their treatment by the King on other scores. Sanger states that - 'The first occurred in 1618 when King James (then king of Scotland) incorporated a number of English, Scots and Zealanders'.

Sanger goes on - 'This charter, appearing to militate against the privileges of the Russia and East India Companies, who had been at the greatest expense in the discovery and establishment of the fishery, was annulled, notwithstanding that ships had been purchased, provisions contracted for, and other considerable preparations made by the different parties, for commencing the fishery.' As a result, The Scottish East India Company sued for damages which were awarded in the amount of £924.10s. As usual, payment was not forthcoming, and the shareholders were 'forced to petition the House of Lords to receive payment of part of the money.' In the meantime, the most distasteful situation for Scotland was being compelled to import its whale oil and bone requirements from English merchants at market rates. So powerful were the London merchants that they had influenced Parliament to go so far as to ban Scotland from taking the less expensive option of importing oil and bone directly from the Dutch.

The elephant in the room, as always, was the unresolved animosity between England and Scotland. It seems the matter of Scotland's entitlement to join in the game had first escalated to a political and legislative crisis way back in 1625 when a Scottish trader by the name of Nathaniel Edwards, a soap factory operator, had - 'attempted to conduct whale expeditions to Greenland under the auspices of the Scottish Greenland Company'. The Muscovy Company challenged Edward's licence as an infringement of their exclusive British patent. At this time Charles I was on the throne, and Nathaniel Edwards and the Scottish Privy Council took steps to petition the King directly for his intervention because they feared there would be no impartiality on the part of the English Privy Council if that Council was set down to deal with the matter. On this occasion the Scots were thwarted by the outbreak of War with Spain.

Charles took advantage of this and made a stance for pseudo-unity. His decree translated into a Britain-wide policy applicable to all three Privy Councils - England, Ireland and Scotland. The King's position was strident, unambiguous and supposedly equally applicable to all parties where henceforth, all shipping movements were to be declared to the Lord Admiral in England. This declaration was to include the name of the port or ports to be visited and the indent of the cargo involved. This directive was worded with a softener at the end, which stated that it was the King's desire that 'all his dominions may be provided and furnished with sufficient strength both for the defence of themselves and the mutual assistance each of the other against attempts of anie enemie.' The Scots would not have swallowed that ruse for a minute and just how this would work in practice is not clear given the time lag with communications.

Sanger goes on to point out that whilst Edwards was awarded his Royal Licence on the 28 July 1625, it was somewhat of a hollow victory as he had neither the finances nor the ships to undertake such a voyage. Ironically, he called upon the involvement of Yarmouth merchants who had expressed a desire to join the whaling fleet but had been previously precluded from doing so given the Muscovy Company's monopolistic franchise. While this could have been an opportunity to break the English strangle-hold the pseudo-Scottish expedition was, at the end of the day, required to sell its oil and fin at market rates to the Muscovy Company. Edwards was also ordered by the English Privy Council in April 1627 to use English ships and wholly English crews. This was a ludicrous situation of monopolistic market control by a handful of greedy English merchants who had the ear of the King. Where Scottish franchise came into this arrangement is impossible to fathom!

Naturally, the matter was in and out of the courts and it only came to a head in 1634 when two Yarmouth vessels set sail and claimed the right to whale 'at Horneslound in Greenland (Spitsbergen) .... Under the authority of the patent granted to Nathaniel Edwards for Scotland'. Upon arrival at the grounds they were confronted by personnel from the Muscovy Company who 'demanded possession of the place and proceeded to remove the coppers of the men of Yarmouth.' A scuffle ensued which resulted in the death of a Yarmouth man and, needless to say, the battles between England and Scotland in matters relating to the right to fish for whales and for restitution were once again set to play out in the Courts.

With more and more vessels sailing for Greenland season after season skirmishes were inevitable as competition grew and the size of the industry grew on an exponential scale. By 1721 the Arctic fishing fleet had been recorded as 251 Dutch, 90 Danish and 55 Germans sailing from Hamburg with a further 24 sailing from Bremen, 20 French Biscayners and 5 Norwegians. Then add to that the English and Scottish fleet and that makes for a very crowded fishery indeed. The Americans too had joined the fleet by 1715 sending 6 sloops from Nantucket. Following their initial success, subsequent seasons, saw other American ships from Boston join their Nantucket countrymen. From this, it is not hard to understand that before long Greenland was fished out and the fleet were being forced to move on to higher and more dangerous latitudes.

In this the British once again proved themselves hugely unsuccessful; so much so that in the period of 1725-1732 their fruitless endeavours produced losses estimated to be in excess of £177,780. The 1725 revival of English investment in whaling saw a new player in the game, the London based South Sea Company who expended an extraordinary amount of money fitting out twelve whalers averaging about 300 tons each. When these vessels proved themselves unsuccessful and the company was required to report on their accumulated losses, the management came in for scathing and unsympathetic criticism. It was argued that the ships were excessively and extravagantly provisioned and managed, their fishing was conducted in a half-hearted fashion and the results therefore were not unexpected. This was in spite of the fact that Commanders, Harpooners, Boat-steerers and Blubber-Cutters, in the order of over 150 men, were hired from Holstein at great expense.

There would have been disgruntled investors, irate shipowners, harassed Masters and malcontents amongst the crews. Many of these sailors and Masters went to sea with their salary largely or entirely based on incentive, so they would have been greatly displeased when receiving nothing for their trouble. These manifestly discordant ventures could have only one outcome; and the decision came at the end of the 1732 season: sell the ships.

The Scots made several other abortive attempts - one was by the Bogle family from Glasgow who put faith in their Dutch connections bringing them success. That was followed by a later attempt by the Glasgow Greenland Company. Seemingly they all suffered the same fate - failure. While there were individual Scots involved in whaling with foreign fleets, the failure of solely Scottish attempts was predicated by a lack of expertise, unsound management and inadequate investment. It was not until Mercantilist Prime Minister Robert Walpole came to power in 1733 that Merchants were once again positively incited to speculate. Gordon Jackson, author of *'The British Whaling Trade'*, contends that it was Walpole's desire for self-sufficiency to Britain that prompted him to agree to pay a subsidy, or a Bounty as it was called. This was designed to reinvigorate the Whale Fishing Industry. Parliament saw this as a last resort. Given that for over a century now England and Scotland had failed dismally where foreign countries had prospered, was this monetary incentive going to guarantee success?

Memories of past failures were still raw in the minds of many Scottish merchants and investors. The initial 1733 offering of a Bounty of twenty shillings per ton did little to excite action so a further ten shillings was legislated. This was responsible for occasioning probably the first documented example of a Cartel, whereby the collective of Merchants and Investors managed to persuade Parliament that greater inducements were necessary given the high risks involved. At this point, the British Government was being held to ransom and was forced to recognise two things; first that the cost of importing whale oil was significant and was increasing year by year; and second, that far greater public subsidisation was required given the increasing demand for whale oil and bone. Decisive steps were taken in 1749 when the Bounty was raised to a whopping forty shillings per ton.

Despite modern day views on Whale Fishing, it can be categorically stated that the Scottish Whale Fishing Industry in the post 1749 era, when the Youngs were guaranteed to be involved in it, was considered perfectly legitimate and quite a prestigious occupation. Many of the fishermen of Leith including some of the Listons and Thomsons became the Whalers of their generation, joining the ranks of those men who risked life and limb and, in

In the beginning 1650-1750

some cases, their own fortunes to go fishing in those dangerous Arctic waters of Spitzbergen, Greenland and Davis Straits. Their well-honed skills in seamanship and their love of fishing which had been so well learned down the generations made them invaluable assets to Scotland's fleet. These were the bravest of men and it cannot be overemphasised how much courage and skill it took to take to those waters let alone succeed. They would have sailed out of port full of hope for a good catch and a safe return so that they too could enjoy their share of the commercial advantage flowing from the King's 40 shilling Bounty.

Notwithstanding our appreciation in hindsight of the great wrong done to these fine mammals, it is clear that for most of history these creatures were considered fish. They were just one of a variety of water based creatures which comprised a normal catch for fishermen right across the world. Ancient evidence of this can be found in an article written by Martyn Gorman of the University of Aberdeen wherein we are given a wonderful insight into the mode of thinking in respect of fishing and seafood around the close of the sixteenth century. Gorman's 2002 work cites a well-documented regal feast in which whale is casually mentioned as one of the items of seafood on a rather lavish menu.

He starts out by reminding his readers that -

'Canon Law requires that Catholics not eat meat on Fridays ...'

'When Princess Elisabeth of Austria made her ceremonial entry into Paris in 1571, one of her first duties was to attend mass at Notre Dame and dine thereafter with the bishop. It being a Friday, she was served with: 4 large fresh salmon, 10 large turbots, 18 brill, 18 grenaulx, 18 trout a foot and a half long, 9 large pike two to three feet long, 18 mullet, 200 cod tripes, 200 white herrings, 200 red herrings, 24 cuts of salted salmon, 9 fresh shad, 50 carp, 18 lampreys, 200 fat young lampreys, 3 creels of smelts, 2 creels of oysters in their shells, 1 creel of oysters without shells, 200 fat crayfish, 1 creel of mussels, 50 crabs, 12 lobsters, 1000 frogs and 50 pounds of whale (probably the salted blubber).'

A feast fit for a King not just a Princess.

Now, we already know the Youngs were part of the Scottish Whale Fishing Fleet from a time pre the 1780s. Therefore, the question arises - did the Youngs understand species identification or did they too act opportunistically?

With regard to the different species, this is what is known today.

The Bowhead [Balaena Mysticetus] or Greenland Right, was the primary target for most fishermen. These are the largest of the Baleen Whales of the Cetacea Group which species includes whales, dolphins and porpoises. They are commonly found in the higher northern latitudes in cold Arctic waters. As well as being the longest living mammal, they are also one of the heaviest, second only to the blue whale which is known to grow to over 100 ft. or 30 mtrs in length and weigh in at a massive 150 tons [152,400 kgs] or more. The main characteristic of the Bowhead is their very large wide skull with a bow-shaped jaw. Their heads are so oversized they can comprise as much as 40% of their entire body length. More important to the fishermen of the day, the Bowheads have the thickest blubber which can measure 17-19 inches, or 43-49 cm.

Typically, a mature Bowhead measured around 66 ft. or some 22 mtrs long and weighed around 100 tons [101,500 kgs]. To put this into perspective of what modern day landlubbers might more easily equate to - a mature male African elephant would be around 4.0 mtrs tall at the shoulder and weigh in at 14,000 lbs. or 6350 kgs, which makes the majestic giant Bowhead roughly equivalent to 16 African Elephants. Bearing this in mind, it is impossible to conceive how mere mortals in flimsy wooden boats armed only with the equivalent of a length of rope and a hand-held spear could have ever conceived how they might overcome such a mammoth beast. The fear which would have consumed the seamen as they rowed their whaleboats in pursuit of this prey would have been palpable and there is little doubt they operated on pure adrenalin. Every chase was life threatening for man and beast: whaling was most certainly not the easiest way of earning a living.

In all fairness, the Muscovy Company's failure was for the most part due in no small measure to their arrogant lack of appreciation of the variation in the species. Therefore, for the

Scots to succeed they had to learn how to identify one species from the other. The easiest way to compare whales was to recognise that the Bowhead was the species with a pair of short narrow flippers and no dorsal fin. They can also be distinguished by their colouring and markings. The Bowhead has mainly dark grey skin with black and white spotted markings especially around the lower snout. Today, we know that Bowheads are filter feeders because of their baleen plates which are a series of bristles which capture the phytoplankton, such as krill, which is their preferred diet. They have been known to swim along with their mouths open, skimming or filtering the water of these microorganisms, hence they were given the nickname 'Skimmer'. The bristles on the 350 baleen plates are so tightly packed they prevent the plankton and krill from escaping.

Unlike other species which migrate to warmer waters in mating season, the Bowheads remain in Arctic waters all year round, simply moving from one feeding ground to another. They are basically solitary animals and have been known to be quite vocal at certain times, but especially when feeding, travelling and mating. They also communicate by breaching and lob-tailing, which is where they slap their flukes on the surface of the water. The gestation period for Bowhead whales is typically 13-14 months and a female will only produce an offspring every 3-4 years. Whilst whales in general are mature at 10-15 years of age, they can live up to 200 years. Their only natural predator is a pack of Killer Whales.

This brings us to the Right Whale. The Right Whales or Black Whales comprise three species of large baleen whale of the genus Eubalaena. They are the North Atlantic Right Whale, the North Pacific Right Whale and the Southern Right Whale. All Right Whale species share several characteristics; namely rotund bodies without a dorsal fin, arching rostrums [beaks], wide v-shaped blowholes and they all have a dark grey to black skin. The powerful Right Whale can blow water 5 mtrs [16 ft.] into the air. In their mouths they have between 200 and 300 baleen plates which are approximately 2 mtrs in length and covered in very fine hairs.

When only a head is visible on the ocean, the Right Whale is more easily distinguished by the patches of rough white skin they develop on their heads due to a parasitism of whale lice. These callosities on their heads and sometimes down their backs have been used by researchers as a kind of fingerprint to help identify and track certain individuals as a part of scientific studies. These giants of the sea can grow to 18 mtrs [59 ft.] or more in length with the longest recorded length a massive 19.8 mtrs [65 ft.]. They have been known to weigh in the vicinity of 135,000 kg. [298,000 lbs]. All three species are migratory and tend to move in line with the seasons chasing their preferred food and preferred birthing grounds. Whilst generally found in the colder waters of the Arctic and Antarctic some have been known to traverse the barrier of warmer water at the Equator.

Generally speaking, Right Whales like to spend the majority of their time along the shoreline, close to peninsulas and bays or on continental shelves which not only offer greater protection than the open ocean but are more abundant in their preferred diet of zooplankton and krill. Like the Bowhead, the Right Whale is known to feed on the move; swimming along with their mouth open they first ingest water and prey, using their baleens to filter the prey as they expel the water. The Right Whales are slow swimmers with a top speed of only around 5 knots or approx. 9.3 klm/hr. However, considering their size and weight they are extremely athletic, and their acrobatics have made them world famous. Their breaching, tail-slapping and lob-tailing have mesmerized both whale fishermen and tourists down the centuries.

The Right Whale was so named because it became known as the – 'right whale to kill'. They have a docile nature and were not aggressive towards their hunters; moreover, they swim slowly so are easily overhauled by men rowing in pursuit. They hugged the shoreline which afforded an added modicum of safety for those who rowed in chase. Ultimately all these factors combined to make them an easy target. Also, similar to the Bowheads, the Right Whale had a high blubber content which not only produced a lucrative yield of oil but also caused them to float when killed. For the very early Greenland whalers this was a real advantage because the whaleboat men could more easily tow the dead whale to the shoreline before hauling it onto the ice for flensing.

In the beginning 1650-1750

The Blue Whale, whose scientific name is Balaenoptera musculus, is a carnivorous mammal with a lifespan of only 80-90 years. A mature Blue Whale will grow to between 85 and 105 feet in length [~50 metres] and weigh up to 200 tons. They are the mammoths of the oceans whose tongues can weigh as much as an elephant and whose hearts weigh as much as the family car. Like their cousins, the Bowhead and Right whales, Blue Whales dine on krill, eating as much as 4 tons a day per adult. They are also baleen whales with a slightly different feeding habit in as much as they utilise their enormous tongue to expel the gulped water. Their mottled blue grey skin earned them their name; although their distinct yellowish underbellies, the result of millions of micro-organisms who have taken up residence on their skin make Blue Whale species identification very easy. Another distinctive feature is their body shape. It begins with a broad flat head leading to a long tapered body and ending in wide triangular flukes.

Observations have shown these graceful swimmers are mostly solitary but sometimes travel in pairs. Like the Right Whale they are happy to cruise along at around five miles an hour except if agitated when they can accelerate to more than twenty miles an hour. These Blue Whales are the more vocal ones, emitting a series of pulses, groans and moans which makes them one of the loudest animals on the planet. As astonishing as it may appear, it is thought they can hear each other at a distance of up to 1,000 miles. Some scientists contend they use their vocalisation and hearing skills to sonar-navigate the lightless ocean depths. The Blue Whales were so aggressively hunted in the 1900s that by the 1960s they were on the brink of extinction with the slaughter of over 360,000 individuals. Since then their numbers have steadily increased. They have few natural predators except perhaps the odd school of Sharks or a pod of Killer Whales. Today, the harpoon is pretty much holstered but man with his large ocean going vessels can cause them injuries which sometimes prove fatal.

Lastly, there is the Sperm Whale or Physeter Macrocephalus. The Sperm Whale belongs to the suborder of toothed whales and dolphins, Odontocetes, and is one of the easiest whales to identify because of its enormous square-shaped head. Combine this with their wrinkly dark grey to brownish skin and they are unmistakable. They also have white markings around their lower jaw and on the underside of their head and body. The head of a Sperm Whale comprises approximately one third of their overall body length and houses the largest and heaviest brain in the animal kingdom. However, it is the enormous cavity in their head, large enough to fit a small sedan car, which holds a yellowish wax known as spermaceti oil, which made them a target species once the virtues of this wax were finally discovered. Externally, the Sperm Whale has relatively short stubby flippers and a low hump rather than a dorsal fin. They are also a lot smaller than the aforementioned whales, with a mature male Sperm Whale measuring only around 55 ft or 18 meters in length. Weight wise they are a sleek 57,000 kgs.

It is inside the mouth that the Sperm Whales varies greatly from its relatives - Sperm Whales have between 40 and 52 thick conical shaped long narrow teeth in their lower jaw. Each tooth can grow to around 20cm and weigh as much as one kilogram. These teeth were favoured by those seamen skilled in scrimshaw - the art of carving, engraving and scrolling designs. Sperm Whales have large triangular tail flukes which assist them when they dive; in fact, they are the deepest diving mammals in the world. While they have been known to reach depths of 2-3 kms typically they hover at a depth of around 400m. Sperm Whales tend to stay submerged for around 45 minutes at a time as a general rule, while some are known to have held their breath for up to two hours.

Sperm Whales prefer to feast on large deep-water squid, and Scientists have observed scars which look like the mark of the suction cups on the tentacles of these giant squid. These whales are called the 'show-offs' because of their gregarious nature and many whale watching businesses follow the Sperm Whale migrations so tourists can enjoy their entertaining breaching, spy-hopping, [rising vertically out of the sea and exposing the head only] and lob-tailing. The females are smaller than the males and are not overly intimidated by their only natural predator, the Killer Whale, except when they have calves swimming with the pod. In that instance, the females will form themselves into what has been termed the 'marguerite' ring

In the beginning 1650-1750

and swim in a head to tail circular formation with their heads remaining on the outside of the ring.

The Sperm Whale was so named by the early whalers because their head contained a milky white substance, wrongly assumed to be sperm. This is the substance which hardens to a yellowish wax when cold and is thought to assist Sperm Whale to manipulate their buoyancy. They are found roaming all the world's oceans except in the very high Arctic latitudes, they prefer deep water and generally travel in pods. Their numbers were seriously threatened by hunting in the past and even today the Japanese have ignored world opinion, refused to sign the International Convention for the Regulation of Whaling and continue to take Sperm Whales each year. This species is still considered to be at risk, not from whalemen hunting them per se but from chemical and noise pollution caused by man. Others have been discovered tangled in fishing nets. While absolute species numbers remain unknown, the Sperm Whale will continue to be listed as vulnerable according to the latest United Nations proclamation.

Man has hunted the waterways and oceans of the world for fish of all shapes and sizes for well over a millennium. The oldest known painting depicting angling of any type comes from Egypt from around 2000 BC. Greek philosophers Plato and Aristotle also mention fishing in their writings. For Britain, the first written legislation in England is dated 1496 in which *'A Treatyse of Fysshynge wyth an Angle'* explains how one should use a fishing rod. First and foremost, fishing was carried out purely as a hunter gatherer activity - food for survival. The scale was small, sustainable and on a basis of need to augment a predominantly land based diet. Down the centuries the scale has changed dramatically. Today, we are hopeful the over-fishing trend is finally being arrested and globally there appears to be a focus on sustainability for what we now term fishing. More importantly, there is also an International Protection Order on whaling which was agreed in 1966. Since then whale numbers have steadily increased, and in 2014 estimates placed the Blue Whale population for one as almost back to pre-hunting levels. Hopefully this will be the case for other whale species over time.

As for those Whalers entering the industry in the 1780s/90s, including members of this Young family, it is fair to say they were joining an industry which looked vastly different to that in the days of the Muscovy Company. They would have had the benefit of species identification and the distinctive commercial properties of each. There had been advances in the design of the whaling ships, in the understanding of the robustness required for whaleboats and in the size and shape of harpoons. It was a time when information about ships, charts and markets was also more readily available. Perhaps this is what accounts for some of the financial success Alexander achieved. We also know that his sons Alexander and John learned the whaling trade from their father. This father and son team went on to establish their own whale fishing company at the height of the industry's 'golden era' which undoubtedly led to their good fortune.

It has been said that timing is everything and that could not be truer than in the case of whaling. It was so important for the fleet to sail north on the cusp of the warmer summer months. At this time of year, the normally clear polar waters experienced a rapid rise in temperature and with the seasonal increase in sunlight hours and day length, these conditions combined to make an ideal environment for the growth of abundant phytoplankton and dependent zooplankton comprising squid and small fish. These Arctic waters became the whale's food playground. Because of the proliferation of a particular type of phytoplankton the area was often described as a pasture because it took on a greenish colour.

Yorkshireman, Captain Scoresby, wrote extensive Logs that have survived and provide an invaluable insight into the life of an Arctic whale fisherman. In his Logs he described the - 'green sea' as equivalent in area to almost one quarter of the Greenland Sea 'between the parallels of 74° and 80°' - where whales, seals and porpoises grazed in great numbers.' From the early days of commercial expeditionary whale fishing, the Bowhead Whale and the Right Whale were the preferred fish and remained so when these Youngs first went whaling.

What can be discovered about the design and construction of the ships the Youngs sailed to the whale fishery?

Fishing for these giants in those far northern latitudes would have been a constant learning experience. Over time lessons had been learned about the optimum size for ships and the proven type of construction. Parliament too had set down rules for those of the Fleet wishing to claim the Bounty. These rules related to the overall size of the ship, the number of crewmembers, the ethnicity of the crew and the number of whaleboats or shallops required to be carried. It was realised that for ships to prevail for longer periods at these latitudes only those of a certain size would enjoy the greatest success. An article published by the Dartmouth University entitled *The Development and Design of Arctic Whaling and Sealing Vessels'* provides a great historical insight. It states that - 'Vessels designed and built for work in the arctic ice were first developed from the Greenland and Spitsbergen whale and seal fisheries some time before 1700.'

Undoubtedly, the earliest whaling vessels were converted merchantmen. One of the most reliable sources of information on the evolution in the design of whalers is the numerous sketches and paintings of whaling scenes pre-1800, and by comparing these, it is clear that the size and weight of vessels was recognised as an important factor. From 1650 to around 1725, converted merchantmen prevailed, then, as knowledge grew, ships were specifically designed and built for sailing in Arctic waters. By the end of this period, Arctic whalers had a far more task-orientated design which was devoid of the decoration and beakheads common to general merchantmen. Later came design updates such as additional wales or guards, doubling, reinforcing and copper sheathing.

The final design change came with the rounding of the sterns and the omission of the high quarterdecks so popular with early shipbuilders. 'However, the square-stern vessel was never wholly replaced, for it was found that a strong hull could be built with this form and the greater room that it provided, compared with the sharp or round-stern hull, had great attraction.' None of these design changes arrested the harrowing loss of thousands of ships and umpteen thousands of men. Add to this the loss of untold thousands of whales and clearly there were no winners. The Whale Fishery was a tough business, stressful, challenging, unpredictable and incredibly dangerous and demanded everyone brings their 'A Game' to the grounds in order to return home safely.

Typically, the length of a whaler was between 60-100 feet [20-30 mtrs] which made them more manoeuvrable when navigating ice floes, and their shallower draft often proved very advantageous in poorly chartered waters. Since their cargo was highly valuable, even smaller vessels could carry enough to make an Arctic season profitable by stowing their casks of oil and furs quite compactly in the hold. Also, with the smaller vessels the cost to the shipowner was less for the provisioning and crewing, and in the case of any loss, there was less investment at stake. Given the massive losses sustained each year, this was most assuredly a serious consideration for many an investor and/or shipowner. And, as we know, these Youngs were set to become Investors and Shipowners as well as Masters.

Then there is the whaleboat. Whaleboats are the chase craft, those smaller vessels transported to the grounds slung in the davits and lowered over the side of the mother ship when a pursuit is on. For this very reason they needed to be built lightweight. They were generally around 28 feet or 8.5 mtrs in length and weighed in at 1000 lbs. or just over 450 kgs. They had to be strong enough to withstand the racking strains of being towed by a whale or the forces at play as they are lowered or raised in the davits. That successful combination of lightness and strength was one of their noteworthy features, with the other being the simplicity and utility of their rigging and fit-out.

The basic whaleboat had one mast and one sail plan, where it is rigged for a gaff mainsail and a jib, giving a total of around 340 square feet of canvas without blocks and only one sheave

In the beginning 1650-1750

in the entire rig. When not employed in the pursuit of whales it doubled as a tender boat for carrying liberty parties ashore, or for retrieving provisions. Whaleboats were even used to tow water casks out to the mother ship. Design variations evolved over time in different parts of the world, reflective of local custom, sea conditions and species fished. As time went on and more was learned about the different fishing experiences, especially in relation to harpooning, the design of whaleboats responded accordingly. Those drawings that have survived tell a great deal about national traditions in whaleboat design and how it varied down the decades.

What is the history of whale oil and other whale by-products?

It has long been known that the burning of whale oil could provide a very useful source of light. The oil was used in the manufacture of candles and lamp oil. Initially, the burning of whale oil is known to have produced a rather unsatisfactory odour. Then came the chance discovery that became a game changer and quickly made the Sperm Whale the new preferred target of Eighteenth century fishermen. It seems the 'spermaceti oil' obtained from the head cavity of the Sperm Whale was a waxier style of oil which not only glowed brighter but did not produce the same nasty odour as that of the blubber of the Bowheads or Right Whales. There were several logical impediments to hunting the Sperm Whale specifically not the least of which being they could dive to incredible depths and thus the pursuers would frequently run out of rope. Secondly, given that hunting was undertaken from wooden shallops, and our understanding that Sperm Whale were known to become agitated, crews were often forced to abandon the chase otherwise they ran the risk of having their shallops smashed to pieces. Unfortunately, if this did occur, all too often crew were either killed or drowned.

Ambergris is another unique by-product of the male Sperm Whale. Ambergris was first discovered and highly prized by the ancient Egyptians and Arabs. Scientists believe the male Sperm

Whale produces a fatty substance in its digestive tract when feasting on the giant squid. It was presumed to be nature's way of preventing the sharp pointy beaks of the squid from abrading the innards of the whale. Eventually this accumulates into a huge lump that is cast out. Lumps of Ambergris have been discovered across the globe and some are known to weigh hundreds of pounds. It is surmised in scientific circles that this Ambergris is cast as faecal matter and not vomit, although to date no one has ever witnessed a 'casting out' event. Hal Whitehead of Dalhousie University in Halifax, Nova Scotia, and others, have joined one groundswell of opinion that contends - when the ambergris is first cast out '..., it smells more like the back end than the front.' An interesting observation!

Once cast out, the Ambergris floats and has been nicknamed 'floating gold'. For the most part it remains at sea until the tide washes it ashore. Some of the more recent discoveries have been made in places like the coast of Lancashire, the Welsh coast and in New Zealand where some Maoris from South Wairarapa Marae made a rare find estimated to have a value of $NZ400,000. The luckiest and largest recorded find was made in late 2016 and is attributed to three Omani fishermen. They found a giant chunk of Ambergris at sea, towed it ashore where it weighed in at an astonishing 80 kilograms. This nugget has an estimated value of $US3 million; however, to date it remains unsold. So if you are walking on the beach and come across a chunk of a waxy substance that has an odour which is - '.... a cross between squid and farmyard manure' - don't walk by, pick it up - it could be your lucky day.

The use of Ambergris is historic, and although it appears to be unknown to the Greeks and Romans, the Arabs recorded it as Ambar for pharmaceutical use wherein they powdered it and ingested it to combat heart and brain ailments. In the Indian Sanskrit Lexicon there are references from 900AD where it is written that the Portuguese - 'took over the Maldives in the sixteenth century in part to gain access to the island's rich bounty of the redolent stuff' although it was the French who first appear to have employed it as a fragrance fixative. Many questions remain unanswered, such as - How did the ancient Arabs determine it was useful as a medicine? What proof is there

In the beginning 1650-1750

that it is only the male Sperm Whale? And, why is Ambergris more prevalent in the southern hemisphere when Sperm Whales range the oceans of the world? And for the purposes of this story the questions remain - Did the Youngs know of this 'floating gold' and did they ever make their own 'floating gold strike'?

There is one final note with respect to just what was driving the Whale Fishing Industry. What we do know for certain is that demand for all whale products continued to increase. By far the greatest demand remained the need of oil, driven by a new innovation - street lighting. As communities across Britain became more citified, so there was a corresponding desire for the amenity of street lighting. Interestingly, it was the traditional and ancient whale fishing port of Hull, in 1713, that led the way in the introduction of street lighting in England. Hull was quickly overtaken by London which boasted in excess of 5000 streetlights by 1750. This speaks volumes about the rise in the demand and its impact on the price of whale oil as a commodity. It also raises the question - could this or would this have occurred when it did if the industry had not been propped up by a massive 40 shilling Bounty?

Despite the acknowledged demand for whale by-products not everyone in England, and probably, Scotland was in favour of the 40 shilling Bounty. To gauge what public opinion was in the day about such a generous Bounty payment we need to once again turn to the social demographers of the era - the essayists and poets. There is one poem which sets out to chronicle the whale fishing industry and records its history from the perspective of an outsider. These opinions come from the pen of Jonathan Swift [1667-1745] who had quite a passion for writing about the sea it seems and is probably best known as the author of Gulliver's Travels (1726). There is a poem he wrote in 1721 which he titled - *'The South Sea Project'* which is of considerable interest and if the contents are truly reflective of public opinion then these whalers were facing harsh opposition at home as well as challenges at sea.

The poem focuses on The South Sea Company, a British joint-stock company founded in 1711 as a public-private partnership in the hope of reducing losses and costs to the public purse. Officially, it was - 'The Governor and Company of the merchants of Great Britain, trading to the South Seas and other parts of America, and for the encouragement of fishing'. Boasting offices on the corner of Threadneedle Street and Bishopsgate in the heart of London, a most respectable address indeed. It could be said that the whale fishing business carried on by The South Seas Company was hiding a dark secret - involvement in the slave trade. Jonathan Swift records his political opinion of the dangers of the Whale Fishing and the folly of those investors who put up their hard earned money.

Swift at first decries the logic of investing and compares the slick marketing pitch to that of a magician's sleight of hand -

> Ye wise philosophers, explain
> What magic makes our money rise,
> When dropt into the Southern main;
> Or do these jugglers cheat our eyes?

then

> Thus in a basin drop a shilling,
> Then fill the vessel to the brim,
> You shall observe, as you are filling,
> The pond'rous metal seems to swim:

As for the financial losses sustained, Swift appears to show little sympathy -

> Thus, the deluded bankrupt raves,
> Puts all upon a desperate bet,
> Then plunges in the Southern waves,
> Dipt over head and ears - in debt.

Then Swift says the mariners too were deluded as to the reality -

> So, by a calenture misled,
> The mariner with rapture sees,
> On the smooth ocean's azure bed,
> Enamell'd fields and verdant trees:

With news of the loss of ships and men fresh in the mind of Swift he wrote of his lack of empathy for the mariners, who he believed were just like the investor: easily duped, dreamers with a romantic notion of reality. So, in the face of mounting losses there must have been a further call for funds. Swift is now decrying the tactics of the Directors who make another hard pitch to investors which he roundly rebuffs -

> Thus, by directors we are told,
> "Pray, gentlemen, believe your eyes;
> Our ocean's cover'd o'er with gold,
> Look round, and see how thick it lies:
>
> "We, gentlemen, are your assisters,
> We'll come, and hold you by the chin."--
> Alas! all is not gold that glisters,
> Ten thousand sink by leaping in.

Swift now employs metaphoric prose to recount not only the untold financial losses to investors but also the loss of the lives of countless mariners -

> There is a Gulf where thousands fell,
> Here all the bold adventurers came,
> A narrow Sound, tho' deep as Hell,
> Change Alley is the dreadful name.
>
> Nine times a day it ebbs and flows,
> Yet he that on the surface lies'
> Without a pilot seldom knows
> The time it falls and when 'twill rise.
>
> Subscribers here by thousands float
> And jostle one another down,

Each paddling in his leaky boat,
And here they fish for gold and drown.

Now buried in the Depth below,
Then mounted up to Heaven again,
They reel and stagger to and fro,
At their wits' end like drunken men.

While the entire poem comprises over forty verses, a few lines relate specifically to the fallout from this flawed South Sea Company of London. It reads -

The nation too, too late will find
Computing all their cost and trouble,
Directors' promises but wind,
South Sea at best a mighty bubble.

This enterprise was such an abysmal failure that it gave rise to the Bubble Act 1720 which was passed by the Parliament incorporating the Royal Exchange and London Assurance Corporation. It forbade the formation of future joint-stock companies without royal charter in order to protect investors but more importantly it gave the power back to the Parliament in such matters. By this it is fair to assume that by the time Alexander Young and others were investing in the Montrose Whale Fishing Company and the emerging steam packet businesses, he could do so under protective legislation.

There is one final footnote on 'The Men' who went whaling. Men like our own Young family members who sailed into these unforgiving waters year after year. These were perilous voyages and countless stories recount the horrors faced by these seamen in the Arctic waters. Perhaps one of the most bizarre and harrowing of all comes from a book written by Basil Lubbock entitled *'Arctic Whalers'*. Once again, Lubbock has used ships logs to chronicle a series of experiences on numerous Arctic

In the beginning 1650-1750

whalers but the one I personally found most arresting relates to the loss of the *Shannon* of Hull on 26th April 1832. It exemplifies what it takes to be an Arctic whaler, how their will to survive and mental endurance was their best stock in trade when it came to survival. It also demonstrates the boundless options men will entertain in the most unimaginable of conditions. And so, in the absences of Logbooks for journeys undertaken by the Youngs, I have decided to include the story of the *Shannon*. This is a most extraordinary tale of mental toughness, physical endurance, and creative thinking by a group of sailors facing certain death.

To set the scene - the *Shannon* had sailed from Lerwick on 4th April in company with the *Comet* and *Truelove* plus others. Then on Thursday the 26th at around 3.30 am in the pitch dark while running under double-reefed topsails before a strong south easterly gale, and with three men on lookout on the fo'c'sle-head, the Shannon ran stem on to an iceberg. It threw the Captain from his seat. He rushed on deck to inspect the damage and discovered 'the bows were entirely knocked in, the main stem broken, the gammoning shackles, bolts and clamp at the heel of the bowsprit were broken and even the catheads forced out of place'. The iceberg struck again on the starboard side and this caused the waterlogged ship to fall over on her broadside.

The Log recounts how 'Two smart men, without orders, got axes and cut the weather lanyards; the masts then broke off 10 feet above the deck, and the ship righted sufficiently to show the starboard side forward above water. Before this happened, all hands were fighting for their lives whilst the seas made a clean sweep over the ship. As she turned over, Captain Davey himself clambered into the main chains, then as the chains went under the water, he lost his hold and was swept away by a heavy sea. He was a good swimmer, and managed to gain the ship's side, catch hold of the main rigging and climb up into the main-top before the next sea could overwhelm him.' 'When day broke, 16 men and 3 boys were found to be missing.'

The Captain's log goes on to explain how both men and ship fought against the elements for the next seven days until on May 1 - 'a strong breeze sent seas rolling over the ship, the survivors being up to their knees in water for hours. The wreck battered by the broken masts which were held by the ice rigging, showed signs of breaking up'. Several men had lost their lives as a result of their injuries or the wrath of the sea and others had died from hunger and thirst. This brings us to the crux of one of the most extraordinary incidents in the annals of sea disasters.

A Shetlander in the crew suggested to the surgeon - 'that he should bleed him, that he might drink his own blood to quench his intolerable thirst.' The surgeon who had his lancet in his pocket opened one of the man's veins and collected the blood in an old shoe. The man gratefully drank his own blood. The surgeon then made an attempt to save another crewman, O'Neil, who though apparently dead was not yet cold. The surgeon opened O'Neil's vein and took a shoe-full of his blood, with which to moisten O'Neil's lips. Though the touch forced the soon to be corpse to make some convulsive movements, as if in an attempt to breathe, sadly the man fell back; dead. The blood in the shoe was then divided amongst the other 17 survivors, and it had an astonishing effect in reviving them. One by one, Captain Davey and the 16 men were then bled in succession, the doctor even bled himself. Some mixed the blood with flour, others drank straight from the shoe, and to a man they found themselves wonderfully refreshed and sated. When night came it was accompanied by a strong gale and heavy sea; and they believed that if it had not been for the strength given them through drinking the blood, they could not have held on.

Lady Luck then played a hand when out of the morning gloom two Danish ships came into view. It is said that - 'the rescue was one of those providential affairs.' So, after seven nights and seven days exposed to the most horrific weather and unimaginable hardship and as far-fetched as this Log appears, all those who did survive came through relatively unscathed except for the Captain who had severe frost-bite.

We can only hope that none of our Men or their crews were forced to take such an unimaginably difficult decision in order to survive. The only Young we know to be placed in such a position was Captain John Young, who along with his men survived the wreck of the whaler *Hero* in the Arctic in 1822.

Introduction - And then 1750-1850

> *'It is not the strongest or the most intelligent who will survive but those who can best manage change'*
>
> Charles Darwin [1809-1892]

With the mere mention of this century, the mind immediately flashes back to the impact of the Industrial Revolution. It was a Revolution without precedent; it delivered change on a grand scale, a scale never before witnessed or imagined. Globally, economists largely agree that, at the outset, Great Britain was considered standing shoulder to shoulder with her European neighbours such as Spain, France and the Dutch Republic. By the end of this century there was a new lexicon of words like 'British Imperialism' and 'world dominance' in order to adequately describe Britain's unrivalled global takeover. The Empire had rapidly expanded to make Britain the pre-eminent manufacturing hub on the planet.

The changes that came as a natural consequence of this Industrial Revolution drove further growth and an evolutionary need for new and bigger markets for raw materials and finished goods, but driving the change was a new kind of commodity - oil. Oil will be extremely relevant to our story in this century, but just as relevant is the fact that these new markets were off-shore and so those involved in the shipping industry found themselves particularly well placed to capitalise on this growth and market expansion. Indeed, we are about to learn how several Youngs adapted to these changes and how they actually embraced the challenges and prospered. But, before we assume a war chest, we need to learn how the Youngs and others did business in this era - exactly what was required, what were the risks and rewards – because there were many on both counts.

Thus far we have learnt about a family with a history of sailing under canvas but all that was also about to change. This Industrial Revolution was about to bring an unforeseen change that would test the Youngs' resolve, strain their family ties and ultimately make moguls and wreck lives. Whilst Darwin was alluding to the animal kingdom in his hypothesis, it can equally be applied to the human species in this time period.

Change came for the Youngs in many forms and affected every aspect of their lives - the men, their ships, where they sailed to and what cargoes they carried when and why. Some Youngs inadvertently fell victim to various well-known pitfalls, and others to foreign powers or avaricious foreigners. Throughout this century they persevered, and all the while they were forced to constantly adapt to an ever changing maritime landscape. This adaptation saw the birth of a new paradigm for future generations and, whilst some proved up to the mark, others fell by the wayside.

This is their story .....

And then 1750-1850

Chapter 5

The Men • The Ships • The Trade Routes
Baltic & Archangel • Jamaica & West Indies
Whaling • Spitzbergen, Greenland & Davis Strait
The Montrose Whale Fishing Company

This is the century where the family will finally take centre stage and begin to drive the narrative. It needs to be said that these Youngs were not in any way celebrities or extraordinary in a twenty-first century tabloid kind of way. They would probably be somewhat bemused by all the fuss but curious nonetheless to learn where their legacy of those early seafaring days has led future generations. These early Youngs were not titled nor did they receive any royal warrants. They were not known to hold high office but willingly took on community leadership responsibilities. They did not hold vast tracts of land, but one did own a large fleet of ships. For the most part they held only shared ownership rights in the ships they sailed but they sailed them with great skill and respect. They did not record their exploits for personal gain or notoriety, nor did they seek any sort of fame. So, when all is said and done, they were ordinary folk going about their daily lives - except for a few individuals whose lives panned out to be somewhat more than ordinary.

Extracting any information about the deeds or misdeeds of such seemingly ordinary folk was going to be an arduous task. And indeed, discovery offered some exhilarating moments punctuated by great frustration. If only one thing was learned along the way, it was if later generations of this family carry any of their forefathers' genes they too would display characteristics like these early seafaring Youngs. They were the quiet achievers whose standout features were their character and life value set. They showed themselves to be exacting and dedicated to their craft, kind and respectful to their men, engaged and loving to their families and above all they would leave their mark for others to discover through positive contributions to their industry, their families and their communities.

Just like the Youngs, my journey of discovery has required traversing the globe many times physically and electronically to uncover what has been learned so far. These revelations will clearly demonstrate that this family did not exist in a vacuum but rather they functioned on land and sea as part of a greater whole. There is however another emerging thread, where from a time prior to the earliest generations taking to the sea, they appear to have consistently married into buoyant seafaring families under whose guidance they began to be seduced and learnt about what was soon to be their new trade. Without exception those families they married into all share a history of making a good living on the oceans of the world, some initially as fishermen and others in the mercantile trade in the era of the first wave of the Merchant Navy. Those same families also enjoyed success on land; they accumulated wealth, and many lived well-to-do lives - all the while enjoying a high level of community respectability. In joining with their well-chosen marital partners, the Youngs became part of a tight familial network of highly capable and dedicated individuals who, through innate ability, learned skills, intuition, daring, bravery and wit, managed to survive the rigours of their danger-ridden but much-loved profession.

The Youngs of this century clearly demonstrated they could move with the times, and from some individual snapshots of their lives we will follow their transition from canvas and wood to steam and steel, from helm to head office, from Scotland to all points of the compass, and rest assured they made these transitions with conviction and certitude. The fathers taught their sons adroitly and most of these lads learned their lessons well. They supported each other and utilised their close connections with family and friends to create enterprises in all sectors of mercantile and maritime business encompassing Trade, Banking & Commerce, Shipping and Insurance. A handful chose to make their career in the Royal Navy for which they appear to have been punished for family disloyalty. Several exercised great entrepreneurship; they thought and acted globally with great determination and, whilst some prospered as a consequence, others fell from grace. For those who succeeded, the affluence of their lives is reflected in the opulence they enjoyed in their later years, those years after the hard work and risk taking. Official records such as Wills indicate the legacy of the more recent generations was abundant in business, property and financial assets which were seemingly equitably and fairly bequeathed within the immediate family including to an adopted son.

With perhaps one exception, the wealth of latter generations is nothing to compare to the likes of the tech-billionaires of today; however, it certainly was what most people of the Victorian Middle Class would aspire to achieve and certainly sufficient to raise the family several layers higher in the British Beehive Model of Society. Initially, I set out to gain specific insight into the Whaling side of their maritime business, and from a 2015 paper written by Martin Breum of the Royal Danish Defence College entitled *'The Greenland Dilemma'* I learned that as an Industry 'Whaling made Greenland the seventeenth century equivalent of an oil state ...'. So, having established that opportunities and financial rewards should have been abundant there was still the dark shadow of the maritime history of the Port of Leith to overcome.

My task then became to try and determine how Robert Young [1723-1797] and more specifically his son Alexander [1750-1817] established their wealth. In Alexander's case it was a fortune large enough to set all his sons on a path to even greater prosperity. Then, before assuming all was right with their personal and commercial behaviour, I felt it was essential to adjudge whether they came by this wealth honestly. This would not only placate a perceived duty to investigate their probity but more importantly would satisfy a lingering curiosity about their character and their business lives. Along the way it will become clear just what it took to stand on the right side of the law at a time and in a port where privateering and smuggling thrived in the later 1750-1850 century in Scotland. Indeed, the Youngs' home-port of Leith was reputed to be heavily involved and many historians and social commentators vehemently maintain, that Leith was the veritable centre of smuggling activity for all of Scotland.

Initially, the two main questions to be answered in this regard were - had the Youngs managed to stand apart? And, were their related families also cleanskins?

Discovery in this century was not going to be an easy task. The first avenue of approach was to peruse the records of the Maritime Courts of Scotland and England as well as the Privy Courts. If any individual had been caught privateering or smuggling their names would most certainly appear. It is not easy to access these records and my searching was not totally exhaustive, but thankfully so far, my investigations have drawn a blank. Indeed, if there were misdemeanours of any kind, they were certainly only minor.

It was now time to turn attention to the Youngs' commercial behaviour and considering the period in question - one option was to interrogate the Accounts of the Burghs. Whilst the records for this period are incomplete those that survive are reasonably comprehensive and are held in the Scottish Archives, albeit principally written in old script. But, before proceeding, it is time for another short history lesson in respect of the Accounts of the Burghs in order to appreciate the scope, function, and appropriateness of such documents.

In the day, the Law of the land was clear - all hard assets of the country were the property of the King. In order to exercise control over all affairs the King and his council had defined fifteen 'Items'

or 'King's By-laws' to be reported annually by each Burgh, a Balance Sheet as it were. The King's Council appointed a team of Baillies who acted like modern day Auditors. Then, just like any auditing team, these Baillies, in groups of two or three, would criss-cross the land visiting the various Burghs to forensically examine the 'Accounts of the Burgh' – looking into income, expenditure and especially any write-offs or losses incurred, as some of these were or could be claims on the King's purse.

These Accounts of the Burghs proved surprisingly detailed, and, more importantly, they record names - names of people, of countries, of ships, plus a detailed folio of any significant losses of ships; be they wrecked or pirated. For the purpose of this facet of the Young story, special emphasis was placed on those by-laws relating to foreign trade and shipping. These encompassed only three of the fifteen, and in this regard, the Baillies had specifics to satisfy for the King -

> '6. Item, In all burghs that they take exact tryall into ther trade both forraigne and inland, and particularly of the wyns and of the vent and consumption of malt for fyve years backward.
> 7. Item, That they take exact accompt of what ships, barks, boats, and ferrie boats they have belonging to them, the names of the said ships, ther burden, and vallow of each of them, and how imployed and by whom.
> 8. Item, That they also take ane accompt of what ships they are owners of or pairtners in, out of ther owne burghs alse weell as in the same. And this to be given accompt of conforme to ther oath of knowledge, and how far they are concerned with the burghs of barrony and regality in the matter of trade.'

In the Accounts for the Burgh of Edinburgh, which included Leith, I came across an entry relating to Margaret Dick's father that is typical of how each vessel, Captain and asset value was accounted for in the 'Balance Sheet section of the Accounts of the Burgh'.

> 'Edinburgh, the eighteen day of May, I^m VIe and nyntie two years. [1692]

This is the trew list of the comon good given up upon by us under subscriveing to the best of our knowledge.—Sic subscribitur Ar"1 Mure prefectus; John Robertson, baillie; PaL Johnstoun, baillie ; Michael Allan, d. gild [Dean of Guild]; Henry Ferguson, theasr [Thesaurer]; Jas. Rocheid; clk [Clerk].

> Accompt of the Ships of Leith, the 7th May, 1692.

> Skippers and Barks

> Gilbert Dick burdine 20 tons Value 0,600' [Scottish Pounds]

It needs to be said that vessels, people and goods were tracked with quite some skill in this computer-less era, as this next partial extract demonstrates -

> 'Accompt of Shiping belonging to the Merchants of Edinburgh for twelve moneths by past.
>
> Kendall's ship twice to Holland with leadure and sheep skins.
> Simson's trade twice to Holland with coall and wooll.
> Alexr Tait twice to Holland with coalls, at present ane transact ship in France with canon.
> Robert Gray twice to Holland with coalls, sheep skins, and wooll.'

To adequately assess any losses to the Crown, including ships and cargoes, the Baillies also prepared a table of events for each Burgh as this sample excerpt shows - 'Note of the Touns Losses.

> At law w' my Lord Lauderdail for 7 years   20,000 00 00
> For building and rebuilding the bulwark
> Of ye toun   20,333 06 08
> It. for cutting the loch of Lundie for water
> to y^c milns   00,333 06 08
> James Davie ship and loadening lost
> at sea to ye value of   05,000 00 00
> Robert Rankine ship, called the Concord,
> And Goodes to the value of lost   20,000 00 00
> Ane other ship and goodes belonging to
> the said Robert, lost sex years yr after   15,000 00 00
> It. ano yr ship of his strand it at Aberdeen,
> Lost   04,000 00 00
> Thomas Patersone, ship and goods lost,
> Valued at   06,000 00 00
> George Adamson's ship lost   04,000 00 00
> Alexr Wedderburne's ship w' a Burdeaux
> Loading   05,000 00 00
> John Fraser's, and goodes lost to the value of   06,000 00 00'

[N.B. – the values quite oddly displayed here are indicative of the manner of expressing Scottish Pounds, Shillings and Pence.]

Names in this extract like Davie, Rankine, Paterson and Adamson are all names associated by marriage or business with this family. The losses were substantial and give us our first definitive insight into the dangers faced by ships and men.

This next extract from Linlithgow shows there were By-law restrictions placed on trade and the personnel involved which would have applied equally to the Youngs and Dicks et al.

> '8. As to the eight article, It is answered that they have only five or six of yr burgers and inhabitants that have interest in ships, and the masters therof are freemen, and obleidged to reside with them, conform to the Act of Borrowes; and these masters being examined upon oath by the saides magistrats, whether or not they hade any unfreemen pairtners with them in these veshells, answered that they, being surprised, could not satisfie them yrin at that tyme, but desired that they have

four months tyme to consider on it, that if ther were any unfreemen concerned with them, they might take them off before the term forsd, and that they are not concerned in matter of trade with unfree burghs.'

Basically, this By-law sets out the guidelines for shipowners, masters and trading. In essence, this town had five or six shipowners who were all Burgesses and therefore required to reside within the town walls. The Masters were freemen and also residents within the town in accordance with Burgess Rules and the King's By-laws. When the Magistrates questioned the Masters as to whether or not unfreemen, as they were termed in the day, were partners in the vessels they mastered, sensibly the Masters declined to answer immediately; instead, they asked for four months to investigate and ensure there were no unfreemen as partners and that they were not inadvertently carrying goods to unfree Burghs. The By-laws were strict and well defined and punishments severe.

As to the disclosure of unscrupulous operators, the Baillies would frequently record quite detailed stories such as this one about a supposed rogue Captain. In this instance they wrote that ' ... after two or three voyadges made with, the owners therof haveing loadening her to Holland, George Fergussone, ther skipper therof, runne away with her and her loadening, and never returned from Virginia again, to the value at least of 10,000 lib.' ['lib' is an abbreviation for the Scottish Pound which was worth less than an English Pound in the day.] If this is typical of the conclusions of the Baillies in these circumstances it demonstrates they were acutely unaware of the inherent dangers on the high seas.

Their immediate response was to accuse Captain Fergussone of absconding to the Americas with the owners' ship and cargo as his personal bank. This conclusion was arrived at without even considering the possibility that the vessel had met with pirates or sailed into a storm, either of which could see the men and the ship vanish without a trace. The Baillies had made a harsh judgement call without evidence and this seems reflective of what Captains, crewmembers and their families were faced with - no Westminster Justice in place in their day.

And then 1750-1850

Given that these Accounts of the Burghs are annual and detailed and given the name of Young has not thus far in my investigations received adverse mention, it is fair to say the family was presumably not acting outside the Law. Additionally, since none of the long list of associated family names received negative comment either, it is likewise fair to conclude that these associated families must have also conducted themselves with a fairly high degree of morality and fidelity. Frankly, this is quite an achievement given the damning profile for the port of Leith, and that, history in general in this century is littered with the names of countless individuals of status and otherwise who managed to find themselves acting outside the law, albeit when the law of the land was quite fluid, particularly during the reign of the House of Hanover.

Having satisfied myself on the probity issue I then decided to explore what could be learned about shipboard life for these Youngs.

It is generally conceded, those who took to the sea during this 1650-1750 century were some of the toughest and most courageous men ever to withstand the many challenges in that era of canvas and wood. Every day they would brace for the dangers presented by the water and the weather overlaid with cramped living conditions, disease, poor food and low pay for the seamen class. Discipline was harshly and cruelly meted out in order to dissuade sailors from mutinying. Punishments such as tarring and feathering, keelhauling and flogging with a cat of nine tails are all well documented. Malnutrition and scurvy were also rife because of two factors: one, a lack of knowledge about what constituted a good diet; and two, the issue of how to properly store the food taken on board in order to prevent spoiling. It has been written that even when quality food supplies were loaded, they were stowed in poorly ventilated spaces where they either deteriorated or became infested with rats and other vermin commonly found on most sailing ships.

Regarding their working conditions, there are ample records to indicate that sailors were required to toil hard on deck and in the rigging in all weather conditions and for long hours at a stretch, with the consequential fatigue contributing to a high number of accidents. Their roles demanded scaling ropes, rigging and masts in fair weather and foul, often to dangerous heights of up to eighty and ninety feet. Injuries were commonplace and shipboard 'surgeons', particularly in the early decades of this century, were not qualified in any real sense and from ships logs and personal stories there are harrowing accounts of medical procedures being undertaken in barbaric circumstances. Surgeons were forced to work in cramped and filthy conditions where patients are known to have endured amputations and extreme operations without the basics we expect today of antiseptic and anaesthetic. Consequently, wounds would frequently become infected and gangrenous. In addition, for the Youngs and their fellow whaler fishermen venturing to the high latitudes, there was the added menace of extreme cold causing severe frost-bite. Additionally, there were icebergs, fog and gales which combined to create specific and unpredictable hazards for men and ships. It was a very hard life suited to only the toughest of men and bravest of boys.

Despite all these negatives, year after year intrepid mariners and passengers travelled further and more frequently as sea routes became established on all the oceans of the world. On every voyage they were forced to face up to these hazards and other unknowns, endangerment and peril. They would have done so in the full knowledge that the dark shadow of a watery grave was their only constant companion. So well understood were these dangers that when seamen signed on for a voyage, they were required to advise the shipowners and masters of their next of kin, and those seamen with property or possessions were encouraged to make a Will. This information was entered into a register held by the shipowners at the vessel's home port and served to ensure that, for those men who did not return home, their families could be notified and the wages due could be paid.

However, perhaps one of the most surprising revelations from this century was the discovery of the level of mobility for crewmembers including Masters. From the humble sailors and mariners to the licensed Skippers and Captains, it appears normal for them to move between ships and trade routes throughout their working lives. This would have demanded a high skill level on the part of the Masters and Captains as they navigated different ports with different vessels. It could also be inferred from the data that work opportunities waxed and waned as much with the level of international political hostility and wars raging at sea as it did with seasonal trade. For those mariners in the Royal Navy, there is evidence to suggest those men would usually remain on board until the end of the expeditionary voyage or sea battle, at which point it appears customary for the Royal Navy to clear out their ships. They would virtually set their crews adrift and leave them marooned to wander the roads as vagrants. From time to time the Scottish countryside has been described as awash with hungry, penniless seamen. Then, somehow these lowly paid, routinely unemployed, sometimes starving and often brutally treated sailors would find themselves drifting back to the docks, bewitched by some invisible force, tempting, almost daring them to join some ship, any ship.

Anecdotally, it could be said that the men who were drawn into this life embraced the adventure caught up in a vortex of what for many, amounted to their shipboard family friendships forged out of their deeply shared fears and extreme adversity.

Now it is time to turn attention more specifically to the men of this Young family and the key related family members who are known to have embarked on seafaring careers. In the process, we will also learn more of what this meant for each of them individually and for Scotland as a whole.

In a publication entitled *'Scottish Seafarers of the Seventeenth Century'*, David Dobson, whilst positively underscoring the importance of seafaring to the Scottish Economy, also took time to highlight the dangers and cruelty experienced. As a framework for this study Dobson created an Inventory of Testaments or Wills which proved quite an eye-opener for two reasons. One, many of the names he listed are familiar in a genealogy sense as they are names associated by marriage or business, like Adamson, Brown, Calderwood, Dick, Ferguson, Gibson, Gourlay, Hay, Lamb, Logan, Lundie, Naismith, Paterson, Petrie, Pirrie, Ramsay, Rankine, Strachan, Thomson, Waddell, Watson and of course he lists several Youngs as well. And two, the occupations of these individuals ranged from humble sailor to skilled mariner, mate, boatswain, foremast-man, surgeon, skipper, captain and master. Overall, the most sobering lesson to come out of Dobson's Inventory was that the sea did not discriminate when it decided to claim a soul.

For those seafarers who became involved in the whale fishing trade there is a whole other story to be told. A major source of information in this regard can be found in the Intent to Claim the Bounty documents held in the Scottish Archives in Edinburgh. These documents are all about accountability and rule compliance and whilst the rules changed over time, especially with respect to the make-up of the crew, the records also proved incredibly valuable in terms of what they could contribute to the genealogy of the families listed. At certain points in British whaling history foreigners could not be legally carried as crew; but, once Parliament acknowledged that the British simply did not possess the right skill set the inclusion of foreigners was enshrined in legislation and reflected in these documents. Regarding the introduction of the Bounty, it was fundamentally designed to encourage the British, including the Scots, to re-engage with whale fishing. Initially a twenty shilling Bounty was offered in 1732 for vessels over 200 tons, but this did very little to stimulate interest and investment, so two subsequent offers were legislated. One in 1740 raised the Bounty to thirty shillings then in 1750 it was increased to a whopping forty shillings. With each of these Bounty increases came a corresponding increase in the level of accountability and the rigour for qualification was consistently enforced.

By the time Alexander Snr was sailing to the Arctic as a Master of a whaler, around 1780, the rules for claiming the Bounty demanded disclosure of not only the size of the vessel but the number of whaleboats carried. This was required to fit a prescribed ship burthen to whaleboat ratio determined by the parliament. It also required particular disclosures be made regarding the attributes of the crew - such as total number, how many were foreigners or apprentice and most recent Claim Forms were required to list the names of the men and boys under their respective job headings. Clearly, this could also be used as proof of Greenland experience when assailed by the Press Gangs because, at various times, crewmembers with Greenland whaling expertise were exempt from impressment. More recently it was only the Officers who were offered exemption from impressment.

Exploration of these Bounty Records also proved insightful as a useful way to track an individual person's career or a particular family's involvement. An ideal example of how whale fishing, like white fishing, was very much a family affair is the Thomson Clan. Their story is punctuated with a Leith whaling ship called the *Friendship*. She was a 237 ½ ton Ship built in 1783 which was sheathed and doubled in 1784 especially for her future in the Arctic whale fishing trade. Her voyage to the Arctic in 1791 comes in for special mention because the Bounty Records show John Thomson was the Mate, Peter & Alexander Thomson were two of the Line Managers, George Thomson was a Harpooner and James Thomson was a Steersman. Sailing from Leith with a 25 man crew including six apprentices, it is gratifying to see they made a safe return on or about the 24 August, which is the date they lodged their Bounty Claim at the Customs House in Leith. One can only imagine what a devastating affair it would have been for the Thomson Clan if the *Friendship* had met with some calamity and that family had lost five of their good sons. A previous sailing from Dunbar in 1780 shows Alexander Thomson on the crew list as an Apprentice. While most apprentices were required to sign on for three years sadly the seasonal Bounty documents do not state details of time served.

Likewise, the Carney Clan are shown on crew lists for sailings of the *Royal Bounty* where John Carney is Steersman and William and James Carney are Sailors. The *Campbelltown* appears to have been a favourite ship with Alexander's mother's Liston Clan too, with three family names cited - Andrew Liston as Harpooner, William Liston as Steersman and David Liston as Sailor included on several Bounty Claim forms. *The Prince of Wales* is another Leith whaling ship with a proud history. Larger than many, it was 344 tons, required a crew of 43-45 men and carried six whaleboats. It was one of the very early vessels to venture to the Arctic and their 1770 voyage proved particularly rewarding. They returned early on 19 July with 213 casks containing the blubber of 16 whales and amongst the crew were Robert and James Young and Richard Thomson who were all listed as sailors, with Robert Young and a Thomas Thomson also listed as Steersmen of a whaleboat. In fact, Robert and James Young remained part of the crew of the *Prince of Wales* for many years. They can be found on the crew lists for both the 1774 and 1775 voyages fulfilling the role of Line Manager, the pivotal position on a whaleboat when in pursuit of a whale. By 1782/83 Robert Young had taken on the role of Harpooner and it is pleasing to report that the *Prince of Wales* achieved notable catch results both seasons.

We have already learned that once the British Government openly acknowledged that British crews lacked the required skills, they legislated for the definite inclusion of foreigners. These foreigners played a vital role as instructors for the English and Scottish crews alike and in order to ensure compliance with the tenet of the legislation, Masters were required to include details of any foreign crewmembers on the Bounty claim forms. At times these details included the crewman's nationality and role. On the occasion of the 1770 voyage of the *Prince of Wales* there were seven foreigners making up the crew of 43 men. Could this account for their outstanding success and very early return?

It is timely now to look specifically at those Leith mariners, Youngs and their relatives, who were the key individuals in this extended family who are known to have been a part of the Scottish seafaring community. Two tables have been compiled, principally from the Registers of the Masters and Mates Certificates held in the National Archives in Kew, one listing Young family members and the other listing related family members. They also include some data extracted from records held in the collections of the National Maritime Museum, Greenwich as well as from the Bounty claim forms.

TABLE 1A – Key Young Male Family Seafarers

Seafarers	Sailing Profile
Robert [1723-1797]	Seaman, Mate, Harpooner, Steersman, Linesman, Greenlandman
Alexander Snr [1750-1817]	Seaman, Master, Greenlandman & Ship Owner, Shipping Company Shareholder & Owner, Steamship Investor & more
James [1755-1796	Seaman, Captain, Shipmaster in Leith, Merchant Navy
Robert [1775-1783]	Royal Navy -Mariner – later Foreman Wet Dock Leith
William [1777->1821]	Seaman. Shipmaster in Leith, Merchant Navy
Alexander Jnr [1782-1848]	Seaman, Captain, Whale Fisherman, Ship Owner, Shipping Company Owner, Lloyds Agent & Ships Surveyor
Robert [1786-1818]	Seaman, Greenlandman and Merchant Navy
John [1789-1836]	Boy, Seaman, Petty Officer in Royal Navy [Trafalgar], Captain, Whale Fisherman, Merchant Navy, died Calcutta, India
Alexander [1806-1863]	Seaman, Mate, Ships Broker Sydney NSW & Macau China, Business Entrepreneur & Manufacturer London England
John [1811-1871]	Seaman, Captain, Merchant Navy, Ship Shareholder Lloyds Assessor Glasgow. Ships Broker & Agent Kirkcaldy

Joshua Richmond [1813-1883]	Shipping Brokerage Firm based in Sydney, NSW, partner & owner, passenger shipping via Ceylon to London, business manager and Entrepreneur London
George [1814-1848]	Partner with brother Liston in Brokerage Firm in Melbourne, Vic., Australia, Stockbroker and Financier, Philadelphia, USA
William [1816-1899]	Royal Navy, Quartermaster, Career Navy - Worldwide retired to Chatham, Kent
Liston [1813-1883]	Shipping Broker & Agent Sydney NSW, & Melb. Vic., Shipping Warehouse London & Liverpool, Shipping Fleet Owner –Offices London
Alexander [1818-1847]	Captain Merchant Navy – Lost at sea
Robert Adamson [1822-1902]	Seaman, Mate, Captain Merchant Navy – Maimed, died in Mariners Retirement Home
John Lamb [1825-1905]	Captain & First Officer Merchant Navy - Australia
David Hill [1826-1902]	Colonial Agent & Broker, Sydney, NSW, London, England
William Wallace [1828-1850]	Seaman Merchant Navy died New Orleans, USA
George Frederick [1829-1860]	Captain Merchant Navy – died at sea
Joshua Richmond [1839-1894]	Seaman, Mariner, Captain, Merchant Navy worldwide, drowned Victoria, Australia
George Alex. [1841-1917]	Marine Engineer
Francis Spittal [1843-1872]	Seaman, Captain, Master, Merchant Navy
John Ellis [1847-1888]	Mercantile Agent, Riga when it was part of Russia
Charles Thomson [1849-1900]	Marine Engineer, Supt of Shaw, Savill & Albion & White Star Line
Samuel Donaclift [1851-1909]	Colonial Merchant & Ships Broker, Colombo, Ceylon

And then 1750-1850

Charles [1858-1936]	Colonial Merchant & Shipping Agent, London
William Main [1860-1885]	Colonial Agent, Blenheim, New Zealand, drowned
George Alexander [1870-1911]	Marine Engineer, Glasgow based shipbuilding companies
David Hill Young [1876-1951]	Marine Engineer, China, Hong Kong & Colombo, Dublin Shipyard Supt. In WW2, Marine Supt. USA
Charles Thomson [1880-1938]	Apprentice, Seaman, Captain, Broker Colombo Ceylon
Charles Purdie [1881-1943]	Chief Engineer, Merchant Navy, Nigeria, East Africa
Alfred Liston [1885-1944]	Steamship Componentry Factory Owner
George Ian 'Ian' [1918-1997]	WW2 & MTB102, Yachts
Robert Tyrrell [1912-1996]	Marine Engineer, Chairman American Bureau of Shipping

TABLE 1B – Those Females Youngs Connected to Seafarers

Wives & Daughters	Seafarer Connections
Margaret Thomson [1651-1709]	John Thomson Father Shipwright
Margaret Dick	Captain Gilbert Dick Father
Janet Lundie	Alexander Lundie Father fisherman
Helen Liston [1756-1797]	John Liston Fisherman
Elizabeth Young [1770-1825]	Captain Thomas Durham
Ann Young [1776-1824]	Captain William Dick
Helen Young [1781-1836]	Captain Joshua Richmond
Jean Strachan [1786-1846]	Robert Strachan ship owner and builder
Penelope Galt [1790-1873	James Galt Father
Jean Lamb [1796-1862]	Captain Dr David Lamb father
Mary Donaclift [1816-1895]	Samuel Donaclift, Ireland Shipwright Samuel Donaclift Brother Appr to Captain John Young

Jean Young [1818-1889]	Captain Francis Spittal
Robina Adamson Young [1813-1892]	Captain Thomas Johnston
Charlotte Anne Wilcox [1827-1897]	Commander Robert Wilcox Father – Royal Navy
Jeanie Renfrew Johnston [1883-1936]	Charles Arthur Hutson, Husb., Marine Engineer & Shipbuilder, Colombo, Ceylon
Margaret Agnew Stewart Young [1887-1936]	John 'Jack' Fullerton of Ship Building

TABLE 2 – Associated Seafaring Families

Family / Person	Profiles
Dick Family Gilbert [C1660-C1704] William [1768-1844]	Skipper and Captain Merchant Navy Captain Merchant Navy
Thomson Family John [1615-1709] Robert [C1610-1633]	Skipper Merchant Navy Skipper Merchant Navy
Liston Family William [C1650-] John [1716-1761] Others	Fisherman Newhaven Fisherman Newhaven Greenlandmen
Lundie Family Alexander [1776-] Walter [C1680-1713] Others	Steersman/Greenlandman Seaman in Leith Fishermen in Newhaven
Carnie/Carney Family Alexander [C1662-] Others	Seaman in Leith Fishermen in Newhaven
Richmond Family Joshua [C1781-1847]	Royal Navy Lieutenant Merchant Navy Captain
Spittal Family Francis [1775-1852]	Captain Merchant Navy, Balast Master & Dock Master in Leith

And then 1750-1850

Lamb Family David [1754-] John [1790-1854]	Doctor, Ships Surgeon, Sea Captain, British East India Company, BEIC Army
Strachan Family Robert [1750-1802] John [1777-1795] Others	Shipowner in Montrose, Shipbuilding in Edinburgh Seaman – lost overboard Cape of Good Hope, Sth Africa Ships Brokers & Lumber Agents – Riga, Russia
Parsons Family George [1729-1812] George [1762-1798] John [1765-1834]	Shipbuilders of note – incl. HMS Elephant which at one time was Lord Nelson's flagship – in all 20 warships for Royal Navy under Warrant 19 Dec 1778.
Willcox Family Robert [1788-1850] Robert [1818-] Scott James Bailey [1848-1907]	Three generations of Royal Navy – Ranks of Commander, Lt. Fleet Surgeon, Lieutenant
Whiting/Bradford Family William Bradford Charles Samuel Bradford Major William Bradford Governor William Bradford	Mayflower arrivals and Governor of Plymouth, seafarers, military, US Navy Commander,
McLean Family Graham Campbell Snr Graham Campbell Jnr Graham Campbell III	Three generations of sailing – Master, Mate and Colonial Agency operations
Dudgeon Family John [1843-]	Mercantile Clerk, Edinburgh
Flood Family William [1835-1885] Otto Barnes Patrick [1878-1940]	Two generations of Royal Navy – Lieutenant OBE, and Paymaster with service in Baltic, Aust., and N.Z. William saw action - Bombardment of Bomersund & Swaeborg – Crimea War 21.6.1854]

These tables demonstrate how individuals from the immediate and extended families have matured from humble Fishermen and Sailors to Sea Captains and from Shipowners to Colonial Merchants and Brokers.

The next task was to delve into the records of Lloyd's Register and others, to learn something about the ships they sailed. For brevity, another table has been compiled representing some of the ships commanded by the four most prominent Youngs of this 1750-1850 century who all enjoyed substantial careers as Masters. As it was customary for the sons in this era to go to sea with their fathers, these instances will become evident when the same ship in the same year is attributed to both people. Lloyd's Register was especially useful here as a cross-reference point because it holds information describing each vessel by type, burthen, decks, ownership details and the name of the Master for each voyage. It also draws attention to certain fraught events because one of its functions is to catalogue damage and repairs. Lloyd's has developed a code for each trade route, port of departure and port of destination. In attempting to verify these voyages with newspaper reports and other documents has highlighted two things – one, that not every voyage is listed in Lloyds and, two - not all records are totally accurate. Despite these shortcomings, Lloyd's Register is considered <u>the</u> primary reference tool, the 'Bible of Shipping' movements as it were, particularly in relation to this century, given few other records survive.

This prestigious company of Lloyd's will feature prominently sometime later in the lives of at least two Youngs - Alexander [1784-1848] and his son John [1811-1871]. Meanwhile, the status of working for Lloyd's is best vouched for by taking a quick look at the organisation's illustrious history. The origins of Lloyd's and its Register can be traced to the late seventeenth century when Londoner Edward Lloyd [1648-1713] first opened a coffee house in Tower Street in 1686. It became a very popular meeting place with sailors, merchants and shipowners alike. Lloyd's coffee shop later became a place where conversations were had and business deals were done involving shipping, insurance, ship-brokering and foreign trade.

When Edward Lloyd relocated his Coffee Shop to Lombard Street during the Christmas of 1691 the shipping intelligence sharing business followed him. Lloyd installed a lectern at his new premises from which merchants conducted maritime auctions and made announcements of shipping news. Lloyd later decided to begin publishing Lloyd's News wherein he reported on shipping schedules and commodity prices. Edward Lloyd was opportunistic, monopolistic and entrepreneurial and his vision led to the formation of one of the most successful and longest continuously operating Companies in the World; currently boasting over 330 years in business. Edward Lloyd would be immensely proud to know his company has moved with the times, broadened its services base, and survives to this very day still trading and tracking shipping movements as Edward Lloyd had intended.

This next table contains data relating to 'The Ships'. The information was either extracted from official registers or discovered in documents held in private family archives –

TABLE 3A – Capt. Alexander Young [1750-1817]

Seafarer	Years at Sea	Name of Ship	Description of Ship
Capt. Alexander Young [1750-1817]	1765-1815	Royal Bounty	Ship – 331 Tons
			Reg. to Leith - Whale Fishing Davis Strait
		Campbelltown	Ship – 305 tons Reg. to Leith
		Tryall	Whaler – Reg. to Leith – burthen unknown, owned Edinburgh Whale Fishing Company 1786

		North Star	Ketch, 150 tons, Single Dec, Built 1772, Thorough Repair 1777, Whale Fishing Davis Strait
		Blessed Endeavour	Ship 150 tons Reb. Leith
		Prince of Wales	Greenland Whaler not listed in Lloyd's Register – sailed ex Dunbar 1776-1789
			Ship 150 tons Reg Leith
		Hero	Whaler – Greenland Ship – 366 tons –
		Raith	Sheathed Keel and Doubled Hull for Arctic Whaling – Sailed ex London then Montrose
			ship 295 Tons Reg Leith Built Kings Yard 1761 – Sheathed and Doubled Hull in 1784, sailed Leith to Greenland & Davis Str.
		Eliza Swan	Ship 241 Tons – Hull doubled sailed ex Montrose to Arctic – Repaired and Lengthened 1806 – Spitzbergen, Greenland & David Str.
		Monarch	Ship 309 tons Reg. to Montrose – Sheathed in Copper, 9 Guns, Whaling Greenland & Davis Str.
		Success	Ship – Whaling Arctic – sailed ex Dundee & Leith 1789-1808, Not in Lloyds Reg. but in Bounty Claims

TABLE 3B – Capt. Alexander Young [1782-1848]

Seafarer	Years at Sea	Name of Ship	Description of Ship
Captain Alexander Young Jnr [1782-1848]	1797+	Eliza Swan	Whaler 241 tons as above
		Monarch	Whaler 309 tons as above
		Jane	Ship 165 Tons – Snow Reg. to Montrose, Merchant Navy sailing Hull to St. Petersburg, Dundee to Baltic, London to Elsinore -Whaling Greenland & Davis Str.
		Hero	Merchant & Whaling 150 tons as above

TABLE 3C – Capt. John Young [1789-1836]

Seafarer	Years at Sea	Name of Ship	Description of Ship
Captain John Young [1789-1836]	1804-1836	Prince of Wales	Appr. With father G/land
		Eliza Swan	Capt. - Whaler – as above
		Monarch	Capt. - Whaler – as above
		Jane	Merchant Navy – as above
			Capt. Whaler – as above
		Hero	Crushed & Lost Davis Str. 1822
		'Fame'? – possible	Merchant Navy – BEIC? Died Calcutta

TABLE 3D – Capt. John Young [1811-1871]

Seafarer	Years at Sea	Name of Ship	Description of Ship
Capt John Young [1811-1871]	1824+	Jane	Apprenticeship with father in the Arctic - father Captain Whaler - Arctic Merchant Navy - Leith to Riga, Russia Merchant – 164 -202 Master - Baltic & Archangel Trade
		Comet	Brig 260 tons - Merch. Newhaven – London
		Byron	Brig 107 tons -Merch. Newcastle
		Tam O'Shanter	Merchant, 383 Tons, Sailed ex North Hylton London to Syd. Australia, wrecked 1837 Tasmania
		Upton Castle	Ship- 600 Tons – Routes - Calcutta for East India Company – Madras, Ceylon, & Calcutta via Cape Town to London + Ret to Australia around 1839
		Huskisson	Barque - 388 Tons – Merch. – Route incl. Liverpool & West Indies via Africa
		Hibernian	Ship - 193 Tons - Merch. Ex Kinsale, Ireland to St John, New Brunswick, Canada
		Emerald	Schooner –171 Tons Merch. - Kinsale to Newport, Cork, Dublin & Bordeaux, France
		Sussex	Ship, 371 tons, Dundee to Montreal, Canada

TABLE 4 – History of the *Jane* – Version 1 & 2

HISTORY OF THE VESSELS - 'JANE' - VERSIONS 1 & 2					
1. Built	**Newcastle 1818**		**Classed -**		
Rig -	Snow		Flag - British		
tons -	143 Burthen				
1818	Young	Young & Co	London-Coasting		Single deck and
to					beams. Classed Lloyds
1826					Draught 23 feet
1827+	No trace of this configuration in Lloyds Registers thereafter				
2. Built	**Leith 1824**		**Classed - A.1. Lloyds**		
Rig -	Snow		Flag - British		
Tons -	net 165 burthen				
Year	**Master**	**Owner**	**Voyage**		**History**
1824	A.Young	Capt & Co	Leith - Riga		Single deck
					with beams
1825	Duckells	A.Young	Hull-St. Petersburg		13 feet Draught
1826	Duckells	A.Young	Hull-St. Petersburg		
1827	A.Young	Capt & Co	Dundee - Baltic		
1828	D.Doctor	A.Young & Co	Waterford - St. Petersburg		
1829	D. Doctor	A.Young & Co	Waterford - St. Petersburg		
1830	D. Doctor	A.Young & Co	Waterford - St. Petersburg		
1831	W.Keith	A.Young & Co	Leith-Baltic		
1832	A.Young	A.Young & Co	Leith-Baltic		Large repair
					carried out

1833	A.Young	A.Young & Co	London-Elsinore	
1834	J.Young A. Strachan	A.Young	Montrose -	Tons net 164
1835	A.Strachan	A.Young	Dundee -	Port of Registry Montrose
1836	J.Young	A.Young	Dundee-St.Petersburg	New deck 1836
1837	J.Young	A.Young	London-Riga	
1838	J.Young	A.Young	London - Riga	
1839	J.Young	A.Young	Montrose-St.Petersburg	Thorough repairs & Lengthening Tonnage 212 net under new act. Tonnage 204 net under old act. Class restored 1839 - 7 years.
1840	J.Young	A.Young	Montrose-St.Petersburg	
1841	J.Young	A.Young	Montrose-Baltic	
1842	J.Young	A.Young	Montrose-Baltic	
1843	J.Young	A.Young	Montrose-Baltic	
1844	J.Young	A.Young		Rig changed to Brigantine
1844	J.Young	A.Young	Montrose-Baltic	New topsides
1845	J.Young	A.Young	Montrose-Baltic	Some repairs carried out
1846	J.Young	A.Young	London-Montrose- & the Continent	
1847	J Young	A Young	London - Montrose	
1848	J Young	A Young	Montrose - Baltic	Ship sold to C. Thomson

1849	J Young	C Thomson	Montrose - Baltic	
1850	J Young	C Thomson	Montrose - Danube	
	W Mearns	C Thomson	Montrose - Danube	
1851	W Mearns	C Thomson	Montrose - Danube	
1852	W Mearns	C Thomson	Montrose - Danube	Ship Wrecked

Having explored the maritime records for the ships and men it was time to take a look at the trade routes sailed and the cargoes carried.

As a starting point, it was timely to refer back to the probate details in Dobson's Inventory of Testaments. This Inventory created a place and time global map of the voyages undertaken by Scots – which includes the Youngs and some of their relatives. Dobson also draws attention to the fact that not all of the men lost their lives as a result of maritime misadventure, or the cruelty of Mother Nature; some of them were among the hundreds of trusting and hopeful Scots who fell victim to that already chronicled failure - The Darien Scheme. The world was still a landscape of frontier territories in this century and one could speculate that when these Youngs and others signed on for a voyage they were on the one hand harbouring daydreams of far off exotic lands spurred on by a sense of adventure. On the other-hand they would all be silently praying that they would once again see their homeland and feel the warmth of their own hearth. They knew the work was hard and the dangers ever present but, with dwindling prospects at home; in the end, the resolute Scots knew that if fate took a hand it would be their desolate families who would be left to blindly wonder their fate.

When contemplating the various Trade Routes, I initially looked east to the Baltic and Archangel knowing it was already a relatively mature route for the Scots by the time this 1750-1850 century rolled around. In a treatise entitled *'Society and Economy in Modern Britain 1700-1850'* Richard Brown devotes much discussion to the subject of Scotland's Baltic Trade. In particular he maintains that Scotland's foreign trade in the Baltic was driven by its own internal deficiencies as it struggled to produce basic items of a suitable quality or in a quantity sufficient to satisfy local demand. Therefore, the cargoes carried on this route would have been made up of mostly everyday items such as cooking utensils, clothing and the like. While Brown contends there were two clear solutions available to overcoming Scotland's manufacturing shortfall, one being to improve methods of manufacture at home, he also acknowledged this would take some time to show measurable improvement and would require the importation of even larger volumes of raw materials. The second was to take the short-term decision to import more finished goods and preferably not from their English neighbours. The upside for the likes of the Youngs and others involved in the Merchant Navy was that both of these solutions would equate to increased demand for shipping services on this prime trade route.

Having learned from previous shipping records that this fluid Baltic Trade continued to be a constant in the lives of several Young family merchantmen throughout this century and following on from Brown's research, it can be concluded that their vessels were initially employed in the importation of essential raw materials such as iron, copper, timber, pitch, tar, flax, as well as finished goods like fine quality linen and woollen goods and metalware. In turn, these same Scottish ships mastered by Scots, Youngs and others, would have carried herring and coal back to the various Baltic and Archangel ports. More important still, Brown's post-1750 Scottish Baltic trade data can also be used as a barometer for the turnaround in Scottish manufacturing success. By tracing certain commodities over time his data shows a definite shift as Scotland begins to flourish on the back of the export of more and more finished goods.

One cottage industry that began to boom in Scotland in the 1760s was the Linen Trade. Scottish ships would carry the raw flax from the Baltic to home-ports whereupon many of these same Scottish ships then carried quality linen and a wide variety of hemp products on their return voyages. Given the general upswing in the variety of goods manufactured from flax during this century it has been suggested that at its pinnacle in excess of thirty per cent of Scotland's manufactured output was being exported on Scottish ships. This trade not only proved vital to the commerce of the cottage spinners and weavers, local manufacturers, merchants and shipowners in Scotland; it also offered vital employment to Scottish sailors.

Historically, this Baltic region was certainly not unfamiliar territory for many Scots. Generally speaking, Scots living and trading in the Baltic can be traced back to late medieval times, and much has been written about those Scots who set up residence and owned businesses in countries such as Prussia, Sweden and Norway. David Dobson in another of his publications entitled *'Scots in Poland, Russia and the Baltic States: 1550-1850'* traces the lives of many of these pioneering Scots and writes of the valuable contributions they made. He includes a long list of names of émigré Scots and the Baltic ports and towns they were aligned with as well as the years of their habitation. He points out that many of these men had initially gone as soldiers to fight in the foreign armies of Prussia and Sweden. Those who decided to remain had taken up residence along the shoreline mostly because land grants were offered in lieu of salary for '[army] services rendered'. Others had arrived as 'chancers'. These were those Scots who saw themselves without any worthwhile prospects at home and who decided to desert a merchant vessel mid-voyage to become itinerant 'cramers' or pedlars.

Of those listed by Dobson, many family names are familiar; names which we can positively identify as associated closely with this Young family from a time pre-1650 - names such as Thomson, Gourlay, Turnbull, Waddell and Lamb. Given that Dobson shows these names can be traced back a century or more it is fair to assume that many of the Scots who sailed to Baltic ports during this 1750-1850 period may well have had family connections going back several generations, particularly in the ports of Danzig and Riga. Maybe some of these early

Scots were the founders of those businesses known to be operating in this century. This would mean these foreign ports were not so foreign after all!

One of the later Young ancestors known to have resided in the Baltic was businessman John Ellis Young [1847-1888], the fifth son of Captain John Young [1811-1871]. This John Ellis Young is known to have operated a lumber business in Riga from a time well prior to 1870. In fact, Riga had quite a community of Scots in the lumber business operating in and around the town and utilising the port facilities. There was another Montrose family in the Baltic at this time, also with close family ties to the Youngs and this was the Strachan Family. One Robert Strachan married a Sarah Lyall in 1815 in Montrose and a few years later around 1830 he moved with his family to Riga where he too operated a lumber trading company which no doubt supplied the Strachan family shipyards in both Montrose and Edinburgh. What remains to be verified is precisely when these businesses of John Ellis Young and Robert Strachan were first established. Given the strength of Dobson's research there is no reason to assume either John Ellis Young or Robert Strachan were the first members of their respective families to live and do business in the region.

In fact, Scots in the Baltic with the Surname of Young can be documented to the late Sixteenth Century, one notable being Captain Abraham Young stationed in Cracow [Krakow], Poland. For a time, he was Commander of the Scots soldiers in the service of the King of Poland in 1604. Alexander, Andrew, John and William Young are names listed in various official Baltic records where they are registered as 'cramers' living in various towns in Prussia around 1615. Unfortunately, so far, no direct link to those particular individuals has yet been established and may never be as records are not definitive enough for certainty, but these are most certainly four family christian names repeated down the generations in our line of Youngs of Scotland.

Alexander Young Snr [1750-1817] and his son Alexander Jnr [1782-1848] both sailed to the Baltic & Archangel in the winter months and sailed to the Arctic in the summer months to go whale fishing. Later on, Alexander Snr's grandson, John

Young [1811-1871], was a regular on this Baltic Route sailing the family owned ship the *Jane*. Even after John gave up shipboard life, and following a stint working for Lloyd's as a Ships Broker and Surveyor in Glasgow, he went into partnership in a ship brokerage business in Kirkcaldy and it was the familiar Baltic Trade that he and their business partner continued to be very strongly associated with.

Other trade routes included voyages south to the Bay of Biscay from where they picked up cargoes of wine and salt. These voyages were reserved for the months on the fringe of winter; however, they were less regular and as the century progressed much longer routes to ports as far afield as the East Indies, Africa, West Indies, Canada, Australia and the Americas became more the norm. Initially, trade with India and the Far East had been monopolised by a group of English Merchants who had the ear of Westminster and so merchant-shipping traffic on this route was predominantly English ships with English crews sailing under the flag of the British East India Company.

Brown and others uphold the notion that Scotland was not integrated into the euphemistically described British Trade System at that time. Avaricious English Merchants did not want Scotland interfering with England's stranglehold on trade in India and Asia in particular and consistently and successfully lobbied Parliament and the King to maintain their preferred status quo. Although the Scots lobbied for change, much to their chagrin, they were consistently unsuccessful which did not sit at all well given the King was their own James VI. Eventually, with the rapid rise in manufactured output once the Industrial Revolution took hold in England, the British East India Company was forced to go in search of new markets, spreading its tentacles to China and the Far East. So strong was their monopoly that at one point these two markets accounted for more than sixty per cent of the Company's turnover. As the demand for shipping services significantly increased so the British East India Company began building its own fleet of ships. All the while, Scottish vessels remained excluded from participation - but not so Scottish Captains.

Interestingly, the commodity of greatest profit to the British East India Company at this time was opium and a twenty-first century country equivalent of this would be Columbia and the cocaine trade with the distinction being that Opium was being legally trafficked back then. Captain Alexander Young Snr owned a very ornate and well-used opium pipe which has been handed down the generations. Whether it originally belonged to his father Robert [1723-1797] or was a personal trophy cannot be properly established, but what is known is that the British East India Company went from strength to strength on the back of its trade monopoly and its vast fleet of ships; some of these were mastered by Scots and quite possibly Youngs. There is a Robert Young listed as Master of the *Vansittart* a vessel that held East Indiaman Warrants from 1768-1826, and then there is Captain John Young [1789-1836], son of Alexander Snr who is rumoured to have sailed for the Company. Whilst that is not conclusively proven, what is known is that he lost his life at Calcutta in the September of 1836 - was it perhaps whilst at the helm of an East India Company vessel?

What is also known for certain is that India was not a foreign port for this Captain John Young who can vouch very strong family connections to India for decades prior to his death. His brother-in-law, Captain Dr John Lamb, was a surgeon and sea captain who married in Calcutta in 1811. His bride was Juliana Crommelin whose grandfather was Charles Crommelin, one time Governor of Bombay. Captain Lamb's eldest son was Colonel Henry Campbell Lamb; in fact, three of Captain Lamb's sons had distinguished military careers in the East India Army [the British East India Company not only had its own fleet of ships it maintained its own army as well] achieving the ranks of Major, General and Colonel. His daughters too married career military officers in India and later they all enjoyed very comfortable retirements in England and Scotland. Just as an aside and as proof of the mobility of people in the day and the strength of the colonisation of India by various European nations, Charles Crommelin, Governor of Bombay, was the son of Marc Antoine Crommelin [1684-1720] of Lyon, France. It was Marc Antoine's father who first ventured to India sometime before 1714 in which year he married a Miss Mary Truman in Mumbai, Maharashtra, India on 5 January. Miss Truman was clearly a lady of English birth.

So, what then were the specific hazards faced by those Youngs who sailed these far-flung Trade Routes?

Without doubt, the biggest threat to ships involved in the Baltic Trade was not the harsh and unpredictable weather conditions at these hazardously high latitudes; rather it was privateering and impressment that posed by far the greatest risk to both men and ships. These risks escalated following the outbreak of war with France in 1756. Ultimately, trade routes worldwide would be affected because France had also expressed a renewed interest in colonising North America. For the Youngs and others sailing to the Arctic or on other international trade routes it gave them yet another hazard to overcome. Around this same time the Royal Navy began demanding merchantmen disclose information on the vessels they encountered en route in exchange for convoy services and safe passage.

On the whole, this arrangement appears to have worked to everyone's advantage and was a means by which the Royal Navy could receive useful enemy intelligence. Scottish Historian Victoria E. Clark refers to one such incident she found in the records of the Port of Aberdeen which stated that 'The white fishers [local fishermen] were valuable at this juncture in collecting intelligence of an approaching enemy. Charles Mackie, the master of a Swedish sloop, informed Captain Antrobus of the *'Surprise'* a Royal Navy man-of-war stationed at Stromness that he had sailed from Gottenburg to the Paternosters in company with Monsieur Thurot, who commanded a French squadron of five ships of 44, 38, 32, 26 and 18 guns, together with two armed cutters. Thurot, who had sailed into Gottenburg for provisions, gave out that he had 2,000 troops on board. His destination was generally supposed to be Ireland. Mackie's story was also confirmed by others.'

Whilst the primary intelligence here was discovered contained in letters sent from the Burgh of Aberdeen in the October of 1759, on this occasion the intelligence did prove to be 100 percent correct. Verification of this comes from another publication by one, Brian Lavery, who in his book *'Shield of Empire'* discloses that 'Off County Down his [Thurot's] remaining three ships met a British squadron and were defeated. Thurot was killed.' Sadly, such intelligence gathering and sharing was not always so clear-cut. Other historical documents demonstrate instances where pirates and privateers were known to fly flags designed to purposely mislead passing merchantmen and thus misinformation was quite innocently and inadvertently passed onto the Royal Navy; but, for a time at least it seems the merchantmen and the naval fleet enjoyed quite a symbiotic relationship.

This brings us to the subject of localised impressment at major Scottish ports such as the Young's home-port of Leith, and the effect it had on the merchant trade in this century specifically.

Once again, I used Victoria E. Clark's publication *'The Port of Aberdeen: .....'* as a reference point because it gives a first-hand account of these issues for that Scottish port. She quotes from various 'Letters Sent from that Burgh', and there is one dated 9th December 1756, wherein the Burgh Council is 'complaining that the hardships endured at the port were greater than those of any other coast town in Scotland, owing to the prolonged visitation of a lieutenant of the navy and a press-gang.' Clark's research shows that fishing and trade were virtually brought to a standstill after the Navy implemented a strategy whereby 'No vessel could enter the harbour without being boarded, and numbers of the crew were captured and carried off to the King's ships.' And whilst the Shipowners in Aberdeen asserted, they were suffering the most hardship of all, rest assured all seaports in Scotland were at one time or another being subjected to the same crippling intimidation. In the case of Aberdeen, it is said that the success of the Press Gang was such that three years on 'not a dozen able-bodied sailors were left in the city'. This was undoubtedly devastating for trade and therefore seriously detrimental to the general revenue flowing into the port Burgh and on to local families. Moreover, it should be viewed as symptomatic of what was occurring in Scottish ports on both sides of the country.

Just as Aberdeen had been plagued by press-gangs in the 1750s Leith was about to suffer a similar fate. When the war with France escalated in 1755 the infamous Captain John Fergusson RN was appointed Regulating Captain in Leith. On one occasion Fergusson planned a dawn raid, where at 4.00 a.m. on the morning of 26 February 1755 he mobilised some one hundred troops from the Edinburgh Castle Garrison. Some were positioned to blockade Leith and others charged with raiding seaman's homes and local taverns. Some 200 seamen were rounded up, of which 175 were ultimately released under the protection order in place at the time in respect of whale fishermen of the Greenland Trade. Given this current exemption it could be presumed that it was a deliberate strategy on the part of the Youngs to blood their sons in the Greenland Trade in order to ensure they could legally avoid Impressment! All of this upheaval was occurring at a time when seafarers with the skill levels and experience of Robert Young and his son Alexander would most certainly have been in the Press Gang's sights.

It was not just the merchant fleet that had to be on the alert for the Press Gangs. The whaler *North Star* suffered a huge loss as she returned to Leith after the 1779 season in Greenland. On that sail Robert Young was Mate and Line Manager and somehow managed to escape the Press; however, the whaler lost the other four Line Managers plus all four of their Steersmen and two of their Harpooners. These are all very specialist roles and the loss of these highly skilled men would have been a great blow to the *North Star* and unsettling for the Leith contingent of Greenlandmen. In 1777 the *Campbelltown* too lost one of her Apprentices. Then matters appear to have escalated from there such that by 1805 the situation had become critical. Our own Alexander Young Jnr was about to turn twenty-five and was Master of the whaler *Eliza Swan* that season. From the information submitted on the Claim for the Bounty Forms, it seems he had quite a challenging homeward voyage.

The season started like this - Alexander and his crew sailed out of Montrose on the 4 March and arrived at Greenland on the 17 April. The fishing was exceptionally good such that they arrived home very early on the 2 June. However, for Captain Young there were several items of paperwork to complete other than the Bounty Claim Form that year. Firstly, there was an incident where a man fell overboard and drowned; but, by far his greatest headache remained reporting on how HMS *Galgo*, a 16 gun Sloop of the Royal Navy had managed to overtake the *Eliza Swan* and impress all five of her Line Managers, together with 15 Sailors and 2 other Greenlandmen. Royal Navy lists for 1805 indicate that HMS *Galgo* had Commander Michael Dod at the helm on that fateful day.

As far back as 1770, huge pressure had been placed on the Press Gangs because the British Government had commenced fitting out a vastly expanded Navy Fleet. In fact, following the unsuccessful raids made in Leith by Fergusson, a communication was sent from the Privy Council in London to the Provost of Edinburgh stating that even greater numbers of seamen were required. The Provost was placed on notice and advised that he would soon be receiving Press Warrants giving his Constables authority to take up 'such seafaring men as shall lurk about the City, Port and Liberties of Edinburgh' and that the Provost was required to deliver such apprehended persons to the Regulating Captains (i.e. those additional Naval Officers who would soon be invading the port en masse). To assuage any misgivings he may harbour in relation to this directive and the legality of enforcing compliance with English law on Scottish soil, come the end of October the Edinburgh Provost felt compelled to write to all the coastal towns in particular warning them of this impending impressment by his Constabulary.

Recognising that local compliance could be an issue, the constables for their part were to be given a shilling, the King's Shilling as it was described, as 'pressed money'; presumably to ensure that they would not overlook or be induced to overlook certain individuals. Meanwhile word came that Captain Napier, the newly appointed Regulating Officer, had already set sail from London in company with several of his most strident Lieutenants. Napier and his men arrived with even further inducements from the King, contained in a more recent November Royal Proclamation, which offered a bounty of 20 shillings to any man who volunteered. In addition, the Edinburgh Council would offer a further bounty of one guinea [twenty-one shillings] for any 'ordinary seaman' or two guineas for an 'able seaman' who took it upon himself to volunteer.

It has been written that the Navy, this time around, had streamlined their 'volunteer' process for Leith and it was proposed it should work like this - firstly the volunteers would report to Lieutenant Walsh aboard *HMS Rendezvous*, then once assessed for their rating (i.e. as ordinary seaman, able seaman, mate etc.), their names were entered upon a list duly submitted to the Council Chamber in Edinburgh. At a later date the men would be required to appear before the Council. For all that no bounty would be paid by either party until such time as the volunteers were secured on board their appointed ship. *HMS Portland* and the sloop HMS *Hazard* were now at anchor in Leith Harbour ready to welcome their new Royal Navy recruits. This would have certainly put the Youngs and their fellow mariner families on notice.

Looking to the lighter side of these events there are several curious pieces of correspondence relating to the impress history of Leith which are quite amusing and whilst not referencing the Youngs in particular, they do say a lot about life in that port for all the sailors and their families. One document sighted is a letter written by Lieutenant Walsh to the Council where he states 'All that is mentioned in the annexed list will appear before you, except James Rennie, who I thought necessary to ship off, being a fine fellow. After examination, if you find them entitled please to send the Bounty per bearer, taking his receipt'. One other missive dated the end of December could be construed as especially comical, wherein it reads 'Peter McDougal, an Edinburgh man and ordinary seaman, is actually on board the tender by some means. He is not marked down for the Bounty of a guinea which the Town allows. His wife is constantly plaguing me ... I cannot give it to her without your approbation'. My personal take on this is that this dear lady was attempting to rid herself of an unwanted husband and he too seems desirous of escaping his nagging wife. In the absence of any follow-up notes we are all left wondering if either got their wish or their money!

By January 1771 reports indicate that only 54 men had volunteered so this left Young family members and other experienced seamen of Leith under dire threat especially given that the Greenland exemption was not always observed. Obviously, this low number fell far short of Captain Napier's target, and just as shown in the Aberdeen example, Edinburgh and Leith Magistrates had to do deals too in order to placate Captain Napier and his Lieutenants. First up, the Provost offered Lieutenant Walsh some of the 'undesirables' currently contained in the Tolbooth as well as those lads who were presumed to be orphans and known to be lurking in alleyways and more importantly being maintained by the City. But this was still not enough for Captain Napier who seemed hell bent on making his quota of experienced seamen.

There was also a harsh stance taken against the poor as exemplified by this next story concerning one Leith citizen by the name of Banks who complained to the Provost about his impressment. When the matter came up for hearing before the Council, Lieutenant Napier could not or did not deem it sufficiently important to attend the Council Chambers on the day. Instead, he sent one of his deputies, Lieutenant Walsh an officer of the 22nd Grenadier Guard, who he maintained 'will appear at the Chamber'. However, Napier did advise the Provost by correspondence that this officer would inform him of the background of Banks and the circumstances of his pressing. He goes on to suggest that 'I think [he will] prove his character to be such, as the Town would be eased by his absence'. Clearly Banks had been deemed an unsavoury character and there was not going to be any reprieve for him.

Actions like this put fear and anger into the hearts of the petty criminals and the poor in Leith who felt defenceless and rightly so, since poverty alone was perceived a crime. Another deeply disgruntled and marginalised citizen took the brazen step of posting a handwritten notice on the gate of St Giles Churchyard decrying impressment by the King. It reads -

'To The Publick

In order to put a speedy end to the present alarming
incrochments on the liberty of the Inhabitants
if Scotland by Impressing etc, Who can say but the
life and liberty of the Meanest Mechanick is Equally
dear to him as that of the Richest or Most powerful.
There is no alternative. We must Distroy or be
Distro[yed]. Let us take the first opertunity [to]
put to Death privily those in [the] highest offices
viz Lord Adv[ocate] Aire and General Skeem
General Aughton both Civil and Military without
distinction as they either[r] are themselves
Villains or their Servants. There will be less loss
t[o] the Publick or their own Famely tho a
thousand of them be pu[t][to Death _____
then it one hun[dred] Plowghmen or Mecanicks
Loss Liberty. Avail yourselves like men.'

Sue Mowat's summation of this public outcry is quite apt, wherein she writes 'The perpetrator of this 'outrage' remained anonymous, and his intended targets remained alive'.

Unfortunately, impressment too remained alive in Leith for another twenty-seven years. Suffice to say as far back as 1739, at the time when Robert Young was taking to the sea, the Royal Navy had been sending cold-hearted unrestrained Officers to Edinburgh, Leith, Aberdeen, Saltcoats, Greenock and Glasgow where, according to Brian Lavery in his publication *'Shield of Empire - the Royal Navy and Scotland'* - these Press Gangs wreaked havoc on seamen in all these key Scottish ports. At the same time, Lavery also became intrigued by the question as to why skilled seamen hated the Royal Navy so much since it was not necessarily any worse than the Merchant Navy in how it treated its men. Indeed, William Spavens, an ex-Royal Navy man and relic of Nelson's era, once wrote 'I would just observe, that His Majesty's service is in many respects preferable to any other; first as when a ship in the merchant navy is cast away, the men and officers lose their pay ..... and second, the provisions are better in kind and generally more plentiful [in the Royal Navy].'

Sadly, this was not the whole story, and ultimately, there were two main reasons why seaman went to great lengths to avoid the Press and both related to wages and conditions. It turns out that in peacetime it is true to say there was little wage disparity between the two, but in wartime many thousands of men were pressed into the Royal Navy, which in turn created a shortage of seamen in the Merchant Navy. With economic supply and demand theory invoked, the wages in the merchant navy sector could be seen to increase by as much as three and four fold. Impressment would prevent a merchant seaman from sharing in this wage bonanza. Besides that, and perhaps most important of all, a merchant seaman always had the option to leave a ship at the end of each and every voyage. Conversely, the situation within the Royal Navy was totally different. With impressment at its highest in war time, men are known to have frequently been 'turned over' from one ship to another year after year without ever setting foot on land. Often this would continue until the war ended. Indeed, the Royal Navy gave no guarantee as to when a sailor might be granted shore leave for fear he would abscond.

A clear case of this Royal Navy 'turn over' is found in the Service Record of our own William Young [1816-1899]. His navy service record shows he was shipboard year in year out without any shore leave. This probably accounts for why he did not marry until quite late in life. William's plight and that of thousands of Navy sailors was well recognised by the Office of the Secretary to the Admiralty as far back as the 1720s, when correspondence was circulating about the detrimental effects this absence of shore leave had on seamen. The then Secretary of the Navy maintained 'This custom is very disagreeable to the seamen and has begot that aversion we have seen in them to the service; It takes from them the freedom of serving where they like, and many times the small [i.e., petty] officers are turned before the mast [ie. lose their status]. It abridges them from the pleasure of seeing their families'.

The Royal Navy simply chose to do nothing to remedy the situation.

And then 1750-1850

Whether or not any Youngs initially volunteered is a point of conjecture but perhaps could account for the exclusion of several individuals from receiving bequests in Wills, especially as these exclusions relate to family members who are known to have abandoned the Merchant Navy in favour of a career in the Royal Navy. One case in point is that of the aforementioned William Young [1816-1899]. Born the son of Captain Alexander Young [1782-1848] and Jean Strachan, William is presumed to have initially gone to sea with his father but later as an adult is found serving in the Royal Navy. William's uncle, Captain Joshua Richmond, in his Will of 1848 left bequests to all of William's surviving siblings and even made bequests to non-family members but in the case of his nephew William he specifically stated - 'except to William, & his proportion to be paid only by and with the consent of his two oldest Brothers for the time being'. This harsh condition was written into Joshua Richmond's Will shortly after the date William appears in Royal Navy records for the first time. Coincidence - maybe?

A full transcript of William Young's Navy career is available at National Archives, Kew. The file was unequivocally identified as our William Young's as it related to a person born at Montrose on 10 June 1816. It lists his Continuous Service Number as 7325, and his last date of re-enlistment as 22 December 1853 and his rating was Able Seaman. A few weeks later on the 17 January 1854 after rating assessment and medical checks he signs on for a further 10 Years. In his file there is a supplementary document notating 'Former Service' which has only two entries - *Raleigh* - 26 January 1846 to 10 November 1849, and *Daedalus* - 11 November 1849 to 13 September 1853. Both of these vessels have been identified as sailing under the flag of the Royal Navy. If this record is complete, it is safe to infer that William first entered the Royal Navy in January 1846 when he was 30 years of age. This advanced age for entry raises many questions and when combined with his rating of Able Seaman it could be rightly construed that he had only general seafaring experience prior to 1846. If this is correct, the question remains – why? And, what was William doing prior to 1846?

With my curiosity raised, I decided to explore the 'Conduct' reports in his file in the hope it could offer another angle as to why he was excluded from his uncle's Will? His entire service record from 26 January 1846 to 11 May 1869 has over twenty vessels listed - several with back-to-back postings, and under the heading of Conduct are the words - 'Good' or 'V.Good' - except for two instances where it is listed as 'Fair' and 'Indifferent'. Unfortunately, no further notations were made in either instance to explain why these less favourable comments were made. When taken at face value, his navy record indicates that early on in life William could have simply lacked ambition. It was not until mid-1856 that he finally achieved the rank of Quartermaster which by the way, is quite a responsible position. Broadly speaking a Quartermaster is equivalent to a Petty Officer on a man-of-war vessel and his role is to attend the helm and binnacle while the ship is at sea and stand on watch for signals [messages] when in port.

His service record shows him serving on a variety of vessels as he makes the transitioning from sail to steam. The list of man-of-war vessels on which he served includes - Raleigh 50 guns, *Daedalus* 46 gun, *Princess Royal* 91 gun screw propelled second-rate, *James Watt* 84 gun Cressy Class, *Impregnable* 98 gun and *Trafalgar* a 120 gun of the Caledonia Class. The April 1861 English Census lists William Young as Quartermaster on board the British Royal Navy ship *Hardy;* an Albacore-class wooden screw gunship which gives its address for the purposes of the Census as 'located near Amoy Harbour [Xiamen]', just off the Coast of China. This census data has been positively crosschecked to his Service Record to verify it is our William Young.

So, do still waters run deep with this family when it comes to perceived disloyalty? We know that at one point William volunteered. We know that he was excluded from Joshua Richmond's Will. But, was volunteering his only crime against his family? Sadly, we may never know the answer.

Time to turn attention to the various Atlantic Trade Routes now to see what can be learnt of their experiences on these voyages.

And then 1750-1850

We know from Lloyd's Register that several Youngs and Dicks as well as Joshua Richmond sailed to the Americas, Africa and the West Indies, including Grenada, a known source of slaves taken primarily to the Americas. What we don't know for sure is whether or not Youngs were participants in the Slave Trade as part of what was termed the 'Triangular Trade' that flourished in this 1750-1850 century. This trade was not only sanctioned by Parliament, it proved very lucrative for Shipowners and Masters. Basically, it worked like this - rum and manufactured goods were taken from Scottish ports on the Atlantic Coast, principally Glasgow and Greenock, to various colonial settlements on the west coast of Africa. From there these same ships were used to transport slaves to the Plantations of the Americas and the West Indies whereupon the ships would be loaded with a cargo of Sugar, Tobacco and Cotton bound for British and European ports which of course included Scotland.

We also know that Youngs visited Antigua and that Captain Joshua Richmond, son-in-law to Alexander Young [1750-1817], had sailed from Greenock to the West Indies regularly, and to the British Island of Jamaica specifically, where he had fathered a child with an Elizabeth Beveridge. So, it is not beyond the realms of possibility that he, or others of them were Masters of vessels transporting slaves, albeit legally.

Another trade arrangement particularly favourable to Scotland in this current century was the Colonial Molasses Trade, which proved to be even bigger than the Slave Trade for Merchants and Shipowners alike. Molasses, a liquid form of sugar, was a major export commodity for the British Colonial Plantations in the West Indies and America. Whilst the molasses was used ostensibly for processing into rum some was redirected for the production of beer as well. The market for Rum was solid and while it had been a fashionable drink in Britain for some time, interestingly, the Royal Navy did not begin its rum tradition until after the Napoleonic Wars when sailors began receiving their daily rum ration called a tot. Previous to this, sailors in the Royal Navy received a beer ration. It is noteworthy to mention that the brewing of beer in Scotland can be traced back some 5,000 years where in the beginning a wild herb called Meadowsweet was used to flavour the ale. It is because of this that the Scots palate was conditioned to favour a sweeter style of ale rather than the hops style preferred by their English neighbours. So popular was this beverage in Scotland that by the mid-19th century Edinburgh could boast forty breweries and was 'recognised as one of the foremost brewing centres in the world' in the day.

The Molasses Trade prospered and as a consequence a trade war broke out between the British Colonies in America and the British, French, Dutch and Spanish West Indies. When The Molasses Act of 1733 was introduced into the British Parliament it was designed to remedy that situation by imposing a tax on New Englanders in order to placate the colonists in the British West Indies who wanted to force all American colonists, but especially those in New England, to import their molasses exclusively from the British West Indies. However, there remained a lingering feeling in Westminster that the American colonies were favouring foreign suppliers anyway, especially given the shrewd New England distillers had openly declared that such a tax would make them uncompetitive. As a result, they not only opposed the tax, they rarely paid it even when it was imposed, and in the end resorted to smuggling, bribery and intimidation of customs officials and ships captains which effectively nullified the Law. Against this backdrop, a retired Professor at Stanford and notable American Historian, John C. Miller, wrote 'Against the Molasses Act, Americans had only their smugglers to depend upon - but these redoubtable gentry proved more than a match for the British.' At another point, with the Molasses Trade being so lucrative, local plantation owners in the Caribbean resorted to selling rum at discounted prices to Navy Captains in an attempt to buy protection from local pirates.

Trade for the Port of Glasgow specifically, in the early decades of this century, was most certainly dominated by the importation of Tobacco. Situated on the Clyde River on the west coast of Scotland, Glasgow for a time became the port of greatest activity for tobacco and that city experienced rapid expansion on the back of the wealth of the so called 'Glasgow Tobacco Lords'. In 1771 a local Merchant by the name of Tobias Smollett is reputed to have advised a group of local merchants that fellow merchant and shipowner, John Glassford, 'had

And then 1750-1850

at one time five and twenty ships with their cargoes - his own property - and to have traded for above half a million sterling a year'. That is Bill Gates Microsoft level business! A lasting legacy of this Tobacco Trade is the neo-classical buildings surviving in Glasgow today, such as William Cunninghame's Mansion on Queen Street, all of which owe their origin to the wealth of these 'Tobacco Lords'.

Another port that shared in the wealth and growth during this period was Joshua Richmond's home-port of Greenock. Way back in 1710 Greenock's port facilities had been enlarged solely to cater to the quantity of sugar and rum moving through the port. These commodities began arriving on larger and larger ships- ships too big to be able to proceed up the Clyde River to the Port facilities of Glasgow.

What was it like to sail the Atlantic in that era of wood and canvas? What were the sailing conditions experienced? And, who were the passengers and what was the cargo these Youngs and others were transporting?

To gain further insight into the nitty-gritty of Atlantic voyaging, conditions on board ship, the weather, the ships and the like it was time to turn to a wonderful journal from 1774 belonging to a Miss Janet Schaw. In it she records her journey from Leith on the Firth of Forth to the West Indies and on to the Americas where she and her brother were voyaging to visit another brother living on a plantation in South Carolina. Whilst her journal offers a passenger perspective of shipboard conditions there is no doubt that her descriptions of the weather and her comments in relation to the behaviour of the owner and the captain, in particular, make an eye-opening read. Her story begins as she embarks the vessel *Jamaica Packet* at 9 o'clock on the evening of the 25th October 1774 whereupon she confides to her diary that she felt compelled to immediately complain to the captain that her cabin was dirty. Alas he fobbed her off by replying all ships were the same and things would settle down once they were under way.

She wrote that her bed chamber 'which is dignified with the title of State Room, is about five foot wide and six long'. This is certainly not commodious especially considering there is a bed on either side, albeit a very narrow one, which she contends will preclude any worthwhile sleep being enjoyed. A short time later her brother arrives on board and proceeds immediately to her cabin to inform her that should she hear any screaming from on deck, not to be alarmed, as it is only Ovid 'our owners poor Devil of a Negro man who has been laid in irons until the ship is out to sea'.

Finally, Janet received word that the ship was about to weigh anchor and she wrote of the great commotion which erupted describing it as a time when 'much hustle, bustle, noise, and confusion raged thro' our wooden kingdom'. Things calmed somewhat for a short time then, before they had even sailed out of the Firth, the captain was announcing a change of course. Apparently, due to the direction of the prevailing winds, it was to be north over the top of Scotland they would sail amid squalls and swells.

Janet complained to her diary that by morning everyone was 'beyond squeamish' and their passage was so rough it was hard to 'keep our feet one moment'. She maintained the temperatures and conditions being experiencing were the worst in the world; the air was bitter beyond expression and they have 'constant dragling rain'. At this point she expresses sympathy for the poor sailors 'who are hardly able to stand out the watch; and as they never fail to be wet thro' and thro'. With all that going on, she chides the captain again about her cabin and conditions; however, her remarks failed to strike a chord with the man who chooses to remain oblivious to her discomfort. Conversely, he brazenly remarked to her on the smoothness of the vessel, which he declares 'so soft in her motion, that one may play at Bowls on the deck'. These descriptions leave the reader in no doubt that the captain was a pompous, sarcastic and indifferent individual.

Janet Schaw is not persuaded in the slightest by his assertions and tells her diary of the possibility of losing a tooth in her desire to enjoy a simple cup of tea and declares once more her disbelief at the captain's overstating of the gentleness of their sail. However, she did honestly confide that the Mate seemed to concur with his Master when he went on to draw comparison to a previous crossing of the Atlantic when they were - 'forced to ly flat on their faces, which the hogs stubbornly refusing, had their brains knocked out against the sides of the ship'. She then chides 'How happy are we, who are only in danger of losing teeth and breaking limbs'. Despite Janet's protestations a check of the Ships Muster Rolls held in Bristol indicates that the *Jamaica Packet* was clearly a sound vessel as these Muster Rolls show it had been making this voyage to the West Indies on a regular basis since at least 1748.

On the issue of the probity of the Captain, once again Janet's diary gives a tremendous insight into what he purports to be 'normal practice' on board. Enticed by her brother to take a turn on deck for a dose of fresh sea air and believing their little party were the sole passengers on board, save for the black slave Ovid, Janet Schaw was immediately confronted with quite a shocking sight; a deck covered with humankind aged, she surmised, from three weeks to three score years, about whom she writes 'Never did my eyes behold so wretched, so disgusting a sight. They looked like a Cargo of Dean Swift's Yahoos newly caught'. The captain confessed that they too were 'smuggled aboard privately' on behalf of the owner. She confides to her journal that she is somewhat distraught now, acknowledging the ship is so overloaded that waves are flooding over the decks, that many people are already soaked through and as if that was not enough, she was made even more anxious by what she saw and felt. As the ship rounded a group of islands the rag tag exiles made it known this was once their home-land which they know they will never set eyes on again. She later engaged in conversation with some of the wretches only to realise their real misery and later wrote with some compassion for their plight.

As the *Jamaica Packet* sailed on past the Fair Isle, which would be the exiles last glimpse of their Scottish homeland, Janet pronounced these Isles were much lacking in beauty, describing them as but a line of perpendicular rugged rocks finally giving way to one well-looking house, which she was told by the wretches, belonged to the proprietor of the Island. Then at a little distance she espied what she described as a poor excuse for a town composed of huts and a church. She later observed several stockyards, but 'neither a tree nor a shrub' was to be seen.

A short time later while Janet and her brother were preoccupied watching a second flotilla of small craft approaching their vessel with supplies, when they hear calls of 'murder, help, murder'. Turning around they observe the captain and several of the crew binding one of the previously-boarded islanders to the mast and stripping off his clothes. She learned that some month's prior the captain had come to grief on the shoreline here and was still angry at losing a chest of his belongings which he was asserting this person or persons known to him had stolen.

Later in her diary, Janet Schaw refers to the captain as 'Supercargo', which is clearly not his real name or an unbefitting nickname. Intrigued by the term I undertook to investigate. It appears that supercargo was a maritime word in common use in the day which is more an explanation of his role on the ship than any superlative describing the man himself. A person described as 'supercargo' was an officer of a merchant ship, more commonly the captain, who was considered trustworthy and therefore duly authorised to arrange the sale of the ship's cargo and was responsible for signing all other necessary commercial and financial documentation as required to secure the said sale on behalf of the owner/s of the cargo.

In comparing this voyage and conditions to similar ones undertaken by the Youngs, it seems Janet Schaw's main concern remained the horrid weather and raging seas. She gives a lengthy description of one circumstance where 'The Vessel which was one moment mounted to the clouds and whirled on the point [of a] wave, descended with such violence, as made her tremble for half a minute with shock, and it appears to me wonderful how her planks stuck together, considering how heavy she was loaded. Nine hogsheads of water which were lashed on the deck gave way, and falling backwards and forwards over our heads, at last went overboard with a dreadful noise. Our hen-coops with all our poultry soon followed, as did the cab-house or kitchen, and with it all our cooking utensils, together with a barrel of fine pickled tongues and above a dozen hams'. And so, the journey proceeded amidst foul weather, wretched exiles soaked to the skin and decks awash day and night, not to mention

And then 1750-1850

grave concern about where their next meal would come from after all their livestock and some of their supplies were washed overboard. Not a pleasant experience for any poor soul; however, it would appear to be typical of Atlantic Crossings. Given these voyages took weeks it is fair to say such voyages were a trying and miserable experience for both passengers and crew.

This provides a convenient segue to explore shipboard life and weather conditions on land, ice and at sea for all those Youngs who braved the Northern Whale Fishery.

This is a much chronicled topic and initially I perused the 1842 publication of Professors Leslie and Jameson and Hugh Murray, Esq entitled *'Narrative of Discovery and Adventure in the Polar Seas and Regions: ... and an account of The Whale Fishery'* which begins the discussion of this region by looking into the climate, geology, vegetation and variety of animal life on land and in the water. It gives a great insight into just what these early Young seafarers would have seen of land and life forms. The publication goes on to chronicle the various exploratory voyages undertaken and relative to this Young story dedicates Chapter IX to *'The Northern Whale Fishery'*. Their book is a compilation publication drawing on a variety of archival material and is dedicated to Sir John Barrow, a one-time Secretary of the Admiralty, who was a graduate of Edinburgh University and a member of the Raleigh Club, a forerunner to the Royal Geographical Society. In 1846 Barrow himself wrote extensively on the Arctic and Arctic voyages and was widely recognised as a proponent of discovery in the Polar Seas and Regions.

Chapter IX - *'The Northern Whale Fishery'* - offers a summary of the earliest knowledge of the Industry -

> 'We have formerly had occasion to notice the great number and stupendous magnitude of those animal forms with which nature has filled the abysses of the Arctic Ocean. The cetaceous orders, which include the mightiest of living beings, belong peculiarly, and in

some respects exclusively, to those northern depths. Confident in their multitude and their strength, they would for ever have rested peaceful and undisturbed amid the vast and dreary domain Providence has given them to occupy, had not the spirit of avarice commenced against them a deadly warfare. Man, ever searching the remotest parts of the globe for objects which might contribute to his use and accommodation, discovered in these huge animals a variety of substances fitted for the supply of important wants. Even after his more refined taste rejected their flesh as food, the oil was required to trim the winter lamp, and to be employed in various branches of manufacture; while the bone, from its firm, flexible, and elastic quality, is peculiarly fitted for various articles of dress and ornament. No sooner, therefore, had the course of discovery opened a way into the seas of the north, than he discerned the benefits which might be derived from snatching the spoil of these tenants of the frozen waters. He commenced against them a system of attack, that was soon converted into a regular trade, but one more full of adventure and peril than any other by which man subsistence is earned'.

Who were the first of the Young family to participate in this Northern Whale Fishing Industry?

There may have been Young family seafarers and indeed whale fishermen before Alexander Young [1750-1817] and his father Robert Young [1723-1797] but at this time that notion remains conjecture. What has been proven, courtesy of the Bounty Claim Forms for 1768-1808 stored in the Scottish Archives, is that both of these men did venture into the icy waters of the Arctic for decades. From what has been learned to date it is clear that Robert Young's early whaling career probably began in the early 1740s. The earliest confirmed seafaring reference in any official record for Robert Young lists him as

'Seaman' in the 1749 Marriage Register for Leith. By 1769 and with over two decades of experience behind him we find he has established a solid career as a Greenlandman. Among the surviving documents the first discovery for Robert Young was as a Steersman on the *Campbelltown* of Leith in 1769. Then in the following year Robert joins the crew of the *Princess of Wales* where he continues to serve, forging a long and successful career as Mate, Steersman, Line Manager and Harpooner right up until 1785. There is one unexplained gap of two consecutive years and on turning to Lloyd's Register it was confirmed that the *Princess of Wales* had sailed to Greenland from Leith with her regular Captain James Muirhead as Master. At this time it is impossible to know whether this gap in the Bounty Claim Records is as a result of the documents being lost or misplaced, or whether the ship returned clean and no Intent to Claim the Bounty forms were submitted; however, it is safe to assume that the crew remained intact.

What is obvious to even the casual observer is that whaling in the Arctic was dangerous work and sometimes it is only the notations in Lloyd's Register which can alert a researcher to a potentially dangerous encounter. For the captain and crew of the *Princess of Wales*, including our Robert Young, the 1775 season was an occasion marred by an event which would have caused the ship to limp home with damage so severe she would be forced to miss the following season. Lloyd's Register indicates that in 1776 the ship was forced to undergo extensive repairs, termed 'Group Repairs'. This repair work kept her out of action for some time, and indeed she was not ready for re-survey until the February of 1777. Thankfully, this would have ensured she was ready for the upcoming whaling season.

Incidents of this nature would force crewmembers to find alternate employment and this is when we see Robert Young sailing to the Arctic as Steersman on board the *Blessed Endeavour* - something he did for only that one season of 1776. Bounty Claim forms for 1777 show the *Princess of Wales* heading north once again with Captain James Muirhead as Master and Robert Young as Steersman. Indeed, this remains the status quo for Robert Young until 1785. By that time, he is 63 years of age and considered a veteran in Greenland terms. Without doubt, he would have been counting himself lucky to have survived and by rights one would expect he would have been looking towards his retirement; however, it seems he had two more seasons left in him – and it was going to be all about family!

1786 Robert Young sails north as Harpooner on the *Friendship* under the command of Captain William Paton, a descendant of his great-great grandmother. His final sail came in 1788 when he sails north for one last memory-making voyage, this time on board the *Royal Bounty* and again under the command of Captain William Paton. On this voyage Robert is listed as both Mate and Harpooner.

What then was the whaling history for their home-port of Leith? What were the precursor events that enticed so many Youngs to risk life and limb in the whale fishing trade?

Harking back to the years when Robert would have begun his seafaring career, the Port of Leith was already a beehive of activity with fishing and shipbuilding well entrenched as well as a buoyant mercantile trade; after all it was the main port for Edinburgh. With the boom in general commerce and whaling came a corresponding boom in jobs for sailors, which would have made it much easier to gain an apprenticeship and for any ordinary or able seaman to find work. With respect to whaling specifically and the newly formed Edinburgh Whale Fishing Company in particular, it all began with the *Tryall* - a 333 ton purpose built and fitted-out whaling ship. Much had been learned down the years about what constituted a bespoke whaler; and, in the day, she was designed and built with her bow either heavily reinforced or doubled. Coppering became quite commonplace sometime later. These various reinforcing options offered protection against the collision forces of icebergs as they were pushed about by the gales and all too often dashed into the path of helpless ship, or worse still, enveloping them and crushing them. All of these dangers are indiscriminate and have proven fatal for many whaling ships. Captain William Allan was at the helm that memorable day of April 17 as the *Tryall* sailed out of Leith boasting an experienced crew of over forty men drawn from Leith, Newhaven, Bo'ness and Edinburgh. I would like to think our Robert Young was amongst their number. Sadly, to this time no crew list for the *Tyrall* has been discovered.

The *Tryall* returned to port victorious on September 22 and the ship's surgeon Dr Gregory Grant came in for particularly high praise. It is said that he not only ministered to the crew sufficient to bring every man home in good health but 'In a case of the greatest difficulty and hazard, he took the command of the ship upon him for some time, and was, in the hands of a kind Providence, the sole instrument of saving the ship and crew'. There is no further mention of any calamity or what befell Captain Allan, however, as an expression of their extreme gratitude the Edinburgh Whale Fishing Company presented Dr Grant with 'a large case of chirugal instruments, the neatest that could be made, with an inscription and device on a silver plate, signifying the intent of the gift'. Despite being afforded the opportunity to nominate his wage for the next season, it seems Dr Grant remained ever mindful of the dangers he witnessed on his last voyage to Greenland and the word is that he not only refused to sign on for another season he quit the whale fishing life altogether.

As for the *Tryall*, she sailed again in 1751 but this time in company with the *Royal Bounty*, which the Edinburgh Whale Fishing Company had only recently brought up from London. Come 1753 and the *Princess of Wales* with Master Matthew King, in company with the *Campbelltown* with Master George Steel, and the *Edinburgh* had all joined the fleet of the Edinburgh Whale Fishing Company sailing for Spitzbergen and East Greenland. These same vessels continued to do so for over a decade, which is a credit to the skill of their respective Captains and crews. Our own Captain Alexander Young's maritime record has his name associated with all of these vessels as well as intrinsically linked to the Edinburgh Whale Fishing Company. In fact, Alexander Young's career in the Arctic can be traced back at least to the *Royal Bounty* in 1768, where he began as an Apprentice and progressed to Sailor, then sometime later he is found as Mate and Line Manager on the *North Star* for the 1780/81/82 seasons then in 1783 he takes on the roles of Mate and Harpooner. Clearly, he learned the business from the ground up.

In the day, the whaling fleet traditionally set sail in late March to early April and depending on catch and conditions would return to harbour anytime from July to September. 1754 proved a bumper year for the *Royal Bounty* who returned with ten fish at a time when the average catch was around five to six. Sue Mowat writes that by 1757 Leith Roads 'had become the habitual mustering point for the vessels of the Edinburgh, Aberdeen, Dunbar and Merse Whaling Companies' who had become acutely aware of the ever-present danger from privateers. Evidence of this activity continuing is contained in a hand-written affidavit by Alexander Young Snr when he was Master of the *Blessed Endeavour* and again when he was claiming the Bounty on behalf of The East Lothian & Merse Whale Fishing Company when he was sailing out of Dunbar in 1784. Of those skippers who preferred to travel in convoy from Leith, only a handful among them took the added precaution of arming their whalers with canon.

In an attempt to gauge Leith and indeed Scotland's success, I became aware that there was a Parliamentary obligation for Scotland to submit an annual return to the Exchequer. It was a statistical account of the whaling season and these records are held at National Archives at Kew in London. The return for 1755 bears the simple title - Account for Scottish Whaling – and was submitted to the Parliamentary Council in the October of that year. It is typical of those that survive. It lists the vessels, their port, burthen, catch and the bounty paid. Evidentially the catches that year were substantial; however, as time went on it is reported elsewhere that the profits of the Edinburgh Whale Fishing Company and others were being significantly eroded by bad weather conditions and heavy losses sustained when ships were crushed and sunk. It was only after a succession of bad luck events that the Edinburgh Whale Fishing Company decided to take action: 1756 they lost a ship due to 'sea hazard', and again in 1757 a vessel had to be abandoned when it became stuck fast in the pack ice. In 1760 Thomas Hogg wrote a letter to London on behalf of the Edinburgh Whale Fishing Company seeking to insure four ships for some £1200. One question that remains unanswered so far is - would such insurance also cover losses inflicted by privateers and smugglers?

In 1760 Alexander Snr is 10 years old and no doubt getting eager to take his first voyage. While this does seem young by today's standards, The Parish Apprentices Act of 1698 had previously reduced the allowable age of entry into Apprenticeship to seven years of age. For later generations of the Young family it seems the norm was more 10-12 years with several lads showing great aptitude and making captain by the age of 24 years. The name of the vessel on which he made his first voyage is unknown; however, during the 1760s and 1770s the *Royal Bounty, Campbelltown* and *Princess of Wales* all sailed from Leith to the Greenland Fishing Grounds. In the case of this Alexander [1750-1817] it is fair to state that since his name is attached to all of these vessels that he may well have sailed to Greenland in the whaling season and to the Baltic the other six months of the year.

Confidence in whaling remained strong once the Bounty was raised to forty shillings in 1750; which also meant there was no shortage of investment. So much so that by 1771 The Edinburgh Whale Fishing Company was boasting over 220 shareholders, holding some 366 shares with nineteen of those investors being Leith residents. Sadly, to date no shareholders Register has been discovered but given the contents of Alexander's Will and his undoubted enthusiasm for investing in all manner of maritime business opportunities, it would be gratifying to imagine that he and indeed his father were part of that shareholder contingent.

As for the general feeling among the residents in Leith, it seems that this increase in whaling activity was not welcomed by many. Records for the Royal Burgh show that during July 1750, while the *Tyrall* was still in the Arctic, there was quite a commotion in the port, not because of privateering or press-gangs this time but because The Edinburgh Whale Fishing Company had petitioned the Council for a stretch of land on which to build the first Boiling House for rendering blubber. The land they nominated was part of the Sands and situated on the outskirts of the north wall of the Bush. Word is that local Leith residents protested loudly about the unpleasant odour that would be produced by a Boiling House and how it would impact residents given the direction of the prevailing winds in that area. But as Sue Mowat rightly contends, it - 'must have been dreadful indeed if it was worse than the normal reek of middens and cesspits, which pervaded the town'. In the end, approval was forthcoming although certain building restrictions were placed on its construct stipulating that 'Any chimney stacks were to be made in their own north wall and not on the wall of the Bush' - [i.e. as far away as possible from the residential area].

Fast forward three decades it is now 1781, and clearly whale fishing and trading was prospering as did privateering. The Royal Navy decided to increase its presence in Leith by building a small Naval Yard on the western half of the land to the east of the Bush. It seems Leith had been identified as a port 'best qualified for cleaning, careening and refitting Her Majesty's ships'. Returning to Brian Lavery's publication *'Shield of Empire .....'* wherein he points out that the advantage of this site was that the area 'was well supplied with all sorts of naval stores from the east country [ie. the Baltic], such as deals, hemp, pitch and tar, iron and of course the Oak which was imported from Lubeck and Danzig identified as 'generally fit for hoys and small vessels ...'.

Notwithstanding that assertion, England remained the preferred supplier of Oak to be used as mast timber. In this, there was a trade-off for the Navy, which may account for some of the 'pleasantries' shared with the Greenlanders sailing out of Leith. In the off-season these whaling ships became part of the merchant fleet sailing to the Baltic and Archangel and often times they enjoyed the luxury of a naval escort. This appears to be purely a matter of self-interest on the part of the Navy given they were one of the largest single consumers of some of the key imports such as tar. Safe passage for any cargo of tar was imperative if the Navy was to maintain their fleet in a seaworthy state. The Navy continued these escort services throughout the Dutch and French Wars but not without mishaps as will soon be revealed.

Meanwhile, business was booming for the Scottish Whaling Fleet, so much so that by 1792 The Edinburgh Whale Fishing

And then 1750-1850

Company had applied for a further extension to their Boiling House premises. Also, by this time, Alexander is 42 years of age, and has earned respect for his success whaling in Greenland and Spitzbergen, and for safely sailing foreign trade routes. His achievements were noteworthy especially when put into the context of the times and the reputation of the port of Leith. His solid career was established in an era plagued with mischief and miscreants, in a port renowned for trouble and strife. From a genealogy perspective it could rightly be asserted that his character was such that he somehow managed to rise above it all.

Time now to consider what constituted a day in the life of a Greenland whale fisherman? And, what can we learn about the voyages of Alexander Young while he was Captain of the famous Leith vessel the *Raith?*

By chance I came across Robert Smith's book *'The Whale Hunters',* which gives a graphic account of the 1791 season for several ships of the Scottish whale fishing fleet. This was a lucky find for our story because Smith actually mentions the *Raith* of Leith and since I already knew that Alexander Young was the Master of the *Raith* that year it is the only firsthand account that could tell us anything of his actual experiences. Smith's book is recounting the experiences of a person by the name of George Kerr, who was Surgeon on board another Scottish whaler that year, the *Christian* of the Aberdeen Whale Fishing Company. George Kerr's original Surgeon's Journal is held in the Special Collections area of the Library at the University of Aberdeen. The *Raith* and the *Christian* were part of the large contingent of vessels that comprised the Scottish Whale Fishing Fleet that 1791 season.

From the outset, Kerr was keen to impress upon Smith that any time at latitude 77°N whalemen can be confronted with two perilous dangers - one is being beset by the ice, the other suffering frostbite or worse as a result of the gnawing and unrelenting cold. When recalling his experiences some decades afterwards it would seem that Kerr's painful memory of the cold searing his flesh and penetrating his bones was as vivid as if it had happened yesterday. Kerr remembered it as a particularly nasty season; a time when he saw 'men carrying shovels laden with hot coals to thaw the spirit casks on the vessel'. 'Water and beer froze on the tables, drugs iced up in the medicine chest, and beef had to be cut with a saw'. Kerr explained that he could not even make entries in his diary because the ink in the inkwell had frozen. Apparently, there was no respite to be found in sleep either, as he recalled that 'his pillow was frozen solid like a block of ice.'

It is impossible to imagine conditions getting any worse but, apparently, they did. As the *Christian* sailed further north beyond Jan Mayen Island [Spitzbergen] the crew began experiencing hoar frost, which blew in clouds, 'like a summer fog in Scotland' he said. The *Christian* had all her sails and rigging dusted with a fine white powder and needless to say the ropes became so stiff that any manoeuvre of them was virtually impossible. They later came upon a mere handful of Scottish whalers as they too made their way north closer to the Arctic Circle. Kerr recalled two of the vessels encountered as the *Raith* and *Neptune* of Leith. The *Christian* in convoy with the *Raith*, *Neptune* and others remained on the heading to push further north as the icebergs became heavier. Kerr estimated one such berg to be 'above a mile in length and about 40 feet thick'. Fishing success so far that season had eluded all the fleet and George Kerr's assessment was 'that unless they had better luck before the end of the season it was likely that fewer than half of them would [survive to] return the following year'.

Kerr's next observation adds significantly to the academic findings from statistical evidence, which states that right from the very beginning the Dutch had cemented their place as the best and most successful fishermen in the Northern Whale Fishery. Kerr's assessment was that the Dutch not only had the best of men they also had the finest of vessels for the task. He backed up his assessment with a detailed description of a cluster of Dutch whalers. He described them as magnificent vessels with three rows of cabin windows 'one story for the harpooners upon the top, the middle for the master, and the surgeon and cook below'. Did Smith detect a touch of envy in Kerr's voice as he related this story? I wonder. Anyhow, Kerr went on to explain that of the seventy-one whalers the

Christian fell in with at the edge of the sea ice, the Dutch were the largest in number and clustered together, held fast by their sea anchors so that at night they resembled 'the appearance of the distant view of a city'.

Kerr remembers the ice was 'stretched as far as the eye could see, ten feet high above the water, broken into pieces about a quarter of a mile to half a mile in diameter.' By the evening of the 21 May the *Christian* is totally beset by ice along with 38 other vessels including the two Leith whalers *Raith* and *Neptune*. A handful of lucky ships had managed to make their way out of the drifting ice; however, word came the next day that sadly the Neptune of Leith had been crushed and lost without word as to the fortunes of her crew. Kerr went on - as another day dawned, he had seen 'a line of men crossing the ice about three miles away, carrying a red ensign with a white cross on it'. He and the crew presumed they were Danes. So, the *Christian* decided to send provisions, assuming these men were in trouble. When the crew of the *Christian* finally reached the men, they were surprised to learn that the presumed 'Danes' were indeed members of the *Raith*'s crew. The story goes they had spotted a dead whale on the ice and had set out to claim it. George Kerr adds that shortly after those men had made their way clear of the *Raith*, disaster struck when ice broke away from the main mass, drifted off taking the *Raith* with it. Kerr reported that the *Raith* and her crew survived on this occasion despite Mother Nature. Was this Alexander Young's first lucky escape?

Kerr then confided some personal memories of the dire conditions that crews endured on every voyage, and this includes the Youngs. He spoke of the fear they endured while lying in their bunks forced to listen to the heart stopping creaking and groaning of the hull under the unrelenting pressure of the pack ice. He also recalled how sleepless nights were constantly punctuated by explosions resembling canon fire as timbers give way or ice breaks off. He described that frightening sight of ice shearing off or when 'huge pieces of ice [were] being thrown into the air. If one of them had landed on a ship it would have had the effect of a stone falling on an egg-shell'.

That season the *Christian* lay captive with the *Raith* and so many others that Kerr could not count them all. He was forced to relive every harrowing moment, recalling how the ice movements would taunt them by easing and flowing but hanging onto them just the same. On one occasion the crew of the *Christian* were so afraid their end was nigh they had 'hauled out their bedding and made ready to abandon ship' only to have the danger ease and the crew return to station onboard ship.

Reading Kerr's account, what comes through is that he was obviously an educated but broken man, his account was lucid, descriptive and philosophic as he related the heartbreak of crisis after crisis. It seems this is the way it was for whale fishermen who took to the high latitudes. At one juncture a contemplative George Kerr, perhaps sensing Smith's incredulity at hearing such an unbelievably distressing tale, offered a final observation to Smith on what it was like for an Arctic whale fisherman to be in these situations when he said it was '... a fine school for an impatient man!'

Kerr explained that on another occasion word filtered across the ice to say as many as ten vessels had been lost that previous night. Almost wanting to dismiss that thought as soon as it sprung to mind, a contemplative Kerr quickly added that often such intelligence was hard to confirm. Clearly, he had not wanted to acknowledge the devastating losses inferred. As for the *Christian*, to a man they had long abandoned any vestige of a hope of fishing, adding that all endeavours were focused on survival as everyone prayed for an escape from what Kerr described as their 'ice-bound prison'. Interestingly, as I read on it seems that even amidst this misery and stress certain rituals were still observed. Kerr recounted one Sunday when he heard the bells ring out from the Dutch whalers calling their crews to prayer. At other times, men could be seen criss-crossing the ice, creating well-trodden pathways as they trudged from ship to ship to exchange gossip, reminisce about home, join in prayer or to simply share a drink - anything to dull the pain of their predicament. It is also interesting to note that while their respective national governments may have been at war from time to time the whale fishermen themselves seemed to subscribe to a fraternity of their own which left international political disputation aside. No doubt an arrangement forged out of their shared condition.

Kerr appears to be on an emotional rollercoaster as he recounted his experiences for Smith. Kerr's mood was once again uplifted for a moment as he related one very happy memory when he crossed the ice to the Dutch vessel *Pro Partia*. Smith captured the essence of Kerr's account when he wrote that Kerr said he 'was welcomed on board by a bluff Falstaffian figure who turned out to be the Captain. He was ..... a great overgrown fellow, scarce fit to totter along the deck. Fifty years old, he was a veteran Arctic whaler, having sailed to Greenland every year since he was ten years old'. Cordiality meant the simple sharing of a coffee and playing the fiddle together - Scots music of course as it was known to be very popular with the Dutch. Kerr became quite emotional as he described in loving refrains the sound of those reels and schottisches echoing across the ice on that sorrowful day.

Then just as quickly Kerr's mood changed, almost as if he wanted to retain some very private images of those moments all to himself. He then got back on track and very business-like as he spoke of rendering medical attention to an Englishman with a gangrenous foot before cautiously making his way back to the *Christian*. While on the surface, this particular portion of Kerr's story starts out like taking an evening stroll, catching up with friends, enjoying some light-hearted frivolity, and returning home; all this belies the reality of their helplessness and melancholy. At this point they had already been stuck fast for months, tormented by the cruel and unpredictable Arctic ice, and all the while hoping and praying that they and their ship would survive.

Amongst the civility it seems examples of uncivilised behaviour were never far away. Kerr recalls one unhappy incident taking place when two Dutch vessels were wrecked. Men from the *Christian* went over the side to try to salvage wood and ropes and were suddenly 'attacked by the Dutchmen, and [likewise] when the Christian was holed by ice they had to fight off Dutchmen who had come to plunder their vessel'. It was all about survival. This is what life was like for these intrepid whale fishermen, including Alexander Young and his crew on-board the *Raith*. Kerr's story is not unique in that sense. He was simply recounting the tragedies these philosophic Arctic seafarers confronted every season and yet we know many of them returned year after year.

Given all we know it is impossible for a twenty-first century reader to fully understand what drew men to this life. For the captains and shipowners, the risks were high, the rewards variable, and it was only the odd good season and the Government Bounty that enticed many to persevere. In the case of the humble seamen, the risks for them were higher as they did the most dangerous jobs and their rewards equally variable. So, in truth, it was probably the threat of homelessness and/or starvation at home that ultimately convinced them to return. Regardless of their reasons they were all impossibly brave, unbelievably stoic, uncommonly resourceful and, above all, the epitome of team players. The shelves of maritime museums and archives across the world tell story after story of men taking to these regions, and as was the case for the captain and crew of the *Christian* their resilience was frequently seriously tested as they were forced to play a watch and wait game with the elements. At times they were teased into believing that a reprieve was coming only to have all their hopes dashed. Far too often we find stories of men compelled to spend weeks or even months wondering if a reprieve would ever arrive in time.

Devastatingly, for the crew of the *Christian* that season, reprieve did not come until 21 July, which was the day she finally gained her freedom. Escaping the clutches of the ice she raised sail to head out into open water, but the going was slow, conditions deceptive and they were far from safe. It would take until 11 August before the crew would get their first glimpse of Scottish home soil. Kerr's final remembrance to Smith is reflective of his mood as the *Christian* sailed up the River Don several weeks later. At a time when you would expect everyone on board would be feeling triumphant; after all they had survived, and their ship had made home-port - in reality the mood was sombre.

Kerr's remark of 'home at last, a clean ship' was a dispirited resignation of defeat; and, despite the passage of time nothing had dulled his pain of failure or dulled his memory of those harrowing experiences. Smith too would have been left in no doubt that Kerr felt survival was not enough.

And then 1750-1850

It is appropriate now to look a little deeper into the history of the Northern Whale Fishing as an industry to see how it progressed and what that meant for the Youngs who participated. In order to prosper, the Youngs too would have been asking themselves what made the Dutch superior whalers. What could be done, if anything, to overcome their commanding position? And ultimately - what effect would this long term Dutch superiority have on Scottish Whaling?

From a genealogy perspective the question arises; how did these issues impact the prospects for Captain Alexander Young Snr?

The undeniable short answer to the first question of Dutch superiority is: Species Identification. Not only were the Dutch more skilled in catching whales they had long been more adept at selecting out those that gave the highest yields in whale oil and bone. Most commentators agree that initially the Scots were no better than the English when it came to whale fishing because they gave no credence to species identification. This attitude persisted despite the availability of catch and cask results from as early as the 1750s, which offered an instructive perspective and should have generated a call to action. For instance, the statistics for Edinburgh alone highlight blatant yield anomalies. For example, in 1753 3 whales produced 60 casks, 1754 1 whale 58 casks, and in 1755 2 whales netted 76 casks. The Government was complicit in this apathy too because they showed a complete lack of understanding of the trade, a wasteful disregard for Exchequer accountability and a myopic view of British knowhow. Shareholders and investors also failed to respond to these anomalies, which clearly demonstrated why catch numbers per se are quite misleading when determining the real profits achieved per voyage. There were no winners, just lessons to be learned - and fast if the industry was to become viable into the future.

Emeritus Professor Chesley W. Sanger makes the point in his book - *'Scottish Arctic Whaling'* - that as far back as July 1749 the Edinburgh Courant newspaper had published an editorial stating that 'The wise Hollanders have continually practiced this Fishery [...] and have thereby added immense Sums to the Wealth of the

People, as well as to the Strength of their State [...]'. The article continues to make the point that '[the value of the products harvested from the sea is estimated [...] A prodigious Sum! Which ought to cover us with shame, considering that we have had at least as great opportunities as they, of making a like advantage of this Fishery; of which for many Years past, we have not made one Shilling.' One could facetiously suggest that perhaps the shipowners and investors were playing the Government's game because they could claim the 40 shilling bounty regardless of whether the oil came from seals, walrus or whales so long as they fished in the Arctic. This attitude created a situation where there was no real incentive to be a better 'whale fisherman'. However, a call to action would soon be forced on the English, who were importing oil from the Dutch at ever increasing prices, which saw the British trade deficit blow out.

Once the English acknowledged the Dutch had long ago perfected the art of species identification and that this accounted for their overwhelming dominance for decades, Parliament acted swiftly. They repealed the old legislation regarding the hiring of crewmembers and framed new Legislation enabling British whale fishermen to hire foreign crewmembers. The Scots were quick to react by initially hiring Jutlanders and while the up-skilling of indigenous Scots occurred slowly, with more and more shipowners now legally able to engage foreigners in the key roles of Harpooners, Line Managers and Steersmen, catch numbers and profitability began to improve. Fortunately for this family, by the time Captain Alexander Young Snr became involved in the trade it had become more commonplace to hire foreign Harpooners and Line Managers for their Arctic crews and here the Bounty Claim records timeline this decision with names like Roluff Dirke, Nanning Janson, Volkart Loranson, and Hendrik Hendriks beginning to appear on Scottish Bounty Claim Forms post 1770s.

While no family records or ships logs survive relating to the whaling days of Alexander Young Snr as Master of the *Raith* we can learn something of his 1786 season thanks to the work of Dr Eric Graham. As luck would have it, on this occasion Dr Graham included a transcript of the 'Notice of Intent' in his article which related to the *Raith* and Captain Alexander

Young. Could this also mean that by 1786 the Scots had sufficient skilled homeland men? -

> 'In her first Notice, the Raith's tonnage burthen for the bounty is stated as 295 1/5 tons and carrying the prerequisite five whale boats for her hull size. Her officers are listed as Alexander Young Master, John Allan Mate and Charles Mackie Surgeon. On her return the captain had to submit an inventory of her cargo - which had to be exclusively Greenland blubber and whalebone - the number of whale boats she had carried and the names of the harpooner, steersman and line manager for each. The Muster Role listed all sailors, apprentices and 'fresh or green men' the ratio of which was also governed by statute. Apprentices had to be fourteen years old but younger than eighteen when signing on for three years with the same Master. In the case of the Raith, in 1786 she carried her full complement of thirty seamen including five apprentices, to which number must be added the officers. The final requirement of the Notice was to note the number of 'foreigners' on board - which in the case of the Raith was a 'nil' entry.'

This 1786 Notice of Intent Bounty claim form also states that 'William Black, green man, was drowned and part of the crew [24 men] left the ship (except William Thomson and John Hall sailors and James Young green man and Thomas Atkins and William Frasier apprentices) on the 24 August a little below Inch Keith for fear of being impressed'. For those not familiar with Scottish geography, Inch Keith is a tiny island in the outer Firth of Forth, situated at the midpoint between Burntisland and Leith and today is an inhospitable bare rock with the only signs of past habitation being the crumbling ruins of a disused sixteenth century fort. It is presumed that once the seamen's families were aware that the *Raith* had arrived into the Forth, they would row out, more than likely under cover of darkness, to rescue their returning kinsmen. Obviously, Alexander was an accessory to this action for two reasons. One, to assist his men avoid the Press, especially critical for those crew members who were not fully accredited Greenlandmen, and two, as insurance that he could count on those same experienced men when set to source a crew for the next season.

With respect to the whaling results achieved by Captain Alexander Young, it is courtesy of Emeritus Professor Chesley W. Sanger that I can present a table of data he specifically prepared for this story. This table gives an invaluable insight into the success or otherwise of Captain Young and the *Raith* while sailing to the Arctic on behalf of The Edinburgh Whale Fishing Company for the Bounty Seasons 1785-1794, with 1794 being the year Alexander was captured by the French. On the face of it one could presume he was one of the very lucky Captains, bearing in mind this shows he sailed to the Arctic for nine consecutive seasons, braving the icy waters and managing to return home safely every time. However, this table also raises the question of - what was happening in those four seasons 1790-1793?

TABLE 5 – Arctic Whaling Voyages – Capt Alex. Young Snr

Year	Whales	Seals
1785	10	72
1786	4	473
1787	5	1440
1788	4	
1789	2	220
1790	1	
1791	0	
1792	0	
1793	1	
1794	3	22

Once again thanks to Sanger's work we can glean some answers. In his publication *'Prologue to Scottish Domination of Northern Whaling: The Role of the French Revolutionary War, 1793-1801'* he writes that 'By the time the French Revolutionary War began in 1793, Scottish Northern whaling, after just forty-two years of activity, was again in decline. Rapid growth following the American War of Independence led to over-expansion, and in the five years leading up to the French Revolution the trade was reduced by more than a third from the record levels of thirty-one whaling vessels during the 1787 and 1789 seasons. It fell a further thirty percentile by 1793, a decline entirely precipitated by the war.' Also, from the start of the 1789 season with a recession looming in Britain and with the fishing grounds plagued by overcrowding 'Attempts to sustain the trade included a greater emphasis on [fishing in] Davis Strait ...'. However, 'Results at both East Greenland and Davis Strait were poor in 1790 ...'. Combine this with George Kerr's horrific account of the 1791 season one could presume that weather was a contributing factor and that the *Raith* was not the only ship to arrive home 'clean' through no fault on their part.

It was a similar story for the *Raith* in 1792 as well. Then, Sanger explains that 'The 1793 season continued the run of generally poor results', and we know this because the *Raith* returned with only 1 fish, and then The Montrose Review carried a report that one crewmember had drowned, so all in all not a good year for Alexander and the *Raith*. Sanger adds that these 'generally poor results, ... were offset to some extent by the fact that the whales taken at both East Greenland and Davis Strait were much larger than those caught in more than a decade. Despite this result and the government's decision to continue the bounty, although at a significantly reduced rate, the 1793 Scottish Northern whale fishery was in essence a complete failure.'

At this point, investors, shareholders and captains would have been weighing up the pros and cons, given the added pressure of the French Revolutionary War and the corresponding incursion of press gangs making it increasingly difficult to put together a qualified crew. Sanger asserts that 'At the onset of hostilities the press became vigorous, and many Scottish whalers lost their crews before arriving home. The bounty documentation for *Royal Bounty* of Edinburgh, for example, contains a note dated 31 August 1793 which provides an indication of what was occurring. It read: "N.B. part of the Crew left the Ship 23 Inst. to the northward off Montrose, for fear of being impressed." Additionally, 'French men-of-war and privateers were about to make their presence felt'. The reality of this would hit hard the very next year when in 1794 Alexander and the entire *Raith* crew would confront their worst fears. Although the Bounty records show 3 fish and 22 seals, and when their catch is considered solely in the context of the catch table, it could be presumed that things were looking up; however, it is what the Bounty Claim Forms don't show that makes for a chapter in itself.

Of far greater significance to this Young Family story is that 1794 was a watershed year for Alexander. His capture and imprisonment marked the end of Alexander's days as Master of the *Raith* and also put an unceremonious end to his long and successful association with The Edinburgh Whale Fishing Company. While this saga is expanded in an upcoming chapter what is clear is that the next seven years would be challenging for the whole Scottish fleet.

When reviewing the early 1800s Sanger suggests that 'The prospects for the Scottish Northern Whale Fishery on the eve of peace in Europe looked promising. The spirit of optimism was shared throughout the country. A report carried by an Edinburgh newspaper towards the end of the 1801 whaling season, for example, provides an indication of the favourable attitude that prevailed.' It read in part 'The [whale] Fisheries become annually more productive...Not a vessel that we have heard of this season returned empty. We are informed of many arrivals in England and Scotland with cargoes of blubber, whalebone, and spermaceti, which must afford to the adventurers in the fishing trade profits for this season far exceeding their most extravagant hopes.'

Despite the dangers and negatives at play Sanger believes that 'The French Revolutionary War was the era in which Scottish whaling entered a stage of maturity and consolidation which permitted further expansion. Not only was a continued presence in Northern whaling ensured, but by the middle of the nineteenth century the Scots would outstrip their English rivals and completely dominate the industry. The stage was set for the beginning of the 'golden age' of Scottish Northern whaling and sealing.'

I am pleased to report that this assessment is totally reflective of Alexander Young's experience - he was one of those Scots who sailed in the Golden Age of Scottish Northern Whaling and succeeded beyond his wildest dreams.

Lastly, it was time to attempt to quantify the financial results achieved by Alexander Young Snr from his voyages whale fishing in the Arctic.

In 1962 S.G.E. Lythe from the Dundee School of Economics wrote a paper for the Scottish Journal of Political Economy and although it focused mainly on the Dundee Whale Fishery, he begins with a chapter entitled *The Establishment of Scottish Arctic Whaling* explaining its value to the Scottish Economy as a whole. There are two salient points to draw from his article: one, that whaling 'illustrates the role of subsidies in the revival of the Scottish Economy', and; two, that 'Between 1750-1788 alone Scotland drew close on a quarter of a million pounds from the [British] Treasury in the form of whaling subsidies, a very substantial boost to the purchasing-power of the maritime communities.'

This windfall seems to be also reflective of the financial outcomes achieved by the Youngs, and whilst Scottish whale fishing revenue started from a low base of £2 per ship ton in the 1760s and '70s, it continued to rise slowly reaching £5 by 1785-90. A decade on and it had taken a quantum leap, escalating to £12.83 by 1795 and finally reached its zenith of £13.08 in 1801. Sometime between 1795-1801 Alexander Snr entered the whale fishing industry as a company shareholder and later a shipowner. This level of financial success goes a long way to explaining the resources itemised in his Will of 1817. I came across another chance discovery from the pen of Gordon Jackson wherein he cites the most successful vessels of the 1801 season as - *Eliza Swan* of Montrose [Captain John Young], the *Raith* of Leith [Captain Lyons] and the *Royal Bounty* of Leith [Captain Alexander Young] grossing approximately £5530, £6323 and £5463 respectively. A bonanza of a find from a genealogical perspective and what a bonanza in financial terms for the brothers and the Young Family coffers.

One of the most outstanding seasons for Alexander Snr and indeed the whole Scottish Fleet was 1799 when the *Eliza Swan* of Montrose returned with 15 fish - the top catch for the season. That same year the *Raith* sailed to Davis Strait under the guiding hand of Burrish Lyons who was Mate when Alexander was Master. Whilst the *Raith* reported leaving the Firth of Forth in company with the *Royal Bounty* [Capt. J. Newton] Lyons said they became separated in bad fog and completely lost sight of each other about 700 miles west of the Orkneys. Upon his return Lyons recounted 'never had [he] seen the *Royal Bounty* to the day of his return on 22 July' when the *Raith* logged catching '9 large whales, each one over 11 feet bone. Besides filling every cask on board to the number of 330, she came home with 10-12 butts of blubber in bulk'. These anecdotal accounts further support Sanger's contention that at this time Scottish results were showing signs of improvement.

What then is the history of whaling out of Montrose? And, why did Alexander Snr believe the port of Montrose offered greater prospects than Leith?

After over thirty years of research, I find it is impossible to say categorically why Alexander is found sailing out of Montrose however the strongest possible clues are derived by looking at the history of the Montrose Fleet. It seems Montrose was one of the east coast ports leading the way at that particular juncture. This shift of port could have been strategic because it certainly marked the beginning of the most outstanding period of his whaling career. Sanger wrote in *'The Dundee-St John's Connection: Nineteenth Century Interlinkages Between Scottish Arctic Whaling and the Newfoundland Seal Fishery'* 'that by the late 1780s England had wrested control of the Northern trade away from the Dutch. In their turn, early in the nineteenth century, the English were supplanted by the Scots.' This proved Scotland was ahead of the game but there was still the question of why Montrose?

I then turned to David Mitchell's *'History of Montrose'* published in 1866, wherein he claims to draw on both historical documents and local reminiscences. He devotes Chapter XI to all things maritime including a segment on whaling. Sadly, he does not timeline much of his script; however, after perusing that text and others it seems that sometime in the early 1780s the first whale fishing operation was founded in Montrose under the guiding hand of a local merchant by the name of John Brown. He purchased the 264 ton *Little Fanny*, one of several American ships recently arrived in Britain and being offered for sale post the American Revolutionary War. She was originally sailed into London, then on to Dunbar, which is where she was sitting in port when permission was sought for her to join the Scottish Arctic whale fishing fleet. Permission was granted which ensured the Bounty could be claimed, and so the *Little Fanny* was sailed on to Montrose from where she was fitted out ready for her maiden voyage in the April of 1785. Unfortunately, her first voyage yielded only one whale so presumably not even the £528 bounty would have covered Brown's costs. Despite the Poseidon superstition about renaming ships it seems Brown shunned that legend and a few years later he renamed the *Little Fanny* the *Montrose*. Shortly afterwards he purchased a second ship, the *Eliza Swan*. There are numerous publications stating that Eliza Swan was the sole property of *Eliza Swan*, the wife of the aforementioned John Brown.

With respect to timing and Brown's ability to source an experienced crew, Sanger states that while Scottish vessels were excluded from the trade in the early days, Scottish sailors had been venturing to the whale fishing grounds on English and foreign vessels for some years. So, once the tide turned and Scottish ships began heading north in the 1750s there were experienced men on hand. Fast-forward to the mid-1780s and this marked the time when ports outside Leith envisaged that they could go it alone and hence the port of Montrose was attempting to join the fleet. Sanger contends that 'the trade became concentrated exclusively in east coast ports where experienced owners, masters and crew employed proven Northern whaling vessels.' Now, the stage was set for Scotland to shine and Sanger believes that it was the last two decades of the eighteenth century that established Northern Whale Fishing as a Scottish tradition.

The Scots Magazine for July 1786 lists two whalers registered to the port of Montrose for the bounty that season and they were the *Little Fanny* and the *Eliza Swan* operated by Brown. Then, sometime towards the end of 1786, on West Pier, a new operator came into being known as the New Whale Fishing Company, which fitted out the *George Dempster*. There is a period of confusion among historical reports for Montrose, with conflicting company names and ownership, but what is clear is that a new company came into being and if Mitchell's 1866 account is correct the two existing operators sold their shareholding to new investors who set up the Greenland Whale Fishing Company. Mitchell states that 'Three vessels were purchased, named the *Eliza Swan*, the *Montrose*, and the [George] *Dempster*.' He further asserts that 'The vessels were fortunate for a number of years'. Gordon Jackson maintained that Montrose's love affair with the Arctic and their preferred ground of Davis Straits produced exceptional results. While geography was one factor, the results achieved also speak volumes about the well-honed skill of the Montrose based Captains and crews. In fact, by 1791 Jackson reports that those three Montrose vessels were 'responsible for 28 per cent of the oil and 33 per cent of the bone imported into Scotland'. Apparently, the *Eliza Swan* was a stand-out as her cargo comprised 60 per cent of the Montrose total.

What has also been learned is that whale fishing is plagued by disasters which present in sporadic and diverse forms. Whilst records around this time are conflicting, the majority view is that increased competition on the back of positive results naturally reduced whale stock. This was followed by an unexpected fall in the oil price due to cheaper colonial imports coming onto the market. It became a constant struggle for shareholders especially when overlaid with the fact that venturing into the fickle Arctic waters could serve up a harsh and expensive lesson at any time. The port of Montrose was about to see how menacing those waters could be when in 1792 the *Eliza Swan* would arrive home 'clean', the *George Dempster* with only 18 tuns [a cask measure] of blubber and the *Montrose* would be reported nipped in the ice and lost in Davis Strait. Fortunately, her crew was rescued. 1794 and the Greenland Whale Fishing Company lost the *George Dempster* and it is thanks to Mitchell's publication that we glean a rare insight into its sad fate. He wrote 'She was commanded by Captain David Christie. When last seen she was under a press of sail, and it was generally supposed that too much canvas had run her down. The loss of so many men was a heavy stroke to Montrose. She had a crew of picked men, and a great many widows and orphans were left destitute.' The Greenland Whale Fishing Company did not replace her rather they sold their 'Greenland Yard' [Boiling House] which became a salt-works. The last straw for Montrose came when *Eliza Swan* was withdrawn from the fishery after the 1795 season.

Undeterred by these events, and clearly believing the future prospects for whale fishing were solid it was 1798 when Alexander Young Snr [not Alexander Jnr as reported by some] purchased a controlling interest in the *Eliza Swan* and set up business as the Montrose Whale Fishing Company. Alexander applied to the Burgh for waterside land close to the port facilities on which to build a boiling house but was pushed up-river to a piece of vacant land adjacent to the salt-works. The new owner of the salt-works, James Dickson, apparently protested about it being a 'fire hazard' and much too close to his salt-works and demanded a buffer zone. The matter was finally resolved, and the remnants of Alexander's building are marked on maps and can be seen to this very day. Alexander continued to sail to the Arctic and by 1801 he and *Eliza Swan* had formed a great partnership and are credited with the 'second largest catch of the Scottish whalers ..... boiling 121 tuns of oil compared to the national average of 73 tuns'. Alexander's estimated earnings for that season alone have been put at £5,530, 'and since *Eliza Swan* was the smallest of the 'well fished' ships, her earnings per ship-ton were the highest in Scotland.'

Gordon Jackson contends the 'Montrose Whale Fishing Company's run of remarkably good catches continued for many years during this period of relatively high prices. There was, however, a countervailing factor - *Eliza Swan* had outlived her usefulness, and an optimistic assessment of future prospects produced a new Eliza Swan of 302 tons (later altered to 306 tons) for the 1807 season.' This is an instance where the Bounty Claim Forms held by the Exchequer Records of Scotland were absolutely misleading and did not and could not tell the correct story.

What is known is that future listings of *Eliza Swan* as a 306 ton ship is reflective of her new burthen after substantial work was undertaken to repair and lengthen the ship and are NOT reflective of a new ship with the same name entering the trade. As a result of damage sustained in the Arctic in 1806 substantial repairs were scheduled. It was decided by the owners that they would take advantage of this hiatus to have her lengthened as well. Once these arrangements were contracted, Alexander sailed her to Leith where the Shipbuilding firm of Strachan & Gavin had been engaged to carry out a prescribed list of works. Matters did not quite go to plan and the whole sordid tale is contained in the Admiralty Courts files. Lloyd's too is incorrect in that they have *Eliza Swan* as 241 tons and departing Leith heading to Davis Strait from 1798 to at least 1816 which we know is completely inaccurate.

So, with Captain Alexander Young Snr as Master 'The Eliza Swan continued in the trade, and in the early part of this century [nineteenth] the company purchased another vessel, the Monarch. About the same time another company was formed, who [over several years] purchased three vessels— the London, the Spencer, and the Hero.' This I believe to be the Union Whale Fishing Company. These new interlopers first sailed north in the antiquated *London*, which in 1814 and 1819 in particular, produced very profitable oil results. Encouraged by this the shareholders decided to purchase the *Spencer* in 1815, which outshone the *London* in its first two seasons. Meanwhile, since 1813 the Montrose Whale Fishing Company had been sailing north with two of the biggest ships in the Scottish fleet - the 306 ton *Eliza Swan*, with 6 whaleboats, and the new 312 ton *Monarch*, carrying 7 whaleboats.

Alexander Young Snr's sons Alexander Jnr and John successfully sailed these vessels year after year which would have made that veteran of the Arctic a very proud father indeed. In the 1814-17 period leading up to their father's death they proved themselves well and truly up to the task and recorded outstanding catch earnings. Estimates one season put *Eliza Swan's* earnings at £5,093 and *Monarch* at £8,315, and to further fill their coffers over the ensuing five years it is reported that oil and bone prices surged to the lucrative levels of £36.10s per ton for oil and £90.0s per ton for bone. And, despite the fact that the Bounty had been reduced to twenty shillings and only paid on the first 300 ship tons the almost £20,000 annual revenue the Northern Whale Fishery would have contributed to the economy of Montrose would have given the town a great financial boost.

Credit for the success enjoyed by the Montrose Whale Fishing Company must rest with Captain Alexander Young Snr who was not only a veteran Greenlandman, he went on to prove himself as astute and skilled in business as he was in sailing and whale fishing. His subsequent decision to hitch the family star to Montrose was necessitated by his changed circumstances following his capture by the French which precipitated his involuntary departure from the Edinburgh Whale Fishing Company. Looking back in hindsight, his decision to purchase the *Eliza Swan* and sail out of Montrose would prove to be a stroke of genius. Then, as the future unfolded he went from success to success in a clear case of - Right place! Right time!

For the purposes of this family's story it seemed appropriate to explore in greater detail just what more could be learned of those early years of Alexander Snr, *Eliza Swan* and the Montrose Whale Fishing Company.

I began with the 1800 season, which had come in for special mention by Basil Lubbock and others. They reported some 50 vessels comprised the British Fleet that season fishing Greenland and the Davis Strait. Fortunately, all but one ship managed to outmanoeuvre the privateers on their outbound voyage, which included Alexander in his *Eliza Swan*. It was reported that the fleet had departed in convoy very early that year at the end of February probably in hopes of outwitting the pirates and privateers. Or were they hoping for a good sealing season ahead of the whale fishing, particularly given the continued strong demand for seal-skins? The first to return full to Montrose was the *Eliza Swan*, with six large fish. As the season went on, many vessels returned early, fully laden with bumper catches whilst others hobbled home with leaky ships after being crushed in the ice. The fact that this 1800 season ended on such a high note for the entire British Fleet seems to have engendered renewed enthusiasm among investors who once again had decided to chance their money in the Greenland Trade.

Seemingly, this buoyant Industry outlook prompted at least one enthusiastic Hull speculator to place this advertisement in the Hull Advertiser on March 20 1801 -

'DAVIS STRAIT AND GREENLAND FISHERY

Wanted to Purchase one-eighth or one-quarter part of the Chance of success or produce of one or more ships on their Present voyage to Davis Strait or Greenland, for which a valuable consideration will be paid immediately on making the bargain. '

That speculator would have been fortunate if he indeed secured a share of the 1801 season, as it was another standout for the entire British fleet. Sanger quotes The Aberdeen Journal as reporting that whales had been found at Davis Strait 'in such plenty that a dozen sail might have loaded.' However, it was not completely smooth sailing because at one stage French Privateers harassed the fleet. On May 16 news came that a dangerous French privateer, the *Active* of 14 guns and 75 men, had been observed lurking around the Shetlands. The whaling fleet would have been put on high alert and from all reports were lucky on this occasion, because before any harm befell a Greenlandman the *HM Lady Ann*, an armed cutter of the Royal Navy captured The *Active*. This was even more fortunate for the Fleet given the abundance of whales and their unprecedented and completely unexpected very early return that year.

Further positive news came from Leith whalers *Royal Bounty* [Capt. J. Newton] and *Raith* [Capt. Burrish Lyons]. They reported that while they were sealing at West Greenland [Davis Strait] they too encountered 'whales so plentiful that they declared a dozen ships could have filled their casks'. Clearly this accounts for Lubbock's report that the *Royal Bounty* was full of oil by May 16. *Royal Bounty* immediately set sail for home arriving into Aberdeen on June 9 and Leith June 10. The *Raith* arrived two days later with 450 butts of blubber and 7 tons of bone, the product of ten very large whales. As an example of what lengths Captains would go to in order to harvest as much oil as possible, the crew of the *Raith* were put on short freshwater rations for their return voyage because every available water cask had been also filled with oil.

Post the Napoleonic Wars there were signs that whale numbers were on the rise in Davis Strait and this was evidenced when in 1802, the Edinburgh Courant reported that the *Raith* had returned with twelve whales and it was 'so full that the boats on deck are stowed with blubber, and the greater part of her beer and water casks are also filled.' Sanger's research indicated that 'This new hunting area, together with improved catches on the older grounds at East Greenland, higher oil and bone prices and peacetime conditions, encouraged the Scots to almost double their whaling effort between 1802 and 1805.'

And so, with investment strong the Scottish fleet continued to take to the high latitudes year after year. From the point of view of this family's story, it is clear all these factors contributed to the overall success enjoyed by Alexander, Montrose and the *Eliza Swan,* who team up to establish a long-standing partnership which would persist to the end of Alexander's sailing days. Emeritus Professor Chesley W. Sanger has produced an amazing table of Montrose results beginning from Alexander's early days sailing in his beloved *Eliza Swan*. So successful was the fishing in this period that not only did Alexander Snr prosper, indeed, he arrived home full and early on numerous occasions. The most notable being - 15 July 1799, 2 July 1801, 13 July 1802, and then in 24 July 1808 which is the first year he is listed as Master and Owner. Clearly a succession of good seasons had ensured that he could own Eliza Swan outright. It should also be pointed out here that those sailings were in the original 241 ton *Eliza Swan* with only 4 whaleboats and a hardworking crew of around thirty-six men. Obviously, what she lacked in size she certainly made up for in profit margin: smaller ship, smaller crew, and big catches producing even bigger profits. This is our first inkling that Alexander must have had a good business mind too.

TABLE 6 – Arctic Whaling Voyages Capt Alex. Young Snr. In the Eliza Swan of Montrose

Year	Whales	Seals	Bears
1798	5		
1799	7.5		
1800	6		
1801	9		
1802	7		
1803	2		
1804	7		
1805	9		
1806	22		
1807	5	116	5
1808	30		
1809			
1810	10		
1811*	20		
1812*	8		
1813*	8		

Although Lloyd's Register (erroneously) lists *Eliza Swan* sailing from Leith to Davis Strait in 1809 there are no catch results to be found. In 1810 Alexander Snr and the *Eliza Swan* bring home ten fish, but there is a changing of the guard in 1811. It is the first year Lloyd's Register lists Captain A. Young Jnr as Master of the *Eliza Swan*. He is now 29 years of age and he returned victorious with twenty fish from his first season in the Arctic as Master. These catch results were achieved despite a delayed departure caused by the ship's late arrival back into the Roads of Leith on February 20 with a load of timber from Quebec. After unloading her cargo at The Bush in Leith, the *Eliza Swan* sailed back to Montrose to take on crew, provisions and casks ready for the whale-fishing season; but it also presented Alexander Jnr with a real dilemma. He would know from past experience how established, overcrowded and downright dangerous the West Greenland fishing grounds of Davis Strait and Baffin Bay could be for any late arrivals. Although Lloyd's records show he fished at Davis Strait it is highly likely that he diverted to East Greenland. Then during the 1812 season reports came back that the ice was treacherous, and again the *Eliza Swan* sustained damage and was forced to return early. She reportedly limped into Montrose in early July reporting a catch of 8 large fish. She was also the first of the fleet to return that year.

The Northern Whale Fishing Industry was riding the crest of a wave in 1813, ports like Montrose were prospering but this upswing in activity does not account for why record keeping became sloppy and assumptions were made. For 1813 what is proven beyond any doubt is that Alexander's brother John was the Captain of the *Eliza Swan* that season despite 'Shipping News' in newspapers and Lloyd's Register, stating to the contrary. There will be more to tell about this 1813 season shortly. What this does bring to light, once again, is that Lloyd's Register and the newspapers are not 100 per cent reliable as a source of information. As a genealogist with forty years' experience it has been my mantra to aim for three pieces of corroborative data before accepting any data as a 'truth'.

While this involves much more work and thoroughness, I can guarantee you it reveals a much more interesting 'truth' as will be revealed in an upcoming Chapter solely devoted to the stories surrounding the *Eliza Swan* from 1809 and 1813.

Looking broadly at the Whaling Industry and the British Economy there is no doubt the real profit for the owners and masters in this period lay in the payments received from the government Bounty. For the government socially, financially, and economically there was an imbedded value in continuing support for the Whaling Trade in general with the quid pro quo being the rising cost of imported oil vs. the benefit to the government of creating jobs given they had long appreciated that there was a social and financial cost to having idle men and idle ships. In the early years of commercial whale fishing there was an ever-increasing worldwide demand for oil, which was driving up the price of imported oil. Once the British Government declared that the Bounty was to remain in place for a further period, a new lease of life and stability was breathed into the Whaling Industry and greater certainty was delivered to investors, masters and sailors alike. All of that was despite catch numbers remaining variable, conditions ever challenging and the inevitable losses of men and ships remaining at staggering levels.

By 1813, Alexander Snr is sixty-three and clearly hankering to take life a little easier and with his sons both well blooded in the Arctic whale fishery we see a new family paradigm coming into play.

It was time for the boys to shine!

TABLE 7 – Whaling Voyages – 'The Sons' – 1813-1823

Captain	Alex. Young Jnr	John Young
Ship	Monarch	Eliza Swan
Year/Catch	Whales	Whales
1813		8
1814	20	11
1815	7	8
1816	7	4
1817	3	3
1818	8	
1819	5	Hero
1820	3	7
1821	19	14
1822	3	Hero Lost
1823	26	

Lloyd's Register in 1814 has A. Young owner [which is not correct as she was still an asset of the Montrose Whale Fishing Company with shareholder ownership] and A. Young captain of the Eliza Swan, and the entry for the *Monarch* also has A. Young Master and 'Capt & Co' as owners. What these entries tell me is the Montrose Whale Fishing Company is still trading but there is confusion between Alexander Snr and Jnr and that sadly, son John is being largely overlooked. From the above table compiled by Emeritus Professor Chesley W. Sanger we can see the sons are sailing year after year with varied success, mostly attributable to weather, diminished numbers resulting in changes in the size of whales. In the same period, losses of ships and men remained high and towards the end of that time the Bounty was being systematically reduced. Firstly, in response to a shift away from whale oil to seed oil; and secondly, the emergence of free trade agreements was influencing the cost of several commodities including oil. The first indication of anything untoward for the Montrose fleet came from an advertisement in the Montrose Review on May 10, 1816, with one investor putting his shareholding in the Union Whale Fishing Co up for sale -

> To be sold by private bargain
> One-32nd part of the capital stock of the Montrose Union Whale Fishing Co
> Comprehending the ships London & Spencer of Montrose
> With the buildings, and apparatus necessary for the manufacture of oil.

The situation then got more serious when in a later issue there was yet another advertisement, but this time it was offering -

One half share of ...... [for sale]

In the end these shareholdings were sold by Roup [auction] and the Montrose whale fishing fleet had some new investors in the game. It should be noted that Scotland had a different ship ownership arrangement to England. The Scottish model allowed for greater shareholder participation, which not only spread the profits it also spread the losses. This probably accounts for the greater investor stability in Scotland, and the fact that many investors formed companies. This provided an added benefit in that ships owned by companies were invariably insured, which logically reduced the shared net loss should disaster strike.

The value of such investments can be assessed by referring to Alexander Young Snr's shareholding values as officially cited in the probate documents associated with his Will of 1817. His Will states that he had retained an interest in his beloved *Eliza Swan* as well as the Company's relatively new acquisition, the *Monarch*. As testament to the shared prosperity being enjoyed by the Company and the Industry in this 'Golden Era', Alexander Snr's 1817 shareholding of 7/54ths [sic – probably meant to be 64ths] of the *Eliza Swan* and 3/32nds of the *Monarch* was valued for probate at £1000 0s 0d which at today's 'economic status value' would amount to something in the range of £975,000.

Partial credit for this must rest with the shareholders, especially those who are known to have been prosperous Montrose Merchants operating independent lucrative businesses in the town. Such shareholder folk included Alex Craw a Montrose Merchant, John Kinnear also a Merchant and Thomas Stewart the local Town Clerk. All of these men had proved themselves astute money managers, and along with Alexander Snr and a succession of Company Managers, including the likes of John Kinnear, David Kinnear and latterly John Paton, had worked together to establish the perfect partnership. Further evidence of this can be found in the 1814-1822 minutes of The Montrose Banking Company, which cites David Kinnear as a Montrose Merchant in attendance at the first meeting of the Bank in January 1814, and who went on to become a Director. A family friend of long standing, David Hill, was endorsed in May 1814 as the Bank's first Accountant. The firm of Thomas Kinnear & Son became the Montrose Bank's Edinburgh Agents. Clearly, Alexander was keeping wise company.

The Montrose Whale Fishing Company continued to operate as usual following Alexander Snr's death, and putting finance aside for a moment, at the end of 1817 there seems to be some unexplained restlessness and a change in son John Young's association with the Montrose Whale Fishing Company and the *Eliza Swan*. Is this the first indication that there was some kind of falling out between the brothers? For some unknown reason John is not sailing to the Arctic at all in 1819 and then The Montrose Review for April 7, 1820 carried this General News story: 'Yesterday, the Hero, a very fine ship, commanded by Captain John Young, Sailed from this port on her first voyage to the Greenland seas. The Eliza Swan, Birnie, and Monarch, Young, are expected to sail this morning.' If the *Eliza Swan* is still sailing as a Montrose Whale Fishing Company ship why is Captain John Young not at the helm?

There are two further articles appearing in The Montrose Review, for that 1820 season, which make interesting reading.

> Friday July 21, 1820 -
> 'The London, Cunningham and the Monarch, Young arrive (sic) here yesterday from Greenland seas - the first with twelve fish, producing 150 tun of oil; and the latter with three fish, about 40 tuns. The following is the latest report of the success of the ships seen, which we regret is rather indifferent. Montrose - Eliza Swan, Birnie, five fish; Spencer, Keith, four; Hero, Young, four.'

Friday August 4, 1820 -
'The Spencer, Keith, arrived here from the Greenland fishery on Tuesday last, with eight fish, which will boil about sixty tons of oil. We are happy to state that there are very favourable accounts of the success of the Hero, Young, who was seen by the Rambler of Kirkcaldy, with seven large fish.'

Clearly Captain John Young and the crew of the *Hero* had achieved even better results since the first intelligence reached Montrose. There are two other notices, which although interesting are hard to explain. One item sits under the heading - *'Sailed from Montrose'* and it reads -

'July 27 - Elizabeth, Young, Gourdon, barrels'.

Could this article chronicle one of the uncles going to the aid of his nephew, because clearly the *Hero* would be struggling to bring back oil from seven large fish. The port of Gourdon is a natural harbour on the coast of Aberdeenshire just south of Inverbervie. Unfortunately, this sailing is not listed in Lloyd's so no further clarity is available.

Then comes the second item listed under Montrose Shipping that reads -

'6 Hero, Young, Greenland, stores'

The '6.' refers to the 6th October 1820 and since John Young was Master of the *Hero* that season and had already returned with 7 fish, it is fair to suggest he was taking stores back to Greenland to assist someone, perhaps his brother Alexander, as the *Monarch* was reported stayed over [remaining behind in Greenland] and with the records showing 3 fish caught, it could be assumed they were very large indeed and Alexander had decided to boil the blubber on the ice. The additional stores would have included food provisions for the crew and probably some additional casks for oil. It has been said that it was these bonanza results that prompted some to remain in the game past the point of viability, abetted by the Scottish shareholder model of spread risk.

Lloyd's, for the three seasons 1820-1822, lists Captain John Young sailing to the Arctic as Master of the *Hero* of Montrose. Then in 1822, there comes a disturbing newspaper report in the Montrose Review that the *Hero* [Captain John Young] was reported as – 'lost, crushed in the ice'. It was later learned that thankfully the crew was saved (all hands) and there is a touching family story to be related later in this regard. The following season saw the *Eliza Swan* beset in the ice yet again, and whether he had a long-range plan or whether he saw the impending downward spiral for the Industry is anyone's guess, but the 1823 season certainly was a watershed year for Alexander Jnr. He retires from all active sailing activities, not just whaling but the merchant trade as well, whereupon his role of Master of the *Monarch* passes to Captain W. Inglis. The *Eliza Swan* continued to be sailed by Captain Birnie.

Two very interesting events occurred in 1824, both of which prove disastrous for the Montrose Whale Fishing Company. Firstly, the Board of Trade announced it was removing the Bounty altogether due to grossly weakened demand for whale oil in the face of the availability of cheaper seed oil in sufficient quantities to satisfy market demand. Secondly, the *Eliza Swan* suffered considerable damage and was scarcely able to limp home after losing her topmast and bowsprit in a vicious gale. Events such as these were hard on crews and costly for the Company. In fact, it was the 1819 and 1822 seasons which would go down in history as standout years for all the wrong reasons. These were two years when the British Fleet, including the Scots, sustained massive losses. Stories of heroism, good luck and outstanding valour are interwoven into frightening outcomes where too many brave men lost their lives and far too many wives and children were set to suffer.

These are but some of the famous ships who with their skilled and fearless crews were now gone to the bottom of the sea -

TABLE 8 – Whale Fishing Ships Wrecked/Lost – 1819 & 1822

Year	Ship	Home Port	Outcome
1819	Diamond	Aberdeen	Wrecked
	Raith	Leith	Wrecked
	Rattler	Leith	Wrecked
	Mary Ann	Dundee	Crushed in the Ice at Lancaster Sound
	Royal Bounty	Leith	Wrecked
	Equestris		
	Sisters	Hull	Wrecked
	Thomas & Ann	Kirkcaldy	Wrecked
	Tay	Leith	Wrecked
	Majestic	Dundee	Lost – fate unknown
	Cherub		
		London	Wrecked
		Hull	Lost during the Autumn in Wingo
1822	King George	London	Lost all hands Greenland
	Lady Forbes	Liverpool	Wrecked – crew saved
	Eliza	North Shields	Lost – fate unknown
	Valiant	Whitby	
	Invincible	Peterhead	Lost – fate unknown
	Calypso	Dundee	Lost – fate unknown
	British Queen	Newcastle	Lost
	Hero	Montrose	Lost – fate unknown
	Eliza	Newcastle	Wrecked – crew saved
			Lost – fate - unknown

1830 was yet another disastrous year, cited by many as the worst in whaling history. Of the 91 ships of the British Fleet that set sail that season some eighteen were lost with ten of those wrecked in the Davis Strait alone. Some crewmembers were rescued and split among surviving vessels; however, many vessels went down all hands. The Montrose fleet was also hit hard - the *Spencer* was lost in Davis Strait, the *London* although undamaged came home clean, *Eliza Swan* arrived clean and in a sinking condition while the *Monarch* had caught only five fish for a meagre return of just 35 tuns.

The other elephant in the room was the Industrial Revolution with the attendant advent of steam as a power source for all manner of machinery, including engines for ships, which was heralding a cataclysmic revolution in shipping. The whale fishing industry was facing a serious dilemma of dwindling catches, poor oil returns, bad seasons, loss of the Bounty and loses of men and ships which all combined to influence the shareholders to come to the decision to wind up the Montrose Whale Fishing Company, which went into voluntary liquidation on 29 November 1833. This would have come as no surprise to the Montrose community given the 1832 and 1833 results were indicative of recent problems with fish numbers and the size of the fish. The figures for 1832 show the *Monarch* registered 24 fish and 205 tuns and for 1833 23 fish and 160 tuns of oil. The hidden truth here is that year upon year now the fish had been getting smaller as were the yields. On these figures the company was barely covering costs, and when these final two years' results followed seven years of similarly poor returns obviously the writing had been on the wall. Notwithstanding all of the above, the 1833 whaling season would have been a memorable last sail to the Arctic for Captain Alexander Young Jnr, the reliable Monarch and her loyal crew.

Such was the dire outlook for the Scottish Whaling Industry that no sale of the ships occurred at the auction. Ultimately, it was John Guthrie, the current Manager of the Company, who ultimately contracted to purchase the *Monarch* and then a short time later decided to also purchase the *Eliza Swan*. The whale fishery continued to decline, Guthrie persevered for six seasons, all of which were a dismal failure. At that point he put the ships to work servicing the year round lucrative flax trade in the Baltic. These two brave ladies of the sea deserved a safe harbour and it is pleasing to be able to report that they continued to sail those familiar routes for many years to come.

Montrose Harbour too was about to take on a very different look, and for many it would be a sad day when no brave whalers could be seen hugging the quayside. With the *Hero* lost in 1822, *Spencer* in 1830 and then the *London* lost all hands in 1834 it was a heavy weight of sorrow for one small community especially given the *London* had enjoyed a long history of success and as such would have carried a very experienced crew of brave locals. But it is the tale of the fate of the *London* which makes frightening reading. Typical of what was printed in the day, this report lays the facts bare: 'The only account of the fate of the *London* came from Captain Bennet of the *Venerable*, who on the 15th April, saw the London in a tremendous storm, lying to windward of an extensive chain of icebergs, among which, it is probable she was dashed to pieces that very evening.' A search of Lloyd's Register revealed the *Venerable* was a fellow whaler of 333 ton built in Scarborough with a sheathed and doubled hull. Captain Bennett was her regular Master.

Knowing that sailors were a superstitious lot I initially wondered if Alexander perceived some of these tragic events as warning signs? Or did he make his decision to retire purely on the basis of economics? Or, was he also influenced by a generous offer from Lloyd's? Whatever his reasoning, Alexander maintained a close association with the Shipping Industry and the port of Montrose as a resident, shipowner, shipping agent and a surveyor for Lloyd's. A further insight into Alexander's post-whaling community and industry involvement comes courtesy of the Montrose Review two decades on when on March 28, 1845, a notice appears for the AGM of the Shipowners & Shipmasters of this Port, signed by the Association's Chairman, Alexander Young.

1847/48 was another memorable time for Captain Alexander Young Jnr. In the February of '47 his brother-in-law, Captain Joshua Richmond died and probate of his Will in March '48 stated that Joshua: 'Appoint[s] Alexander Young

And then 1750-1850

my Brother-in-law, late Shipmaster now Surveyor for Lloyd's in Montrose' as Executor. A mere six months later, on the 29 October 1848, Alexander's long and adventurous, and dare I say successful and rewarding life comes to a close with only his eldest surviving son, Captain John Young, by his side. John was the only one of Alexander's six surviving sons to remain resident in Montrose and to share his father's lifelong passion for sailing under canvas.

So, what path did his other sons take?

Chapter 6

The Pre-Napoleonic French Connection
Unarmed Arctic Whalers Vs Mighty French Navy
A Courageous Tale of Capture & Political Will
Imprisonment Détente Escape & Daring

Millions of people travel to Paris every year to stroll the Avenue des Champs-Elysées, to wonder at the exhibits in Musée du Louvre and Musée D'Orsay, to scale Le Tour Eiffel or to picnic in Jardins du Trocadéro. Some take in the 360 degree view from the roof-top of the Arc de Triomphe and of course almost everyone pays a visit to Les Invalides. For the majority of these tourists, a visit to Les Invalides remains focussed on the hallowed resting place of that well chronicled and lauded French Emperor and General, Napoleon Bonaparte. The exploits of this slight statured man are so venerated in France that even in death he is immortalised by a shrine so oversized one can only wonder at the enormity of the tribute. His colossal sarcophagus of red-quartzite commands the room as he once commanded his troops. It dwarfs anyone who enters, and its elegance belies the ugly truth of the deeds of the man and it also hides a secret - Napoleon is cocooned in the heart of no less than six concentric coffins. These coffins are elevated on a plinth of green granite symbolising his exaltation in the eyes of the creator of this artistic edifice. His massive monolith dominates the room and stands centre stage under a classic frescoed baroque Dome whose designer was reputedly inspired by no greater godly building than St Peter's Basilica in Rome. Seemingly all this grandeur is in line with the level of adoration

Napoleon enjoyed in life. He rests surrounded by vaults bearing the name plaques of Admirals, Marshals and Generals, men who also gave their lives in the name of France, but scarcely a handful of visitors would give them more than a cursory glance and even fewer of them would recognise the names. Such is the immortal reverence for this one man whose nickname was 'le petit caporal' - The Little Corporal.

If Française is your mother tongue you will probably be in no doubt that Napoleon was the greatest Military General of all time, spoken of by his christian name only; it's personal - it's Fraternity. However, down the centuries historians of all nationalities have remained curious, passionate and divided about the Man and the General. Napoleon has been variously characterised as a *'Traitor to the Revolution'*, as someone who retarded democratic progress and as a *'Warmonger'* - who, even after battle success, failed to create an enduring peace. Perhaps the harshest criticism of all comes from those detractors who describe him as - *'a corrupt individual, bereft of morality'*. It has been said that his success in war *'made him rely on war as an instrument of policy'* but even more arresting is the fact that he appeared to remain completely and utterly insensitive to the human cost of his commands.

In publications entitled - *'The Napoleon Series'* author Max Sewell contends that 'The execution of d'Enghien [Louis Antoine de Bourbon, Duke of Enghien] was criminal, the imprisonment of the Pope immoral, and Napoleon's quest for total dominance a reflection of his warped psyche. Lord Acton's adage "power corrupts, and absolute power corrupts absolutely" has come to be permanently identified with Napoleon as its foremost example of voracity.' There is a contemporaneous example of adoration versus ego to be found in the writings of Ferdinand Ries, a German composer who was at one time a student of and later both biographer and Secretary to a much more famous Pianist and Composer than himself, Ludwig van Beethoven. Reis states that Beethoven so admired Napoleon that he was planning to dedicate his career defining Symphony No. 3 to the esteemed French General; however in 1804 when the megalomaniac Napoleon declared himself First Consul for Life and Emperor of France, Beethoven reportedly - 'flew into a rage and cried out: 'Is he too, then, nothing more than an ordinary human being? Now he, too, will trample on the rights of man, and indulge only his ambition!'

On the other hand, if you are English speaking, your view of Napoleon would likely be entirely at odds with that of your near neighbour and historically errant foe, France. As for the poor Scots, they were perennially drawn into England's wars with France since a time well before that of Oliver Cromwell and his army of Roundheads. For a century or more both Scotland and France followed the Catholic religion, had been sound trading partners, and it could be said that for a greater part of history both of them saw Protestant England as their enemy. In fact, Scotland and France shared a distrust and resentment towards England which had endured from the time Edward I of England installed John Balliol as Scottish Regent around 1292. The most controversial doctrine of the precursor period to our story is when James VI of Scotland [1567-1625] developed what was termed 'the theory of divine right' which he imposed on England from 1603 when he succeeded Elizabeth I and became James I of England. Interestingly, King James VI of Scotland had been tutored by a Sir Peter Young since he was a lad, and Sir Peter's pupil clearly embraced his lessons on religion and power such that he asserted that a monarch is subject to no earthly authority, deriving the right to rule directly from the will of God and as such the King is not subject to the will of his people, the aristocracy, or any other estate of the realm for that matter. Despite the obvious religious difference between Scotland and France it seems France believed that the Auld Alliance held strong. In fact, Charles de Gaulle spoke of it in Edinburgh as recently as 1942 even though most historians would have us believe that the Treaty of Edinburgh of 1560 and Scotland's conversion to Protestantism ended their accord.

Now fast forward to the last decade of the eighteenth century, England (including Scotland), France and Spain - were once again on a war footing. The period so relevant to this segment of our story and Captain Alexander Young Snr in particular is 1792-1797, encompassing what Historians call the War of the First Coalition which in turn is part of the society redefining French Revolutionary Wars. Included in this period was the Battle in the Vendee fought as a Franco-British battle 1793-1796. These wars may appear to be all about international political intrigue at a high level and bear no relationship to this family, but what needs to be appreciated is that these battles signalled a very difficult time for ordinary citizens in these key countries and more especially for our merchantmen and Greenlandmen. What will soon become clear is that these little known scrimmages would have helped shape the lives of these early generations of Youngs and been the subject of much family folklore and many a family roundtable.

It cannot be stressed too strongly how these battles were responsible for much unrest and uncertainty and came at a major humanitarian cost. The real statistics remain unknown, but estimates put the figure at between two and four million lives lost. Young family ancestors on land and sea would have been forced to act as spectators to this ebb and flow of cordiality and war. These are not incidents played out in some Shakespearian drama; they are real and embroil everyday people. It is unequivocal that our Youngs and their extended families living in Edinburgh and Leith at the time would have felt the fear, endured the helplessness, suffered the loss of loved ones and livelihoods and then were forced to brace themselves for the grief and hardship inflicted when one of their own was captured by the French Navy.

What were the actual precursor events which led to the capture of Captain Alexander Young Snr?

France, Spain, Holland and England had all amassed significant naval forces, and were pushing the boundaries of world exploration for territorial supremacy, aided in no small measure by improvements to ships, navigation equipment and horology. However, the threat of war or the incidents of war were forever hanging over the heads of all those who were doing business on the oceans of the world and sailors and Masters alike were acutely aware that a dangerous enemy encounter could lurk in the swell anytime, anywhere, with the added challenge being that these foes might employ the deception of flying the flag of a nation other than their register. This strategy became commonplace and many a merchantman fell victim to this clever deception.

While our Scottish family would have endeavoured to stay out of the firing line in order to safely sail as usual to Greenland and the Baltic, in the middle of all this treachery and strife, a new kind of battle had emerged in France, a fight for human survival: literally. In fact, what began as a groundswell was now a full-blown Revolution set to change the face of France for ever. The Peasant's Revolt began smouldering in 1788 when it was announced to the people that the French Treasury was empty. People were already starving to death right across France and naturally many had resorted to crime in order to feed themselves and their families. Their resultant apprehension and incarceration caused severe overcrowding in the prisons and all the while the royals and social elite were known to be still dining 'high off the hog'. The general populace were drawn to action out of desperation and disgust. The first event in a long line of sorrowful tales occurred on the 14 July 1789 when the peasants stormed the Bastille in Paris. However, there was much more blood to be shed before the 'perfidy, corruption and abomination of the French Government' was finally arrested and exposed to the world.

There was much treachery on both sides. Many in high places were soon to see the inside of a prison as the aristocratic elite as well as prominent social commentators were systematically apprehended by the Revolutionary Forces and imprisoned only to become victims of Madame La Guillotine. One by one the doyen dominos fell - King Louis XVI, Queen Marie-Antoinette, the Mayor of Paris Jean Sylvain Bailly, Maximilien Robespierre and his brother Augustin who were both close friends of Napoleon, Georges Danton and Camile Desmoulins. Then came the apprehension of a rogue General, Jean-Baptiste Carrier who was charged with being singularly responsible for the death of as many as ten thousand of his French countrymen. These victims were peasant prisoners ordered to be deliberately drowned whilst being transported on barges en route along the Loire River. These were extraordinary times. No one was safe.

The year that is so crucial to our story and Alexander Young is 1794. In Paris on the 27 July 1794 people witnessed the 'Thermidorean Reaction' which brought about the apprehension and death of the Robespierre brothers and is considered by many to be the pivotal event which defined the end point of the French Revolution per se; however, it signalled the beginning of trouble for many. Napoleon for one finds himself at the centre of serious allegations and is placed under house arrest. He is eventually cleared of any wrong-doing and released to once again send the French Army on the march. Napoleon, for his battle success of driving the English out of Toulon is promoted to the rank of General by Lazare Carnot. It is very important that one remembers this man's name!

All the while the French Navy was forced to remain at sea. In 1794 there were two major maritime events involving the French Navy. First, on 1 June Admiral Villaret Joyeuse had a victory over the Royal Navy and was successful in gaining safe passage for a convoy of American ships bringing much needed grain to the starving French people. While this sea battle was playing out in the Bay of Biscay on the south coast of France, other vessels of the French Navy were engaged in a battle of their own in the North Sea – a battle of piracy to be precise. One of those who fell victim to these French Navy Privateers was none other than our very own Captain Alexander Young Snr.

For some weeks the English Navy had been aware the French Navy were masquerading as Privateers and marauding the Atlantic Ocean and creating havoc for the Merchant Navy and the Greenlandmen. The Royal Navy had made sundry efforts to protect all classes of shipping but the dire circumstances in France combined to conspire against several Greenlandmen that season. With the French Government Treasury empty the French Navy was not being paid. Napoleon was so totally pre-occupied with his land army at this point that the French Navy was forced to resort to Piracy in order to survive. In this year of extreme violence and terror right across Europe, Alexander finds himself caught up in the fracas. This was a time when ordinary people became victims of a greater international political struggle which was none of their making and certainly outside their control.

There was no twenty-four hour news channel to warn citizens of events being played out on foreign soil let alone at sea and no Foreign Affairs Department to issue Travel Advisories. Danger was everywhere and survival was on everyone's mind while large helpings of despair, uncertainty and helplessness were being served up daily while ships and crews attempted to go about their regular business. Greenlandmen like Young and his crew had a job to do and it cannot be over-emphasised, the courage they exercised for the level of threat they faced from these heavily armed French Privateer Men-of-war vessels.

And so begins the tale of the capture of the *Raith* of Leith, an innocent Greenland whaling ship as it headed home after surviving the rigours of a successful fishing voyage in the treacherous waters of the Davis Straits. Laden with a good bounty in the form of blubber and bone, the crew, elated by their good fortune and buoyed with the promise of a substantial reward for their hard work, would have been feeling confident as their ship sailed homeward, regardless of the weather conditions. With the northern isles of Scotland in plain sight their world imploded. It is not hard to conjure up the feelings of dread and tension on board the *Raith* that fateful day. To a man they would have had a sinking feeling low down in the gut, the kind that seems to suck the life out of your body. It would have been one of those moments when you suddenly gasp for air because you had forgotten to breathe. Everyone would have known the taste of fear that day as each crew member quietly wondered to himself, too fearful to speak out loud - 'why us and why now?'

Then comes the questions and recriminations. Had they simply become complacent? Were the lookouts gazing forward with home and hearth occupying their minds rather than to port, starboard and aft with Press Gangs and Privateers in mind? Alas, there was no obvious answer, but what was true in the end, they were helpless to defend themselves and worse still, they were about to come face to face with the reality that home and hearth were a long way off.

It all began on July 21, 1794. They were sailing in the North Sea at roughly 60°N, 5°W just off Duncansby Lighthouse. Unbeknown to Captain Young a squadron of seven heavily armed French Privateers, already known to the Royal Navy to be cruising around somewhere between Newfoundland and Spitzbergen, had decided to put the *Raith* in their gun sights. In fact, all the unarmed English, Scottish and Dutch Greenlandmen returning from Davis Straits and East Greenland made easy targets. Whaling vessels were strong not sleek, and were heavily laden thus slowed in their progress, and their crews were trained to lookout for whales not sharks! In a nutshell, they were easy prey!

It should also be highlighted at this point that it was a well-known fact that these whalers were well provisioned because of how long they could potentially be forced to remain at sea. These stores would be a welcome prize for any sea-locked penniless Privateer. Lubbock reports that in desperation this season *Le Tartare* had actually taken the fight to several Dutch Greenland ships right up to the ice edge. It later came to light that a short time after the capture of the *Raith* a list was posted in Amsterdam of no less than 37 Dutch whalers which had been captured by the French Navy that season. The Caledonian Mercury printed a list of the vessels in the French Squadron which captured the *Raith* and according to shipping intelligence from the Royal Navy, had sailed in convoy from Brest on the 7th July past.

TABLE 9 – French Warships – North Sea - 1794

Ship	Guns	
Le Taste	44	A Rear Admiral on board
La Bellone	44	Frigate
La Brutus	50	Formerly a line of battle ship but now cut down
La Reputlicaine	36	
La Vengeance	24	
La Montagne	24	
La Neriade	16	Brig

On Monday, July 21, the *Raith* was overhauled by one of that Squadron, the French Privateer frigate *Bellona*, just off Duncansby Head, the most north-easterly part of mainland Scotland. As previously mentioned, Burrish Lyons was Mate on that particular voyage with Captain Young. As events transpired Lyons was not taken captive and after reaching Lerwick he wrote a letter to one of the *Raith's* owners under date 28 July 1794 explaining the situation with Captain Young and the crew. This letter, which was eventually delivered to Leith by the *HM Royal George*, Excise Cutter, stated that the French had loaded 'sundry of the stores along with Mr Young and the ship's crew into a frigate, excepting myself and two of the people who were left on board with sixteen Frenchmen'. What later came to light is that the French had taken two prizes that day. The other vessel, another Greenland whaler, was the *Dundee* of Dundee. Since the holds of both whaling ships were piled high with butts of valuable blubber and whalebone there was no possibility of negotiating a ransom deal because it was their cargo and food stores which were the obvious target. At this juncture on their return voyage neither Greenlandman had yet off-loaded any crew in the Orkneys or Shetlands, so both ships were sailing with a full complement of men who, once taken prisoner, were consigned to various French prisons in the vicinity of Dunkirk and as Eric Graham contends: 'to await the remote possibility of a prisoner exchange'.

Several crewmembers from the French privateer were put aboard the *Dundee* and *Raith* with the intention of maintaining French Navy control and with a plan to later sail the vessels to a friendly port whereupon the cargo and ship could be sold to the highest bidder. In the case of the *Raith*, the three crew who remained on board were the Mate, Burrish Lyons, the Cooper and a boy apprentice. Their instruction from the Captain of the *Bellona* was to sail the *Raith* to Bergen, a port on what we now know as the coast of Norway and whilst it was a known Danish stronghold in 1794 the Danes were collaborators and friendly toward the French.

In his open letter published in the Scots Magazine, Lyons recounts that the sixteen Frenchmen aboard the *Raith* 'were imbued with the Revolutionaries disrespect for Officers and did very much as they pleased'. He recounted that when the *Raith* was about fifteen miles off the coast of Norway seven of the French crew were so 'badly drunk on whiskey' they clambered below decks to sleep it off in the hammocks. The other nine men from the *Bellona* who were supposed to be on watch remained on deck drinking. Lyons regaled that for some unexplained reason these men decided to clamber into one of the *Raith's* whaleboats hanging on the davits. It was there they passed out, drunk!

Here the resourcefulness of Lyons and his two crewmates proved outstanding. They decided to take advantage of the inebriated state of the nine and carefully lowered the whaleboat over the side and set the drunken Frenchmen adrift. Next, they rushed to nail down the hatches and companionways on the *Raith* in order to entomb the remaining members of the prize crew sleeping it off below deck. In the end it was Lyons and the apprentice who sailed the *Raith* safely into Lerwick harbour to a tumultuous welcome. Lyons later reported that sadly, the cooper, an Englishman, had fallen overboard on the 24 July and drowned. In the circumstances Lyons may not have been able to attempt a rescue either or he may have decided it more prudent to nose the *Raith* high into the wind and set course directly for Lerwick. HM Excise Cutter, *Royal George*, was at anchor in the roads of Lerwick on that jaunty day.

From there on the Royal Navy took command of the situation. A boarding party removed the prisoners from the hold, placed them in irons and transported them to Edinburgh for imprisonment in the dungeons of Edinburgh Castle where they would be in company with a great number of their fellow countrymen. But there was even more good fortune for the Scots that week when word eventually came that on the 24th July the eighteen gun *HM Kings Fisher*, under the command of J. Le M. Gosselin, had managed to recapture the *Dundee*. Imagine Gosselin's surprise when he discovered the cast adrift French crewmembers from the *Raith* were also on board.

Unfortunately, for these French sailors, all of their number were about to enjoy the same fate as the rest of the *Bellona* crew: set to languish in a dank cold Scottish dungeon prison. Meanwhile, the Captain of *HM Kings Fisher* reported his last sighting of the French Privateer squadron had them setting course 'fleeing for the Noze of Norway, to intercept the Baltic ships.'

What then of the *Raith* and Burrish Lyons?

Burrish Lyons was fittingly rewarded for his incredible presence of mind and undeniably magnificent seamanship. Bell & Co., on behalf of the owners of the *Raith* and the Edinburgh Whale Fishing Company, promoted Lyons to Master as a mark of their gratitude. Lyons first duty as the newly appointed Master of the *Raith* was to assemble a crew in Lerwick and sail the vessel to her home port of Leith and disgorge her rich cargo of some 160 butts of whale blubber still quite intact in the hull. According to an article printed in the Caledonian Mercury of the 25th August 1794, the *Raith* did arrive safely into Leith harbour that very day. It would not be too hard to picture the welcome Lyons and the *Raith* received, although it would have been somewhat overshadowed by the sadness and uncertainty being experienced by the families and friends of those Scots taken prisoner. Alexander's wife Helen Liston would have been there with their brood wondering if any of them would ever see Alexander again.

As for Lyons, he went on to prove himself a competent and successful whaler over several seasons both with the *Raith* and her sister Leith whaler, the *William & Ann*. The 1802 season would prove to be yet another lucky escape for Lyon. While Master of the Raith and fishing in Davis Straits on the Labrador coast, it was observed by Scoresby that a whale breached and threw Lyons whaleboat fifteen feet into the air. Scoresby's account stated that it 'came down into the water with its keel upwards, yet all the men except one were saved'.

Lyons survived on this occasion, but alas, as for so many, his luck would eventually run out and there is a monument inscription in the Cullen Churchyard near Inverness, which tells the last chapter of the Burrish Lyons story -

'Sacred to the memory of Burrish Lyons,
sometime Shipmaster in Leith, aged 41 years,
who was lost in the brig Mary of London, of
which he was owner, wrecked on this coast on
the night of 7th September 1807, when all
on board perished. This marble is erected
by Mathias Lyons, Writer to the Signet, in
testimony of his esteem and affection for a
much-beloved brother, 1822.'

So what then was to be the final chapter in the life of the *Raith*?

After Burrish Lyons moved on she passed through the hands of a succession of Masters including Robert Kellie, James Davidson, Peter Baillie and most recently William Duncan. It was on Duncan's maiden voyage to Davis Straits at the helm of the *Raith* that he and his crew unfortunately encountered a very strong south westerly gale and the *Raith* was nipped up in the pack-ice and crushed. All told eleven ships were similarly crushed that season, and along with the *Raith* other Leith vessels familiar to this family's story including the *Rattler, Royal Bounty* and *Thomas & Ann* also met their fate. Such was life for the brave fishermen who dared to confront the harsh and unpredictable environmental conditions at those high latitudes. Lamentably, Lubbock's report of these events does not include any information regarding the fate of any of these crews after their ships were crushed and sunk.

Now we turn to the plight of Captain Alexander Young and his crew.

Their capture certainly drew wide attention. The story of their encounter with the French can be found in newspapers as far afield as the Hampshire Chronicle, Newcastle Courant, The Scots Magazine, Saunders's News-Letter, Universal Magazine, Caledonian Mercury, Kentish Weekly Post, Cumberland Pacquet and Ware's Whitehaven Advertiser, the Derby Mercury, Reading Mercury, Bury and Norwich Post, Hull Advertiser, Chester Chronicle, Stamford Mercury and probably many more not yet discovered. This demonstrates not only the newsworthiness of such events but highlights the perceived gravity of the situation. Reading the circumstances of the capture of the *Raith* would have been not only difficult and heartbreaking for the families of all the men taken prisoner, it was a reminder to every merchantman and Greenlandman they were helpless pawns in this international game of War.

Caught up in a storm of mixed emotions, the kinsfolk of Young and his crew would have been hoping for the best but preparing for the worst - as they contemplated life without their husbands, brothers and sons. The human cost is often not printed but is nonetheless real. In Alexander's case, he had just turned 44 years of age on the 3 July and was in the prime of his life. He and Helen Liston had a family of eight children. Anne was almost 18 years of age and probably considered not a child as such, Helen was 13 and in school, son Alexander was 12 years of age also at school but more importantly almost of the age to take his place as an apprentice alongside his father and Master. Then came the youngsters - Robert 8, Margaret 6, John 5, William 3 and Janet 20 months. Two of Alexander's sons Alexander and Robert also had birthdays in July, on the 22nd and 24th respectively which leads me to believe that this was normally a month of great celebration for this family. Surely a father would remember those important dates and just maybe he was distracted too and busy counting his blessings to be full and headed home early and for once he would be on hand to celebrate these memorable occasions with his boys. Alas, it was not to be. In fact, no one in the family had the slightest notion as to whether he was alive or dead.

Apart from the newspaper archive material, the only other direct information available comes contained in two letters held in the personal archival collection of Lord Henry Dundas in the National Records of Scotland, in Edinburgh. One letter was penned by Mr James Pirie WS [Writer to the Signet], a Lawyer in Edinburgh, and addressed to Lord Henry Dundas, and the other by the hand of John Stephens, Clerk in His Majesty's Service stationed on-board *HM Brilliant*. What was James Pirie's involvement in all this you wonder? Well, his only son, James Pirie Jnr happened to be Surgeon aboard the *Raith* on that particular Greenland voyage. Upon hearing the news of his son's capture and being known to the Captain of the *Brilliant*, James Pirie Snr took it upon himself to write to the Captain under letter dated 12 September 1794.

In his letter Pirie expressed grave concerns for his son's welfare and enquired whether the Captain had received any intelligence of his son and Young. This is the reply that James Pirie received from John Stephens

'In answer to your letter of the 12th instant I have to inform you, the Raith Greenlandman was captured on the 21st July in the North Sea, on the 3rd day after leaving Shetland, by a French Squadron, as stated in your son's letter. The treatment of the crew on board the [French] squadron was humane and lenient as the rigours of war would admit, not aggravated in any measure from national or hostile antipathy. Their treatment after being landed and imprisoned at Dunkirk was conformable to the decree of the Convention, acted up to in France universally, Captain Young and your son being considered and treated upon an equality with the rest of the unfortunate crew and deprived of their clothes etc. etc., except that wherein they stood. When marched to St Omer they were (as at Dunkirk) indiscriminately confined and your son, not having any money, was restricted to the established allowance of the prison, viz. 1 lb bread, and of aqua pura 2 litres per diem- a small portion of beef, which was affected them at Dunkirk, being here curtailed from their subsistence.

Tanner (the writer's informant) being obliged to remain some time at Dunkirk after escaping from St. Omer, before an opportunity offered from his escape from thence, was then joined by one of the crew of the Dundee Greenlandman of Dundee, captured at the same time as the Raith. From this man he learned that your son, Captain Young and others of the prisoners at St Omer were removed about 150 miles further in the Country, the day before he effected his escape, where, no doubt, if confined their treatment would be the same, but as their situation was hereby removed so far from the sea as to render their escape less practicable, a stronger probability exists of your son and Captain Young obtaining their parole, in which case their circumstances would be (and I hope are) considerably ameliorated.

Permit Sir, the only Son of an Affectionate aged parent tho' a stranger to offer his cordial condolence on this unfortunate and melancholy event. Tho were I not aware that any attempt to remove your present natural affliction, by any means whatsoever than the restored liberty of your only son would be inconsiderate and ill timed. I would presume to remind you that your son is still under the Protection of the Almighty and that in [...illegible handwriting.....] to the Hardships of his Captivity will heighten his enjoyment of liberty, and filial Feelings and affection, while I trust you will soon have to rejoice upon his restoration to his Friends in a degree equal to what you doubtless did at his Birth. That you may soon mutually enjoy the happiness of each others Society is as ardently wished as the Certainty of the Event would contribute to the pleasure and happiness of your Son

                              Your most obedient
                              Humble Servant
                              J^{no} Stephens

                              Clerk in His Majesty's
                              Ship Brilliant

PS Your letter tho' dated the 12th instant was only received this day having been to 'Chatham' and the Downy before it came to Sheerness.'

To say that those poor wretches were caught up in something way outside their management is no understatement. To put the predicament of Young and his crew into perspective it is important to appreciate the role Dunkirk and Lord Dundas played in this scenario. About a year earlier, between 24 August and 8 September 1793 to be precise, the Duke of York had led coalition troops from Britain, Hanover, Austria and Hesse-Kassel to lay siege to Dunkirk as part of the Flanders Campaign. After defeat at the Battle of Hondshoote the Duke of York and his troops withdrew to the northeast. In defence of the Duke of York, and to add a twist of irony, York may have been field commander of the troops, but he was not a party to the decision to besiege the fortified albeit dilapidated Port of Dunkirk. Nor was the decision taken by his military commanders; indeed, it was the decision of then War Minister, Lord Henry Dundas, reputedly Prime Minister William Pitt's closest advisor.

Dundas was not only devoid of any military expertise, he had completely underestimated the military nous of Prussian born French Military Commander Lazare Carnot, a man known to be an astute military strategist and the same person who had promoted Napoleon to the rank of General. Carnot stealthily survived the Revolution and was now head of the Committee of Public Safety for France in Paris. Carnot was a Politician, Engineer and Mathematician, and his glorified reputation as the Organizer of Victory in the French Revolutionary Wars lay in his ability to size up an engagement and to arm and supply his troops accordingly, and in a manner which far outshone the lacklustre performance of the English. He was blindly abetted by Henry Dundas who certainly had the ear of Pitt, but was non-military, and, as highlighted by the Duke of York in his scathing despatches to Parliament in London, Dundas was making decisions which were counter to success.

Subsequent to this attack, Dunkirk was seen by the French as an enemy target, and accordingly the garrison's fortifications were improved, making any chance of escape by the crew of the *Raith* suddenly all the more difficult and unlikely. To add to Alexander's woes, as a result of these recent battle victories by the French, Dunkirk Prison had become grossly overcrowded and as a consequence Alexander and his crew were moved to Saint-Omer. John Stephens' letter states that they were marched from Dunkirk, and bearing in mind it was high summer, temperatures in this part of France can reach upwards of 30°C. When such conditions are compared to the below zero freezing temperatures the men were experiencing so very recently in Davis Straits and the mild maximum of 15-18°C they could expect in Leith at that time of year, their march would have been difficult and debilitating and a circumstance they were ill-prepared for in many respects. We also learn from Stephens' letter that their clothes were taken leaving them with only the bare essentials of apparel, and most certainly without a change of clothes. Were they reduced to simply wearing under garments as further humiliation?

Either way it would have been a very disagreeable journey indeed, as Saint-Omer is some 24 miles inland and slightly to the south of Dunkirk. The fact they were later removed even further inland would not have rested easy with Alexander and his crew who would have realised that their chances of plotting an escape were evaporating with every mile they marched. Exactly where they ended up after their second relocation is a point of conjecture. Due to the current physical state of Stephen's letter it is unclear whether this second march took them 15 or 150 miles further into rural France. In the worst case this could have placed the men in the vicinity of, say Reims, if they were headed east or Rouen if marched to the south.

Now we need to overlay their predicament with the fact the period of their imprisonment coincided with what Historians have labelled as the 'Reign of Terror'. This name was coined because in the twelve months leading up to Alexander's capture in July 1794 over 16,500 death sentences were carried out in France, with over 2,500 of those so sentenced being executed by guillotine in Paris. One can only wonder at the stress levels these desperate men were subjected to as their minds played tricks on them while contemplating their fate. There is no doubt

And then 1750-1850

the events at Dunkirk leading up to their arrival would have set the tone for their treatment and movement. It could go part way to explaining why James Pirie decided to write directly to Lord Dundas which was certainly not normal protocol for the time. Then again desperate people will resort to desperate measure if their children's lives are in jeopardy.

While deténte was being played out in England what were these Scots prisoners enduring within the walls of Saint-Omer Prison?

Well, thanks to a series of letters written by an anonymous English Lady living in France at the time we can learn exactly what life was like for Alexander and his men. These letters made their way to England and into the hands of one, John Gifford, a student of French History and the author of several papers on French Politics. He assembled her letters into a two volume publication with the descriptive title - *'A Residence in France during the Years 1792, 1793, 1794, and 1795; described in a Series of Letters from an English Lady: with General and Incidental Remarks on the French Character and Manners'*. In these letters the English Lady wrote her own account of conditions at Saint-Omer as a place where - 'prisoners were frequently disturbed at midnight by the entrance of men in[to] their apartments, who, with the detestable ensign of their order, (red caps,) and pipes in their mouths, came by way of frolic to search the pockets, trunks, &c. - At Montreuil, the Maison d'Arrêt were under the direction of the Commissary, whose behaviour to the female prisoners was too atrocious for recital - two young women, in particular, who refused to purchase milder treatment, were locked up in a room for seventeen days. - Soon after I left Arras, every prison became a den of horror. The Miserable inhabitants were subject to the agents of Le Bon, whose avarice, cruelty, and licentiousness, were beyond any thing a humane mind can imagine.'

This does not bode well for Alexander and his men. Even supposing they could manage to make good their escape, what impediments would they be faced with in making good the footslog to the coast?

Again, this English Lady and her letters describe in detail how people's movements were now being controlled and monitored. It seems that as a result of the Duke of York's invasion and recurrent Austrian incursions, restrictions had been put in place for all travel within France, and these were being more strictly employed near the seacoast and frontiers. The rules decreed that no person could pass through a town without the equivalent of a 'passport' from the Municipality he or she resided in. This document needed to specify personal details such as age, place of birth, destination, height and facial features. So, it seems even if a prisoner should be fortunate enough to gain his freedom, achieving safe passage to the coast would have been very fraught indeed. In another of the English Lady's letters, she wrote that Georges Danton, who was at one time President of the Comité de Surveillance, or Committee of Public Safety, was such an unscrupulous character and so untrustworthy that 'You will not be surprized at such occurrences, when I tell you that G_____, whom you must remember to have heard of as a Jacobin [a Political Club of the elite formed during the Revolution] at_____, is President of the committee above mentioned - yes, an assassin is now the protector of the public safety ...'.

Her accusations were later exposed, and Danton's actions saw him meet his fate at the hands of Madame La Guillotine.

Treachery was everywhere.

There is just one more letter available. It does shed some further light on how Alexander and his men could have possibly found their way back to Leith. After James Pirie received that lengthy reply from John Stephens, which presumably was around 29th or 30th September 1794, Pirie set about writing to Henry Dundas who, as previously mentioned, was War Minister in the Parliament of William Pitt the Younger. Henry Dundas was a fellow Scot from Edinburgh, and at one time he too had been a Scottish Advocate like James Pirie. Clearly, from this information there is every possibility these men were known to each other professionally; however, it was still baffling me as to why Pirie would take such an audacious step, given the social and political protocols of the day. Could there be another reason why Pirie took it upon himself to write directly to the War Minister? Was there something more to their relationship which could more readily explain Pirie's action and the tone of his letter?

Evidence in this regard was obtained from the Proceedings of the 1787 Edinburgh Dean of Guild Court Records which suggest the Pirie and Dundas families are in fact connected by marriage and therefore these men were more intimately known to each other than was initially thought. One particular entry mentions a David Pirie, soldier in Lord Robert Manners Regiment of Foot. This Lieutenant-General Manners later became Chief Equerry and Clerk Marshal to the King. Meanwhile, David Pirie on the other hand was the only son and heir of the deceased Alexander Pirie but more importantly he was the grandson of the deceased Elizabeth Dundas who was spouse to Thomas Pirie, sometime Writer in Edinburgh. Whilst these records establish a definite family connection they also go some way to explaining James Pirie's audacious actions.

Clearly Pirie recognised the power resting in the hands of his relative Henry Dundas and so took it upon himself to write directly to this high ranking official. It is also an obvious sign of his growing desperation; and in this, Pirie's action only makes sense if there was a pre-existing relationship especially given that the opening sentences of Pirie's letter are written in a manner indicating he had previously briefed Dundas on the circumstances pertaining to the capture of the *Raith*.

Sadly, no correspondence in the form of Dundas' reply appears to have survived, however, Pirie's second letter is concise. He quickly cuts to the chase and immediately appeals to Dundas for help. He writes very presumptively, given the protocol of the era, and even goes so far as to almost direct Dundas to organise a prisoner exchange. Obviously, ever since Pirie first became aware of the capture of the *Raith* he has kept himself busy scheming and negotiating a prisoner exchange.

In his letter he advises Dundas that he has already made the acquaintance of a reliable man on the ground in France capable of handling the money side of the transaction. Notwithstanding his very personal grief and anguish Pirie shows himself to be a very fair man indeed as he pleads the case not just for his only beloved son, but also for Young and indeed the whole of the crew of the *Raith*.

Pirie's letter reads -

'Edin^b 30 Sept 1794

Sir

The situation of the Crew of the Raith Greenlandman of Leith Captain Young is particularly described in Mr. Stephen's Letter to me sent with this. Words cannot describe the distress of the Wives of the unfortunate Crew and in particular Mrs. Young who has a family of six helpless children and separated from one of the best husbands. They wish if possible that their husbands should be exchanged. The French prisoners in the Castle here earnestly wish for the same thing and one of them whose father is a man of consequence in Dunkirk has sent a Letter of credite in favour of Captain Young and my Son.

From your well known humanity I have no doubt but you will exert your whole power to bring about the exchange so wished for by us all. I have the honour to be Sir

Your most obed^t humble servant

James Pirie

In. Mr. Stephens
Sept 24th '

Pirie's second letter directly raises the matter of Prisoner Exchange. What is it and how did it work in the day?

Reports of Prisoner Exchanges taking place in our 1794-5 timeframe are sketchy at best and lists of names, if any existed, do not appear to have survived or are so far not discovered in official archives. So, rather than rely on official government records some of the most enlightening documents are the journals written by actual prisoners. Several of these have come to be published, some immediately upon the prisoner's return to Britain whilst others were held within private family collections and published by later generations. One such publication bears the onerous title of *'An address to the People of the United Kingdoms of Great Britain and Ireland, Containing an Account of the Sufferings of Thomas O'Neill, a British Officer, While Confined in the Prison of the Conciergerie, At Paris, For Two Years and Ten Months; And of His Escape from Thence, During His Second Imprisonment as a Prisoner of War, Written by Himself. (London, 1806)'*

Thomas O'Neill recorded a diary of his experiences and those of his fellow prisoners wherein he records how they were abused by the residents of towns as they were marched through, were required to sleep in comfortless conditions, had their personal effects stolen and at times saw prisoners shot dead purely as an example to those forced to bear witness. All in all, the situation was dire; it would not be tolerated in civilised society but was symptomatic of the unruly behaviour at play in post-Revolutionary France. Academic J. David Markham makes the point in his paper; *'British Prisoners of War in France during the Napoleonic Wars'* that merchant seamen were the 'Men in the Middle'. They were not Officers or Military men and were not 'Travelling Gentlemen' which was the title given to those English who were living in France for business, academic or other personal reasons, and innocently caught up in these political struggles and their aftermath.

Prison conditions appear to have changed throughout the years of the Napoleonic Wars as evidenced by several other publications. Peter Bussell tells of his imprisonment as a Merchant Seaman in an essay entitled 'The Diary of Peter Bussell (1806-1814)'. Bussell's story was edited by his great-grandson and first published with illustrations and original drawings by author, G.A. Turner, Editor (London 1931). It explains that Peter Bussell, like Alexander Young, was a ships Master. Bussell was part owner of the unarmed trading sloop

The Dove which was captured by the French in 1806. It seems his experience was markedly different from that of British Officer Thomas O'Neill. It seems that 'Bussell was given substantially more freedom of movement and of sleeping arrangements than common prisoners of war were afforded.' Markham points out that Bussell's stories of some of the French gaolers and other persons were often quite amusing. One such story related to a gaoler in Cherbourg about whom Bussell wrote: 'Our gaoler was an elderly man, very friendly to us, but he loved the bottle. His wife and he often had words betwixt them, particularly when the old woman catched him at the bottle, which he would get to on every opportunity'. Bussell goes on to explain that he had some money and at times could: 'buy his way unto more private quarters and better beds'.

There were two other curious sources of funds to help prisoners. One came about when the French paid what was termed 'marching' money and the other was when prisoners were sent funds from the Lloyd's Patriotic Fund. This Lloyd's Patriotic Fund was set up in England and received money by subscription, mostly from shipowners and fellow seamen. We can only hope that Alexander and his crew were recipients of some of this benefaction. We know that the crew of the *Raith* were marched inland and similarly Bussell tells of his experiences on one such occasion. He wrote - 'When we reached the prison where we was to take up our night's abode we had marched twenty-seven miles this day. We was as hungry as half-starved hounds, and at last we succeeded in getting for our refreshment half a sheep's head, a little soup maigre [thin], and some bread. They charged us three livres [approx. half a crown]. So much for their humanity! Our night's rest was very uncomfortable, we having only but a little dirty straw to lay our weary bones on and being likewise both wet and cold.'

Markham then relates the tale of Alexander Stewart as extracted from 'The Life of Alexander Stewart, Prisoner of Napoleon and Preacher of the Gospel'. Stewart was born in Lochleven and later settled with his family in Kirkcaldy. He ran away from home to become a cabin boy on a merchant ship but sadly his vessel was captured within clear sight of the coastal guns of Brighton. They were boarded by a French privateer, the crew taken prisoner and the vessel sailed to France. Stewart described his experience thus - 'We were marched off to Dunkirk, each carrying the few clothes he was allowed to bring with him from the ship, slung on his back. We were tied to each other with a string chord [sic], much as you may see a number of horses coming to Smithfield [a market in central London], and escorted by a party of soldiers headed by two Drummers, beating what, I suppose, we should call the Rogue's march, to give dignity to the scene. Before we reached Dunkirk we were much fatigued, partly from want of food, but chiefly from depression of spirits'.

All told Alexander Stewart spent 10 years in captivity being marched from depot to depot. He said at times he was joined to other prisoners by a cord or on other occasions they were chained; either at their feet or by the neck. He goes on to explain that when the chains were removed he quite: 'forgot he was a prisoner'. As for life within the prison walls, Stewart writes: 'The whole was tedious, wearing and depressive beyond what I could well describe. The frequent boisterous rioting, gambling, drinking, swearing, and fighting, especially when shut down in the middle of the day (they were locked up for 3 hours each midday) often made the place a little hell on earth.' 'If your next neighbour chose to swear or to sing close to your ear when you wanted to read or write, or keep quiet, there was no remedy but your fists.' One can only imagine what kind of hellishly harsh treatment could have been meted out to the crew of the *Raith* and the desperation and depression they felt.

On the finer point of Prisoner Exchange there is one publication entitled - *'Prisoners of War in Britain 1756 to 1815 - A Record of their Lives, their Romance and their Sufferings'* by Francis Abell, which takes a look at just this subject and in our precise time period. The taking of prisoners has long been a natural event of war, in fact Patricia K. Crimmins in her paper entitled *'Prisoners of War and British Port Communities 1793-1815'* suggests that 'Prisoners were a muted and secondary - but not negligible - part of war policy.' There were rules agreed in the eighteenth century about what prisoners were to be allocated as a food allowance as per a prior agreement between countries. It also outlined that an agent be appointed by each combatant nation to oversee the treatment of their prisoner nationals, and these agents could visit prisons, hear complaints and organise prisoner exchanges as per a cartel system.

As far back as March 12, 1780, a Scale of Equivalents had been devised and agreed between England and France on how they would deal with Prisoner Exchanges in the future. It is a cold and inhumane approach which did see some men returned to their families. The Scale of Equivalents highlights class in the worst possible manner wherein it sets the rate as 'sixty men for an admiral or field-marshal to one man for a common sailor or soldier in the regular services, and from four men for a captain to one man of privateers or merchantmen.' These were cruel times and equality for human-kind was not part of the belief system of the day.

Unfortunately for Alexander and the crew of the *Raith*, sometime in 1793 the game changed and the French altered the equivalents and decreed that 'henceforth the exchange should be strictly of grade for grade, and man for man, and that no non-combatants or surgeons should be retained as prisoners of war.'

As a reader you are now thinking this is out of step with the previous summation but do read on! Timely to the opportunity or otherwise for Alexander and his crew to make good their escape, release, or exchange the English Admiralty had sent a deputation to France on 4 February 1795 authorised to settle the vexing question of Prisoner Exchange because the French were known to be violating their own rules.

Several meetings were set up on both sides of the Channel but the parties failed to come to a resolution primarily because French Military Strategists had ultimately concluded that France had quite sufficient manpower to defeat its enemies therefore no further soldiers or sailors were required. Furthermore, they realised if they were to release prisoners to the English, be they army or navy personnel, this action would only strengthen the English enemy ranks to the detriment of France. Plus, taking their own soldiers and sailors back into their various forces would have resulted in even greater numbers of mouths for the French to feed.

And then 1750-1850

This base level of strategic thinking reeks of General Lazare Carnot the Mathematician!

So where did this decision leave our crew of the *Raith*?

It is my greatest disappointment to report that to date the manner of the release of Captain Alexander Young, James Pirie Jnr or any or all of the crew of the *Raith* remains a total mystery. However, we do know that Alexander did make it home to Leith and to his beloved wife Helen. He was reunited with his sons, and since the birth of his 10th child George Young occurred on 15 Feb 1796, presumably Alexander returned to Leith sometime prior to June 1795. From this we can extrapolate that Alexander, James Pirie and his crew spent up to a year in captivity, and what a horrid year it would have been. It was their own - 'annus horribilis'.

On the positive side, Alexander does not appear to have sustained any injury or suffered any serious long term health issues as a result of his incarceration. Indeed, Alexander lived on for another twenty years and continued to do what he loved (roam the seas under canvas) and of course impart his well-honed skills to his sons, three of whom we know went on to become significant seafarers in their own right.

Chapter 7

Proceedings in the Admiralty Courts
The Ransoming of the *Eliza Swan*
America Vs Britain • Rodgers Vs Young
It's a Whale of a Tale!

A decade or so ago I felt there could be more to the Young's story than had been discovered so far so I decided to go in search of further details in respect of the ships known to be associated with the family. My search began with the *Eliza Swan*. Whilst my initial motivation was to satisfy my curiosity about these men and their ships - as sometimes happens in Genealogy the rewards in the end can be so much more than one could ever have imagined. In the case of the *Eliza Swan* I knew something about her whaling voyages, but I went on to uncover two very different but equally intriguing stories which turned out to be hallmarks of her life. These stories are impregnated with danger and intrigue as this ship, her captain and her crew of forty-eight fight battles both on land and sea.

Modern day researchers who put *'Eliza Swan'* in a search engine will be absolutely astounded by a hit count in the hundreds of thousands. Words like 'Battler of Montrose', The War of 1812, folk songs such as 'The Bonny Ship the Diamond', Books entitled 'In Pursuit of Leviathan:...' and 'Sixpence for the Wind: ...' all come to the fore in the synopses. Enter it into the British Newspaper Archives and again there are over fifty thousand hits; a staggering number of those are tagged to just three publications in one timeframe. *Eliza Swan* can also boast countless entries in the Shipping and Mercantile Gazette, the Scots Magazine and a Scottish regional newspaper: The Montrose, Arbroath and Brechin Review. These were all very popular print media in their day as they were the publications the general public turned to for information of local or national interest in respect of events, places and people. As such they were popular reads for most Scots.

The *Eliza Swan* also made it onto the pages of other tabloid newspapers like the Dundee Advertiser, Dundee Courier, Caledonian Mercury, York Herald, London Evening Chronicle, John O'Groat Journal, London Morning Post, Forfar and Kincardineshire Advertiser and the Derby Mercury and for many years her voyages were recorded in Lloyd's Register. She has been variously linked geographically with ports and places as noteworthy as Davis Strait, Greenland, the Gulf of Danzig in Poland, Riga, Russia [now part of Latvia] and St Petersburg in Russia, the White Sea port of Onega, Narva in Estonia, the infamous Elsinore Island of Vonved fame, Copenhagen, Leith, London and of course her home port of Montrose.

In fact, this grand old lady received very honourable mention in that previously referenced book entitled *'History of Montrose'* written by David Mitchell and published in 1866. At one time Mitchell had received a commission from then Acting Secretary to Government in Scotland, Mr. A.D. Robertson, to record the history of the ancient port town of Montrose and in his Chapter XI relating to 'Ship-Building, Shipping Trade, Wood Trade, Cabinet Making, Shipping, &c.' Mitchell included several paragraphs relating to the *Eliza Swan* with one early reference mentioning Mr. James Strachan and Mr. James Petrie, Shipbuilders. [The Petrie name will become more relevant shortly!] Mitchell continues with his insight that 'Montrose, some forty years ago, had about forty sail of sloops, a fleet of Greenland whalers, and three brigs, about 80 tons register, which were the Baltic and Archangel fleet. An improvement commenced when a brig of 150 tons was brought from Shields by Captain John Young, and it was such a wonder to see such a large ship bought for the Baltic trade, that people came from far and near to see her.' This Captain Young is none other than our own John Young, son of Alexander Snr and Helen Liston.

Some years prior to my inquiries, Robert T. Young, of the American branch of the Young Family, had made enquiries at Lloyd's Register. They replied to him by letter dated 27 July 1961, wherein Lloyd's advised their 1800 Register held the following survey data in relation to this ship -

ELIZA SWAN - Full-rigged Ship
Hull - doubled
Master - A. Young
Tonnage - 241
Built at Shields in 1785
Deep Repairs - 1798
Owners - Brown & Co
Draught - 13 feet
Voyage - Leith to Davis Strait
Classed - E1

Lloyd's Register also shed light on some of her ownership history with a notation in 1802 where she was purchased by Miller & Co., and then again in 1807 when A. Young became her Owner and Master and according to the records, he remained so until 1816. Whilst Lloyd's has Alexander Snr and Alexander Jnr's names ascribed as Master at various times, this is not the whole story because we know from various validated sources that Alexander and John often swapped ships and that at one point John Young was most definitely the Master of the *Eliza Swan* and a very successful Master indeed for many many seasons in the Arctic. There was one further note in Lloyd's Register which sparked my interest and it stated that she had been lengthened and tripled in 1806. Further investigations revealed that this work was such a major undertaking it took over six months to complete and the *Eliza Swan* was not re-floated until well into 1807.

The saga of this event constitutes story #1 for the *Eliza Swan*.

The said modifications and repairs were significant and set to become the subject of a protracted court action which achieved dishonourable mention in the House of Lords in 1828. In charting a path through the documentation of this case one garners an amazing insight into the workings of the Scottish and English Admiralty Courts, shipbuilding practice in the day, the art of doing business in the early 1800s and of course the character of Alexander Young Snr. This work was undertaken at a time when both shipbuilding and whaling were thriving. This would have seen most credible shipbuilders operating under a great deal of pressure; and, in the circumstances, it seems their overall quality of workmanship sometimes suffered. When a project goes awry and shortcuts are taken, in the end it is never a positive outcome for either party.

From the outset of negotiations, Alexander Young Snr was the owners' nominee and he played a pivotal role in liaising with the shipbuilders and overseeing the work. But more importantly from a genealogical point of view is the fact that the extensive documentation in respect of this court case adds to and supports what we already have come to understand about the character of this man. What this story exposes yet another layer of fact regarding the respect he commanded, his professional expertise, his staying power, his strength of conviction and above all his sense of fairness and rightfulness. The whole sorry saga was set to play out over almost a quarter of a century; and, would have impacted not only Alexander Snr and his close family but his broader Leith family of relatives, friends and business associates, as he pursued justice for *Eliza Swan's* original shareholders/owners and later for himself as Sole Owner. The Appellants were Strachan & Gavin [S&G], Shipbuilders in Leith, and the initial Respondents were Paton & Others on behalf of the then shareholders/owners.

The records dealing with this case which were found in the collections of the Scotland Admiralty Court and the Court of Session files in Edinburgh are extensive and so, for the purposes of this family narrative, only the final Appeal Hearing documents will be quoted. In a nutshell, the opening salvo to this particular document states the owners of the ship corresponded by letter with S&G shipwrights, regarding the lengthening and repairing of the ship, and requesting them 'to furnish an estimate of the probable cost, and also to note the prices of timber, and the rate of wages'. The owner's letter also contained this passage of clear instruction - 'the timber must be all English oak, and if you have a sufficient quantity on hand for the repair of the ship, besides her lengthening'. S&G replied in writing, stating that the cost of lengthening, on a rough calculation, would be in the vicinity of £900; but bearing in mind the vessel also required other repair work to be carried out, it would be in the best interest of both parties for the work to be done on a day rate basis. S.&G.'s letter goes on to confirm - 'The captain will have it in his power to keep an exact account of the articles expended, and to turn off any workmen that does not please him. We have on hand an excellent assortment of English oak timber of a suitable size for the vessel.'

A cost agenda was added wherein they stated that 'wages per day, 3s.4d ... common English oak timber per foot, 5s.' To a letter from the owners, announcing the dispatch of the ship from Montrose to Leith, this postscript was added 'As it is understood that nothing is to be put into the ship but English oak timber and Dantzic oak plank, to which you must bind yourselves by letter, &c.' To this, S&G replied thus 'With respect to the materials, we have a good stock of English timber and Dantzic plank, and little or no Hamburg; so that Captain Young will have it in his power to take what he likes best.' In a subsequent letter from the agent for the owners it is stated that 'I hope you will put on her the best of materials, and also the best of workmanship.' This makes it perfectly clear that *Eliza Swan* was a highly valued ship and was expected to receive only the very best of material and workmanship.

The repairs and lengthening did not go to plan and the owners were ultimately forced to pursue justice in the Courts on three complaints. One related to the materials used, another to the quality of the workmanship, and their final grievance related to the amount of the wages due to be paid to the carpenters employed on the job. On the matter of the timbers to be used, all the documentation clearly states that S&G gave major assurances in this regard, even to the point of stating that 'Captain Young will have it in his power to take what he likes best.' With respect to the wages issue, it appears that while *Eliza*

Swan was in Leith undergoing this work it was legislated that the wages for carpenters were to increase by 6d. per day. This pay-rise is set to become a major bone of contention because the owners believed they had a contracted figure quoted and S&G believe they had a right to claim for the additional wages. The issues surrounding the shoddy workmanship were indisputable and could have not only cost lives but could quit easily have resulted in the loss of the ship.

Also, the work took much longer than expected to complete and so immediately the *Eliza Swan* was released from the dry dock in Leith, Alexander set sail for Montrose where it was intended the vessel would be very quickly fitted out, crewed and victualled for the upcoming scheduled voyage to the whale fishery, albeit a little later than planned. On the short voyage from Leith to Montrose the *Eliza Swan* sprang a leak of alarming proportions. The owners would later contend that she only made Montrose 'because of the moderate sailing conditions prevailing at that time.' Once safely into Port, there was no alternative for the owners but to undertake the repairs to the *Eliza Swan* themselves. A notice to this effect was sent to the shipwrights S&G, who subsequently sent their Foreman to inspect.

The *Eliza Swan* did eventually set out for the whale fishery but because she was detained for an additional twenty-two days on account of the gravity of her unscheduled repairs, it was now too late to join the fleet in Davis Strait. Captain Young's years of experience would have told him there would already be overcrowding in the Strait. Therefore, it is highly likely he decided to try to fish the waters to the north of East Greenland which are several days sailing short of Davis Strait and far less crowded. In documents submitted by the owners to the Court they further contend that these protracted delays and enforced change of plans were solely responsible for the *Eliza Swan* arriving home with a short cargo. She sailed into Montrose with a very odd catch indeed: 5 fish, 116 seals and 5 bears. This further supports the notion that she did not sail to Davis Straits.

Additional documents were presented to the Court which demonstrated why the owners were standing a loss on several grounds and why they were therefore haggling over the payment of the full amount of their residual debt. They highlighted the several flaws in workmanship and related these directly to S&G's lack of attention to the Terms of the Contract. One of the most serious breaches of Contract related to the timbers used. Whilst English oak had been stipulated in the contract of work, after closer examination it appeared that American oak had been substituted for the repair of the *Eliza Swan*. There were several other points of shoddy workmanship cited: one in relation to two bolts which had been driven and clenched imperfectly; and another where there was actually a hole in the hull as a result of the omission of a tree-nail which was the cause of the serious leak. Finally, after the lengthening and repair work was finalised, the vessel had inadvertently been increased in the mid-ships five feet in width. This was not part of the terms of work originally agreed.

The owners contended under their pleadings and evidence that they were claiming redress for all these faults, nonconformities and losses. They also contended the shipwrights had no authority to charge on their account the additional 6d per day for wages. Nor were the owners prepared to pay the price charged for superior English oak timber when S&G had substituted inferior American Oak. In addition, the owners were claiming damages on account of their fishery losses which they attributed solely to their enforced delayed departure occasioned by the detention of the vessel for essential remediation repairs. S&G were arguing that they were entitled to full payment and after much toing and froing for over two decades and several court actions the case was finally up for hearing in the Appeals Court in order to resolve the matter once and for all.

Bearing in mind the initial contract was signed in July 1806 it is staggering to realise that the final day of the Appeal Hearing was set to be held in the 1st Division of the Admiralty Court on February 22, 1828. To say this case was a very long and drawn out affair is an understatement. What is patently obvious from the various data is that man for man those involved were obstinate men and each held the conviction that they had right on their side. At no point was either party prepared to give ground. The Appeal Hearing in this instance was presided over by Lord Meadowbank. At the time, Lord Meadowbank was Lord Ordinary and as such he was the sole judge of the

Outer House of the Scottish Court of Session charged with making determinations in civil cases such as this one. The legal representatives nominated were Solicitor-General Tindal and John Campbell Esq. appearing for the Appellants and Lushington and Keay appearing for G. Paton & Others, current shareholders/owners in what is the Montrose Whale Fishing Company which was by that time owner of the *Eliza Swan*.

Closer scrutiny of the legal representatives in this case revealed it had gained quite a high profile indeed, with some equally high profile legal professionals set to argue their respective opinions. Sir Nicholas Conyngham Tindal PC [Privy Counsellor] was representing Strachan & Gavin and was a man of considerable legal clout. Today, his commandingly judicial portrait hangs large and prominently in the prestigious Great Hall of Lincoln's Inn, London - the hallowed hall for lauded legal minds. He is described by many as the 'celebrated English lawyer who successfully defended the Queen of the United Kingdom, Caroline of Brunswick, at her trial for adultery in 1820 ... [and] was also responsible for the inception of that special verdict option "Not Guilty by reason of insanity".' This was the innovative defence Tindal mounted on the occasion of the murder trial of Daniel M'Naughten wherein Tindal argued that M'Naughten was insane at the time he shot Edward Drummond. Drummond was working as Secretary to Prime Minister Robert Peel at the time M'Naughten shot him in the back of the head. Once it was established that Robert Peel was the intended target of the would be assassin Tindal made the assertion that only insanity could account for M'Naughten's action of mistakenly identifying Drummond as Prime Minister Peel. This verdict stands as legal precedence today in countries inside and outside the British Commonwealth. Such was the clear and creative legal mind of this Privy Counsellor.

Opposing Counsel was Stephen Lushington, appearing for the 'Owners' of *Eliza Swan*. He appears to be a legal professional of equal status and merit. Born the younger son of the powerful Chairman of the British East India Company, he was a staunch Whig who also emerged as a prominent figure in the Queen Caroline of Brunswick affair but was more commonly characterised as someone of strong convictions, not afraid to openly criticise the Government for its arrogant and oppressive conduct in matters where he disapproved of their stance. His profile was enhanced in the day as a result of his extraordinary friendship with Thomas Fowell Buxton, renowned Abolitionist and Social Reformer. Lushington was a powerful and persuasive voice within the anti-slavery cabinet, and later took on the role of Vice-President of the Anti-Slavery Society. Whilst he was a close collaborator of Abolitionist William Wilberforce, Lushington's lasting legacy of character is that of a man not afraid to stand tall and reproach the establishment. He was a known quantity to his opposing counsel but a force to be reckoned with for sure and certain.

So, it was - Game on!

Detailed evidence was presented to the court asserting the *Eliza Swan* arrived into dry dock in Leith on the 15 August 1806. Captain Young was noted as 'the master, the ship-carpenter: and Mr. Young, a part owner, superintended the workmanship'. [The sidebar here is we now know that Alexander Snr did his apprenticeship as a Ships Carpenter]. The *Eliza Swan* remained in the dry dock until the following 26th January, almost seven months, at which time she was delivered over to the captain. The total agreed cost of the work was £2685.9s.8d of which £1350 was paid in advance. Due to the passage of time ownership of the vessel had changed several times, such that by 1828 when the matter comes before Lord Ordinary Meadowbank Alexander Snr was deceased. In the interim Alexander Snr had purchased the Montrose Greenland Whale Fishing Company, renamed it the Montrose Whale Fishing Company and 'as a major shareholder of the company' was one of the owners of the *Eliza Swan* along with his sons. Notwithstanding these ownership changes, the crux of the matter remained; the current Respondents, namely the company headed by Alexander Jnr, were steadfastly claiming damages for their costs and losses.

At various times down the decades the 'owners' had offered a settlement whereby they would agree to pay the balance outstanding less their damages claim, but S&G declined their settlement terms hence the matter went all the way to the Appeals Court. S&G were now seeking the full balance of their debt plus interest which they contended amounted to some £435 15s 10d giving a grand total of £1771.5s.6d. The great minds of legal persuasion put their respective sides of the argument to Judge Admiral and Lord Ordinary Meadowbank. After viewing all the evidence and hearing the arguments in this Appeal Case Meadowbank delivered his verdict via this detailed judgment:

> 'In respect that, by the letters of agreement entered into between the parties in July 1806, the repairs in question were stipulated to be made by days' wages, and at a rate of fixed sum per day, and that no satisfactory proof has been brought (independent of the objections to the pursuers' witnessers) of any such general practice in the trade as will justify a higher charge in the event of a rise of wages; finds, that the pursuers are not entitled to charge for carpenters' work at a higher rate than 3s.4d per day; therefore sustain the objections to the over charge of 6d. per day, amounting in whole to £69.0s.6d sterling. In respect of the final interlocutor of 8th June 1815, finds, that the pursuers are not entitled to charge for timber at a higher rate than that specified in the letters of agreement; and therefore sustains the objections that a part of the timber is charged at 6s. per foot instead of 5s., and allows a deduction accordingly to the amount of £35.8s.6d sterling. With regard to the objection that some American oak was substituted in place of English oak, finds, that by the letters of agreement the whole timber was to be English oak, and that the pursuers ought not to have made use of any other oak in the repairs; but in respect that some persons were

employed by the defenders to superintend the work, and that the vessel was benefited to the extent of the oak furnished, finds, that the pursuers are entitled to charge for the price of American oak, and appoints each party to give in a short minute on the question what these charges should be: Repels the objection made to the period occupied in repairing the vessel, in respect that there were some persons employed by the defenders to superintend what was going on; and that satisfactory evidence has not been brought that there was an unreasonable delay: Repels the whole other objections stated to the pursuers' account. And with respect to the defenders' counterclaims stated in the defences, and in the supplementary action, finds it sufficiently instructed by the evidence of the carpenters who inspected the vessel, by the leakage of the vessel on her voyage from Leith to Montrose, in the attempted voyage to Davis Strait, and in the voyage to Greenland, that the repairs made upon the vessel by the pursuers were insufficiently executed, and that the defenders are entitled to all reasonable damages which they sustained in consequence of the insufficiency of the work. Therefore finds the defenders entitled, 1st, To the expense of the repairs which the vessel received at Montrose before she sailed for Davis Strait (Greenland), amounting to £44.9s.1$^{1/2}$d sterling: 2nd, To the expense of wages to the captain and crew of the vessel for the twenty-two days occupied in repairing her at Montrose, amounting to £248.7s sterling: 3rd, To the expense of the repairs which the vessel received after her return from Greenland voyages, amounting to £194.12s.7d. sterling: Repels the claims of the defenders, founded on the damages alleged to have been sustained by the unsuccessful fishing at Greenland, in respect the voyage appears to have been pretty successful, and that a claim of this kind partakes too much of the nature of consequential damages: Repels also the claim of the defenders, founded on the demand for the vessel being now repaired with English oak instead of American oak, in respect of the long period which elapsed before this claim was brought forward, and that it ought to have been insisted in when the vessel was repaired at Montrose.'

In addition, the judge also awarded The Montrose Whale Fishing Company costs in respect of the judicial actions heard in the local Montrose Court over the last 22 years. These costs amounted to a further £31.5s.0d. After Meadowbank finished handing down this final judgment; and, taking into account the expenses accrued to date by *Eliza Swan's* owners in attempting to settle the matter, The Montrose Whale Fishing Company was ordered to pay a meagre settlement of £250.14s.7d. This left Strachan & Gavin with a crippling loss of £1520.10s.11d on their counter claim or £1084.15s.1d without the calculation of any interest on their account for the past almost a quarter of a century. Either way, a financial loss of that magnitude would have been extremely damaging for any business. Just what it meant for Strachan & Gavin is not entirely clear nor is it known how these events impacted relations between the parties, their families and businesses associated in the small and close knit shipping communities of Montrose and Leith. Add to that the negative fallout from the ongoing bad publicity for S&G and one would have to assume S&G paid a very high price for their stubbornness.

So protracted was this case that by the time it was finally determined, Alexander Snr was deceased some eleven years which meant Alexander Jnr was charged with the responsibility of seeing the case through to a satisfactory conclusion. That being the situation, I was left wondering how did this impact the life of Alexander Jnr and what can it tell us about his strength of character?

All told, Alexander Jnr and his father had lived and worked out of the Port of Leith for half a century prior to taking up business opportunities in Montrose, which seems to have necessitated Alexander Jnr relocating to that ancient Burgh port. What has been learned so far is that the Leith waterfront was a melting pot of intrigue wrapped up in a cloak of family and friends which would have made this long drawn out affair of the *Eliza Swan* lawsuit, countersuit and appeal all the more conversation worthy as well as stressful. To help understand how this may have impacted on the lives of Alexander Snr and his sons as well as Strachan & Gavin I initially turned to Sue Mowat's book where she gives some insight into the business background of Strachan & Gavin, and the principals Crichton Strachan and John Gavin as well as their connections within the Leith community.

Mowat states that Crichton Strachan and John Gavin initially learned their trade whilst in the employ of John Sime Snr, a premier shipbuilder in Leith and the man credited by many as having built the first Dry Dock there in 1720. As employees, these men were so well respected by Sime that he went so far as to nominate them as Executors in is Will of 1776. It was only after John Sime Jnr joined his father's business that both Strachan and Gavin decided their future prospects were limited within the family company, at which point they left and set up their own operation.

Strachan & Gavin were rubbing shoulders with fellow shipbuilders such as Robert Dryburgh and Robert Menzies, who are also known to have had business dealings with Alexander Snr. Mowat reports that at one point Dryburgh rented out his dry dock to John Sime Jnr who had just been awarded a major Navy contract to build a sloop-of-war, the HMS *Fury*, which was to be around 350-400 burthen; too big for the Sime's current dock facilities. Clearly, all these men were plying their trade in close proximity to each other and enjoying respectful relationships. So close and inter-related were these families that Robert Menzies named his second son Robert Dryburgh Menzies. That's close – that's like family. That's how it was in Leith in the day.

Despite these intertwined relationships and the massive loss S&G sustained, the company of Strachan & Gavin managed to remain in business, probably for two main reasons. One, Leith shipbuilders were enjoying a great upsurge in business activity thanks to the buoyancy of the shipbuilding industry as a whole brought about by England's goal to have an even bigger and stronger Navy. And two, Strachan & Gavin were ship owners as well as shipbuilders and this meant they had diversified and spread their exposure to loss and risk.

Flying in the face of the shoddy workmanship carried out on the *Eliza Swan*, it appears S&G had achieved quite a reputation for building ships which were specifically designed for the Polar Regions. One article which appeared in the Scottish Geographical Magazine as recently as 1965 talks about the Antarctic exploits of a Captain James Weddell, Master of the Brig *Jane* of Leith, built by Strachan & Gavin. The article gives these shipbuilders a glowing endorsement. The writer argues S&G's contribution to Polar Expedition is equal to that of the much lauded Messrs. Enderby of London. The article reads in part 'Weddell Sea perpetuates the daring voyage of a merchant seaman of Scottish ancestry', and then the author goes on to lament that there is nothing to substantiate the work of either Messrs. Enderby or Strachan & Gavin. Reading this high praise, it is fair to consider that S&G may have pursued the *Eliza Swan* case so vigorously because they wished to protect their business reputation.

Or, is that all there was to it? Interestingly, I uncovered yet another insight into the behaviour of these shipbuilders where they were embroiled in another protracted court action. This one began in 1811 and relates to the loss of a vessel owned by S&G which was covered by an insurance policy. An action was brought against them by the Sea Insurance Co. of Scotland but this time it took only sixteen years, with judgment being handed down in 1827. Again S&G suffered a major loss. The case came down to yet another point of contract law in that the port at which their ship was wrecked in a hurricane was not one of the ports cited in their policy. In all fairness, in this instance, there were extenuating circumstances. It reads like a for-shortened version of the *Eliza Swan* incident where S&G felt they had right on their side and were determined to pursue the matter through the Admiralty Court and wound up facing a final judgement in the Appeals Court with costs awarded against them yet again.

These long drawn out cases seem to have taken a toll on the men personally, and whilst John Gavin was still alive when the final judgment was handed down in the *Eliza Swan* case, his partner Crichton Strachan was deceased, and court proceedings show his side of the partnership was being represented by his Executors. Of course, Alexander Young Snr was also deceased, and The Montrose Whale Fishing Company was now solely in the hands of Alexander Young Jnr. Since John Gavin was also found cited in several other court actions, one involving John Sime Jnr and his sister Margaret, it is clear that he was no stranger to the inside of a courtroom. Plus, given the close familial circumstances in Leith, one is left to conclude these occurrences could well have divided the community.

It seems this lady of the sea, *Eliza Swan*, was never far from controversy - in fact, while the legal wrangle about the work done by S&G was being thrashed out inside and outside the courts, she was involved in yet another legal wrangle - this one would be recorded in the books as maritime legal precedent.

Many of the discoveries surrounding this story of the 'Ransoming of the *Eliza Swan*' came about yet again by chance. One of these chance discoveries was made by Maritime Lawyer, Donald Petrie. So passionate was his pursuit of the legal facts in this matter that in the end he felt compelled to write a book which he dedicated to his wife, Mary Stewart Petrie. Renowned American Broadcast Journalist, Walter Cronkite, described Donald Petrie's account of these events as '... an extraordinary book. All the romance and adventure from the age of piracy and privateers told from a hitherto unexplored perspective - that of the law of the time so constructed and interpreted that it fostered and protected what otherwise would have been an era of lawlessness at sea. A wonderful addition to our nautical lore'.

Petrie's book is entitled *'The Prize Game - Lawful Looting on the High Seas in the Days of Fighting Sail.'* Another literary critique was offered by Peter Stanford, one time President

Emeritus, Founder and generous benefactor of the National Maritime Historical Society in New York. He proffered, if you attempt to read 'The Prize Game' you should 'brace yourself for high adventure, sailing with some of the most dashing and dedicated captains of the age of sail, [and] the privateers men whose experiences are set forth in ...' this book.

In his Preface, Petrie writes he had suffered some health issues and, like many people 'of a certain age' he decided to take time out from his hectic professional life as a New York based Maritime Lawyer to explore his genealogy. He had always been a keen lover of sail, and he and other family members had enjoyed sailing but admitted he knew almost nothing of the antecedents of his large American family. He goes on to say that his American family had '....been seafaring people and, not surprisingly, my trail led to the ancient port town of Montrose on the North Sea coast of Scotland. There I learned that my great-grandfather and namesake had gone to the Arctic for twenty-five summers hunting whales on board a local whaler, the *Eliza Swan*.' This was to prove to be a life changing discovery for Donald Petrie in ways he had not imagined.

This decision also prompted another chance encounter which would change Petrie's life forever. His quest led him to conduct research at the Montrose Museum where he met Mary Stewart Cook, a meeting which in turn led him to make two major life decisions. Firstly, it was because of Mary that he was alerted to the events surrounding the ransoming of the *Eliza Swan*, the existence of the Ransom Note itself, and it was Mary who made him aware of the fact that the ransom was never paid. This latter fact excited Petrie's inquiring legal mind and ultimately is what made the writing of 'The Prize Game' such a necessity. Secondly, as a delightful consequence of their close working relationship Donald Petrie developed an admiration and affection for Mary and having had a chance encounter with Mary in Montrose in 2014, it is clear why he fell in love with her and later married her. Donald and Mary returned to New York where Donald set about completing his research and writing his book. Mary started a new chapter in her life too. On a personal note, let me say here that Mary Stewart Petrie has been very supportive of my project and still holds a passion for this story.

When I met her in Montrose she declared she still holds a deep affection for Scotland and for Montrose and endeavours to spend time there every year.

This is not a tall tale but the true story of a ransoming on the high seas involving Captain John Young and the *Eliza Swan* of Montrose. It is an intriguing adventure overlaid with the War of 1812, the Law of Nations, Insurance and Legal Precedent. In the end, Petrie had to admit that even well credentialed experienced lawyers still have something more to learn.

In the course of his researching, Petrie learned the *Eliza Swan* had been taken by an American frigate and released on the basis of a five thousand pounds ransom note. At this point his legal training led him to seriously question Mary's account of events that the ransom was never paid; in fact, he openly admitted his scepticism. On the other hand, it seemed equally as ludicrous that Young would be carrying large sums of cash. After all, 'what was a frugal Scottish captain doing with that much money in the Arctic where there is nothing to buy?' Mary politely informed him that in reality Captain John Young did not carry that much cash, and the sum was only contained in the Ransom Note. Then Petrie's legal mind took over and he vehemently contended that '.... a note given under duress, would be utterly worthless' in the eyes of the law.

At this point, Donald Petrie felt compelled to return to New York, and once there he hastened to the Association of the Bar Reading Room, from where he writes '..... to my astonishment, learned that in the days of sailing ships, Bills of Exchange and Bonds, given for the release of enemy ships captured in wartime, were valid legal documents, enforceable in courts throughout the world.' This sent him in hot pursuit of further evidence relating to the *Eliza Swan* case. By now Donald Petrie was of a single mind, family genealogy aside he was now searching for corroborating answers to the legal conundrum. He delved into the archives of International Law, and specific documents relating to these events in the American Maritime Legal Archives. He wrote that he 'Unwittingly .... began to study the doctrine and practice of maritime prize taking under the Law of Nations, as international law was formerly called'. Along the way he also met with Gordon Jackson and Eric Graham whom he sought out in his quest for validation and a need to learn more of the related Scottish Maritime History from these well published Maritime Historians.

Petrie's book largely embraces the legal perspective and the differences in the legal boundaries of responsibility as they pertained to the United States and Britain in the nineteenth century. These differences highlight the difficulty in the day for sea captains such as John Young, his brother Alexander Jnr and indeed their father Alexander Snr. What Petrie also brings to front of mind is that sea captains in the day were required to shoulder a great deal more responsibility than just that which related to sailing their ships, delivering their cargoes and managing their crews. They were also required to understand and act within the Law in jurisdictions other than their own in order to ply their trade. This involved not only the law relating to Ransoming and Bills of Exchange, but all matters bound by the Law of Nations as it applied to the Merchant Navy worldwide. Is it any wonder some ran foul of the law at times!

The story of the Ransoming of the *Eliza Swan* began in the year 1813. *Eliza Swan* had been at the whale fishery in Davis Straits and was on her homeward voyage to Montrose when she was boarded. To understand the how and why this ransoming occurred as well as the when and where, we need to look at the whale fishery for that season, the issues arising out of the American War and how these conspired to impact Captain John Young and place the *Eliza Swan* in the line of fire.

Were they lucky or unlucky? You decide.

Lubbock reported that 'After several years of good fishing, the British whaling industry was riding the high tide of prosperity when war with America broke out and made the seas still more dangerous for the peaceful traders.' It has been variously recorded that the value of the fleet heading north for that 1813 season was valued at a staggering one million and a half pounds sterling, 'and manned by between 5,000 and 6,000 seamen.' In total one hundred and thirty-eight British ships sailed to the Arctic of which only 3 departed from Montrose and 10 from Leith. This fleet included a number of newcomers mainly from Hull and Aberdeen - so competition was fierce, and expectations were riding high. The first to leave port as usual was the *James of Whitby* on the 14 February but the blustery weather and gale force winds reported in March and April caused significant damage among the fleet. These severe storms caught several vessels in Gray Hope Bay off Aberdeen where they were all dragging their anchors for a time and one, *Oscar*, was complete wrecked. Fortunately, she went down within clear sight of land and reports are that the crew were saved. The rest of the fleet were more fortunate except for the few who lost their foremasts and bowsprits and were forced to return to home port.

Even Captain Scoresby in his treatise entitled *'The Arctic Regions and the Northern Whale-Fishery'* contends that the weather was rather 'boisterous' as he called it. His Ship's Log for 25 April 1813 records that a 'hard gale from the north-east' had blown the ship away from the edge of the ice and strangely the cold eased. He says that '... when a ship, which has attained the edge of the ice, under a southerly gale, is exposed suddenly to a northerly breeze, the change in temperature is so great and rapid, that the most hardy cannot conceal their uneasiness under its first impression.'

The dangers imposed by the ice floes were never far away and on the 17 June 1813 several Greenlandmen were seen penetrating the ice in pursuit of a number of whales. While some whales were secured, as time went by a strange situation developed where the 'sea was as smooth as the surface of a pond; but the ice ..... was in a strange state of disturbance.' Scoresby wrote elsewhere in his later book *'An Account of the Arctic Regions'* - 'Some floes, and some large pieces, moved with a velocity of three or four miles per hour, while other similar masses were at rest.' He later observed great sheets of ice completely detached from the main body beginning to float south at speed such that they were leaving an eddy like a 'strong current in a shallow river'. Suddenly there were five or six whale boats along with their mother ships beset in the ice. There were crewmembers in these boats who lived in fear for three days until the ice slackened. By then the mother ships had been released and blown out of sight and the crews were forced to row for many hours to the south-east to discover their ships. Such events did not always end so positively.

Another report states a heavy gale blew up on 11 May 1813 and fourteen crew from a Whitby ship were put off to set an anchor in a large piece of ice. The ship then approached on a signal, a rope was fixed to the anchor but the ice 'shivering with the violence of the strain when the ship fell astern, the anchor flew out, and the ship went adrift.' Under the force of the wind and sail she 'scudded a considerable distance to leeward, and was then reached out to sea.' The fate of the crew was sealed at that point, as the air temperature was 15-16°F [-9 to -10°C], and Scoresby observed 'these poor wretches were left upon a detached piece of ice, of no considerable magnitude, without food, without shelter from the inclement storm, and deprived of every means of refuge.'

In the absence of any logs or diaries for Captains Alexander and John Young for 1813, Scoresby's account explains conditions well. He reports that 'many whales were seen near the same latitude [80°N]; but the weather being tempestuous in an almost unprecedented degree, few were killed'. The greater number that year were fished in the open sea and in the greatest abundance about the end of June and beginning of July. What we do know about the *Eliza Swan* and *Monarch*, the two vessels of the Young's Montrose Whale Fishing Company, is that, according to The Montrose Review of the 16 April 1813, they sailed from Montrose on the 12 April in company with the *London* with Captain Flockhart as Master. They were setting course for Spitzbergen with many of their regular crew on board including Donald Petrie's great-grandfather, Archibald Petrie. It is not hard to imagine that spirits were high as they made their way north. It is fair to say they would have experienced the same conditions as Scoresby described for his voyage north and while at the fishing grounds. Finally, a positive report appeared in the local newspaper stating all three vessels returned safely to Montrose and by all accounts they had reasonable catches - *Eliza*

Swan 8 fish, *Monarch* 5 but no details for the *London*. On the face of it for anyone reading just the statistical returns for the Port of Montrose, everything appears perfectly normal. However, it is what these newspaper articles and the raw data don't tell the reader that constitutes the real story.

While *Eliza Swan* and *Monarch* were fishing in the Arctic, the situation for the American Navy ships forced to remain at sea had become pretty grim. By 27th June 1813, the *USS President* under the command of Commodore John Rodgers had been at sea for two months raiding, or privateering, in the North Atlantic. Short of provisions and water at one point Rodgers was forced to put into Bergen and despite his declaration of famine on board, he was given only water and very meagre provisions. He sailed out of Bergen on 2 July heading west towards the Orkneys with an initial plan to then change course to North Cape for the purpose of intercepting a convoy of 25-30 merchantmen returning from Archangel. The USS *President's* first encounter was with the snow, *Daphne* of Whitby, skippered by Captain Gales. It was 18 July and the *Daphne* of Whitby was bound for Archangel in ballast. [A 'snow' is a particular class of Merchant Navy ship specifically rigged for Arctic conditions, hence its name.]

The captain's Log from the *Daphne* records her capture in detail. William Gales wrote 'At midnight on the 18 July a frigate with English colours hoisted hove in sight to leeward in lat. 71.35°N long. 26.51°E fired a gun to bring us to. We bore down to him. At two a.m. the fourth Lieutenant boarded us under pretence of impressing men and gaining intelligence'. The Lieutenant proceeded to order the Master of the *Daphne* to take his Logbook and papers and go on board the frigate. 'As soon as the Master was on board, the President hoisted American colours, and the Lieutenant ordered the mate to deliver up the ship's keys, and the men to pack up their clothes and be peaceable, and they should have everything belonging to them, as the brig was a prize, and they prisoners to the United States frigate President, Commodore Rodgers.' A scurrilous act perpetrated in copybook style, so typical of the day, especially given the privateers knew these defenceless unarmed merchantmen were easy pickings.

On the same day, 18 July 1813, the *President* is joined by American privateer *Scourge*, a New York based Schooner. Subsequent Maritime records for 19 July give the *President's* location as near the North Cape at position 71°51'N and 20°18'E, when Rodgers sights two sails. He continues to sail toward them until he identifies them as a British line of battleship and a frigate. He hauls by the wind on the opposite tack and flees toward the Southwest. The British ships are, in fact, the frigate *Alexandria*, 32 guns 12-pounders, Captain Robert Cathcart and sloop-of-war *Spitfire*, 16 guns 9 pounders, Captain John Ellis. At this point, Rodgers orders that the prisoners from the *Daphne* be sent into the hold under strict confinement, and as the *President* prepared for action Commodore Rodgers promised 'three days extra grog allowance for any man willing to fight till they sink because the English should never be allowed to carry the President to England.' The English men-of-war sail in pursuit for a period variously described as between 80 hours and four days. Early on in that encounter the USS *Scourge* decides to break away fleeing upwind to the Northwest; where she is not pursued.

On the morning of 20 July, Rodgers' log records the English vessels are continuing the chase and the prisoners remain confined in the hold. There is no known entry for the 21 July, and it is presumed the status quo remained. Dawn on 22 July and the *Alexandria* comes up with the *President* 'very fast, the prisoners are confined below as the crew prepare for action. The men loaded the stern chasers with iron bars and bolts over and above the common charging, and swore they had rather sink than be taken.' Meanwhile, the treble allowance of 'grog' had gone down well and spirits were high. 'During the chase they hove the Daphne's two guns overboard. The master saw a great number of iron bars and bolts made fast at the ends with a great deal spun yarns. &c. and also small shot put into the wads, ready to load the guns should they come into action.'

It is said the Second Lieutenant on board the *President* approached Commodore Rodgers to 'come to an action'. Rodgers was thinking more strategically and decided to play a waiting game. At this point the *President* is flying two fighting flags both large and white with black lettering; one saying 'No impressment' the other saying 'This is the haughty President, how do you like her?' The *Scourge* on the other hand was known to fight under a flag boasting 'Free Trade and Sailors Rights'. To a modern day non-maritime reader this may seem a strange tradition; however, it was part of maritime culture back then for each crew to have their own fighting banner.

Yet another day passed without any action, and ultimately the *President* runs the English out of sight and the prisoners can at last enjoy a long-awaited liberty on deck.

From here we will take up the story as told by Donald Petrie that includes excerpts from Commodore Rodgers Log -

> 'In late morning of 24 July 1813 the whaleship *Eliza Swan* sailed south through the Norwegian Sea en route from the Greenland whaling grounds to her home port of Montrose on the east coast of Scotland. John Young the twenty-four-year-old Scottish Captain, drove his ship under full sail in a moderate southeast breeze. His noon reading showed that he was approaching the sixty-seventh parallel. He had every reason to be satisfied on that July morning. The *Eliza Swan*, 306 tons, with six whale boats and a crew of forty-eight, had upheld her reputation as a 'lucky ship'. Having caught eight whales, she sailed home laden with 146 tons of whale blubber for the ravenous British oil market. John had left the Spitzbergen ice line a week before in company with his older brother, Alexander, captain of the *Monarch* and a partner in the Montrose Whale Fishing Company, which owned both vessels. Although the *Monarch* was a newer and larger ship and carried a lighter cargo, the *Eliza Swan* had managed to outsail her and she was now out of sight. The brothers were nearing home and no threat stood in their way that morning except the ever-present danger of forcible recruitment by Royal Navy press gangs.

Britain was still at war with Napoleonic France, and the Royal Navy had French fleets tightly blockaded in continental ports from the North Sea to the Mediterranean. For the past year, the British had also suffered the nuisance of another war with the United States and maintained a blockade of all the major ports on that distant shore as well. These blockades were complicated and costly exercises in ships, men and supplies.

So, as Captain John Young neared Scottish shore his thought would have turned to the ever-present danger of the Press Gangs of the Royal Navy. It seems the protections once enjoyed by Greenlandmen under the old legislation had now changed and the law as it stood in 1813 only offered immunity to impressment for the Officers on board whalers not for their crewmembers. Petrie's view on this is shared by many in that 'The British government subsidized the whale fishery in order to create a bank of trained seamen on whom their press gangs could forcibly draw if needed. Although the government exempted Young and his officers from seizure, the loss of even one man to a lifetime of involuntary naval service was a tragedy felt by all in the close-knit burgh of Montrose. In 1811 an apprentice was seized, and six years earlier the Eliza Swan had suffered the calamity of losing a third of her crew to a seaborne Royal Navy press gang.'

Unbeknown to John Young the *Eliza Swan* had been under surveillance for some time by the hungry frigate *USS President* who, according to her Log, recorded their surveillance thus 'strange sail in sight; they take her to be a man of war, and prepare for action: the prisoners sent into the hold. We come up with her, and find her to be the Eliza Swan, of Montrose, Captain Young, from Greenland to Montrose .'

Petrie makes two salient points here - one, that the *Eliza Swan* was a whaler, and her lookouts were accustomed to looking for whales in the foreground not ships in the far ground. And two, the towering mastheads on men-of-war vessels like the *President* were specifically designed for the latter purpose unlike the much shorter masts on the whalers. Besides, Young and his crew were headed home and would have been looking forward toward Scottish shore with great anticipation and longing - not backwards to the cold inhospitable North. The situation took a dramatic turn mid-afternoon when the crew of the *Eliza Swan* finally became aware that a large frigate was suddenly bearing down on them on their windward side; and approaching at speed. John would have realised this was no ordinary frigate despite the fact she was flying a British Ensign. She was advancing with her guns manned and ready and it was clear the eight small canon on his vessel would simply be no match for the mighty fighting power of the fifty heavy guns on the advancing warship.

At this point, John Young had no real reason to suspect it was a hostile American frigate since no American vessel since John Paul Jones in 1779 had been known to venture that far north. Therefore, in accordance with sailing procedure, John Young 'put his helm over and hove to'. The frigate lowered a boat and 'sent a lieutenant in the uniform of the Royal Navy on board the Eliza Swan. At the gangway the boarding officer identified his ship as the HM frigate Alexandria and directed Young to accompany him to the man-of-war with his ship's papers.' Once Captain Young and the Lieutenant reached the frigate's quarter-deck Young was immediately ushered into the Day Room.

Right there and then, the gravity of his situation would have been all too apparent as he came face to face with Commodore Rodgers of the US Navy. Rodgers' uniform would have been an immediate give-away. John would recognise it instantly as not a Royal Navy uniform, since he and his brother Alexander had grown up in Leith, where there had been a Navy base for many years and on numerous occasions he and the entire Young family would have rubbed shoulders with members of the real Royal Navy and been totally familiar with their various uniforms and insignia according to rank and role.

John Young knew he was in serious trouble!

Petrie's research revealed that in reality the two men had quite a deal in common. At the same age as John Young was that day, Rodgers too had been 'four years master of the *Jane*, a ship about the size of *Eliza Swan*, which traded between Baltimore and European ports.' Both their fathers were Scotsmen - Commodore Rodgers father was Col. John Rodgers of the Harve de Grace of Maryland, John's we know was Captain Alexander Young of Montrose and Leith. Both their fathers had taken them to sea as boys and their natural talents meant they rose to command at a very young age. They were also accustomed to shouldering responsibility for their ship, men, cargo and owners. As they sized each other up they were doubtless also thinking about the provisions of the Law of Nations 'as it then existed among the maritime powers and [John] would have concluded that the Eliza Swan and her cargo were a valid prize of the American and that he and the crew were prisoners of war.'

Unbeknown to John Young, the *President* was desperately short of provisions. Rodgers had not only his own crew of over four hundred to feed but he had taken on board a further twenty-eight prisoners, comprising the Captain and crew from the *Daphne*. To make matters worse, over the last month while cruising the colder high northern latitudes of the Norwegian and Barents Seas, Rodgers' men seem to have consumed more than their usual rations. What Rodgers did not need at this point was another forty eight whale fishermen to feed; therefore, this made Rodgers very kindly predisposed to making a deal.

John may have been very young; however, he proved his strength of character by maintaining a clear head. What he ultimately decided to do may well have been a strategy discussed with his father given Alexander's experience with the French Navy. Or was it a simple matter of being aware of and understanding the ambit of the Law of Nations? Either way, on the day, as luck would have it, it was an option particularly attractive to Rodgers. It is written that ' ... even if this Young achieved something of a coup. It seems that disturbing rumours surrounding the escapades of this American frigate's presence had reached Britain, and with the implied threat President posed to the returning Greenland whaling fleet oil prices had risen considerably.' Every cloud has a silver lining.

Appreciating that frugal Scottish Captains did not carry massive amounts of cash, Rodgers was quite prepared to accept John Young's Bill of Exchange for five thousand pounds drawn upon David Kinnear and the other shareholders of the Montrose Whale Fishing Company. In the day a Bill of Exchange was an instrument similar to a cheque today 'but instead of being drawn on a bank it was drawn on a commercial company which was instructed to honour it when presented.' It was further backed by 'John Young's personal bond so that if the company did not pay on demand, Young would be obliged to do so.'

The final gesture required by Rodgers of Young was a 'Sea Cartel'. In the day this was the name given to a formal exchange of prisoners at sea. Rodgers was keen to divest himself of those additional twenty-eight unwanted mouths and as part of their arrangement, Young agreed to transport Captain Gales and the crew of the *Daphne* back to Scotland. Once having agreed the terms they were almost done, but not quite. Considerable time was spent handwriting multiple copies of the salient documents which were counter-signed by both Rodgers and Young. Once the document side of the ransom transaction was completed all that remained was the expedient co-ordination of the prisoner transfer. Rodgers was astute enough to realise time is of the essence and he should be on his way. His final logbook entry of the day stated the *President* was standing toward the southwest while the *Eliza Swan* continued on her course directly south toward home port.

Scottish Admiralty records reveal that a short time later John Young fell in with two ships of the Royal Navy, His Majesty's frigate *Alexandria* and the sloop-of-war *Spitfire*. The first step for Captain Young was to deliver over to the *Alexandria* Captain Gales and the crew from the *Daphne*. The Montrose Review of 13 August 1813 reports that the *Eliza Swan* made it safely into home port on Monday August 9. The journalist from the Review interviewed Captain John Young on this occasion and wrote an article which appears very prosaic and nonchalant. It reads 'Young first reported on the success of the fishing and the extent

And then 1750-1850

of his cargo and then described his encounter with Commodore Rodgers.' That was it! The full extent of the reporting. So commonplace was rogue Navy privateering the reporter wrote it up as if it was all in a day's work.

Petrie's observation at this point was this should have ended the matter, except for one other event which took place a short time later and surely must have been a rare if not unique event in nineteenth century naval warfare and privateering. Not to mention the look of utter consternation which would have come over the face of Captain John Young when the local postman in Montrose delivered a personal letter sent to him by Commodore John Rodgers. It had been mailed from Liverpool on August 14 and addressed to 'Mr. John Young, Master of the Eliza Swan, Montrose, Scotland'.

It reads -

'U.S. Frigate <u>President</u>
At Sea August 2nd 1813

Sir,

I have been induced to forward you the enclosed certificate in order that you may be enabled to account with your Insurers for the ransom of the Ship Eliza Swan and Cargo of which you are Master.

Respectfully, etc.
Jn Rodgers

[Enclosure]

U.S, Frigate <u>President</u>
At Sea, August 2nd 1813

This is to certify that having captured on the 24th ultimo the British Merchant Ship the Eliza Swan belonging to Montrose, Scotland with a cargo of fish blubber it was my intention to have destroyed her had not John Young ransomed said ship and cargo for five thousand pounds Sterling money of Great Britain signing a bond and giving Bills of Exchange on his owner David Kinnear Esquire of Montrose for said amount.

Jn Rodgers '

Sometimes life turns out to be stranger than fiction, and it seems there would be yet another lucky chance encounter in the North Atlantic that summer to add further intrigue to an already amazing tale. After parting from *Eliza Swan* on July 24, the USS *President* later changed course and stood toward the Irish Sea. Five days later, in company with the USS *Scourge* she captured the merchantman brig *Alert* of Peterhead, Captain George Shand. Unfortunately for the *Alert*, she was discovered to be carrying pitch and tar from Archangel en route to Oporto Spain; and so, for her it was not going to be such a positive encounter. Commodore Rodgers was forced to make a more strategic military decision because whilst a ship full of whale oil for civilian consumption was no threat to Rodgers or the American Navy, a ship full of pitch and tar, vital Navy Stores, most definitely was. Rodgers saw it as his duty to prevent these crucial supplies reaching an enemy Navy, so he set about taking the Captain and crew prisoner and burning the *Alert*. Once again Rodgers was faced with the pressing dilemma of how to feed these unwanted prisoners. A solution presented itself just a few days later when on August 2, off the Faroe Islands, he laid siege to the English barque *Lion* of Liverpool, a whaling vessel under the command of Captain Thomas Hawkins of 8 guns and 52 men voyaging south from Greenland bound for Liverpool.

For Rodgers the solution was clear he would repeat the transaction he had made with Captain John Young. On this occasion he ransomed the barque *Lion* for £3000 and took a Bill of Exchange on Samuel Staniforth, owner of the *Lion*, as well as a personal Bond signed by Captain Hawkins. Donald Petrie asserts that Commodore Rodgers' astuteness in business matters was further illustrated by the people he selected to witness the signatures of Captains Young and Hawkins. He employed, for this purpose, Captains Robert Caldwell [Master of the *Jane and Ann* of Salt Coats, voyaging from Cork to Archangel in ballast on 12 July when run down by the *President* and sunk.] and Captain George Shand, both of whom were masters of the ships he had recently sunk. They were not only his prisoners; he was now sending them back to Britain so they would be available to testify as to the validity of the documents and to the veracity of the events surrounding these ransoms if they had to be adjudicated in a British Court. Rodgers happily released all his prisoners from the *Alert* and the *Jane and Ann* and required Captain Hawkins to convey them all directly to Liverpool.

At this point, Captain Thomas Hawkins demonstrated his own astuteness by asking for and receiving from Rodgers a written statement testifying the only way Hawkins could save his ship and cargo was to agree to pay the ransom. Whilst ransoming was a relatively new phenomenon, Hawkins must have been aware the owners of the *Lion* had some form of insurance policy and that by obtaining this statement from Rodgers it would prove beneficial to his owners when they made a claim on their insurers. But it is what occurred next which proved a bizarre example of honour among thieves. One or both of Hawkins and Rodgers resolved in hindsight that such a statement may also be advantageous for Captain Young should his owners also hold some form of insurance. So, Rodgers wrote out and signed a similar statement to cover Captain John Young and the *Eliza Swan*. One further condition of safe passage and freedom imposed on Captain Hawkins, his crew and the crew of the *Alert* was the extraction of an undertaking from Hawkins that immediately after the *Lion* reached Liverpool, he would mail the said insurance letter to Captain Young in Montrose.

This tale has so many twists and turns, all of which give us a wonderful insight into the life of the Youngs and others of the merchant fleet. As you can imagine matters did not quite end there either. After Captain Hawkins and the *Lion* set their course south into the Irish Sea on a heading for their home port of Liverpool, the *Lion* fell in with the British naval frigate HMS *Fortune*, 36 guns, under the command of Captain William Goate. It was now August 5 and the *Fortune* was sitting at her position west of the Orkneys, presumably to provide escort duties as protection for any Greenlandmen passing en route south. In the same way as Young had reported his encounter with Rodgers to Captain Cathcart of the *Alexandria* so Hawkins did likewise to Captain Goate RN. The reason why this action was so imperative is revealed by Petrie who discovered that the British Admiralty's law of the day provided for severe penalties to be meted out to anyone found carrying communications on behalf of an enemy of Britain. At this time Commodore Rodgers had undoubtedly been flagged as a notorious enemy and given the war with America was still raging on land and sea Hawkins prudently handed over all the letters by the hand of Commodore John Rodgers of the US Navy.

The exact timeline of events from there is not known with any certainty but what is documented is that the insurance letter from Commodore Rodgers to Captain John Young was eventually delivered to him in Montrose. The original of this letter found its way into the hands of the Montrose Museum, who framed it for the purpose of public display. This is where it remained untouched for one hundred and seventy-eight years until a member of the Museum staff removed it from its frame in the summer of 1991 for the purpose of photocopying it for Donald Petrie. Mysteriously a faint legend, previously invisible to the naked eye, appeared in the margin of the photocopy and it reads -

'This letter was opened by the Capt of the <u>Fortune</u> Frigate 3 Days after the Lion was boarded by the United States Frigate President & is now forwarded by Samuel Staniforth Owner of the <u>Lion</u> Augt 14 1813'

Putting his legal hat on once again, Petrie's overarching opinion was that such were the civilities which existed 'between enemies at sea in the years before the ferocity of unrestricted warfare, by submarine, brought to an end the profitable and rather civilised business of prize-taking'.

Despite all these events and civilities, it was War, but in the case of the *Eliza Swan* - the ransom was never paid.

So, whilst both Walter Cronkite and Peter Stanford believed Donald Petrie's story of the *Eliza Swan* to be extraordinary in many respects, it is clear those journalists living in Scotland and indeed Britain at the time had come to see privateering and prize taking as quite common place and not especially newsworthy. The contemporary reporting of such events was prosaic to say the least, and as previously stated, the return of the *Eliza Swan* in 1813 was reported in several newspapers as normal shipping news. Those articles which did make any mention of Rodgers only did so in passing and then simply reverted to reporting catch size in the usual way.

For instance, the Saunders' News-letter in Dublin Ireland printed in part 'The Eliza Swan, Young, master arrived yesterday Montrose from Greenland, with eight fish; will boil about 120 tons of oil.' The Montrose Review, in their column headed 'Greenland Fisheries', simply states 'The Eliza Swan, Captain John Young, arrived here on Monday from Greenland with eight fish - 110 tons of oil.'

So, with sailing in their blood and the lucrative whaling trade riding the crest of a wave, for the brothers Young there was no turning their back on what they clearly loved to do. *Monarch* and *Eliza Swan* are discovered setting sail for the Arctic the very next season. Harbour Logs show both Greenlandmen sailed out of Montrose on 6th April 1814. It was to prove a particularly successful voyage; they caught twenty whales between them. And this life would be mirrored for years to come.

Believe it or not there is yet another piece of intrigue relating to the *Eliza Swan* which has been the basis of much conversation over the years. It surrounds a very elaborate Silver Tea Set in the possession of one branch of the family. It is large and quite ornate, clearly intended as a grand gesture and designed to impress. Its origins are clear but the reason for the presentation has never been fully explained. The only insight into its providence comes from an inscription which reads -

To
Capt. Alexr Young Junr
From the
Montrose Whale Fishing Company
As a mark of appreciation of
His conduct while commanding
THE ELIZA SWAN
1814

For many years the family assumed that Alexander had excelled in some individual way whilst he was Master of the *Eliza Swan*. All efforts to uncover any evidence of a noteworthy event just prior to or during 1814 have failed to produce any tangible evidence. At one point, Linda Fraser of the Montrose Museum perused some of the uncatalogued material in the Museum's archive on my behalf, but to no avail.

Another line of enquiry taken up related to the results posted for 1814, and whilst Gordon Jackson cites that year as the most outstanding for the period 1814-1820 for the Montrose Whale Fishing Company, in the end the figures posted were Eliza Swan £5,093 and Monarch £8,315. Knowing that most newspaper media state that John Young was master in 1814, and since we have already established that the newspapers and Lloyd's have been proven notoriously inaccurate on numerous occasions, we are left to wonder whether perhaps Alexander was at the helm of Eliza Swan for the 1814 season. Then, if he did not post the best results what is it that Alexander is supposed to have accomplished that demanded the presentation of such a gracious and generous reward?

From a distance of two hundred years it's frustrating in the extreme that no hard evidence has come to light either anecdotally or from news media or via the Bounty claim forms. Then, if it was in recognition of the splendid action taken in ransoming the *Eliza Swan*, why was the presentation made to Alexander? Worse still, could it be the case of the eldest brother prevailing? We are left to ponder the why as we gaze on a beautiful remembrance of a bygone era.

As for the *Eliza Swan*, she received many plaudits in her lifetime; she enjoyed an illustrious career as the longest serving Montrose whaler and for much of that time she was reported as the most successful of the Montrose fleet. This measure of her success is set by comparing her to others not just season to season but within a season. Her best figures were –

TABLE 10 – Best Whale Fishing Seasons for Eliza Swan

Year	Catch	Tons of Oil
1805	9 Large	225
1806	Full	
1810	10	130
1811	27	165
1823	33	190

But it was never all smooth sailing in the Arctic for even the so called 'lucky ship', and there is evidence that *Eliza Swan* experienced her fair share of misadventures in those far northern Latitudes. At least twice she found herself icebound in the Davis Strait; the first such occurrence was in 1822 when her sister ship from Montrose, the *Hero*, mastered by the Captain John Young of *Eliza Swan* Ransoming fame, was crushed and lost, and again during the disastrous season of 1830 when eighteen of the British fleet of ninety-one were crushed in the pack ice and lost in Baffin Bay.

That year a strong south-westerly wind blew unrelentingly for days and virtually filled Baffin Bay with ice floes. It has been reported that the *Eliza Swan* and five others were trapped on the east side of Baffin Bay from the 10th of June to 10th of September. At one point, the vessels unsuccessfully attempted to navigate through a narrow opening in the pack ice, only to be struck by huge ice-masses driven on by a raging south west gale. The *Eliza Swan's* mizzen mast went in one collision and on another day, while attempting to escape, the crew had lowered one of their whaleboats preparing to use manpower to attempt to tow her through the ice. Alas, to no avail. Thankfully for the *Eliza Swan* and her crew, early September brought a change in the weather and she, along with several others could finally unfurl some canvas and make their way out into open water. Newspapers tell us that the 'Eliza Swan limped home empty and in a sinking condition.'

Lyricist A.L. Lloyd made comment about the events of 1830 on the sleeve notes to his record *'Leviathan! Ballads and Songs of the Whaling Trade'*, as the time when 'a fleet of fifty British whaleships reached the grounds in early June, a month before they expected. But the same winds that had helped them also crowded the Bay with ice floes and locked most of the fleet in, including the *Diamond*, the *Resolution*, the *Rattler* (not *Battler*) *of Leith* (not *Montrose*), and the *Eliza Swan*. Twenty fine ships were crushed to splinters and many bold whaler men froze or drowned. The *Eliza Swan* was among those that got free and brought the sad news home.' Many of those who managed to sail back to port did so under the weight of significant damage and with heavy hearts having witnessed the greatest loss of life for any single season.

Sometimes it is from the most unexpected sources the most enlightening stories emerge. There was not a great deal written at the time about that horrific 1830 season, but a seemingly unrelated headline in 1897 excited my interest. It relates to an editorial which appeared in the Montrose, Arbroath and Brechin Review on Friday 11 June that year. It is recalling the days of the Montrose whaling fleet as told by a local Montrose whale fisherman. Vowing never to leave a stone unturned and armed with a renewed subscription to the British Newspaper Archives, this article was in my sights. Imagine my delight when it brought two elements of this story together; the magical *Eliza Swan* and Captain Archibald Petrie, ancestor and namesake of the American Maritime Lawyer, Donald Archibald Petrie.

The editorial was a memoir relating the life story of old salt Captain Archibald Petrie, his first-hand recollections of sailing to the whale fishery from Montrose and his long and proud association with the Montrose Whale Fishing Company.

'Whale fishing was carried on for a number of years from this port, giving employment to a goodly number of seamen and others at the fishing and also to a number of men at the oil-boiling yards. The slaughtering of cattle and the curing of beef for the whalers was carried on in the upper part of the yard now belonging to Mr Alexander Mearns fishcurer. There are few now alive to tell of the whaling adventures connected with the Montrose fleet, which comprised among other vessels the Eliza Swan the Monarch and the London.

Captain Petrie, who died at Broughty Ferry in March last when almost a centenarian, having been born in Montrose in the beginning of the century, was wont to tell a very exciting experience he had in the Arctic seas on board the Eliza Swan in 1830. They sailed from Montrose about the middle of April, and experienced a very stormy passage across the Atlantic. The fishing was begun on the Greenland side of the strait, but the weather was bad, and the condition of the ice was unfavourable. Fish were seen in abundance, but very few were caught by any of the fleet. About the middle of June sail was made for Melville Bay. The fleet got amongst the floes, and endeavoured to force a passage through to the fishing ground when a strong south-westerly gale sprang up, and increased the dangers of navigation.

To secure the safety of the ships, docks were cut in the ice by some of the crews. Captain Fulton, of the Eliza Swan, sent several boats' crews on the ice with saws to cut out a dock for his ship. While the men were engaged working the great ice saws, a great upheaval arose amongst the ice, caused by a strong tide or current. Many of the men had barely time to reach their vessels when the masses of ice set in, and came crashing on the ships, crushing their timbers and spreading terror and disaster throughout the whole fleet. The Archilles of Dundee was a total wreck, and sank in a few minutes. The Eliza Swan was thrown on her beam ends and terribly damaged.

In all, twenty vessels - eighteen British and two foreigners - were lost by that fell disaster. It was an appalling scene - the roaring and crashing of the immense ice fields, the shouting of the sailors, and the heaving sinking vessels reeling before the irresistible foe. The crews escaped from the doomed ships to the treacherous ice as their only hope of safety. The Eliza Swan did not go down. She righted herself, and the crew set to work to repair the damage. In a patched-up condition the fishing was pursued till the 25th September, when they bore up for home. After they were fairly on the Atlantic they encountered a succession of heavy gales accompanied by rain, hail and snow. On the 12 October, Cape Wrath [the most north westerly point of Britain] was sighted, and on the 4th they were running through the Pentland Firth [the strait which separates the Orkney Islands from Caithness on mainland Scotland] with a fair wind.

They were nearing home now, and all hands were eagerly looking forward with joyful hope of seeing their friends once more. At last Girdleness [Girdle Ness is the headland that guards the southern side of Aberdeen Harbour on which a lighthouse stands] hove in sight. But here a new disaster befell the voyagers. A squall of wind carried away the foretopmast and the ship was crippled. This unfortunate accident occurred about noon on Thursday, the 19th. The Captain bore up for Aberdeen, and at 3 p.m. the ship was brought up in the bay, with the best bower anchor in seven fathoms water. The carpenters set to work and made a new topmast. The ship was now making two feet of water per hour, with the pumps going hard.

The new mast was got up, and the yards slung and sails bent, and by noon the following day the anchor was weighed, and sail made for Montrose. It was the last run for home, but the leak was widening and the water gaining on them fast. Montrose Ness [the Scurdie Ness lighthouse of Montrose] was sighted, and a pilot came on board in the bay. In sight of home at last but the ship almost breaking beneath them and the water rising at the rate of three feet per hour was a very trying situation for captain and crew. If they had been compelled to make another tack in the bay of

Montrose they would have had to run her ashore. But her head was turned for the mouth of the river, and she was run in and brought up alongside the London with nine feet of water in the hold.'

A frightening experience well recalled. It reminded me of George Kerr's opinion of whale fishing after a similar Arctic misadventure in 1791, where he described it as 'a good school for an impatient man'.

The last word on the *Eliza Swan* -

Fighting Atlantic gales and navigating the hopelessly unpredictable ice floes for a succession of years not only resulted in very high losses of ships and men and often accounted for some very low catches for those who were lucky enough to eventually escape the clutches of the ice and limp home. In fact, we have already learned that in the worst of seasons many a ship arrived home clean. So, it is no wonder that the 1830s once again saw a decline in whale fishing internationally. The Youngs had also seen the writing on the wall and Alexander Jnr is known to have liquidated The Montrose Whale Fishing Company in 1833 whereupon the *Eliza Swan* was sold to Montrose Textile Manufacturers, John and George Paton, who, as previously written, used her to import flax from the Baltic for their mills in Montrose. In 1839 the *Eliza Swan* and *Monarch* along with the premises of The Montrose New Whale Fishing Company were purchased by Charles Birnie, a local Timber & Wood Merchant. In fact, the Birnie family at the time could boast three to four generations involved in shipbuilding, wood and cabinetmaking trades in Montrose. *Eliza Swan* reportedly made her last Arctic voyage in 1839 and later that same year Birnie advertised the old blubber rendering facility down by the harbour - 'to let as fishcuring premises'.

From 1840 onwards the Birnie family operated the *Eliza Swan* as a merchant trading vessel. Interrogation of Lloyd's Register shows her fully employed sailing for Memel [East Prussia, Germany now known as Kalaipêda, Lithuania] on 19 Mar in ballast, passing Elsinore Island on 31 March, arriving 4th April. She later departed 19 April for London re-passing Elsinore on the

28th arriving London 12 May. There she unloaded and reloaded ready for a voyage to Archangel [a port on the banks of the Dvina River near the exit to the White Sea in Arctic Russia]. She departed London 30th May but did not arrive in Russia until 10 July only to depart again on the 31st bound for Dundee. Her next voyage listed in Lloyd's shows the *Eliza Swan* still braving the Arctic waters; arriving St Petersburg 21st Sept from Dundee but this time she had a long wait in port as she did not depart Kronstadt [St Petersburg's main seaport on Kotlin Island at 60°N 29°46'E] until 12 October when she was bound for Lynn [King's Lynn is an ancient Dock situated in Norfolk established in the 13th Century].

The Birnie family in Montrose can be found in Piggot & Co.'s trade directories of 1837 under various headings of Merchants, Ship Builders, Ship Owners, and Marine Insurance Agents but in the neighbouring column under the heading of Shipping Companies there is an ominous entry which would sound the ultimate death knell for the future of the *Eliza Swan* and ships of sail like her. It reads - Montrose & London Steam Navigation Company. Sail was being forced to finally give way to steam. We know the Birnie family persevered in the merchant trade with *Eliza Swan* because there is a continuous record of her voyages in Lloyd's Register right up until 1845. Clearly by then her opportunities were dwindling, and she was forced to operate in a smaller and smaller niche market as there was no way she could compete for general business given the expectations of merchants now that steam and speed were the order of the day.

She made her last voyage in 1845 when she was lost off the French Coast. The Shipping Gazette of 2 February 1845 carries the story that 'the Eliza Swan was feared totally lost on Point de Combre on the 28th January and that the crew had perished.' The Nautical Magazine of 1845 states that while en route from Newcastle to Bordeaux the *Eliza Swan* was wrecked near Gironde on January 5. From these and other conflicting reports it is fair to say there were no witnesses to her calamitous end; and she died alone. Sadly, she took all hands with her to her dark watery grave.

The Lucky Ship had run out of luck!

Before we close this chapter there is one lasting memory precious to the *Eliza Swan* which proves she is far from forgotten; in fact, she lives on to this day forever regaled in song and intrinsically linked to those brave men and ships of the whaling trade.

While the by-products of the Whaling Industry are many and varied there is one which is intriguing and educational at the same time and that is - Music. Many of the Sea Shanties of yesterday were the work songs created during the age of sail which served several purposes. For the poorly educated sailors required to work in teams doing the many and varied backbreaking repetitive tasks such as hauling up rigging, these Sea Shanties provided a means by which they could rote-learn their tasks but even more important, it helped them to keep their rhythm.

The Kendall Whaling Museum in Massachusetts published a monograph series in 2000 entitled - *'Sea Chanteys and Sailors' Songs'* wherein author Stuart M. Frank makes the point that there are four 'species' of hauling sea shanties. The 'Long-drag or long-haul halyard chanteys were used for hoisting topsails, the largest and heaviest aboard a square rigger.... and [also sung] occasionally for rowing and other rhythmic chores of long duration.' 'Short-drag or short-haul chanteys were for hoisting smaller topgallants, royals, skysails, and other lighter sails.' Next came the 'Furling chanteys [which] were a small family of songs intended for furling sail aloft, which requires a unified haul among several hands to gather, fold, and tuck the bunt.' The 'Heaving chanteys are ... used for working the capstan, brake windlass, and pumps - thus for weighing anchor, cutting-in whales, uploading or offloading cargo, and pumping ship.'

Foc'sle, forecastle or forebitters are the names variously attributed to those ballads sung after the work is done. These are not technically considered sea shanties as they are not work songs, however, historically they are just as important to the sailors because they tell the more personal stories of sailors' lives. The name ascribed to this group of songs is symbolic and derives from the name given to the sailors' living quarters onboard ship: that place where they would gather to sing and drink. The lyrics would generally describe things like their harsh living conditions, the abuse they receive from captains and crew, alcohol, friendships, dreams of home and of course girls and dry land. There is even an old sea shanty about a cross-dressing sailor entitled - *'The Handsome Cabin Boy'*.

Sailors were simple brave souls who endured unimaginably harsh conditions while being surrounded by immeasurable camaraderie. For George Kerr, Archibald Petrie and the like of our Youngs who went whale fishing in the Arctic, music provided a rare pleasure. However, these same brave sailors were also known to be quite a superstitious lot and adhered to a strict protocol for when and where certain types of shanties were to be sung. Those songs with themes of work and life at sea were only sung on the outward journey while those about family, sweethearts, coming home and dry land were reserved to be sung exclusively on the homeward voyage. The true tradition of Sea Shanties ended with the age of sail when most of the music became part of folklore; however, there are some modern day lyricists and musicians endeavouring to keep the genre alive.

I have included some sample songs which capture the spirit of the men - young and old. The first example is most certainly a song which draws on the reminiscences of a man who left home as a boy but was quickly drawn up in the excitement of the chase. It is simply titled –

'When First I went a Whaling'

When first I went a whaling,
I left my home, a boy,
And 'mongst
the gleaming ice-fields,
That home was still my joy;
For when, below the North-lights,
The polar winds blew shrill,
Dreams of my loving mother,
Those dear dreams warmed me still.

Amid the clashing icebergs
My whaler rolls to-day,
And keen the Arctic ice-blasts
From the snow-floes round me play;
But fond dreams of another

My thoughts with summer fill;
One, dearer than a mother,
My heart is warming still.

This next lyric is a modern day Sea Shanty written in 1993 by Ken Graydon, a Poet and Storyteller. It is entitled - 'A Whaler's Tale' and tells a passionate tale of the job of a whale fisherman, of the dangers encountered and why so many sailors are believed to be superstitious.

I signed aboard this whaling ship
I made my mark it's true
And I'll serve out the span of time
I swore that I would do
But I'll not man your boats again
Though you cast me in the sea
For I tell you sir, them fish can think
As well as you or me

Just yesterday the lookout's call
Had bent us to our work
I took me place like all the rest
I'd not be one to shirk
Now thirteen men's been drownded
And no more of them we'll see
I'd take an oath, them fish can think
As well as you or me

We'd pulled our boats abreast the pod
The steersman took his stand
He'd had no time to make his throw
When the oar flew from my hand
Just then a great fluke smashed our boat
The whale I didn't see
Now I believe them fish can think
As well as you or me

For then them whales destroyed our boats
They rammed them one by one

They stove them all with head and fluke
And after they was done
We few poor souls left half-alive
Was clinging to debris
I'd stake me life them fish can think
As good as you and me

The way them whale fish went for us
It seemed as though t'was planned
For each one had his target boat
They played us man for man
Just knowin' now they think so clear
My heart says let them be
I swear to God them fish can think
As good as you or me

Now John is blind, Jim's lost an arm
And Caleb's lost below
My leg will heal but other men
No more aloft can go
So I'll not man your boats again
Though you drown me in the sea
For I tell you sir, them fish can think
As good as you or me

There is another entitled 'Greenland *Whale Fisheries*' which bears testament to the fact that the life of a whaler did not improve over time -

'Twas eighteen hundred and fifty-three and on June the thirteenth day,
That our gallant ship, her anchor weighed,
And for Greenland bore away, brave boys,
and for Greenland bore a--way.
And for Greenland bore a-way.

Our captain stood on the quarterdeck
With a spyglass in his hand,
"It's a whale, and a whale, and a whalefish," cried he,

Where she blows at every span, brave boys,
Where she blows at every span.

Then the boats were launched and the men on board
With the whalefish well in view,
And well-prepared were all our jolly shipmates
For to strike where the whalefish blew, brave boys,
For to strike where the whalefish blew.

Then the whale was struck and the line played out,
But he gave such a flourish with his tail,
He capsized our boat, and we lost five men,
And we never did catch that whale, brave boys,
And we never did catch that whale.

Well, then, the loss of that whalefish,
It grieved our hearts full sore,
But oh! The loss of our five shipmates,
That grieved us ten times more, brave boys,
That grieved us ten times more.
"Up anchor, up anchor," our captain cried,

"Let us leave this cold country,
Where the storm and the snow and the whalefish do blow,
And the daylight's seldom seen, brave boys,
And the daylight's seldom seen."

The final musical contribution to this Sea Shanty segment is left to be told as the wonderful story of three famous Greenlandmen: the *Diamond*, *Resolution* and the lady of the moment - *Eliza Swan*. It is entitled -
'The Bonny Ship the Diamond'

The Diamond is a ship, my lads,
for the Davis Strait she's bound,
the quay it is all garnished

with wee bonny lasses 'round;
Captain Thomson gives the order
to sail the ocean wide,
Where the sun it never sets, my lads,
nor darkness dims the sky,

Chorus:
For it's cheer up my lads,
let your hearts never fail,
While the bonny ship, the Diamond,
goes a-fishing for the whale.

Along the quay at Peterhead,
the lasses stand aroon,
Wi' their shawls all pulled around them
and the salt tears runnin' doon;
Don't you weep, my bonny lass,
though ye'll be left behind,
For the rose will grow on Greenland's ice
before we change our mind.

Chorus:
For it's cheer up my lads,
let your hearts never fail,
While the bonny ship, the Diamond,
goes a-fishing for the whale.

Here's a health tae the Resolution,
likewise the Eliza Swan,
Here's a health tae the Battler of Montrose
and the Diamond, ship of fame;
We wear the trooser o' the white
The jackets o' the blue,
When we return tae Peterhead,
we'll be sweethearts wi you

Chorus:
For it's cheer up my lads,

let your hearts never fail,
While the bonny ship, the Diamond,
goes a-fishing for the whale.

It'll be bricht both day and nicht
when the Greenland lads come hame,
Wi' a ship that's fu' of oil, my lads,
and money tae oor name;
We'll make the cradles for to rock
And the blankets for to tear
And every lass in Peterhead sing
"Hushabye, my dear"

Chorus:
For it's cheer up my lads,
let your hearts never fail,
While the bonny ship, the Diamond,
goes a-fishing for the whale.

There is one final custom which was close to the heart of every lad taking to the whaling and this related to the May Day wreath. It is often depicted in Huggins paintings of whaling ships. With the Scottish fleet leaving port around the end of March, sailors were away from home for May Day Celebrations so the ladies would get together to make a wreath of bright coloured ribbons made from pieces of their bonnets, shirts or petticoats. En route to the Arctic one of the men would whittle a small model of a ship to be hung either above or in the middle of the wreath. Doreen Young explains 'when May Day came and the ship and the crew found themselves amidst the colourless Arctic waters, they would hoist this brilliant little circle of colour amongst the rigging and think of their ladies and the wildflowers in the Scottish lanes. The wreath remained aloft until they returned.'

Chapter 8

**The End of Sail • Beginning of Steam
A New Family Paradigm Emerges
Sons take Voyages to New Frontiers
Maritime Adventure Or Mercantile Plan**

The Leith Patriarch, Alexander Young [1750-1817] thrived and did business not only in the Golden Era of Sail but also in the Golden Era of Whaling - the classic example of right place right time. He also lived long enough to appreciate he was witnessing the end of the glory days for the sailing ship. At the time, those charged with the task of designing vessels for the international mercantile fleet in particular were embracing the latest evolutions in steam power and iron. From what we have learned from Alexander's Will we know he welcomed these changes, in fact, he was so convinced about their long term future he actually invested in the changes. However, I cannot but think that deep down he would have felt a tinge of sadness at times when he realised future generations would never feel that awesome power of the wind in canvas so intoxicatingly familiar to himself, his father, his great-grandfather and so many other old tars inside and outside his extended family.

Those halcyon days of sail are not so much defined by dates as by deeds. Many of the old timber vessels which have endured were now weary and so many more are long gone just like the brave sailors who voyaged in them. For the humans and the ships, the seafaring journey had been long but what a history that combination of timber, canvas and man had managed to create. From the Bronze Age to the midpoint of the nineteenth century wooden ships have dominated international and coastal trade and naval warfare and enabled human transportation on a scale never envisaged possible. Looking back over those centuries this was but the curtain raiser for what was to follow.

Down the ages, ships were being built larger - wider, deeper and longer. Some of the designs from this 1750-1850 century incorporated multiple masts carrying an ever-increasing square footage of sail in new and various rigging designs. These adaptations meant that ships could travel faster, more robustly face the rigour of hazardous sailing conditions whilst at the same time provide greater security for cargo, more comfort and safety for passengers and above all be more hospitable for the daring and brave souls who crewed them. The early seafarers of the Young, Dick, Richmond, Liston, Thomson and Carney families would have sailed in some of the most basic of sailing ships, particularly the fisher folk.

They put their faith in vessels of all shapes, sizes, designs and rigging and would have travelled to places so culturally diverse from their Scottish homeland that it could only have added to the excitement and adventure of the voyage. They would have eaten foods in foreign ports which challenged their traditional oats and herring diet, heard languages unfamiliar to the ear, witnessed traditions that seemed alien in their own world and all the while they would have been enriching themselves and the lives of those around them by sharing this new-found knowledge of these global frontiers. Along the way they would have encountered dangers so diverse that no learning could prepare them for every circumstance. Still they sailed on because once seduced by the sea it seems that to a man they remained loyal to their calling.

During the present century under review, the design and construction of ships for the Merchant Fleet was seen to undergo change and dramatic change at that as shipowners were forced to embrace new design criteria. Some of these criteria were tried and proven and had been in place for naval vessels from as far back as the time of the 1706 Establishment when iron fittings were incorporated for the very first time. In the early stages, the - 'wrought iron [now known as cast iron] produced was very brittle and subject to fracture. This was mainly due to the impurities introduced from coke [used] during the smelting process.' Once the coke infusion issue was resolved by Abraham Darby II around 1750 it should have followed that iron achieved wider acceptance but English shipbuilders in particular remained reluctant. This is partly because English iron had been identified as poor quality and not fit for purpose which in turn had forced English and Scottish shipbuilders to be reliant on imported material from Sweden and the American colonies. This imported iron was most certainly of a far higher grade and it added significantly to the end cost.

Much to the chagrin of the British, at one point the French were leading the way in the design and construction of new generation sailing ships. This can be time-lined to three important events that took place in 1733, 1752 and 1754 which when combined, forced change on the British. The first event was triggered in 1733 when the French Minister of the Navy, Monsieur Blaise Gislain, made a visit to three of England's premier dockyards - Chatham, Deptford and Woolwich. Following his tour of the yards M. Gislain produced an extensively illustrated report which included several sketches for iron fittings. The second event occurred almost two decades later when M. Gislain's original drawings were discovered to have been enhanced by another Frenchman, Duhamel Du Monceau, and published in Monceau's treatise of 1752. The most significant of these design changes credited to M. Monceau related to the shape and fabrication of 'knees'.

Knees have always been a major component in the building of any wooden vessel and remain so to this very day. Knees come in many shapes and sizes depending on their application. Basically, they are a type of reinforcing bracket used to strengthen and support many and varied parts of a ship, from the deck beams and masts to the keel. When used vertically they are called 'hanging' or 'standard' knees; laterally positioned they are either 'lodging' or 'bosom' knees. The knee is the most widely used single named component in any wooden sailing ship and the strength afforded by these components is paramount to the rigidity of the final structure. As a result, the timber utilised needed to be well seasoned; anything from one month to four years depending on the thickness of the piece of timber making up the particular knee. This is where the introduction of iron was seen to make a positive impact; not only on building and repair time but more importantly for the likes of these Youngs, iron offered that additional structural strength demanded by those whaling ships and merchant ships voyaging at high latitudes among the gales and ice floes.

When it comes to the design and incorporation of iron knees, the French remained on the front foot, and it was not until three further events occurred that any long term change was embedded into English and Scottish design and shipbuilding. The first big breakthrough came when English shipwright Mungo Murray translated Duhamel's 1752 document into English. The second discovery was accidental; and occurred after the French vessel *Invincible* foundered and sank off Spithead, England in 1758. When Royal Navy carried out an inspection of that wreck they discovered it was fitted with Duhamel's revised iron knees. But there was an even bigger surprise awaiting the British, the iron knees on the *Invincible* were considerably larger than anything previously seen - they were 5ft5ins long, 4ins wide and 1 1/2 ins thick or in the metric measure of the modern world - 1.67mx10.16cmx3.81cm.

Change happened slowly, and there is well documented evidence to support the view that English shipbuilders still remained reluctant to adopt alternate materials irrespective of the proven advantages. This has widely been ascribed to their conservatism and their espoused view that timber was preferable to iron; however, that is not the whole story. These shipbuilders were being persuaded to persevere with timber by many of the key decision-makers in merchant circles and in Government, including some individuals in the Royal Navy, all of whom had an undeclared personal financial interest in the lucrative Timber Trade. Although eventually, other events would force change; the main issue remained the escalating shortages and difficulty in procuring good compass timber which was also driving up the price of new builds. This was collateral damage in the aftermath of the French Revolution and the Napoleonic Wars - both of which had seen unprecedented construction of timber warships.

These factors plus the dire need for advances to be made in smelting methods combined to bring about the opening of the first iron rolling mill at Fareham in the south of England in 1754. For the first time England could boast a mill which was able to economically produce stronger iron bar, an essential material when it came to the fashioning of high need components such as bolts. Also, with the mill situated in close proximity to the Royal Dockyard at Portsmouth it was set it prosper. Peter Goodwin, Keeper & Curator of *HMS Victory* wrote an essay entitled - *'The Influence of Iron in Ship Construction: 1660-1830'* - in which he draws on all this history and in fact he contends the greatest influencer of all was Henry Cort who first became aware of the poor quality of English iron while working as a Royal Navy agent in London.

Firstly, Cort is credited with developing a new method for making better quality iron bar; so important for shaping into vital componentry such as eyebolts. He did this by using the steam-powered grooved roller process which he patented in 1783. Perhaps, the most significant breakthrough of this era came in 1784 when Henry Cort patented his balling and puddling furnace which hallmarked a new method of converting pig iron into malleable wrought iron. Henry Cort combined two previously known processes into one, whereby - 'the iron is stirred to separate out impurities and extract the higher quality wrought iron. The "puddler" extracts a mass of iron from the furnace using a rabbling bar. The extracted ball of metal is then processed into a shingle by a shingling hammer, after which it is rolled in a rolling mill.'

Notwithstanding the above, one should not discount the powerful influence of the British East India Company [BEIC] in this argument. Gabriel Snodgrass, Marine Surveyor for the BEIC, was one who had already embraced the French innovations; in fact, he went one step further and incorporated not only iron knees but also iron riders and braces in the design for all the BEIC ships built in the 1780s. These ships quickly earned a reputation as the biggest and fastest ships afloat and on the back of the BEIC innovations Snodgrass is known to have made a lengthy submission to the Admiralty in 1792. Some Maritime observers have suggested it was from this point onward that England took the lead over France whose innovation was slowed by crippling debt after supporting the American cause abroad and in the aftermath of the Napoleonic Wars and the Revolution at home. However, despite the demonstrated success of the BEIC design changes, the Royal Navy was still lagging behind, probably as a direct result of the personal pecuniary reasons already cited. In fact, it took Seppings, who was the Marine Surveyor for the Royal Navy at the time, until 1813 to fully incorporate iron knees and other iron fittings into the designs for future naval vessels.

Those Youngs investing and mastering ships in this era would have been following these matters very closely and would have realised the benefits to be had from engaging with the new technology because it would affect them all in their everyday lives.

Pushing design improvements were two other factors - Cabotage and Cartography. Cabotage in the day related to a long held international maritime legal agreement first established by the French wherein a country held exclusive rights to the navigation route between their home ports and any foreign country where they held colonial rights. Enforcement of this restriction to a single power on many of the developing international trade routes gave added impetus to Britain to extend its Empire not only in order to expand its trade opportunities but to overcome the impediments of Cabotage. Prior to this principal being adopted, these trade routes were navigated by stealth and mapping was basic at best. Once any Cabotage arrangement was in place cartographic knowledge was equating to economic and political power.

As far back as the 17th-Century the Dutch, French and English had begun a concerted push to join the lines on navigation maps; however, this was a mammoth undertaking which was not completed until the mid-18th Century by which time all the world's shorelines not encumbered with sea ice were fully charted; with the exception of Antarctica. This would have been particularly helpful to Alexander [1750-1817] and those of his sons who followed in his footsteps. In celebration of this cartographic achievement and the British Empirical expansion, in 1740 Scotsman James Thomson composed that well known song - 'Rule Britannia'. These lyrics became the fighting song of the Royal Navy and Army as England continued to spread her tentacles far and wide. The chorus is a stirring reminder of another issue driving their fight for Empire -

'Rule, Britannia!
Britannia rule the waves
Britons never, never, never shall be slaves'

As a manifesto to the overwhelming dominance achieved by the British Merchant Fleet and the Royal Navy worldwide, the Victoria and Albert Museum produced a publication entitled - *'Ancient and Modern Ships'* - in 1906. It came in two parts, where Part I was devoted to the era of the Wooden Sailing Ships, including those which were steam powered. In it, author Sir George C.V. Holmes quotes statistics on the size of the British combined Fleet in relation to her enemies. Holmes points out that of all the sailing vessels over 100 tons known to exist in the civilised world in the year 1898, those sailing under the flag of the United Kingdom and her Colonies equated to 39% of the world total by number, and a staggering 50% by gross tonnage of vessels. The next nearest was America with almost 11% by number but only 9% by gross tonnage.

Although 1898 is a little outside our present century it is a clear indication of the massive growth in overall fleet numbers made in the aftermath of these initial design developments. It also underscores the level of activity in shipbuilding prior to this 1898 analysis. No wonder the British Empire prospered - it forged ahead purely on weight of numbers. When looking back over these prosperous years of economic activity in shipping it is pleasing to note there were Young family members involved as shipwrights, shipowners, investors, masters and sailors - all of whom would have benefited in one way or another. However, their commercial success would have required them to excel at their craft, move with the times in skill and technology and compete on the world stage. We are about to learn that they seem to have done all this with ease.

Having gained a general insight into the global Shipping Industry and given the recent design evolutions to sailing ships, it is time to put this Young Family in the mix and assess how these innovations impacted not only the Scottish Merchant Trade as a whole, but the Youngs and their associated families in particular.

Traditionally, the Scottish Merchant Fleet had relied on capital investment on a shared ownership basis. Alexander Snr's Will and others mentioned so far, substantiate this fact. In the early days of Alexander's involvement there were virtually no non-mercantile investors. All funding came from within the mercantile industry - merchants, shipbuilders, shipowners, ships masters and mariners. Then, along with the new generation of vessels incorporating iron and steam, came a new class of investor. For the first time, funds began to flow in from very diverse quarters outside the industry; people such as writers [solicitors], coal dealers, bankers, gentlemen, corn merchants and farmers. It seems the shipping industry had proved itself not only vital to global commercial success, more importantly it was beginning to be considered as less high risk, investors were not only financially supporting the industry they were, for the very first time, espousing belief in its future viability.

As the steamship era took hold, services were expanded and although these vessels were far more expensive to build and operate, they were faster and more reliable hence the financial returns were there in support of the higher cost base. Traditional supporters like Alexander Young Snr were so convinced of the future viability of the shipping industry they too invested solidly. In his case, as we learned from his Will, he had decided the Steam Packet niche market offered greater reliable returns in the short term; hence he and others like him are known to have invested broadly as this new commuter transportation option which had captured the imagination of the British traveller in particular who, until that time, had relied on horse and coach travel.

Mark Howard wrote a treatise on the history of shipbuilding wherein he states the United Kingdom's Merchant Fleet doubled between 1775 and 1790 and doubled again by the end of the Napoleonic Wars in 1815. Britain's continued naval dominance and its ever expanding international trade routes were pushing existing shipping resources to their limit. While Howard suggests the 1707 Act of Union enabled Scotland to 'share fully in Britain's economic growth' in reality we know that, for many decades to follow, English merchants were known to be successfully lobbying Westminster and the King in order to maintain their monopolies at the exclusion of Scotland. One small gain for the Clyde and Greenock shipbuilders and Glasgow merchants in particular was the building of the Clyde-Forth Canal which was completed in 1790.

This initiative gave Glasgow merchants better access to the Baltic trade route and Greenock shipbuilders the opportunity to build a number of specifically designed narrower steam-boats to satisfy the requirements of this particular canal. Howard's research further shows that - 'between 1750 and 1800 Scotland's overseas trade increased by three hundred percent compared with two hundred percent for England.' This was also the time when the port of Greenock outstripped Glasgow in importance because the newly designed larger ocean going sailing ships, when fully laden, could not easily negotiate the upper Clyde. This would have been a timely positive for Alexander's son-in-law, Captain Joshua Richmond, because prior to relocating to Leith, Greenock was his home port, and it was from here that Captain Richmond is known to have sailed to the West Indies.

Locked out of the British Trade System, Scotland continued to push its own mercantile agenda. The port of Greenock continued to thrive, and by - '1800 there were 377 ships based in the port employing four thousand men.' - these are massive numbers and would have been tremendously significant in the day. So strong was Greenock's Shipping Economy, the collapse of the Tobacco Trade does not appear to have had a detrimental affect on the port at all because Greenock virtually survived on the back of its firmly established Shipbuilding sector, which was by now being supplied with cheaper timber from Canada and the Baltic, imported on Scottish vessels. We also know these are two countries where several Young ancestors had sailed to and returned with cargoes of timber, and where they were already financially invested with lumber business operations and would remain so for several generations into the future. Names synonymous with Greenock Shipbuilding such as John Wood, Robert Napier Snr and Robert Napier Jnr will feature in this family's personal story in years to come as will several other notable Clyde shipbuilders.

Looking at the first generation of merchant vessels incorporating steam power, it seems they were mostly successful on shorter coastal routes where coal supply could be organised. Concessions needed to be made for the larger ocean going vessels, which were initially fitted out as a combination of sail and steam. Solely steam-powered boats had been traversing the inland waterways of France and Britain since the late 1700s; all thanks to the creative genius of the Marquis Claude de Jouffroy who in 1783 built the first paddle steamer *Pyroscaphe* in which he installed the English designed and built Newcomen steam engine. The next leap forward came when a Czech born Austrian, Josef Ludvok Ressel, invented the first screw propeller in 1827. This was a real game changer. His invention not only revolutionised internal barge trade and people transportation, it also heralded the arrival of a new form of recreational tourism. Later iterations were designed to facilitate the needs of larger long haul vessels and put shipping and shipbuilding once again at the forefront of global expansion and industrial development.

The broader acceptance of the steamboat initially suffering somewhat from the negative publicity generated by several explosions and sinking's and it was not until the mid-1780s that substantial remedies were identified. This turnaround is attributed to another Scotsman, William Symington of Dumfries, who took the steamboat to a safer level by combining the efficiency of the Watt engine with the simplicity of that devised by Thomas Newcomen. Symington patented this design in 1787. While these steam-boats were for non-ocean travel, it is clear that even from the early days of Alexander's [1750-1817] ocean going career in sailing ships the signs were there that change was on the horizon. From there, steam-powered design gained momentum and Symington alone is credited with over thirty-two evolutionary designs for steam engines for use in industry and shipping. The romance with steam was being fully embraced and the transition to steam was now moving forward at pace thanks to the inventiveness of some Scots.

It is timely now for another Lord Dundas to join the Young's seafaring story. He too was a Scot from Edinburgh who made his first fortune by supplying goods to the British Army during The Seven Years War [1756-1763] when they were fighting the Jacobites in Flanders. He was Sir Lawrence Dundas, 1st Baronet [1710-1781] described as - 'a cunning shrewd man of the world' - he was also a major financier and supporter of the building of the Forth and Clyde Canal. This project provided the already mentioned vital canal route across central Scotland. It joined the Firth of Forth in Edinburgh to the Firth of Clyde in Glasgow by utilising the existing waterways of the Rivers Clyde and Carron plus the addition of a manmade section that just happened to traverse his Dundas estate of 'Grangemouth'. This Canal proved to be a major financial windfall for Lord Dundas who charged a fee to all who used it. For the likes of those Youngs who were engaged in the Baltic trade it probably proved a life saver for some. Records indicate that the canal received a great deal of support because it truly was a safer, speedier and more reliable route for moving goods and coal between these two major Scottish cities. This was particularly so in the winter months, those non-whaling months, when merchantmen had been accustomed to wrestling with the thick fog, howling gales, rough seas, treacherous currents and unpredictable wind systems when traversing the top of Scotland.

In the early days, this canal proved so successful that not even the arrival of the railways stopped it from surviving for almost two centuries. Ultimately, mass consumerism, a by-product of the Industrial Revolution, would make it no longer viable for goods transportation. The simple reason here being that the canal was built too narrow, which in turn restricted the size of vessel to the point of non-profitability and when the industry was faced with rising maintenance cost for the numerous locks along the canal and a corresponding fall in revenue from freight services, the canal was closed to freighting.

However, the Forth and Clyde Canal did remain a very popular choice for passenger traffic and by 1812 it was carrying upwards of 44,000 passengers annually. 1828 saw the introduction of a steamboat passenger service on the canal. There was one other event for which the Canal became famous and was known to draw quite a crowd. It occurred once a year when the east coast fishing fleet would traverse the Forth & Clyde Canal to fish the Irish Sea.

All the while, the rail network was expanding as a matter of national priority, not just for the distribution of trade goods but rather for the strategic distribution of that new high need commodity - coal. Coal for factories, power plants and steam ships. The Youngs now find themselves operating in a new highly competitive and rapidly changing mercantile marketplace. The question them arises – are the next generation up to the challenge?

First up we will look at the international trade routes –

Sailing ship requirements for those operating on long haul International Trade Routes had a completely different set of needs to those of short haul and coastal freighting vessels. Indeed, in this same era, the design for long haul vessels went against the trend as it spawned a new design of sailing ship and two new words were entered into the mariner lexicon: Clipper and Windjammer. These words are interchangeable, and their mere mention conjures up images of those goliaths of the sea with their tall and numerous masts and massive sail area. By the end of the Eighteenth Century the Merchant Fleet was largely comprised of these Clipper Ships, a word coined to encompass the new look Schooners and Brigantines being designed and built to be faster and sleeker.

These vessels became synonymous with maritime beauty, grace and speed and at the same time as steam was infiltrating design for smaller vessels, so sail designs were being reborn for these Clipper Ships. The word 'windjammer' seems so befitting when describing these vessels with their multiple tall masts and ever increasing square footage of sail, so typified by the design of the British East Indiamen. On those long haul trade routes to India, Australia and indeed the East and West Indies it was impossible to entertain steam at that time because of the lack of coal bunkering facilities. As knowledge and skill improved, it is recorded that many of these fast East Indiamen were being built in India as it was felt that utilising local teak timber was far more suitable for hulls traversing those tropical waters.

We know that at least one of the Youngs was sailing these routes because Captain John Young lost his life in Calcutta in 1836. What is not identified as yet is whether he was Master of a Clipper Ship or one of the faster, sleeker and slightly smaller Blackwall Frigates. These frigates had been specifically designed and built for the so-called premium end of the India and China Trade and are typical of the 1830s 'workhorse' sailing vessels which were around 150 ft. in length and 950 tons burthen. The Blackwall Frigate's name derives from their place of construction – Blackwall, on the Thames in London, in the shipyards of Wigram & Green with whom this family has an established connection.

These Blackwall Frigates were a three-masted fully rigged ship carrying a crew of 60 men plus boys and sporting a characteristic black hull with a white stripe at the plimsoll line. They were also considered ideal for training future officers for the Merchant Navy and in their heyday they could be seen crowding the East India Dock on the Thames. The Blackwall Frigate also proved popular in the lucrative Opium Trade where speed was essential in order to outrun the pirates and privateers.

For those Youngs sailing the India and Australia routes the next milestone was the 1869 opening of the British-sponsored Suez Canal. Originally planned as a means of shortening voyage times, it should have marked a major turning point for the Clipper

Ship era; however, sail got a reprieve on two accounts. Firstly, the lack of coal bunkering facilities and secondly, and more relevant still, was the problematic wind systems which blew across the Suez. This delayed the phasing out of sail on these particular routes for almost a decade. Eventually, bunkering facilities were established, and steamships took over the tea and mail trade routes. Henceforward, the Clipper Ships were exclusively employed on the very long haul broad ocean voyages to Australia.

Now it is time to turn attention to the fourth generation of the Young Family, to learn how they coped with these industry wide changes and to see if anyone was able to capitalise on the lucrative commercial opportunities which were about to flow from this major expansion of the fleet and the Empire. Clearly, this would have been an incredibly demanding period for all sectors allied to the Shipping Industry as they grappled with a constant flood of new concepts, processes, work functions and regulations. For those Youngs who were at sea at the time, whether they were involved in Whaling, Merchant Navy or Royal Navy the game was in a constant state of flux; they were all on a steep learning curve - nothing would be the same ever again.

But remain the Youngs did, and for those with careers on the high seas this meant coming to terms with new steel ships, steam power plants, associated monitoring equipment and so much more. This generation was faced with an ultimatum - get with the program or get out of the game. For the Youngs on land, these changes signalled new lucrative commercial opportunities. What is even more illuminating is that this fourth generation was about to become the 'Change Generation' and for them education, attitude, aptitude and seizing opportunity had become more important than ever. By embracing the new order, they would have to think and act creatively in order to get into the business and to remain relevant to the market, they would need to innovate and invest. This is a long way from the sailing experiences of their great-grandfather Robert Young [1723-1797], grandfather Alexander [1750-1817] or indeed their own fathers Alexander [1782-1848] and John [1789-1836].

Several family historians have suggested the first Robert Young, great-grandfather, was the Captain Robert Young who was Master of the British East Indiaman, *Vansittart*. It is possible but not proved. All that is known for certain is that our Robert Young remained a mariner until his passing in 1797. This Robert would have witnessed first-hand the radical front end period of these changes, and of his five sons who grew to manhood, son Robert became a sailor but sadly he died at just 18 years of age. Sons James and William are variously listed as shipmasters in Leith but little else has come to light on their activities; his youngest son, who was also named Robert [1775 -] rose to the Rank of Lieutenant in the Royal Navy, and of course we already know a great deal about his eldest son, Alexander [1750-1817] arguably the most successful of them all.

When looking into this fourth generation, the crucial period is between 1805 and 1830. We already know that brothers Alexander and John had moved from Leith to Montrose, that they both married there and between them they welcomed no less than thirteen sons into the world. Seven of these lads are known to have followed in the seafaring footsteps of their forefathers, forging careers on the high seas and achieving Master status. One carved out a career in the Royal Navy and another became a significant shipowner with a fleet of vessels of considerable size and latterly steam powered of course. Four others set up ship brokage businesses. They were; indeed, the Change Generation and about to establish a new family paradigm. In embracing global expansion, this generation of Youngs were looking to position themselves in strategic locations to take advantage of emerging mercantile opportunities.

In the process of finding their individual place in this new look Shipping Industry, they were required to think more commercially than practically and act more entrepreneurially than their forebears while all the time remaining true to their seafaring roots. By far the greatest change for this generation of Youngs was the geographic reach of their interests and home ports. Until now, Scotland, and more especially Montrose, Leith and to some extent Edinburgh had been 'home port' for the

Youngs. From all we have learned so far, for the period 1650 through to around 1830, they had remained a tight-knit family unit; however, all that was about to unravel in a way that would have shaken the parents and grandparents to their very core.

Alexander and Helen Liston's eldest son was also named Alexander. He was born July 1782 in Leith, lived with his family in Leith, was educated in Leith and only became acquainted with Montrose through his father's association with the *Eliza Swan*. Henceforward his world changed, he began his sailing days in Montrose, and his voyages to the whale fishery were exclusively out of Montrose. So, it was no surprise that Montrose is where Alexander Jnr decided to reside permanently, and it was in Montrose he met and married Jean Strachan, the daughter of the local Butcher, Robert Strachan. Robert also held shares in several ships involved in the merchant trade as well as a financial interest in shipbuilding in partnership with his son Robert. Most important of all, Robert Strachan Snr was much loved by his family and well respected and admired within the Montrose community. His epitaph describes him as a - 'man of a remarkably kind and friendly disposition'. From the data to hand, only one of Jean Strachan's siblings became a mariner and that was her youngest brother David.

Jean was one of 13 children and then Alexander and Jean had 14 children of their own, which would have made Sunday family gatherings a very noisy crowded affair indeed. Of their brood of 14 three are known to have died young and possibly a fourth, as nothing is known of Thomas Glover Young, apart from his christening in February 1828, and where he is found living with his family at Panmure Place at the time of the 1841 Census. No connections to a Thomas Glover have come to light either, so the reason for this son to be so christened is a mystery. Of their ten surviving children, eight were sons and as remarkable as it seems for the time they all survived to adulthood and to a man did remarkably well in life. Being born 1806 to 1830 in a small provincial Burgh in Scotland was not what one would naturally perceive as a great kick start in life; but Scotland, and indeed Montrose in particular, was renowned for its shipping history, its harbour and the quality of its education. We know that both Alexander Young and Robert Strachan valued education highly because they are listed as financial contributors, and substantial ones at that, to the funding of the Montrose Academy. They also financially supported other community facilities such as the Montrose Royal Infirmary & Lunatic Asylum [Hospital].

Education has long been at the core of the Young family success story, and official records for Montrose date education in that town to as early as 1329. The current Montrose Academy was built in 1815 from publicly raised funds. Those students fortunate enough to attend were enrolled on a fee-paying basis; however, there are also numerous examples where a local lad from a poor family, who had come to be noticed for his natural talents, was sponsored by the local church minister or a benevolent landowner. It has been written that The Montrose Academy employed teachers with excellent credentials and in fact the institution has long been recognised for its notable educators and broad subject offering which led to its reputation for turning out learned men. It is thanks to the solid and well-rounded education this generation received that they were enabled to carve out good lives at the peak of the Victorian era when work, society and culture were seen as essential partners.

The captains and masters in this family could not succeed without a sound knowledge and skill in mathematics which is associated with astronomy, geography and map reading. They had to be adept in the use of navigation equipment, have knowledge and understanding of the function of armaments, the vagaries of climate, the cycle of the seasons, the strange movements of ocean currents, and at the same time they needed to be able to comprehend legal documents, work within the Law of Nations, know how to hire and manage good men, how to adequately and healthily provision a vessel, the physics of loading and so much more. Whether in their own home port or a foreign port there were customs and harbour officials to communicate with and ship owners and merchants to negotiate with. At a community level there were social events where good manners, adherence to dress codes and knowing the correct social protocol were essential if one was to climb what those of the Victorian era had termed the Social Ladder.

These observations raised so many questions: Was their success born out of the achievement of their ancestors or their own driving ambition? Was it the love and support of family that enabled them to push the boundaries, to have enough confidence and self-belief to be able to succeed? And then, what role did the family network of connections, established by the father and grandfather, play in opening doors for this generation?

On this occasion, I intend to follow just one line of the Young Family – the children of Alexander Young and Jean Strachan with a view to demonstrating where this generation ended up. Frankly, at this point it is not hard to imagine all of these scenarios playing a part in their lives to a varying degree. As for their father, Captain Alexander Young Jnr [1789-1848], from all the research data available he most certainly led an exemplary life as a contributing member of the Montrose community and along the way made some well-positioned personal and business friends.

This does not usually happen for those who have a serious character flaw or for those who have not been upstanding in their dealings with others. Alexander also married into a well-respected, long established local family already involved in ship building, ship ownership and the merchant trade. He also held positions of trust and respect in the Montrose community, including the Montrose Harbour Trust and the Montrose Academy. Alexander proved himself successful in business without having to venture outside the law and from all accounts he was also a fair man and an accomplished sea captain who appears to have moved with the times, much like his father before him.

All of these things mattered and proved to be the vital ingredients for creating this family's new paradigm!

So, it was - look out world here they come .....

The eldest son, Alexander Young [1806-1863], was born in Montrose, took to the sea at fourteen, can be seen renewing his Mates Certificate in September 1824 and remained at sea until sometime in late 1837 when we find him bound for Australia. He sailed as a passenger on the 596 ton vessel *Upton Castle* under the command of Master Thomas Williams on that particular voyage. His journey would take him from London via the Cape of Good Hope in South Africa all the way to Sydney, New South Wales. The Log for the *Upton Castle* shows they departed London on 16 October 1837, The Cape 1 January 1838 and arrived into Sydney Cove on 24 February 1838.

Alexander Young travelled as a First Class passenger, and it goes without saying that his four month journey provided ample time for him to become properly acquainted with his fellow travellers in First Class. The *Upton Castle* passenger manifest boasts some illustrious individuals on that auspicious voyage, the most notable being His Excellency Sir George Gipps, Lady Gipps and their only son Reginald. Sir George was heading to the Colony to take up the post of Captain-General and Governor-in-Chief of New South Wales and Van Diemans Land. More important to this story, as Governor-in-Chief, Sir George Gipps was about to become an outspoken proponent of the 'free passage' programme for Bounty Immigration, an initiative which will soon see the colony's population double and put substantial revenue into the coffers of more than one enterprising Young. More on that later.

Wife Lady Elizabeth is known to hold strong Scottish connections as the daughter of the Earl of Dalhousie GCB. Another career military man he was at one time Governor of Nova Scotia and went on to become Governor General of British North America and later Commander-in-Chief in India. These were notable military families and so it is no surprise to learn that Sir George's only son Reginald was destined to serve in the military like his father and grandfather. At some point young Reginald is known to have returned to England where he graduated from Eton College. His career defining role was as General Sir Reginald Ramsay Gipps GCB, Military Secretary in the British Parliament. Clearly Alexander was in excellent company.

Two other passengers with whom Alexander would have enjoyed seafaring dialogue, were Captain Gordon R.N. and Captain Bordes R.N. both of whom were sailing to take up navy postings in Sydney Town. However, it was the final passenger on the manifest, Robert Burnett Ramsay, who, in the very near future, is about to play a pivotal role in the life of this Alexander Young and, sometime later Alexander's brother Joshua. It has been written by other researchers that these three men were known to each other back in Scotland, yet no real evidence was offered to support their assumption and in reality it is highly improbable. My investigations reveal that Robert Burnett Ramsay was born into a Scottish military family in Kolkata [Calcutta], West Bengal in 1818. His father was Captain Robert Ramsay of His Majesty's 14th Regiment of Foot of Bengal. Young Robert received his initial education in Edinburgh before heading to Harrow [now known as the University of Westminster] in Middlesex, London. Sometime later he attended the L'École Spéciale Militaire de Saint-Cyr which is most notable as the French military academy founded by Napoleon.

It transpires that a military career was not what young Robert Burnett Ramsay had in mind for himself, and perhaps that decision was influenced somewhat by his father. By 1838, Captain Ramsay had already retired from the Army to take a partnership role in Cruickshank Melville & Co, a mercantile firm with its Head Office in London. This firm is known to have owned plantation operations in the West Indies as well as doing business in Australia. Interestingly, the publication, Allen's Indian Mail, for 1846 printed an article mentioning Cruickshank Melville & Co wherein the Company is listed as co-signatories to a letter from the East-India and China Association of London to His Highness Ibrahim Pacha, the then Royal and Military leader of Egypt, which reads in part - ' ... beg leave to approach your Highness with sentiments of great respect. We feel so sensibly the benefits which have for a series of years been derived from the protection afforded by his Highness Mehemet Ali to travellers passing through Egypt, and for the facilities given for the transmission of the India Mails....'. This letter relates to a time prior to the opening of the Suez Canal when mail and passengers alike utilised a train line connecting the port of Alexandria to the southern port of Tawfiq [Suez] on what we now know as the Gulf of Suez on the Red Sea. This was the first step in shortening transit times of Europe and Britain to India and the Far East.

To explain how Captain Ramsay found himself taking a partnership role in this firm in particular it is important to mention that his wife, and Robert Burnett Ramsay's mother, was none other than Margaret Gerard Cruickshank, the daughter of Patrick Cruickshank of St Vincent in the Caribbean who was a Planter and Slave Owner in the West Indies. She was also the grand-daughter of Sir Donald Cruickshank of Stracathro, Scotland. Today, the residence on the Estate, Stracathro House is described as 'a find A-listed Palladian style mansion, overlooking the Cruick Water.' This Estate, comprising over 800 acres, was purchased in 1775 by Patrick Cruickshank who had made his fortune in Jamaica. So given this background information it is highly unlikely their paths had crossed, but they would have had some geography and history to share in conversation.

There is no doubt that young Robert Burnett Ramsay was heading to Sydney full of ambition, armed with great family credentials and established business connections in the Colony. Alexander too would have been full of ambition, albeit that he lacked Ramsay's illustrious family credentials, but most certainly he came armed with a solid education, sound family values and a good work ethic. On the face of it, one would have to say it was a stroke of luck for Alexander that he travelled on that particular *Upton Castle* voyage. It has also been erroneously reported by some Young family historians that it was Alexander's brother Joshua Richmond who travelled on the *Upton Castle* with Ramsay, and therefore was behind the establishment of Ramsay, Young & Company. The vessel's passenger manifest for the voyage is available and definitely shows quite clearly that this was not the case and that assumption too is incorrect.

What is more likely, is that Robert Ramsay and Alexander Young struck up an acquaintance on that voyage and as a result of their numerous conversations en route decided they shared some common goals and therefore it made sense to go into business together. With this plan in mind, very soon after they disembarked at Port Jackson on 24 February 1838, they set about putting their plan into action. On 5 March the business of Ramsay, Young & Co. was registered with the New South Wales government. From all reports Alexander and his partner Robert quickly settled into their new mercantile venture quite probably using Cruickshank Melville & Co in London as their agents. A short time later they entered into another partnership. This time with another local Sydney firm styled J.B. Holdsworth & Co. This company appears in the Sands Business Directory for Sydney for 1870 as a Wholesaler & Retailer of some size. John Holdsworth is listed as the principal of the company which was well established as a major importer of Furnishing and General Ironmongery and as such, Holdsworths were potentially major clients for Ramsay, Young and Company. Newspaper advertisements and New South Wales Government Gazette records all indicate that both these companies were very successful although they remained trading as separate entities.

Again, it is from The Sands Business Directory of Sydney that we learn the Shipping Agents and Brokage business of Ramsay, Young & Co. was initially situated in Hunter Street where they had a Stores Building and an Office block with a residence above. A short time later they acquired an additional warehouse building in George Street. A decade or so on and we get a real sense of their prosperity and business expansion from another publication entitled - *Sydney in 1848* written by Joseph Fowles. In Chapter XI headed 'Hunter Street - Early History Continued' Fowles writes - 'The portion of Hunter Street represented in our accompanying plate {page 45} extends from Pitt Street westward as far as Castlereagh Street. The upper line contains [one side of the street] the extensive Stores of Messrs. Flower, Salting, and Co.; the private residence of Mr. Young, and Stores belonging to the firm of Young and Co.

While from various newspaper notices and advertisements it is clear that Ramsay, Young & Co. continued to trade for some five years or so it seems the timeline for both these initial two partnerships Alexander Young had entered into with Robert Ramsay and John Holdsworth had run their course and were set to be dissolved by mutual consent. The requisite Legal

Notices appeared in the Sydney Morning Herald; the first on 22 February 1843 stated the dissolution of these partnerships was effective as of 27 January of that year. The reason for the Ramsay Young partnership dissolution is simple, Ramsay had his eyes set on a far bigger prize - land - and lots of it, plus he saw advantages in becoming part of the political machine much as his grandfather had done.

Ramsay then set about building his political career and his personal business empire. Initially, after establishing himself as a Magistrate, he spent a short time sitting on the bench in Sydney, but this could not hold his interest as his real intention was to avail himself of the land grants on offer in the prosperous north of the Colony. Ramsay headed off to take advantage of the development of what was to become the State of Queensland. He was a man with a new-found vision and high aspirations - hungry for success. At one point Robert alone held some 64,000 acres of prime grazing land on the Darling Downs and its fringes on which he was grazing upwards of 37,000 sheep and 1,200 cattle. This area today is still considered the Dress Circle of agriculture in that State.

Ramsay went on to form several new business alliances and later a personal alliance. In 1855, Robert Burnett Ramsay was discovered sailing back to London where he married Susan Lindsay Carnegie, the daughter of William Fullerton Lindsay Carnegie of Inverkeillor, Scotland and Jane Christian Carnegie, daughter of William Carnegie 7th Earl of Northesk. Returning to Australia, Ramsay and his new wife set about raising their family of fourteen children on his premier landholding of 'Rosalie Downs'. Eventually, politics beckoned, and his first electoral success came following the Queensland Colonial Election of 1867, when he became State Representative for the seat of Western Downs. This move into politics saw him rise quickly through the ranks to become the 8th State Treasurer of Queensland. Robert Burnett Ramsay remained a Legislative Parliamentary Member from 1867-1877. All the while Alexander and Robert maintained a close friendship.

Around the same time as the Ramsay Young partnership was dissolved, Alexander cited his brother Joshua Richmond Young as his 'Attorney' in a Legal Notice in The Sydney

Morning Herald. This is the first indication we have that the two brothers were about to be re-united and become business partners in Young & Co. at 46 Hunter Street, Sydney. Apart from the expected assortment of newspaper advertisements for their brokerage business little is known of Alexander Young's professional life except that he did remain focused on all things mercantile. The best indication of the early success he enjoyed in this Ship Broking business can be found in the Will of his uncle, Captain Joshua Richmond, who died in Scotland in late 1847. Even at that early stage of his time in Sydney, word of Alexander's success had reached Scottish shores, because his Uncle Joshua had added a codicil to his Will excluding Alexander from inheriting on account 'he was not in need'.

On the other hand, Alexander's family life had not enjoyed the same sweet success. In 1840 in Sydney he had married Miss Louisa Davies recently arrived from London. Alas, this union was to be the source of a great deal of pain and sorrow for Alexander and Louisa too. Their first born son died at three weeks of age, their next child, a daughter, has her birth and death registered on the same day in 1842. Then a year or so later Alexander and Louisa were in Macau, China when Louisa gives birth to twin boys, Alexander Richmond and William Broughton. Sadly, only William survived. At this point I have no idea why they were in China and can only assume they were en route to England because son William's christening is registered in Sonning, Berkshire in the October of 1843. Alexander and Louisa's movements are a little erratic for the next few years, until more bad news is learned when in 1852 Louisa dies of Consumption. At that time the family were residing at Brompton Crescent, London; however, her death was also reported in the Sydney Morning Herald, indicating that Alexander still had strong connections in that city.

Alexander remained in England to pursue new business opportunities, and it is not long before we find his name associated with a very innovative product. In the intervening years he had met and married a lady by the name of Mary Papworth who was some 20 years his junior. They had married at Clerkenwell, London, in 1855 and when next we find them, Alexander, Mary and his son William are listed in the 1861 Census living at 'Fair Mead Cottage', Waltham Holy Cross, in Essex. It is from this Census that we learn more about what Alexander has been doing. He is listed therein as proprietor of a substantial manufacturing factory in Bow, London employing some 32 men involved with the manufacture of an innovative product - Bitumenized Pipe. The London Daily News carries several stories on this new style of pipe which is apparently made from paper and strengthened by admixing bitumen under pressure. The original concept was patented by Parisian Monsieur Jalonreau and Local Authorities in Paris had embraced it and utilised it for the reticulation of water and gas in that city.

At this point we see that Alexander Young has developed a thirst for innovation and knowledge, lost none of his ambition, and was confident to be at the forefront of anything and everything new. The next time his name appears in British business records it is discovered that Messrs. Paul Joske and Alexander Young are nominated as the patentees of the Bitumenized Pipe in England. Shortly afterward there was a court case regarding ownership of the said patent in Britain and the case was settled in Alexander's favour. It appears that Alexander and his partner had acted shrewdly in that they realised M. Jalonreau had failed to take out a worldwide patent; which left the door open for entrepreneurial thinkers like Alexander and his partner to capitalise on the invention outside of France.

Alexander has now established himself as an international businessman and a manufacturer. He subsequently made several visits to Australia to promote this innovative product of bitumenized pipe. To maximise the business opportunity of these visits he placed advertisements in newspapers across the country espousing the products virtues and announcing the dates for his impending visits.

One such advertorial appeared in The South Australian for Wednesday 5 September 1860, which displays a cunning form of marketing indeed. It reads –

'We have before us a circular signed by Mr. Alexander Young, Secretary to a Company recently formed in London for the manufacture of these curious pipes, and for this circular we extracted the following:-
The original inventor was M. Jalonreau, and his patent has been tested by actual use in Paris for more than three years. The basis of the pipe is paper - another instance of the wondrous diversity of application - of which that substance is now capable.

Indeed, to such perfection is this invention carried, that the patentees will be able legally to cheat the House of Lords itself, inasmuch as the "patent bituminized pipes," though made in reality of paper, are only paper for a passing moment, and never assume that form to the eyes of an Exciseman.

'The 'Patent Bituminized Pipes' are neutral, non-conductors of electricity and consequently are not exposed to any of the deteriorating influences mentioned above. ....these pipes have been proved in Paris up to a pressure of 15 atmospheres, equal to 480 feet of water; and in London they resisted the pressure of 220 lbs. to the square inch, equal to 506 feet head of water....'.

Alexander's venture thrived and made the global tabloids many times over the years. When Alexander died in 1863 the Sydney Morning Herald carried a public notice advising of his passing at the age of fifty-seven whilst a resident at Palace Gardens Villas, London which today is a street in Central West London reputedly boasting some of the most expensive properties in the world and has long been known as 'Billionaire Row'. Today, the palatial homes of Palace Gardens Villas are either occupied as private residences by persons of extreme wealth or as national embassies and ambassadorial residences. Properties changing hands for prices in the vicinity of £100 million is not an uncommon occurrence.

Alexander's various achievements stemmed from his hard won rewards for his entrepreneurial thinking, risk taking and good sound business acumen, combined with a big dose of hard work. Alexander set about embracing the opportunities on offer in the new world landscape of international mercantile business. He used Sydney as a stepping-stone to his higher goals, and along the way he outwitted a Frenchman and wound up creating his own family fortune.

Next comes Alexander's brother, John Young [1811-1871] the second surviving son of Alexander and Jean. John too was born in Montrose, educated at the Montrose Academy and went to sea as a young lad. By 1824 he is apprenticed to his father, shipping out of Montrose on voyages to the Baltic, Archangel and the East Indies and West Indies. Currently in the possession of a family member is Captain Young's metal Lodge Case in which he kept his personal handwritten inventory of his voyages. Beginning with his days as an Apprentice sailing out of Montrose, he makes Seaman by June 1828, Mate by June 1829 and Master by March 1832. At one point in 1830-31 he was found sailing out of London for Bombay as Mate on the same *Upton Castle* which in 1838 took his older brother, Alexander, all the way to Sydney, Australia. The difference here is that John is working on the vessel as crew whereas big brother Alexander travelled as a First Class passenger. John's next vessel, the 300 ton *Hodgkinson*, was also engaged in the West Indies trade. He was only twenty-one years of age when he first qualified for his 'Certificate of Competency as Master' and overall he had a proud 30 year career in the Merchant Navy criss-crossing the globe. Among the handful of Certificates that do survive at National Archives, Kew, is a recent copy of his Master's Claim for Certificate of Service submitted at the Port of Dundee on the 31st Feb 1850 and another such Certificate N° 49.470 dated 26 December 1850 when he was still known to be sailing the lucrative Baltic and Archangel routes.

TABLE 11 – Capt John Young [1811-1871] Career Table

Vessel Name	Port of Sailing	Capacity	Date of Joining	Date of Discharge	Length of Servitude		
					Yrs	Mths	Days
Jane	Montrose	Apprentice	1 Jun 1824	31 May 1828	4	-	-
Jane	Montrose	Seaman	1 Jun 1828	10 Mar 1829		9	10
Comet	London	2nd Mate	15 Mar 1829	3 Jun 1829		2	19
Byron	Dundee	Mate	10 Jun 1829	Left sick at Elsinore Is.		3	
Tam O"Shanter	London	3rd Mate	15 Mar 1830	Left in Jun w/o proceed. to sea		3	
Upton Castle	London	3rd Mate	Jun 1830	Left in Jul 1831	1	1	-
Hodgkinson	Liverpool	Mate	Jul 1831	Jan 1832		7	-
Jane	Montrose	Master	26 Mar 1832	8 Sep 1834	2	5	22
Hibernia	Kinsale	Master	Sep 1834				
Emerald	Kinsale	Master		Sep 1835	1	1	
Jane	Montrose	Master	21 Mar 1836	6 Mar 1851	14	11	28
Sussex	Dundee	Master	27 May 1851	3 May 1853	2		
Sussex	Dundee	Master	23 Aug 1853	21 Mar 1854		7	
					28	3	19

I make the above declaration conscientiously believing the same to be true and in virtue of the Act made, and passed in the Fifth and Sixth Years of the reign of his late Majesty William the Fourth, entitled an Act for the more effectual abolition of Oaths.

Sgd. John Young

This is a transcript of John's own list of his voyages -

This document carries a mention of Kinsale in Ireland. His time in Kinsale was totally unplanned - it was a matter of any port in a storm - literally. He was sailing as Master of the snow *Jane* when he was caught in a severe gale in the Irish Sea which snapped the mast and destroyed much of the *Jane's* rigging. John managed to limp into Kinsale Harbour where he met with Samuel Donaclift of Donaclift Shipyards, the man who he subsequently engaged to carry out the extensive repair work on the *Jane*. At this time, mast timber was not easy to procure in Ireland, or England for that matter, and John was delayed in Kinsale for a lengthy period as he awaited suitable mast timber to be sourced; probably via the Strachan family lumber operation in Riga. In the meantime, John kept himself busy sailing Irish ships the *Hibernia* and the *Emerald*. Lloyd's Register lists these vessels sailing between Kinsale, Cork, Dublin and London. The original of the Donaclift Shipwrights Work Order/Invoice from 1834 with its Certification by a Representative of Lloyds Surveyors of London survives to this day and is a treasured part of a private family collection. [See Website].

It was during his time in Kinsale that John met his future wife, Mary Donaclift, daughter of the shipwright of the same name. John and Mary married in Kinsale in 1834 and their first born, Alexander Donaclift Young, arrived into this world on the 3rd October 1835 in Kinsale. Very shortly afterwards the family set sail for Montrose, where baby Alexander was christened on the 7th October. At this point John takes time out, probably to settle his new family into life in Montrose. We know this because Lloyd's Register confirms all of these events with entries in their 1832-1836 Register for the initial voyage, for 1835 when the *Jane* is returned to home port but sailing without John at the helm and finally for 1836 when the status quo returns and we find John and his beloved *Jane* reunited. These entries are cited as examples of Lloyd's entries. They read –

1832
Jane Sw Young 164 Leith n.Kl&drp Young&Co Lo.Elsn 1C11
A 10   SDB   26

[This tells us that the Jane was a Snow class ship, Capt Young, 164 tons Burthen, single deck with beams, sheathed & doubled, built in Leith, new Keel and damages repaired, owned by Young & Co, last surveyed in 1826, sailing out of London, of cedar construction, due for survey in November 1832, and classified as A or First Class]

1835
Jane Sw Strachan 165 Leith 1824 A. Young Montrose Dun., AE1
Drp 35 3

[This tells us that this is the same Jane of Snow Class, now with Captain Strachan at the helm, 165 burthen, built in Leith 1824, Damage Repairs completed 1835, A. Young Owner, home port is Montrose, sailing for Dundee, and it is now rated Level2 of AE of First Class]

1836
John Young is back as Captain.

Montrose is where John and Mary were to make their home for the next twenty years or so and it is where we find Mary's young brother, Samuel, in early 1837. At age 16 year Samuel Donaclift Jnr has decided on a career at sea and after journeying from Kinsale to Montrose we discover that on the 17 February 1837 he enters into a formal apprenticeship arrangement with his brother-in-law and serves out his time sailing on the *Jane* with Captain John Young. This partnership of John and the *Jane* is a long and successful one until John finally retires from active sailing in 1853 and becomes a Ships Broker firstly in Montrose, followed by a short stint in Glasgow where he also acted as a Surveyor for Lloyd's Shipping. His final move to Kirkcaldy around 1858 is when John enters into partnership with a local established Kirkcaldy Shipowner, Ships Broker & Insurance Agent by the name of George Turnbull. Sadly, by June 1866 Turnbull has died and then the 1871 Census shows John has decided to remain in Kirkcaldy and hangs up his shingle as - John Young, Ships Broker - at 511 High Street, Kirkcaldy. He also maintained a warehouse facility down by the harbour-side.

Just like his father and grandfather before him, John was a community minded and church going person as well as a member of the Freemasons Lodge of St Peters Episcopalian Church while resident in Montrose. John also donated money to The Montrose Academy and supported community projects both in Montrose and Kirkcaldy where he is discovered involved with a little known Parliamentary Petition for the Greenwich Sixpence Fund. The Fife Herald, for Thursday 4 Feb 1869, published the following story under the heading of - 'Greenwich Sixpence'. 'We are glad to observe that the movement on behalf of the merchant seamen for the recovery of what is known as 'Greenwich Sixpences', is now being warmly carried on. Petitions to Parliament lie for signature at the office of Captain John Young, Ship Broker here, and elsewhere, which we understand will be forwarded to the member for the burghs for presentation. There is every prospect that this important matter will be taken up at the ensuing session of Parliament, and consequently it is desirable that the petition be largely signed by all who have an interest in dealing out justice to our brave tars.' Having no prior knowledge of the Greenwich Sixpence Fund it was time to explore its significance.

It transpires that the genesis of this Fund lies in an offer made by Queen Mary to establish the Greenwich Hospital for old and disabled sailors just as Charles II had established the Chelsea Hospital for old and disabled soldiers. This was not done for humane or altruistic reasons rather as a means of gaining popular favour for her husband William III. But things did not quite go to plan, progress was slow and unfortunately Mary died before her plans for the hospital could be properly formalised, despite there being records indicating that she had organised for the land to be set aside. William III subsequently endowed the building to be built; however, the British Parliament decreed that the seamen themselves would be held solely responsible for funding the running costs.

Historical records highlight the inequality between the Chelsea soldiers' facility and the Greenwich sailors' facility entitlements. This put the Government into damage control and it soon became a clear case of legislation on the run. Several Acts of Parliament later and the persisting inequality remained a matter of grave concern for the merchant sailors who were intended to benefit from this regal largess. But there was worse to come. From the outset there was clear favouritism shown to Navy personnel because of the introduction of complicated paperwork. The higher levels of illiteracy amongst merchant sailors meant they simply could not complete the forms and satisfy the requirements for inclusion.

It was not until 1747 that a partial resolution was reached via the - 'Act for the Relief and Support of Maimed and Disabled Seamen, and the Widows and Children of such as shall be killed, slain or drowned in the Merchants Service' - a wordy title which gave mere lip-service to the problems being faced and so once again matters were left to roll along. All the while discontent was on the rise among the merchant sailor ranks and the lack of resolution and tardiness on behalf of the Government meant their voices were now being raised louder and louder about this and other issues causing dissatisfaction.

Next came the Act of 1834 which - 'made Scottish and Irish seamen eligible for pensions and granted Awards to widows so that by 1843 seamen's widows comprised over half of the pension list'. This too was a flawed initiative in that the seamen's funds were collected centrally and distributed locally which simply did not work. By 1835 a seaman's' contribution had been raised to a shilling a month and at the same time these contributions were redirected to the newly created Merchant Seaman's Fund rather than passed directly to Greenwich Hospital. Without a resolution in sight unrest continued to fester and with shipwreck numbers on the rise and thousands making claims, the viability of the Fund was under serious threat.

Right about now the Youngs and their fellow sailors would have been very frustrated watching these events unfold but then the game changed. The next major milestone occurred in 1840 with the establishment of a Parliamentary Select Committee Hearing into the complaints raised by the sailors – the long suffering merchantmen had decided enough was enough. Submissions were not confined to pension and hospital care issues either, but included topics such as dangerous working conditions, cramped and unhealthy foc'sle accommodation, the lack of sanitary provisions, poor quality and inappropriate food rations, the low standard set for medical services on board ship and more.

Continued government inaction finally led to the seamen's strike of 1866. This should have heralded the beginning of serious long term change in response to the grievances raised over the two decades prior; but, as is the case so often with government initiatives, they are designed to quell conversation, not offer solutions. Further evidence of this came to light in an answer from the First Lord of the Admiralty, Mr. George Shaw-Lefevre, in the House of Commons in 1866 when he advised in part - '3,400 claims had been sent in, of which 1,115 were from men who went to sea before 1815, so that at present no person who was of less age than seventy would have much chance of receiving a pension.' Very disappointing!

Harking back to that article in the Fife Herald it can be concluded that Captain John Young fully supported the Fund and indeed he lived just long enough to see his activism rewarded. From Hansard for 21 February 1870 it is revealed that in the October of 1869 The House Commons did make an Order in Council under the 'Greenwich Hospital Act' designed to streamline the process of allocating pensions. The power of the people won out - finally!

There is one remaining Fife Herald article for Thursday 11 November 1869 which gives further insight into the person of Captain John Young and the respect and regard he enjoyed in the Kirkcaldy community. It reads - 'TOWN COUNCIL - INDUCTION OF THE NEW COUNCILLORS - The Council met on Friday night in the Town Hall - Provost Swan in the chair - when the newly-elected Councillors made the necessary declarations as to the faithful discharge of their duties as Councillors. [Other matters were dealt with then ...] The Council next appointed Councillors Gow, Bogie and Wemyss, as members of the Dean of Guild Court;

And then 1750-1850

re-appointed Captain John Young and Captain Isles to be assessors to the Admiralty; and also re-elected Mr. Sloddart and Mr. James Beveridge as assessors to the Admiralty.' Black's Law Dictionary broadly defines this role as - 'An officer chosen or appointed to appraise, value, or assess property. In civil and Scotch Law. Persons skilled in law, selected to advise the judges of the inferior courts. A person learned in some particular science or industry, who sits with the judge on the trial of a cause requiring such special knowledge and gives his advice. .... it is the practice to call in admiralty business to call in assessors, in cases involving questions of navigation or seamanship. They are called 'nautical assessors', and are always Brethren of the Trinity House.' Recognition well deserved.

In the final analysis, Captain John Young was a good man. He was the only son to follow the family tradition of taking the helm, of feeling that exhilaration of wind in canvas for his entire seafaring career. In fact, he was the last Young to do so and remained forever engaged with sail and the sea, and apart from his enforced stay in Kinsale, he was the only son of Alexander and Jean to live out his days in Scotland. As to his character, John had unconditional trust placed in him by his uncle, Captain Joshua Richmond, who appointed him an Executor and bequeathed to him and his father 'any nautical books charts or instruments found at [his] death...'. As well, the various positions of trust he held in Montrose, Glasgow and Kirkcaldy required the assignation of his peers. Such was his maritime reputation that Lloyd's appointed him to their own prestigious organisation. Notwithstanding all of his achievements John seems to have been the quiet and unassuming one of the family who spent much of his life in the shadow of his father and uncle. John was someone who never shone brightly but was a lasting light. He died at Kirkcaldy in October 1871 at the age of 59 years. A Death Notice appeared in the Fife Free Press on 21 October, and his name appears on the Family Carfax in Old Cathcart Cemetery in Glasgow. It is sobering to realise that his passing also brought an end to this family's connection to Montrose.

Alexander and Jean's third surviving son was Joshua Richmond Young, born April 1813 in Montrose, and was so named to honour his esteemed uncle. Although he was raised at a time when his father was extremely successful at the whale fishery in the Arctic this career was not to be for him. Like his big brother before him, after attaining his education in Montrose, he too left home in his mid-twenties and probably lured by the positive stories related to the family back in Montrose by Alexander, Joshua is found heading to Australia. He travelled to Sydney and met up with Alexander around 1840/41 which was right about the time Alexander and Robert Ramsay were planning to dissolve their partnership and it could be surmised that this was a proposition put by Alexander to Joshua. The three men worked together for a short time, and these early business arrangements have been mentioned previously. Socially, Joshua quickly settled into Sydney life and it is not long after his arrival that we find his name on the social pages of the Sydney Morning Herald advising of his marriage to Mary Scott, daughter of the late Robert Scott, Esq., of Turin, Forfarshire. Their marriage took place at St James Anglican Church, King Street, Sydney in the August of 1842.

Joshua's association with Robert Ramsay might appear brief but their personal friendship was a connection which remained solid, close and enduring. In 1850 Joshua christened one of his daughters Margaret Ramsay Young, to honour Robert Ramsay's family. Their personal connection did not end there either because another of Joshua's daughters, Jane, is found marrying Edwin David Donkin who was Robert Ramsay's trusted Station Manager. Donkin had responsibility for Ramsay's massive pastoral holding of 'Eton Vale' where the newly- weds made their home for almost a decade before returning to New South Wales to take up a holding of their own in the Bowral district. Edwin Donkin was the third son of the highly esteemed Reverend Thomas Donkin of Yorkshire who came to Sydney in 1853, and has a plaque dedicated to him and his work in St. Andrews Cathedral in Sydney. Edwin's brother also distinguished himself as a prominent sheep and cattle pastoralist in the Wyalong District, and is noted as one of the pioneers in water irrigation and mechanised shearing.

And then 1750-1850

As Joshua and Mary's family expanded to seven children, they moved from the original house over the Offices in Hunter Street which he once shared with brother Alexander, to take up residence in 'Hereford House', on the Bishopthorpe Estate on Glebe Road, Sydney. After his brother Alexander returned to England Joshua wisely retained the stores buildings and company offices in Hunter Street as well as the new warehouse in George Street. These were in prime locations, close to the burgeoning commercial hub of Sydney Town yet still in close proximity to the busy wharf facilities of Port Jackson.

Like his big brother Alexander, Joshua had an entrepreneurial approach to doing business and The New South Wales Government Gazette is littered with the name of Joshua Richmond Young in relation to his diverse business interests. One set of examples covers the period 1851-1857 where Joshua gave £1000 Sureties annually to cover his numerous Gold Leases and there quite possibly could be earlier instances not yet uncovered. Whilst gold had been discovered in the early 1820s in New South Wales the Colonial Office in England decided to suppress the news as it was believed it would destabilise the Colonial economy which was solidly focused on a building program. It was only after the 1848 California Gold Rush saw significant numbers of newly arrived settlers leaving Australia that the Colonial Office in London changed its tune and permitted the exploitation of local resources and offered rewards to those who found 'payable gold'. Once news got out of the 1851 gold discovery at Orange in New South Wales the 'Rush' was on and towns such as Braidwood, Araluen, Orange and Bathurst quickly became epicentres, alive with gold prospectors.

With Sydney's rising prosperity came an opportunity for Joshua to speculate in land development, and we see he takes up 10 allotments for residential development [the NSW Register does not contain any date but it is thought to be C1850]. 1850 was a busy year for Joshua, he was granted and purchased land in central Sydney for additional warehouse space and he also formed a new business partnership known as - Young, Lark & Bennett. Francis Bennett and Thomas Lark were not only business partners; according to the Historical Electoral Rolls for New South Wales they were also near neighbours of Joshua's in the fashionable suburb of Glebe. Some early editions of The Sands Business Directories for Sydney also indicate that Messrs Lark & Bennett already owned business premises at 376-378 George Street on the corner of Margaret Street.

To learn a little more about Joshua's business activities it's time to turn to the later 1870 edition of the Sands Directory which carries two display advertisements, the first relates to the English, Scottish and Australian Chartered Bank [which, for Australian readers over 60 years of age, will be recognised as what was set to become known as the E.S. & A. Bank]. This Bank was originally formed in London by Royal Charter in 1852 and continued to trade in Australia until 1970 when it merged with the ANZ Bank. The London Head Office of the E.S, & A. Bank was situated at 73 Cornhill, a building that still stands as an elegant Georgian property in the heart of London's banking precinct. Their Sydney Office had four Directors, one of whom was Joshua Richmond Young.

The second item appears in two parts - a one page spread and a two page spread regaling the prestige and virtues of the Pacific Fire & Marine Insurance Company. The London Offices of this firm were in the prestigious Cornhill Chambers, a classic example of Victorian Architecture, built very ornately as an outward show of wealth. Messrs Young & Lark were listed as their Agents in Sydney. The Pacific Fire & Marine Insurance Company boasted offices in London, Sydney, Melbourne, Bombay and the Mauritius, with their Sydney Office located in Pitt Street. The Company prospectus advises £1Million capital of which £793,550 was subscribed and Joshua Richmond Young Esq., is listed as Chairman of that Insurance Company.

Business success for Joshua seems nothing short of stunning and even after the dissolution of his partnership with his brother Alexander the business of Young & Co continued to prosper right up until around August 1855/56 when the partnership with Messrs. Lark & Bennett tends to take centre stage. It is unclear exactly why these men decided to continue to trade separately for a time; perhaps it was a strategic decision in an attempt to gain a greater share of the market. In many ways their businesses were complimentary, with Lark &

Bennett being described as Wool Brokers & Mercantile Agents, and Young & Co listed as Merchants and Mercantile Brokers. There is a possibility that they held government contracts which needed to time out, or maybe they felt a silent amalgamation afford them a business advantage given clients previously saw them as separate operators.

Right about this time the Wool and Gold markets were set to boom in Australia. While the first Spanish Merino sheep had arrived from Cape of Good Hope, South Africa in 1797 it was not until a selective breeding program was undertaken by John Macarthur and the Rev. Samuel Marsden [remember his man's name], that the Australian Wool Industry was born. The first auction of Australian fleece was held at the famous Garraway's Coffee House in Change-alley, Cornhill, London, in 1821, and by 1840 Australia was producing more than two million kilos of wool each year. Success here invigorated exploration to establish a road to the rich grazing land known to exist on the inland side of the mountains to the west of Sydney.

While Explorers, Blaxland, Lawson and Wentworth, had found a way over the Blue Mountains in 1813 the track was far too rugged for bullock drays. Along came George Evans who surveyed a more suitable pathway. Meanwhile back in January 1800 a Dorset engineer and mariner, William M. Cox, had arrived in the colony. He came with his sons as Captain of the *Minerva* arriving into and by 1803 Cox owned 1300 acres of land, 100 cattle and 2,000 sheep and £4,000 of trading property. He then took up a further 4000 acres in the Mulgoa Valley near Gregory and John Blaxland. Obviously neighbourly conversation at some point extended to roadmaking whereupon Cox advised he had experience of roadmaking in the County of Cumberland. Once word of this reached Governor Macquarie he moved quickly, and by letter from Government House dated July 1814 he appointed Cox Superintendent of Works for the construction of the new road over the Blue Mountains.

Cox set to with a team of 30 convicts and 8 guards and they built the first trafficable road to cover the 100 mile distance from Emu Plains in western Sydney over the Blue mountains to the hub town of Bathurst. This project had many drivers from within and outside Australia. There was a strong push for colonial expansion, a deterioration in the quality of English wool and the rising cost of German imports. Overlay these primary fuels with the insatiable demands coming from Yorkshire Mill owners and English Merchants all eager to find a new source of raw material in order to expand their businesses. It has generally been conceded that Australia rose to prosperity on 'the sheep's back.' None of it would have been possible without Cox and his road. Even greater success was to follow for these graziers and squatters west of the Blue Mountains who by 1870 had combined to make Australia the world's largest wool producer. The point here is that this was great for business for Young, Lark & Bennett.

What then of the human transportation side of Joshua's mercantile business. While the transportation of convicts to Australia ceased in 1840, the arrival of Governor Gipps on the *Upton Castle* was set to see the passenger side of the Shipping Brokerage business boom on the back of his initiative to encourage mass immigration. The New South Wales Government appointed representatives to Britain to offer incentives of free passage and more to any skilled and able bodied men and women eager to head to the Colony. Meanwhile, the Government in New South Wales were drawing up plans for the next wave of colonial expansion. Firstly, it was Alexander who prospered here, and later Joshua's companies were in a prime position to contract to the Government on the basis of their expertise and established Agency connections. There was also a homeland connection for these lads with Scots arriving into the Colony in significant numbers. Mostly, the Scots who signed on were those still displaced as a consequence of the 1785-1820 Highland Clearances and 1760-1830 Lowland Clearances. They were followed by those who fell victim to the 1846/56 Highland Potato Famine. Hence there were large numbers of Scots who out of desperation set sail for Australia and the Americas. Alas, we will soon learn that some of these new arrivals were Joshua's cousins. At one point in the mid-late 1840s over 12% of Australians were Scots-born emigrants.

This next newspaper article appeared in the Sydney Morning Herald, for Friday 20 March 1857, and is one of many which appeared over the next few years. Under the heading of Shipping Arrivals, it says -

'March 10 - Mary Ann, ship 1057 tons,
Captain Phelan, from Southampton
29 November. Passengers – 330 immigrants,
Dr. Spicer, Surgeon Superintendent.

Young, Lark and Bennett, Agents.'

Unless your ancestor is a major public figure, uncovering any information vouching for his or her character in this era is rare indeed. However, as luck would have it, the Trove Newspaper Archives in Australia has provided a window into the character of our Joshua Richmond Young. The article in point relates to a court case where Joshua's partner, Mr Francis Bennett, of Young, Lark and Bennett appeared at a sitting of the Insolvency Court in April 1861. Bennett's petition relates to the Estate of Mr William C. Rush wherein Bennett stated that Rush should be allowed to retain his household furniture and wearing apparel. As incongruous as it may seem, it was the norm in the day, that, should a person default on the payment of a debt, his or her creditor or creditors could take court action to confiscate all the person's worldly possessions in settlement of said debt. This includes their wearing apparel. Quite extraordinary but it does reinforce the notion that these were different and cruel times, and in all fairness, it was also a time when the marketplace was rife with speculators and the risks to Merchants and Bankers were high.

Now, it is pleasing to report that Bennett did manage to persuade his fellow creditors to agree to his petition and from this unique insight it is fair to suggest two things - one, that partnerships were generally formed between like-minded individuals with shared values; and two, since Bennett was attending the Court on behalf of Young, Clark & Bennett that this was a clear indication of the sense of fairness and humanity that all three partners subscribed to. The last known entry for any of these partners is for a firm styled Young & Lark in 1873.

Probably 1868 was the year that Young, Lark & Bennett became Young & Lark as this year marks the death of Francis Bennett. Bennett's epitaph appeared in The Sydney Morning Herald stating that he died on 19 July at his home 'Cliff Lodge', Victoria Street, Glebe at age 51 years. Francis Bennett was a descendant of the Bennett's of Tankerville, a town in the Industrial Heartland of England. His family had operated a Silk Manufacturing factory in Macclesfield. It was so large and successful that at one time the Bennett's had their own fleet of ships employed in the importation of the requisite raw materials. The Bennett's factory held substantial contracts with the British Government and the East India Company; however, they lost most of their fortune when the Silk Industry collapsed due to the removal of Government tariffs. This family's story was symptomatic of so many manufacturers in the whirlwind days of Industrial England. Many inefficiencies were identified, and businesses suffered as a result of the removal of tariff protection and the establishment of free-trade agreements. With no business future at home, all three of the Bennett sons are known to have left England in the March of 1838 on board the vessel *Wave*. Two decided to disembark in Tasmania while Francis Bennett sailed on to Sydney.

Young men like Thomas Lark, Francis Bennett and Alexander and Joshua Young all shared that youthful Victorian dream - a dream that would see them leave their homeland, saying lasting farewells to family, friends and everything they knew to risk their lives on perilous voyages to an unsighted frontier land way down in the southern hemisphere in the hope of making their fortune. The driving force behind this speculation was a desire for a more advantageous life fuelled by a thirst for success and an ambition for social acknowledgement. All these men proved themselves very successful in their commercial pursuits and their personal lives and like so many of those who came to Australia to make their fortune, Robert Burnett Ramsay, Alexander Young and Joshua Richmond Young decided in the end to return to the 'old country'. However, it was in England and not Scotland or India that these three decided to see out their final days.

And then 1750-1850

In retirement, Joshua shared his time between a residential property on fashionable Westbourne Terrace, Kensington, Central London and a country estate 'Higham Lodge', just outside Colchester in Essex, which is where he died in 1883. Their good friend and business partner Robert Ramsay retired in 1887, returned to England and settled into 'Howletts', a property near Bekesbourne, Kent. He lived a very long life and died at the advanced age of 92 years.

Next comes the fourth son George Young who, like his brothers with the exception of John, saw a brighter future outside Scotland and indeed outside the Britain Empire. George was born 19 October 1814 at Montrose and would have undertaken his early education there. At some point he gained qualifications as an Accountant perhaps in Montrose or maybe at a college in Edinburgh. Unlike his brothers, George like so many Scots was soon to be seduced by the lure of the Americas and while his movements are difficult to timeline in his early twenties, there is a George Young listed on a New York bound voyage from Greenock in 1840. The vessel is the *Jane Hadden* which arrived into New York on the 11 July 1840, and the passenger of interest is a 25 year old single male by the name of George Young. It is conceivable that George arrived in New York with a Letter of Introduction either from close family friend and Banker, David Hill of Montrose, or perhaps from a family connection within the Ramsay, Bonnar Banking Group in Edinburgh, his grandfather's Bankers.

A Letter of Introduction was a document, quite common in the day, and served as both an introduction and a personal reference. It was usually provided by the hand of a high ranking official or someone in a respected position and designed to vouch for the character of the holder, his employment and his family. Census records show George initially works as an Accountant in New York, and judging from the direction his career took, it is fair to suggest it was within either a Bank or a Stockbrokers Office. New York is also where he met Harriet Lathrop Whiting and whilst no marriage documents have been identified it is presumed they married in New York around 1842/43.

In true Victorian fashion, George has chosen an excellent marriage partnership. Harriet is a member of the well credentialed Federation family of Whiting with links to the Sons and Daughters of the Revolution and the Mayflower. For those unfamiliar with American history the significance of such connections cannot be overstated for the likes of an up and coming Scottish Stockbroker looking to manage the funds of the elite in society. Harriet's father, Judge Daniel Whiting, studied law at Old Columbia Academy, Kinderhook, New York State. He also established the renowned Backus & Whiting publishing house in Albany, New York State which is best known for its academic publications. Her brother was Commander William Bradford Whiting, an esteemed Navy Officer variously described as a 'blameless Christian Gentleman and Patriot'. Her great-grandfather Colonel William Whiting retired from the Military and embarked on a political career which began in 1798 as Clerk of the Connecticut House of Representatives, then Representative for prestigious constituency of Hartford from 1712-1714 and again from 1716-1718. He also held the post of High Sheriff of Hartford County from May 1701 to October 1722.

Commander Whiting was named after his grandfather Colonel William Bradford Whiting of Hartford Connecticut whose mother Elizabeth has her birth recorded in Mayflower annuls. Elizabeth's grandfather, Major William Bradford of Yorkshire, England, was Governor of the Colony of Plymouth from 1621 until his passing in May 1657. Down the generations Harriet Lathrop Whiting's family boast numerous Lieutenants, Majors, Colonels and Commanders with illustrious careers in both the Army and Navy.

Getting back to the Young family - George not only fulfilled his Victorian aspiration in the marital stakes such that he also proved he had an excellent head for finance and investment. He partnered with brother Liston in many National and International ventures in Melbourne which proved successful and it was surely George's knowledge of banking, broking and world markets plus his business associates in these spheres which enabled these two brothers to take some daring steps. More is written about this in the Liston segment of this story.

And then 1750-1850

As for George, he remained a life-long American resident and the last official entry for him is in the 1880 Census where his occupation remains as Stockbroker.

George is now 66 years of age still actively engaged in commerce and of his four sons and one daughter who survived to adulthood, not one joined the business, and to the best of my knowledge, only one daughter married. This family remained living together in relative comfort in the family home at 1112 Fitzwater Street, Philadelphia. We know that George remained in communication with his family back in Scotland thanks once again to that 1848 Will of his uncle, Joshua Richmond, wherein it is stated that George was not in need of any financial bequest and Joshua directed that George's share should be redistributed. Bearing in mind, this was only eight years after George had sailed to America, it could be inferred that his rise to sound financial status was quite rapid indeed.

George died at his home in Philadelphia in the September of 1885 at the age of 71 years. Harriet lived on until 1906. While no evidence has been found of George ever travelling back to Scotland to visit his family, he was most certainly lovingly embraced by Harriet's extended family. A later generation erected an endearing monument to the memory of their much loved aunt and uncle. These family members knew George well, and his tombstone is inscribed - George Young born 19 October 1814, Scotland. Clearly they didn't know him well enough to know it was at Montrose, but then again he had been living in America for 45 years.

Son William has been discussed, his supposed fall from grace; his Navy career - and although he was made to look like some sort of an outcast by the comments in Joshua Richmond's Will, William's Royal Navy Service Record does not support such an assertion. William spent the greater part of his early life at sea with back-to-back stints on a wide variety of well-armed fighting ships. In 1874, at the age of 58 years, he retires from the Navy and later that same year he marries Miss Ann Cutting a 48 year old spinster from nearby Ospringe in Kent. The couple can be found living in Chatham, for the next two decades and more. Census records list William as a Naval Pensioner. Chatham is in the district of Medway, Kent, and is deeply steeped in Naval History. It was established as a dockyard during the reign of Henry VIII, and it was here that HMS *Victory*, Lord Nelson's flagship at Trafalgar, was built and launched in 1765. William should have felt right at home.

The 1891 Census has William and his wife Ann living on High Street, Chatham, where he remained until his death in 1899 at the ripe old age of 83 years. William should be justifiably proud of his navy service record, and of his ability to embrace change as his role moved from sail through the infant era of steam and beyond. Sadly, no discovery to date can sheds any further light on the reason for his exclusion from his uncle's Will despite the fact that his financial position was such that he could not be considered 'well fixed'. Notwithstanding his global travels, there is no evidence that William ever returned to Scotland or had contact with any of his siblings or other family members.

This was a serious family rift!

James Sandilands Young is a total mystery. He was born in Montrose on 1 September 1823 but not christened until 25 September, which was most uncommon for the time. If he was a sickly child then he would have been christened urgently. There is a distinct possibility that Jean was waiting for Alexander to return home from the Arctic so he could attend the christening; however Alexander was late that season because the *Eliza Swan* had been beset in the ice for some considerable time.

James was not living with his parents at the time of the 1841 census when he would have been 16 years of age, nor did he follow a Merchant Navy or Royal Navy career, or at least there are no surviving records to indicate anything of that sort. There is a death entry in the Montrose Register for 19 November 1833 for a James Young but there is no data regarding the person's age or a notation with respect to his parents. It is entirely possible that James Sandilands Young died as a young lad.

Next is son David Hill Young who was born at Montrose in 1826. It was traditional for the Youngs to name their children initially after family members and latterly after close family friends or valued business partners. David Hill Young appears to be named after a local Montrose friend and banker of his father's acquaintance. David Hill Young came into this world the twelfth child to Alexander and Jean. His namesake David Hill was also Montrose born, the only son of Thomas Hill and Katherine Wright. Both boys grew up in Montrose where David Hill was a fellow Shipowner and respected Banker to Alexander Jnr. At one time, David Hill worked for the British Linen Company's Montrose branch which carried on business similar to a lending and investment bank; however when The Montrose Banking Company, better known latterly as the Montrose Bank, opened its doors in 1814 David Hill was appointed the first Accountant on a salary of £150 per annum. David Hill and Alexander Young were not only near neighbours and fellow Shipowners in Montrose they were also been found being re-elected year after year as Trustees of the Montrose Harbour Trust.

At this point in the life story of Alexander and Jean's children a theme has already emerged - leave Montrose if you want a future which does not involve the whale fishery. It is not hard to imagine that conversations were had along these lines because as each of their boys reached maturity, one by one they embarked on mercantile based careers in commerce outside Scotland. Despite the undoubted encouragement and support Alexander would have extended to all of his sons, as a father it is fair to say he would have lamented their departure. As for this David Hill Young he does not appear in the 1851 Census for either Scotland or England but is listed in London in 1861. The what, and where of his life for the previous decade is soon to be revealed but a more burning question is - why London?

Well, obviously there was a whole lot more enterprise and enlightenment to be experienced in London. To appreciate this one only has to turn to contemporary descriptions of the capital in the day. There is a wonderful 1850 publication entitled - *'Hogben's Strangers Guide to London or a Brief Account of all the Principal Palaces, Government Offices, Sacred Edifices, Public Buildings, Hospitals, Clubs, Parks and Gardens, Museums, Bazaars, theatres, Statues, Colleges, Schools, Docks, Markets, Prisons and Places of Amusement in London, &c., &c.'*, and really the title says it all.

Prior to his London experiences David Hill Young had journeyed to Australia. He sailed from Plymouth on the 27 September 1850 on the *Roman Emperor* a 793 tons vessel in the hands of Captain Champion. The vessel arrived into Port Jackson, Sydney on 6 January 1851 and having departed England on the cusp of winter and arriving into Sydney at the height of summer, it would have been his first harsh lesson of the rigour of colonial life. While en route from Montrose to Plymouth it is fair to assume that David stopped off in London and enjoyed long and fruitful discussions with his eldest brother Alexander on the how, when, where and why of doing business in Sydney, Australia. Soon after meeting up with brother Joshua and his business associates in Sydney, it appears David had determined there were far greater opportunities on offer in Melbourne, Victoria. After all, Victoria had just been granted statehood which signalled that business opportunities there were about to explode. In fact, not long after he arrived in Melbourne regional Victoria was set to boom on the back of a major gold discovery at Ballarat in mid-1851. David Hill Young, just like his grandfather, was in the right place at the right time.

Networking was certainly not a word in common in polite society use in 1851, but for those in business in that Victorian era it was a time when cordiality and connections were managed with much more decorum than today and these Youngs proved they understood its real value. David for his part certainly made the best of his strategic alliances in business, government circles and within the church community as well. He also ingratiated himself into the wider community by supporting community projects and contributing to charitable organisations. It was as if he was fulfilling the family mantra. Shortly after he arrived in Melbourne he called upon family expertise in the mercantile and banking arena and set about establishing a place for himself in the social and business fabric of this brand new capital city. He hung out his shingle as D. Hill Young & Co and by June 1851 he is listed in the prime newspaper of the day, The Argus, on two counts. One is as a donor to the Friendly Brethren Society, and the second was a tout for business -

'F O R S A L E

BEST STAFFORDSHIRE CROWN IRON
Ex Lancastrian, assorted sizes, imported
Expressly for Blacksmiths use

D. HILL YOUNG,
11 Little Collins Street, west.'

Next we see that David Hill Young was about to get a lesson in colonial business protocol and why it is not always wise to take the moral high ground. These advertisements from Friday 10 October 1851, explain -

'L O S T
FROM the Queen's Wharf, on or about 25th August last, a Case of Beads, marked B R § I landed from the 'Tron harbour' by the lighter Kate, and supposed to have been removed in mistake by a Mr. P, Robinson, consignee by that ship, and receiving goods similarly marked by the same lighter. Should Mr. P. Robinson, or any other person be able to afford any information respecting the above, they are requested to communicate with D. Hill Young, 11, Little Collins Street West.'

Mr. P. Robinson was not having a bar of this insult and on the same date he placed his own notice, twice, which incidentally appeared directly below that of D. Hill Young. This is Robinson's rebuttal -

'NOTICE
MR P ROBINSON begs to inform Mr. D. Hill Young, that he is totally ignorant respecting the case of beads mentioned in his advertisement of yesterday, which it is supposed was taken, in mistake, from the Queen's Wharf, on the 25th of August Last. Had such been the case Mr Young would have assuredly, before this, have heard of them; and Mr. Robinson hopes that in future, if Mr. Young wishes any communication with him, he will seek a personal interview before publishing his name to the world upon such mere supposition

115 Flinders-street, East
Melbourne, Oct. 8 1851'

These new generation Youngs were proving themselves very socially astute, in possession of a fair degree of business savvy and somewhat more entrepreneurial than might be expected given their backgrounds. Prepared to seize any business opportunity which came his way, David is embracing non-mercantile agency work as well. This next advertisement appeared in The Argus, for Saturday 15 November, and Wednesday 20 November 1851, and highlights his scope of business -

'WANTED

WANTED to purchase, a station in the un Settled district, with about 5000 sheeps [sic] one to the westward would be preferred. The Station must be capable of carrying at least 12,000.

Apply by letter, stating particulars, to G.C. W., care of Mr. D. Hill Young, No. 11, Little Collins-street, Melbourne.'

And then 1750-1850

[N.B. - Either David or the typesetter did not understand that 'sheep' is both singular and plural.]

It is once again time for a short history lesson to achieve a basic understanding of just how well entrepreneurial David Hill Young and his brothers were doing in 1850s colonial Australia. When brothers Alexander and Joshua first arrived in Sydney Town, it was still regarded as a penal colony, ticket-of-leave transportation although scaled back in the 1840s to New South Wales was not totally suspended until 1 June 1850. The British Government had passed the Australian Colonies Government Act in 1850 to enable Victoria and Moreton Bay [later to become the state of Queensland] to be separated from New South Wales which signalled the development of Sydney and Melbourne as independent commercial hub cities. These lads had no terms of reference for what they were experiencing, they had come from Montrose, a Burgh steeped in over a thousand years of recorded establishment to arrive in an open marketplace with less than one hundred years of penal settlement. The speed with which vacant landscapes were transformed into thriving and cultured cities would have been mesmerising. Elegant and ornate civic buildings, attractive tree-lined and paved streetscapes and gothic revival and neo-classical style townhouses were appearing everywhere. The level of building activity was relentless, such that by the end of the 1850s there were Art Galleries, Museums, Zoos and Universities; and the streets were lit by gas lamps.

It has been written that - 'During this decade, the wealth from gold transformed Melbourne into one of the world's largest and wealthiest cities and funded many grand new civic buildings such as the Parliament House, the Treasury Building, the Free Public Library, the National Museum and the University of Melbourne. In 1858 the National Bank of Australasia opened its doors in response to the wealth of the gold rushes.' 'The 1850s was a decade dominated by the discovery of gold, particularly in New South Wales and Victoria. The gold rushes and the subsequent riches that came from these significant finds changed the social, political and economic fabric of the colonies.' Joshua and David Young invested and traded heavily in gold and Joshua held Gold Leases during the 1850s.

What is relevant to consider with this segment of the Young story and Australia's colonial past, is that these lads and others like them were there and played a part in the transformation of the colony of New South Wales into the nation that Australia has become. It was the likes of Alexander, Joshua and David Young and indeed their partners like Ramsay, Lark and Bennet who helped facilitate that boom. They resolved to arrive and do business in a whirlwind economic environment, such as Australia was in these early days, and they and the country prospered. It would have required solid business acumen, intelligence, vision and base funding as they rode an emotional roller-coaster between exhilaration and stress in a 'Boom and Bust' marketplace. Rest assured for everyone who made a fortune there was someone who lost everything. These men are the success stories - the lucky ones.

In a way they are the 'modern day Cramers' - the chancers who left their homeland in expectation of finding that pot of gold at the end of the rainbow. One by one we have seen these lads followed each other to Australia. This was no accident; what's more, I firmly believe that letters would have flowed back to Montrose full of positive reports about colonial life and what could be achieved. These men were the first in the family to fulfil what became known as the Victorian dream. They are real life examples of that emerging social belief that anyone can achieve wealth, prosperity and social standing purely on the back of his or her own endeavours. As the sons of a whale fisherman they knew all about what constituted hard work and saw first-hand the success which could flow from it. Essentially, these family examples would have been their best asset and given them a firm foundation. Any assumptions made about their family values and examples setting the tone is reinforced by the knowledge that every one of them succeeded handsomely. This was no accident either!

Harking back to David Hill Young, the gold discoveries and urban development taking place in Victoria translated to - Wealth and Opportunity. The pages of Melbourne's newspapers in the day are awash with stories of the gold rush and it is important here to reinforce the scale of these discoveries and what it could possibly have meant for those like David Hill Young who were brave enough to enter the ultra-competitive market of buying and selling gold. This next extract comes from the Earth Resources page of the Victorian Government's own website and explains absolutely why David Young chose to move to Melbourne and how he made his fortune in less than a decade.

> 'It was the discovery of gold at Ballarat in 1851 that resulted in Victoria's gold boom. Ballarat was recognised as probably the richest alluvial goldfield in the world at its peak between 1852 and 1853. The rush spilled over to the Mt Alexander field at Castlemaine and by December 1851 the field had attracted 20,000 diggers and was yielding 23,000 oz of gold a week!'

David Hill Young became a wealthy man on the back of his gold dealing, and this next sample advertisement was placed by him in The Argus, Melbourne on Saturday 6 December 1851. In fact, it became his regular weekly tout for business -

> 'G O L D
>
> THE undersigned is a purchaser.
> D. HILL YOUNG,
> 11, Little Collins-street.'

Short, sweet and to the point, this advertisement can be found repeated week after week for years. As time went on David was finding himself operating in an increasingly competitive market as new players entered the game and began running similar advertisements. This placed David in an extremely price sensitive market situation where excellent product and market knowledge, steely resolve, business credibility and a good poker face would have been the order of the day. While bargaining over the gold price continued, the threat of growing competition began infuriating the established Melbourne dealers. It is not long before some action was required and so we then see David plus twenty or so of his fellow gold dealers, band together to put their names to the following Notice which appeared in The Argus on Friday 27 February 1852 -

'TO W. WESTGARTH, ESQ.,
Chairman of the Chamber of commerce,
Melbourne.
Melbourne, 25 Feb., 1852

SIR - We, the undersigned merchants and traders, beg to inform you that we have been given to understand that it is the intention of the two English Banks to commence purchasing gold on their own account. This, in our opinion, scarcely comes within the legitimate business of a Bank. We therefore request that you will call a meeting of the merchants and traders of the Colony, for the purpose of considering the subject.

We are, sir,
Your obedient servants,
[20 merchant and trader names –
including David Hill Young]

Melbourne, 26 Feb., 1852'

Gentlemen - I have the honour to acknowledge
your communication of yesterday's date, and, in accordance with your request, invite the attendance of the merchants and traders, on Tuesday next, the 2nd March, at the new offices of the Chamber, opposite the Bank of Australasia, at Two o'clock p.m. for the purpose of considering the subject alluded to.

I am, Gentlemen,
Your most obedient servant,
W. WESTGARTH'

There is another little known consequence of the Victorian Gold Rush that would have impacted Ships Brokers like David and Liston in Melbourne and given the New South Wales gold discoveries were not as significant it would have impacted Joshua to a lesser degree. It relates to the difficulty for masters and shipowners to hold their crews onboard for the return voyages. In the Victorian example, once a vessel made port in Melbourne, crewmembers were jumping ship in large numbers and high-tailing it to Ballarat in hopes of striking it rich. The hysteria was fuelled by world newspaper headlines reporting the size of the Ballarat strike, and with upwards of 23,000 ounces of gold being extracted each and every week, these seamen were induced to try their luck. Whilst it has to be said that by and large sailors were a simple and mostly uneducated lot, even they deduced there was more money to be made panning for gold than they could expect to earn in the Merchant Navy.

For some time past, the world had been told that Australia was currently the place where a quick fortune could be made and given sailors were well accustomed to the hard life - living rough and working hard, in some ways they were ideally suited to the harsh living and working conditions on the goldfields. However, their lack of education and general social vulnerability saw many fall victim to some of the less scrupulous Gold Dealers who are known to have bankrolled these absconding often penniless sailors. They would supply them with a kit of tools and utensils wrapped up in a piece of canvas which they would later utilise as a makeshift tent. Ultimately, these unscrupulous dealers planned to handsomely recover their expenses by offering a much lesser gold price - but not our Young brothers.

In fact, as news of the gravity of this mercantile employment situation spread, their seafaring heritage came to the fore, and the brothers decided to become personally involved. It should also be remembered that they too were in the mercantile trade which makes this next editorial all the more important. It appeared in The Maitland Mercury and Hunter River General Advertiser on Saturday 7 Feb 1852 under a column headed, 'From the Empire'.

'We notice some additional extracts from private letters, touching the Australian gold fields, the most interesting, perhaps, being from the firm of Messrs. Young and Co., of Sydney, and Mr. D. Hill Young, of Melbourne. In reference to this subject, it will be gratifying to many of our readers to find such sober view taken as appears in the following extract, which is from the Plymouth Herald, October 25th:-

The last advices from Sydney give some satisfactory assurances against the probability of any extensive desertion of their vessels by the seamen in the port in consequence of the discovery of the gold mines. The desertion at San Francisco when the Californian gold was discovered was universal, because there was no marine police, but at Sydney there is an organised and efficient police for the protection of the harbour and the prevention of offences. There is a water police magistrate specially appointed to decide maritime disputes, to whom a jurisdiction, most important to the commerce of the colony, has been recently given under the Mercantile Marine Act to hear and determine certain cases summarily which were previously sent to a jury.'

Their father would have been very proud!

Newspapers in this period were not only a way for people to communicate, it was where Public Notices were placed. In fact, it was a requirement of Government that certain matters of public interest were to be publicly advertised, and so the Notices column along with general advertisements can be quite a treasure trove of information. In the case of David and Liston Young in particular, the Australian Newspaper Archives permit a researcher to track the brothers' movements and business dealings very succinctly. For instance, these next few snapshots tell such a great deal about what they were doing as well as where and when they were doing it. One such Notice printed on the 20 March 1852 is where we first learn Liston Young has joined his brother as a partner in D. Hill Young and Co. A further Notice on 26 May 1852 advises that D. Hill Young & Co is running a Packet Service between Melbourne and Sydney. Then on 7 May 1852 David is advertising for an - 'active lad to make himself useful in a store and take charge of a horse'; 15 Jul 1852 finds D. Hill Young placing an advertising aimed at those who are desirous of shipping gold to Sydney.

'The fine A1 brig SARAH Lewis Grant, Commander will be despatched on Thursday next ... and presents a favourable opportunity for shipping gold'.

'On 26 Jul 1852 under the column headed 'EXPORTS' - July 24 - *Abberton* for London: Cargo .... Gold .... 300 ozs. D. Hill Young...'; 6 Aug 1852 in the Empire Magazine, published in Sydney, Mr. D. Hill Young is listed as a passenger for Melbourne in First on board *Conside*, a screw steamer of 259 tons with Captain W. Appleby at the helm. David had obviously made a familial visit to Joshua and his family in Sydney, maybe for the Christening of their daughter and his niece, Alice. 27 Sept 1852, in the Shipping Intelligence, and under the heading of 'EXPORTS' - Sept 20 - *Kent*, barque from London ... 38 quarter-casks, 4 casks, 194 cases, 9 hhds [hogsheads], 78 quarter-casks, D. Hill Young; 8 Oct 1852 NOTICE - The undersigned have this day moved to their Stores, No. 7, Market-square, lately occupied by Messrs Turnbull Brothers. D. HILL YOUNG & CO.; 13 Oct 1852 Shipping Intelligence again, October 12 - *Flying Squirrel*, schooner, 74 tons, Mr. Abson, Master, from Hobart Town ... D. Hill Young & Co, Agents. 5 Aug 1852 in Shipping Intelligence, Arrived - Aug 4. M-Chowringhee, ship, 870 tons, George T. Browne, from London April 17th. Passengers - two hundred and fifty-three in the intermediate. D. Hill Young, Agent.'

From this small sample it can be gleaned that success had come their way, they now had several streams to their business operations, and from this fabulous insight into the products they were importing and exporting one can look deeper into how life in this new country from going from strength to strength. Newspaper archives are one of the greatest treasure troves for tracking people and business in any generation – and a must source for any family historian. For the Youngs, business and life continued in this vein until the next 'Notice' came to light which establishes the time markers for two poignant events - the dissolution of the David and Liston business partnership and the decision by brother George to enter into partnership with Liston in his Melbourne ventures; probably as an investment partner only since he is still living in Philadelphia.

First, on 21 Jan 1853, a notice appears in The Argus, Melbourne which reads -

'NOTICE

THE Partnership carried on by David Hill Young and Liston Young, trading at Melbourne as Merchants and Commission Agents, under the firm of D. Hill Young and Company, having been dissolved on the 30th day of September last, the undersigned have entered into partnership, and intend to continue the business on their own sole account, under the firm of George and Liston Young. All debts due to and by the late firm will be received and paid by the new firm. Dated at Melbourne, this 1st Day of January, A.D., 1853.

GEO. YOUNG
LISTON YOUNG
Witness - Hugh J. Chambers.'

At this point it is unknown just when or in which vessel David Hill Young returned to London in 1853. What is known is he maintained his Australian business connections and continued his Merchant business from Offices he established in London in Riches Court. It was there, in London, that he went into a new partnership with one Frederick Dealtry Lewin as Young, Lewin & Co., Commission Agents. So far it remains a mystery as to how David and his partner made their acquaintance, given Frederick Dealtry Lewin was born in Calcutta, Bengal, India in 1835, and his family remained there until the late 1860s. However, they do share a seafaring connection. Frederick was the son of Commander William Henry Lewin, R.N. and Jane Elizabeth La Primaudaye, also born Calcutta. Frederick's mother Jane had died August 1877 and since the probate of her will describes her as a Widow of St John's Park, Blackheath, Kent, it is fair to say Commander Lewis was also deceased. Whilst there is no obvious prior association via Frederick's parents, of far greater interest to me was the fact that one of Frederick's mother's Executors was none other than Henry Green of Blackwall Frigate Shipbuilding fame. Henry Green was a partner in the firm of Wigram & Green. Was this the vital link? Was David's uncle, Captain John Young [1789-1836], in some way connected to that firm after all?

Looking further into the background of David's partner, Frederick, it seems his brother was Commander William Henry Lewin, R.N., his cousins were Brigadier General Henry Frederick Elliot Lewin, CB. CMG. DL. JP RFA., Rear Admiral Charles LaPrimaudaye Lewin R.N. It also came to light that Frederick Dealtry Lewin was married to a Christina Hutchinson and they had three sons - Francis Hutchinson La Primaudaye Lewin R.N., Willian George Lewin, Attorney-at-Law and Priest, and Edward Hale Lewin, a Captain in the Royal Navy. So, whilst, Frederick Dealtry Lewin came to the business partnership with solid family credentials and a shared maritime history so far no other connection to David Hill Young or the Young family has yet been positively identified. It would not be at all surprising if in the final analysis their initial introduction was in fact related to Captain John Young, his Calcutta military connections and his association with Henry Green and those Blackwall Frigates because after all we know this family are very astute in establishing and maintaining 'contacts'.

As for David Hill Young, Esq., he had already achieved the Victorian dream; he had gone out to the Colony of Victoria, made his fortune in just a few years, established those all-important solid business and social connections and returned to London with full pockets and the title of Gentleman - all prerequisites for taking the next step of making a good marriage. It is not long before he makes the acquaintance of Miss Lavinia Eliza Phoebe Hurst, the daughter of respected London Publisher, Daniel William Stow Hurst. They wed on 7 October 1854 in the grand church of St Luke's in fashionable Norwood in West London. Notices of their nuptials appeared in several newspapers including the Morning Chronicle in London on Tuesday 10 October 1854, as well as the London Evening Standard and the Morning Post on the same date.

The reason for the newsworthy publication of the Hurst Family's social events and their obvious social status, only became clear when Lavinia became sole heir to her father's substantial estate. It seems Daniel W.S. Hurst was a founding partner in Hurst & Blackett, a reputable London Publishing House founded in 1852. Messrs. Hurst and Blackett had at one time worked for one Henry Colburn, a London Publisher since 1812. When Colburn retired, Daniel Hurst & Henry Blackett, the son of a London shipbuilder, purchased Colburn's business and changed its name. Down the centuries the firm has remained at the top of its field, and after several subsequent changes of ownership it now bears the familiar name of Random House, a mega-publisher in today's world.

Following their marriage, David Hill Young and his wife Lavinia settled down to life in leafy fashionable Surrey, then a peaceful and quiet alternative to the hustle and bustle of overcrowded and polluted London. Today Surrey has been swallowed up in the urban sprawl of Greater London. In the 1871 Census David's occupation is shown as Commission Merchant and it looks like the couple are still on an upwards social climb as they are now found residing at 'Gloster Taverse', White Horse Road in Croydon. By 1881 they have moved to 'Holcombe House', Lewisham and latterly they are discovered residing in a house called 'Enderley' at 116 Auckland Road, Croydon. David Hill Young died in 1902 leaving a very sizeable estate which included two substantial properties: one his business premises in East India Avenue, Central London and the other his private residence of 'Enderley'.

David and Lavinia had four sons and one daughter. Eldest son Daniel became a London Stockbroker like his uncle George, son Charles took over the family Commission Merchant business in London. Son William inherited the family's lust for adventure and travelled to New Zealand where he set up his own Commission Agency operation. Sadly, he accidentally drowned in 1885 near Blenheim on the South Island. According to newspaper stories of the incident, there was a storm raging at the time and as William was attempting to ford a flooded, fast-flowing river on horseback, the horse shied, tossing him into the torrent. Fourth son, Frederick, did work in the family business for a time but the world of publishing was more to his liking. At one point, Frederick was living and working in Buenos Aires, Argentina, where he was a Newspaper Editor. He married a Spanish lady in Buenos Aires, and then around 1900 they all relocated to New York. Daughter Lavinia married an Irish Land Agent and is known to have settled in Dublin. Once again, we see find examples of that Young family tradition where the parents see their children well educated and then set them free to chosen their own career pathways and points of the compass to call home.

Despite their 13 year age difference, and the geography which separated David from his brother Joshua for most of their lives, they obviously maintained contact and enjoyed a close brotherly bond. The foundation for their extraordinary relationship is bound up in the high level of trust and respect each had for the other as men and as business operators. After Joshua's return to England he not only settled close to his brother but also named brother David Hill Young as the Executor of his will.

This brings us to Alexander and Jean's youngest son, Liston, born in the February of 1830 in Montrose. He was the fourteenth and youngest child in the family. There is nothing to suggest that Liston had anything other than a normal childhood in Montrose.

He would have attended the Academy just as his siblings had done. He too would have heard the stories of the Young family's sailing exploits and grown to manhood acutely aware of the larger than life figures of his father and grand-father, the Captains Alexander Young Jnr and Snr. Being the youngest in the family, Liston was living at home with his parents in Montrose as one by one he watched his brothers leave home. Come the 26 March of 1846, just a month after his sixteenth birthday, he sustained his first bitter blow - Liston lost his dear mother. Two years on, Liston has turned eighteen and it is now about to set off on his first big adventure, and what a life he was set to carve out for himself. We will follow him as he leaves home, leaves Scotland – never to return.

The first leg of his journey in 1848 sees him bound for Australia where he meets up with his two older brothers. The Australian Passenger & Crew Lists Register for 1848 and The Port Philip Gazette and Settler's Journal for Monday 16 October 1848 both carry articles advising of Mr. Liston Young's arrival at Port Phillip, Melbourne on 15 October 1848 on board the 332 ton Barque *Globe*. This vessel had sailed from Leith on June 24th under the command of Captain John Liddell. It was no surprise to see passenger Liston Young occupying a First Class Cabin.

The timing of his departure is a little difficult to completely understand given the date of his father's death in October that year. Did Liston not realise his father was quite so frail? Or did his father encourage him to move on with his life and join his brothers knowing that his own days were numbered? At the time, mail arrived in Australia by ship, and therefore it would have taken several more months before the sad news of their father's passing would have reached any of the brothers in Australia. In a way, Liston's voyages to Australia and those of his brothers were not dissimilar to the ones taken by their father when he sailed to the Arctic or the Baltic for that matter. Each one of them would have embarked with love in his heart, a dream in his head and carrying the treasured images of the faces of the loved ones they were forced to leave behind; never knowing if they would ever see them again.

Letter writing was commonplace back then, and in this regard, there is an interesting story involving the mail and

Liston Young. It concerns a curious item published in the New South Wales Government Gazette for Sydney which relates to an historical list of 'Unclaimed Letters' held at the Sydney General Post Office as at the 14 October 1851. Appearing on page 1,649 is the name - Mr. Liston Young. Could his Unclaimed Letter be from someone close to the family in Montrose, perhaps his brother John, advising Liston and his brothers of their father's passing?

Liston sailed on to Sydney where he remained for a short while working in the business of his brothers Alexander and Joshua; clearly, they were teaching their kid brother the ropes as Alexander was preparing to depart the colony. When next we pick up his trail, Liston Young is heading back to Melbourne. Ahead of his arrival brother David had already placed a Notice in The Argus in the March of '52 announcing that Liston was joining his firm. Is it now David's turn to take baby brother Liston under his wing in order to upskill him in the ways of the gold business? Liston settles into colonial life and is soon discovered doing business in Melbourne. A Public Notice for October 1853 shows that Liston too is following the family tradition of supporting community charities. A prior notice in The Argus for 25 May 1852 lists Liston Young as a donor to the Queen Victoria Birthday celebration fund. And, again on 8th October 1852 there among the list of donors to The Houseless Immigrants Fund we find Mr. Liston Young making the sizeable donation of £10.0s.0d.

David's reason for inviting Liston to Melbourne becomes obvious a short time later when in early 1853 David is seen selling up his personal belongings and heading to London, leaving Liston to take over his business in Melbourne. This brings us to some of the earliest documents discovered linking brothers Liston and George Young. They date from February 1854 when their business entity registered a lease with the Victorian Government in respect of what is described as 'wharf land' currently the property of the Peninsular and Oriental Company - or P&O for the modern day reader. The George and Liston Young partnership company also signed Victorian Government lease documents as representatives of the firm of Willis, Merry & Co., another local Shipping Brokerage firm. Although George is in Philadelphia and Liston in Melbourne it is clear they are in close communication, sharing business and 'opportunity' intelligence. The company operation of George & Liston Young continues to trade and do business in shipping and warehousing in both Melbourne and Geelong. One advertisement in the Geelong Advertiser and Intelligencer for Saturday 5 August 1854 gives an insight into the wholesale side of their mercantile operation.

'On Sale - at the Stores of the undersigned.
Evans bottled ale and porter
Swaine, Boord, and Co.'s old tom,, in 1 dozen cases
Brandy, in bulk cases
Geneva, in 4 gallon cases
Sherry, in 3 dozen cases
Claret
Assorted liqueurs and Syrups
Sardines, in half and quarter tins
Salmon, in tins
Red Herrings, in tin
Preserved ginger
Sugar
Currants
Raisins
Sugar candy

GEORGE & LISTON YOUNG, Ryrie Street, Geelong,
5th August 1854.'

Advertisements along these lines appeared on a regular basis throughout the years 1854-1857, for both business addresses - Ryrie Street, Geelong and 7 Market-square, Melbourne. In Geelong, south of Melbourne, they built a major warehouse partly for their own use and partly for customer storage equivalent to a bond/wharf store. This next classified advertisement also appeared in the Geelong Advertiser and Intelligencer, but this time it was Thursday 24th August 1854 -

'Storage - The undersigned are prepared to store
500 tons goods, at 1s 6d. per ton, at their warehouse.

And then 1750-1850

GEORGE & LISTON YOUNG, Ryrie Street, opposite O'Farrell's sale yard.'

What then of Liston's personal life?

Well, while in Melbourne, Liston meets and marries Charlotte Wilcox, in the May of 1854. She is the fourth daughter of Commander Robert Willcox, R.N. but more importantly she is the great grand-daughter of George Parsons Jnr [1762-1798] and great great- grand-daughter of George Parsons Snr [1729-1812] two of Britain's most famous shipbuilders. George Snr held a Royal Navy Warrant from 1778 for the building of man-of-war gun-ships; perhaps the most famous of the 30+ ships he built is HMS *Elephant* which at one time served as Lord Nelson's flagship. Come October 1855 these newly-weds are listed on the passenger manifest for the famous Scottish vessel, *Donald McKay*, one of the same that will soon transport nephew, Alexander Donaclift Young to Port Phillip. Liston and Charlotte are heading back to Britain, bound for the bustling port of Liverpool. The following advertisement appeared in The Argus on 4 September 1855 and was one of several offering for sale all of Liston's household possessions. He may have only been in Melbourne for three years or so but his ambition and hard work have clearly paid off.

'TUESDAY, 11TH SEPTEMBER

Preliminary Notice

Sale of Elegant Household Furniture, Carriages, Harnesses, Horses, &c.

W. M. TENNENT and CO. are instructed by Liston Young, Esq., (who is about returning

To England) to sell by auction, at his residence St. Heliers, adjoining Abbotsford, and near to Hodgson's Punt, on

Tuesday, 11th September, at eleven o'clock, the whole of his superior imported English furniture, consisting of -

Very handsome drawing-room furniture, in rosewood and satin damask, cheffioneers, sofas, lounges, chairs, loo and card tables, very handsome pier glass, splendid semi-grand pianofortes, tapestry, carpets, &c. Dining room furniture, in Spanish mahogany, consisting of - Sideboard, telescope table, chairs, tapestry, carpets, pier glass, &c. Bedroom furniture consisting of - Mahogany Arabian beds, marble washstands, wardrobes, escritoires, dressing tables, glasses, &c. Kitchen utensils of all useful kinds

Also

Carriage
Harness
Horse
Cow
Poultry, &c.

The whole will be on view on Monday, 10th September, and catalogues will be prepared and issued prior to the day of sale.'

This sale did not mean the end of his business in Melbourne. The Argus, Melbourne Friday 30 January 1857

'Clerk - Wanted a situation as Clerk in a Merchant's Office, or in a wholesale house, by a young man who has been for eight years in the first-rate house in London,

and who can give unexceptionable testimonials and references of character.
Address
EDWARD C. BATTY, care of
Messrs. George and Liston Young,
7 Market-square.'

While the firm continued to trade for many years under the banner of George & Liston Young, Liston's move to England was the precursor to his next big business venture.

From the sale of his belongings it is clear that Liston and Charlotte were not simply embarking on the Victorian Grand Tour of Europe as a belated honeymoon, rather they were selling up and leaving Melbourne for good. It proves to be a strategic business decision; Liston had plans, and big plans at that. By the time of the April 1861 Census Liston and Charlotte are living in prestigious Cheshire with two lads five and three and an infant of one week of age, plus no less than five live-in servants. Liston Young's fortunes are manifold and just how he accomplished so much in such a short space of time is staggering to imagine, but it is what follows on from this point which is even more astonishing.

In brief, Liston Young goes on to create a Fleet Manifest which would be the envy of his father and grandfather. Exploration of the Merchant Navy Lists for the years 1868-1880 alone disclose quite an inventory of vessels with their Registered Owner as Liston Young. Riding this tidal wave of success, Liston will soon boast offices on prestigious Cannon Street in Central London, a street made famous as the location of St. Paul's Cathedral. Some of the numerous merchant ships which Liston owned include the *Bayard* and *Vernon* both of 1319 tons, *Bolingbroke* 1259 tons, *British Lion* 1162 tons, *Cornwallis* 1214 tons, *Marlborough* 899 tons; along with the *Dragon*, *Lloyd Rayner*, *Rinaldo*, *Robert Lees* and many more in a list which simply goes on and on.

This newspaper editorial from the Liverpool Mercury for Wednesday 8th April 1863 clearly demonstrates how quickly fortunes and status were created in Victorian England -

'LAUNCH

On Saturday, there was successfully launched from the building yard of Messrs. Thos. Vernon and Son, Brunswick Dock, an iron sailing vessel of 1200 burthen, named the Robert Lees, intended for the East India Trade. The dimensions of the vessel are - 205 feet long between perpendiculars; 34 feet 6 inches beam; and 23 feet depth of hold. Her model, construction, and equipment are all of the very first class. She will be classed A1 at Lloyd's for twelve years, and twenty years at the Liverpool Underwriters Association. She is a sister ship to the Cornwallis, launched from the same yard last year, and which vessel attracted so much attention at the time. The owners are the enterprising firm, of Messrs. Liston Young and Co., of this town, who are also the owners of the Cornwallis. The ceremony of christening was performed by Mrs. Liston Young, and after the launch a select party were entertained at the elegant déjèurner, served in one of the mould rooms of the establishment. We understand that Messrs. Vernon have another large ship on hand for Messrs. Liston Young and Co, already in an advanced state of construction and several, other large merchant ships are being constructed in these extensive works.'

Buoyed by his success it is no surprise that by April 1871 Liston and Charlotte have moved to a new more commodious residence - not in Liverpool, no indeed, now they are residing at 'Southbank Lodge', Kingston on Thames, London; but where are the children? It seems in true Victorian style, especially for the very wealthy and upper classes, the children have been sent away to Boarding School. The corollary was the richer the family the more prestigious the school one's children would attend. So, while all three of Liston's sons can be found away at Boarding

School the four family servants - Cook, Housemaid, Parlour Maid and Groom are still living in but now catering solely to the whims of their Master and Mistress.

Liston Young remains focused on establishing a shipping empire, his name is aligned with the like of the Hall Line, Sun Shipping Co Ltd., the Ellerman Group and so many other hallmark organisations. Any student of Victorian wealth creation or curious about the History of British Merchant Shipping would gain a great deal by simply following the life of Liston Young and his various partners in a case study. One quite interesting observation arising out of my investigations is that the Mercantile Sector seem to have a nervous disposition to partnership arrangements. The first example related to Alexander and Joshua Young in their early days in Sydney, and it comes to the fore again with Liston and his arrangements with Robert and James Alexander in particular, with whom he formed and dissolved partnerships and company structures on several occasions during the 1850s and 60s. In all there are over a thousand media articles in Australia and Britain in which the name of Liston Young receives mention, some are for his community financial support, several are where he has taken a debtor to court and unlike his brother Joshua, Liston is not so generous of spirit. Liston, on more than one occasion, leaves the Debtor with only his - 'wearing apparel and necessaries to an amount not exceeding £25' and claims the rest. How times and attitudes changed? For Liston Young it seems there is no place for sentiment in business.

To say that Liston Young has left his mark is clear and nothing highlights that more than a story which was written over sixty years after his death. While the editorial was circulated worldwide it was printed in Sydney in a publication entitled - *'The Daily Commercial News and Shipping List'*. It is headed up - *'Eighty Years of the Hall Line - Ellerman Group Merged Developments Recalled'*. While it is well known that the company had a global focus to its extensive commercial activity this editorial goes on to tell the story from 1864 through the WW1 era and all the way to WW2. This excerpt is enlightening not only because it affords a further insight into Liston Young, but it also offers a priceless insight into the men he partnered with and their character. It is a fine example of what it was like doing business in Britain in the late 1800s; how fortunes were made and how people could dare to Dream and wind up with wealth beyond their imagination. The article reads -

'In 1864, the firm of Liston Young and Company change the title to Alexander and Young when Robert Alexander joined Liston Young in partnership, and to that change 80 years ago can be traced the beginnings of the Hall Line section of the present Ellerman Group (writes a correspondent in the Liverpool 'Journal of Commerce').

Robert Alexander was a native of Northern Ireland, where his family had been connected with shipping for many years, although in 1855 James Alexander of Liverpool had taken over the business of Robert Alexander Snr and had run a number of big sailing ships, many of them built in British North America, wherever cargo offered.

Some 3 years later, Liston Young of London took over James Alexander's business and his fleet, with some added iron-hulled sailing vessels with an increasing tendency to cover regular services, including the Indian and Australian. But he was still principally interested in tramping. Robert Alexander Junior who became Liston Young's partner had already owned coasting tonnage with James, but the partnership was his first entry into the distance trades.

The new firm started by building the fine iron and sister ships Bayard and Vernon dispatching one to India and the other to Australia. With offices in Cannon Street, London, the partnership continued for only 4 years when Liston Young & Co reverted to its old name. Robert Alexander commenced to own ships separately with headquarters at Liverpool, although he still remained in the most-friendly relations with his old partner and did an immense amount of business with him.

System of Nomenclature

His first action was to start the whole system of nomenclature with the iron full-rigged ship Haddon Hall, 1491 tons gross followed by the 1356 tons, Locksley Hall. He still maintained any interest in the Australian Trade and loaded ships on that berth, but his real interest was becoming centred more and more on India.

In 1871 in consequence of the opening of the Suez Canal, two years previously, which threatened to hit the sailing ships hard, he had his first steamer build on the Clyde. The 2144 ton Rydal Hall, and Liston Young followed his example next year. Alexander did not, however, give up sailing ships with the advent of the early steamers. He wisely decided to learn the steamship business by engaging in small scale operations while he stuck to his sailing ships in case the estimate of the canal's potentialities proved too optimistic.

In 1874, Alexander and his associates formed the Sun Shipping Co. Ltd., which was the official name for the Hall Line for many years afterwards. He sold the pioneer Rydal Hall, but acquired the very much better City of Baltimore, once a crack Inman liner on the North Atlantic, and despatched her to Bombay with results so promising that plans were made for a steam fleet. This was rapidly built up in the 70s, mostly with unpretentious screw steamers of rather more than 2000 tonnes gross which were very economical for the day and it was not until they had sufficient steam tonnage that they advertised a regular passenger and cargo service between Liverpool and Bombay.

In 1883 the fleet was split up under three separate ownerships: The Sun Shipping Co Ltd., Messrs Alexander and Radcliffe, and Messrs. Robert Alexander & Co., but they were all in the same offices in Liverpool and worked in close cooperation. The Alexander and Radcliffe partnership was dissolved in 1885, and Robert Alexander & Co. became the sole managers of the Sun Company, with its own ships running along-side theirs. The various changes made no difference to the policy of the Concern.

Triple expansion engines, with their greatly improved economy, came in with the Methley Hall and Worsley Hall of 1886, which were followed by the well-remembered Branksome Hall, Locksley Hall and Rufford Hall. These were immensely popular among their particular section of the Indian travelling public.

The cargo side of the fleet was also improved the tonnage of many of the ships approximating to that of the passenger steamers, and cargo really formed the backbone of their business so that in 1894. They were willing to sell the Branksome Locksley and Rufford Halls, which had been maintaining the passenger service between Liverpool, Bombay and Karachi, to the P & O Line, with an agreement that they would retire from the passenger side to India for a certain number of years.

The ships were renamed Tientsin, Pekin and Nankin respectively, the P & O scrapping their passenger accommodation and running them on the Eastern cargo business. The Hall Line did not re-enter the Indian passenger trade until well after the expiry of their agreement, when they had joined the Ellerman Group.

In 1899 the Hall Line Ltd. was registered with capital of half-a-million pounds, Mr. Robert Alexander being the principal shareholder and first Chairman. It took over the fleet of the Sun Shipping Company, but Robert Alexander & Co continued to own some ships independently. In the Boer War five of their ships were taken up for transport purposes and proved very useful.

Sale to Ellerman Group

In September, 1901, the shipping world was astonished by the announcement that the Hall Line had been sold to Mr. (later Sir) John R. Ellerman and his associates, including all the ships in the Alexander fleet, for £32 for each £10 share.'

As a consequence of his success, it is obvious that Liston and Charlotte Young would have enjoyed life to the fullest in their retirement. April 1881 sees them residents at 'The Spa', Speldhurst in Kent, wherein Liston describes his occupation as 'Gentleman'. Today this venue is as prestigious as it was in their time. The main building of 'The Spa' dates back to 1766 when a country mansion on the outskirts of what is now known as Royal Tunbridge Wells. Today, the mansion is better known as - The Spa Hotel and offers all the modern facilities within the grandeur of its original Georgian Architecture. There was a time when the high iron content of the waters of Chalybeate Spring were believed to hold special healing properties. Chalybeate Spring was originally discovered and made famous by Dudley Lord North, the 3rd Baron North and has been frequented as a health restorative 'spa' for over 400 years.

On the matter of family, Liston had three sons - none of whom had the slightest interest in shipping. Eldest son Arthur joined the Matabele Mounted Police in Rhodesia where he served under the command of Captain Southey. Sadly, his service record shows that Arthur was out on patrol when he was murdered at Lo Magondi, in the Umvokwe Mountains. He is buried in Africa. Middle son Leonard initially worked in the mercantile sector as a Commission Agent but later decided to followed in the footsteps of his uncle George and ultimately became a wealthy London Stockbroker. Youngest son, Ernest Thomas Liston Young, embarked on a career in the Military. He made Lieutenant by age 20, Captain a short time later. He retired his Army commission in 1911 and lived out his days in Rochford, Essex.

As for Liston and Charlotte. It seems Liston Young maintained his interest and lust for business and was in semi-retirement in Devon at the time of his death in 1883. He was just 53 years of age, so maybe the stress of those years at the forefront of high-risk business ventures took their toll. Following Liston's passing, Charlotte decided to return to her home county of Hampshire, where she lived on in 'Argyle House', Victoria Road, Southsea for a further fourteen years in familiar surroundings and among Wilcox and Parsons family and friends. Charlotte passed away on April 4, 1897. Probate of her Will was given to son Leonard Douglas with no mention of youngest son Ernest.

Now it is time to turn to the four daughters in Alexander and Jean's brood of fourteen. Two of their daughters died young. Their eldest surviving daughter was christened Jean on the 4 Jun 1818; however, either that is a mistake in the Register or somehow they forgot her name because all future records for her are entered as Jane. Or was it purely an example of that quaint Scottish naming custom where, in instances when the mother and daughter share the same Christian name of Jean, one seems to be called Jane, presumably to avoid confusion? Jane married Captain Francis Spittal in 1845 and does appear to have made a good marriage, or rather her father secured a good partner for her because records show that Alexander Young played a key role in the drawing up of Jane's Contract of Marriage. This document was ultimately entered into the Books of Session in Leith on 19 July 1845. Francis was the son of Sir James Spittal who was known to be in the employ of Her Majesty's Customs and was at one time a resident at Hanover Square in London. Francis was 43 years Jane's senior; in fact, a similar age to her father and most certainly was a person well known to Alexander.

Captain Francis Spittal had arrived in Leith pre-1841 when he is listed as Ship Master. He later took on various land based roles at Leith Harbour. In the 1851 Census his occupation is listed as Ballast Master, and another document from 1852 lists him as Dock Master for the Docks of Edinburgh. Following their marriage, the couple resided at 3 Hamburg Place, Leith. The 1845-46 P.O. Directory contains several Spittal listings - one for Francis as Dock Master, John as General Agent, Dr Robert F.R,C,P. as Medical Officer for Edinburgh for Palladium Life Assurance Society of Pall Mall in London and other Insurance Houses, and Lady Spittal as residing at 2 Minto St.

Jane Young was one who received positive mention in the Will of her uncle, Joshua Richmond. He bequeathed to Jane his gold watch seal and key [a small topaz seal] as formerly worn by her aunt, one gold finger ring set with moon stone, red coral eardrops, one pebble brooch and a zebra woodwork table. She would also receive a round mahogany table once the property of her Grandfather, Alexander Young [1750-1817] on the proviso that she kept it as a family heirloom. Her uncle, Joshua Richmond, went one step further and in a codicil attached to his Will he gave definite instruction to his Executors - 'Leith 20th June. 1842 - Considering these circumstances, it is my positive desire that Alexander Young Jnr and Joshua Richmond Young's proportions in this Settlement devolves now and shall be divided, share and share as follows namely One to their sister Jane Young and the other to their Brother John Young and that neither Alexander or Joshua has any claim here but struck off, and also that Ann Young is to have no participation whatever in the division of the funds in this Settlement being also struck off. Signed Joshua Richmond.'

[This Ann Young [1823-1910] is the daughter of Captain John Young [1789-1836] and his wife Jean Lamb. Joshua's reason for passing such a harsh judgement on Ann is unknown. Ann was at one time a carer for Joshua Richmond's wife, her aunt Helen Young, and although there are surviving family letters belonging to Jean Lamb and others, none of these contain anything indicating the genesis of his dislike for his niece.]

Jane Young's husband, Captain Francis Spittal, died on 23 August 1852 and after probate, Jane was left very comfortable indeed. One could surmise that it was her father's plan that she be the sole beneficiary of her husband's quite sizeable estate, comprising the splendid house in Hamburgh Place, plus all the furniture and chattels and a good sum of money. Jane was 34 years of age when she found herself a widow, so it is no surprise to see her remarry. She weds widower Charles McGlashan, at 10 Cassells' Place Edinburgh, the home of her cousin, Helen Dudgeon, in the May of 1854. Quite soon afterwards the newly married couple depart Leith and can be found residing in Whitehaven, Cumberland. Charles a Mercantile Accountant had two grown-up daughters from his previous marriage who seemingly welcomed Jane into the family. In April 1881 Jane and Charles are found living at a residence called 'Fell View' in the village of Beckermet in Cumberland where they remained to their final days. Sharing the house with them was Charles's spinster daughter, Margaret Kilgour Henderson McGlashan, and one domestic servant. Jane passed away in 1889 and Charles died the following year.

Alexander and Jean's daughter Robina Adamson Young was the only other daughter to survive to adulthood. Robina was also to receive honourable mention in the February 1848 Will of her uncle wherein he bequeathed to her several treasures which had belonged to her aunt Helen. These included - 'a Calamander India work box, as used by her Aunt one East India finger ring, one ditto brooch and one Trichinopoly Gold Chain for the neck'. Given Joshua's penchant for disavowing those whose behaviour he found to be wanting we can assume that Robina most certainly was not one to give him cause to exclude her.

In that same month in 1848 Robina married Captain Thomas Johnston, shipmaster from Academy Place, Montrose. Thomas was originally from St Monance, Fifeshire and the final listing for him in The Maritime Register of Certificates was for the renewal of his Masters' Certificate on 6 May 1851. The couple's two children, Isabella and Alexander, were born while they were still living in Montrose but shortly after the birth of son Alexander Young Johnston in October 1853 Thomas decided to give up the sea. This was probably because steam was pushing sail out of the foreign trade routes and work opportunities were shrinking. Thomas, Robina along with their children set sail for Canada where they made their home in the province of Ontario.

They settled in the farming community of Raleigh on the outskirts of Chatham-Kent Township and close to the shoreline of Lake Erie. The town had a strong Scottish connection and was previously known as Wallaceburg, named in honour of that great Scottish hero, Sir William Wallace. With so many Scots deciding to settle there the district was often alluded to as 'New Scotland'. The Johnston family took up land and became farmers. They remained working the land to their dying day and can be found listed in the Canadian Census for 1871, 1881 and 1891. Thomas passed away in August 1892 and Robina in January 1897. Neither ever returned to Scotland.

It is now time to turn attention to the other famous son of Alexander and Helen Liston – that of Captain John Young of *Eliza Swan* fame. Was it going to be a similarly positive story for his children? We know that John and his brother Alexander had both been raised in Leith, gone to sea with their father albeit John spent some time in the Royal Navy. They later joined their father in Montrose and became partners with him in the Montrose Whale Fishing Company. In their youth they would have listened intently to the stories of father Alexander and grandfather Robert, so all in all a very similar background had brought them to the point of establishing their own families, passing on their family value set and business prospects.

John Young is rumoured to have spent some time in the Royal Navy and been present at the Battle of Trafalgar. It is possible given that in the day lads as young as eight could be enlisted as 'boys' and since John was born in June 1789 and the battle in question took place on 21 October 1805, it would make him just over sixteen years of age. The family story goes that he was a Petty Officer at the time but after meeting Jean he decided that the Navy life was far too dangerous for a family man, so he resigned and joined the family business. John Young is a very common name and suffice to say to date no definitive evidence of this has been uncovered by myself or any other family member directly connected to his line of the Youngs.

John Young and Jean Lamb were married in Montrose on 4 Sep 1814. They had a family of nine children born between June 1815 and July 1829. Despite his heroics in the Arctic and his success whale fishing and with the ransoming of the Eliza Swan, John sadly lost his life at Calcutta on or around the 13 September 1836. To date it has been impossible to locate any evidence of his passing, whether on land or at sea. All that is known for sure is that this left his wife Jean a widow with a very young family to care for, educate and set on future pathways in life. So, despite growing up without their larger than life father figure to guide them, the boys did have their uncle and cousins in Montrose to ensure the salt-encrusted family maritime mantle would not slip far from view. Sadly, what has been discovered will show that John Young's family were about to have quite a different life thrust upon them, and although all five of his sons took to the sea, with four achieving Captain status and one becoming a First Officer; these boys' lives and those of their sisters were constantly touched by misfortune, sadness and sometimes absolute despair.

Eldest son, Alexander [1818-1847] had a short Merchant Navy career. He is variously listed by some descendants as Shipowner and Ships Captain in Canada up to 1846/7. To date no records have been positively identified to verify their claim of ship ownership, and I contend that he has been confused with another Alexander Young in that regard. This Alexander Young came into the world in Montrose in March 1818; received his education there and was likely put to his apprenticeship by his father a year or two before John mysteriously lost his life. Records of his apprenticeship are not proved; however, an Alexander Young, born 1818, Seaman of Montrose is entered into the British Merchant Seamen's Register as sailing on the *Newport* in Dec 1842 and again in June 1843, with both these voyages positively cross-referenced to Lloyd's Register. The *Newport* was a Schooner of 73 tons built in Dundee in 1837, owned by a Mr. J. Fulton, with its home port listed as Montrose. This seaman is registered for the period 1841-1844 which would equate to an apprenticeship.

A family biography has been discovered which states that Alexander was a Captain, and I suspect that he must have served his time on merchant ships trading between Canada and Scotland because Quebec is where he met his future wife, Margaret. He spent enough time in the company of the Buchanan family that they gave him the affectionate nickname of 'Sandy' on account of his shock of red hair. His wife, Margaret Jane Buchanan was an Irish Canadian, born in Omagh, Ireland and known to have migrated to Canada with her parents as a babe in arms. The family settled at Port Levis, in Quebec Province where Margaret attained her education. Alexander and Margaret's nuptials took place at Point Levis, Quebec on the 30 Jun 1846.

Regretfully, very soon afterwards fate was to take a hand. It is generally reported that Alexander was voyaging from the Canadian Maritimes across the Atlantic when his vessel struck bad weather. He was rescued and taken aboard the Inconstant, which sadly also fell victim to the weather and sank somewhere off the coast of Canada. There is no record discovered thus far which relate to the loss of the *Inconstant*, but Lloyd's Register for 1846, covering the period July 1846 to June 1847, shows a listing for the *Inconstant*, as a Ship owned by Fairbanks & Co, with Captain G. Beacon in command. The voyage cited in this instance relates to a sailing from Halifax, Nova Scotia to the British West Indies. Since there are no listings for that same vessel for the following two years it is fair to assume that this was the fateful voyage alluded to in Sandy's Story. Margaret and 'Sandy' had been married for less than one year.

The aforementioned Margaret Buchanan's biography states that following Alexander's death Margaret decided to sail to Melbourne to meet up with Sandy's relatives and look for employment. This was not out of character for this adventurous young woman. She finally made the journey in 1852 accompanied by her good friend and travel companion, Miss Blake. Sandy did indeed have family in Melbourne at the time, his cousins David Hill Young and Liston Young. Not long after her arrival Margaret secured employment as Head Matron at the Emigration Depot where a Dr Thomson was Medical Officer in Charge. To end on a more positive note, Margaret did find happiness again, she married Alfred Millwater Caldecott in 1855 in St Kilda. Sadly, he too lost his life at sea whilst en route from Mauritius to Australia in the March of 1875. There are several other segments in the biography which have been verified and it is fair to say that the descendants of this family are proud of their association with Captain Alexander 'Sandy' Young [1818-1847].

The story of the life of Robert Adamson Young, John's second son is a rather complicated tale. He was born at Montrose in the August of 1822 right about the time his father John had his lucky escape in the Arctic when the *Hero* was nipped in the ice, crushed and sank. This seems somehow to be a metaphor for what was to come for this poor lad. Robert was barely fourteen when his father did not return home from India, which was right about when he would expect to be signing on as his father's apprentice on his next sail, so the death of his father will prove to be a life changing moment for Robert. Also, from the codicil attached to Joshua Richmond's Will, it seems that Robert's mother Jean Lamb was struggling to cope, and all the children were considered to be suffering one way or another. Joshua made provision for a £505 bequest to Jean [Lamb] Young with strict provisions attached regarding the children's future education in particular. It was worded such that no reader would be in any doubt that Joshua was neither fond of Jean nor did he feel that she was a reliable person.

From all reports, life for Jean and her brood was indeed a struggle, she made several overtures to family for assistance, and so it was no surprise when records were discovered showing Robert and his sister, Ann, migrating to Australia. Unfortunately, they did not travel First Class like their cousins, rather they were found travelling as Assisted Immigrants on board the *Anne Milne*. Robert Adamson Young was listed as an Unmarried Male Immigrant whose passage was paid for by Robert Home & Co. of Sydney, Migration Agents. His trade was listed as Carpenter, he was 19 years of age, and his personal details were vouched for by a Mr James Hay, Session Clerk of Montrose. His character was stated as 'Good' by both John Brown and William Mitchell also of Montrose. To the best of my research none of these individuals had any direct connection with the family. Then, in the column headed 'bodily health, strength and probable usefulness' there are cold and impersonal comments of - 'good' and 'likely to be useful'.

But why migrate to Australia? Was he seduced by the Government Immigration Officers inducements? Or had he heard word of the positive experiences of his cousins? After what appears to have been an uneventful voyage, the *Anne Milne* arrived into Sydney Cove on 17 Jan 1842. Nothing is known of Robert's short stay in the Colony or what drove him to sail back to Scotland, or indeed how he got there or who paid his fare. But return he most assuredly did.

There is one small personal snippet about Robert recorded by Doreen Young following her meeting with the Misses Dudgeon, Euphemia and Helen, in 1963. They are the great granddaughters of John and Jean Young, and great grand-nieces of Robert Adamson Young. What was told to Doreen at that time I believe now to be a case of family Chinese whispers! The Misses Dudgeon apparently told Doreen that Robert was the 'black sheep' of the family, that he had been engaged to a Miss Reid but at the last minute abandoned her, and ran off and married an Emily 'someone or other' who they described as a 'harsh and greedy woman'. The Misses Dudgeon said that Robert and Emily had a daughter Betty, and then Emily left Robert and went to America. The Misses Dudgeon's final salvo about Robert was that he died in the poorhouse in Liverpool.

For anyone else who has read this same account I feel it is time to set the record straight because reality could not be further from their story. Indeed, the only part of the Misses Dudgeon's story that carries the slightest modicum of fact is that he did marry a woman named Emily; Emily Gordon Smart to be precise. They wed in Leith in 1863, and although she was fourteen years his junior, they remained together throughout his life and they had a son not a daughter. Robert Campbell Young was christened in Edinburgh in 1866. There is absolutely no record of a daughter Betty or Elizabeth born anywhere in Scotland or England to a Robert and Emily Young nor was an Elizabeth or Betty found living with Emily or her family in any subsequent Census Records. Mistaken identity or sour grapes - you decide!

As for the character of Emily, all indications are that she was from a very respectable family; her father Robert Smart was a Master Engraver employing 5 men and a boy according to the 1861 Census, when Emily's family could be located living in South Leith with their two servants. Conversely, Robert Adamson Young was a poor mariner, so there was obviously nothing for Emily to acquire by greed. Further discoveries reveal Emily's brother was none other than the highly acclaimed Scottish Landscape Artist, John Smart. John holds the distinction of being a founding member of the Royal Scottish Society of Painters in Watercolour and was elected to the Royal Scottish Academy in 1877. There is absolutely nothing to indicate that this family was anything other than upstanding, and to date Emily and her siblings display only first class personal credentials.

This brings us to a painting the Misses Dudgeon had hanging on the wall in their home in Musselburgh. It certainly grabbed Doreen's attention and she described it as a dramatic and dark scene depicting a ship fighting the waves in a fierce storm. When she enquired as to its providence the Misses Dudgeon informed her that it was the *J.E.H.*, a ship associated with Robert Adamson Young, and the painting was the work of an artist friend of his. Well, this 'artist friend' was most probably Emily's brother and watercolourist, John Smart. Doreen's own words give this graphic description of the work - 'By far the most dramatic painting in the room is of the J.E.H., the ship of Robert Adamson Young. The J.E.H. is depicted in the middle of a tempest so terrible it defies description! The height of the waves, the angle of the ship, the stark black and white colours and the strange eerie light, all contribute to the drama. All the masts are broken, the sails are torn to ribbons, the deck is a mess of tangled wreckage. Apparently, Captain Robert Young was in such a storm. He was sure the ship would not survive. By some miracle it did. And when they reached port, Robert described it all to an artist and engaged him to paint it. This painting, I believe, is being left to the Edinburgh Museum'. Following up on Doreen's advice I have made enquiries with Edinburgh Museums and Archives and it is not listed in any official holding.

Lloyd's Register lists the *J.E.H.* as a wooden ship of some 706 tons, built in Quebec and registered in Liverpool. The Encyclopaedia of Australian Shipwrecks tells a fascinating story about the *J.E.H.*'s final voyage when loaded with passengers, general cargo and gold; in fact, 10,920 ounces of gold after departing Melbourne for England on 16 July 1864, the J.E.H. was never seen again. While her route for the voyage was not logged with Lloyd's Register it is known that at certain times of the year ships would take the shorter and riskier route around Cape Horn. If that was the route taken by the *J.E.H.* on that last fateful voyage it would explain notes discovered which state – 'she probably collided with an iceberg'. Thankfully Robert survived his own stormy encounter and was not on board for the *J.E.H.*'s final voyage.

It was probably late 1840s when Robert returned to Scotland whereupon he took up a seafaring career. Whilst no records of his apprenticeship appear to have survived, the first confirmed documents of his sailing days were found when he was granted his Masters Certificate #5351 at Leith on 23 Feb 1853. Lloyd's has numerous entries for a R. Young as Master and these include regular sailings of the bark *Emperor* from Leith to India in the 1850s, the aforementioned ship the *J.E.H.* sailing Liverpool to India from 1862-64, and the 406 ton ship *Hero* sailing Cardiff to India during 1865/66. There is a curious entry for 1872/73 where R. Young is Master of the Kirkcaldy registered *Triad* sailing Leith to the Baltic - could Robert have been associated with his uncle John's business at one time? Robert's last Masters renewal was 6 April 1882 with the issue of Certificate #11362 at Liverpool, England.

While Robert was at sea Emily and their son remained living with her family, initially in South Leith, until they all relocated to Yorkshire where Emily's father died at Bradford March 1871. Emily, along with son Robert, are then found residing with her mother Emily and two sisters Annie and Maggie in the village of Horton just outside Bradford. Emily was using her married name and keeping herself busy assisting her sisters, who were teachers, with the operating of a Private School. But there is more good news and to set the record straight - Emily did not leave Robert, rather sometime after he last renewed his Masters Certificate he was seriously injured and could no longer work. In the 1891 Census he is listed as 'Master Now Disabled' and was residing at a stately property, Andrew Gibson House on Seabank Road, Wallasey near Birkenhead.

This was a bequeathed property set aside for the care of Aged and Injured Mariners. Robert remained living there until his death in 1902. The Echo newspaper in Liverpool ran an article in November 2017 citing this historical property is a Maritime

Landmark and confirming the Wirral Council had recently stepped in to halt its demolition. The current owners, Nautilus Welfare Trust, had previously stated the building no longer met the requirements of its residents; however in order to save the building the Council agreed to partner with a developer to restore it to its original glory which would then complement the new residential housing estate being established nearby. I am certain Robert Adamson Young would be delighted to know that the property which was his home for many years was so valued that it too was to be rescued.

Just to put the last chapter of the Miss Dudgeons' story to rest, we turn to the Census records where for the entirety of his life Robert Adamson Young advised the Enumerator that he was a married man and his wife Emily Smart advised likewise. For some years Emily and son Robert can be found living only a short distance away from Robert's mariners' retreat of Gibson Home and it is positive to imagine that this was so Emily and Robert Jnr could visit Robert Snr from time to time. Son Robert Campbell Young received a solid education and clearly shone academically. By the time of the 1901 Census, Robert Jnr has qualified as a Consulting Engineer (Mech.), has married, and he and wife Rhoda have two young children. Emily remained living with her son and his family in Guiseley just outside St. Oswald, Yorkshire right up until Robert Adamson Young passed away in early 1902, at which point Robert Jnr took his young family and his mother to Canada. This equates to a far more positive story about the life and trials of Robert Adamson Young than that told to Doreen Young all those years ago.

Not all family stories have such a happy ending and it is timely here to make a general observation about the disadvantage caused to the children of mariners lost at sea. For many it became life changing and in the case of this Captain John Young's children, it is clear his untimely death caused them to face a harder and more challenging life than their cousins. However, it was symptomatic of life for tens of thousands of children of seafaring families in that era. There were thousands of families just like theirs all over Scotland; in fact, all over the world - all suffering the same disadvantage. For some a new start in a new country was their way of disassociating themselves from the grief and hardship at home. Their new community became their new family in a circumstance where everyone was a stranger in a strange land, and this became their shared bond of camaraderie.

Regarding Robert Adamson Young, it is wonderful to see that his wife and son remained loyal and a part of his life despite their enforced separations because of his career choices and his injuries. Further research shows that Robert Jnr, his mother and his young family found peace in Alberta, Canada. Clearly, they harboured hopes and dreams which they bravely followed and were rewarded with long and fruitful lives.

John Lamb Young was the third son and only eleven years of age when his father failed to return home. Born in Montrose in 1825 we already know that he and his younger brother George were found living as Boarders in Constitution Street, Leith, at the time of the 1841 Census. Since they were both undertaking apprenticeships as Seamen/Ships Carpenters it is not unreasonable to presume this was in part facilitated by the £505 bequeathed by their uncle, Joshua Richmond. Once John completed his apprenticeships, he too left Scotland and sailed out to Australia, but as an Unassisted Immigrant Passenger departing from Southampton on the *Argo* which arrived into Sydney on 14 Dec 1854.

In all probability correspondence was going backward and forward over the years, and so once in Sydney John would have first of all met with his cousin Joshua before travelling to the Kiama District in New South Wales to pay a visit to his married sister Ann in Gerringong. It is there he would have met brother-in-law, Hugh Mitchell, for the first time. It was also in Gerringong that John met and married the recently arrived Mary

Stevenson, daughter of a Scottish farmer from Wigtownshire who had taken up land in the Kiama District. Mary was one of seven children and she and the entire Stevenson family were identified in the shipping records travelling via New York to Australia. They had arrived in Sydney on board the *Glen Isla* where they arrived on 2 Jul 1857.

The newlyweds remained in the district close to family until after the birth of their first child at which time it seems John had resolved that the farming life was not for him; whereupon he and Mary return to Sydney. It is there that John finds employment in his preferred seafaring profession. His name is linked to coastal ferry and freighting work and the most recent records show him as First Officer on the Steamship *SS Murray*, a 59 ton vessel travelling between Sydney and Rockhampton on the Queensland Central Coast. John lived a full life and died in Sydney in 1905 at the age of 80 years.

John and Jean's fourth son, William Wallace Young, was born in Montrose in 1828. He was a wee lad of eight when he was left without a father. His life remained a total mystery until a recent chance discovery of a Death Notice in the British Newspaper Archives. The Scotsman for Wed 3 April 1850 and the Stonehaven Journal for 9 April 1850, both carried the following Death Notice –

> 'At New Orleans, on the 14th January last, William Wallace Young aged 22, fourth son of the late Captain John Young of Montrose. Friends will please accept this intimation'

Why William was in Louisiana or how he got there is unknown. Given his family more than likely inserted the notice, it is possible that William too became a Seaman. We know that it was a requirement for shipowners and masters to complete pre-departure paperwork listing all crewmembers who had signed on for a particular voyage. This document itemised a sailor's personal family details including next of kin and was retained by the Shipowner at the departure port. Its purpose was designed to ensure that in the case of the death of a crewmember the sailor's family could be properly advised and his wages could be paid.

This scenario also fits timing wise, because the notice was printed some three months after William's death; which is about the time it would take for a vessel to make the return voyage from New Orleans to Scotland.

The youngest and fifth son in this family is George Frederick Young born 1829. A mere seven years of age when he saw his family's world turned upside down, he was twelve when he was separated from his mother and sent to Leith to board so that he could undertake an Apprenticeship, albeit in company of his

TABLE 12 – Capt. George Frederick Young Career Table

Name	Port of Sailing	Capacity	Date of Joining	Date of Discharge	Length of Servitude		
					Yrs	Mths	Days
Indenture							
Rajah	Leith	Apprentice	3 Oct 1842	3 Oct 1846	4	-	-
Chieftain	Siclly	Able Seaman	8 Nov 1848	23 May 1849		6	2
Protector	Bristol	ditto	29 Sep 1849	4 Jul 1850		9	0
Countess of Durham	Newcastle	ditto	23 Jul 1850	7 Nov 1850		3	2
Vittoria	London	ditto	22 Nov 1850	9 Jun 1851		6	2
Idas	Bristol	2nd Mate	17 Jul 1851	19 Dec 1851		5	2

Harlequin	Glasgow	ditto	12 Mar 1852	26 Aug 1852		3	2
Harlequin	Glasgow	ditto	6 Sept 1852	7 Dec 1852		3	0
Service without Certificate							
Rajah	Leith	Able Seaman	5 Nov 1846	4 Nov 1847	1	0	0
Socrates	Liverpool	ditto	20 Jun 1849	21 Sep 1849		3	0
Union	Launceston	2dn Mate	10 Jun 1848	9 Oct 1848		3	0
Brittania	Glasgow	1st Mate	20 Feb 1853	19 Jul 1853		5	0
Walter Baine	Greenock	ditto	25 Jul 1853	4 Oct 1853		2	1
Othello	ditto	Master	6 Oct 1853	26 Apr 1854		6	3
					9	10	2

I make the above declaration conscientiously believing the same to be true and in virtue of the Act made, and passed in the Fifth and Sixth Years of the reign of his late Majesty William the Fourth, entitled an Act for the more effectual abolition of Oaths.

Sgd. GFY

brother John. By 1854 George is 25 years of age, already has his Masters ticket and is using his sister's house at 10 Cassels Place, Leith Walk as his postal address for correspondence. In fact, both of her brothers, Robert Adamson Young and George Frederick Young, registered her address with the General Register and Record Office of Seamen for the mail-out of their Maritime Certificates. Neither appears to have ever had a residence of their own and it is highly likely, especially in their single days, that they took a room with William and Helen Dudgeon between voyages.

There are records held by the Office of Register of Seamen which accounts for some of George's career, namely the period 1842-1854.

Lloyd's Register lists several of these vessels. The first is *Rajah* a 352 ton Barque built at Whitby in 1835 and owned by a Mr. J. Smith. This was the vessel on which George served his entire four year Apprenticeship plus his first year as an Able Seaman, sailing under Captain C. Ferguson. This experience would have been a great eye-opener for a young Scots lad sailing those long haul voyages from Leith to Sydney and Hobart. In 1849, George is found sailing from London to Mauritius on the Barque *Protector*, followed by the *Socrates (a 419 ton Barque)* out of Liverpool sailing to Calcutta. 1850 he is found on board the *Vittoria* sailing out of London en route to Sierra Leone. George then sails as 2nd Mate on the *Idas* out of Bristol to the West Indies in 1851. This is followed by two stints on vessels named *Harlequin* out of Glasgow, and after cross-referencing George's personal records with Lloyd's Register, it appears these are two different vessels with the same name. The 1851 voyage was on board a 199 ton Barque listed as sailing from Clyde to the West Indies and the 1852 vessel *Harlequin* appears in Lloyd's Register as a 702 ton Barque sailing from Clyde to Montreal. This brings us to the *Windhoven*. There are several vessels in Lloyd's Register with the name of *Windhoven*, with one registered to the port of Kirkcaldy. This was a 228 ton Brig (Iron) of A1 Class, owned by Staig & Co and in 1855, on its maiden voyage, it lists G. Young, Master en route to the Mediterranean.

At this point I became intrigued as to why George was so inclined to sail on a Barque as against the Schooners and Ships that were also multi-masted vessels. As a non-aficionado of sailing vessels this required some further investigation to satisfy my curiosity. It seems the origins of the Barque date back to the end of the 18th Century and they can be identified by a particular set sail plan. The design of the Barque has a minimum of three masts, fore-and-aft sails on the aftermost mast and square sails on all other masts. They were the workhorses of the Golden Age of Sail in the mid-19th century and popular with owners and masters as they could be sailed with a smaller crew. Also, the Barque could outperform the Schooners and Barquentines going to windward. Most of the ocean-going windjammers were four-masted Barques with their mainmast being the tallest of any vessel afloat. The mast on the *Moshul*, for example, extended

58 meters off the deck. So, with only a third of the numbers of crew needed, and the ability to achieve comparable speeds and better performance when headed high into the wind, it made the Barque the fast high-performance Formula 1 vessel of its day.

After the five years George sailed on the *Rajah* he seems to have gone through quite an unstable period of rolling-on and off ships voyage after voyage. Promotions came along and he finally sat his Masters' Ordinary Examination at Leith in 1852, and on 26 May 1854, at the age of 25, George Frederick Young received his Masters Certificate #10.316 at Leith. There is another little consequential snippet about George which I personally found intriguing. Throughout his life he entered his birthdate as 31st July 1829 instead of 30th July as in the official Birth Register of Scotland. This is quite possibly a legacy of his father's early death and Jean's inability to cope. I know of another similar family example for a young lass whose mother died when she was only six years of age and her father and siblings never remembered her actual birthday. For young Sarah Dawes this meant she too celebrated her birthday on the wrong day.

There is so much more which could be said about George, his career, his mobility, his back-to-back sailing, his obvious dislike for attending to paperwork etc. which all go to define the character and personality of the man. However, there is another painting that Doreen Young reported seeing at the Misses Dudgeon's house in Musselburgh which Doreen was given to understand was a portrait of George Frederick Young. She goes on to describe him as having a shock of red hair, like his brother Alexander, and a cheeky 'twinkle in his eye'. From these conversations and others' descriptions of George we get the picture of the man as a typical salty tar, happiest when at sea doing what he loved. There are several hand-written notes in National Archives in Kew, sent by George to the Registrar of Seamen where he proffers the same old excuse for his tardy paperwork - 'he was at sea!'.

George never married, he was in love with the sea, and any wonder when you look at his career and the beautiful Barques he sailed down the years - it is enough to put a twinkle in the eye of any passionate mariner. According to Doreen Young, his portrait was to be donated to the Edinburgh Museum along with a presentation bowl which belonged to George; the providence of which is unknown. Again, my enquiries to the various museums managed by Scottish Archives have born no positive results to date. Perhaps all the artwork mentioned by Doreen still remains in family hands.

George spent decades sailing through equatorial waters at a time when Tropical Diseases were at plague proportion. Sadly, Captain George Frederick Young became one of those to die of Yellow Fever. His death on 7 September 1860 was reported in the Montrose Review as local information related to the village of Durris in Kincardineshire. In the absence of any marriage or death entries in the Scottish Records for George the reason for linking his death to the village of Durris thus far remain yet another unsolved mystery.

Finally, it was time to see if the lives of the daughters of John Young and Jean Lamb were any happier or easier than those of their sons?

They had four daughters. Their first born daughter was christened Catharina Juliana after her grandmother and great grandmother. Sadly she died as an infant. Their second daughter, Helen Young, was born 18 July 1816 in Montrose. Helen married William Dudgeon, a Flesher from Musselburgh, in November 1837. A Flesher or Fleshmonger was the old name for a Butcher or Tannery worker – basically someone who fleshed animals. This William Dudgeon was in fact a Butcher. Helen and William initially resided at H Street, Musselburgh where they can be found in the 1841 Census, along with two servants. Sometime afterward they moved to the aforementioned property at 10 Cassels Place, Leith Walk, where Helen was still residing on the night of the 1861 Census.

In all, Helen and William had four children, two girls and two boys between 1838 and 1847. Then a deep sadness struck this family too. Helen's husband William died at just 46 years of age in the November 1847, which was just three months after the birth of their son William Alexander. Their two boys went into the Merchant business and are variously listed as Commercial Clerks and Grain Merchants. Daughter Annie died of Tuberculosis at age 23, and to the best of my knowledge their eldest daughter Jane never married and died in 1877 in South Leith. Helen Young was someone Joshua Richmond looked upon favourably. He bequeathed to her a Silver Tea Pot, Milk Jug and Sugar Dish to be preserved as a family relic also - 'one common finger ring' - belonging to her aunt Helen. These preservation clauses more than likely refer to items previously inherited by Joshua's wife, Helen Young, from the estate of her parents Alexander and Helen Liston. The conditions imposed were there to ensure the items remained in the hands of Young descendants. This Helen Young, daughter of Captain John Young and Jean Lamb, was the grandmother of the Misses Dudgeon.

John and Jean's second surviving daughter was Susanna or Susan as she came to be known. Susan was born in Montrose in 1820 and married Reverend Duncan St. Clair of Assynt on the 7 Oct 1844 in Musselburgh, Edinburgh. Their marriage was reported widely with notices appearing in the Aberdeen Press & Journal on 23 Oct 1844 as well as the John O'Groats Journal for 25 Oct 1844 and others. Presumably there were folk in these communities outside of Edinburgh with an interest in hearing this news. Susan and the Reverend St Clair had seven children with their youngest child, Duncan Charles Colin Campbell St. Clair born 1858. As happens all too often with this branch of the Young family, the lives of these folk too are set to be touched by great sadness. Firstly, two year old William St Clair dies in 1852, then in the December of 1860 the Rev. Duncan St. Clair dies and Susan, who had been suffering from Tuberculosis, died just four months later.

It seems Susan knew she was ill and had recently travelled down from Loth, Sutherlandshire where the Reverend had a parish, in order to be closer to her mother and sister in Edinburgh. She was residing with her sister Helen Dudgeon at the time of her death and it was seventeen year old nephew John

Dudgeon who signed the Death Register as the person present at the time of Susan's passing. What subsequently happened to Susan's children is quite a sad story – Archibald dies in 1861, Rachel dies in 1864. Henry and Anna go to live with their aunt Helen, then Anna moves to Yorkshire with Uncle Robert's wife, Emily Smart et al, while eldest son John moves to Edinburgh, sets up in business as a Merchant, marries Lilias Dudgeon, and then seems to become responsible for his siblings and a nephew as well. Duncan is found at age 15 signing on to the vessel, *City of Fee Chow*, in Glasgow on 31 May 1873, supposedly with a view to serving an apprenticeship in the Merchant Navy with the firm of George Smith & Sons. This vessel was wrecked on the 17 Mar 1877 with no mention of the fate of the crew. It is unclear whether Duncan was part of that crew, but curiously around this time he decided to give up the sea. When next we find any trace of him, he is living close to his aunt, Ann Mitchell, in the Kiama District of New South Wales. Duncan Charles Colin Campbell St. Clair remained in New South Wales, married an Isabella Johnstone Walker and settled down to enjoy family life in rural Australia. He died at Gerringong in 1931.

This brings us to Ann Young, and the one really happy story for a child of John Young and Jean Lamb. We have already learned that their daughter Ann, had migrated to Australia with her brother Robert on the *'Anne Milne'* in 1842. Fortunately, on that voyage, Ann met a fellow by the name of Hugh Mitchell. Hugh was a Scot from neighbouring Perthshire, and they wed at St Andrews Scots Church in Sydney just a year after arriving in the Colony. Sydney was teeming with Scots, in fact almost 10,000 of their countrymen and women had migrated to Sydney between 1837 and 1842. This number was composed of 1500 Unassisted, 5200 as Government Bounty Emigrants, and the group of most interest is the 3300 who were sent out by Private Operators under the Colonial Bounty System. One historian wrote - '[This] migration was to have a profound effect on Scottish attitudes to Australia, and was to influence the growing class of investors, who regarded it as a sign that Australia might have a bright future as more than a despised penal colony or a droughty sheep-run from which ambitious adventurers could make quick fortunes.' Adverse publicity in Scotland caused the Bounty System to be drastically curtailed around 1841-42, in which case it is highly likely the *Anne Milne* was one of the last ships to arrive for almost a decade. In those intervening years there was a shift in migration which saw some 2,000+ Scots head to Canada and the United States.

The Australian Immigration Records give Ann Young's occupation as Nursery Maid and her age as 17 years. There is very little other detail other than a Mr Wentworth of Vaucluse sponsored her and paid her Twelve Pounds passage. As for her husband, Hugh Mitchell, his shipping record on the other hand occupied a full page and is an example of the more extensive and thorough paperwork completed by the Private Migration Agents. Hugh, like Ann's brother Robert, was brought out by Robert Home & Co., Sydney, a Scottish Agent appointed under the Colonial Bounty System. Hugh is described as a native of Kinnoul, Perthshire; his parents being Hugh Mitchell, Farmer and Janet Brackenridge, mother deceased. His occupation is given as Agricultural Labourer which is contrary to records found in Scotland for the 1840s where Hugh and his brother are both listed as Bakers.

How can this be? Is it the right Hugh Mitchell? Well, what we do known is the Government Bounty Scheme were offering 'free passage' to nominated numbers of persons who had certain occupational skills. From the statistics of Bounty arrivals contained in an article on Australian Emigration; Farm Labourers, General Labourers and Shepherds accounted for almost 750 emigrants whereas Bakers accounted for only 7. Clearly the false declaration was made in order for Hugh and his brother to qualify for free passage.

As to the question of why leave Scotland? It seems conditions were dire for many of the folk in Scotland at that time and consequently local officials became complicit and sympathetic to their plight, thereby assisting them to leave Scotland in search of betterment even if it meant they lied on the official forms. A Journalist from the Inverness Courier wrote an article which appeared on 30 May 1838 headed up - *'Australian Emigration - Fort William'* - and it reads

'After some months of expectation and anxiety, Dr. Boyter, the Government emigration agent for Australia, arrived at Fort William on the 8th current. The news of his arrival, like the fiery cross of old, soon spread through every glen of the district, and at an early hour on Monday, thousands of enterprising Gaels might be seen ranked around the Caledonian Hotel, anxious to quit the land of their forefathers and to go and possess the unbounded pastures of Australia. . . . While we regret that so many active men should feel it necessary to leave their own country, the Highlands will be considerably relieved of its overpopulation.'

In the case of Hugh Mitchell, his hometown Session Clerk in Kinnoul, William Murdock, simply signed his paperwork as true and correct as he probably did for many a local lad. The 'Remarks' section states - Nineteen pounds with initials. Sydney – Certif. S. Walcott. Then, following their marriage in Sydney, Ann and Hugh Mitchell took up land in the Gerringong District, of New South Wales, which was fast becoming a rich dairy farming area. Ann had eleven children all of whom had their births registered in the Kiama District Registry. Ann Young's descendants have prospered and can be singled out as the most successful and happiest of all of John and Jean's descendants.

A Scottish Family Tale 1650-1950

Introduction -
In the end 1850-1950

> 'Success is not final, failure is not fatal:
> it is the courage to continue that counts.'
> Winston S. Churchill [1874-1965]

With this observation Churchill has virtually summed up what has been learned of this Young family so far. They have displayed 'Courage' in many ways, in many places and in many different forms which has kept them relevant to their times and enabled many to prosper. They showed the courage to not let success go to their head, courage to not let failure define them and, above all, they showed the courage to be flexible in an ever changing world. Alexander Snr and Alexander Jnr exemplified courage for their families and associates by maintaining strong conviction about the future whatever shape it may take, and by unerringly maintaining a high moral code. They respected and were respected by the families they married into, and this helped to cement them in their communities and their industry. For all family members, this became a positive path to follow and would have engendered a tremendous sense of belonging. Alexander Snr and Jnr did this with the courage to stand apart from the lesser elements in their respective communities, namely the privateers and smugglers, regardless of the personal financial cost involved - which is not so easily accomplished when times are hard, but further demonstrates their resolve and strength of character.

In the end 1850-1950

Words like brotherhood, solidarity, kinship and community always spring to mind when summing up what I have learned about this family. Early on, the Youngs developed a strong fraternity which, when overlaid with elements such as education, natural gifts, legacies and the like, permitted both Alexanders and their sons to look at the changing face of Industrial Britain and the ever-expanding British Empire and exercise the courage needed to wholeheartedly embrace a completely new direction and to take a global perspective. The individuals who prospered in the early decades of the nineteenth century did so for all of these reasons. Their actions do not appear contrived or engineered but innate, as they pursued success, fairness and family.

Now, heading into this final 1850-1950 century it is time to explore how future generations sought to continue the family legacy. This timeline begins with the latter half of the nineteenth century when the world saw society changing even more rapidly and not always for the better. There were ever-increasing pressures on individuals, families and businesses which were sometimes offset by innovative opportunities at home and abroad. Family life as they had known it was about to become more fractured, new family connections would be established. The one constant being that when choosing life and business partners like value sets were paramount.

This generation of Youngs grew to adulthood during Britain's Victorian Era which saw the emergence of a new social class, a class of chancers who were opportunistic and hence fortunes were made and lost. Charles Dickens, an author prone to social commentary, found this phenomenon so intoxicating that he created several memorable characters who did not possess the wisdom of Churchill. However, Dickens' characters were reflective of life in the day, in that they were individuals who chose to see failure as fatal and demonstrated their lack of courage by creating false personas and anonymous lives. Dickens' message was simple – these people lacked courage and were not comfortable living their own truth.

By the dawn of this 1850-1950 century the number of family members in our particular branch of Young has swelled into the hundreds if not thousands. Given their strong moral legacy, it could well be felt that they would become homogenous and boring, but not so. Most lived their lives with conviction and defined their own success. Others had to exercise great courage in the face of failed opportunities, but the one stand-out feature of this family remains their strong moral code. Well, except in the case of one individual - the family 'black sheep' - who is a standout for all the wrong reasons. For this man, failure proved fatal. What is even more damning is that, from the evidence accumulated so far, his was a self-inflicted fall from grace which he compounded by his own actions and inactions until it defined his miserable life and person. No sympathy should be felt for a man whose life story demonstrates he held no affection for, obligation to or respect for his ancestral roots, his spouses or his children. And, from what is about to be revealed, it is impossible to see a day in his life when his decisions made the sun to shine on him.

Whilst families, generally speaking, are a melange, across any parent child group there are identifiable givens in terms of various shared characteristics, shared values, levels of intellect, etc. Bearing this in mind, once again my thoughts turned to the Nature vs. Nurture controversy. So, to satisfy my own curiosity a plan was made to genealogically examine the lives of three individuals from one family and, given there was one 'black sheep', it made sense to include him in the mix. The three people selected are Alexander, Samuel and George Young who are the eldest, youngest and middle sons of Captain John Young and his wife Mary Donaclift. To take the notion of DNA one step further it was decided to extend the reporting to include the children of these three brothers in the hope that this additional evidence could satisfy this vexing question.

In the end 1850-1950

Chapter 9

**The Pirate Son • Rogue & Scoundrel
Trail of Destruction Across the Oceans
Scotland, New Zealand and Australia
Bigamy • Prison • Bankruptcy and More....**

Life experience tells us that families are complex units of individuals not all of whom behave in a manner reflective of their family's standards nor do all of them feel obliged to abide by any shared set of family values. These individuals who don't quite fit the mould get labelled as 'the black sheep' or 'the colourful characters'. By and large they are the stand-out individuals who sometimes engender the broadest curiosity and initiate the greatest detective work by any Genealogist. They most certainly create the most interest and are always the most memorable. Overall, these people show themselves to be more adventurous; they are the highly spirited risk takers who show little or no concern for their own personal welfare or for the sometimes dangerous consequences of their actions. Loveable rogues as it were; who, for the most part only hurt themselves.

On the other hand, there are some among these rogues who stand apart for all the wrong reasons – they are the loners, the shadowy characters who show a flagrant disregard for their family, their fellow man, common decency, and the laws of the land, and will without the slightest waiver blatantly lie in all manner of circumstances and whose actions overall are self-focused. Some are found to be calculatingly deceitful, and often uncaringly involve innocent others in their single-minded quest to achieve their own selfish ends. For the researcher these are the people who by their very nature provide some of the most seminal moments. Just when you think you have discovered all the truth a whole other surprise comes out of left field. This was my experience with this serial offender whose life story is about to be laid bare.

Of the hundreds of individuals researched in connection with this Young family of Scotland, Alexander Donaclift Young is the one person who stands out as the worst kind of 'black sheep'. There is no doubt he brought shame, disgrace and great sadness on his parents and probably his siblings too, if word of his misdeeds ever reached them. He was an abuser to his several wives, an absent father to at least two innocent children, and much worse. He not only committed crimes for which he was imprisoned but had the audacity to commit further crimes whilst in prison. His entire persona is completely at odds with his entire family and it would need the skill of a Forensic Profiler to explain such a flawed personality.

This is Alexander's story -

As we already know, Alexander Donaclift Young came into this world on 3 October 1835 in Kinsale, County Cork, Ireland, the first born of the youthful Captain John Young and his new Irish wife, Mary Donaclift. Shortly after his birth, he and his parents departed Ireland and sailed for Montrose, where just four days later, on the 7th October, baby Alexander was christened. Being the eldest son of the last of a long line of Sea Captains, infant Alexander Donaclift Young represented the future for this seafaring family, and as such the entire Young clan would have gathered in St Peter's Episcopalian Church in Montrose that baptismal day; in celebration and to offer thanks. He was given the christian name of Alexander after his famous grandfather and his even larger than life doyen great-grandfather. Donaclift was to honour Mary's family, her rich Irish heritage and to serve as a constant reminder to Alexander of his Irish connections. Whilst these may seem big shoes to fill, these new parents would have had much love in their hearts and held high hopes for their beloved first born son.

These Youngs of Montrose have already shown themselves to be a very warm and close knit family; well respected in the Montrose community as competent Ships Masters, trustworthy Shipowners, dependable Shipping Company Shareholders, successful Whale Fishermen, reliable Harbour Board Trustees and proud community contributors. The Strachans, especially Jean's father Robert, has been described by his peers and family as a kind and gentle man. He too was well respected and well-loved, and a long-time resident of the town. Robert Strachan was not only the town Butcher, he was also a Shipowner, Ship Builder, Merchant, community contributor and more.

So, as Alexander grew to manhood there would have been a great deal for him to be proud of and to all intents and purposes, the stage was set for a whole new generation of positive family seafaring heritage to play out. There is little doubt that Alexander Donaclift Young was fully expected to take the helm. Basically, his future was assured, there for the taking as it were, and from what has been learned about this family there is no doubt that, along the way, he would have received all the education, guidance and support he needed in order to succeed.

During those early years he and his family made their home in a well-positioned and comfortable property in Ferry Street, Montrose; close by the harbour. Right from the very earliest days they had the services of live-in servants to help Mary with her growing brood. After visiting this property in the 1980s it was evident they had some of the modern conveniences of the day which included their own well for fresh water, stables for the sulky and horse, and a wonderful airy house with lots of windows - for which John was required to pay The Window Tax of course. Clearly, they could afford to do so and were in a position to place a high value on fresh air and light, unlike so many other families who could not afford the tax and were forced to brick up some of their window openings.

From everything we know, John was a good provider, and this enabled the family to continue to upgrade to bigger and better homes over the next few years. First, they moved to

Gibson Street in early 1847 and then to Panmure Place sometime prior to the March 1851 Census. This may have occurred shortly after John's father, Alexander Jnr, passed away in late 1848. Their property at 12 Panmure Place was a far more commodious residence at a fashionable address; in fact, it is in one of the loveliest streets of Montrose to this very day. In April 1851, at the time of the Census, Mary is pregnant and now managing her family of six children with the help of two live-in servants: a Domestic and a Nursemaid. Just three months later she gave birth to another son - bringing the family to seven children by the July of that year.

Alexander grew up with all the benefits that come with such familial security - parents, grandparents and siblings, albeit in a busy bustling household of young energetic children. John was not at home with the family at the time of either the 1841 or 1851 Census - symptomatic of a Sea Captain's life but from all reports he sailed to the Baltic and elsewhere without any further misadventure. By March 1851 Alexander has turned 15 years of age and is listed as 'Joiners (App)'. This was the first indication that something was not altogether as one had rightfully come to expect with this family, and it raised questions as to why Alexander was not undertaking an apprenticeship as a 'Ships Joiner'. Had Alexander already demonstrated those behaviours and traits that are about to be revealed? Behaviours and traits which would set him apart from his own family's values. Had his father, John, already identified that his son did not possess the intelligence, or the perhaps the temperament demanded for the rigour and responsibility of a seafaring life, let alone the additional weight of responsibility of master or skipper?

This was the mid-1980s and my feeling was that the answers would lie in Scotland and more especially Montrose. This made a visit to Montrose an imperative and whilst everyone at the local Archives, Town Library and Montrose Museum was extremely helpful to the enquiring Australian, alas, that first visit provided no answers, just generated more questions. Then, as often happens, I got a lucky break. An unplanned visit to Sydney with my wheelchair-bound mother accidentally provided the first clues. She expressed a wish to take a promenade along Sydney Harbour shoreline at Circular Quay which led us to the Genealogical

Research Centre at Sydney Cove. It was here I made the chance discovery that Alexander had married Jane Donald twice - once in Sydney and again in Brisbane. First there was the question of why and then the question of why several years apart. Obviously, my detective instincts went into overdrive; my mind was racing with possibilities - there was definitely a story to be uncovered! I needed to find the reason or reasons warranting such unexpected and unusual behaviour.

After arriving home, it seemed appropriate to clear my mind of what I knew, rid myself of all preconceptions and start afresh. I began by firstly revisiting his early family life. Still nothing untoward came to light – Alexander was with his mother and siblings in the 1841 and 1851 Census and the family remained living in Montrose where Alexander had initially attended school. Neither the Census nor other official records gave the slightest hint of anything out of the ordinary. There were the usual family tragedies like losing his grandmother in 1846, his grandfather in 1848 then sister Margaret who died of a heart complaint in 1850. All these events were easily explained, none involved trauma, and should not have had a serious negative impact on a lad growing up in a happy household. After all, such events were a part of everyday life.

So, to this point, Alexander's life seemed almost boringly normal; father John had been safely sailing to destinations in the Baltic and not experienced any dramas. I was left to conclude that whatever occurred to make Alexander the person he became and the self-imposed outcast of his entire family, was either intrinsic to his personality or occurred between 1850 and 1855 because from that time onwards his life goes into a downward spiral. There was one person alive in Brisbane at the time who may be able to shed some light on these matters and I set up a meeting. She was a dear lady in her eighties and after quite a cordial afternoon tea she transformed into an irate threatening person appalled that I would pose a question related to Jane and Alexander's marital arrangements. Passionately protective of what she felt was the truth, she told a story which has since been thoroughly disproved but goes to show how family whispers can become someone's truth.

In an effort to track Alexander's movements, I broadened my search and despite years of looking in Scotland and indeed right across Britain, he was nowhere to be found, not with his family, not in Montrose nor elsewhere in Scotland for that matter. He had mysteriously disappeared. Just to be sure no stone was left unturned, I set about exploring the lives of all of Alexander's siblings, but that drew a blank too; at least with respect to Alexander's whereabouts. However, what I did learn was that as Alexander's brothers came of age, their lives were far more positive and predictable - normal really. They completed their education then headed off to find their place in the world, with some following logical pathways while others began by embarking on seafaring apprenticeships for a time before transitioning to the commercial side and setting up mercantile businesses.

The only other timeline marker of interest was that sometime around 1852/53, Alexander's father, John, had retired from active sailing and had sold up in Montrose and moved to Glasgow along with Mary and the four youngest children who were still living at home – but no Alexander. After a stint of 4-5 years in Glasgow, the family return to the east coast but to Kirkcaldy this time, where we know John hangs up a shingle as Young & Turnbull - Ships Brokers. There is still no sign of son Alexander, not with the family, not in Montrose, in fact to this day he has still not been discovered anywhere in Scotland, England or Ireland. Meanwhile, life continues as usual for the rest of the family; in 1859 Mary gives birth to her youngest child, a daughter Mary Jane, in Abbotshall, a suburb of Kirkcaldy - a little sister Alexander will never meet.

By now I was quite puzzled and, taking the Nature vs. Nurture notion on board, I began to wonder whether there were environmental factors to explain Alexander's absence. At this point, broadly speaking, life in Scotland was in the grip of upheaval brought on by the juggernaut of the Industrial Revolution; the infamous Clearances were continuing, there was a second Cholera Pandemic, the railways were expanding their tentacles across the land and the shipping industry too was in for a major shake-up. The first oceangoing steamship was launched on the Clyde and the Merchant Shipping Act of 1854 came into being. None of which should have had any effect on Alexander.

At the same time, in the antipodes, citizens there too were witnessing expansion and development on a grand scale. With opportunities aplenty for everyone, we have already learned that several of Alexander's uncles had ventured to the Colony and that two remained, well entrenched in the Sydney business fraternity with thriving Brokerage operations. With Australia coming of age, and in order to support its second major growth spurt, various State Governments were once again offering free passage and other incentives to those able bodied men and women willing to take their chances. These programs also provided an ideal opportunity for those miscreants and misfits wishing to 'escape' their past, to set sail for either Australia or America for that matter, where they could begin a afresh.

About this time, I recalled having in my possession Alexander's book of Common Prayer which he had inscribed with -' A.D. Young, Ballarat, 17/7/1858'. [Ballarat is in Victoria, Australia – Gold Rush territory and the place for chancers!] Having already established that he had arrived in Australia some years prior to July 1858, I speculated that he probably left the family home sometime post the March 1851 Census and as late as early 1856/57. At some point he would have travelled to Liverpool, England from where I know he found passage to Australia. It is quite possible that he met up with his uncle Liston and it was with the benefit of his uncle's connections that Alexander managed to secure a passage on the famous ship, the *Donald McKay*.

The *Donald McKay* was the largest of the four Black Ball Line ships owned and commissioned by expat Scot, Mr. Donald McKay, and indeed the largest ship in the world at that time. It had been built by James Baines and Company at their East Boston Shipyard and with a gross weight of 2646 tons and carrying 14,214 sq. metres of sail she was a giant Clipper Ship setting new benchmarks in comfort for her 591 passengers. She even boasted a piano in the Ladies Lounge. Owner Donald McKay was onboard for her inaugural voyage when she sailed out of Boston on 21st February 1855 and despite encountering strong gales and difficult seas she performed well and arrived safely into Liverpool. With no time to waste, passengers and supplies were loaded ready for her first scheduled long haul voyage to Melbourne, Australia where it was reported that 'After just 81 days the ship arrived at Port Philip on the 26th August with her load of new settlers.' It is interesting here to note that the *Donald McKay* departed on route back to Liverpool on '3rd October carrying amongst other things, 104,000 ounces (2,954 kg.) of gold.'

Alexander was a passenger on the third voyage of the *Donald McKay* which sailed out of Liverpool in the July of 1857. Even before he sets foot on land, he has been demonstrating those behaviours and traits which will define his life. Obviously, a clean slate and a fresh start were outside his capabilities. Looking back over his early days in Melbourne, it is clear that he over-inflates his skills and abilities by calling himself a Building Contractor and later boasting to others that he had hung up a shingle in South Melbourne to that effect. How embarrassing would it have been for Liston and Charlotte if their nephew Alexander had made himself known to the Wilcox family. Was it via letters from aunt Charlotte's family that word reached John and Mary that Alexander was in Melbourne or did Liston write to his brother, John?

Then came yet another chance discovery - the Victorian Government legal file relating to Alexander Donaclift Young. A Victorian Researcher was engaged to attend the State Archives to obtain a copy of the full dossier comprising some 200 pages. This file was a legal window into his life from the time of his arrival in Australia to the time of his release from prison. This was extremely exciting, intriguing and answered so many questions but raised yet another more pressing one - why was Alexander Donaclift Young masquerading as Andrew Young? This is the first inkling of his baseline character flaw – he was a consummate liar.

In the end 1850-1950

After absorbing the contents of his legal file, I maintain the firm belief that it will require forensic examination of the court records in Scotland to disclose the real truth surrounding the years unaccounted for and hopefully expose the reasons why he needed to escape Scotland. To date I have only been able to consult online resources which have not revealed anything of substance, but given his assumed names, it is also possible that the reality will be overlooked because of yet another assumed identity. In fact, as his life story unfolds he is seen taking some absolutely bizarre steps to pretend to his parents and others that he is no longer alive.

These actions are radical in the extreme and were clearly aimed at closing the door on his family and Scotland. But why? Why did he feel that it was necessary to do so? What did he do that was so unacceptable to his family? Why did he recognise he would never be welcomed back into the fold? For reasons known only to himself, he accepted his fate. Was he told that his behaviour was out of line and totally unforgivable? And finally, what level of shame possesses a man to publicly announce his own death although he is well and truly alive? Was it shame for his past and shame for his present?

Many of the other answers sought came to light in that rather hefty legal file. The sordid tales of his early years in Australia are contained in the trial brief lodged in the City Police Court in Melbourne 31 December 1873. The details leading to the initial charge and the premise behind the documents are in witness statements which were taken in the first case in relation to a Bigamy Charge being brought by a Jane Eliza Penman Young. Now, any researcher perusing an index searching for Alexander Donaclift Young and seeing an entry for an Andrew and Jane Young would be forgiven for glossing over it as irrelevant and unrelated to their search. This is why obtaining that trial dossier proved so crucial and invaluable. It was crucial to not only unravelling the question of 'Andrew Young', but the myriad of convoluted questions which arose during the course of previous searching. Among the over 200 pages of material there is a mountain of damning evidence of deceit, wife beating, lies and more. There are now three wives involved in this intriguing tale of deception. It transpires that the one bringing the charges is not the first wife at all but the second. However, it was Jane Eliza Penman Young who set the legal process in motion by citing Jane Donald, the lady Alexander married twice, as the person with whom he commits bigamy.

The trial notes and further searches stretch this story all the way from Montrose in Angus and Moffat in Dumfrieshire to Cardiff in Wales, Sydney and Yass in New South Wales, Melbourne and Ballarat in regional Victoria and across the Tasman to New Zealand before ending up in Bald Hills in Queensland. The evidence contained in the witness and victim statements is damning and compelling. These are first-hand accounts offered by those who knew Alexander alias Andrew, including an account from his estranged wife #2, Jane Eliza Young nee Penman who was initially unaware of wife #1. Jane Eliza Penman Young was relentless in her pursuit of Alexander. It was only her desire to see Alexander answer to the Courts and pay for what he did to her that his other marital indiscretions and more came to be fully disclosed.

Alexander was at last having to face up to what he had done. The matter was brought before the Supreme Court of the Colony of Victoria as Case No. 239 of 1873 in Unit 24 of the Court and served before The Honourable, The Attorney General, James Wilberforce Stephen, M.A., on the 25 September of that same year. In the opening paragraphs of her Statement to the court Jane Eliza Penman Young advised that she was petitioning for divorce from Alexander Donaclift Young whom she married at the Presbyterian Church, in Sale in the Colony of Victoria on the 8th July 1865, where they were wed by the Reverend William Spence Login. A copy of their Marriage Licence was presented in evidence. Jane testified that she was the daughter of an Edinburgh Cabinetmaker and that Alexander had stated to her that he was born in Montrose, Scotland but that his parents' whereabouts were unknown.

At first read one could be excused for feeling some sympathy for Alexander: no parents and no family. But, when the reality is exposed it is Alexander's parents who indeed deserve our sympathy, for they must have suffered greatly at the hands of their eldest son. So incredibly deceptive was Alexander that his most outrageous deception was not discovered until 2018 when a very strange newspaper Notice came to light. It is clear that Jane Eliza Penman Young believed Alexander when he declared to her that he had no siblings and no parents. In the day this was not an unusual situation for any of a number of reasons: pandemics, general high mortality rates, hunger and starvation – all resulted in death for the masses. However, over the past forty years if there is only one thing I have learned about Alexander, it is to take nothing at face value and to question everything.

Thus, when his premature Death Notice came to light, courtesy of the British Newspaper Archives, it was not entirely unexpected. After all, liars are constantly forced to cover their tracks, and this gives credence to the notion that he knew exactly what he was doing. Yes, audacious Alexander had placed his own false Death Notice in the Dunfermline Saturday Press on 18 November 1865. How can this be you ask - well it was quite common in the day for family members estranged from their roots by the mass migration which had taken place to send information in respect of births, marriages and death to newspapers back home. These were published without question, more or less as a community service. It was one way of disseminating such information to the wider community.

In this instance, Alexander is the only person who could have sent the notice to Scotland. Sadly, the truth of the why he did it died with him, but from what I have subsequently learned about him it would not be inconceivable that he sent the Notice for two reasons. Firstly, to put paid to any further enquiries being made by his parents or siblings, which infers that he knew they were aware he was in Australia. And secondly, to put the Police in Victoria off his trail – the reason for this is coming up shortly. What is certain is the Notice was meant to be taken seriously; it was accurate for the date and place he had lived, and more importantly, it reveals one more very surprising fact - Alexander knew his parents had moved to Kirkcaldy. How, I wonder?

The Death Notice reads -

> 'YOUNG. - At Beechworth, Australia, Alexander,
> aged 31 years, eldest son of Captain John
> Young, Kirkcaldy.

From here the story gets even murkier, probably because Alexander had a trail of lies to conceal and in an attempt to cover his tracks he just kept muddying the waters. Jane's evidence in respect of Alexander was predicated on what he had told her and what she had subsequently learned for herself. She stated that Alexander told her that he had arrived in Melbourne in 1855 and that he had been working as a building contractor in Castlemaine, Melbourne, for some time and was still doing so at the time she met him in 1864. Jane added that he also told her that some twelve months prior he had spent time in Sale carrying on the same business.

As for Jane, she swore she migrated to Australia in 1863, and upon arriving into Melbourne had gone into employment as a domestic and was still working at the time she first met Alexander. Her statement continues, that following their marriage they lived firstly at Stratford in Sale and then at St. Kilda in Melbourne. In July 1867 Alexander left Melbourne for Sydney on the pretext of looking for work, leaving Jane in Melbourne without any financial support. This forced her to return to work as a domestic; this time she found employment with Capt. & Mrs. Hindson of 10 George Street, East Melbourne.

Just a month later in the September '67 Alexander returned to Melbourne and invited Jane to accompany him to Sydney; but, he required her to pay not only her own passage but his as well. She continued working in Melbourne for a time and once she had sufficient savings put aside they took ship to Sydney. They arrived in November, moved into furnished lodgings, then after only six weeks Alexander declared that he could not afford to pay the rent and suggested to Jane that she should 'take a situation' and look out for herself for a while. Once again Jane found employment in service, this time with a Mrs. Roberts, the wife of James Roberts, Esq., Squatter and Grazier at 'Currawang', Harden in the Colony of New South Wales. Jane deponed [an old legal term for giving evidence in a court] in her statement that she repeatedly sent money to Alexander who was now living in Yass in rural New South Wales.

At one point, Alexander sent correspondence to Jane stating he had a house at Nanama [Nanima] at which point Jane quit her employment to go and join him. When she arrived, she learnt that he had lied; he did not have a house nor was he earning sufficient to maintain her. She further stated in her deposition that, with the consent of her husband, she returned to her position with the Roberts family, where she remained until returning to Melbourne in August 1873.

For those who have already learned something of Alexander and Jane Donald, you will now know the couple certainly knew each other in Yass way ahead of their 1871 marriage at Balmain in Sydney. For those unfamiliar with the geography of this part of the story, Nanima is about 19 miles to the south-east of Yass and Harden is 40 miles to the north-west. Yass is also about 180 miles south-west of Sydney. Since travel in the day would have been either on horseback or by Cobb & Co coach, it was a long dusty trek at 15 miles per hour maximum speed for a horse drawn coach to reach any of these destinations.

Jane Eliza Penman Young's discovery that Alexander had married Jane Donald of Yass, at Balmain in Sydney on the 21 July 1871, was the basis for her Bigamy Case. She presented a copy of that 1871 Marriage Certificate showing that Reverend Colin McCulloch of the Presbyterian Church had officiated. Jane Eliza Penman Young further asserted that Alexander and Jane Donald had quickly left the Colony on board the steamship 'Hero' bound for New Zealand. Indeed, several newspaper advertisements have been identified in The Sydney Morning Herald for 1871 and 1872 vouching for the fact that the SS Hero was sailing regularly between Sydney, Melbourne and Auckland at that time.

Jane Eliza Penman Young advised that although she received word of Alexander's marriage to Jane Donald on or about the 25 July 1871; unfortunately, she lacked the financial means to take any action in the Court until the current time. As such it became incumbent on her to swear an oath that she was not complicit in any way with the actions of Alexander Young and Jane Donald nor did she condone their adulterous affair. Jane Eliza Penman Young's legal documents were lodged by one John Wesley Dickinson, Clerk to Proctor Henry Hale Budd, of No. 69 Chancery Lane, Melbourne. Budd petitioned the court for a non-jury hearing date of 10 December 1873.

The next items in the trial documents were the affidavits of several Victorian citizens. First is that of Emma Smith of Elgin Street, Carlton, Melbourne, wife of Frederick Thurgood Smith, a local Saddler. She swore that in late 1864 she and her husband were residents in Sale and had employed Alexander Young to erect a house there. At that time Jane Eliza Penman was in the employ of a Mr Patten, Solicitor in Sale. Emma further stated that Alexander would often spend his evenings in conversation with herself and her husband and that he spoke of living in Castlemaine and that among the work he had done there was to build a hotel. He declared to them that he liked Sale, and when asked if he had any thought of returning to his native Scotland, he replied that he had no wish to do so. He further stated that he liked Victoria, had purchased land in Stratford and intended to build a house thereon and marry Jane Eliza Penman. Emma Smith also declared in a separate statement to David Rourke, Policeman 1st Class of District 1108, that she was bridesmaid to Jane Eliza Penman, and had signed the 'Books in the Church' along with the other witness, Samuel Chinn.

The next document in the collection states that the case was finally set down for an initial hearing on 15 December 1873 in the Divorce and Matrimonial causes Jurisdiction of the Court of Melbourne. Then came yet another affidavit by a Richard Hassett of Castlereagh Street, Sydney, stating under oath that he had on the 6 October 1873 personally served on Alexander Donaclift Young a copy of the Petition in this suit bearing the seal of the Honourable Court of Victoria along with a true copy of the Citation and swearing also that he had showed Alexander Young a copy of the original documents. One further document of a legal nature contains advice from Thos. Howard Fellows, suggesting Budd should add a paragraph which asks - 'that Your Honors [sic] do Order that the said Alexander Donaclift Young do pay the costs of the Incident to these Proceedings and that Your Petitioner may have such further and other relief in the premises as Your Honors may seem fit'. Budd's Clerk, Dickinson, duly complies and resubmits Jane's Petition. Alexander is given 21 days to appear.

Now, at this point one could rightly assume this was the whole story, but being Alexander, let me assure you there is yet

In the end 1850-1950

another roller-coaster of deception and despicable behaviour, lavish lies and physical violence about to unfold.

Will Andrew Young please stand up!!

It is now time to turn to the Supplementary File segment of these Court documents. Disclosure here revealed so much more than was ever expected - it was a real bonanza. The first item is by the hand of a William Borrowman, brother of a Margaret Borrowman, who incidentally are all new names to the Alexander story. William identifies himself as currently residing at 'Sidmount Cottage', Rotherwood Street, Richmond [Melbourne]. He wrote that his sister, Margaret, had landed [in Melbourne] around 1st October 1857 on board the *Donald McKay*. The vessel departed Liverpool on her third voyage to Melbourne on the 8 July 1857, under the command of a Captain Joseph Mundle, and had duly arrived in Port Phillip on 29 September 1857. The delay in disembarking was due to mandatory medical checks being carried out prior to anyone being permitted to proceed ashore.

The duration of that voyage was some 83 days and, that journey time provided ample opportunity for many if not all the passengers to become well acquainted. William Borrowman further deponed that an Andrew Young and his sister Margaret Borrowman had met on that voyage and were married on the 3rd October 1857 in St. James Church, Melbourne. He offered that he is very well acquainted with both parties as they came to live with him for a while as 'man and wife' at his then residence in Spencer Street, Melbourne. He confirmed they had continued to live together 'as man and wife' in Melbourne and elsewhere in Victoria for several years. The marriage was troubled and not a happy union, and despite the birth of a son at Richmond in 1859 Andrew [aka Alexander] Young was accused by Margaret of maliciously and habitually beating her. Sometime later, Margaret confided to her brother in her letters that she believed it was these beatings which caused her to lose her sight.

William was aware that Margaret had also written to her parents about the circumstances of her abusive marriage.

William added that his parents ultimately sent [money] for her to return home. Despite being heavily pregnant Margaret and her then four year old son, John, set sail on the long and difficult voyage back to Scotland. So desperate was Margaret to escape Alexander's malicious beatings that she embarked on this arduous journey very near her confinement date. To put her misery and fear into context, consider how difficult this journey was for anyone in good health let alone the unbelievable difficult experienced by a heavily pregnant mother with a four-year-old at her side. Her second son Robert Norfolk Young was born 18 November 1863 and, according to the UK 'born at sea' Register at National Archives at Kew, the parents' names submitted to the Captain for entry into his log were - Alexander Young father and Margaret Young mother. The child's name could offer a clue as to where he was born as the ship would have sailed past Norfolk Island, only 3-4 days out of Sydney; or 4-5 days sail from Melbourne. (For the non-Australian readers, Norfolk Island is a 13 sq. mile Australian Protectorate located at grid position 29.03°S and 167.95°E.)

Returning to Alexander, so serious had this case become, William Borrowman was ordered to make a personal appearance at the trial and at one point was required, for the purposes of the Court, to identify the man he knew as the Andrew Young who was the husband of his sister. William Borrowman pointed to the man standing in the dock – Alexander Donaclift Young. The presiding judge requested a verbal declaration for the Court records that the man in the dock, Alexander Donaclift Young, was known to William Borrowman as Andrew Young. William declared aloud the prisoner was the man he knew as Andrew Young, the husband of his sister Margaret.

Next comes a statement by a Robert Denholm. Robert identified himself as a carpenter residing at 46 Lonsdale Street, Melbourne. He stated he was well acquainted with Margaret Borrowman as she was his cousin. The last time he had heard from her was on the 22nd October 1866 at which time she was residing under the name of Margaret Young with her two children in the home of her parents in Moffat, Dumfrieshire, Scotland. Robert Denholm fully corroborated all the evidence contained in the statement of William Borrowman especially that which related to a similar conversation Denholm had had with his cousin Margaret regarding the dreadful beatings she sustained. In relation to the physical violence she had endured, Denholm swore that Margaret had gone one step further by confiding to him that she believed the loss of her sight was intentional on Alexander's part.

Next came a statement by Susannah Terry, wife of John Terry, Draper of Fitzroy, Melbourne. She testified she knew both the prisoner and Margaret Young. She further advised the Court that all three of them had travelled to Australia back in 1857, and my investigations have verified this with the passenger manifest of the *Donald McKay*. Susannah Terry also formally identified Alexander Donaclift Young, the man in the dock, as the same person she also knew as Andrew Young from that *Donald McKay* voyage. The final witness, Thomas Ellis, a resident of Sandhurst in Melbourne. He too was a fellow passenger with the accused and Margaret Borrowman on the Donald McKay voyage in 1857. He swore under oath before the court that to the best of his knowledge he was the only person to have known both of them on board the voyage and to have been present at their wedding. His testimony was that the Reverend John Freeman married the prisoner and Margaret Borrowman at St James Church, Melbourne, and that an Isabella McLean was the other witness. He also deponed that both he and Isabella had - 'attached our signatures to the Books in the Church'. Thomas Ellis also swore under oath that Alexander Donaclift Young was the same person he knew as the Andrew Young who had travelled on the *Donald McKay* in 1857 and who had subsequently married Margaret Borrowman.

Patrick Tracey, Clerk in the Registrar General's Office Melbourne attested that he produced a Certified Copy of the entry of marriage for Jane Eliza Penman and Alexander Donaclift Young from the Books in the Registrar General's office which he had handed to Jane Eliza Penman Young on the 10 December 1873. The final piece of evidence offered to the Court in this case came as a sworn statement by the Reverend John Freeman himself, who confirmed the said marriage had taken place, the names of the witnesses thereto were indeed Thomas Ellis and Isabella McLean and that they had duly signed on the day in accordance with the rules of the Church. There was further evidence in the supplementary file which was not presented to the Court. This included a note of an interview conducted with midwife, Mrs. Campbell, who had been in attendance to Margaret Young at the birth of her first son. Mrs Campbell confirmed that Margaret and her husband 'Andrew Young' had been residing in Richmond at the time this child was born.

As for the initial case of Bigamy being brought against Alexander Donaclift Young by Jane Eliza Penman Young it is fair to say that Jane had done her homework thoroughly and presented a very incriminating account of events. However, by the time the case was set down to be heard in December 1873 Jane Eliza Penman Young was living back in Melbourne, at Bevan Street, Emerald Hill which for the modern day reader is an area now known as South Melbourne, and for any Formula One devotees it encompasses those streets which surround Albert Park, the site of the famous motor race. She produced for the Court the previously mentioned Certified Copy of her Marriage Certificate of 8 July 1865 which verified the place of marriage was Sale in the Gippsland District of Victoria, and that the person officiating was the Reverend W.S. Login of the Presbyterian Church.

Jane told the Court that when she and Alexander attended the Government Office to apply for their Marriage Licence all the usual questions regarding previous marriages and children had been asked by the Clerk and that Alexander had denied ever being married or ever having any children. She added this could be attested to by her bridesmaid Enid Smith, if required, as Enid was also present with them when they completed these pre-marriage formalities. Jane told the Court that after their marriage she and Alexander had cohabitated as man and wife for just over two years in Victoria and later in New South Wales, which is where he finally deserted her.

Sydney, New South Wales, was where Alexander and Jane Donald were residing at the time of his arrest for extradition to Melbourne. There is a Police Report written by a Detective Patrick Lyons which lays bare the details pertaining to Alexander's apprehension and some associated events and comments. The Police had located Alexander living on Glebe Road – curiously, this was the same suburb as his Uncle Joshua.

Detective Lyons wrote that he went to the premises on or about 9 o'clock on Saturday evening 20 December 1873 and told Alexander that he had a Warrant for his arrest, whereupon he took Alexander into custody and transported him to Sydney Central Police Station. The charge warrant was read out and Alexander acknowledged that he was the person so mentioned but denied ever being married to Jane Penman, stating that they were just living together. Now this is not very smart since he had married her as Alexander Donaclift Young and it was in the official records. All liars eventually trip themselves up; either they assume they can lie their way out of everything; or, they forget the lies they've told. In Alexander's case, it was all of the above.

Lyons then produced a photograph of a man and Alexander admitted the person in the photograph was himself. Lyons then produced a Certified Copy of a Marriage Certificate of an Andrew Young and a Margaret Borrowman, as well as one pertaining to Jane Eliza Penman, and yet another pertaining to Jane Donald. Piece by piece the evidence was mounting. Then came the depositions of all the deponents which were produced one by one. By now Alexander would have known it was game up and that he was going to find it impossible to lie his way out of this mess.

From here, Alexander was remanded to Melbourne with Bail allowed as self only and set at £150. Clearly he would not have had any such funds at his disposal. Legal notices show the previously mentioned witnesses were not bound over to appear; they were subpoenaed along with several new ones. There was a James Campbell who met with the prisoner and his first wife Margaret in Melbourne, shortly before she returned to Scotland; in fact, he had invited them both to come dine with him that evening. Margaret had attended but Alexander did not. Campbell swore he knew the prisoner when he was living with Margaret in Richmond in 1859. Isabella Ellis, who was a fellow shipboard passenger on the *Donald McKay* in 1857 and bridesmaid to Margaret Borrowman, appeared in person to give her damning evidence. Isabella's evidence held a further revelation; Isabella was married on the same day and Margaret Borrowman Young had acted as Isabella's witness at her marriage. Isabella too confirmed this Andrew Young [aka Alexander] and Margaret had been resident in Sandhurst, Melbourne, in 1860.

At this point the trial had been escalated to The Crown vs. Young, as it is no longer just a simple bigamy proceeding but, as a multiple offender, it was now a criminal matter. Alexander is held on remand in jail in Melbourne; there are police file notes regarding subpoenas for Dr. William Crooke and Mr. William Handfield Wheelan to appear on Thursday 19 February 1874 before 9 o'clock in the forenoon before the Justices in Melbourne at The Court House, Latrobe Street. There is also a handwritten note dated 17 January 1874 by Alexander Young written from Jail to the Clerk of the Peace requesting copies of his deposition and the others shown to him in Sydney. Furthermore, the Supplementary File indicated Alexander had decided to plead that since he had not lived with Margaret for seven years, he could claim he was therefore free to marry. But, being the fool he was, he got the conditions of this provision totally wrong.

Why did he believe he could plead freedom to marry? Well, he was misguided of course, because such provisions did not apply to him anyway. In the day Divorce was the province of the Church Court, it was rarely exercised, and clearly Alexander was not fully conversant with the provisions set down by the Church. There were two conditions for Divorce - Divorce *from Bed and Board* [known as - a mensa et thoro] -which literally defined a situation where one party was absent from table and hearth, but this did not permit either party to remarry during the lifetime of one or other. Next, *Divorce from the chain or bond of matrimony* invalidated or annulled a marriage when a list of circumstances could be proved which included non-consummation, impotence, frigidity, lunacy, incest or bigamy.

Now, there is nothing in the file to indicate that Alexander sought legal advice before so pleading. If he had taken counsel he would have been rightly informed regarding the Church Court conditions and the ambit of the precedent to which those conditions refer. This precedent actually relates to the 1720s case of a Mrs. Bell where 'seven years' desertion or separation was cited as grounds for her Divorce. However, in such circumstances it is only the 'desertee' not the 'deserter' who has the legal right to remarry. Notwithstanding this precedent, resorting to this action was uncommon for the ordinary class and still rare for the upper class. Utilising this provision also demanded legal deed documents be drawn up and registered. So, Alexander did not have the law on his side when he decided to make such a foolhardy plea.

His actions took up Court time, and in typical Alexander fashion he tried to push the boundaries. In the end, the delay allowed two very clever policeman in Sydney to uncover even more evidence; this time in relation to his prior arrest and his absconding from the Law. Detective Lyons and Policeman Rourke uncovered new incriminating evidence in the Police Files of New South Wales. This evidence was contained in the notes of two other police officers who confirmed for the Court that - 'Young is identical with a man of the same name who had been committed for trial at Beechworth in 1862 re an assault on his first wife. The depositions would most likely be in the Crown Law Department.'

Clearly, this was in connection with the Margaret Borrowman Young beatings which until now were not known to have ever been a police matter. Finally, there was a plausible explanation for the bogus Death Notice which Alexander placed in the Dunfermline newspaper. Being, the selfish self-centred liar we have come to know, it is clear that he was not only trying to put his family off his trail but he wanted to escape the Law as well. It should be pointed out that in 1862 Alexander is still only twenty-seven years of age and has committed so many crimes that he has found it necessary to leave Scotland forever, and take on an assumed name. Even the opportunity for a fresh start in Australia is marred with lie after lie, physical and mental abuse of poor Margaret Borrowman, false death claims and now bigamy twice over. Add to this his hare-brained plea and his level of ignorance reaches new heights as he attempts to use a legal defence he does not understand to try to weasel out of serving jail time.

This story demonstrates once and for all that Alexander's character is very seriously flawed that he has no self-respect, or respect for humankind. He believes he can flout the law without regard for the consequences for himself or his family, and when push comes to shove his first line of defence is always to use lies and deceit to find a way out – he lied to the police, the court, and everyone he came in contact with. The man is a blaggard and a fool!

The case was iron-clad, the evidence showed he was guilty as charged on all counts. Liars like Alexander, in my experience, eventually incriminate themselves because they are not smart, forget the lies they've told and in some instances maybe even take the falsehoods as their truth. In Alexander's case the various Marriage Licences reveal part of the complex web of deceit which he clearly lost track of. In the case of his first marriage to Margaret Borrowman in 1857, Alexander uses the alias of Andrew Young but brazenly cites his parent's names and his birthplace correctly. On the Marriage Certificate of 1865 pertaining to himself and Jane Eliza Penman, Alexander cites his father as John Young, Shipowner and mother as Mary Donaclift with his marital status as Bachelor. This brings us to his first marriage in Sydney to Jane Donald in 1871 and that Certificate has blanks where the names of the parents of the bride and groom should be noted. This is unfathomable given Jane's sister signed as one of the witnesses and her father had died in Yass only 17 months prior. Could it be that Jane Donald was not entirely an innocent party in Alexander's deceptions?

The Crown Prosecutor then called for every piece of evidence available to prove Margaret Borrowman Young was still alive in 1865. A letter was produced which had been addressed to William Borrowman in Melbourne and written by his nephew, Margaret's son John. It was dated Scotland, June 1873. John's letter was full of family news including information which showed that his mother was alive and in good health despite her blindness.

On the final day of the hearing, Alexander was transported back to the Court room and in the case of Regina v. Young the Judge instructed the Jury in this manner -

In the end 1850-1950

'Questions Jury required to answer in giving their Verdict as to 2nd Marriage only

1. Are you of opinion Mr. Login was an officiating minister.
   [file note - 'Yes']
2. If you think not, Do you think the parties at the time of the marriage honestly and in good faith believed he was an officiating minister.
   [file note - 'No necessity to consider we having answered the first.]
3. Are you satisfied that the parties agreed or contracted before Login to become man and wife.
   [The verdict of Guilty covers that.]

Tried before Justice Fellows, Alexander Donaclift Young was found Guilty as charged and sent to prison. The Prison Register VPRS 515 Unit 19: for Prisoner No. 11680, Page 159 - Alexander D. Young reads as follows -

Height:	5 ft 7 1/4 inches
Weight:	11 stone 12 lbs.
Eyes:	Hazel
Complexion:	Fresh
Hair:	Light Brown
Mouth:	Medium
Nose:	Broad
Eyebrows:	Light Brown
Chin:	Medium
Forehead:	Medium
Visage:	Square
Date of Birth:	1837
Trade:	Carpenter
Native Place:	Scotland
Religion:	Presbyterian
Read and Write:	Both
Date of Conviction:	16 Feb 1874

Conviction Affirmed: 26 Mar 1874

Sentence to Date
From: 13 Mar 1874
Offence: Bigamy

Where & Before
Whom Tried: Melbourne Criminal Sessions
Justice Fellows

Description: Bald crown of head, scar right side of Head, scar centre of forehead, scar over left eyebrow, scar bridge of nose, boil mark right jaw & boil mark right side of neck, long scars over front armpits JB outside upper left arm, scar left thumb, & scar left side of neck.

Per: 'Donald McKay' from Liverpool to Melbourne in 1857.

MARRIED. Wife (maiden name Margaret Borrowman or Boorowman) in Scotland.
Transferred to Pentridge Jail: 17 April 1874

Offences:		
	18.07.74	2nd Class
	20.11.74	3rd Class
	13.05.75	4th Class - pay
	28.11.75	5th Class
	04.04.76	6th Class

22.1.1875 - Not accounting for timber - 7 days H L [Hard Labour]
May 1876 - Warrants to Discharge 10 prox.
10.6.1876 - Freedom by Remission
Pay rec'd - £3. 4.3.

In the end 1850-1950

What then was the collateral damage of Alexander's actions?

Victim #1 - Margaret Borrowman - her story and that of her two sons is by far the saddest and most tragic of all. Thankfully, she and her two sons did survive the voyage back to Scotland, they eventually found their way to her parent's home in Moffat, Dumfries, probably after a short visit with her sister Agnes in London. All the while she had to care for and protect four year old John and little Robert as a babe in arms. Margaret is still a young woman of twenty-eight years and life has dealt her a poor hand. All things considered, Margaret needs to be commended for her courage to speak out and contact the police, her courage to leave her abusive marriage and take her children to safety, for her ability to cope as a single parent and all the while nursing the burdens of a broken heart and failing sight.

The first Census after returning to Scotland was held on 2 April 1871 and it lists Margaret and son Norfolk [as Robert came to be called] living with her mother in Moffat, Dumfriesshire. Sadly, her father had already passed away. Son John, now twelve years old, was absent and later discovered living in Pembroke Dock, Wales with his two uncles, John & Robert Borrowman who were both unmarried and working as Drapers. As a positive to their story, John Young is listed as a Scholar, so some level of education was being acquired. A decade passes before next we find further legal records relating to this broken family. Margaret and Norfolk are still living in Moffat in 1881, then three years later Margaret's mother, Janet, now 77 years of age, also dies. We know Margaret was declared totally blind in the '81 Census and in need of fulltime care so it is no surprise to discover Mother and son leaving Scotland for Wales where they will join her siblings; two brothers and a sister. It also meant that for the first time in over a decade Margaret would have both her sons close by.

Margaret's son, John Young gets married in 1879 to an Annie Gardner O'Brien. In 1881 he is found working as a Shipfitter in the 'Ship Refit Industry' at HM Dockyard, Pembroke Dock. John and Annie's fourth child was born on 12 May 1890, but by 5th April 1891 John is listed as a 'Pauper Inmate' in the Cardiff Union Workhouse on Cowbridge Road, Cardiff. He advised the Superintendent at the Workhouse that his occupation had been Sea Chief Engineer and that he was born in Melbourne.

Perusal of the Workhouse register shows it is overflowing with ex-dockyard employees. After some investigation two further items were uncovered which go part way to explaining John's predicament. Firstly, on 27 March 1889 the South Wales Daily News ran an advertisement on behalf of Bowling Brothers, a firm of Pembroke Auctioneers, regarding an auction sale at the HM Dockyard at Pembroke. Then on 26 Sept 1890 another Auction notice appears in the South Wales Daily News – this notice appears 'By Order of Lord Commissioner of the Admiralty' – and lists for sale all the old stores of Oak, Teak and Elm timber right down to the chairs, carpets were all to be sold off. Timber and sail had gone forever, new shipyards were being built and sadly so many of the old workers could not or were not being upskilled.

Life was just not offering John Young a break! He had endured the childhood trauma of watching his father beating his mother, his later childhood in Scotland saw him without a father, then he was sent away to live with his uncles in the Pembroke Docks which has been described as an overcrowded area of hard work and hard drinking, and now he is out of work and penniless. In an attempt to see if there were any positives for Margaret's son John Young my searches uncovered a very interesting document, written by a one-time Commander of the H.M. Dockyard Pembroke, John S. Guard, which is a brief but proud history of the Yard where John Young had worked. In his story, Guard charts the establishment and evolution of the Royal Navy Dockyards in Pembroke and noted the first ship launched went into the water on 10 February 1816. Pembroke was established in the era of wood and canvas; and as a consequence, it maintained a huge stockpile of timber and now, with the weight of change associated with the Industrial Revolution and the new direction in shipbuilding destined to be iron and steam, Pembroke was deemed inadequate for the task and not suitable for reorganising. At one point there looked like a reprieve was possible when the docks were tasked to bridge the gap with the construction of what were termed composite vessels, which were those used in the transitional phase. They were rigged with sail and carried steam engines. Pembroke built the Barracuda-class cruisers which were fitted with screw propellers. Guard's melancholy memory of those final days states - 'The last composite built ship, the sloop *Blonde*, was launched in 1889 and the following year saw the final end of the use of wood for ship construction when the training brig *Mayflower* was launched. It must have been a sentimental occasion for many.'

Now it seems entirely possible there is a little more to John's story which is not all positive. On the upside John was clearly a good student because competition for apprenticeships at the Dockyards was fierce and 'places were subject to quotas and only the best students would be successful'. It is therefore baffling as to why he was not offered retraining. Then looking into the history of the Cowbridge Road Workhouse records it seems that an infirmary was added in 1872 and then other major refurbishment work was done in 1880-81; so, it would appear that at the time John was in residence around April 1891 it was not only catering to the poor it was also available for those in need of medical attention. Given that there were rules governing the length of stay available to those entering the Workhouse, and given the length of John's stay at Cowbridge Workhouse, it is entirely possible that he suffered an injury and was unable to work which could account for the fact that he remained a resident for almost a year.

With the closure of the old HM Dockyard Pembroke the township of Pembroke went into decline; schools were closing, and the community was bracing for the inevitable. Shipbuilding as it had been carried on had ceased, so where did this leave John and many of his fellow workers? For many families it would have meant being out of work and struggling to survive on relief. In the case of John Alexander Joshua Richmond Young, his final release from the pain of his plight came in the form of death in mid-1892. He was aged just 33 years. His wife, Annie, was left with four children under 10 years and no income. Also, if John's circumstances were solely a matter of being a pauper, one would expect that John's wife and his children would have followed him into the Workhouse, but not so.

Thankfully, by the time of the 1901 Census I see good fortune has finally been visited upon Annie and her children. Annie appears to have married a Worcestershire man by the name of George Handley - or has she? They certainly advised the enumerator they were husband and wife. George was a Stonemason and their blended families are living at Bryn Cottage, Coychurch, South Glamorganshire. Annie and George have another four young children of their own before the time of the 1911 Census; however, something has gone awry. Annie's eldest son John is listed as Head of the house and there is no George Handley in sight, Annie is listed as Annie Young once again and the children she had with George Handley are listed as illegitimate, although 'ILLEGITIMATE' is later crossed out. All round there was great confusion because their surname was shown as Young, then Handley, then both names were lined through. We can suppose from this that Annie and George were definitely not married. Did Annie accept this 'relationship' situation purely as security for her children and as a means of keeping them out of the Workhouse? I suggest there is a case for such an argument, given the Workhouse in Victorian times has been painted as a place of doom and gloom reserved for the desperately poor and displaced who were subjected to penal labour regimes and physical punishment. No mother would want that for her children.

Now it's time to turn to Margaret's son Robert Norfolk Young, who seems to have used the Christian name Norfolk, in family circles at least. After completing his education, he served an apprenticeship as a Ships Joiner and continued to care for his mother. In the autumn of 1897, he marries his first cousin, Emily Phoebe Pascoe, in Cardiff. They have one son the following year who they named William Alexander Young; William after Emily's father, a Chief Mate in the Merchant Navy, and Alexander after the father Robert never knew. One can only surmise from this that Margaret was not disparaging of her estranged husband, at least in front of the boys, because each of her sons named children after their absent and largely unknown father. Despite all of Margaret's best intentions, hers was a family destined to remain broken – broken by Alexander, broken by lack of opportunity and broken because they simply never got a lucky break and lived in very poor circumstances.

In the case of Robert and Emily, the 1911 Census shows them living at 1 Aberystwyth Street, Spott, Cardiff, and although Robert told the enumerator that he was the father of six children with five surviving, there is something not quite right there either – there are no children living with the parents and none to be found anywhere else in the Census, except for their eldest, William Alexander Young, who spent his early years living with his Aunt Janet. Robert and Emily have two further children in

In the end 1850-1950

1913 and 1916, and sadly Robert is decreased by 1927. Emily lived on for another twenty years although all was not straight forward there either, as this family too seems to be fractured, for reasons so far unknown. What has been discovered is that Emily Phoebe Pascoe Young died in 1947 but probate was not finalised until 1963; at which time her daughter, Queenie Stoker, the wife of a George Stoker of Middlesex was cited as sole beneficiary. Why were mother and daughter so estranged that it took 36 years to resolve Probate? Why did Emily disinherit her other surviving children and grandchildren?

This brings us to victim #2 - Jane Eliza Penman. Jane was born the daughter of William Paterson Penman and his wife Catherine Grieve of Wester Clerk, Dumfrieshire in 1844. Her father was a Journeyman Cabinetmaker, and the family were found living at 13 Dublin St., Edinburgh, on 31 Mar 1851 but later moved to 6 Pirrie's Close. Jane had eight siblings and from the records it seems they all received a decent education before taking up a trade. The exact reason for why Jane travelled to Australia without any of her family is uncertain, but what is known is she travelled from Southampton, England, on the *Ivanhoe* at age 19 years and arrived into Melbourne on the 26 February 1863.

On reflection, the one thing Jane would have been grateful for was the fact that there were no children of her marriage to Alexander. Following the Trial, Jane moved on with her life and very positively indeed. Trove Newspaper Archives carry a notice for The Argus newspaper, (Melbourne Vic.) for Wednesday 25 Feb 1874 which reads -

> ROBERTS - PENMAN - On the 23rd inst., at the Manse Of The Scots Church, Melbourne, by the Rev. I. Hetherington, James Roberts, Esq., J.P., of Harden, New South Wales, sixth son of the late William Roberts, of Sydney, New South Wales, to Jane Eliza, fifth daughter of the late William Paterson Penman, of Edinburgh, Scotland.

Jane married her long-time employer and wealthy Grazier James Roberts in the Feb 1874. It transpires that Mrs Roberts had died in the December of '68, and it is fair to say that Jane was retained to run the homestead and care for the children. A relationship seems to have blossomed with James Roberts although he was some 28 years her senior. This was undoubtedly the impetus for her to pursue the divorce in the first instance, and there is little doubt James Roberts provided financial assistance to see it through. Jane Eliza Penman Roberts appears to have not worn the deep scars of Margaret Borrowman and her two sons. Although she would find herself a widow by November 1876, Jane became a very wealthy woman and more importantly was welcomed into the fold of a family who are recorded in Australian Historical Archives as 'Australian Royalty' - such was their pastoral wealth and social position.

Lastly, there is victim #3 - Jane Donald. Jane was born at Yass, New South Wales, the 10th child of George Donald of Galston, Ayrshire and Jean Galbraith from Dalrymple, Ayrshire. She was christened Jean but after the death of her sister, Jane seems to have been her preferred name. Her parents had sailed to Australia on the *'John Barry'* in 1837. George Donald was a Master Stonemason and can be found listed in the NSW Blue Book for 1 November 1837 at which time he is appointed to the Public Service by the Supt. of Works, Fort Macquarie, on a salary of £146 payable by the Department of Colonial Engineers. However, George was not happy with the harsh treatment he was required to mete out to the convict labourers supplied by the Colonial Government for his 'work gangs' and he consequently gave up this appointment and moved to Yass where he went into business contracting as a Stonemason. His name is associated with several local structures in the town, including the Court House and the first Rail Bridge, both of which still stand today, and are fine examples of his work and bear testament to his skill and craftsmanship. Shortly before Jane married Alexander the first time in 1871, her father tragically drowned in the river at Yass. His body was found near where he was accustomed to taking his ablutions and this explains why her sister Susan signed as her witness.

In the end 1850-1950

There is quite a deal of family folklore and misinformation floating around regarding Jane Donald and Alexander, but what is factual is they absconded to New Zealand very shortly after their July wedding in 1871, and their first born son James Buckland Young was born in Auckland, 30 November 1871. The New Zealand register reads - 1871/17057 - 'Young, James Buckland Mother Jane Father Alexander'. Sometime afterwards the new family of three arrive back in Sydney, where they remained residing at Glebe until the birth of their second son Donald Galbraith Young on 3rd July 1873.

Then, following Alexander's arrest and extradition to Melbourne, Jane and the two boys moved to Bald Hills on the outskirts of Brisbane in Queensland where they lived with Jane's sister Janet and her husband John Patterson. John Patterson was the first schoolteacher in the area; he later established the first school and recently a Municipal Park in the Brisbane suburb of Chermside was named in his honour. Jane and her two sons remained with the Patterson Family until Alexander came to join them following his release from prison. But even in this Alexander is not as honest, diligent or urgent as one would have expected. According to an entry in the Police Gazette for Victoria - 'Alex. D. Young Prisoner #11680, DOB 1837' achieved his Freedom by Remission on 10 June 1876 and was subsequently released from Pentridge Goal that week. [N.B. - Considering he was born 1835 was this another of Alexander's deceptions or a clerical error? You decide.] For reasons best known only to himself, he did not arrive at Bald Hills for over a year. What was he doing and where? And with whom, I wonder!

Alexander and Jane then married for the second time on 28 Nov 1877. They went on to have a further six children but Jane was clearly the matriarch of that family and from all reports was well loved and respected by all who knew her. Eventually, Alexander built a home at Bald Hills but even in that he was something of a failure. A set of house plans has been uncovered which shows it resembled more a land ship than a house. The rooms were tiny like cabins and the stairways were steeper than normal - similar to what one would encounter on a ship. No strict Building Code in their day!

After my 1980 meeting with one of Jane's grand-daughters I concluded that the story related to me was probably the convenient truth which Alexander and/or Jane concocted to hide the shame and to protect their children? Clearly Jane knew of his arrest in Glebe, Sydney but never spoke of it. As for Jane Donald, she had been forced to face up to a great many embarrassing and disappointing moments throughout her married life, and Alexander most assuredly gave her many occasions for deep regret.

As for Alexander, he remained a tumbleweed drifting through life - one minute he is listed in the Post Office Directory as Builder then a Storekeeper and later Mineral Oil Manufacturer. He had no qualifications for either of the last two. He had absolutely no savvy when it came to business or money management either and there are several newspaper clippings to prove it. One, from the Brisbane Courier Mail for 5 May 1883, just five years after his return, shows he has not learnt one single lesson from his past. Under the heading of 'Insolvency' is a list of names and there we find Alexander Donaclift Young, Contractor of Sandgate. In fact, there are several Insolvency Notices for Alexander Donaclift Young listed in the Supreme Court of Queensland Registers, the first appeared in March 1883 by order of Pring Roberts, Deputy Registrar. Solicitor for the Insolvent was J.R. Baxter Bruce, of George Street, Brisbane. Then in May 1883 a dividend of 3s 6d in the pound was declared in that case. His disregard for lawful commercial behaviour and absolute lack of financial skills sees him go Insolvent for a second time in July 1889 with another series of Notices registered in the Supreme Court of Queensland. This time he is being sued and legal firm, Chambers, Bruce & McNab, are seen acting for his creditors.

Despite all of the above, the children of his marriage to Jane Donald were found to be fortunate and faultless throughout their lives. Obviously, it was the morals and values inculcated by their mother Jane which set them on the straight and narrow; she was a strong woman, who from all reports ruled with a rod of iron. At the same time, she was immensely proud of her children, and if family photos, diaries and letters are anything to go by, she was very much a part of all their lives. James Buckland Young, Montrose Markham Stanley Young and Alexander Donaclift Young Jnr lived close to their mother all their lives. These three boys and their two brothers grew to manhood in difficult and trying circumstances but were all upstanding, God-fearing honest people who also served the Empire with distinction in times of war. Montrose M.S. Young was a decorated Captain in the Australian Mounted Infantry. The girls too were extremely close to their mother and remained so to the very end. Release for Jane, from the shame and burden of her marriage, came on 6 November 1890 when Alexander Donaclift Young died. He was buried the very next day in Bald Hills Cemetery.

It is also pleasing to report that Jane had a second chance at happiness. In 1907 she married Alfred George Keith, her widowed brother-in-law. He was much adored by the family, and Alfred and Jane happily spent their twilight years together in Sydney. Alfred died in July 1929 at the age of 93. Jane returned to Queensland where she died peacefully at her home in Bald Hills at age 90 in November 1942. Her dear friend and relative by marriage, Sarah Dawes, wrote in her diary of Jane's passing - 'Grandma died at 10 o'clock this morning'. Sarah made one final entry after Jane's funeral the following day, Tuesday 2nd June - 'We went to Lutwyche, Mum's funeral was a quiet and peaceful one. I think just what she would [have] wished herself.'

Alexander Donaclift Young defies the parameters for Nature and Nurture. There is absolutely nothing about his personality or character that resemble his antecedents or descendants in any way. He was not just a 'black sheep' he was a complete enigma. One can only wonder at the great dissatisfied he must have felt throughout his 55 years as he continually hurt himself and those around him and from what has been learned so far it is impossible to conceive a single moment in his adult life at least when he was happy and behaving like a normal human being.

He does not deserve any sympathy or pity, that should be reserved for all the people he hurt and the collateral damage he created.

Chapter 10

**Model Son • Exemplar of Victorian Success
Scotland, England, Siam and Ceylon
Exotic Kings & Oxford Dons - Linked to
Famous Gardens & The Flogging Parson!**

The life story for Samuel Donaclift Young has unfolded as a classic example of how sometimes, attempts to unearth simple answers about an individual, and his/her associates, can expose a completely unexpected bonanza of information. Once again this vindicates a long held conviction that those family historians who simply record names, dates and places are deluding themselves if they think for one moment they know anything at all about those whose names they blindly add to a family tree. It is paramount to uncover the person's real life – put flesh on the bones as it were; because then, and only then, can one begin to know anything at all about the real person.

This is also a second step in the process of attempting to put Alexander Donaclift Young's life in perspective within his family; although, it is probably fair to say these two brothers would not have known each other as teens or adults, given Samuel was born only months after the 1851 Census. The night of that Census is the last time we know for certain that Alexander was living with his family, and by October 1857, when Samuel has just turned six years of age, his big brother had already landed in Melbourne.

Samuel is the youngest surviving son of Captain John Young and Mary Donaclift, and what was ultimately discovered about Samuel will prove him to be the absolute antithesis of his big brother. It is astonishing that these two lads - same parents, same upbringing, same set of family values, same family environment - could evolve to be two individuals so diametrically opposed in their value set and life outcomes. Families are a group of individuals connected by birth and marriage who share a time and place. Most children will say their earliest childhood memories of family and home represent security, love and learning. Ultimately, it is what they take on-board, the values they hold dear and the aspirations and dreams they carry into adulthood which define each person's respective pathway through life.

This is Samuel's story .....

His life journey began in Montrose on 16 July 1851. He was named after Mary's father, the Irish Shipwright Samuel Donaclift from Kinsale Harbour, County Cork. By the time baby Samuel was born this Young family's circumstances were what we have come to understand as comfortable in that Victorian era. Samuel would have enjoyed a lifestyle much the same as that of his older siblings, just much later on and, perhaps more importantly, at a time when his father, John, was on the cusp of retiring from sailing. The family's financial security was assured; in fact they had moved into the more commodious property on Panmure Place not long before Samuel was born. There were now two live-in servants to attend to the children's needs and to assist Mary to keep the household ordered and functioning.

John gave up the sea when Samuel was three years old, and so a positive for this young lad compared with his brothers is that he would have known a more present father, a father who was at the table most evenings. But that advantage should be taken on balance with the disruption and unsettling times that result from multiple relocations. The family made three moves in fairly quick succession: Firstly, to Panmure Place, then to Glasgow for a few years where John worked as a Ships Broker for Lloyds. Glasgow was also where Samuel would begin his schooling, but then in 1858 a promising business opportunity arose for John in

Kirkcaldy, and so the family moved for the third time and Samuel would find himself in another school in another town.

In Kirkcaldy, Samuel and his family lived initially on Abbotshall Road, where his baby sister Mary Jane was born in the March of '59. Whilst living in this house Samuel would have attended the nearby Chapel School. Sometime between then and April 1861 John, Mary, Samuel and Mary Jane moved to a residence on the High Street, of Kirkcaldy. From all accounts John's business continued to do well – they had an office on the High Street and Young & Turnbull also maintained a warehouse on the pier of the inner harbour. This warehouse was across the road from the Sailors Refuge and, of more relevance to John's business success, it was very close by the Michael Nairn & Co.'s linoleum factory, a major client for the flax they were importing from the Baltic. If Francis H. Groome's 1861 statistics for the port of Kirkcaldy are correct, John Young made a very prudent business decision to join George Turnbull in Kirkcaldy because in that year the tiny port boasted a whopping seventy-four sailing ships registered, moving 7,458 tons of goods. There were also two packet steamers servicing the coastal freight and passenger needs of the town.

Why was Kirkcaldy booming and, why now? Well, in '61 Michael Barker Nairn joined his family's company of Michael Nairn & Co, and in the same year was granted patents for his latest invention. His concept was to use specifically designed power looms to streamline and semi-automate the manufacture of floor cloths and linoleum. For his vision as an inventor and entrepreneur he was awarded a knighthood and became Sir Michael Barker Nairn, 1st Baronet of Rankeilour and Dysart House. This recognition was not only for his achievements at home but also for his international business acumen and entrepreneurship, for his business had now established branches in the United States, with a factory in New Jersey, as well as France, Germany and Australia. So substantial was the initial Kirkcaldy manufacturing operation that at the height of its success it offered employment to over 1300 local townsfolk. Later on, in 1870, Kirkcaldy saw the old factory replaced with a new six-storey manufacturing plant on the same site close by the railhead and port. Remnants of this building still stand today.

After the railway came to Kirkcaldy, a harbour redevelopment program was needed to handle the volume of ships and cargo passing through the port. Clearly John Young was well positioned to take advantage of some incredible business opportunities, given Nairn's was importing all their raw materials. Perhaps early word of this impending development by Nairn's proved to be the major drawcard for John? After all, he had spent half his working life servicing the Baltic, and one of the major commodities he imported into Scotland during those years was flax. In his early sailing days, flax was essential to the linen and hessian weaving trade but now there was a massive quantity required for the production of this completely new products - floor cloth and linoleum. John Young not only had the connections in the Baltic with shipowners but also the mercantile know-how. All this was presumably table talk while Samuel was growing up.

As previously mentioned, John's original business venture was as Young & Turnbull, Ship Brokers and Merchants, in which he partnered with an already established local business operator of good repute by the name of George Turnbull. Turnbull had various arms to his business which included operating as a Shipowner, Ships Broker and Insurance Agent. This is not only relevant to the John Young family story, but it was a life example which will prove relevant to Samuel in the years to come. In fact, it will become a business model Samuel will duplicate. Whilst the family and their business interests were riding the crest of a wave of success, Samuel was about to get his first lesson in dealing with unforeseen circumstances.

George Turnbull died on the 26 Jun 1866, and so the partnership of Turnbull & Young (Commission) Agents of 511 High Street Kirkcaldy appeared in the 1866 Westwood's Parochial Directory for the very last time. It was now John's turn to shine. He decided he would go it alone and for the very first time in his fifty-five years of life he would not linger in the shadow of his father or his uncle, rather he would hang up a solo shingle as - John Young Ships Broker. Records for the port of Kirkcaldy from 1866-1871 indicate that John was to experience some excellent trading years particularly for the import of raw jute and hemp for the 18 weaving mills operating in the town by 1867, plus there was Michael Nairn's new linoleum factory.

Whilst the locals initially called it 'Nairn's Folley' he would soon prove them wrong and put Kirkcaldy on the world stage as the linoleum capital of the world and the port and its operators such as John Young would benefit handsomely. Five years on and Samuel had completed his secondary education and leaves home about 1870 to pursue career opportunities in London.

Come April 1871 we know from Census records that John continues operating his business both on the High Street and down by the harbour. All seemed to be sailing along quite smoothly; but, unfortunately one never knows when life is about to toss a curved ball, and for John Young and his family it would be all too soon. Just six months later at 11.45 a.m. on the morning of 15 October 1871, John would pass away quite suddenly at home not as a result of the Hepatic Disease [Liver Disease] he had battled for over two years but from Phrenitis. Unfamiliar with this term I consulted The Lancet Medical Journal which explained its ancient origins thus – 'Phrenitis, the origin of our word frenzy, meant just that: for Hippocrates, the patient with phrenitis might exhibit a high fever and chill, void a scanty urine, feel a heaviness of his head and neck, and eventually lapse into delirium and trembling, before death releases him. All four of the cases that the Hippocratic author of *Epidemics* carefully recorded died between 17 and 34 days of the onset of their illness' – John died just 4 days after diagnosis. Whilst son George did rush to his father's bedside, sadly for Samuel there was no time for him to receive this news and return to Kirkcaldy. John's passing was the precursor to a most unsettling future for Mary and her daughter Mary Jane and with Samuel set to forge his career elsewhere and only George residing full time in Glasgow, it makes sense that very soon afterwards we see Mary and her daughter returning to Glasgow.

By the time of his father's passing, Samuel had already left home, as he was now 20 years of age and naturally eager to forge his own career path. We find him drawn to the bright lights and pandemonium of the vibrant and booming trading city of

London where he is working as a Bankers Clerk and living in the then fashionable Borough of Hackney. Once a quiet rural area on the outskirts of London, the 1860s saw this ancient hamlet transformed by the accelerated development of lines of stylish terrace houses. Life in London in general in the 1870s would have seemed so high powered and dynamic compared to the conservative provincial port town of Kirkcaldy.

Working as a Banker's Clerk was quite a positive achievement for Samuel too, because, believe it or not, in his day a degree of prestige was attached to such a position. The era of financial services growth began around 1861 with the establishment of the Post Office Savings Bank, such that by 1900 deposits sat at £191 million. This was the catalyst for so many new and interesting careers in Banking and Finance. Looking back on the 1870s the role of Banker's Clerk was more commonly reserved for the sons of wealthy families, as a lad's first step on the ladder to achieving a role as say a modern-day Merchant Banker.

This development coincided with the emergence of the 'White Collar' brigade - a band of well-educated office workers who were in very high demand right across Industrial England. To gauge the growth in the sheer number of clerical positions being created there are census statistics which show the number of Clerks rose from 20,000 in 1841 to over 119,000 by the time of the '71 Census. Samuel helped to make up that growth in numbers.

Was this a lucky break for Samuel or was he following on from past behaviour by using family networks of business associates? After all, David Hill was a local Banker in Montrose and a very close friend of grand-father Alexander Jnr and Alexander Snr had strong ties to and was a long-time customer of the prestigious private financiers, Ramsay Bonnar Bank in Edinburgh. In reality, what would achieving such a position mean for Samuel? To help answer this question, a paper by Ingrid Jeacle, of the University of Edinburgh Business School, explores - *The bank clerk in Victorian society: the case of Hoare and Company*. For the record, Hoare & Company is a highly successful private bank founded in the seventeenth century which has remained in business to this day and is the oldest surviving independent bank in Britain. While it is not known which bank employed Samuel, it is fair to say that, given the competition for good Bank Clerks,

Hoare & Company could be seen as setting the benchmark for all the financial houses operating in London at the time Samuel was seeking employment.

Jeacle's paper takes a two-fold approach. Firstly, she explores employment from the bank's perspective and, across subject headings such as '.... recruitment, house rules, acts of paternalism and the overwhelming concern with maintaining respectability', she takes more than a cursory glance into those heady days of Victorian England's financial operations. Secondly, she looked at employment from the employee's perspective, whereupon she asserts a Bank Clerk - 'generally enjoyed a higher salary, longer holidays and more favourable working conditions than his clerical counterparts. It was therefore a highly sought after position. Only those of impeccable character; however, were recruited into its ranks.' Very insightful deduction indeed, however it's Jeacle's quoted anecdotal evidence from the files of Hoare & Company, which is even more elucidating. One comment reads - 'while Hoare's [bank] clerks humorously referred to themselves as the Association of the Sons of Toil, the records [of Hoare & Company] support the literature in revealing the relatively cosseted career of the bank clerk within Victorian clerical circles.'

Hard work and handsome rewards with indulgence and pampering tossed in for good measure - well done Samuel, great career choice. You are on your way!

To further understand Samuel Donaclift Young's life, we need to look at the social mores which made his achievements possible and, to some degree, normal in Victorian times. It would be nice to know how a wee laddie from an obscure provincial port town in Scotland could go all the way to rub shoulders at the highest levels of academia, be actively involved in international big business and comfortably socialise with foreign chieftains and ancient and exotic royal families. Most demographers and social commentators would agree the middle and latter part of the Victorian Era was a time which coincided with radical social change. Professor Kathryn Hughes has made a life study of this phenomenon and she points out that Victorians from the mid-1860s onwards had become preoccupied with class and status and this would have most certainly included Samuel. Victorians had not just a need but a real fixation for placing people in a particular social class. Hughes contends the main reason for this was that the pre-existing simple order of 'the privileged' and 'the poor' had literally been torn apart.

The populace in general were coming to terms with the social ramification of the Industrial Revolution whereby a new multi-layered social stratification was emerging on account of changed working conditions and changed opportunities. There was this new Middle Class. Hughes makes the point, that for the first time in history - 'people were getting rich in new ways' and so by the time Samuel came into the workforce there was a new society, a new class structure, a new class of wealthy, and a Middle Class who did not inherit its wealth and privileged position in life and business, rather created it by their own endeavours. For the very first time, people like Samuel, who were not born part of the nobility, could move up the social ladder purely as a result of having a good education and their own work effort. These new ways of creating wealth came about because people embraced the new age pursuits of Manufacturing, Production, Banking and Brokering. This in turn spawned new age occupations such as Engineers, Stockbrokers and Investment Bankers such as Samuel.

London too was experiencing a transformation. It was a burgeoning and invigorated City somewhat overrun by newcomers, migrants and transients all jostling with each other as they looked to make their mark. Essentially they were people just like Samuel, disconnected from their family roots and attempting to make sense of their place in the wild maelstrom that was London. There was a social and business belief that demanded a conscious effort should be made to mix with the 'right' people and thus all these new contacts were seen as having two potential virtues: one, as a person who would help shore-up one's own social status; and two, as being of paramount importance to one's future business opportunities. In making his move to London, Samuel had set his sights a lot higher than his brother Alexander.

Along with the perplexity and uncertainty of this situation came a need to keep abreast of the dynamics of the 'new economy' and the 'new business society'. Business was being conducted in new ways, there was a divergent marketplace moving away from control by the landed gentry via church and state to one based on a strong belief in free trade and in the free movement of people, goods and services. These beliefs were fundamental to the success of the growing number of those making up the Middle Class.

The old model of monopolies and cartels controlled by the Lords had been cast aside. Success was only predicated on effort and a calculated risk. Consequently, the old establishment of the landed gentry were suddenly feeling under threat and their first reaction was to vocally rebuke those who adopted the new business model, whereby the Lords and their cohorts postulated that these new chancers were setting themselves up for failure. The contrary became the majority outcome for the likes of Samuel and his uncles Joshua Richmond, George, David Hill and Liston who were part of that army of new frontier business entrepreneurs making up the early ranks of this successful Middle Class. We will soon see that Samuel and his uncles are not the only Youngs to prosper with this as their vision.

Professor Kathryn Hughes contends that this prediction of the Lords placed an - 'extraordinary burden on the new Middle Class Business Entrepreneur[s]' who had been brainwashed into thinking that they did not deserve any good fortune which came their way. Hughes feels this new ideology encompassed aspects of what we know today as the free market concept of - 'beating the next man, undercutting the opposition, and making a bigger fortune'. The dynamics of this were beginning to be played out in a new commercial world of free exchange, intense commercial opportunism and stiff competition. Hughes goes on to contend all this was seriously at odds with previously held Christian beliefs in the - 'brotherhood of man and not damaging anybody else by your actions' - although such a motherhood statement would be seriously challenged by the old-time Scottish Whalers and Traders marginalised by their nationality and geography due to successful lobbying of the English Lords and English Merchants during the reign of James I.

Hughes believes these changes caused great angst amongst some of the traditional Lords businessmen as well as many of the new Middle Class businessmen, especially those who held strong Christian beliefs, and who were struggling to deal with the hypocrisy of being a Sunday morning Christian. To save face, many of these men resorted to a very sexist form of deception. To cover-up the inopportune disclosure of any of their misdeeds in business dealings, they kept their wives and daughters completely ignorant by isolating them at home. As a result, Middle Class home life became all about outward Christian kindness, sweetness and gentility in an environment where wives and daughters were encouraged to specialise in conspicuous consumption and polite etiquette to give an outward sign of their family's upward mobility.

There was another complication for men like Samuel who were not born into Nobility or High Society; they had an obvious knowledge shortfall when it came to acceptable behaviour protocols so necessary in polite circles. Whilst the simple achievement of worldly success was no guarantee they would be welcomed into a higher order social set, clearly these new business men and technocrats still had to swim against the undercurrent of - 'don't rise above your station' - as the establishment struggled with the loss of certain privileges previously exclusively their domain.

For those like Samuel who were striving to achieve this new 'Gentlemen' status there were some lessons to learn before they could properly navigate the maze. Awareness of this imperative spawned the publication of a range of self-help books which steered these up-and-coming young men through the darkness and into the light, especially in terms of personal and business matters. Books with topics relating to work behaviour and the requirements of social protocol in the workplace filled bookshops across London.

In relation to Samuel's vocation there is one publication whose frontispiece is so wordy it is almost a Table of Contents. It reads -

'The
Young Clerk's Manual;
or,
Counting-House Assistant,
Embracing
Instructions relating to Mercantile Correspondence,
Book-keeping, Bills, and Promissory Notes,
Foreign Bills of Exchange, Protests, Invoices, Etc.,
The Funds and Course of Exchange, Banks and Banking,
Interest and Discount,
Tables of Foreign Coins,
Marine Insurance, Laws of the Customs with Reference
to Shipping, Partnership and Bankruptcy;
and a
Dictionary of Commercial Terms.'

This just about encompasses the totality of Samuel's work environment. Then, with regard to matters of personal behaviour, there were books addressing subjects like etiquette, dress and personal hygiene. With titles like - 'How to Behave' and 'Hints from a Gentleman' - they were all about the finer points of life in Victorian England. Many of the behaviours discussed are things we take for granted today such as: how to shake hands, how to bring polite conversation to a close, how to sit, how to stand gracefully and the meaning and protocol attached to R.S.V.P. On the subject of personal hygiene, topics covered included dirty fingernails, bad breath and beard management. There were instructions on how to conduct yourself at dinner parties, at picture galleries and in church. These self-help books became the behaviour bible; a one stop shop full of remedies to avoid making social gaffes.

It would seem Samuel and his peers may have had a great deal to learn, and fast!

London aside, it seems Samuel saw his future guided by a bright star shining in the East. He became part of the caravan of Brits who sought to make their fortune in the Far East and for Samuel it was the dizzying, far-flung and exotic country of Siam he was about to call home. Records show he lived in Siam from 1873-1879. But why Siam? As with so many things in life, it was all about opportunity and timing. The Kingdom of Siam was one of the few countries in the Far East that managed to resist being colonialized by a foreign power, whilst at the same time embracing westernisation and modernisation. This was largely due to two extraordinary Siamese Kings, Mongkut and his son Chulalongkorn. Life remained raw and evolving for some time and it was the radical political leanings of the son which saw the enactment of several major reforms in 1872-73, including the appointment of the first Royal Privy Council, the sale of government-owned opium and gambling houses and the abolition of slavery, which signalled a major turning point in Siam's social and political history. By the time Samuel arrived in 1873, his entré was into a society and business world which was somewhat more mature but completely foreign to his experiences. He was only 22 years of age and it is not hard to imagine that his elation and excitement would have been palpable.

In an attempt to understand what Samuel was doing work wise, it is necessary to understand exactly what was taking place in Siam and the involvement of the British in this region in the 1870s. It has been written that - 'The presence of the British became an integral part of King Chulalongkorn's programme for reforms and modernisation. The British established trading houses and banks; they were involved in the extractive industries; and participated in a portfolio of investment. This opening up of the Siamese market to world trade required the Siamese administration to establish exchange banks, telecommunications and mail services and of course review Customs Regulations'. This insight is courtesy of Peter Sek Wannamethee, who conducted extensive research into his homeland as part of his PhD Thesis. Fortunately, for our story, he focused specifically on – *'Anglo-Siamese Economic Relations: British Trade, Capital and Enterprise in Siam, 1856-1914'* which very conveniently overlaps the period of Samuel's residence in Siam.

Since Samuel was a Bankers Clerk in London, it is fair to assume that it was through this employment he was first offered a position in Siam. The three banks operating in Siam in the 1870s were - the Hong Kong & Shanghai, the Chartered Mercantile and Banque de L'Indo-Chine. These were all inter-related at times but in the 1870s the Chartered Mercantile was a British constituent bank of the Hong Kong & Shanghai giant set up specifically to pioneer banking in the Far East. It - 'became the leading exchange bank in India and South East Asia whilst all the time retaining its head office in the pivotal London market.' It has experienced many name changes and amalgamations down the decades, but modern day readers would recognise it today as the HSBC Bank. In 1873 the Chartered Mercantile arm of the now HSBC was under the ambit of their Singapore Office, and Windsor, Rose & Co were the local agent in Siam and quite possibly the agency where Samuel was first employed on behalf of Chartered Mercantile. My reasons for making that connection will be addressed shortly.

In a publication entitled *'British Exchanger Banks in the International Trade of Asia from 1850-1890'*, edited by Webster, de Bosma and de Melo, it is stated that - 'The office's [of the Chartered Mercantile Bank] routine activities also included advances on opium and spirits farms'. Whilst the majority of these Agency Houses could trade largely on their own resources - 'their long-distance trade frequently required banking services such as overdrafts, packing credits, advances against shipping documents and the discounting of bills.' Samuel had the benefit of learning about these dealings initially from a banking perspective and later on from the merchant perspective. He would have also received a solid grounding in the Siam market workings of the Teak and Opium trades and seen first-hand how lucratively these commodities were traded. Bank records show that at one time the trade in Teak and Opium alone were sufficient to influence the Chartered Mercantile bank to seriously consider establishing their own operations.

As for Samuel's career prospects, it is written that - 'those assistants who showed their worth did not have to wait long before they faced the real responsibility of being placed in charge of one of the bank's sub-agencies or smaller offices, or indeed before they were promoted to the rank of Accountant.' Apparently, this could eventuate within two or three years of arrival because that first tour of duty was seen by Head Office as a - 'weeding out [of] those who did not measure up to the abilities and character needed to fulfil the bank's expectations.' In the case of the Chartered Mercantile Bank, promotion in the 1870s to the rank of Accountant would occur by the time one was in their late twenties, and Agent or Manager by mid-thirties. Meanwhile, the living conditions and social life for these young men was also controlled by the bank to a fairly large extent. Accommodation was situated on the floor immediately above the bank and below the Manager or Accountant who, along with his family, were accommodated on the top floor.

A further characteristic of British trade and presence in Siam in Samuel's day was the establishment of trading entities termed Agency Houses, in which the Banks played a vital role. After many years in eastern markets like Hong Kong and India, the parent Banks had honed a proven methodology to garner influence through trade: they fostered the establishment of Agency Houses which were essentially trading houses acting as bankers, bill brokers, shipowners, freighter and insurance agents who would buy and sell on commission. These Agency Houses could and were constantly expanding into new markets in the 1860s & 70s. This came about principally because 1858 saw the anachronistic monopoly of the British East India Company come to a close on the Indian sub-continent and in the Far East, which paved the way for other British and foreign Merchants to not only embrace the India and China trade but trade throughout the whole of the Far East.

When Samuel first arrived in Siam he entered an established expat community, albeit one still in its infancy. Whilst an initial agreement between Britain and Siam had been signed way back in 1826, little happened until 1855 when a more formal commercial document was signed, cementing cordiality between the two countries, which is popularly referred to as the Bowring Treaty. Described by many as a treaty of friendship and commerce between the British Empire and the Kingdom of Siam, it re-stated and expanded on the 1826 agreement and got its name from Sir John Bowring, the then Governor of Hong Kong who signed as British Envoy.

Wannamethee's research makes two further valuable observations which would have applied to Samuel and his early employment in Siam. Firstly, the nationality of the Agency House did not always correspond to that of the firms it represented: for example, a British Agency House may well represent American, German, Dutch and Danish businesses; conversely, British firms could be represented by Agency Houses from Germany or America and so on. Secondly, the local representatives for these Agency Houses were considered to be well respected 'Gentlemen' and astute business identities and as a result were often appointed to be the local Consular Representatives of foreign countries. For example, in 1867, Paul Pickenpack of German Agency House, Pickenpack Thies & Co., was appointed Consul for the Hanseatic Republic [the Baltic States] which at that time encompassed Sweden, Norway and the Netherlands.

Why is this relevant to Samuel? Well, after his time in Siam, Samuel took a short posting back in London after which he returned East, but this time to Ceylon where he embarked on a long and successful business career as the Managing Partner of his own Agency House. Trade had been the backbone of Industrial Britain's economic growth and if this was to continue it was imperative that new markets be identified and their potential fully exploited, particularly as more and more markets were required for Britain's ever-increasing manufactured output. The Far East had remained of paramount importance to Britain since the 1860s when some 33% of British exports were shipped to Asia. The new and expanding markets of the smaller Far East countries would have been identified as prime targets. It seems that Samuel had positioned himself in the right place at the right time because the second half of the nineteenth century was considered mutually important to Britain and Asia, and that included the tiny countries of Siam and Ceylon.

More important to this part of the Young Family's story - Samuel Donaclift Young was sufficiently respected for his character and his business reputation in Siam that King Chulalongkorn appointed him as the first Consul for Siam in Ceylon - a post he held for many years. Evidence for his appointment was discovered in a pictorial publication entitled – *Twentieth Century Impressions of Ceylon*', published in 1907, which has an entire section dedicated to listing the personal profiles of Consuls.

In the end 1850-1950

The entry for Samuel gives details in relation to his current and past business activity and describes his connection to Siam in particular. It reads -

SIAM

> Mr. Samuel Donnaclift Young, partner In the firm of Messrs. Clark, Young & Co., General merchants, is the Consul for Siam in Ceylon, and is the first to hold that position. He comes from Scotland and has been in Ceylon about seven-and-twenty years, and has Been Siamese Consul for ten years. In the Old Country he was in the banking business.

It is known that Samuel arrived in Colombo some time in 1879. Ceylon at that time was under British rule and had been since 1815. It is written there had been a British presence in Ceylon since 1796, but initially Ceylon was nothing more than a strategic military outpost of the Empire. The arrival of the British ended over 2300 years of Sinhalese monarchical rule; but, Ceylon's transition to Empire was not totally harmonious. A potted history of Ceylon shows the first significant foreign incursion was when the Portuguese arrived in 1505. They easily overlorded the peaceful Buddhist Kingdom, such that when the Dutch arrived around 1660 they were oddly welcomed by the locals who set about encouraging their new Dutch allies to oust their nemesis, the Portuguese. This new equilibrium persisted until 1802 when, as a consequence of Anglo-Dutch fighting, the Treaty of Amiens saw the Dutch cede authority over Ceylon to the British. Then came the Uva Rebellion of 1817-18 in retaliation for the high-handed British takeover, with the end result that the Kandyan peasantry were stripped of their lands. The British immediately set about establishing their plantation form of agriculture. In their haste, the British made fundamental errors – the most serious was the importation of significant numbers of Tamil indentured labourers from south India, which rightly upset

Ceylon's Buddhist majority and has left Ceylon with a legacy of religious unrest to this very day.

Fortunately for Samuel, he arrived into a somewhat less hostile Ceylon. To learn something of Colombo in that precursor period to Samuel's arrival, I turned to Dr. G.C. Mendis' publication - *'Ceylon Under the British - 1869-1879'*. Mendis states that during the decade under review - over 400,000 acres of crown land was sold, and the area covered by European plantations rose in 1878 to 275,000 acres. Speculators flocked to take up land; but. in their haste to establish coffee plantations they failed to give proper credence to the type of soil and methods required so it was not long before the Colonial Executive's plans suffered a major setback due to a fungus infection that decimated the coffee industry.

While this setback received much publicity, probably because some of the investors were wealthy Brits, in actual fact it turned out to be only a minor glitch, given that at the same time Import/Export trade for Ceylon rose from £500,000 in 1837 to £10,000,000 by 1877. Once it entered the global market, Ceylon's economy became subject to external factors such as the 1876-80 trade depression in Europe which ultimately brought on the collapse of the Oriental Bank Corporation in Ceylon, in 1884. Despite these economic woes, local expansion had already prompted the development of roads, railways and telegraph communications. As for Colombo itself, the British Colonial powers had decided it should be the capital and commercial hub and funds had been allocated for the maintenance of the Dutch canals which had historically been used to carry goods and people to the port. This continued expansion in Colombo would have created quite the chatter in banking circles in the region, including Samuel's circle in Siam. Was this the catalyst for Samuel deciding to head to Ceylon? On reflection, it seems several entrepreneurial Youngs have shown they have a knack, an instinct, which sees them in the right place at the right time. Had Samuel inherited the family 'gift' of business acumen?

Trade needs ships and ships need harbours, so it came as no surprise when Mendis commented - 'Perhaps the greatest event of this period [1869-1879] was the construction of the Colombo Harbour.' Governor, Sir William Gregory, is credited with building the first breakwater which was completed in 1882;

just three years after Samuel arrived. Other commentators have mentioned the increase in shipping movements from 1883 to 1893 when further harbour work was sanctioned, which enlarged the sheltered water area from 415 acres to 660 acres. This prompted the building of a 700 feet long graving dock for the cleaning and repairing of ships. By the time all this work was completed in 1899, Colombo Harbour was considered the largest and finest port in Asia. As a gauge to the growth in port activity tonnage wise, the 1891 figure was estimated at 5,696,948 and by around the time Samuel retired in 1907, that figure had risen to 6,196,116 tons. Trade figures for Ceylon at the same time rose from, Rs. 117,342,259 in 1891 to Rs. 346,434,756 by 1912. Mendis believes - 'Ceylon was never more prosperous.' Samuel was in business in Colombo and most certainly prospered.

Samuel lived on Slave Island, Colombo which had become quite a sought after address. Thanks to the Rev. James Selkirk, a British clergyman who wrote a story about Slave Island in 1844, we can glean an insight into life for a British expat like Samuel. Selkirk described Slave Island geographically as having - 'A lake [which] almost insulates the fort. In the centre of this lake is a tongue of land called Slave Island, being the place where the Dutch used to keep their slaves.' That lake is Beira Lake. Slave Island in Samuel's time had become joined to the mainland so in reality it was more a peninsula than an island.

At one time in the black past of this island, the Dutch had used it to corral their slaves by stocking the waters of the lake with crocodiles to prevent slaves from escaping under cover of darkness. In its grand colonial days Slave Island was a green oasis for picnics and promenading on the site of the first Royal Botanic Gardens. Another insight comes from John Deschamps, a British Army Officer stationed in Ceylon in the 1840s. In his - *Scenery and Reminiscences of Ceylon* (1845) he describes Slave Island as - 'being pleasant and commodious, with some elegant residences by the lake, foremost amongst which was the one called 'Kew'.' In Samuel's time Slave Island boasted parks, gardens, wide roads, a bazaar and several colonial Clubs designated 'Members Only'. In Colombo in 1881 came the building of the famous Koch Memorial Clock Tower and 1884 was the year the Kelani Valley Club opened its doors. Situated on the banks of the Seethawaka River, this is one of the oldest British Planters' Clubs in Ceylon, a favourite for planters and businessmen.

In 1894 Samuel founded the firm of Clark, Young & Co. in partnership with Messrs. T.S. & E.S. Clark. Allister Macmillan wrote in - *'Seaports of India and Ceylon'* - that the company conducted business as Importers, Exporters and General Commission Agents, from their Head Offices in Prince Street and warehouse facilities in Lauriston Stores. Macmillan says - 'It grew to be one of the most noteworthy mercantile undertakings on the island.' The firm embraced technology and can be found, at the turn of the century, listed with the telegraphic address of 'Centrum'. It acted as agent for over 25 diverse businesses from London, Paris, New York, Edinburgh, Carlisle, Manchester, Schledam [South Holland], and Belgium. Samuel also maintained his Far East agency connections with companies from Rangoon, Saigon, Batavia and Hong Kong.

Ceylon was a frontier favoured by several Scots. In 1867, James Taylor had started the first tea growing enterprise on just 19 acres of land at Loolecondera Estate. Taylor is generally considered to be the Father of the Tea Industry for Ceylon. Amazing success was to follow in 1873 with the export of the first consignment of Ceylon Tea to London. It was a mere 10 kg. but it created quite a deal of attention because of its outstanding flavour and quality. A decade later, on 30 July 1883, the first Public Auction of prime Ceylon tea was held in Colombo at the premises of Somerville & Co. under the auspices of the Ceylon Chamber of Commerce. In 1884 the Central Tea Factory was built on Fairyland Estate in Nuwara-Eliya, and in 1891 Ceylon Tea set a record price at the London Tea Auctions.

The previously mentioned failure of the Coffee crop saw the Tea sector set to boom, and from information contained in the 1894 edition of the Ceylon Tea Traders Association Journal the tea industry truly had come of age, offering new export opportunities for Samuel and his partners. Expanding trade meant increased numbers of ships - steam ships, and what they needed was coal. Clark, Young & Co.'s principal line of business was the importation of coal from Bengal and Cardiff in Wales for bunkering. So significant did this operation become their stock on hand was recorded as in excess of 15,000 tons, which was held at the company's coal-grounds on Kochchikade Island. The area of this island is said to be approximately one and a half acres and the firm employed over 300 'coolies', the local name given to the Ceylonese native labourers. While these native workers were supervised by Europeans, they were kept busy year-round, forced to load by hand the quantity of coal needed to satisfy the massive demand of the growing long-haul steamship movements in and out of Colombo Harbour. Once again, from the pages of - *'Twentieth Century Impressions of Ceylon'* - we learn that Samuel's coal bunkering business was significant and that Clark, Young & Co also acted as Agents for the Indian firm of Bengal Coal Company Ltd as well as the local firm of Colombo Coaling Company.

Clark, Young & Co. had a Financial Services side to their business which incorporated banking and brokering as well as fire, marine and accident insurance. The firm also had a trading arm to its operations, which had interests in the export of plumbago, tea and citronella oil as well as oyster and tortoise shells. The oyster shells found a ready market in Hamburg where they were manufactured into those well-known buttons sold as mother-of-pearl, which were in high demand by the fashion houses of Europe at that time. Indeed, Clark, Young & Co has been singled out as a significant supplier. One of the chief products on the firm's import manifest was timber - teak logs came from Siam and were principally used for ship repair/building and furniture manufacture.

Samuel's firm also had a value-adding side to its portfolio. It maintained its own citronella oil extraction factory at Galle, a port town just south of Colombo. The firm would purchase citronella grass from local growers, process, distil and filter it then pack it in drums and cases for shipment to markets worldwide. Another of their value-added businesses involved the extraction of the milk of the papaya fruit which was likewise processed and packaged largely for markets in America and London where it was highly sought after as a medicinal ingredient used in the manufacture of papain and pepsin preparations. These were touted as beneficial in breaking down proteins in the digestive tract and stomach. The need for such medicinal products was created by the affluence in Victorian times. Greater wealth saw diets changed to include a high consumption of protein which had a negative effect on the digestive system. In this pre-pharmaceutical era people looked to natural remedies to ease their discomfort, and this need saw 'medicines' the likes of papain and pepsin quickly grow in popularity.

There are two further curious exports which required careful management by the company's staff. The first relates to tortoise shells. The firm achieved special mention and was renowned for its careful attention to the sorting, sizing and classification of these shells prior to packaging for export. Next is the curious item of plumbago. This plant was also recognised for its medicinal properties. Originally a native of Madagascar, it was not traditionally grown in Ceylon but was introduced and fostered as a crop for native farmers. It was so successful it ultimately became a significant revenue earner for Clark, Young & Co. But this was not the only innovation the firm brought to their business and the island nation of Ceylon. Theirs was one of the first firms to make export shipments of India rubber – the milky colloid substance drawn off by making incisions in the bark of rubber trees. This substance was used mainly in the production of latex products and at one time these India rubber exports were so significant they were considered by some economists as strategic to the commercial success of Ceylon and Clark, Young & Co. Clearly, both the country and the company were seen to thrive.

In the midst of all this undoubted hard work, and flushed with his incredible success in business, Samuel must have realised that something was missing from his life in Colombo. At age twenty eight he took account of his personal situation and marriage was on his mind. Historians have written that Marriage for men in the Victorian Era was all about finding the 'best looking woman' around. Men apparently had very little respect for women by and large, being more consumed with business success. For the upwardly mobile *nouveau riche* Middle Class

Gentlemen it appears to have been more about making the right choice - finding a partner with the right pedigree and family status: status that is at least equal to or preferably slightly superior to his own.

To help understand this a little more, one can turn to the George Cruickshanks hierarchical model of English society which is affectionately known as The British Beehive. Essentially, Cruickshanks used this traditional layer model of a native hive, and placed people into the layers according to their job category to create his model by classes. He placed the Royal Family at the apex of the Societal Beehive and the likes of cabmen, shoeblacks, coal-heavers, sweeps and dustmen at the bottom. Cruickshanks philosophised this was a static model, inferring people could only change their level by changing their job, which reflects totally what was occurring in Industrial England. Charles Dickens is a perfect example of how the Beehive Model was seen to work. From Dickens' humble beginnings where, at the age of twelve, he was forced to work in a 'blacking factory' after his mother died and his father went to debtor's prison, Dickens got on with learning to improve his chances. He initially took a job as a roving legal reporter and wrote short stories on the side before he ascended to literary genius status as a full time author. Changing jobs was clearly Dickens' ladder to success.

As for Samuel, he too had done the hard yards; he had climbed his own ladder and now it was time for the next phase of his life to begin. Sometime around 1885-87 he travels from Colombo to London. Did he time his arrival for the 'Social Season' – which was basically April to the end of June? It would indeed make good sense to do so as these are the hottest months in Ceylon, a time when a mass exodus of expats was the order of the day. Some would voyage to England and other parts of Europe to visit with family and friends while others took refuge in the mountains; anything to escape the oppressive heat and humidity of a Monsoon Season in Colombo.

Whilst the custom of 'coming out' and the presentation of young ladies to Society had waned somewhat by the latter half of the nineteenth century, the debutant balls remained a social highlight. By that time, they were confined to the gentry and generally hosted at the grand houses of the aristocracy.

The popularity of such elitist events was disparaged by many, including poet Lord Byron who described them in very unflattering terms as very disagreeable 'Marriage Marts'. In the mid-late 1880s when Samuel visited London, less pretentious families held more intimate tea parties and dinner parties to introduce their daughters into Society.

Whether or not his journey was for the sole purpose of finding himself a wife, find a wife he most certainly did. When Samuel lived in London back in 1870-73 he resided at 114 Southgate Road in the Borough of Hackney, and it is pleasing to report that even today on his side of that road there remains a row of three story Georgian terrace houses which amazingly survived the Blitz. Not too far away on swanky Finsbury Square lived a young lady by the name of Florence Harriette Looker. She was soon to become Samuel's life partner. Samuel and Florence married in December 1888 at St George's Church on fashionable Hanover Square in London. This is quite a grand Anglican Church in the City of Westminster whose Vestry faces Mill Street in Mayfair. Florence was twelve years Samuel's junior and the daughter of Richard Billingsley Looker and Harriet Elizabeth Bobart.

Did Samuel achieve the Victorian Gentleman's dream of making the right choice for his wife? Did Florence come with a suitable pedigree? Would her background offer social status which would help to further the ambition of this young man who was already a successful colonial businessman?

My first line of enquiry was in respect of Florence's father, Richard Billingsley Looker [1832-1905]. He was discovered to be a well-educated man who had worked his way up the Victorian Beehive ladder from Articled Clerk in 1854 to Merchant in 1859 to Company Secretary, firstly of a Land Company around 1871 and later, in 1891, of a Railway Company. Likewise, Harriette's grandfather John Looker [1796-1869] did his Article Clerkship in 1817 with Attorney Thomas Roberson in Oxford. Later in the 1825 Poll Books & Electoral Rolls for the parish of St Peter Le Bailey, Oxfordshire, John Looker is listed as Attorney-at-law. The Billingsley name goes back to the first Sir Thomas Billingsley [1660-1670/80] who was a horseman of note with connections to the likes of Prince Rupert of the Rhine, godfather to Rupert Billingsley [1644 -] who distinguished himself for holding the town of Berwick-upon-Tweed for William of Orange during the Glorious Revolution of 1688. This certainly showed that Florence's credentials on her father's side seemed to support the expectations. Her father's family also boasts at least one hundred years of well-educated legal minds and two centuries of military distinction.

What then of Florence's mother, Harriet Bobart? Now, anytime an unusual surname crops up it excites curiosity about its origins, particularly when it is a surname like Bobart which is distinctly non-British. So, what were its origins? What can we learn about this Bobart family and their history? Did they too possess status and wealth? Researching the background of Florence's mother, Harriet Elizabeth Bobart [1788-1856] revealed that her father was Tilleman Hodgkinson Bobart [1770-1838], described as Bedel at Law of Oxford. Now that sounded impressive! However, it raised more questions than answers! What is a Bedel at Law? How did he come to achieve such a title? And - what of his family's lineage?

To my absolute surprise and delight - *'The Dictionary of National Biographies for Great Britain'* – was about to reveal all. The Bobart Family story begins with Jacob Bobart the Elder [1599-1680], who was a soldier in Saxony before turning his hand to gardening and botany and moving from Continental Europe to Oxford, England. The Bobart Story in England begins to take on more significance around 1632 when the first Earl of Danby donated £5,000 to the University of Oxford for the purpose of establishing what would initially be known as the Oxford Physic Garden at Oxford University. Herbal medicine was the order of the day back then and Danby's lofty ambition was to create a medicinal garden which would enhance plant knowledge through research and thus strengthen mankind's understanding of those species used in Medicine.

As happens so often in life, circumstances dictate outcomes, and for the Bobart story this is a truism. The initial appointment for the position of Head Gardener was accepted by a John

Tradescant the Elder who sadly died before commencing in the position. Instead, the position of Horti Praefectus went in 1641/2 to Jacob Bobart the Elder, described in historical documents as an eccentric retired soldier of the German wars, and a very capable gardener and botanist. He was also the Keeper of the Greyhound Inn in Oxford. Bobart the Elder had come to the notice of those persons at Oxford charged with the responsibility of selecting Tradescant's replacement. As luck would have it the Greyhound Inn was situated opposite the site chosen for the proposed Garden and Bobart's own successful garden was on clear display. Jacob Bobart the Elder accepted the role and began by establishing a small plot some 100 metres by 115 metres located just outside the Oxford city wall. He reputedly added some - '4,000 loads of - 'mucke and dunge' - from the college cesspits to transform the barren riverside space into a spectacular Italian quadrant garden. Later, the area was extended to some 2 acres, walled in, and local Master Mason, Nicholas Stone, fashioned the magnificent entrance gateway which is so admired to this day.

Jacob Bobart's work progressed methodically and in 1648 he published a detailed catalogue in Latin of the Garden's sixteen hundred plants entitled - *'Catalogie Plantarum, horti medici Oxoniensis'*. It includes detailed botanical drawings by his own hand, and his descriptions are equally impressive. The Catalogue was expanded and updated in 1658 by his son Jacob Bobart the Younger who took over as Gardener upon his father's death.

Next I discovered a set of diaries recording - *'The Life and Times of Anthony Wood, Antiquary, of Oxford., 1632-1695'*, edited by Andrew Clark, M.A., Fellow of Lincoln College, Oxford and Vicar of St. Michael's. Anthony Wood's assemblage of documents includes numerous passages about the Bobarts, which go part way to further explain who Jacob Bobart the Elder was, his status and social respectability.

This first snippet relates to an Elias Ashmole, unfamiliar to most people; however, he is the person after whom the Ashmolean Museum at Oxford University was named, and it turns out he was a long-time acquaintance of Jacob Bobart the Elder. Ashmole [1617-1692] was an antiquary, politician, officer of arms, astrologer and student of alchemy, a royalist supporter during the English Civil War who was well rewarded at the restoration of Charles II. He was also a founding Fellow of the Royal Society, an early Freemason with links by marriage to the Baron of the Exchequer the King's Commissioner of Excise. After being widowed he married Lady Mainwaring, a wealthy thrice married woman twenty years his senior. After their divorce he retained her late husband's Estates in Berkshire which provided him with the great wealth necessary to enable him to pursue his interests. Anthony Wood's diary states -

> 'July 6 - Elias Ashmole, Esq came to Oxon to spend some time there, and to see the solemnity of the great Act approaching. He lodged in the Greyhound Inn without the East-Gate of Oxon, and then he very kindly sent of Anthony Wood to come to him, purposely to deliver commendations to him for his father in law, Dugdale Norroy Earl of Armes. He continued in Oxon y or 6 dayes and Anthony Wood attended him every day in seeing many curiosities, as the painting in Alls. Coll. Chappel, the paynting in Magd. Coll. Chappell, and the paynting in the Theater. They were often in the Physick Garden with Jacob Bobart the keeper (an old acquaintance of Mr. Ashmole), who shewd them many choice plants, herbs, grafts, and other curiosities to Mr. Ashmole's great content.'

There are over 200 mentions of Bobart in Wood's diaries. Noteworthy is one in the December of 1670 which is a notation regarding a visit by the previously mentioned Prince of Orange, King William III, to Oxford, where -

> 'about ten of the clock, the prince, his retinew, the Vicechancellor and bedles, went in sevrall coaches (borrowed of some of the Heads of Houses, for their owne were all dirty with travelling the day before) to visit these places following, viz.,' - then item three on the visitation list was - 'The physic garden, where (Jacob) Bobart the gardiner also recreived him with a Dutch complement.'

Among the many notes regarding events and medicinal experiments is this item from October 1667 -

"24 Oct. 1667., M.A. 9 July 1670. Stabnl., secxetarius juratus anlicus, ac * in Wood MS. £.32 fol. 23 is this intimi cubicula familiaris S.R.M. in anecdote: - 'Jacob Bobert senior, keeper Swecia, eques Polonus;* and notes 'if of the Physick Garden Oxon., used to this be meant of him who was usually weare a long beard. Wherupon Mark called the lord Coreskie, it should have colman, a melancholy distracted man, been written about 1654 when he came sometimes a singing man of Ch. Ch., first to Oxon.' Walking in the Physick Garden.'

Clearly some herbal concoctions made men very merry indeed. All done in the name of medical science I am sure!

There are a number of surviving images of Jacob Bobart the Elder which depict an extremely characterful person with a kind face bordered by a shock of long curly fair hair and equally bushy fertile beard, soft eyes and angular features. Outwardly, he gives the impression of a Germanic man of contemplation and gentleness. It is written that - 'on rejoicing days he used to have his beard tagged with silver'. Several sketches include his pet goat which reputedly followed him around like a dog. Jacob Bobart the Elder died on 4 Feb 1680 at the Garden House, and Anthony Wood once again made two personal diary notes on the occasion of Jacob's passing -

'Feb. 4, W., Jacob Bobert of Brunswick, Germany, put in 2 gardiner of the Physic Garden by the founder (the earl of Danby), died at his house in the Physick Garden. In Fasii 1655.

Feb. 4, W., Jacob Bobart died: servant to the University: an understanding man: the best gardiner in England: hath a book extant.'

Jacob Bobart the Elder is buried in St Peter in the East Churchyard, Oxford. His grave is marked by a massive tablet to his memory. Throughout his life he managed to accumulate considerable wealth and property. In his Will he leaves houses and the Inn to his two surviving sons, Jacob Bobart the Younger and Tilleman Bobart. One passage from his Will reads - 'to my eldest son Jacob Bobart all my garden plants and halfe my Books', and 'to my son Tilleman the other moietie or halfe of my Books'. There were also sizeable legacies to each of his six daughters and to his second wife Ann who was cited as a residuary legatee. Portraits and engravings, one full length, provide a wonderfully warm, thoughtful remembrance of this inspiring man. Also surviving him is a poem he addressed to his deceased son and another which was printed in the *Oxford Almanac of 1719*. His talents were boundless, and his legacies cherished.

But the most outstanding remembrance of all is the comparison made to the painting 'Vertumnus' by Mannerist Giuiseppe Arcimboldo of Milan, which was used on the cover of a book written to celebrate the life of Jacob Bobart the Elder. The original of this painting is of the Holy Roman Emperor Rudolf II reimagined as Vertumnus, the Roman God of Metamorphosis who is depicted with fruit and vegetables as a symbol of the abundance of life which had returned in the Golden Age of his rule. The book's title page reads – *'Vertumnus: An epistle to Mr. Jacob Bobart, Botany Professor to The University of Oxford, And Keeper of The Physick-garden - By the Author of The Apparition.'* It was printed in 1713 for Stephen Fletcher Bookseller: And are to be Sold by John Morphew near Stationer's Hall, London.' Extraordinary!

Jacob Bobart the Elder achieved status and recognition on a majestic scale whilst remaining true to himself. In an Addendum to Anthony Wood's diary collection there is a noteworthy regal and political remembrance -

'Vol. I, p. 314. - As to the destruction of the Royal arms in Oxford during the Civil war, I may refer to a jest in William Hickes' Grammatical Dollery, Lond. 1686, p. 81. 'Upon the taking down of the king's arms at Oxford in the time of the Rump, viz. 1649; who instead of plucking down them on the gate of the Physick Garden in Oxford, they were such excellent Heralds that they pluckt down the Earl of Danby's arms who was the founder there.'

Whilst Jacob Bobart the Elder clearly chose to leave his mark on this world, not even he would have ever imagined that over 350 years later he would continue to be fondly and professionally acclaimed. Jacob Bobart the Elder was not only a highly skilful Horticulturalist and Botanist, he was a wonderful father and husband and a devoted animal lover and anyone visiting Oxford in 2019 will see Bobart's botanical legacy on show at what is now the Oxford Botanic Garden which has been expanded to include the Harcourt Arboretum and seven huge Glasshouses. Jacob would be immensely proud to see that what he created from - '4,000 loads of mucke and dunge' - has been enlarged in his name and attributed as his original work. In 2004, in further recognition of his contribution to Horticulture and Oxford University, 'The Bobart Group' was founded whose tenet is to ensure Jacob's work is never ever forgotten and that the learning continues. The University celebrates Bobart Day in April each year which highlights the Arboretum. One other of the numerous events on the Oxford Botanical Calendar is the Bodleian Botanical Art Collection Day with displays of precious works in the Weston Library, Oxford. It is curated to include some of Bobart's original drawings.

Son, Jacob Bobart the Younger, was equally as eccentric as his father. He distinguished himself as a Professor of Botany at Oxford, but it was his comical anatomical exploits for which he was to receive international notoriety. Zachary Grey's Notes on Hudibras explain - 'Mr. Jacob Bobart, botany professor of Oxford, did about forty years ago (in 1704) find a dead rat in the Physic Garden, which he made to resemble the common picture of dragons by altering its head and tail, and thrusting in taper sharp sticks, which distended the skin on each side till it mimicked wings. He let it dry as hard as possible. The learned immediately pronounced it a dragon, and one of them sent an accurate description of it to Dr. Magliabechi, librarian to the Grand Duke of Tuscany. Several fine copies of verses were wrote upon so rare a subject; but at last Mr. Bobart owned the cheat. However, it was looked upon as a masterpiece of art, and as such deposited in the museum of the anatomy school at Oxford.' This misdeed was his way of showing disdain for his peers and his wicked sense of humour.

When Jacob Bobart the Younger died he made what has been termed a 'noble benefaction' to the University. In fact Item 1 of his Will reads - 'give to the Chancellor Masters & Scholars of the University of Oxon all my seeds books & dryed plants with the Catalogue of the same 4 other my books & furniture of my study to be kept together [sic] in hopes of my Successors improvement of the same for the better service of the University As also the stock of Plants Potts & other instruments in the Garden all which have been by me procured with considerable trouble and charge.' In describing this collection it is written that - 'The catalogue of Bobart's library is in the Archives of the University, and there are two copies of it in the Library at the Botanic Garden. It consisted, apparently, of 218 vols., together with thirtyeight folio vols, of Hortus Siccus, as well as eight other vols, of dried plants, volumina minus accurate digesta.' But there was more largesse to come - 'to our three public librarys Bodleian, Ashmolean and Bobartian, if it be lawful to give that title to his collection, which by will he hath bequeathed to the garden, with an estate of 5£ per annum for a Salary to a Botanic Professor, at the same time we build him a very pleasant house to inhabit in.'

Subsequent generations continued to uphold the family's fame including Florence's grandfather, Tilleman Hodgkinson Bobart. His unique characterful portrait hangs proudly today in the National Portrait Gallery in St Martin's Place in London. *The Gentleman's Magazine,* an English publication where the life of the social elite was chronicled, carried a notice in February 1839 which was the obituary written upon the death of Florence's grand-father, Tilleman Hodgkinson Bobart. It reads - 'Dec 30. At Oxford, suddenly, in his 67th year, Tilleman Hodgkinson Bobart, Esq. Superior Bedel of the Faculty of Law, and formerly

Commoner of University College, of which Society he became a member, May 5th 1790. Mr. Bobart was much beloved by his private friends, and highly respected by all who knew him. He obtained the appointment of Esquire Bedel in 1815. He has left a widow and a numerous family.'

From these incredible accounts of social position and respectability, it could be said that Samuel took the Victorian marriage model very seriously indeed and found himself a wife of considerable standing and pedigree.

Samuel's life seems to have panned out just about as perfect as life could get in his day and a dramatic contrast to that of his eldest brother Alexander. Following their marriage Samuel and Florence returned to Ceylon, and from scant family letters and official records it seems they set about enjoying all the privileges and varied opportunities colonial expat life had to offer. Samuel had the benefit of his years in Siam and Ceylon to develop strategies to cope with the heat and humidity but for his new bride this was a lesson she still had to learn. As with many people in the Far East, Florence would find herself seeking refuge in the mountains when summer descended to sap the life out of all who remained. Whilst Trincomalee and Anuradhapura are favourite stations, other areas near Nuwara Eliya are the most beclouded districts. Arnold Wright tells us that - 'Ceylon - affected as it is by the monsoonal changes - is no less varied than its soil; and throughout the year, while no fixed seasons are remarked, variations may be found to occur from chill winter to overpowering heat.' In the grip of the monsoon, parts of coastal Ceylon can receive between 150-200 inches of rain.

Social life for Samuel and Florence centred around the various Clubs, such as the Nuwara Eliya Golf Club founded in 1890. Local business identities were prominent among the membership and fellow Scot Mr. W. Somerville of Somerville & Co was a founding member of the Colombo Golf Club. A Ladies Championship was instituted in 1895 and Club records show a very competitive tussle for the 'Gold Bangle' trophy. Cricket was a firm favourite at the Slave Island Club which was established in the 1860s. In fact, the first Colombo Cricket Club played on Rifle Green on Slave Island and, looking through the Players Board, the names of prominent merchants feature strongly as do the sons of District Judges, Politicians and Military heavyweights as well as Sinhalese businessmen - but alas, not Samuel. Integration seems to have been the social order of the day, at least for the wealthy elite.

One element of social conviviality shared by the poor and rich alike was the tradition of - 'Arrack and Toddy'. [Arrack is the fermented juice of the coconut and - 'is to the Ceylonese what whisky is to the people of the United Kingdom.' Toddy was the local name for fresh juice. It is said to - 'furnish some measure of relief, not to say sustenance, to the thirsty traveller wandering under the fervid heat of a tropical sun.' So popular did this refreshment become that a whole industry grew up around it, such that at one point it was described as - 'one of the most flourishing trades pursued in Ceylon.' Since Samuel and Florence were known to enjoy a tipple or two one wonders if Arrack and Toddy was their beverage of choice.

In Florence's day Slave Island has been variably described as a place of factories, forts and fabulous residences. Pettah District was the hub where bazaars, temples, mosques and theatres could be found side by side with coconut desiccating mills, military garrisons, lighthouses, post offices, banks, business premises and mercantile houses. This diversity extended to places of worship too with Hindu, Buddhist, Muslim, Dutch Reform, Wesleyan, Anglican and Roman Catholic sites dotted throughout the island. The varied styles of architecture offer a mirror into Ceylon's past history with traditional designs interspersed with Portuguese and the Doric style of the Dutch. One of the oldest remaining examples is the edifice of a building dating from 1749, constructed as a place of worship for the Dutch Governor. The Tamil Theatre in Pettah is another standout and has been described as the most massive building on Slave Island. It forms part of a quadrangle including elegant Braybrooke Hall, the official residence of the Officer-Commanding, hard up against the Police Headquarters in the Corinthian style rubbing shoulders with the newer and characterless modern Law Courts.

Samuel's business continued to thrive - prosperity was his for the taking. It was the geographical position of Ceylon which could be said to be its greatest natural advantage. Ceylon was referred to by the British, especially Londoners, as - 'The Clapham Junction of the ocean'. Just as all trains travelling in and out of London had to pass through Clapham Junction, similarly all ships travelling to and from London en route to Australia and the Far East had to pass through Ceylon. Wright wrote - 'Coal in these days is the breath of the nostrils of shipping' and Samuel and his partners were at the forefront of supply. As a guide to the huge prosperity this provided to Ceylon and Samuel, Arnold Wright provides a table of Harbour Dues from the time collection began in 1883 to the end of 1905 and the figures are staggering. Revenue rose from Rs. 379,000 in 1883 to Rs. 1,187,00 by 1905. He cites 2,000 steamers alone in 1905. Samuel had clearly achieved beyond his dreams.

Despite the rigour of business Florence and Samuel found time for family as well. They had two sons, Richard Donaclift Young [1889-1976] who was born on Slave Island and Jack Bobart Young [1893-1915] born in Sussex, England. Very little has been discovered about their early years but it is safe to say they would have been raised principally by an Ayah, the name given to those local domestic servants who acted as Nursemaid to the children of expats. Author N. Maisondeau wrote in his - *'Summer in Ceylon'*, (1909) that "some ladies require an ayah or lady's maid, one of the most vexatious though useful creatures that one can add to an eastern household." This is a sample advertisement published in 1889:

> 'AYAH_SINGHALESE AYAH. Cornelia, at Ayah's Home 6, Jewry-street is open to engagement, for Ceylon or India. Crossed 25 times. Excellent sailor.
> September 23, 1889.'

Unlike Alexander, Samuel maintained strong ties to his family and to Scotland. These were very important to Samuel and down the decades the couple are frequently discovered in shipping records which makes it clear that Scotland was one of their holiday destinations of choice. They can be found taking a respite there in 1901, residing at the newly opened Shandon Hydropathic, a converted private residence originally built by notable Clyde Shipbuilder Robert Napier. These trips also provided an opportunity to visit with Samuel's sole surviving sibling in Scotland, elder brother George and his family who were living close-by in Largs.

However, while records show these new parents are expensively ensconced in the Shandon Hydropathic, there was initially no sign of their children. A wider search finds the boys residing in the house of an Edith Sturrock, at 32 St Augustine St., Bedford St Peter. But why? The Census declares that Edith was a Ceylon born widow who was also caring for 2 other Indian born children by the surname of Shaw. Given the Ceylon connection, Edith was surely known to the Youngs in some way. At the time private boarding schools and private tutors remained a popular choice for the wealthy Middle Class, and at first glance it was possible Edith Sturrock was providing one or both of these services for possibly two expat families. Edith is listed as a widow, she does not have an occupation listed against her name in the Census, but she does have a Singapore born daughter to support, so one would imagine that some form of income would have been essential in the absence of a husband and social security.

However, things are not always as they first appear. A little further detective work reveals an entirely different story. It came to pass that these families were very well acquainted indeed. Edith was Edith Constance Mary Amelia Dalton, the wife of John Patrick Sturrock who, according to his probate records, was an Accountant in the Chartered Mercantile Bank of India London and China ex their Colombo office, and who was later transferred to Djakarta, Batavia [Indonesia] where he died of Cholera - 'on or about 30 April 1886'. His estate papers were sealed at Edinburgh on 26 October 1886 – but why so? In the archives of the Chartered Mercantile Bank there is cited a - 'rather macabre Court minute [which] records that, following Sturrock's death at Batavia in 1886, the doctor had given orders for some furniture to be destroyed and that the Court of Directors gave approval for it to be replaced at the bank's expense.' The author who extracted this citation states this does not make sense when the cause of death recorded in the Court minutes was Heart Disease. Rightly so, but when the truth of his death is finally revealed as Cholera it is clear that the bank was trying to cover up some impropriety and a lack of duty of care on their part. It also highlights the dangers presented by the climate, living conditions and inadequate medical services available in the Far East, and in John Sturrock's case all of these were found wanting.

The Chartered Mercantile Bank provides an understandable link between Samuel and Edith's husband John Sturrock. At one time they would have been work colleagues at the Chartered Mercantile Bank in Colombo. When Edith passed away in 1957 her residual estate was valued at £3,365.8s.8d so she was certainly not in need of funds in 1901. Getting back to that 1901 Census: all of the children listed were around a similar age, so most likely knew each other in Ceylon and were simply enjoying their summer holiday together. There is one further painful memory these two families would share. During World War I Edith's nephew Bernard Silvester Sturrock fell at Loos, Flanders one day after Samuel's son Jack was killed at Loos. Both of these young men died in the September of 1915.

Samuel and Florence returned to Ceylon, and it was business as usual until 1903 when Samuel, perhaps aware of his failing health, decides to finalise his Last Will & Testament. Whilst Samuel and Florence made several visits to Scotland, by early 1909 they had made a permanent move back to the Motherland, becoming residents at West Shandon House, at Shandon Hydropathic in Dunbartonshire, Scotland. This is where they remained until 31 March 1909, the day of Samuel's passing. He was in the 58th year of his age and is buried in the family plot in Old Cathcart Cemetery, Glasgow, one of the few in his family known to be actually interred there despite their names being engraved on the headstone. His Will turned out to be a complex legal document involving property and business holdings in two countries and probate was delayed until April of 1910. Both his sons were under-age at the time so special provisions had to be made. He nominated his Executors as William Caldwell Young and Alexander Renfrew Young, two sons of his brother George. They were charged with the onerous task of dealing with the protracted and complex legalities. It speaks volumes as to the honesty, respect and level of trust these men shared.

It was a sad and difficult time for Florence who immediately departed Shandon Hydropathic to take up residence in Hillhead, which is still a real estate mecca and renowned as a fashionable and leafy area of the West End of Glasgow. There are strips of elegant Terrace Houses standing proud today as remnants of a glamorous past and testament to the wealthy who lived there. In 1911, son John is living there with his mother, with his occupation listed as Stockbroker's Clerk; however, Richard is absent once again. Less than a year later Florence too passes away, leaving the two boys reliant on family patriarch, Uncle George, and cousins William and Alexander, as their life guides.

Sadly, the grief and dislocation brought about by the loss of their parents, the necessities of work, war and life in Victorian times saw the lives of these brothers take very different directions. Richard is known to have been working as a Cashier [Accountant] when war was declared in August 1914. Following family tradition, he is drawn to the sea, and so it is no surprise to find him enlisting in the Royal Naval Air Service in the September. This was the air arm of the Royal Navy administered by the Admiralty. Richard's service papers state that he was a very tall slim fellow with a fresh complexion. He was of very good character and superior ability. His service record shows he served on board *President II*, a 'stone ship' or 'land establishment base' under the control of the Admiralty and had responsible for accounting and administration duties. A 'Stone Ship' or 'Land Ship' was a physical ship no longer seaworthy which was put into use as administrative offices. The *President II* was permanently moored in the Thames as the London HQ for the RNAC.

His young brother Jack also served in WW1. He enlisted in the Queens's Own Cameron Highlanders. Records show that he too enlisted in September 1914 like his brother and had been promoted quickly, rising to the rank of Corporal by the time of his death a year later on 25 September 1915. He was killed on the fields of Flanders during the Battle of Loos, which was the first time the British had used poisonous gas on the battlefield - he was only 22 years of age. There is mention of Jack in the De Ruvigny Roll of Honour which completes his story. It reads -

'YOUNG, JACK BOBART - Corp., No. S. 12216, B. Coy., 5th (Service) Battn. The Queen's Own Cameron, son of Samuel Donaclift Young, of Slave Island, East India Merchant, by his wife, Florence Harriet, dau. of Richard B. Looker; employed as a Clerk with Messrs. Wingate & Waters, Stockbrokers, Glasgow; enlisted in Sept. 1914, after the outbreak of war; served with the Expeditionary Forces in France and Flanders from April 1915, and was killed in action at the Battle of Loos 25 Sept following. While at Kelly College he won his Cap in the Football XV 1908 and 1909, and the Cricket XI 1909; died unmarried.'

The final segment of the Samuel Donaclift Young story brings us to his curious connection, by marriage, to 'The Flogging Parson' of Australia. This snippet is for those Australian descendants who recall their 6th Grade history.

Who is the Flogging Parson?

As a proud Australian I felt compelled to include this interesting sidebar which goes to the heart of Australia's dark Colonial past, and at a time when Samuel's uncles were in the colony, so not entirely unrelated. The person so nicknamed is a man of the cloth, the Reverend Samuel Marsden [1765-1838] who was born the son of a Yorkshire Blacksmith. As a young lad he was heavily influenced by the Methodist Religion in his home village of Farsley, in Yorkshire. At the late age of 24 Marsden went to Hull Grammar School, and met members of the Clapham Sect and William Wilberforce, the doyen of Humanitarianism and the person most closely associated with the abolition of slavery. It was on Wilberforce's recommendation that Marsden accepted the position of Chaplain of New South Wales, but little did Wilberforce realise Marsden had a very dark side to his character.

Marsden's clerical career had evolved quite quickly - he was ordained a deacon on 17 March 1793, he married on 20 April,

In the end 1850-1950

was ordained priest in the May and by 1 July 1793 he and his new wife were departing England on board the *William* bound for the new colony of New South Wales. Governor Lachlan Macquarie was heading up the colony at the time of Marsden's arrival and it was he who ordered Marsden to reside in Parramatta to take up the position of Chaplain. Marsden's list of associates in Australia is littered with influential and notable men of the time like New South Wales Governors King, Bligh, Darling and Hunter as well as botanist Sir Joseph Banks. But not one of these insightful men saw Marsden as anything other than an extremely pious man. Had they been privy to the contents of any of his numerous letters to England they would have become aware of his disturbing comments regarding the high level of immorality and crime that prevailed in Parramatta. He blamed it on the dilapidated state of the 'factory' [work house]; however, what he failed to mention or take responsibility for was his prolonged and inexcusable lack of action on behalf of the inmates.

Quite the contrary, under his supervision life for the convicts in Parramatta was about to get a whole lot worse. At that time in England and Australia, clergymen were often appointed to judicial positions, and in this instance the newly arrived, equally pious, New South Wales Governor John Hunter decided to appoint Marsden as a Magistrate and Superintendent of Government Affairs at Parramatta. Marsden's solution to quelling crime and non-religious behaviour was to mete out severe floggings to every convict who came before his court. His decidedly unchristian behaviour estranged him as a clergyman from his convict flock and free-settler parishioners alike and his pastoral work was done irreparable harm.

Excuses were offered attributing his behaviour to his high-mindedness, his passionate detest for sin and his conviction that Parramatta was such a den of iniquity that morality could be preserved only by the most rigorous disciplinary measures. In the end he was forced to resign from the church, his magisterial position was suspended, and he took up a block of pastoral land and became a sheep farmer. His best known reputation is his association with Grazier John MacArthur and Merino sheep. His unflattering but fitting epitaph reads -

Rev. Samuel Marsden
Puritanical to the emancipists
Cruel as a magistrate
Grossly Materialistic

How does this connect to Samuel? Well, Florence's uncle, Henry Hodgkinson Bobart also became a minister of religion after studying Theology at Oxford University. Believing his vocation would best be served by removing himself to the settlement of Parramatta in New South Wales, he took a ship in the late 1820s. In Parramatta he met and married Elizabeth Mary Marsden on the 28 September 1837. Elizabeth was the second surviving daughter of the unchristian Rev. Samuel Marsden of Yorkshire, the infamous 'Flogging Parson'.

In the end 1850-1950

Chapter 11 – Part 1

**Transition • Sea Captain to Silk Manufacturer
Darwin's Commandment & Religious Fervour
Enduring Friendship & Business Partnership
Son Husband Father Lay Preacher • Believer!**

This chapter is the part one of the final family group to be explored in connection with this Young story; in fact, so incredible is this branch of the family tree, that it is not only worthy of inclusion, it demands greater exposure – hence it will be told in two parts. It's the story of the 'middle child' of John Young and Mary Donaclift: George Alexander Young and his descendants. Colloquially we have all heard tales of 'middle child syndrome' where that child is supposed to harbour feelings of exclusion and/or isolation within the sibling/family circle. In 2010 Psychologist, Daniel Eckstein et al, conducted a review of some 200 Birth-Order Studies which by and large upheld that broad opinion; but, on balance their findings also indicate the middle child was likely to be more sociable, more faithful in their relationships and better at relating to both older and younger people. Their findings also suggested the middle child tended to be the family peace-keeper and often possessed traits like agreeableness and loyalty. From what has been learned about George Alexander Young [1841-1917] it is clear he inherited a very healthy dose of all those positives and more. As we follow George's life journey we will bear witness to the marvellous life he enjoyed. George was the temperate quiet achiever who patiently embraced opportunity, steadfastly believed in the future and showed great determination and resoluteness, all tightly interwoven into a mantle of loyalty and faith. And finally, the juxtaposition of George to his eldest brother Alexander will leave readers flabbergasted.

George's life story will not only confound the professional psychologists, his achievements and those of his children will outshine those of his siblings, especially in the maritime stakes. If George's parents had lived long enough, they would have taken immense pride in their middle son George, his children and the values he and Penelope imparted to them. Above all else, George and his descendants upheld the Young Family standards for business and personal behaviour and the consistency of their humanitarian contribution to community and employees alike. George's branch of this Young family has remained proud and strong down the generations; in fact, a great many of the items of personal memorabilia and documents of unique historic family significance presented within this manuscript are treasured pieces of history residing in the hands of descendants of this truly admirable man.

George, like so many Youngs before him consistently displayed that rare combination of initiative, drive and innate ability which ultimately rewarded him with all the success he could ever have imagined. He showed himself to be highly intelligent but practical at the same time, a characteristic he shared with his sons. He possessed a keen business mind but was always fair in his dealings with others, he was loving and caring to his family and christian kind to those he encountered but most important of all, George led from the front and set the example so all of his children could stand proud and strong in whatever they pursued and wherever their lives took them. This is not only my personal assessment of the man, but a synopsis of the views expressed by others who knew him and could speak first-hand about his personal and working life. We are also privileged to have some of his writings to draw on, samples of which will be presented here. They will combine to define the man, the father, the husband and the friend that was George Alexander Young.

In the end..... 1850-1950

This is George's story -

For patriarch George, it all began in Montrose on 10 May 1841 where he was born the fourth child and third son of Captain John Young and Mary Donaclift. Three months before George was born there was a notice posted in the Montrose Review on February 5 offering for rent the family's previous house on Ferry Street, cited as the residence of Shipmaster John Young as if everyone would know which house it was. The family had decided to move just one street north to Gibson-place where they remained for the greater part of a decade. For George, during his pre-school years, it would have been a comfort and a joy to have his grandparents living just around the corner. Five years on and the serenity and stability of family life was set to change when, in the March of 1846 he lost his grandmother, Jean Strachan, and the family moved into the grandparents' home at No. 12 Panmure Place. Grandfather, Alexander, had retired to a smaller property on Bridge Street in Montrose, which is where he was residing at the time of his death on the 29 October 1848. Whilst these were clearly sad events, ultimately it was the death of his sister, Margaret, in 1850 which will leave the most lasting impression, a scar that simply refused to heal, and caused George to question his faith for decades. This was a life event which he spoke of much later on in adulthood as a defining moment, a turning point in his thinking about God, life and the Universe.

In terms of the family's standard of living, it is clear that his father John was a good provider, and Panmure Place is situated in what was the dress circle of Montrose at the time. It is still a much sought after address today and the property at No. 12 is still standing and overlooks the beautiful town Green. On the other side of the Green on Melville Gardens stands the Montrose Town Hall which is flanked by the most architecturally pleasing double fronted properties in the whole of Montrose. Mary and the children would have enjoyed strolling and playing on the Green where they could, from time to time, either enjoy the entertainment or partake of the refreshments on offer at the wonderful Victorian Pavilion located at the northern end of the Green. Panmure Place is also the address for the Montrose Museum and with the Montrose Academy quite close by, it meant just a short walk to school for George and his siblings.

By the time George reached school age there were five children in the family and Mary was pregnant with her sixth child, so there is no doubt George would have grown up in a very active, noisy and bustling household where he was never short of a playmate. In appreciation of the family's financial status and the work involved raising such a large family, Census records from 1841 onwards show a constancy of live-in servants assisting Mary with the day to day running of the household and domestics as nursemaids helping with the childcare. Father, John, is noticeably absent on those occasions and from his personal Captain's Log we can see he was continuously sailing to and from the Baltic and Archangel as Master of the trading brig *Jane* early 1836, just after he and Mary returned from Ireland, until March 1851, then the *Success* until March 1854.

Taking this into account, it is safe to say during his formative years George would not have seen a great deal of his father so it is fair to assume that much of George's character and the value set he carried into adulthood was imparted to him by his mother Mary Donaclift and of course his grandparents. Although he was seven and a half at the time of his grandfather's passing, George would have been fully aware of the larger than life shadow, Captain Alexander Young Jnr cast on the family, within the seafaring fraternity and the broader Montrose community. The pages of the 1846 & 1847 Directory for Montrose, for instance, list Captain Alexander Young as a Parliamentary Elector for the Burgh, Ships Master and Shipowner.

By this point the Young family has become well and truly part of the fabric of Montrose, albeit from a mostly maritime perspective. The importance of this should not be underestimated because the town of Montrose had, by then, established a solid reputation as a leading east coast whaling port as well as an international trading port of significance to the Scottish economy. George's grandfather had no doubt made his strong contribution to these achievements: as a pioneering and successful Northern Whale Fishing master, as a successful shipowner and merchant master, as well as a long-time member and Chairman of the Harbour Board Trust and as a Trustee of the Merchant Seamen's Fund. Latterly, under the heading of - 'Vessels Registered to the Port of Montrose', we can see Captain Alexander Young cited as owner of the vessel *Jane*, a brig of 212 tons burthen built in 1824. For a time, Alexander Jnr was the only Surveyor of Shipping in Montrose and sole Agent for the prestigious Lloyd's Shipping Co. Given this family's history in Montrose, George must have felt safely cocooned in a cloak of family respectability and pride. Growing up, Montrose was George's personal safe harbour, and with most of his extended family having some connection with the sea, one could be forgiven for thinking that his life direction was pre-ordained. But not so!

George's father, like his grandfather before him, had long ago recognised that sailing in wooden ships with canvas sails was doomed to history. In fact, March 1854 was to be the next watershed moment for young George and his family. He had just turned eleven, his father had retired from the sea and John's vessel, the *Jane*, had been sold. Since that sale was negotiated on condition that John remain as Captain for a time, it was only after the satisfaction of that obligation that John could take steps towards carving out a new future for himself and his family. After all, John was only 43 years of age and presumably not ready for retirement, so it was no surprise to discover the family had decided to sell up in Montrose and head to Glasgow where John takes on the role of Ships Broker for Lloyd's of London. Life carried on as expected in Glasgow for a time and George was enrolled in school in order to complete his education. Then in the words of one publication - 'he [George] was put to business.'

George's working life got off to quite a shaky start for he had only been employed for about a year when he suffered a serious illness which necessitated a prolonged convalescence. George was sent to the south of Ireland to recuperate under the watchful eye of his mother's family in Kinsale. He spent some months living with his Uncle John and Aunt Mary where thankfully he makes a full recovery and subsequently returns to Glasgow and to his employment. George was very happy with his employment and would not have had any inkling at the time, that his family's move from Montrose to Glasgow was set to describe his future and change his life in ways no young man could ever have imagined possible.

Obviously, when most of us accept our first paid employment position it is with some trepidation and a fair degree of experimentation; albeit a calculated leap of faith given the ebb and flow of economic climates. This was certainly not the case for George. For him, all indications are that he was extremely fortunate to find his first position was in an industry very much to his liking and with a well-established company owned and operated by people with whom he quite quickly established solidarity and affinity. Clearly, these feelings were mutual because such was their level of satisfaction with George, they very kindly kept his position open for him until such time as he was fully recovered. Fortunately, for George, everything seems to have naturally and easily fallen into place.

Employment for George Alexander Young would not be in any way related to the sea; nor would he follow in his uncles' footsteps and head into a branch of mercantile business either. However, just like his father and grandfather before him George starts at the bottom and works his way up. The first company he worked for was James McAulay & Co. and his first role was as a 'Warehouse Boy' under the supervision of a Mr. William Caldwell. This company were Silk Manufacturers in Glasgow which, incidentally, was not this Young family's first association with the Silk trade. George's Aunt Jane had married Captain Francis Spittal whose brother was Sir James Spittal, a Silk Merchant in Edinburgh. In fact, Sir James is listed in the 1810 Post Office Directory as having a Silk & Shawl Shop at 12 St Andrews Square, New Town, Edinburgh, as well as a Haberdashery Shop at 55 South Bridge St., Edinburgh City. Perhaps he purchased some of his stock from McAulays. Whilst these retail occupations are of minor significance in today's world, Sir James enjoyed great respectability and at one time was Deputy Lieutenant of Edinburgh, a Magistrate in Edinburgh and fulfilled the role of Lord Provost from 1833-37. What's more, since George's sister, Margaret, died in Leith, it is entirely feasible that George accompanied his mother and Margaret when they visited Edinburgh and Leith and that they visited Sir James' shop on popular St Andrews Square.

Although George's work aspirations were put on hold at one point due to a serious health issue it seems his passion, friendship and perseverance would see his career plan not only get back on track but blossom. Once back in Glasgow he progressed with ease from Apprentice Clerk, to Salesman, Traveller and then to Mercantile Clerk by 1866; all of which suggests he was an ambitious young man, eager to please and a fast learner. Working alongside George A. Young was a young man by the name of John R. Caldwell; who was the son of the Manager, William Caldwell. George and John were not only work colleagues, they were soon to establish a friendship which we will follow closely as it develops into a close life-long personal and business partnership. These young lads had more in common than either of them would have first realised. They had both had to face up to death at a very young age, they were both intelligent, ambitious, energetic and not afraid of hard work, compassionate and devout. In fact, it was probably their shared spiritual quest, at a time in the Victorian era when religion and social life were closely intertwined, that initially spawned their friendship.

Under what circumstances George, or indeed his father John, made the acquaintance of local businessman William Caldwell is unknown, but it was to be a very important meeting for this young lad. The influential role William Caldwell was about to play in the life of George Young cannot be overstated, and once this fact became evident it made me want to explore the Caldwells further to see just who William Caldwell was, and why he was set to play such a pivotal role in George's private and professional life?

The first snippet of information I found in respect of William Caldwell, was a listing in the 1856 Scottish Post Office Directory for Glasgow. It appears as - 'Caldwell, William, of James McAulay & Co., house Hillhead.' A cross-check of the Hillhead Directory shows William Caldwell and his family living at No. 8 Bloomfield Place [now known as 44 Gibson Street]. That listing reads - 'Wm. Caldwell, silk manufacturer (of James McAulay & Co., silk manufacturers, printers & commission agents, 18 St. Vincents Lane).' [N.B. - some entries have Lane and some Place - Old Maps shows it as St. Vincents Lane running from North Street parallel to St. Vincent Street which leads to St. Vincents Place]. St Vincents

Place in its day was described as spacious and open with many fine buildings occupied by the likes of the head office for the Bank of Scotland, the New Clydesdale Bank, Phoenix Assurance and the grand but gothic St Columba Church of Scotland which dates from 1770. Interestingly, this church was built to cater to the spiritual needs of a large number of Gaelic speakers from the Highlands and Islands who had come to settle in Glasgow long before the clearances. Because of this, in its day, it was referred to locally as the Highland Cathedral.

While company owner James McAulay was still alive when George first joined the firm, it was not long before he was found going into retirement whereupon ownership of the firm passed to William Caldwell. William's background and qualifications are that he was born in Staines, Middlesex, England the son of Scottish parents who a short time later moved to Dublin as part of their personal religious crusade. William first learned the weaving and printing trade in the Cotton Mills of Ireland alongside his father William Snr. When the Caldwell family first arrived in Dublin, the Cotton Industry was quite buoyant then by the 1840s disaster had struck and the industry went into a fairly rapid decline. This was brought about by several factors: a lack of local coal for the new steam powered machinery, unreliable supply of raw material from the Americas and finally, the overwhelming competition arising from the massive expansion taking place in Manchester, England. By that time William Caldwell Jnr was married and consequently decided to relocate his young family to the thriving industrial hub of Glasgow where cotton and linen were still prospering.

When next I located the Caldwells it's 1851 and William Jnr is now a widower of 48, with him are his two sons William 16, John who is 11 and William Jnr's unmarried sister, Janet Caldwell, 33, is listed as the family's live-in Housekeeper. In Victorian times it was the norm for a spinster sister or aunt to move in with a family following the untimely death of a wife or mother. It was frowned upon if such a void was filled by a single female servant from the local town or village. In the case of William Caldwell, he did have his personal and business reputation to protect. In 1857, shortly after George Young joined James McAulay & Co., William Caldwell remarries at Blythswood, Glasgow, a residential area first opened up by Textile Manufacturer, William Harley around 1802 and is an address which will remain significant to George and his family for almost a century.

William Caldwell's bride was the wealthy Miss Jane Arthur Blackburn a near neighbour at Hillhead. She was living on Great George Street. Jane is related to the Blackburns of Glasgow who were Hosiery & Glove Merchants. Jane and her sister Agnes are described in the 1851 Census as 'Proprietors of Properties', which was an uncommon status for women in those days. It transpires that sundry properties were part of an inheritance they received following the death of their father. This came about because the family solicitor had been unable to successfully trace the whereabouts of their brother, Robert Blackburn whose last known movements were when he set sail for Newfoundland.

No word of his safe arrival was ever received and despite sundry notices being published in the London Gazette and elsewhere as far back as 1836, offering a handsome reward to anyone who proffered information regarding his whereabouts and suggesting that - 'he will hear something to his advantage' no useful information was ever forthcoming. Eventually, the two sisters were granted probate of their father's estate. William Caldwell is yet another example of a Victorian Gentleman marrying well. In the 1861 Census we find the new family unit residing at 10 Royal Terrace, Glasgow, and the new family unit consisted of William, wife Jane, William's son John who is now 21 years of age and Jane's sister Agnes along with one servant.

On the work front, George continues to prosper, and on the personal front George is doing what all would be young Gentlemen of the Victorian Era aspired to, and that is moving in the privileged circles of the upper social class. At this juncture, George's prospects were looking very promising indeed: he was working for a well-respected firm in the business hub of bustling Glasgow, he had made new acquaintances in William and John Caldwell and seemed set on an optimistic career path. Or, so he thought. Little did he realise his dreams were about to be shattered with his father's announcement the family were moving to Kirkcaldy. As we have already learned, this is the occasion when John went into partnership with George Turnbull. Son George was rumoured to be very upset having to decamp with his family; and, all the while his heart remained in Glasgow and he maintained a regular correspondence with both William and John Caldwell, and from family documents it is clear George's sojourn in Kirkcaldy was relatively short-lived.

Moreover, George's memorial states John Caldwell was his most regular correspondent and it was indeed he and not his father, William, who ultimately badgered George about returning to Glasgow. Either way, George would have had to put a persuasive argument to his parents, and they in turn would have most certainly sought assurances from William Caldwell regarding George's employment prospects before agreeing to their young lad's return. George did return, and November 1858 finds him once again working at James McAulay & Co., but it was not until the 1861 April Census there is any inkling as to George's new living arrangements. It shows him residing as a Boarder in the home of a Mrs. Isabella Jarvie at No. 95 North Court, Glasgow. This is just a short walk from his place of work in St Vincents Lane, and for young George, his dream now looks more like becoming a reality!

From here on George's friendship with John Caldwell flourishes and eventually he becomes very closely aligned with the entire Caldwell family. George embraces their family's religious values and more particularly their belief systems. While this is the subject of several anecdotal stories from inside and outside the family the most poignant evidence relating to George and John's shared religious zeal is contained in memorials composed to celebrate the life of two of the Caldwells. The first relates to Robert Caldwell, brother to William Snr which proves the strength of the Caldwell family's religious conviction and boasting an ancestry dating all the

In the end 1850-1950

way back to Oliver Cromwell. The second is a memorial written to acknowledge the life of George's dear friend and eventual business partner, John Robert Caldwell.

In the case of William Jnr's brother, Robert Caldwell [1814-1891] he was one of seven children, born at Clady, in Belfast, Ulster, Ireland to Scottish parents. Both Robert and his brother William were brought up in a Presbyterian home. Their father, William, was a calico printer and their mother, Isabella Hamilton, was from a noted Glasgow family remembered for maintaining very strong religious and commercial connections in that city and to the Cotton Industry more particularly. Robert initially trained as an artist for three years in Dublin, and despite some success with his painting, he gave up that career to devote himself to God's work. Returning to the family home in Glasgow, he first of all worked with the Congregationalists then, after being granted a study scholarship by the London Missionary Society (LMS), he studied Theology at the University of Glasgow. He proved himself a brilliant student, winning a half share of the Robert Peel prize for graduating top of his year.

Robert Caldwell felt his true calling was working in India as a Missionary and after his ordination in Glasgow as a non-conformist minister he set sail for Madras, arriving four months later in the January of 1838, which was just five years after the British East India Company had relaxed its prohibition on Christian evangelism. Robert worked for four years in Madras before transferring from the LMS to the [Anglican] Society for the Propagation of the Gospel (SPG). Robert subsequently formed the view there was good ministry work to be done amongst India's poorest in the more isolated rural communities, so he headed to the SPG's southernmost village of Tirunelveli in Madras Province. He undertook that long and arduous journey on foot - 'to get acquainted with the people and their ideas, manners, and to talk in a way in which I could never expect to do if I travelled in a palanquin or even a cart' - the normal European conveyances. He did not arrive until December 1841, by which time he had covered over 800 miles, walking mostly in the mornings and evenings. Incredibly, the last part of his epic trek was undertaken during the rainy season, and while considered an extraordinary feat by many, this was even more so when it is realised that, back home in Scotland seven years earlier, he had been told by the family physician that he was: 'unlikely to be ever able to bear the trials of a tropical climate'.

It was in Madras Province that Robert made the acquaintance of Charles Mault and his wife, Martha; fellow missionaries under the auspices of the LMS. Martha had a reputation for being an extremely devout and formidable woman, not unexpected given she is a direct descendant of Oliver Cromwell who had been accorded the reputation of a 'religious firebrand'. Robert and the Maults are set to become very close. Charles Mault originally hailed from Shropshire, was ordained in Portsmouth in 1818, a week later he married Martha Mead and one month later the newly-weds left England by ship for the five month journey to Bombay. They both took their missionary calling very seriously and by 1821 Charles had established the first printing press at Nagercoil while Martha had started the first of many schools she establish exclusively catering to Indian girls.

By 1844 the Maults had their own family of five children and as was the case for missionaries in foreign lands, their children were sent away to boarding school in England. These cruel separations combined with frequent outbreaks of Cholera, were part of the inescapable lot for missionaries in India. Disease was not the only issue, it seems the LMS treated their remote missionaries like Robert and the Maults with unchristian disdain. Desperate at one point, Martha wrote to the LMS pointing out that - 'it is five years since my husband had permission to go to England on leave but he is still awaiting a replacement'. But no Christian charity was forthcoming for these out of sight out of mind folks: and so, Martha's plea went unanswered. Unbelievably, they tolerated it for another seven years, when eventually Charles wrote a stern letter to the LMS. Again, there was no response. It was 1854 when matters finally came to a head Charles Mault's health broke down and he and Martha were forced to return home to England.

In the end 1850-1950

Meanwhile, the Mault's eldest daughter Eliza had completed her education and returned to India to work with her parents. It was there she met and married Robert Caldwell in 1844. Raised in Travancore and fluent in the Tamil language, Eliza was not only a very devout Christian, she was also the ideal partner for Robert Caldwell, who had established a reputation as a linguist of note. She joins him in Idaiyanguidi to assist in the advancement of his missionary and linguistic work. Robert Caldwell is credited with launching the Dravidian movement and is recognised as 'a pioneer Dravidian linguist'. His work was posthumously acknowledged in 1968 when a statue of Robert Caldwell was among eight installed on the Marina Beach at Chennai (Madras).

Eliza followed her mother's example in that soon after her arrival at Idaiyangudi; she set about expanding the girls' day school which had been previously established by Robert. It transitioned into a boarding school and, at the same time she took over control of the existing boys' boarding school. Eliza and Robert were a formidable partnership, their reputation grew and much of the financial support required for their work depended on their personal following at home in England and donations from private benefactors. The remainder of their funding came from the SPG, SPCK and other sources in India. One biographer stated - 'Their campaign[ing] continued unabated in the following years while Eliza gave birth to four sons and three daughters.'

At Calcutta in March 1877, after nearly forty years in India preaching and educating and at the age of 63, Robert Caldwell was consecrated Bishop of Madras. Whilst his brother William achieved success in the commercial arena in Glasgow and remained a faithful servant of God and the church, Robert Caldwell stood taller and for him the accolades and awards just kept coming. His biography lists Rt Rev Dr Robert Caldwell, DD, LLD (1814-91) of Glasgow, Missionary Chaplain to the Bishop of Madras (GJT Spencer) 1844-48, LLD (Glasgow) 1857, DD (Durham) 1874, Senior Fellow of the University of Madras, consecrated (SPG) bishop, coadjutor of the Bishop of Madras, 1877. Robert was globally published on a wide range of topics from religion to the antiquities: put simply he had a wonderful mind, was a tireless worker and a high achiever. Not everyone was gracious about Robert's achievements and professional jealousy crept into the ranks of the SPG which by 1883 had become intolerable and drove Robert and Eliza into reclusive retirement at Tuticorin on the south east coast of India.

Robert, through his work and his writings, continued to be a great influence on many lives including his Caldwell family in Scotland, and dare it be said, George Young as well. Eventually, it was left to others in the family and elsewhere to carry on Robert's work because at Kodaikanal in the Palani Hills in 1891, Robert died at the age of 77. Eliza stayed on in India until her passing in 1899. In recognition of their contributions and sacrifices both 'Robert Caldwell and Eliza are buried beneath the chancel of Holy Trinity, Idaiyangudi, the church which he took 33 years to build.' These stories are presented as an important backdrop to the depth of the conviction within this Caldwell Family and to show the powerful influence this would have had on George Young.

What is so arresting to contemplate at this juncture in our story of these three brothers is how divergent their lives really were. For instance, by the age of thirty-five Alexander Donaclift Young was in prison in Australia having been found guilty on three counts of bigamy and worse, Samuel Donaclift Young had already achieved Victorian Gentleman status, aided in no small measure by the support of the Siamese Royal Family and the success achieved with business operations in Colombo, Ceylon. Although George Alexander Young had remained in Scotland, he had conscientiously pursued his ambitions in the Silk Manufacturing Industry, established a great marriage partnership with Penelope and was raising a wonderful family while all the time remaining true to his religious convictions.

So, what is there to know of John Robert Caldwell, George's close and dear friend and eventual business partner?

Not only does this lad share a name with his famous uncle, he shared many of the traits attributed to his uncle who in turn, obviously inherited his religious zeal from his father William Caldwell Snr and his mother Isabebella [sic] Hamilton. The

In the end 1850-1950

Hamiltons of Bonhill and Glasgow were renowned in Glasgow circles for their strong religious views. At the same time, they were hard at work establishing their fortune in the Cotton Industry when it was at its zenith. In fact, Bonhill on the River Leven, where they had their factory, had been a prosperous hub for the cotton manufacture boasting spinning, textile and print works. While John Caldwell's grandfather, William Snr, is best remembered for his missionary work, like the Hamiltons, he also spent many years working in the calico production side of the cotton industry. John's father, William Jnr, like his uncle Robert, gained more recognition as a leader of the independent church movement than for his work in either the silk or cotton trade. So much so that it has been written that John Robert Caldwell was raised in 'the nurture and admonition of the Lord'. From a very young age John was enveloped in his family's passion for the scriptures and had taken part in readings and debates on interpretation. Gatherings of this kind were quite commonplace as mid-Victorian Britain struggled with christian ideology.

The relevance of all this to our Young story is that we will soon learn how such events were the catalyst for blurring the lines between George's work and personal life as he became more and more aligned to the thinking of the Caldwell clan. In a memorial written about John Robert Caldwell there is mention of the family's principal place of worship became the Ewing Place Church. This church stands today and presents as a grand edifice in an otherwise characterless part of Glasgow. It became known as a meeting place for born again Christians which included the faithful like John and George. John taught in the Sunday School there and was also a member of the Young Men's Christian Association. He became fully engaged with lay preaching and often led Evening Services in order to preach the gospel.

John's memorial goes on to say that around 1859-1860 - 'the Caldwells, father and son, came into contact with a noted group of men leading meetings on behalf of the Scottish Baptists. Bible reading sessions were held in the home of William Caldwell, when specific passages of doctrine were debated, and the scriptures were examined. It was at this point that John Caldwell, and his friend George Young, committed themselves to be baptized by immersion.' We should remember that in 1860, George is still only nineteen years of age. He was certainly swept up in the enthusiasm of the Caldwell's religious zeal and has now joined with them in accepting the preaching of noted Sectarian, Gordon Forlong as his own truth. The Caldwell family then took steps to sever ties with the Congregational denomination, and along with their dear friend George Young ' .... began to meet in simplicity, according to the scriptures.'. This memorial to John R Caldwell also bears witness to the maturing fraternity between these two lads.

All these inclusions could suggest too much emphasis has been placed on the religious links between John and George, but it needs to be understood that their friendship was forged out of their very deep spiritual and ideological connection. This was occurring at a time when Glaswegians, like those in congregations right across Britain, found themselves in spiritual limbo in the wake of Charles Darwin's proclamation of 1859. Indeed, Darwin's publication 'On the Origin of the Species' was the sole reason for a period of religious and social upheaval as people began openly debating the absolute truth about creation. On the one hand the christian community much maligned Darwin and his followers for their views and consistently disavowed his argument caught up in the momentum of counter-lobbying by Darwin and his supporters. These were perplexing times for all christians.

John felt more should be done to spread the word, so his next initiative was to begin editing an evangelical magazine he called, 'The Witness', wherein he stridently defended the fundamentals of the Faith. So strong was his passion for evangelising his beliefs that he remained its editor from when the magazine began in 1876 right up until his failing health forced him to stand down in 1914. Not satisfied 'The Witness' would reach as wide an audience as he had hoped, he frequently travelled to countries across Europe to address groups and, like his uncle Robert, John too had numerous editorials and essays published. Shortly before John's passing, one of his disciples, a self-declared admirer of the man as a spiritual leader, penned a piece to share his impressions of John Caldwell. It reads - ' there was something about [his] demeanour and movements which impressed one even more than [his] address - a fact which indicates that a man is more than his message'. Ultimately, it is what has been written about him by those closest to him that best tell us what type of man John Robert Caldwell truly was.

Having gained a firm appreciation of where their friendship was heading it was then time to turn attention to what lay behind their extraordinary business partnership. In this twenty-first century of online research, one begins by inputting a suitable phrase into Google and then hope for the best. Numerous items appeared which proved marginally beneficial, mostly confirming what was already known. However, included in the long list of results was what appeared to be a random synopsis. Had Google got it wrong? No indeed, after closer examination it turned out to be the <u>most</u> valuable snippet of all. Hidden away in a May 2013 blog entitled 'Complicated Evangelical' and under the heading of - 'A life in letters: Brackenridge, Alexander (1854-1919)' - was a story relating to Alexander Brackenridge. At first it did not have any obvious connection; but I decided to read on and was so glad I did. What I discovered was that pot of gold at the end of the rainbow. It is the kind of discovery researchers hope for but so very rarely find. Call it providence, kismet or serendipity; whatever it was that put that blog on my computer screen that day it was propitious for it contained information which would never otherwise be discovered. The blog tied the subject person Alexander Brackenridge to John Caldwell and George Young, to James McAulay & Co. and to Caldwell, Young & Co. across several decades. It is hard to express in words my level of excitement as the story of all three of these men unfolded with the common theme being - religion.

I learned that Alexander Brackenridge had been born in Maybole, Ayrshire 21 Oct 1854 the son of the local Postman and Lay Preacher, John Brackenridge, whose nickname was: 'The Maybole Post'. As I read on, I learned that John Brackenridge would preach on street corners as he walked around the village and his young son, Alexander, was known to join him. On one such occasion the young lad was witnessed giving himself to Christ. By all reports, Alexander was academically bright, and this is substantiated by the

1871 Census, wherein he is just 16 years of age with his occupation listed as Engineer. Initially Alexander had found employment in Stranraer where he joined the Christian Brethren. Then around 1875/76 Alexander returned to Maybole, was instrumental in establishing a local Brethren Assembly there in 1877 just ahead of his next move to Glasgow. It could be said that Alexander was following in the footsteps of his maternal grandfather, Alexander Currie who was a Hosier [someone who works in the stocking manufacturing sector and sells long wool or silk stockings] because in Glasgow he found employment in the silk weaving industry within the firm of James McAulay & Co. Being dislocated from his christian family in Maybole he joined a local fellowship group in Glasgow, the Young Men's Christian Association, and began worshipping at the Assembly in Bridgeton. From this point forward these three young men, John Caldwell, George Young and Alexander Brackenridge struck up an acquaintance which led to a lifetime of shared employment and zealous christian homage.

The blog previously mentioned was written as a memorial to Alexander Brackenridge citing the most important milestones of his long life and in so doing included a detailed account of his employment. To do so the author drew on information contained in the 1888 Glasgow Directory which provided a description of the evolution of the firm of James McAulay & Co into Caldwell, Young & Co. This is that story:

> 'The manufacturing house whose well-known name appears above was founded as far back as the year 1850 in Glasgow, under the style of James McAulay & Co., and nearly five years ago assumed the title under which its operations are now conducted. The present premises (at 178 Buchanan Street) comprising a commodious suite of rooms on the first floor, and constituting offices, salesrooms, and warerooms, with a large and valuable stock, have been occupied for the past two years. Previous to the removal to this convenient address the business had been for twenty years carried on in St. Vincent Place.
>
> The personnel of the present firm includes Messrs. J. R. Caldwell and George Young, two gentlemen of high

standing and recognised ability in connection with the important industrial branch to which their attention is now so vigorously and successfully directed, and both of whom have been connected with the firm for thirty years.

Caldwell, Young & Co. have erected an extensive and well-equipped factory at Larkhall, Lanarkshire, and are the only Scottish silk manufacturers, who have a factory of their own. Their operations are conducted upon a large scale and embrace the manufacture and printing of silk handkerchiefs and other classes of silks for the markets of the world. These goods are made in all classes and qualities, from the best and most expensive down to the commoner and cheaper grades, and their production calls into requisition the services f a large staff of skilled silk-weaving and printing operatives, whose labours are assisted by a valuable plant of improved modern machinery.

Two years ago, Messrs. Caldwell, Young & Co. inaugurated a metropolitan depot at 2, Angel Court, Friday Street, London, E.C., and important branches are also controlled at 10, Lever Street, Manchester, at 6, Faubourg Poissonniere, Paris, and at Rangoon. The house is thoroughly representative if every department of the industry it so well and credibly exemplifies, and its manufactures have acquired an international reputation, leading to a universal and constantly increasing demand. The business is capably and enterprisingly conducted upon principles which have won and retained the confidence of an influential home and export connection, and their wholesale and shipping trade takes effect directly and indirectly in every quarter of the globe.'

What a sensational find!

Although the blog was intended as a lasting tribute to Alexander Brackenridge: the good community citizen, the hard working and loyal employee and declared christian, in telling Alexander's story we also gained a very precious insight into the business reputation of John and George. Indeed, in normal circumstances it is nigh on impossible to learn anything of employees or companies of this era as records simply do not exist. In the case of Caldwell, Young & Co there are some records from a time after the firm was sold but the documents are not open access. Certainly nothing else has ever come to light linking Alexander, John and George and given the most important ingredient of any successful business is its people, there is no doubt that employing Alexander Brackenridge was the soundest hiring decision John and George ever made.

I know it was their hiring decision because William Caldwell Snr had already stood down as the head of James McAulay & Co in 1865. As part of the McAulay succession plan, 1865 was the year when John and George formally confirmed their business partnership and assumed joint control of the Silk Manufacturing operations of James McAulay & Co. From all known records it would appear they continued to trade as James McAulay & Co. until after William Snr's passing in 1870; probably out of deference due this family patriarch. But why did John decide to partner with George Young? Well John's only sibling was his brother, William Henry Caldwell [1835-1920], who obviously had no interest in the silk manufacturing business. Brother William had other plans which saw him departing Glasgow for London in 1870 where he rose to a very senior position as a Merchant within the prestigious British East India Company. As to William's character, it is interesting to note that he was appointed guardian for his uncle Robert's children while they were at boarding school in England.

Curious as to why George felt that Silk Manufacturing would provide a sound career future, I decided to learn a little more. I discovered that the mid-point of the nineteenth century was a time when the textile industry was thriving in Scotland, but it was cotton and linen and not silk which were at the forefront of Scotland's manufacturing expansion. In fact, the Silk Industry was so small by comparison it is reputed to have employed less than a thousand people while Cotton boasted 50,000 and Linen 26,000 employees respectively. Then I turned to the 1921 publication of Sir Frank Warner, K.B.E. [1862-1930] entitled 'The Silk Industry of the United Kingdom - Its Origin and Development' in which he cites two towns noted for silk factories in Scotland; Paisley and Glasgow. He also makes the point that as far as the Silk Industry was concerned there was initially a predominance of hand-loom weaving in Larkhall, a circumstance which will come to prominence a little later in this story. Warner further states that 'Two of the Glasgow silk manufacturing firms whose names appear in the Glasgow Directory for 1860 may be especially mentioned. James McAulay and Co., who in 1848 were drugget manufacturers, and who started their silk trade in 1850, were succeeded in business by Caldwell, Young and Co., who are at present the principal silk manufacturers in Scotland, and have their factory at Larkhall, Lanarkshire. The business of Alex. Henry and Co., makers of silk gossamers, survives, and is now carried on as a branch of Caldwell, Young and Company, Ltd., whose primary business is the manufacture of mufflers and handkerchiefs.' [N.B. - drugget was a coarse fabric made of wool, silk or linen on a cotton warp and was used for rugs, tablecloths and the like.]

Clearly, Messrs Caldwell and Young were making smart business decisions in a fickle marketplace which had transitioned from burgeoning Industrial Revolutionary Britain to a post-industrial society where producing ideas was the new growth sector of the national economy. As one facet of their business strategy George and John capitalised on the goodwill of James McAulay & Co. by continuing to trade under that name right up until 1883/84. This is when the first entry for the firm of Caldwell, Young & Co. appears in a Glasgow Trade Directory. John and George had finally decided to stand tall and tell the world they had arrived in their own right. Whether to hedge their bets, avoid confusion or out of respect for the old firm this is how that first listing appeared:

> 'Caldwell, Young & Co. (late Jas. McAulay & Co.), silk manufacturers and printers, 13 St. Vincent Place'

This move was probably precipitated by the fact they were formulating ideas for further expanding the business, which they obviously wished to occur under their own names. Plans were finalised, and three years later step one was to establish a second premises at 178 Buchanan Street, Glasgow. This was an area of central Glasgow which had recently been transformed from a street of merchants' villas, small holdings and sundry trade workshops to a street of fine Victorian buildings including the Glasgow Stock Exchange which opened in 1877. 'The street acquired a reputation for elegance and specialty shopping which continues to this day.' An example of this can be found in the Stewart & McDonald building where jeweller, Robert Stewart, conducted his business. Stewart held Royal Warrants as Goldsmith, Silversmith and Jeweller to Queen Victoria. It was not long before grand Victorian multi-storey buildings lined both sides of Buchanan Street and it became <u>the</u> address in Glasgow for businesses of distinction.

On the practical side, there was another advantage of this address for Caldwell, Young & Co. and it lies in the fact that Buchanan Street was very close to the Queen Street Railway Station. Built in 1842 and redesigned and expanded in 1878, to cater to the increase in traffic due to the reinvigoration of the Buchanan Street precinct, this railway station served Greater Glasgow and was the terminus for several services radiating out across Northern Scotland. It was ideal for those wishing to shop in Glasgow and for the distribution of finished goods, but, more relevant still, it provided direct access to and from the port on the Clyde for the movement of the raw materials required for silk production, arriving from foreign parts, as well as the distribution and export of finished goods.

With their business riding the crest of a wave, even greater expansion was on their minds, and this is what ultimately connects Caldwell, Young & Co with Larkhall. The best clue available for the timing of this move to Larkhall was found in an article in the Lanarkshire Upper Ward Examiner for Saturday 3 May 1879. So newsworthy was this to the local community, an abridged version of this article also appeared in the Alloa Advertiser on the same day. It came at a time when the general employment landscape was somewhat depressed and many of the hand loom weavers in the district were unemployed. One could also speculate that the women of Larkhall and surrounds would have taken great comfort from this story too as they were now comprising the greater proportion of silk factory employees.

'LARKHALL

> THE WEAVING TRADE. - The silk trade of this district, which has been in a state of unprecedented depression for a considerable time back shows little or no signs of improvement. In the weaving district around Larkhall, the number of idle hands (engaged almost wholly in the silk trade) is not far short of a thousand, and it is believed that it will be a month or two yet before there is any improvement. Amidst the general depression which exists, it is somewhat cheering to learn that Messrs. McAulay & Co., silk manufacturers, Glasgow, are making arrangements for the building of a Silk Factory here, which as an additional source of employment, will prove a great benefit to the place. We understand the work is to be carried on by hand and steam power, and it is expected to commence in the month of August. Building operations will be started immediately.'

Whilst the Company continued to maintain a presence in Glasgow, these ambitious partners were about to take a great leap of faith and build a brand new factory operation at Larkhall. Why choose Larkhall? Well, probably for two main reasons. Firstly, it was widely recognised that Larkhall already had a workforce of skilled loom operators. Secondly, it had gained the reputation as a stronghold for Sectarianism; a beliefs system which both Caldwell and Young subscribed to. So, with guaranteed access to a community of skilled workers with shared religious values it would have been a logical choice given there was also local infrastructure in the way of coal mining to power their steam driven machinery. As we already know, Caldwell, Young & Co. charged Alexander Brackenridge with the responsibilities of Operations Manager at this new factory, and he repaid their trust by making their dream a reality. The factory operation thrived, and at the height of its success it employed over 240 hands; which was surely a significant proportion of the town's available workforce.

As a measure of their success, and as a tribute to the esteem they had engendered across the community, there are several funeral notices that appeared in the Hamilton Advertiser mentioning the deceased person's association with Caldwell, Young & Co. as a very proud and positive part of their lives. One such Death Notice from April 1897 was for John Scott of Victoria Street, Larkhall, and it identifies him as 'for many years with Messrs. Caldwell, Young & Co. Ltd.'. Another for Mr James Longmuir from February 1917 describes him as 'A native of Strathaven, he was a handloom weaver to trade, and after being with various firms came to Larkhall, where he had been in the employment of Messrs. Caldwell, Young & Co. Ltd. silk factory for 33 years. He was foreman in the beaming and twisting department, and as such came in daily contact with the workers, with whom he was highly esteemed and respected.' James Longmuir would have been one of the earliest employees hired to work at the Larkhall factory and personal remembrances such as these say as much about the firm and the people responsible for its management as they do about the deceased.

Everything went along quite smoothly for a while; 1886 saw them establish their London Office, followed shortly afterwards by a branch operation in Manchester, a known thriving cotton weaving centre. Other offices followed: one in the fashion capital of the world, Paris, with another in the exotic city of Rangoon. Paris made complete sense given it was and is the fashion epicentre of the world and where designers would have been demanding quality silk fabric and accessories. To the casual reader, Rangoon would appears random; but realising George's young brother Samuel Donaclift Young had worked there in the 1870s, received a personal appointment by the King to act as Consul, it made perfect sense to utilise this entré to develop a new export opportunity with an important and established British trading partner. After all, new markets provided the opportunities required to account for the increased production from the bigger and more efficient Larkhall factory.

By 1889 Messrs Caldwell, Young & Co was not only firmly entrenched into the commercial life of Larkhall but into the community as well. John Caldwell used his personal finances to set up and support the Young Men's Christian Association and its Library. He also paid for guest speakers to visit for lecture evenings. One such evening lecture was the subject of an advertisement introducing the Rev Mr. Turnbull of Lesmahagow as an upcoming Guest Speaker. The Rev Turnbull's topic was to be 'Sweethearts and Wives'. Needless to say, the community notice which appeared after this lecture, stated it was very popular with the locals. The reporter wrote that Mr J.A. Beattie in his introduction of the Rev Turnbull suggested '.... The very large audience assembled on the present occasion, would justify steps being taken to have a series of lectures in winters to come. He asked them to give close attention, as he felt sure something would be said of interest of all assembled - married or unmarried.' 'The rev. gentleman then proceeded, in an interesting and graphic manner, to deal with the many phases connected with sweethearting and the married life. Not only did he deal with the humorous sides of the question, but gave sound, practical advice to those married and unmarried. His closing advice, -'Get married as soon as you can do so.'

Whilst the lecture was obviously appreciated by the residents of Larkhall it affords a twenty-first century reader a window into village life in Victorian Britain especially given these further comments regarding the evening's entertainment. 'During the evening Messrs Ramsay, Hunter and Hugh Cowen added in no small measure to the entertainment by rendering several solos in a manner which brought forth repeated encores from the audience. Miss Frame ably accompanied the soloists on the organ. On the motion of Mr. Beattie, a hearty vote of thanks was given Mr. Turnbull for the treat offered them. Rev. Mr. McCallum, before closing the meeting proposed a vote of thanks to the chairman and to the others who had contributed to the gathering, which was heartily responded to.' Oh! To have been a fly on the wall that night.

Other Larkhall community meetings are listed in the local newspaper from time to time, most of which are of a more general nature, such as one regarding the changing of the date for the Larkhall Fair Holiday to a date in July to coincide with the Glasgow holidays. Another on 22 January 1889 relates to a Merchants' Committee meeting attended by 'Mr. Lightbody, for Caldwell, Young & Co, silk factory' where a letter was read out on behalf of the company submitted by its author Mr. A.G. Blackburn who appears in the 1881 Census as 'Manager - Silk Manufacturer'. This gentleman is listed as the cousin of John R. Caldwell in 1871 Census, and nephew to Jane A. Caldwell nee Blackburn in 1881 Census. The Caldwells, like the Youngs, were developing a reputation for keeping it all in the family. I am pleased to report that the town vote was carried unanimously.

John and George were also on the same page when it came to innovation and technology. Caldwell, Young & Co.'s Larkhall factory was steam powered which could account for their reasoning to position themselves on land in relative proximity to the water resources of the Avon River. Likewise, lighting in factories had been an issue since the dawn of the Industrial Revolution. Initially, factory owners were forced to wrestle with the dangers and dullness of whale oil lamps, then gas lamplight but it was not until 1879 when Thomas Edison invented the electric light bulb that workplaces around the world were set to see a revolution in illumination. In Britain in 1882 Parliament legislated for electricity supply companies to be established. Investment lagged and progress was slow until 1888 when the initial Act was amended to reinvigorated investment. However, another three years of planning and construction would be required before the London Electric Supply Corporation would fire up its Deptford Power Station in 1891. This was a London first, but Scotland was set to quickly follow. From the archives of The Glasgow Evening Post we learn that Larkhall too was embracing this latest innovation.

> 'ELECTRIC LIGHT AT LARKHALL. - Mr John Bennie, electrical and general engineer, Star Engine Works, Glasgow, has just completed an electric light installation for Messrs. Caldwell, Young & Co., at their Clydesdale silk factory Larkhall. The installation is upon the low-pressure system. A special feature of the installation is that in the event of the factory engine breaking down or being under repair the motive power of the installation can be utilised for working the factory.'

What about the looms they used? It would appear that loom evolution would be somewhat slower. Rev Edmund Cartwright had invented the power loom way back in 1785; it was steam powered, mechanically operated and remained in common use until 1889 when the Americans made a major innovative step forward with the invention of the Northrop Loom. The industry was set to endorse this fully automatic power loom, which was a very smart machine even by modern standards, especially considering its many in-built labour saving and production enhancing features. For instance, when a warp thread broke it stopped; when a shuttle ran out of thread it loaded a new one without the need to stop the machine. These innovations would have translated into great savings for factory owners like Caldwell, Young & Co. because as a consequence staffing levels could potentially move from one person per machine to one person for up to sixteen or more machines. As grand as it sounds, it will be sometime before these new looms were installed in Britain.

As demand for silk commodities increased it seems it was now George Young's turn to be 'Right Place Right Time'. Silk thread and silk fabrics of all kinds were being demanded right across the clothing sector - fabrics, gloves, hats, hosiery and umbrellas were now all being offered in silk. Towards the end of the Victorian Era colouring and dying techniques were improved too. There were now bright blacks and a full range of colours being demanded by High Street shoppers for everything the fashion conscious of the day could possibly desire. The demand was endless and not restricted to ladies' fashion either. Peter Robinson's Men's Outfitters on fashionable Oxford Street in London can be found advertising, in the London Evening Standard, their new range of Rich Silk Undershirts. The silk arm of the textile industry was experiencing unprecedented demand and Caldwell, Young & Co. with their international connections were well positioned to capitalise on the popularity of their production worldwide.

Given the catalogue of successes enjoyed by the company so far it was hard to understand why opposition firms were failing. One is left to surmise their competitor's operations were either not as well run or failed to move with the times. Or, were Caldwell & Young formidable business opponents? One such competitor with operations in nearby Motherwell and Glasgow was forced to close as per this next story which was printed in The Motherwell Times on Saturday 3 Mar 1894. It read: 'work will be suspended at the end of the present week for an indefinite period. The stoppage is due to the dullness of trade and upwards of 120 girls will be thrown out of employment....'. Sadly, a similar notice was posted for the lay-off of staff at this firm's original mill at Govan in Glasgow.

The 1890s were rolling along quite positively and life could not have been better, which makes the devastation caused by the fire of Thursday 15 April 1897 all the more acute. The total destruction of the Caldwell, Young & Co.'s factory at Larkhall was so newsworthy that media in Lincolnshire, Hampshire, South Wales, Wiltshire and London along with others in Belfast and Tyrone in Ireland all printed stories about the fire. They all told a similar story, that 'The extensive silk factory of Messrs Caldwell Young & Co of Larkhall has been totally destroyed by fire. The damages are estimated at £20,000 and 250 hands will be thrown out of employment. The workmen's houses narrowly escaped being consumed also.' The piece printed in The Dundee Advertiser carried additional information which stated the fire had broken out late on Wednesday night at the factory in Miller Street, Larkhall. It started in the winding and faking department which occupied a two-storey block of buildings, and the flames were fanned by a strong north-westerly wind which caused the fire to spread rapidly. The fire engulfed the top part of the building, then spread to the warehouse and then down the side 'forming a square [of fire] and completely gutting the weaving shed'.

The Hamilton Fire Brigade were first to arrive on the scene and it seems they were ill-equipped to deal with such an intense inferno in a multi-storey building. Despite the factory's proximity to the Avon River it was reported their pumps and hoses were found inadequate for the task at hand; not to mention the probable lack of suitable high rise ladders. The local newspaper says the Larkhall Volunteer Brigade arrived shortly after their Hamilton counterparts and immediately swung into action. According to all the reports, the fire had a solid hold by the time any help reached the scene, even thought it was reported both fire services 'speedily arrived'. In the end, all efforts were concentrated on saving the engine house and dynamo shed. This was successful, and they also managed to save several of the workers cottages which for a time appeared in imminent danger. One news report recounted - 'Nothing was saved from the conflagration but the engine house and some silk. There were nearly 300 looms, which gave employment to 250 hands, mostly girls.' With the estimate of damage sitting at £20,000 it is most fortunate for George Young and John Caldwell that they were fully insured.

Matters moved quite swiftly from that point because only a month later, on the 14 May 1897, both the Hamilton Herald and the Lanarkshire Weekly News printed some welcome and uplifting news for the silk factory workers of Larkhall. The factory was going to be rebuilt. Just a few lines buried among curious community notices for the upcoming Horse Races, The Football Club, Parish Council announcements and the statistics for the Penny Savings Bank for the previous Monday, can be found this seemingly important news.

> 'REBUILDING SILK FACTORY. - On Wednesday, operations were begun at the Silk Factory which was recently destroyed by fire, to enable the rebuilding of the structure to be gone on with as soon as possible. It is to be hoped that this will be speedily accomplished, and that the workers presently idle may soon be able to get started again.'

Construction proceeded with haste and only four months later, in the September of 1897, there was more promising news reported in the Hamilton Advertiser -

> 'LARKHALL
>
> THE SILK FACTORY. - The work of rebuilding the Silk Factory is being proceeded with as quickly as possible, and before long a number of the unemployed workers will be fully engaged.'

Fortunately for Caldwell, Young & Co this was not the single event which defined the end of their business. All the while they still had their original Glasgow site plus Buchanan Street, and they maintained operations from there in the interim. The last of the Post Office Directories accessed for this story relates to the year 1911/12 and therein can be found an entry showing they have not only survived the calamitous fire they have signed up for the new communications technology as well. Their listing reads:

> 'Caldwell, Young, & Co., Ltd., Silk Manufacturers and Printers, Registered Office, 178 Buchanan Street, Telegraph address, "Foulard", Glasgow; telephone Nos. - National 701; P.O. Box 1307.'

In that same 1911 Directory John R. Caldwell is listed residing at 'Courtallam', Upper Helensburgh, which is on the north shore of the Firth of Clyde to the west of Glasgow. This is where he remained absorbed in his evangelical pursuits. George Young is now residing at Blythswood, 17 Monreith Road, Newlands, Glasgow. Whilst both men have the company name alongside their own it is not known if they still played an active role in day to day affairs or whether this was done purely out of respect for these men and their shared history with the firm. It would seem reasonable to assume they were both enjoying their later years. George was known to relish spending time with family at their holiday home 'Stonefield' on Ardberg Road in Rothesay on the Isle of Bute. Some years ago I travelled to Bute in company with Young descendants and we discovered 'Stonefield' still stands today, it is a most charming property overlooking the waters of Rothesay Bay offering an abundance of fresh sea air, peace and tranquillity. Down the years it was a family favourite holiday destination and for George it would have provided a welcome relief from the noisy clatter and bustle of the factory floor, not to mention the pressure of business in the age of ever increasing competition.

Sadly, as the years marched on John Caldwell was reported to be in failing health and continued to decline. At one point in 1905, he was thought to be so poorly, that on 20th November, just before he was due to leave for France, some fifty-two brethren, presuming he would not survive his intended pilgrimage, 'met him in a room of the Christian Institute ...... Thinking they might not have another occasion, they desired to confirm their love and return thanks for the help he had given.' He did survive that journey and for a time afterwards he made 'somewhat of a recovery' but his deterioration then became more rapid, and it is said he was 'losing many of his faculties'. Sadly, he endured many months of pain and weakness leading up to his passing on the 14th January 1917. His epitaph reads 'He had been a liberal giver, a wise counsellor, a devoted servant, and a fearless minister of the truth and defender of the faith.' John R. Caldwell was 77 years of age.

Six months prior, George and Penelope had celebrated their Golden Wedding Anniversary with a splendid dinner party gathering where George paid a heartfelt romantic tribute to his dear wife Penelope Galt Renfrew. Notices of their milestone were printed in the Social Column of several newspapers including the Lanarkshire Daily Record on Thursday 20 July 1916 and the Hamilton Advertiser on Saturday 15th July. One example reads:

> 'Mr & Mrs George Young, Blythswood, 17 Monreith Road, Newlands, Glasgow, have completed the fiftieth year of their wedded life. Mr. Young who belongs to a Montrose shipping family, is a member of the firm of Messrs. Caldwell, Young & Co. silk manufacturers, while his wife is a daughter of the late Mr. Alexander Renfrew cotton spinner, Bridgeton.'

One year on and the Dundee Evening Telegraph is printing quite a different story:

> 'Mr George Young, Blythswood, Monreith Road, Newlands, Glasgow, has died at his coast residence, Bromlea, Largs, in his 76th year. Mr. Young who belonged to a Montrose and Kirkcaldy shipping family, was a member of the firm of Messrs. Caldwell, Young & Co. Limited, silk manufacturers, Glasgow and London. Mr. Young and his wife, by whom he is survived, celebrated their golden wedding in July of last year.'

Other tributes in a similar vein appeared in the Lanarkshire Daily Record and the Hamilton Advertiser. The light had finally gone out for these two incredible friends, they had shared over fifty years working and worshiping together, and in the end died just seven months apart. What a remarkable and enduring friendship they created and nurtured; and in return it undoubtedly gave strength to each of them. They had much to be thankful for, and would have rested easy, content in the knowledge, that they lived long enough to see the firm they built, now styled Caldwell, Young & Co. Ltd., prosper and provide many proud moments. Now they could go their rest, knowing full well the next generation were at the helm, the ship was pointing high, and business was smooth sailing.

After placing George Alexander Young, business-man and friend under the microscope, we now know that, just like his key ancestors, George's commercial and personal dealings were conducted with a high degree of integrity, morality and fairness as well as being financially rewarding. While we also have our answers to the questions posed in relation to the middle child issue and the comparison of George's life outcome to that of his brothers especially Alexander; this is only one part of George's story: there is so much more to share about George and his descendants. Their achievements are quite remarkable, and for many there is a wealth of evidence relating to the main ancestral theme of the Young family: their legacy of seafaring. Despite the fact George was not a seafarer himself, his favourite pastime was spending time with family by the waters of Rothesay Bay, either at Largs or on Bute. From this it is a given the family legacy was not lost or forgotten, and by exploring George Alexander Young the husband and father, and then looking into the lives of his children and grandchildren, it was heartening how this family had continued that seafaring legacy all the way from Alexander Snr [1750-1817] in Scotland to a great-great-great-grandson Robert Tyrrell Young in America. Some family members flirted with the sea, others married into maritime families, most travelled on the new generation of ocean liner at every opportunity and one rose to the pinnacle of this profession.

It is now time to take an extraordinary journey with George and Penelope Young and explore the path taken by their children and grandchildren.

When I began my research into George and Penelope's relationship and family what struck me first and foremost was the amount of memorabilia surviving to this day in various family holdings. It has been my privilege to meet with folk from right across the world who have been extremely generous in allowing access to all manner of material held dear, and from this experience alone it is right to say categorically that George and Penelope were greatly loved and admired. At the same time, these remnants of their lives show that they set a fine example for their children in terms of what constitutes a good marriage, what family life should be and how to cherish such a very special partnership. George and Penelope brought thirteen children into the world, ten of whom survived them, which is an amazing achievement in itself; and, if George's Golden Wedding Anniversary tribute to Penelope is anything to go by, there is little doubt he absolutely adored his wife. Being the avid student of the scriptures that George was, perhaps in this George took his cue from Ephesians 5:25 which says 'Husbands, love your wives as Christ loved the church and gave himself up for her'. From George's own words in a little booklet entitled 'Believers Pathway' he makes it clear that not only was his Faith important and shared, he strived hard to be a loving and supportive husband and a present and encouraging father.

So, then the question became: what did Penelope Galt Renfrew bring to their marriage partnership? Apart from a loving heart and her faith, I learned she already understood the value of resilience and perseverance. While growing up, her family life had been punctuated with success and failure. She witnessed her parents suffer the highs and lows of business and the cruelty of reliance on international markets for the supply of raw materials, which would have made her an ideal partner for George, who was exposed to all the same business challenges. Penelope was born 1845 the eldest daughter of Alexander Renfrew of Glasgow and Penelope Galt Young [a different and unconnected Young family] of Stewarton, Ayrshire. Her father, Alexander, was a Cotton Manufacturer in Glasgow. The last listing in any directory for Alexander's business appeared in the Post Office Directory for 1857-58 where it was described as 'a wadding and girth manufacturer and cotton-yarn twister, 103 Duke Street, house 173 George Street' in Glasgow'. Alexander could not be found in Scotland in the 1860s; and it was only after perusal of his half-brother's Will that it became clear he was abroad for a time. Whilst his cousin's business of Andrew Renfrew & Co. had survived, and was still trading a decade on, clearly Alexander had experienced great misfortune because he not only lost his business but was now in paid employment as a Salesman Rope & General.

To put his dilemma into perspective, Alexander Renfrew had begun his business in that 1830s-60s boom time for the cotton weaving industry in Scotland; in fact, at its peak Scotland boasted almost 200 cotton weaving mills. Unfortunately for Alexander Renfrew and many other mill operators, from the early 1860s onwards the Industry went into rapid decline as a direct consequence of a lack of supplies of raw cotton from America due to the outbreak of Civil War in that country. Penelope's father was one of a large number of mill owners in Glasgow who fell victim to this collapse. This forced countless numbers of unemployed mill-workers to seek alternative employment, and Alexander, like so many, would have been forced to take whatever job was available. Times were tough and whilst Penelope's father persevered the family never really recovered. Evidence for this was found in the probate file for Alexander's Will of 1880 declaring an estate value of £48.9s.7d.: a meagre sum indeed. From that time forward Penelope's mother spent her remaining years living with either Penelope and George or with Jeannie Young Johnston, Penelope's married sister. Amazingly, her mother outlived her father by two decades, during which time she proved to be a frugal Scot as probate of her Will of 1900 valued her estate at £949.0s.8d.

George and Penelope's marriage partnership began in Glasgow on 19 July 1866. The newlyweds first home was a flat in Gordon Chambers, a grand Victorian Building at 82 Mitchell Street. Later they moved to 362 St Vincents Street, where they remained until around 1872/73 when the family moved into 'Bellevue Cottage' in Clydesdale Street, Hamilton. Of the thirteen children born between 1867 and 1887 eleven survived to adulthood. Their eighth child was a daughter they named Jean Johnston Young: sadly, Jean died at the age of 18 months. Infant son James, Penelope's eleventh baby was born on the 16 September and was buried on the 17 September 1884. As to day to day family life for the children in this Young household there is no doubt they were more fortunate than most youngsters in middle class Victorian households, many of whom were raised by nannies, rarely spoken to by their parents and were frequently described as living 'sad, redundant and affection-less existences'. Winston Churchill [1874-1965] once said he could 'count the times he had been hugged by his mother' as a child. On the contrary, the profusion of family photographs featuring George and Penelope with their children show this family very much together, relaxed, smiling and looking anything but sad.

Of their three daughters who grew to adulthood, the eldest was Penelope Renfrew Young [1869-1947], affectionately known to one and all as 'Nellie'. Penelope was very close to her mother and remained living in the family home until she was 31 years of age, no doubt kept busy helping her mother raise her siblings. This was a role often taken on by the eldest daughter. As a result, this mother and daughter definitely shared a very special bond and it was Nellie who was by her mother's side when she passed away. Eventually. in June 1900 Nellie did marry Manufacturers' Agent, Alfred John Hobson and the newly-weds settled into married life in a property at 62 Cadder Street, Pollockshields, Glasgow where they remained for decades. They had three children, a daughter who died in infancy in 1903 and two surviving sons. As a Manufacturers' Agent Alfred travelled widely and on one occasion in 1899 he was found returning from a visit to Quebec on board the *Cambroman* bound for Liverpool. In 1934 both Penelope and Alfred take a family vacation to visit their married son Alfred who was now living in the USA. They departed Glasgow for Boston on board the *Tuscania*, then returned home on board the *Caledonia*, once again voyaging from Boston and disembarking in Glasgow on 6 August.

But it was Penelope's son, Alfred Gardner Hobson born 1901, who would be the first in this family to move to America where he became involved in the Shipbuilding Industry. After serving an apprenticeship as a Ships Carpenter in Scotland his ambition carried him all the way to Marine Engineer. At the time he completed his apprenticeship in Glasgow the economy of post-WW1 Britain was depressed and in decline, so Alfred decided to try his luck in the USA. He sailed for America in 1925, disembarking at Ellis Island in New York, before travelling on to the shipyard district of Norfolk County in Massachusetts. There he found the shipbuilding industry and the national economy were strong indeed. It truly was the Roaring 20s as the Shipbuilding Industry there was literally roaring, supported by the Jones Act, a federal law requiring all goods shipped between US ports must be carried on ships built, owned and operated by United States citizens or permanent residents.

Alfred settled in the city of Quincy where the biggest shipbuilding firm was NASSCO, National Steel and Shipbuilding Company, a division of General Dynamics Corporation. At that time the GD Corporation owned and operated three shipyards across the US in San Diego, Norfolk and Mayport. The GD Corporation's NASSCO Shipyards were the biggest employer in Quincy. This is also where Alfred met and married a Scottish lass, Catherine Garvie Campbell in 1925. After two very rewarding years, Alfred recognised that the US offered the better employment and life opportunities, and so in 1927 he gave up his Scottish citizenship to become a naturalized American. In 1928, Alfred and Catherine took their young family on holiday to Scotland on board the *Cameronia*. Alfred forged a successful career with NASSCO and when he decided to retire, he and Catherine settled on Staten Island, New York. Today, shipbuilding is no more, but the 113 acre Fore River shipyard site in Quincy where Alfred spent his entire working life is now the subject of a $US1.6 Billion redevelopment project.

Penelope and Alfred's son George Young Hobson, born February 1906, began an apprenticeship as a Seaman although it would seem he was not destined to spend his life at sea. The last record showing his occupation as Seaman was in 1924 when he was discovered sailing as a passenger on board the *Columbia* from New York to Glasgow. Perhaps on that occasion George was taking a vacation with his brother and met Alfred's fiancé. On the manifest George gave his address as 62 Cadder Street, Pollockshields, his parents' home. Little else is known about

George Young Hobson except he did not follow a life at sea, nor spend his life in Scotland, rather he moved to London where for the majority of his life he worked as a chauffeur. George is known to have married four times between 1931 and 1979, with various Electoral Rolls showing his residential address in some of the most fashionable parts of London: like Chelsea, Kensington and Fulham.

Next was daughter, Mary Donaclift Young [1875-1950], so named in honour of George's mother. Mary married James Love MacKay, the Superintendent of a Ladies Mantle Factory. They were wed at the Windsor Hotel in Glasgow on 7 Jul 1899 and then settled in Govan a suburb of Glasgow. They had one child, a son, James Donaclift MacKay in 1911. James married in Essex, England in 1937 before sailing to South Africa to make a life there in Kynsna, Western Cape Province. There are no online records of their son James ever returning to visit his parents in Scotland, and sadly, Mary and James likewise never visited South Africa. Mary and James died within a few months of each other in 1950, and despite their Wills being sealed, there was a legal notice discovered in The Scotsman for Saturday 10 Jun 1950 stating that probate for Mary Donaclift MacKay amounted to £7,109 but oddly no beneficiary was mentioned. From what is known from within the family there was no rift here as several of Mary's American cousins corresponded with both the parents and their son and are known to have visited with those in South Africa.

The last surviving daughter of George and Penelope Young was their youngest child, Margaret Agnes Stewart Young [1887-1936], or Madge to all who knew and loved her. Madge was a strikingly attractive woman; and, if surviving family photographs and stories are any guide, she was a free spirit enjoying all the female freedoms prevailing in post-Victorian Britain. In 1915 she married the suave John Fullerton, affectionately known as Jack. Jack grew up in what could be classified as upper middle class circumstances. His father, James Fullerton, was the owner and operator of the Merksworth Shipyards up the Clyde on the River Cart at Paisley. John Fullerton Snr, Jack's grandfather had begun building steel ships in these shipyards in 1866: the first vessel launched was the *Kyles* in 1872 from Yard No. 11. That

In the end 1850-1950

vessel is still seaworthy today and is part of a live exhibit within the Scottish Maritime Museum in Glasgow. Fullerton's shipyards specialised in building smaller ships such as coastal steamers, tugs and trawlers and achieved quite a reputation by the time John Snr died in 1905. The business John Fullerton & Co then passed to his son James who successfully ran the shipyard until his passing in 1925. The Merksworth Shipyards launched their last coastal freighter in 1928 after which the yards were closed, and the buildings demolished.

As a measure of the success, prosperity and social status the Fullerton family enjoyed it has been written the Fife Family, of Fairlie, shipbuilding royalty in Scotland, were closely associated with the Fullerton family – personally and in business. William Fife III, born 1857, left school at the tender age of 14 to take up a shipwright apprenticeship under the watchful eye of his father William Fife II in the family shipyards of William Fife & Sons, which had been established by William III's grandfather, often described as a natural genius of ship design. William III also spent time working in the Paisley yards of John Fullerton & Co. learning about composite construction before being appointed Manager of Culzean Shipbuilding Company founded by the Marquis of Ailsa. When his father, William II, took control of the family shipyards he took it in a new direction. First up, he built the famous paddle-steamer *Industry* but refused to build more, stating he wanted to build sailing boats, yachts, which were 'fast and bonnie'. His first real success came with the *Stella* in 1849 and with business booming on the back of the wealth created by the Industrial Revolution both he and the business were set to prosper.

Willian Fife III followed in his father's footsteps and went on to establish an international reputation for his racing yacht designs. His clientele included European Royalty and Australia's wealthy. In all, he designed over 600 yachts, for the rich and famous who made up the cruising and racing fraternity. Clients included the King of Spain. It is said that Fife was able to perfect his hull designs by utilising the 'steam hammer' designed by fellow Scot, James Naismyth. Maritime historians telling the story of the Fifes of Fairlie and their success have made special comment that the villagers of Fairlie were superb craftsmen.

Likewise, Clyde maritime historian, James Pottinger, in his book 'Clyde Built Ships' also makes special mention of the 'teams of talented craftsmen at work ...' at John Fullerton's shipyards.

There is another thrilling connection here which is incredible to have established. It runs like this - George's eldest son is John Ellis Young and one of John's very best friends was Sir Thomas Lipton of Lipton Tea fame. Now, William Fife III is most famous for his designing of racing yachts, and in particular for two he designed for Sir Thomas Lipton: Shamrock I and Shamrock III which competed in the Americas Cup Challenge. So close was the abovementioned friendship between Sir Thomas and John Young that we will shortly see where John Ellis Young accompanied Sir Thomas Lipton to America on more than one occasion when the America's Cup challenge races were being sailed. So highly respected was William III in American yacht racing circles that the New York Times ran a feature on his life on 12 August 1944 to commemorate his passing and to remind readers of that particular Scot's outstanding yachting accomplishments. Even more recently, in 2004, William III was inducted into the America's Cup Hall of Fame. William III also received an Order of the British Empire in the 1919 New Year Honours.

So we continue to see how these Young descendants never lost their passion for all things maritime, which continues to reward them in new and different ways. They are also found living the Victorian dream: mixing with the rich and famous and for those whose adult lives were spent in early post-Victorian decades they too grasped every opportunity to become acquainted with the new world order.

This brings us to a discussion of the eight surviving sons of George and Penelope Young. What I have come to know about these lads is extensive, with the standout feature of their lives being they matured to be an eclectic group of individuals with divergent interests. One could rightly speculate their boundless confidence and self-assurance would have made family roundtable conversations lively and challenging. These lads, like their sisters, grew up in the security and pride of their seafaring history bolstered by a solid education, and with parents who encouraged them to follow a career path of their own choosing. Perhaps George was forever grateful for the fact his father afforded him that opportunity. While some of George's children and grandchildren were involved in the family Silk Manufacturing business others did pursue maritime careers. What has emerged so far and will continue to do so as their individual stories unfold, is how many of George and Penelope's children and grandchildren took advantage of global opportunities.

Time now to explore the multifaceted lives of George and Penelope's sons.

Beginning with their youngest son, Alfred Liston Young [1885-1944], he like all his siblings, remained living at home until it was time to take up employment. Alfred was a keen recreational yachtsman and for many years kept his private yacht moored on the Clyde. Alfred's career ambition led him to join the Military, where he served with the British Army Royal Engineers Regiment pre and post WW1, receiving several medals for distinguished service and retired having achieved the rank of Major. Towards the end of the war, in April 1917, Alfred met and married Christina Mitchell Leadbetter. Christina was the daughter of a Roxburghshire Farmer and a woman of style and a free spirit. She was not unlike Alfred's sister Madge in that she too was busy energetically taking advantage of the new female freedoms available in post-Victorian Britain. Family members have described her as an adventurer and a real character which seems a little tame for this lady. Among other passions, Christina was a keen aviator, she sat her pilot's exam in September 1929 in a Bluebird Genet and continued to fly various private aircraft for years to come as a member of the Suffolk Aero Club at Hadleigh. That Club's Membership Register for 1929 has Christina Young and Lady Finola Somers as two of only a mere handful of female pilot members.

Perhaps it was because Christina was so foot-loose and carefree that she and conservative Major Alfred L. Young became estranged not long after their second son was born. They separated and eventually divorced early in 1930s. Around that same time Christina purchased her own private plane, a De Havilland Moth, which she called Chyrsalis. One family story which perpetuates is that on more than one occasion, when Christina was running late organising her boys for school, she would telephone the Headmaster to arrange to have the goal posts taken down on the football field so she could fly the boys to school in Chyrsalis. Christina took several sea voyages over the years, some with the children and some alone. One such voyage was from Gibraltar on board *SS Madura*, another in November '48 was from Calcutta to England. On that passenger manifest she gave her address in the UK as 'Yacht Joyce', Burnham-on-Crouch, Suffolk. This was a vessel belonging to Commodore Rogers, her second husband whom she married in 1937. Alfred Douglas Rogers, RN, is remembered as also a real character, full of life and every bit the adventurer himself: they were kindred spirits by all reports. He was an active Member of the R.A.F. Club in Piccadilly and was affectionately nicknamed 'Commodore'.

After he retired his commission, Major Alfred Liston Young, went to live at St Edmunds Lodge, Great Cornard and purchased a manufacturing factory/foundry in Sudbury, Suffolk, England specialising in the design and production of brass propellers for ships and yachts. The company has had several names over the decades. In Alfred's day it was styled Bruntons (Sudbury 1919) Ltd and was located within the Stour Valley Ironworks complex on Station Road. The factory was noted for its brass propellers, steering gears and non-ferrous castings for the marine sector. Bruntons was at the cutting edge of technology in the day and as such was a lead Exhibitor at the 1922 Marine and Small Craft Exhibition. Bruntons are still trading, have relocated their operations to Clacton-on-Sea and remain award winning designers and manufacturers of brass propellers, folding and static, in all shapes and sizes for all styles of ships from workhorse Naval ships & Super Yachts to any sized leisure craft. Later Alfred settled quietly in retirement

In the end 1850-1950

in Sudbury, Suffolk where he was an active member of the Stour Valley Lodge until his death in 1944.

As to Alfred and Christina's two sons, the eldest was George Ian born 1918 known as Ian within the family. Ian spent the greater part of his life either by the sea at Burnham-on-Crouch where he had a sailboat and was active in the local Yacht Club or on the Isle of Wight where he also spent his leisure time sailing. When WW2 broke out, Ian volunteered and in recognition of his Marine Engineering skills, he soon found himself working in a developmental role within the Navy Reserve. Ian was given a commission as Lieutenant Commander and served the bulk of the war years as part of the Royal Navy Volunteer Reserve. The most noteworthy maritime development project of his wartime experience was undoubtedly his involvement with the MTB102. Designed by Commander Peter Du Cane and launched in 1937 the MTB102 had an all-wood hull of double diagonal Honduras Mahogany over Canadian Rock Elm. Besides her torpedo tubes she was built to carry depth charges, machine guns, and the Swiss Oerlikon 20 mm anti-aircraft canon.

She was purchased by the Admiralty at the outbreak of the war. Stationed in the English Channel, during Operation Dynamo in 1940, i.e. the evacuation from Dunkirk, she made eight crossings of the Channel. The MTB102 was the fastest wartime British naval vessel capable of an incredible 48 knots. She distinguished herself as the one-time flagship of Rear Admiral Wake-Walker when his destroyer HMS Keith was disables. Then in 1944 the MTB102 carried Winston Churchill and General Eisenhower to review the fleet for Operation Overlord – the invasion of Normandy. This vessel was sold post war and was almost lost to time but was firstly refurbished for the making of the film – The Eagle has Landed, and then more recently the 102 was given a major rebuild courtesy of a charity trust set up in her honour so that she could appear as herself in the 2017 war film, Dunkirk'. Ian and his family are all very proud of his association with this unique ship.

Ian's brother, Donald Harper Leadbetter Young on the other hand, clearly inherited his mother's wanderlust and need for adventure. After serving as a Lieutenant in the RN during WW2 he struggled to settle back into civilian life in

England so decided to set sail for Nigeria where he worked as an unqualified veterinary. Donald remained restless and numerous shipping manifests list Donald Harper Young as a passenger for voyages between Africa and Britain in 1948, 1949, 1952 etc. More recently, he sailed as a First Class passenger from Tika, Cameroon on board the *Tilapa*, arriving at Southampton on 1 May 1958, just in time for his brother's second marriage in the June.

Unbeknown to his family, at some point he had made the acquaintance of a Miss Jeanne Harvey, because soon after his brother's wedding Donald travelled down to Poole in Dorset, and quietly married Jeanne early in the September of that same year. Then on the 18 September 1958 Donald and his 'new family' were identified sailing as passengers on the *Nicola* out of Liverpool. Along with Donald Harper Young and Jeanne Elizabeth Young there is a Jeanette Young, Scholar, born 18 November 1944. Was this Donald's 'love child'? After all he was stationed in the south of England during the war which included an extended period on the Isle of Wight. When I enquired of family members regarding Jeanette, they confessed she was a total unknown in family circles. It was later discovered her birth was registered as Jeanette Harvey [her mother's maiden name] at Bournemouth with no father's name entered.

It is generally conceded in family circles that Donald remained a restless fellow. One family member advised that Jeanne confessed after their wedding, 'that she was not sure she could hold Donald'. Jeanne remained with Donald in Kano, Northern Nigeria where Donald worked as a Veterinary Surgeon while teaching the natives animal welfare. Just before Nigeria achieved Independence on 1 October 1960 Donald and Jeanne moved to neighbouring French Cameroon. One year on and French Cameroon is granted Independence and the couple are on the move again, this time to South Africa. Around this time, they made one last voyage back to England, this time from Tika, Cameroon. On that passenger manifest Donald lists his occupation as Snr Livestock Superintendent.

This time, Donald and Jeanne remained in England for a time living on a rented farm in Diss, Norfolk. Ultimately, dissatisfaction with life in England saw Donald, Jeanne and

Jeanne had a brother Peter, who was the same age as Donald. Although Peter had served an apprenticeship as a Motor Mechanic prior to enlisting, he was deployed to maritime service and when demobbed went and worked as a Ships Engineer and was on the passenger manifest on a ship sailing from Nigeria to Liverpool in September 1951. Yet another maritime link was found with Jeanne's maternal grandfather who was a Chief Stoker in the Royal Navy. No one seems to know anything further of Donald's later life.

By contrast, George & Penelope's second-youngest son Francis 'Frank' Naismith Young [1882-1946] lived a very quiet life indeed. Frank was born at Clydesdale Street, Hamilton at the time his father, George, was busy establishing his new factory just down the road at Larkhall. Frank's initial education was at the Hamilton Academy, and after completing his education around 1901 he takes up a role in the Banking sector as a 'Bank Clerk Apprentice' – quite an odd job description really. Somewhere along the way Frank determined the world of finance was not suited to him so he returned to further his study at University where he graduated as an Electrical Engineer. In 1920 he married Grace McKendrick Reid [erroneously recorded as McKean in several places including on the family tombstone] by which time we know he was fully qualified. Frank and Grace had one son and one grandson, who not only shared the same name of Douglas Naismith Young, but both qualified as Electrical Engineers too and can be found working in Scotland and France. Without any evidence surviving in relation to where Frank was employed, it is impossible to know whether or not he worked in the maritime sector. His son and grandson most certainly did not.

Next comes a very colourful character, son Charles Thomson Young [1880-1938]. Affectionately known as Charlie, he is the youngest of George's sons to take on a maritime career. In fact there are four Charles Thomson Youngs in this Young family and they all carry the name of the original owner of the

Jane, the ship which Captain John Young [1810-1871] sailed for the majority of his seafaring days; and they all at one point had maritime careers. This Charlie, was born in Hamilton, educated at the Academy, and began serving his apprenticeship as a Seaman in 1893. By early 1907 he is in Colombo with his uncle Samuel, calling himself a Broker and Merchant. He was not there just for a visit either as he has a constant entry on the membership registers for the St. George Lodge, Colombo, from 3 January 1907 to post 1921. Then on 4 Feb 1929 he is listed among passengers sailing on the SS *Tenyo Maru* from Colombo via Japan to Honolulu with his new wife, Gladys De Gruchy. After a short stay they sailed from Honolulu to San Francisco and on to New York where they arrived on-board the *Lewiston* on May 21. The final leg of their voyage they sailed on Cunard's *'Caronia'* from New York to London, when on that manifest it is stated that England was their intended place of permanent residence. Their future address was to be 'Colley Cottage', Reigate, Surrey. In 1939 Charles did travel from Suva to Vancouver en route to London, giving his address as Ceylon, Occupation as Broker, and his wife's address was the Cumberland Hotel in London. Little else has been discovered about this mysterious couple.

The fourth child in this family was William Caldwell Young [1872-1933], affectionately known as Willie, and born in Glasgow while his parents were still living in Gordon Chambers. He was named after John Caldwell's father, the man who gave George his first job in the Silk Industry well over a decade prior. William must have been very proud to carry the Caldwell name because in his adult life he described himself as W. Caldwell Young in his commercial listings. Willie completed a Law Degree in Glasgow and obviously decided a career in commerce was preferable to one inside a courtroom. He ultimately found employment in the Insurance Sector, where he clearly applied himself. An entry in the 1911/12 Post Office Directory shows he is already Assistant Manager for Scotland for the prestigious Norwich Union Fire Insurance Society Limited, a Company founded in 1797.

In the meantime, he had met, and married Jacobina Annie Robin and they were living in Broomhill Street, Hillhead an old Caldwell family address. Willie remained living in Glasgow, had a very close relationship with all his family, especially his brothers Charlie and Alexander. His ethics and trustworthiness are vouched for by the fact his uncle, Samuel [Samuel Donaclift Young of Colombo, Ceylon] nominated Willie and his brother Alexander as Executors of his Will. Ultimately, Willie's career path took him all the way to Manager for Scotland, and he lived out his retirement in a beautiful property at 160 Great George Street in Hillhead. Willie died at the Crichton Royal Hospital Dumfries on 15 April 1933 leaving an estate in excess of £10,500. Jacobina lived on until 1954. Willie and Jacobina did not have any children.

Now, this brings us to George Alexander Young Jnr. [1870-1911]. Named after his father and born in Glasgow July 1870, he completed his education at Hamilton and Glasgow where he graduated as a Marine Engineer. George remained living in Glasgow, found employment in and around the port on the Clyde with one of the many Shipbuilding firms. George appears to have suffered health issues from an early age which could explain why he never married. He remained living with his parents in Hamilton until around 1890 when he and Willie were undertaking their tertiary studies in Glasgow and residing as boarders at Ardoch Lodge in Cambuslang. A decade on George is living with his brother Alexander at Largs. George dies on the 6 January 1911 at his parent's home 'Blythswood' on Monreith Road, Newlands, Glasgow. His cause of death is cited as 'Syncope', an old medical term related to a sudden fall in blood pressure. George is buried in the family plot, Lair 2117 in Old Cathcart Cemetery, Glasgow. He was only 39 years of age.

As for any insight there may be into George's character, the best evidence of this comes from his Will which also gives a hint as to how that family felt about extending loans to each other. George used his uncle's firm of Solicitors, Wright Johnston & Orr of 178 West George St., Glasgow, to draw up his Will wherein he acknowledges a debt owed to his father in the order of £1,000 for which he was being charged interest at the rate of 5%. This debt was to be recovered from sundry life insurance policies George had taken out, probably purchased on the advice of his brother Willie. While George's Will was brief it did outline a loan made to his young brother Charlie [Charles Thomson Young of

Colombo, Ceylon] in the order of £10, 'the sum contained in IOU dated 27th August 1909', which may be money Charlie borrowed from George while in Scotland on a holiday from Colombo. Like his father, George made that loan to his brother conditional on the payment of interest, and it seems Charlie's liability was then standing at £10.3s.6d. George Jnr. was a chip off the old block it would seem! He nominated his brothers Alexander Renfrew Young, Silk Manufacturer, of 178 Buchanan St., and William Caldwell Young, Insurance Manager of 125 St. Vincent Street as his Executors. These addresses are familiar in that one is a business address for Caldwell, Young & Co. Ltd. and the other an address for an apartment where George and Penelope once lived.

This brings us to the two sons who took active roles in Caldwell, Young & Co. First up there is Alexander Renfrew Young [1873-1930] who was named after his maternal grandfather, the Cotton Mill owner from Glasgow. Alexander remained living in Lanarkshire all his life and there he married a local lassie by the name of Jeanie Thorburn Wiseman, the daughter of a Hamilton Jeweller and Watchmaker. Jeanie was born the eleventh child of James Wiseman, a Watchmaker, and his second wife Jeannie Scott Thorburn. Her maternal grandfather was a Master Confectioner and her paternal grandfather a School Teacher. For Jeanie's family too, education is a solid theme. As for Alexander, at various times in his early life he was a resident of Glasgow, Hamilton and Largs depending on what his study and work commitments were at the time. He also supported his younger brothers, George and Alfred who are found living with Alexander and his wife Jeanie in 1901 at their home at 2 Douglas Terrace, Largs. His entire working life was spent in the family business where he assumed the role of General Manager of Caldwell, Young & Co. Ltd. at their Head Office in Glasgow. Several family members nominated him to be Executor of their Wills, which would indicate he was an ethical, moral and trusted person. In the case of his uncle Samuel's Will, he also assumed the role of mentor to Samuel's two young sons, which would also imply a high degree of familial responsibility, parenting skills, common sense and strength of character. It seems Alexander's role was to shoulder responsibility for business and family. Alexander and Jeanie also had their own family of four to raise; but, sport and education not sailing would be this family's legacy.

Their son George Frederick Young [1898-1982] was born at Larkhall and followed in his father's footsteps and joined the family business. 1930 documents list George as Silk Manufacturer; however, his specific role in the Company is unknown. In 1928 George married Mary Ann Nimmo Adair at Blythswood, and they had one daughter. George's sister, Jean Kathleen Thorburn Young [1903-1991], was a National and International Champion Hockey player. At one international meet Jean was the only Scot on the British Ladies Hockey Team when it toured the USA. Next is Penelope Gault Young [1910-1982] named after her paternal great-grandmother. As a young woman Penelope was involved with Guides which enabled her to take an exchange in Poland for a time. However, Music and Education were more suited to Penelope's character, and after achieving qualifications in both of these areas she devoted her life to children's education in both academic and musical pursuits. With music as her private passion as well, she was not only proficient in the classics and jazz but frequently accompanied singers in local concerts. Penelope married John W.J. Robertson and they had two children.

Alexander and Jeanie's youngest daughter was Madge Alexandra Young [1913-2001], who was another high achieving athlete who went on to distinguish herself in the International Athletics arena. The Glasgow Herald published a lengthy obituary in January 2001 laying out Madge's long list of achievements among which they cite President of the Scottish Women's Amateur Athletics Association, Team Manager for the Scottish Women's Athletics Team at the 1974 Commonwealth Games in Christchurch, New Zealand, and National Coach for Athletics Scotland. During WW2 Madge organised sports for evacuated children before enlisting in the ATS where she was appointed Physical Training Instructor and rose to the rank of Captain. Madge may have been barely five feet tall but what she lacked in physical height she made up for with her strong personality and wicked sense of humour. Madge spent a number of years as Athletics Coach at the Westbourne School in Glasgow and is credited with leading that school to victory in the Paisley Shield points competition at the Scottish Schoolgirls Championships four years in a row. She also inspired her own daughter and a niece to excel in athletics.

This brings us to the second son who joined the family firm. He is the first born child of George and Penelope, John Ellis Young. He shares that name with an uncle who was a Trader and Steamships Mercantile Agent in Riga, Latvia; but, of more importance still this family's association with the name John Ellis can be traced all the way back to his great-uncle, Captain John Young [1789-1836], and the events surrounding the ransoming of the *Eliza Swan*. Captain John Ellis was commander of the Royal Navy vessel '*Spitfire*' who met up with the *Eliza Swan* after that unhappy encounter with Commodore Rodgers. Captain Ellis relieved Eliza Swan of her additional cargo of the crew of the *Daphne* and they sailed in convoy thereafter to enable safe passage to the port of Montrose. However, the closest this John Ellis Young will come to seafaring or outracing the Americans would be on one of his many trips to the America's Cup races with Sir Thomas Lipton.

Every now and then one child in a family stands out from their siblings and John Ellis Young most certainly does that. He is fondly remembered for the shape of his character, his enthusiasm for life, his boundless energy, his quirky sense of fun, his competitive streak and in terms of this family's values displays a distinct lack of conservatism. For this generation of George & Penelope Young's family it was definitely their eldest son John Ellis Young, born 1867 at Anderston, Glasgow, who remains the colourful character. He spent his early life living in the Gordon Chambers flat in central Glasgow. After the family moved to Hamilton, just like his brothers, John's school days were spent at the nearby Hamilton Academy, which was begun by Lord Hamilton after whom the town was named. By 1891, John and several brothers are boarding at Ardoch Lodge, Cambuslang, Glasgow, where he and Alexander are already listed as Silk Manufacturers. At the time it was decided to expand the reach of the business, it is son John who relocates to head up

In the end 1850-1950

the firm's operations in London. This obviously included making sales and marketing trips to New York because he is found sailing back and forth across the Atlantic from around 1898/99 onwards. Whilst the usual ecclesiastic and government records told something of John's life including his Army service with the Royal Scots Labour Corp, it was the discovery of his obituary in the British Newspaper Archives which has enabled his story to take on a whole new dimension.

This John Ellis Young memorial appeared in the Bexhill-on-Sea Observer on Saturday 14 May 1932. Many column inches we taken up with describing and celebrating this man, his life, his character, his work, his hobbies and his achievements in business and sport. The article carries three main headings: 'Loss to Cooden', 'Sudden Death of Mr. J.E. Young', and 'City Freeman's Distinguished Career' with sub-headings of 'Pioneer Racing Cyclist', 'Motoring Record', and 'Scottish Funeral custom'. There is also a very dashing photograph of a tall stylishly dressed distinguished looking Gentleman in Plus Fours. John's sudden death had '... occasioned a profound sense of shock, for he was at his business in London the previous day, and returned in the afternoon to play a round of golf at the Cooden Beach course'. He complained of feeling unwell on the Saturday morning, and succumbed to a massive heart attack that very day.

The obituary makes it clear John was a much loved and respected member of the Cooden community, having moved there from Barnet, London in 1917. A keen competitive golfer, he joined the Cooden Beach Golf Club in 1921, was Captain in 1924, appointed to the Board of Directors when the Club was formed into a company, and in 1928 was the winner of the Automobile Golfing Society Dunlop Cup which would have taken his mind back to his own cycling days when he was the first Scotsman to race on one of Dunlop's first pneumatic bicycle tyres.

John's business interests extended outside the family company. Whilst he was a partner in the firm of Caldwell, Young and Co. Ltd., and Managing Director of their London

Office which by 1932 had moved to larger premises in Gresham Street, he was also Chairman of the Bowden Wire Syndicate in Willesden. John was '... one of three men who introduced the Bowden cycle brake, claimed to be the safest of its kind in existence' and to this very day Bowden remains a name synonymous with professional cycle racing across the world. It transpires that as a young man John was 'an enthusiastic cyclist and had a successful racing career from 1887-1891. During that time he held the tricycle and one mile bicycle championships of Scotland and also dead-heated with R.A. Vogt for the five mile bicycle championship.' R.A. Vogt was a member of the Clydesdale Harriers Club and was their 20 mile Cycling Champion. John was a frequent competitor at Herne Hill and other English cycling tracks and is known to have taken '... great pride in the fact that he was the first cyclist in Scotland to ride a pneumatic-tyred machine in a cycling race.'

In his day cycle races were incorporated into athletics events as there were no dedicated cycle tracks as we know them today. Whether a separate passion or as a means of developing leg strength for his cycling, John also achieved recognition as a track and cross-country athlete at which events he was a regular competitor. In a publication entitled - 'The Origins of Scottish Cross-Country' John Ellis Young is mentioned as: 'Another survivor of the first season, 1885-86, is Young (CH) [Clydesdale Harriers]. Although a sprinter of much ability on the track, Young seldom missed a run across country.' As a member of the Clydesdale Harriers, John spent many years cycling in the summer and running cross-country and sprint racing in the winter. In September 1886, at the age of nineteen, he joined the West of Scotland Harriers whose membership was mostly cyclists and rowers. John maintained his love of cycling and his association with the sport extended well into his adult years.

Apart from his modest achievements in the sport of cycling, it seems John was able to combine his sense of fun with his sport of passion - cycling. In an 1890 edition of the Scottish Cyclist I found the following excerpt: ' ... J.E. Young has been a personality without which our championships would have appeared very bald indeed. He had the enterprise to order a pneumatic racer when it was to many of us little beyond a dream of Utopia, and this enterprise brought its reward.' It could be suggested it was his family's financial resources which would have made such a purchase possible. Most of his fellow competitors would have been racing the 1888 Townsend Juvenile Tricycles or Cripper Tricycles fitted with the old solid tyres making for a rough ride and affording less manoeuvrability.

When John moved to London he continued his association with cycling but now it was on a social and recreational level; indeed, he became a member of the prestigious Pickwick Bicycle Club. This Club had originally come into being back in 1870 in celebration of the life of Charles Dickens. It seems a group of cycling enthusiasts who were also Dickens lovers met over an ale or three at the Downs Hotel in Hackney to lament the recent death of Britain's favourite storyteller. It was decided that to commemorate Dickens life and his many comic episodic creations, the group would form a club and call it the Pickwick Bicycle Club.

The idea was that members would be assigned a nickname aligning their character to one of the characters created by Dickens, and those nicknames must be drawn exclusively from 'The Posthumous Papers of the Pickwick Club'. John Ellis Young was given the nickname: 'Tom Wildspark'. For the non-Dickens aficionados, I should explain. Tom Wildspark managed to escape a manslaughter charge because he was given a false alibi. This is despite the prosecution, and 'all the big wigs to a man said as nothing couldn't save him.' In John's case he had a reputation as a speed demon in his motorcar and although John had been caught speeding on numerous occasions, mostly he managed to escape being fined. But not always! One of his offences was reported in the Hendon & Finchley Times newspaper on Friday 12 May 1916 stating he was fined 15s. [fifteen shillings] for doing a speed of 27 m.p.h. when the speed limit was 20 m.p.h. Apparently the thrill of speed was something shared in the family, his cousin, Jeanie's husband, Charles Hutson, was similarly hauled up before the Court in Bedfordshire on 2 Jul 1907 for 'Driving a motor-cycle at a speed dangerous to the public on the Midland Road Railway Bridge on the 19th Ultimo'. He too was found guilty and fined. Another cousin, George Liston-Young, a wealthy businessman, who also indulged speed as part of his hobby of racing expensive Italian cars. He is associated with the most prestigious events in England including Goodwood and Silverstone. It seems George confined his racing to the track not to road.

It seems speed in all forms was a passion for John Ellis Young, initially on his bicycle and latterly in his cars, and along the way he engaged with innovation and new technology. It was written that 'when his cycle racing days were over, Mr. Young manifested a keen interest in the development of the motor car, the industry being then in its infancy. He was a member of the Scottish Automobile Club and the Royal Automobile Club, and under the auspices of the latter participated in a speed event, with passengers on board where he managed to set a petrol consumption record. This was in 1907, when he drove his two-cylinder 10-12 h.p. Argyll for 39 1/2 miles on one gallon on the outward journey and 40 m.p.g. on the return.'

It transpires John had a closer connection to this motorcar and its designer, Alex Govan, than might first appear. Alex Govan was a fellow Glaswegian raised in the slums of Bridgeton, an area very familiar to John's forebears and Alexander Brackenridge. Govan worked in the cotton mills during the day and to further his education he attended night school at the West of Scotland Technical College in Glasgow, where he excelled and gained distinctions. In 1893 Alex Govan and his brother-in-law John Worton went into partnership manufacturing the Worvan bicycle, and it is at this point Govan and John first became acquainted. This bicycle business failed due to a glut in the market and so Alex then went to work for Eadie Manufacturing Co. in Redditch. Eadie's wanted to build cars, and they had a cunning strategy to short-circuit the R&D by copying other cars. So, to get their business off the ground in 1897 they decided to import three cars from the continent: a Vallee, a Mors and a Benz. The plan was to strip them down and then set to designing and building their own car with Alex Govan as their Principal Designer. Two years on and with his skills well honed, Govan returned to Glasgow where he took over as Managing Director of Hozier Engineering Co. Ltd. whose core business was focused on the designing and building of the Argyll motorcar. Motoring Journalists felt the 10-h.p. Argyll 'Fosters motoring because it contains fascinating problems, and because it is the 'best sport on earth'. This is the car that John Ellis Young drove to win the fuel consumption event.

Intrigued by the heading 'City Freeman's Distinguished Career', and knowing that John was not a tradesman, I decided to investigate the role of Guild membership pre and post the Victorian era. Originally, Guilds were established by charter to represent various trades, to regulate quality of workmanship, monitor training and provide support and welfare to members' families much like Nautilus International does for seafarers and their families today. The power of these Guilds declined greatly in the nineteenth century and became more about social prestige, business contacts and having a political voice. Throughout this period the Guilds continued to provide support to members funded largely by charitable bequests. As membership became more expensive these Guilds and Liveries became little more than Gentleman's Clubs where members could pay a redemption fee in lieu of practicing a particular trade.

Later, the Guilds became absorbed into what became known as Livery Companies of the City of London, and today there are over one hundred representing trade associations and guilds and styled as the 'Worshipful Company of ....'. So, for business, and one would like to think for charitable reasons too given the Young family's history in this regard, John Ellis Young became associated with several Livery Companies. One of those being the City Livery Club, which was relatively new, only founded in 1914. The primary objective of the City Livery Club was to bring together liverymen from the various Guilds 'in defence of all that citizens hold dear...in service to the ancient Corporation [of the City of London] and in maintenance of the priceless City churches.' Now, even John's father, George, would have approved of that contribution to the social and charitable fabric of London. Another was The Worshipful Company of Glass Sellers; a more prestigious organisation founded way back in 1664, which has maintained a strong focus on pastoral care, charitable work and working in support of civic leaders. For John that would mean the London Lord Mayor and the Corporation of the City of London. John was also a member of the Worshipful Company of Loriners, which is considered one of the ancient Guilds. It dates from 1261 and was originally established as a guild for the makers of metal parts such as bridles, harnesses, spurs and the like – Lorimers in nineteenth century census records [note the spelling difference]. Membership of this Worshipful Company was restricted to 500 by the Court of Aldermen and in modern times it is more closely associated with Equestrianism. Princess Anne has been one of its Masters, along with Samuel Vestey, Master of the Horse in the Queen's household. It was by virtue of being elected as a Liveryman that John Ellis Young was also made a Freeman of the City of London. This was how Gentlemen like John conducted business in his day. Today we have business associations and chambers of commerce and it is openly called networking.

Men like John E. Young stood out in a crowd, they were the fun loving people that others wanted to get to know and as a consequence his circle of friends and acquaintances - ' ... was naturally a wide one, and he numbered among them such distinguished personalities as the late Sir Thomas Lipton, and the late Lord Dewar. He was a particular close friend of Sir Thomas Lipton and went with him to America for the first yacht race for the Americas Cup.' We have already established John's connection to Lipton via his sister Madge and Sir William Fife III; but, it seems these men were kindred spirits on other bases as well. While they both loved living life to the full they also shared a competitive streak. Lipton was a Scotsman of Irish parentage, a self-made man, merchant and yachtsman who sailed with King Edward VII and King George V and was a five time challenger for the America's Cup through the Royal Ulster Yacht Club between 1899 and 1930. He also made the cover of Time Magazine in November 1924.

Sir Thomas Lipton was quite a complex character who was openly homosexual at a time when it was scarcely spoken about and widely unacceptable. But this was no impediment to his achievement of high status social credentials. He was created Knight Commander of the Royal Victorian Order in March 1901 and created a Baronet in 1902. He died in 1931 and bequeathed the majority of his fortune to his native Glasgow, including his yachting trophies which are currently on display at the Kelvingrove Art Gallery and Museum. It is known that Lipton visited Ceylon in 1890 to establish his tea connections, at which time Samuel

Doneclift Young was already imbedded into the elite business world of Colombo and was a known associate of James Taylor the man credited with the birth of Tea Farming in Ceylon. So, given what has been uncovered so far about the various Youngs and Sir Thomas Lipton it would appear capitalising on family connections remains a theme repeated down the generations: it is something those early generations of Youngs did so very well!

This brings us to another example of high level business and social connections. John's friend Lord Dewar [1864-1930] or Thomas Robert Dewar. Tommy to his friends, he was the 1st Baron Dewar of Scotland, and heir to the Dewar's Whisky empire. Like John and his brothers who joined the family business and took it to the world, Lord Dewar and his brother, John, joined the family business and after putting their own stamp on the product by blending their whisky to ensure wider palate appeal, they took Dewar's Whisky to new markets and achieved great international success. Lord Dewar openly declared no interest whatsoever in the factory side of the business but developed quite a reputation for marketing as he travelled the world to identify and develop new opportunities. He is also credited with - 'exploiting romantic images of Scotland and tartan in his advertising.' From this it seems he and John Young shared a passion for the marketing aspect of business, a flamboyant approach to marketing and indeed a love of international travel: by ship of course.

Lord Dewar's two major sporting interests were cycling and thoroughbred horse racing. We know cycling was very close to John's heart and perhaps it was to honour his friend that Dewar in 1901, created the Dewar Challenge Shield to be awarded to the winner of the Five Mile Cycling Championship, one of John's pet events. These Gentlemen would have also rubbed shoulders at Livery events as Lord Dewar was at one time a Lieutenant of the City of London and a Sheriff of London.

These remembrances so far help draw a picture of John the businessman and friend; however, it seems that John's Scottish roots remained top of mind for those organising his funeral. One of the sub-headings in the Bexhill-on-Sea obituary was 'Scottish Funeral Custom'. This segment of the obituary went on to describe one of the customs observed at the 'interment in St Mark's Church graveyard silken cords were attached to the coffin and held by the mourners. The releasing of the cords as the remains were lowered into the grace was a symbol of the severing of earthly ties between the departed and those who remain.' In searching for an explanation for this unfamiliar tradition I discovered a current Scottish funeral director's website for a business which has been operating since 1870. Thomas McKellar & Sons burial options explains the tradition in Scotland was for eight cords to be attached to the coffin, each to be held by either a family member or close friends as they assist in the lowering of the coffin. The first cord is held by the chief mourner, the person nominated as next-of-kin, then the funeral director calls forward the remaining seven persons, men or women, who are placed in position in a set order. Silk cords were used on the occasion of John's funeral which was so very appropriate.

The obituary included a very long list of attendees and among them was a Mr Alan Young, described as John's adopted son. Also, in attendance were his brothers Alfred and Frank, his brother-in-law John Fullerton, with a special notation stating that his wife was ill and unable to attend. The list of family members was followed by a long list of distinguished mourners named as close and personal friends some of whom are mentioned already, as well as representatives from his beloved Golf Club and the local community. 'The Cooden Beach Golf Club was largely represented among the sympathisers, and members present included Councillor E.W. Bowrey and Colonel A.A. Messer, Brig-General C.G. Pritchard, C.M.G., D.S.O., Councillors H.G. Coughlan and H.J. Mulliner, Captain S. Wyvel Thompson and Captain A.H. Hollins'. Those staff members from the Golf Club who could not attend because of work commitments sent apologies and were all noted by name in the newspaper as a mark of respect to John. It was reported some 135 floral tributes were received in addition to family wreaths and those from Caldwell, Young & Co Ltd., the Directors of Bowden Wire, the

In the end 1850-1950

Pickwick Cyclists, the Cooden Beach Golf Club, with a specific note stating floral tributes came from both the inside staff and the greensmen of the Golf Club. John Ellis Young lived a heady life, was certainly much loved and respected and obviously made a positive and lasting impression on those he met.

R I P.

One final note regarding the previously mentioned Mr Allan Young, the adopted son. John Ellis Young had married Elizabeth Foster Hornby in Marylebone Parish Church in 1901 but sadly they did not have any children of their own. Their adopted son was born 1905 Henry Allan Hornby the youngest son of Elizabeth's brother William Richardson Hornby but sadly the young lad was left an orphan following the death of his mother in late 1907 and his father just a few months later in early 1908. Alan was only two years old at the time and was initially taken in by his aunt and uncle, Henrietta and Frederick Hornby, Elizabeth's young brother. Years passed and as Henrietta and Frederick became parents to their own growing family; it appears sometime after Henry's fifth birthday he went to live with his uncle John and aunt 'Betty'. Whilst no official adoption documents have been discovered John's Will indicates the boy was officially adopted. For some unknown reason John and Betty decided to switch the lad's christian names around; which I dare say would have been somewhat confusing for the child. Clearly this was not official as his marriage record in September 1932 shows him listed as Henry Allan Hornby Young. The price a child pays for being orphaned at a young age!

Chapter 12 – Part 2

**Seafaring Legacy • Six Generations & Going Strong
Father & Son • Marine Engineers with Global Reach
WW2 • Liberty Ships & the Sinking of *Andrea Doria*
Pinnacle • Chairman, American Bureau of Shipping**

It is hard to believe this family could have more to add to their seafaring story, but the strongest connections are yet to be revealed. There is one further son of George and Penelope who has not been mentioned to date and that is David Hill Young. Just like his eldest brother, John Ellis, David too carries the name of a person who clearly meant a great deal to this family. Indeed, his great-uncle was the first David Hill Young and was so named by Alexander Young Jnr [1782-1848] to honour his long-time friend and trusted banker, David Hill, a fellow shipowner in Montrose. As we have learned, the Youngs have a tradition of remembering those whose actions have had a positive impact on the family in some way; and, by perpetuating these names it tells us that at least some family stories of bygone days were shared down the generations and not lost to time. It also reinforces the significance of and the appreciation due to those special individuals they chose to acknowledge.

This David Hill Young [1876-1951] just like his father before him, was born the middle child in a large family and does not appear to have suffered from being so positioned among his siblings. He spent his early years living with his family in 'Bellevue Cottage', Clydesdale Street, Hamilton where he later attended the Hamilton Academy before completed his secondary education as a student at the High School of Glasgow, an educational centre steeped in history and tradition. Originally founded in 1124 as the Choir School of the Glasgow Cathedral, the Highschool of Glasgow in the era of David's attendance had moved to the premises of what is now The Glasgow Academy. It operated as a selective, independent, co-educational, christian school and prospective students were required to sit an entrance exam to be accepted. David went on to study Marine Engineering at the Heriot Watt College in Edinburgh, an equally prestigious educational facility. Established in 1821, it was the world's first Mechanics' Institute; and so, named to honour two great Scotsmen - James Watt an Engineer and George Heriot a Goldsmith and Philanthropist. It was the only College with a charter to appoint Professors. Today, it has campuses in Dubai, Malaysia and the Orkneys and still enjoys a global reputation for the quality of its research in Science and Engineering. In 2018 it was named International University of the Year. Yet again we have evidence that education was highly valued.

We have already learned that on the night of the 1891 census David was with his family at their island retreat in Rothesay on Bute, the family's favourite holiday escape; however, it is from the subsequent 1901 records we get our first glimpse as to what David's future career path may be. He is with his mother and siblings, Frank and Margaret at 30 Albert Drive, Govan and on that census evening mother Penelope has listed David's occupation as 'Marine Engineering Draughtsman'. He is now 25 years of age, has graduated and in his first paid employment. His career choice will lead him on quite a journey and not in his wildest imaginings could he have dreamt where that vocational decision would take him. Fortunately, courtesy of a resume he submitted to the War Office towards the end of WW1 we have a complete record of his employment up until the outbreak of the war.

That War Office document states that David initially signed up for an apprenticeship with John Bennie of Star Engine Works a Hydraulic, General and Electrical Engineering company. At that time, they had a Head Office located at 151 Moncur Street, Glasgow and factory premises located at Balloch Landing on the River Leven. Star Engine Works was principally involved with the design and manufacture of horizontal engines for slipways, haulage equipment and elevators installed on land and on ships. As David's career unfolds it will become clear that right from the very beginning he had a passion for design. His next position was also in a Drawing Office, this time with Muir & Houston, located at Harbour Engine Works, Portman Street, Kinning Park in Glasgow. Muir & Houston specialised in Marine Engineering and Boiler-making for steam powerplants on merchant vessels. There is a company profile in 'Grace's Guide to British Industrial History and Index to Firms for 1891'. The publication begins with an overview of the Engineering Industry in Scotland in the day citing 'The steady and substantial progress of the engineering industries in and around Glasgow has been marked by the rise in development of many firms that have become known and distinguished over a wide area in connection with some special branch production.' It goes on to say that '.... among the many prominent houses that have played a part in building up the city's reputation in this respect, a high position is held by that of Messrs. Muir & Houston, of Harbour Engine Works.'

The scope of work for a Marine Engineer is quite broad, but for David it seems his penchant for design was swayed more towards the steam engine side of the business. This is reinforced when it was explained that 'The firm [Muir & Houston] has greatly distinguished itself in the manufacture of all descriptions of marine engines and steam boilers. The works are of a very considerable extent, fully two-thirds of the area being covered by the buildings, offices and workshops. ..... Some of the most powerful machine tools are here to be seen in operation - drilling, boring, cutting, and performing prodigious feats in a few minutes which would have occupied our grandfathers for several days. The blacksmith's shop, engine and boiler houses, the pattern shops, and the various stores ... [and the] air of busy activity which pervades the establishment will not fail to impress. .... The firm devotes a large share of its attention to the introduction of boilers of the leading types, and contracts in this department are carried out in the most thorough manner, Messrs. Muir & Houston embodying in all their work the latest improvements that mechanical science has been able to devise.'

From this it could be said David had truly found his niche, his dream job, and was on his way! It could also be assumed he was a quality employee as he is found working for highly respected professional firms at the top of their game. In fact, this will not be the last time we find David Hill Young's name mentioned in association with world benchmark organisations. Furthermore, Grace's Guide also states that 'The firm altogether has developed a business and industry of exceptional magnitude and influence, and it will universally be admitted throughout the engineering world that Messrs. Muir & Houston have won a splendid position in the line of operations they follow. They employ five hundred hands, and in addition to the large and valuable home connection maintained, control also an immense export trade, and send their machinery to win added fame and extended renown in every quarter of the globe.' Firms of this stature most assuredly hired only 'the cream of the crop' in order to maintain their prestigious position at home and abroad.

This brings us to certification and seagoing experience. Marine Engineers in the Merchant Navy in the day were required to become certified and demonstrate expertise in both land and shipboard practices. This was a new requirement and so perhaps a little clarity here will explain why this was necessary and how Merchant Engineering careers differed from those of Royal Navy Officers doing the same work. With the inclusion of the stream ship in both Royal Navy and Merchant Navy fleets came a corresponding need to employ Engineers. In the early days, these men were drawn predominantly from the ranks of land based civilian industry environments. All that changed in 1837 when Navy Engineers were finally given Warrant Officer rank and were Certified. However, there were no such standards or recognition for those Engineers employed in the Merchant Navy. The one major impediment influencing this was the age old British Class System. Generally speaking, Royal Navy Engineers were considered to be from the upper class whereas their Merchant Navy counterparts were considered to belong to the lower middle class of the working class. This remained the status quo until 1863 when the first set of regulations were developed.

These regulations used a formula related to the relevant horsepower capacity of the steam engines to denote levels for qualification for Engineers Certificates of Competency.

Henceforward, it was mandated that Marine Engineers should be designated as either First, Second and Third Class. Manfred Grignard, a Chartered Engineer, wrote a paper entitled 'The History of British Marine Engineers Licensing', which was published in the Royal Belgian Institute of Marine Engineers magazine in 2006, where he goes into great detail as to the history and parameters defined for licensing Marine Engineers. In the case of the Royal Navy, Grignard makes the point that prior to 1863 those employed as Engineers although highly skilled, highly valued and considered an integral part of any steam powered vessel's company were never counted or listed as part of the crew nor did they hold any title or status - officer or otherwise. Given it was recognised they were indispensable to steamship operations it is hard to understand why it took so long for certification to be implemented.

In order for David to gain his seagoing certification as a Marine Engineer, he initially signed on with Alfred Holt & Co. Again, this is a landmark Scottish firm involved in engine design; in fact, Alfred Holt were at the forefront of the development of a revolutionary compound tandem steam engine concept which was set to make merchant vessels considerably faster and therefore more profitable. The main impetus for Alfred Holt & Co. to pursue this line of innovation was clearly self-interest as they had their own fleet of merchant ships. Alfred Holt & Co. provided a regular service between Liverpool and Shanghai carrying a mixed cargo of cotton and woollen goods on the outbound voyage and commodities such as tea, tin and tobacco on the homeward voyage. David was now combining his design passion with hands-on shipboard engineering.

It was this work with Holts that provided David with an entré to career opportunities in the Far East via one of Holts' associated companies which in his day was styled China Merchants S.N. Company. Founded in 1872 in Shanghai and operating in the China Japan Vladivostok triangle of textile trade, at one point China Merchants S.N. Company controlled a whopping 42% of the Shanghai Yangtze trade, with the other two major players being Swires with 38% and Jardines 20%. Make no mistake, these were all significant organisations in David's time and remain major players today. China Merchants

S.N. Company is now styled China Merchants Group with total assets in excess of 8 trillion RMB. Jardines revenue for 2017 was $US39.5 billion, and Swires with its diversified product offering and market penetration had a market capitalisation in 2017 of $HKD30.54 trillion.

What is true is these companies were always serious players and whilst David Hill Young was there almost a century ago one could rightly say he was in the 'right place at the right time' for two main reasons. Firstly, the Merchant Industry was experiencing a particularly buoyant period; and secondly, and perhaps even more importantly, China Merchants S.N. Company were about to place an order for a twin screw steamer to be built in Scotland by Messrs J. & J. Weir of Glasgow. It would be David's work experience here in 1903 that enabled him to secure his First Class B.O.T. Engineer Certification. [B.O.T. = Board of Trade; the controlling and issuing body when it came to Merchant Marine Engineer Certification.]

Working in the Far East was challenging on many levels and to make matters worse, several unforeseen world events were about to influence the path David's career could take. Firstly, his move occurred at the height of the Sino-British trade war, which saw China Merchants Stream Navigation Company branded as China Merchants S.N. Co. on one side and the abovementioned British antagonists on the other, all fighting for mercantile supremacy. Secondly two Scots had founded Jardine's in 1832 following the end of the East India Company's monopoly on trade with China. The other was The China Navigation Company Limited (CNCo) who traded under the name of Swire Shipping. Swire's had their head office in Singapore - a major shipping crossroads in the East. At one point John Samuel Swire attempted to get David's previous employer, Alfred Holt & Co. to partner with Swire's to gain market dominance of the Yangtze River trade but that offer was refused despite Alfred Holt personally holding a financial interest in Swire Shipping as a contributor to the £360,000 investment capital raising done in London in 1872. Maybe Alfred Holt was being shrewd and decided to hedge his bets; after all, it was a fickle market where partnering with a China company while investing in a British one made sound investment sense.

Then, not long after David arrived in the East, the Russo-Japanese War was declared between the Russian Empire and the Empire of Japan. The date is 5 February 1904 and the objective was to gain control of trade in the Yellow Sea. David decided to stay on and then found himself caught up in these events and for about eighteen months was ostensibly working for the Russian Government out of a base in Shanghai overseeing the fitting out of transport ships and carrying out logistical design work. This Russo-Japanese War continued until July 31, 1905; at which point David and several other ex-pat Marine Engineers appear to have been seconded to the Chinese Imperial Maritime Customs Service, the equivalent of the modern day Coast Guard Service.

These Engineers were initially engaged to work on the Custom Service's Cruiser Fleet then at the end of the Russo-Japanese War some, including David, transitioned to the Cotton Industry. This may seem a little out of step with his career direction, but 1906 was a turning point for the implementation of steam mechanisation into China's Cotton Mills, and with the removal of tariffs on cotton production British companies were the first to invest. One China Yearbook for the latter period of 1913/1914 lists numerous Cotton Spinning and Weaving Works including the Kwang Yu Spinning Mill of Changtefu where David was stationed for a time. Interestingly, that same Yearbook lists John Johnstone of Jardine's as Chairman of the Shanghai British Chamber of Commerce, and there is also a listing for David's employer Holts as: A. Holt & Co (British) – Blue Funnel Line.

Looking back over David's working life to date it could be said that while his time in the shipbuilding and mercantile arena in Scotland was a period of stability, conversely his time in the burgeoning Far East marketplace was a time of instability where speculators made business activity susceptible to boom and bust. Opportunism and entrepreneurship had focused on consolidating diverse businesses into mega-organisations in order to more rapidly grow businesses in what could be considered a highly competitive foreign commercial environment overlaid with all the political issues that was China and the Far East in the day. Whilst the cut and thrust of this can be exciting at times it can also be very destabilising and stressful for those employed who, more often than not, found themselves persisting under a cloud of uncertainty. In David's case this translated to employment ambiguity right up until the outbreak of WW1 as takeover, restructuring and redeployment of assets, including people assets, became the norm. In his case, we will soon learn this uncertainty continued after the end of WW1 but for a different set of reasons: the British Exchequer was exhausted and shipbuilding orders completely dried up.

It is appropriate here to digress a little as we pick up the first threads of David's personal life - circa 1900. Prior to going out East he had made the acquaintance of a Miss Emily Harriet McCaw, the daughter of Robert McCaw, a successful Linen Manufacturer of Lurgan, Ireland. Once the Russo-Japanese war was over and David was posted on contract to Kwang Yu Spinning Mill at Changtefu, he sent for Emily. Among the vast collection of documents held by David's family there is a wonderful collection of personal letters exchanged between the pair as they maintained their long distance romance. There is also Emily's travel diary recording her experiences and events as she journeyed from her family residence of Teghnevan [various spellings exist], in Lurgan. First of all, she visited with David's family in Scotland, then escorted by David's youngest sister Madge, the ladies took the train to London, where David's eldest brother, John Ellis [Jack] met them. For the duration of their stay, they were house guests of Jack and his wife Betty at their then property in New Barnet, North London. Prior to Emily embarking for China there were numerous social events planned by David's siblings and friends. These included taking in a Drury Lane pantomime, attending various theatre performances, having dinner at Frascati's, taking tea at Harrods and much more. Emily writes very favourably about one very special event, a Dinner Dance held in her honour hosted by Jack and Betty in the Venetian Room of the Midland Grand Hotel in St Pancras. Now this hotel was the place in its day. It is a very grand 1873 Gothic Revival building denoted as a George G. Scott masterpiece of architectural design which in recent years has been fully refurbished and rebranded as the St. Pancras Renaissance Hotel. Of that Dinner Dance evening, Emily writes, 'supper was announced about 9.30 and headed by the piper, who had been specially engaged for the Scotch Reel, we went down to supper'. Later, the MC gave a speech and then all 120 guests rose to their feet 'and with glasses raised sang the chorus of "Aileen Alannah" [Eileen Alannah is an 1870s Irish Ballad] – "Faithful I'll be to the Colleen I adore" [is part of the chorus to Eileen Alannah], and "For he's a jolly good fellow". Jack responded on Emily's behalf and she wrote he described her as a 'plucky Irish Girl'. Plucky will sound like an understatement once the trials and tribulations of her journey from London to inland China are retold.

The very next day Emily was to embark on the ship which would sail the following morning on the first leg of the long journey to Shanghai, China. Emily's travel diary gives a wonderful insight into sea travel in 1908. It all begins on – 'Saturday, Feby 15th - Left New Barnet by the 12.00 train, (Madge accompanying me) and reached Broad Street Station, where we were met by Jack. After luncheon in a hotel, we started for Fenchurch Street Station, where we were to join the train for Royal Albert Docks. At the station we met Jim MacKay [David's brother-in-law], Llorne Reburn, Harry Allan, and Mr. Wilson, so as they all accompanied Jack, Madge, and me to the docks. I had quite a jovial party to see me on board the good ship 'Nore' on which I was to embark for China. My friends all had afternoon tea on board with me and as the ship was not sailing till Sunday, they spent quite a long time with me on board, so I felt quite at home....the goodbyes however had to be said again, and once again I was left alone, to realise again that I was indeed leaving home and all the dear familiar faces behind me, going out to a strange land to make a new home there for myself.'

Emily also gives a fine account of some of the day to day issues such as how mail was dealt with, the joys of sharing a cabin, the comparison of the *S.S. Nore* to other ships of the P & O Company, and with respect to her vessel the *S.S. Nore* her final assessment was that she was pleased she was not a 2nd Class passenger! Emily wrote at length about how she and many of her fellow travellers suffered from the dreaded mal-de-mar for several days as they sailed on through a windy and foggy Channel and into a wet and windy Mediterranean. Conditions were so dire at one point she confided to her diary she felt they would die. Sailing through the gloom and grey of stormy weather any kind of visual relief was rare in those early days of her voyage save for an occasional school of porpoises; and of course, the charming Captain whom she positively describes as 'cheery'. Emily discovered that one of her fellow passengers, a Mr Wells, worked in inland China and she was pleased when he and his wife struck up a conversation offering her a first-hand insight into what life would be like. She reported the Messrs Wells' account was more encouraging than that of another female passenger who had made Emily quite 'frightened ... telling her [about] ... all she had to do in the interior of China'.

As they sailed on into the Mediterranean the *S.S. Nore's* first port of call was Gibraltar, then Malta, Port Said and Cairo. On each occasion Emily ventured ashore with her new shipboard companions, taking in the sights and sounds and recording all she experienced. Her intrigue with the disembarking and boarding of passengers took on a different hue once she was required to shuffle from cabin to cabin as the Captain attempted to accommodate as many passengers as possible. She was also intrigued by the concept of bargaining with local traders. At one point she commented that 'Miss Darling was asked 7/6 for a blue bead bracelet, which she got in the end for 6d.' It was also the first time Emily had seen women with their heads and bodies completely covered, something she found a little strange.

As the ship traversed the Suez Canal it was slowed to 6-7 miles an hour for that 87 mile stretch of congested waterway. At one juncture a special pilot was taken on board to deal with upcoming navigation hazards. All the while she confessed her boredom at the monotonous scenery, just sand on both banks, as far as the eye could see, dotted with the occasional terrace house on the shoreline or the odd commercial building accompanied by a cluster of palm trees. Although the railway line ran parallel to the Canal it was rare to actually see a train. As the *Nore* sailed on south through Great Bitter Lake they passed several ships heading in the opposite direction, one of which was a troop carrier that Emily later discovered was heading from Bombay to London.

Sailing from London to Cairo the weather had been inclement and cool; now, as they neared the end of the Suez the days were becoming warmer, and the nearer they came to Ceylon the more oppressive Emily found the hot tropical conditions. As the *Nore* exited the Red Sea and sailed through the Gulf of Aden she began to look forward to meeting up with David's brother Charlie in Colombo. At first, she was a little concerned she may not recognise him after eight years, so she asked a Mr Halloway, a business associate of Charlie's, to point him out to her to save her any embarrassment. In the end, that was not necessary as Charlie had his own plan and made a grand solo entrance. Not content to wait to arrive on the tender boat, Charlie had hired his own boat to go out to meet the *Nore*, and Emily described it as 'rowed by six native boatmen in white tunics.' Charlie came on-board and she later wrote how the ladies were quite taken with him. Introductions over, Emily and Charlie 'went ashore ... [in their privately hired vessel] arriving much sooner than any of the other passengers'.

Once at the dock, she had to climb a ladder to the quay where Charlie had a rickshaw waiting. It was so very hot Emily was pleased when their rickshaw finally arrived at 'Wentworth', a rambling house Charlie shared with some single male friends. She described it as definitely a single men's house. However, she was most grateful for the cool shade and to Charlie for having his personal houseboy arrange refreshments. They then paid a visit to Mr & Mrs Clark. Mr Clark was David's uncle Samuel's business partner in Clark, Young & Co. She writes that Mr Clark has taken over the role of Siamese Consul now that Samuel has retreated to Scotland due to ill health. Overall, Emily appears quite taken with Colombo and described the harbour as very grand, the general landscape as picturesque and the streets of Colombo and surrounding areas as utterly charming. She also noted how surprised and somewhat overwhelmed she was by the life, habits and customs of the native people.

Charlie was shortly whisking Emily off to meet yet another group of folks at the Galle Face Hotel. Again, they travelled by rickshaw and on this occasion, Emily confided to her diary that with Charlie being over 6 feet tall and 14 stone, his coolie had the worst of it! At the same time, she appears mesmerized by the number of cars and bullock wagons sharing the roads with the rickshaws being pulled along the red sandstone roads at speed by their 'copper skinned human steeds'. She felt this was made all the more astonishing given the oppressive heat under the blazing sun of Ceylon. While at the Galle Face Hotel, Emily espies the Captain and some of his Officers also enjoying dinner. Meanwhile, Charlie goes to his Club to change then after dinner they retire to the verandah to enjoy some band music and take their coffee.

Emily appears quite taken with the colourful electric lights strung up all around and while this is something we would take for granted today clearly it was still a novelty in 1908. However, she is even more taken with the Devil Dance, the foreign music of the Indian band, their flaming torch throwing antics and their even stranger native dancing. En route back to the jetty they make one final stop at the Grand Oriental Hotel for a farewell drink. Obviously, it was Charlie's plan to show Emily a grand time in Colombo, and the evening hours did not disappoint either as she describes it as a perfect moonlight night. Charlie had organised to have the same boat and oarsmen on standby ready to row Emily back out to the *Nore* in plenty of time before the ship was due to sail.

The memory of that pleasant evening was soon to fade because the *Nore* immediately hit more bad weather, this time a nasty thunderstorm, and it was their first night out of Colombo. Emily wrote it was so severe it woke everyone on-board. The next day was March 17, St Patricks Day, and being the only Irish lass on board, Emily improvised by wearing a parsley bouquet instead of the traditional shamrock. This was also the day the *Nore* arrived in Penang, Malaysia, and although she went ashore with a group of ladies late in the afternoon she felt it was the hottest day so far. So hot in fact that even the thought of a walk in the Botanical Gardens felt like it would be a risk to one's health. Later that evening while a group of passengers took a moonlight row in a sampan, Emily fell under the spell of the sound of native drums in the distance, which somehow reminded her of St Patrick's Day in Lurgan. For the second time since leaving London, Emily confided to her diary she was more than a little homesick. After departing Penang, they had a sea day when the passengers could enjoy playing deck games.

Their next port of call would be Singapore and here plans would go awry. For some unexplained reason the *Nore* anchored five miles out and this caused no end of confusion for a Mr Robertson who had arranged to meet Emily at the regular P & O dock. Unfortunately, the message regarding the change of docking did not reach Mr Robertson which meant their paths did not cross until her second day in Singapore. Confused but undaunted Emily did manage to see some of the local sights and was very impressed. Thankfully the *Nore* was not sailing until late in the evening on that second day so she had ample time to enjoy Mr Robertson's hospitality and that of Mr and Mrs Weir. Apparently, Mr Weir had travelled down from Shanghai to meet his wife in Singapore. Mrs Weir had become a favourite travel companion of Emily's and they had shared many a conversation and shore excursion since embarking together in London.

With the end of her journey just a few days away, Emily expressed she wished her journey to be ended sooner rather than later. The *Nore's* arrival into its penultimate port of Hong Kong saw the Captain manoeuvring in a busy harbour shrouded in dense fog which was more than a little unnerving. Later, when the fog lifted, Emily ventured on shore with some friends and they took a rickshaw and cable railway to the Peak, the premier lookout on Hong Kong Island. For their return journey they chose sedan chairs pulled by coolies who took them all the way to the main shopping precinct. Emily had strict instructions from David to purchase sets of silver teaspoons for the wedding party. Ever since the *Nore* had left Singapore and began sailing north Emily had noted another distinct change in the weather. Temperatures had cooled and, realising it would become even cooler as she reached Shanghai, she decided to take advantage of the 'special day' set aside for passengers to access their trunks. She packed away her summer garb and retrieve warmer attire.

From Hong Kong they sailed north towards Shanghai, and once the *Nore* arrived in the Yangtze River the ship was delayed for a few hours in Woosung while medical checks were completed. Then she slowly made her way the twelve miles upriver to the port of Shanghai. Speeds on this section of the Yangtze were dramatically reduced due to the huge volume of shipping on the river. Along the way Emily noted ships flying flags of England, Germany, Austria and France, there was even an Italian man-of-war, as well as cruisers, gun boats, river steamers and small passenger boats along with clusters of Chinese junks and sampans. It was a well-known fact that collisions were frequent along this stretch and so tensions were high and progress annoyingly slow. Emily was understandably anxious to see David and the Captain had very generously offered his private cabin for her reunion with her fiancé - a lovely romantic gesture.

And so, with David and Emily finally reunited, their wedding date was set for 7th April in the Cathedral in Shanghai. As custom and protocol would decree, Emily had been invited to spend the preceding day as the guest of Mr & Mrs Weir at their home of 'Woodlands'. Although lamenting being far from her Irish home and her dear Irish family on her wedding day Emily was extraordinarily complimentary about the warm hospitality extended by so many complete strangers. Their big day came and so did the heavy rains, a thunderstorm in fact. The ceremony went on regardless, followed by a dinner at 'Woodlands' after which the newly-weds finalised their packing and were escorted to the jetty ready to embark on their first adventure as husband and wife. They boarded the *S.S. Loong Wo* to journey up the Yangtze River to Hankow [Hankou] a distance of some 445 miles. From there the plan was to take the train to their final destination of Changtefu.

Overall, Emily's diary describes that journey as uneventful save for the torrential downpour that greeted them as they arrived in Hankow [today known as Wuhan]. Their luggage was taken ashore, suspended by ropes from bamboo poles and two Chinamen then transported it to the 'Hankowville Railway Station' [Hankou Railway Station]. This is where David and Emily planned to board the 'Pekin-Hankow' train [now known as

Beijing-Hankou Railway] en route to Changtefu. Emily described the scene at the Railway Station as utter pandemonium.

Curiously, in China at that time train passengers had their luggage weighed, and so when this luggage fee was added to their train fares the total cost amounted to £40 no less; a tidy sum given it is 1908. It was still pouring rain at 4.30 a.m. when they reached their final destination. As they alighted from the train it was pitch dark and they were most grateful David's friends from the Mission Compound were there to greet them. Little did Emily realise but the worst transport experience of her entire journey was yet to come. This is best described through an excerpt from her own diary.

'Dr MacKenzie, Dr. Leslie and D.H.Y. preferred to walk in spite of the rain. I was installed, however, in the special coach which was sent from the Mission Compound to meet the new bride! Never will I forget that ride my first one, in a spring-less Chinese cart in the interior of China, I had read about these carts, but one needs to travel in one to thoroughly appreciate it! The roads, to begin with, baffle [sic] description, the wear and tear of centuries to repair which would evidently be a breach of the law, has made them almost impassable. Ruts, rocks, rivulets, rain, nothing daunts the celestial driver as he urges on his sure-footed mule and rattles the poor traveller's bones over the stones. You look ahead and see deep ruts, or high boulders obstructing the way, to cross which must surely mean a complete over-hauling of cart, mule, driver, passenger, but still the dumb animal between the shafts plods on and finally we get over the difficulties some way, and land safely on the other side.'

However, there was a colourful and noisy reward waiting at the end of her most uncomfortable ride as Emily's diary explains. 'As our mule turns towards the entrance gate it stops short amid a volume of crackers and fireworks and pealing of the mission bells, which are evidently meant to announce the arrival of the bride and bridegroom!' A lovely greeting, but it was still only 5.30 a.m. Now, prior to travelling to Shanghai, David had accepted an invitation for he and Emily to be house guests of Dr. Douglas MacKenzie and his wife at the Mission Compound. This was necessary because the house they had been allocated in the Company Compound still needed to be thoroughly cleaned.

In the end 1850-1950

Unfortunately, the man David had previously engaged as Cook & Cleaner had left when he heard a new 'missi' was coming and so it would be a few more days before the new staff, a cook and a cleaner, would arrive. Eventually, they set to and had the house in 'fair order' by April 13, the date set by David for when he and Emily would move in.

According to Emily's diary, David's employer had a compound of their own located some two miles from the Mission Compound and all up some 612 miles into inland China. Emily lamented having to leave her new friends at the Mission as they had been so kind and welcoming. She was on the move again to another strange house in another strange compound with more strangers to get to know. Plucky Irish lass indeed! She describes it as quite a civilised compound in that their house had six large rooms and a cook-house as well as separate quarters for their Chinese staff. There were one and a half acres of gardens with ample water available from fifteen wells supplying crystal clear water - albeit Emily is advised to boil their drinking water. The newlyweds finally get to unpack and settle into their new life together. For social activities they journeyed back and forth to the Mission Compound where they enjoyed Sunday Services, tennis matches and dinners parties with friends. They found it preferable to walk the two miles rather than take that horrid Chinese spring-less cart. Their coolie would walk along with them and wait to escort them home by lantern light.

They had been married for only six weeks when they were about to experience their first disappointment. David knew his contract was up for renewal on June 15, but fully expected renewal was a mere formality given the equipment installation he was hired to oversee was not yet complete. But this was not to be the case. It probably did not come as a total surprise as Emily confided to her diary that David had heard the company was in some sort of financial difficulties. This is also a point made by several academic papers exposing the unstable history of early twentieth century British cotton mill operations in China. So, after all the expense of Emily coming out to China, the wedding and travelling inland and setting up house they were about to pack up and move again. On their final day they enjoyed 'Tiffin' with friends at the Mission Compound, before Emily, David and all their worldly possessions were delivered back to the railway station. This time they were headed for Hong Kong.

David's next position, which incidentally, would be his final role in the Far East, would be working for Shewan, Tomes & Co., one of the leading trading house companies in Hong Kong and China. They are featured in a publication entitled 'Twentieth Century Impressions of Hong Kong, Shanghai and other Treaty Ports of China' edited by Arnold Wright and published by Lloyds Greater Britain Publishing Company in 1908.

> 'The firm of Messrs. Shewan, Tomes & Co., of Hongkong, Canton, Shanghai, Tientsin, Kobe, London, and New York, with its agencies, in Amoy, Foochow, Formosa, Hankow, Manila, and the Straits Settlements is an example of the widespread character of the business in which a modern house may find itself engaged.
>
> Messrs. Shewan, Tomes & Co., are general managers of the China and Manila Steamship Company, Ltd., the American Asiatic Steamship Company, the Green Island Cement Company, Ltd., the Hongkong Rope Manufacturing Company, Ltd., the China Provident Loan and Mortgage Company, Ltd., the China Light and Power Company, Ltd., the Equitable Life Assurance Society, of the U.S.A., and the Canton Land Company, Ltd.; whilst they are agents for the "Shire" Line of Steamers, Ltd., the Yangtze Insurance Association, Ltd., the Insurance Company of North America, the Batavia Sea and Fire, North British and Mercantile, Reliance Marine, Union Marine, World Marine, Law Union and Crown, Yorkshire Fire and Life, Fireman's Fund, and Federal Insurance Companies, the Electric Traction Company of Hongkong, Ltd., the Chinese Engineering and Mining Company, Ltd., the Shanghai Pulp and Paper Company, Ltd., and the Tacoma Grain Company.

All these divergent interests are controlled from the head office in Hongkong, an imposing structure known as St. George's Buildings, with a magnificent frontage overlooking the harbour.'

The firm of Shewan, Tomes & Co originally traded as Russell & Co., once headlined as the largest American trading house in mid-nineteenth century China. Founded in 1824 and dealing mostly in opium, silks and teas the company prospered until 1891 when as Russell & Co. it began experiencing financial difficulties and a few years later declared bankruptcy. This is when two former employees, Scotsman Robert Shewan and Englishman Charles A. Tomes, pooled their resources to purchase the remnants of Russell & Co in 1895 whereupon they put their own names to the firm. This duo was so successful that within two decades they had offices in Hong Kong, Canton, Shanghai, Tientsin, Kobe, London and New York with agencies in Amoy, Foochow, Formosa, Hankow, Manila and the Straits Settlements [Singapore]. It is interesting to note raw silk was one of their chief export commodities and it would be wonderful to know if any of that raw silk ever found its way to Caldwell, Young & Co. in Larkhall.

David fulfilled a dual role within Shewan, Tomes & Co. He was the Manager of their Engineering Department in the Hong Kong Head Office, and also Assistant Superintendent of China Manila S.N. Co. Once again it was from the pages of 'Twentieth Century Impressions of Hong Kong, Shanghai and other Treaty Ports of China' that this latter company's profile was discovered. China Manila S.N. Co. was a passenger and cargo steamship operator providing weekly services between Mainland China, Manila and the Philippine Islands. They had two steamers, the *Zafiro* and the *Rubi*, each of 3,000 tons offering first-class accommodation for fifty saloon passengers. The ships were officered by Europeans and carried a doctor. Shewan, Tomes & Co acted as general managers and booking agents. Of greater interest to David and his work, the *Zafiro* was a single screw compound surface-condensing steam powered vessel built by Hall, Russell & Co of Aberdeen, Scotland and was launched in 1884. The *Rubi*, built by David J. Dunlop & Co., Port Glasgow, was launched in 1901 and was put into service in Hong Kong by the China Manila S.N. Co. [China & Manila Steamship Navigation Co Ltd] where it continued in service until the outbreak of WW1.

The Far East was a melting pot of intrigue and opportunity for many individuals at the time David Hill Young ventured to that part of the world and there is one person with whom he would have crossed paths but been blissfully unaware that they were in any way related. David would have read newspaper editorials written by and had his work life influenced by the political opinions expressed by one particular Hong Kong journalist. Today, we are quite familiar with the adage 'six degrees of separation' but often we are blissfully unaware of the connection. The dots to join in this instance are Hong Kong, Shanghai, the Russo-Japanese War, Chiang Kai-shek and an Australian born journalist by the name of William Henry Donald: the nephew of Jane Donald wife of Alexander Donaclift Young, who was the estranged uncle of David Hill Young.

W.H. Donald [known as Don] was born in Lithgow, New South Wales and spent his early journalist days working on the Lithgow Mercury before accepting the role of editor on the Bathurst National Advocate. Undoubtedly a very ambitious fellow he soon moved to Sydney to take up a role of Editor on frontline newspaper Sydney Daily Telegraph and later in Melbourne he was Editor on The Melbourne Argus. In 1901 he was enticed to leave Australia by The China Mail, the oldest English language newspaper in Hong Kong. There he rose to Managing Editor before his ideological inflexibility saw him at odds with company thinking and after he resigned in 1908 he engaged in global freelance journalism while writing a 'History of the Press in China and Hong Kong'. There is no doubt David Hill Young would have read many of Don's articles. Along the way, Don had earned a reputation as not just a prickly, controversial and provocative journalist but as someone whose articles inflamed an uprising against Japanese Imperialism. In fact, he is said to have significantly influenced the 1904-05 war between Russia and Japan. He felt strongly about China and the jostling of Russia and Japan for supremacy over China or more importantly control of the Yellow Sea between China and Japan.

In 1911 Don moved to Shanghai where he became key Editor of the Far Eastern Economic Review. Firstly, he befriends 'Charlie' Soong, a Chinese born American educated Methodist missionary known to be a member of a secret society dedicated to the overthrow of the Qing Dynasty. Charlie accorded Don the family status of 'uncle', and Don made no secret that his favourite in the Soong family was Mei-ling, the daughter who will later become Madame Chiang Kai-shek. It was right about this time that he also befriended Sun Yat-Sen who is referred to as the 'Father of the Nation' because of his instrumental role in the overthrow of the Qing Dynasty. After the overthrow Sun served as provisional first President of the Republic of China and the first leader of the Nationalist Party of China. Don became a trusted advisor to Sun Yat-sen and it was through this friendship he first made the acquaintance of Lt Chiang Kai-shek. Although Don never learned to speak Chinese and openly showed a dislike for Chinese food it did not affect his friendships with these military leaders or their families. Later Don became advisor and military strategist for Generalissimo and Mme Chiang Kai-shek. These were powerful people in high places and Donald remained on the inside of the upper echelons of Chinese military leadership for many years and this is how he first met Zhang Xueliang, nicknamed the 'Young Marshal' and who as General Zhang would later kidnap General Chiang Kai-shek in the December of 1936. This coup is referred to as the Xi'an Incident. It is said that W.H. Donald's 'finest hour' came when, at the behest of Madame Chiang, he played a pivotal role in convincing his old friend Zhang, the man he had cured of his opium addiction, to release General Chiang Kai-shek.

William Henry Donald remained a part of General Chiang Kai-shek's inner circle until May 1940 when they fell out over China's policy on Germany. Meanwhile, the outbreak of WW2 had seen Japan declare William Henry Donald 'the evil spirit of China' and indeed offered a handsome reward for his capture – dead or alive. In 1942 Madame Chiang requested Donald to return to China; however he was captured by the Japanese whilst en-route from the Philippines. Don was able to masquerade as someone else and the Japanese never became aware of his true identity. He lingered in a Manila Prison Camp until February 1945. After his release he made a short visit to New York City before returning to Shanghai where he died in November 1946, but not before he could recount much of his life to fellow Hong Kong journalist and friend Earl Albert Selle who recorded his memoires in a book entitled 'Donald of China'. Such was the level of respect and gratitude this Australian Journalist enjoyed in China he was farewelled with a state funeral organised and paid for by the government of the Republic of China. Columbia University Library in the United States holds a collection of his surviving papers from 1942-46.

What would David Hill Young have thought of his second cousin? More important still, the life story of William Henry Donald has many more chapters to be told but what can be seen from this snapshot is that he lived an extraordinary life and regardless of his political views it is unanimous this individual certainly left his mark.

Time now to return to David and Emily. While living in Hong Kong their first child, Mary Penelope Galt Young, known as Penelope within the family, was born in December 1911. Then, shortly afterwards the family were on the move once again but the impetus for this move is not entirely clear; however, word from within the family is that 'work in the Far East was drawing to a logical conclusion for expats' and so next we find them living in Colombo, Ceylon. The why of Ceylon is perhaps easily explained in the context of; firstly, David's uncle Samuel, but more relevant still is his cousin Jeanie Renfrew Johnston. We know David had visited his uncle several times as he travelled back and forth to Scotland from the Far East. It is entirely possible that at the time his contract was not renewed at Changtefu, David contacted his network seeking a new position. Also, it should be remembered that not only was his young brother Charlie still in Colombo operating a business as a Merchant of even greater relevance is his cousin Jeanie had married Charles Arthur Hutson of London, a Mechanical Engineer who was now living in Colombo. Their residence at that time was 'Brentham', 3 Cambridge Place, Colombo 7 which, in 1961 was the grand residence of the Australian High Commission. Following the death of Charles Alfred Hutson in 1908, Jeanie's husband Charles Arthur Hutson took over as owner operator of his father's business: C.A. Hutson & Co. History has told us time and time again this Young family are known to be great communicators within the family circle and outside, and to use these connections as a means of seeking out opportunities. This time David has secured the role as Managing Partner, within the firm of Messrs C.A. Hutson & Co.: Shipbuilders, Marine Engineers and Boilermakers, a business previously established by Charles Alfred Hutson. Just like Clark, Young & Co., Hutsons were a significant business in the Colombo commercial marketplace and while images have been included of their entries in the 1917 Ferguson's Directory for Ceylon there is also an illuminating write-up in the previously mentioned publication of 'Twentieth Century Impressions of Ceylon'. That book describes Hutsons as:

> 'Founded in 1886, this firm, who own the Ceylon Engineering Works, Colombo, with a branch in Kandapola, have recently erected new and commodious premises at Mutwal, immediately facing the entrance to the harbour, having outgrown their old premises on the seashore. This well-known landmark had to be removed owing to the harbour improvements. The firm's new engineering shop is fitted with the latest machinery, also with the electric-lights for the night work rendered continually necessary owing to the large amount of ship repairs undertaken. The firm engage in engineering work of all kinds. They have built the large oil tanks seen from the harbour, also several of the launches and tugs for use in the harbour and many of the factories of the island. They are agents for Messrs. Ruston, Proctor & Co, of Lincoln, England, and Messrs. Crossley Bros., Ltd.,

of Manchester. Their fine new foundry has a moulding floor of 4500 sq. ft. and contains three cupolas as well as three brass furnaces and can turn out castings up to 10 tons each in weight. A full set of propeller blades, each weighing 2 1/4 tons, for the *S.S. Istria*, may be specified as a typical piece of work turned out here. There is also a smithy, with forges, steam-hammers, and bending-rolls, and a carpenter's shop, thus enabling the firm to take up any construction work. The business is under the direction of Mr. C.A. Hutson and his manager Mr. W.R. Burnett, assisted by five European engineers and about 350 native employees. The firm are on the Army and Admiralty lists as capable of undertaking contracts for those great department of State.

Obviously, this was a great move for David and Emily, and with close family around them, their integration into the local expat society would have been a lot easier.

Like most ambitious men of his era, David spent the first period of his working life gaining broad experience and trying to carve out a career. He had clearly proven himself to be a well-credentialed fellow who secured roles within benchmark organisations but all the while he was forced to wrestle with the uncertainty and stress created by the corporate ambitions of these organisations eager to garner a greater and greater market share in what was a highly politicised environment. Now that he had landed a senior role in a great firm in a stable marketplace he and Emily could finally relax a little. At this point he must have reflected on those tough years and quietly acknowledged that perhaps it was all worthwhile.

Whilst C.A. Hutson & Co. was yet another firm of distinction it could offer the stability and certainty this young family needed and at the same time reward this growing family with a good lifestyle. Even though his uncle Samuel had died some years prior, David was well acquainted with Edwin Stanhope Clark, his uncle's partner in Clark, Young & Co. And, with the Clarks also firmly entrenched in Colombo's social circles this would have made David and Emily's integration into the social fabric of Colombo almost seamless. While their residential address is unknown there are numerous family letters relating to Kandapola and at one time there was a family anecdote that suggested David had perhaps worked on a Tea Plantation there as a Chief Engineer. The more likely scenario is that David worked for a time at the Hutson business premises in Kandapola and as such could have consulted to any number of plantation clients on behalf of his employer. It should also be noted that Kandapola is an idyllic respite location for those Europeans wishing to escape the humidity of a Ceylon summer. Situated at just over 6,300 feet above sea level it enjoys the reputation as being the coolest place in all Ceylon. Conveniently, the narrow gauge railway line covering the 31kms from central Colombo to Kandapola had opened in 1904 and would have provided easy access for those expats who did not return to Europe when the monsoon summer weather was descending on the populace.

While in Colombo David and Emily welcome two more children into their family; the first was Robert Tyrrell born in the December of 1912, then their youngest child, Doreen Isabel, was born on the 26 August of 1914. This was just three weeks after England declared war on Germany. With the whole of Europe now on a war footing and uncertainty surrounding the future of Ceylon, Emily and David would have had many a conversation about how best to protect their family. In their first six years of marriage David and Emily had faced many obstacles but now they were faced with the biggest dilemma of all. Watching helplessly as events unfolded in Europe it must have been an agonising decision to have to make. Stay or go? When to go? Was it safe to travel? Ultimately, the decision was made. The year is 1916 and once again they were packing up, but this time it was David, Emily, Penelope, Robert and toddler Doreen who sailed for the homeland where David immediately joined the war effort to do his part serving King and country.

Aware that David's strengths were with the installation and commissioning of steam engines it would be a given that this is where his talents would be best employed by the War Office. Family correspondence from around this time indicated David and Emily were living in Belfast where they remained for the duration of the war and from David's resume, we learn he was commissioned by the War Office to work in the shipyards of Workman, Clark & Co. But who was this company and what did this appointment mean for David and his career? Most of the answers were found in a wonderful little booklet entitled 'Belfast Shipbuilders' published on behalf of the Ulster-Scots Community Network. That story begins by stating the golden era of Belfast Shipbuilding was from 1880 to the outbreak of the Great War where by 1914 Belfast accounted for nearly 8% of world output. The booklet states that 'A Financial Times supplement in March 1914 described Belfast as "the premier shipbuilding centre of the entire world". It went on to advise that 'Belfast possessed two great shipyards: Harland & Wolff and Workman, Clark & Co. The former was the 'big yard', while the latter was affectionately known as the 'wee yard.' The article makes it clear that 'To describe Workman, Clark & Co. as the 'wee yard' was to seriously understate the scale of the operation. Indeed, in 1901, 1909, 1910 and 1913 the wee yard's output exceeded that of the big yard.'

Astonishingly, Belfast's shipbuilding success was achieved despite them not having ready access to local sources of iron and coal and without an established tradition in shipbuilding. This confounded the experts, and at one point a Dr John Lynch set to exploring why this was so. His findings were published in a paper entitled 'An Unlikely Success Story: The Belfast Shipbuilding Industry 1880-1935' published in 2001, wherein he attributes 'the success of the industry to a "happy coincidence of timing, luck, nepotism and the Protestant work ethic". What also seems to have been in their favour was that Belfast entered the industry without the impediment of a shipbuilding past, leaving it free to develop 'largely on the basis of "new technology".' Maybe it was timing, maybe it was luck, but I believe nepotism paid a strong part because the partisanship they exercised translated into a highly skilled and highly motivated local workforce not only capable of undertaking the work required but they quickly earned for Belfast an enviable reputation for their 'state-of-the-art design and construction methods.'

This is the backdrop to David's entré into the Belfast shipbuilding arena during WW1. He was stationed in the 'wee yards' of Workman, Clark & Co. Ltd. who receive honourable mention in another publication on the history of shipbuilding in WW1 entitled - 'British Shipbuilding Yards, Vol 1,2,3, by Norman L. Middlemiss, published in 1995. This later profile on Workman, Clark & Co. reads as follows -

> 'Workman, Clark & Co Ltd., Belfast, Co. Cork - mercantile, plus 2 small monitors, 3 Flower-class sloops, 7 patrol boats, boom defence vessels, 'War' cargo ships Workman Clark, Belfast M.29-class monitors M.32 (22.5.15), M.33 (22.5.15) Arabis-class fleet sweeping sloops *Pentstemon* [sic] (15.2.16), *Petunia* (3.4.16), Anchusa-class convoy sloops *Syringa* (29.9.17), *Wildflower* (12.4.18), P-type patrol boats P.15, P.16, P.17 - PC-type decoy patrol boats PC.60, PC.61, PC.69, PC70'

According to the 'Belfast Shipbuilding' booklet 'During the Great War Workman, Clark & Co built 35 vessels for the Admiralty and also many standard merchant ships to replace those lost to German U-boats. The latter ships were built at break-neck speed: [with the] south yard ...... finishing a standard ship, an 8,000 ton vessel, being completed in 3 ¾ days from the time of launch.'

The early history of Workman, Clark & Co is one of compounding success, and in 'Grace's Guide to British Industrial History' there is yet another report on this firm which reads, in the '1900s Workman, Clark and Co began to establish their reputation for innovative transatlantic liners. The Company had also expanded, with seven berths in the North Yard and five berths in the South Yard.' 'A number of companies established long term relations with Workman Clark and Co. including Irish Star Line, Cunard Line, Alfred Holt and the United Fruit Co plus others.' That last business will eventually become extremely relevant to David's working life and go part way to explaining the incredible connection about to be revealed between David Hill Young, Workman, Clark & Co., Alfred Holt and the United Fruit Company.

At the time David took up his position with the War Office's Ministry of Shipping, the firm is listed thus - '1914 ..... Shipbuilders and engineers. Speciality: steel screw steamers of large dimensions for passenger and cargo service; also, builders of turbine machinery under Parsons' patents. Employees 9,000. WWI - This was perhaps the peak output time for the yard. At this stage the yard employed 12,000 people. The work consisted of repairs, naval orders and merchant ships. Alongside this, the demand for fruiters, cargo-liners, cargo-ships, and standard "B" tramps continued. The yard also set a world record for the number of rivets driven home by one man in one working day: 11,209.' Throughout the war, production continued unabated, was highly profitable and David was there not only doing his bit for the War but was also gaining invaluable experience and making very useful contacts.

There is one final profile item in respect of this firm that explains the situation within the shipbuilding industry at the end of WW1:

> '1918 - The Furness Group sold the Howdon yard to new owners led by R. A. Workman of Workman, Clark and Co Belfast who were associated with Sperling & Company, London Merchant Bankers. Sperling and Company used the Northumberland Company to create a shipbuilding combine, the largest in Britain under Sir Alex Kennedy. As a public company, The Northumberland Shipbuilding Co Ltd acquired majority holdings in William Doxford and Sons of Sunderland, followed by Fairfield Shipbuilding and Engineering Co of Govan; Workman, Clark and Co of Belfast;

In the end 1850-1950

Blythswood Shipbuilding Co; Monmouth Shipbuilding Co and the Lancashire Iron and Steel Co.

1920 - The value of the company rose from £2.4M [in 1918] to £7.0M by 1920.

Never content to rest on his laurels, we learn a little more about David's level of ambition from a letter he sent to the War Office towards the end of the war wherein he explains he - 'Came from Colombo to join the Army, and for the last 2 1/2 years stationed in Ireland, as the Representative of the Controller General of Merchant Shipbuilding, Director of Auxiliary Vessels, War Office, and the Ministry of Shipping.' This letter was all about David attempting to apply for higher officer ranking. I am pleased to advise he was successful, and the family archives hold a Certificate issued in the Reign of King George V stating that as of the 1st January 1917 David was promoted to the rank of Lieutenant in the Land Forces. A short time later he was promoted again, this time to the rank of Captain. Clearly his work was recognised as vital to the war effort especially considering those auxiliary vessels carried out a vital service in the distribution of men, equipment and food supplies as well as carrying out decoy and reconnaissance missions. His role was responsible for overseeing all work undertaken and to ensure that it satisfied the design and maintenance criteria as set down by the Royal Navy. Given all that, his promotion to Captain was entirely justified. For the benefit of those non-military readers a Captain in the Navy is equivalent to a Colonel in the Army - so one has to say - well done!

While a promotion and pay rise would have been welcome it was the uncertain future for the industry that would have been of greater concern. With the war at an end and without forward contracts, more and more workers were being laid off, and once again the Shipping Industry was about to be littered with the casualties of boom to bust outcomes. Shortly, the firm of Workman, Clark & Co. would fall victim to this disastrous downward spiral that was post-war industrial Britain. For David Hill Young, his world came crashing down on 30 August 1921 when a letter was delivered from Whitehall advising he would be demobbed on 13 September next. He was informed he could retain the rank of Captain and outlining the conditions for wearing his uniform. There is little doubt David would have preferred a job and no rank considering unemployment in this sector would soon reach a staggering 30% against a national labour figure of 8.5%. 1923 saw Workman's record profits spiral into a loss of £3.12M with the ramification that Northumberland Shipbuilding Co defaulted on guaranteed debenture interest, which in turn led to litigation with shareholders seeking damages for deceit, conspiracy and statutory liability.

Notwithstanding the above, David must have seen the writing on the wall because over six months prior, he began to get his credentials in order to update his resumé. One step in this process required that he write to the Hong Kong office of Mercantile Marine requesting a copy of his Certification as a First Class Engineer. Certificate #3865 was issued in lieu of #1982 of 25 April 1904, which he declared as lost. The replacement was issued on 1 March 1921 and posted to his residence at 87 Cliftonville Road, Belfast, which, it turns out, is only about a mile from the Docks. Assuming this is where the family were living since arriving in Belfast, it is fair to say that when local transport was interrupted or non-existent, David would have had an invigorating but comfortable half hour walk, from his home to the Docks.

David remained in Britain and persevered until 1925 but in the face of continued high levels of unemployment and the scale of social decline it is no wonder, he decided to immigrate to the United States. Hoping it truly would be the land of opportunity, David, Emily and the children left their latest home at St Johns Park, Ormeau Road, Belfast, and set sail for Boston on 30 November 1925 aboard the RMS *Celtic*, a vessel of the White Star Line. The *Celtic*, like David Hill Young, was indefatigable and a WW1 survivor. In 1917 she had struck a mine off the Isle of Man that took the lives of seventeen onboard, but the vessel survived. She was then torpedoed by German U-Boat UB-77 in the Irish Sea in March 1918, and again remained afloat despite the damage and the loss of six lives. After that incident, the *Celtic* was towed into Liverpool for repairs. It is pleasing to note that in December 1925 she voyaged across the Atlantic without incident and the family disembarked in New York on 8th December. They did not receive the warmest of welcomes given it was a chilly 4°C that day.

Family reminiscences around this move to America are that it was forced upon David and precipitated by the long and painful struggle he had trying to secure worthwhile long term employment anywhere in Britain. Ever resourceful and resilient this survivor did what any self-respecting Young would do - he used his connections. This ultimately led to finding employment with a firm associated with both Holts and Workman's: the United Fruit Company of Boston. The calibre of the man is vouched for by the fact that yet again he had secured a position with a company who were a market leader in their field. United Fruit at this time was cashed up and on an acquisition drive. In fact, by 1930 it had absorbed more than 20 rival firms and had a capitalised value in excess of $US215 million. It was also the largest employer in Central America and owned over 3.5 million acres of land there and in the Caribbean devoted to the production of fruit, especially bananas. One of their fruit carrying vessels was the *Tivives* built in 1911 in the yards of Workman, Clark & Co. Whilst several of their vessels had been requisitioned by the US Navy during WW1 they now had big plans to restore their fleet to commercial operational status. This would have kept David and others very busy.

In March 1927, Captain D.H. Young seized the opportunity to return to Ireland, but this time on behalf of the United Fruit Company not the War Office. He was there for the launch of a new vessel. Accompanying him was his daughter Penelope who had the honour of breaking the bottle of champagne at the launch of the *S.S. Tela*. The Belfast News-letter newspaper for Friday March 25 1927 carried the story along with several photographs of Superintendent Engineer David Hill Young and his daughter. He was back again in 1930. This time for the launch of the *Musa* also built by Workman, Clark & Co. as a refrigerated banana vessel of the United Fruit Company fleet. It was another triumphant return for him and on this occasion launch honours fell to daughter Doreen. The *S.S. Musa* was 5833 GRT in burthen, 416 ft. long with a beam of 56ft. and came equipped with state of the art oil-fired boilers, turbo-electric transmission, single screw, echo-sounding and had a top speed of 15.5 knots. She sailed under the Panamanian flag of convenience. At this point we can only wonder what his grandfather, Captain John Young, and his great-grandfather Captain Alexander Young, would have thought of this man whose skill and knowledge were well employed in supervising the building of such a stupendous state-of-the-art vessel.

From this point forward, his working life remains on the up and up and the family were next discovered comfortably residing in Brookline, Massachusetts. US Government archives show that on three separate occasions David made Petitions for Citizenship of the United States. The first was as early as April 1926 when he was refused on the grounds of insufficient residency. He applied again in July 1931, but again refused. Finally, in January of 1933, his application was accepted, but sadly by then his personal life had taken a downward turn when on 1 May 1929 he lost the love of his life - his beloved Emily. Family photographs and letters remain chronicling their life from the time of their long distance courtship, which nurtured to become an outstanding marital partnership. From those shy beginnings they became global citizens, endured and prevailed, and surely David's only regret would have been they were deprived of growing old together.

Despite renouncing his Scottish Citizenship David remained close to family and friends in the home country. He made numerous Atlantic crossings and was a regular correspondent. At one point David did remarry an Australian living and working in New York at the time. Her name is Blanche Suttcliffe and from my meetings with her descendants I have learned that she was a nurse and a very adventurous woman. There is also a story in The Sydney Morning Herald for Monday 7 September 1914, Blanche and her friend Clara Fairland, both nurses, decided to sail on a P & O steamer to London at their own expense and offer their services to the British Red Cross - there they joined the war effort.

The 1930 Census for New York State has Blanche living at Brookhaven in Suffolk County, and working at the Mather

In the end 1850-1950

Memorial Hospital, Port Jefferson in Brookhaven. This is probably where this couple met since around that time David was hospitalised. They married in November 1932 in New York and then on 8th December they took a delayed honeymoon voyage on board *SS President Hoover* to Honolulu where Blanche had many friends. They arrived on the 5th January 1933. Sadly, by the April Blanche had fallen ill and this is where she passed away on the 11 April 1933.

David returned to Brookline, Massachusetts and remained close to his three children and their families. David's stories so inspired his daughter Doreen; that, in the 1960s she made visits to Scotland and ultimately write an account of his seafaring Young ancestors of whom he was so very proud. There is so much more that could be written about David Hill Young but suffice to say he lived a long and adventure filled life. He earned huge respect in the industry for his Marine Engineering abilities and undoubted personal qualities, but it is now time to hand the family maritime baton over to his only son, Robert Tyrrell Young.

> "What connexion can there have been between many people in the innumerable histories of this world, who, from opposite sides of great gulfs, have, nevertheless, been very curiously brought together!"
> *Charles Dickens, Bleak House*

This virtually sums up my feelings at this point as I continue writing the tale of this Young Family whose lives are so curiously interwoven with other people and world events. With only a broad chronological outline in mind at the outset, my overall intent was to attempt to add to what had already been written about these largely unknown Scots. I also wanted to explore how these Young family sailors' and sea captains' experiences meshed with Scottish whaling and seafaring history. As research progressed I was constantly surprised by the length, breadth and strength of their generational involvement. However, the most seminal moment came when it became apparent the father and son at the beginning of this family's story should be in the mould of the father and son who fall at the end. What we have, in both instances, are fathers whose sons not only follow in their footsteps they build on their father's legacy to reach even greater heights and achieve even greater recognition. These men embody the true legacy that defines the character of these seafaring Youngs. Along the way, except for one individual, they never lost sight of the practicalities of life, the importance of family and community or the value of their humanity. That very famous Scot, William Wallace, is quoted as saying - 'Every man dies. Not every man really lives' - and that just about sums up my impressions of the game-breakers in this clan and brings me to the story of Robert Tyrrell Young.

Robert did not realise as a young lad in Ceylon and Ireland that even his name set the benchmark high. Robert is the name he inherited from his 5th great-grandfather who was the very first sailor in the Young family. Tyrrell is a connection to his mother's noble ancestry in Ireland. The family have watercolour miniatures of the Tyrrell line with one inscribed: Adam Tyrrell, Grange Castle 1781. Such ancestral history can often embody great responsibility, which can sometimes be overwhelming, but this Robert Tyrrell Young was neither awestruck nor submerged by the weight of any leadership responsibility; moreover, throughout his life he embraced any opportunity to step up and lead the way. In arriving at the point of building on his father's legacy it is fair to say that he was not only close to his father, but fascinated by the work he did, and with almost two centuries of maritime history coursing through his veins there is no doubt that Robert's life's work could be considered preordained.

Throughout this story there is evidence to show that education remained the cornerstone of the Young Family's success. Right from those early days when they offered their financial support for the establishment of the Montrose Academy they have ensured that all the children received the very best education available. In Robert's case he attended Thayer Academy in Braintree, Massachusetts before going on to Tufts College's School of Engineering in Medford where he was awarded a Bachelor of Science degree with a Civil Engineering major. Thayer and Tufts are institutions of quality and Robert proved to be a quality student, graduating with Honours. He was accordingly awarded membership of the prestigious Tau Beta Pi Association, the oldest Engineering Honour Society in America and the second oldest Collegiate Honour Society in the entire United States. The benchmarks required to qualify for such an Award are: *Integrity and Excellence in Engineering.* Membership is restricted to those who have 'conferred honour upon their Alma Mater by distinguished scholarship and exemplary character as students in engineering.' Institutions with the calibre and history of Thayer and Tufts also instil a sense of pride and for Robert there was the added bonus they were a great fit for him personally. He once wrote that they gave him a sense of belonging and at the same time offered quality and opportunity in education. These institutions enjoy a formidable reputation to this very day.

Robert's first paid employment came in 1935 when straight out of Tufts he went to work for Bethlehem Steel Co. in their shipbuilding division at Quincy in Massachusetts. Shadowing his father, Robert's role was as Hull Structural Designer in their Central Technical Department. The Bethlehem Steel Co. was previously known as Fore River Ship & Engine Company and was established by Alexander Graham Bell's famous assistant, Thomas A Watson, in 1886. Bethlehem Steel took over Fore River Ship & Engine Company in 1913, expanding the shipbuilding side mostly on the back of Government contracts to build destroyers and submarines for the US Navy during WW1. They remained fully operational post-war and gained the reputation as one of the world's great shipbuilders. Their capacity was expanded pre-WW2 by the healthy injection of $US21M from the US Navy. Back in 1932 they had built three vessels for the United Fruit Co., David Hill Young's employer, and it is highly likely that this was the conduit needed to settle Robert into his first job. These three vessels were launched in the April, June and August of '32 and were identical ships of 6983 tons. Christened - *Antigua, Quirigua* and *Veragua*, they were designed to carry passengers and cargo on those all-important US/Central American routes. These vessels remained in service until 1964 when they were unanimously scrapped. Curious coincidence or planned obsolescence?

While at University, Robert had made the acquaintance of Miss Virginia Belliveau. Virginia was a graduate of Radcliffe College Class of '35. Whilst this is yet another link to prestige and quality in education, it also says a great deal about the lady herself. Radcliffe was established in 1879 as the 'Harvard Annex' for women. However, it was the respect and leadership of Radcliffe's third President, Ada Louise Comstock, which set that college on its path to greatness. Since Ada Comstock was President pre- and post- Virginia's time, and a vigorous supporter of women's higher education in America and overseas, it is fair to assume that Virginia and her contemporaries were influenced in some way. Robert and Virginia wed in 1937 in Medford and Robert always paid credit to Virginia for her unwavering support and he proudly stated so in his resume. The couple enjoyed an enduring partnership and having met Virginia in her later years I remember her as a worldly, elegant and intelligent woman always eager to recount stories of the family's international experiences and travels. At the same time, she was clear about the pride she took in Robert's achievement.

1938 was set to become the turning point in Robert's career; this was the year he joined the American Bureau of Shipping. Little did he realise but this new working partnership would last for over forty years. For those who are unfamiliar with the ABS a potted history is required. The ABS was originally charted in 1862 in New York to certify Ships and Sea Captains much in the way Lloyds did in Britain. It published its initial 'Rules for Survey and Classing Wooden Vessels' in 1870, which was the first real means by which a previously self-regulating industry could look to setting technical standards for shipbuilding design and for shipbuilders. Right from the outset, the Bureau recognised it needed to move relevant to the changing requirements of the industry, so when wood gave way to iron the ABS established new standards and published them as 'Rules for Survey and Classing of Iron Vessels'. By 1890 the industry had transitioned from iron to steel and once again the ABS was on the front foot and published the latest ABS Rules for 'Building and Classing Steel Vessels'. The ABS Rule Book has remained a dynamic document under constant review in order to uphold the organisation's mantra of involvement in the 'development and improvement of safety standards in shipping.' Since its foundation in 1862 it has remained a not-for-profit organisation in order to fulfil its augmented role as an agent of the US government on matters of government vessel classification.

When Robert Tyrrell Young joined the ABS his initial role was as a Marine Surveyor. Interestingly, it was his great-great-grandfather Captain Alexander Young [1782-1848] who was the first Marine Surveyor in the family and can be found listed as Lloyds Surveyor in the 1846 and 1847 Directories for Montrose. A further notice in the March 28 1845 edition of the Montrose Review carries his name in relation to harbour management, and as Chairman of the Shipowners & Shipmasters Association at the Port's A.G.M. His great-grandfather Captain John Young [1810-1871] also acted as a Ships Surveyor and Broker for Lloyds in Glasgow. While it would seem, the apple had not fallen far from the tree, these facts were unknown to Robert at the time he joined the ABS. Today, the ABS has a Mission Statement that reads - 'To serve the public interest as well as the needs of our members and clients by promoting the security of life and property, and preserving the natural environment.' In truth this is an objective that has been shared by the British and the Americans and has not changed since Lloyds began over three centuries ago at Edward Lloyd's humble Coffee House in London in 1688.

While ABS headquarters in 1938 were on Lower Broadway in New York City, Robert's first posting was with the Technical Division located at 24 Old Slip, New York. He would spend two years there familiarising himself with the 'Rules' before being sent to the Federal Shipyards in Kearny, New Jersey where a number of the U.S. Maritime Commission's C-2 type ships were being built. At the completion of this project the Bureau transferred Robert to Bath Iron Works in Bath, Maine, to overseer the building of four new cargo ships for American Export Lines. Robert found this an interesting assignment considering this shipyard had not built a ship of this type since WW1. Their output since 1920 had been confined to destroyers, trawlers and luxury yachts and indeed Robert's first survey job was on a yacht that had been sold to the British Royal Navy. Britain had just declared war on Germany and the Royal Navy planned to convert it to an anti-submarine patrol craft for reconnaissance duty around Bermuda.

Once the last two American Export Line cargo ships were delivered Robert was posted to South Portland, Maine, where U.S.M.C. [United States Marine Commission] had constructed new shipyards with a view to building Liberty ships. The original Liberty ship was designed as a cargo vessel by the British as a part of their supply fleet. It was simple and easy to build, had a coal burning power plant because Britain had substantial coal reserves, and was designed to fill a void in merchant marine shipping. In 1940, Britain placed an urgent order for 60 more units from American civilian shipyards to replace their war losses. The urgency and obvious size of this order meant that very soon the design was modified; predominantly, so that it conformed to American construction practices as defined by the US Marine Commission and pass the rules set for marine surveys to be conducted by Robert and others of the ABS. Greater production efficiency was achieved by replacing many of the rivets with welds, and whilst this amounted to a 30% saving in labour cost it came at a high cost of life because ships were literally breaking in half and sinking. There were two main issues; one was that the grade of steel used suffered from embrittlement; and two, the welding methods employed were inadequate. British Professor of Engineering, Constance Tipper, identified these issues as particularly relevant to those ships operating in the North Atlantic where below critical temperatures were causing cracks to propagate across very large distances; an issue that would not arise in riveted ships.

It's now December 7 1941 and Japan had just bombed Pearl Harbour. The US joins the war and American women, like their British counterparts, are now entering the factories to fill those jobs vacated by their menfolk. The new look Liberty ships were designated as EC2-S-C1 class of cargo ship, their coal-fired engine had been replaced with an oil burning powerplant and these were then being mass-produced on an unprecedented scale. The Liberty ship came to symbolize US wartime industrial ingenuity and production. Because of its unsafe early history, the Liberty Ship had acquired a poor public image which was further exacerbated by its unglamorous workhorse appearance. US President Franklin D. Roosevelt once described it as a 'dreadful looking object'. Time magazine and others alluded to it as an 'Ugly Duckling'. In an attempt to overcome these negatives, improve its public image and reinvigorate public subscription, September 27, 1941 was dubbed Liberty Ship Day. In all 480 Liberty ships were produced at South Portland, and Robert wrote that in his view they contributed in no small measure to the Allied victory. Many of these vessels were supplied to the British as part of the notorious Lend-Lease Scheme, some found their way into the Russian Fleet and the remainder went into service in the US Navy Fleet.

The value of Robert's contribution to and expertise in the work carried out at South Portland on behalf of the ABS was recognised in 1944 when he was appointed to a Board of the U.S. Navy chartered to 'Investigate the Design & Construction of Welded Steel Merchant Vessels'. The findings of the Board ultimately had far reaching implications and brought together for the first time the standards set by the ABS for Merchant ships and the standards set by the Maritime Commission on behalf of the US Navy for what they termed 'their specific requirements'. Rear Admiral Harvey F. Johnson of the US Coast Guard was Chairman of that Board. Just how the lessons learned would translate into useful contributions to the Merchant Fleet in a post-war environment was yet another task for the Board. While the first edition of the new Manual was issued back in August 1943 it was subsequently amended to incorporate the Board later findings in 1944. The American Welding Society and the American Bureau of Shipping approved these new guidelines.

There is so much more to the story behind this game-changing ship but the final chapter for now is devoted to Robert Tyrrell Young and the *SS Jeremiah O'Brien*. All up some eighteen American shipyards built just over 2700 Liberty Ships between 1941 and 1945 but the *SS Jeremiah O'Brien* remains one of only two fully functional Liberty Ships afloat. She was restored to be historically accurate to her original build and on the Bridge is the original ABS Seaworthy Certificate signed by Robert T. Young and Bob MacGregor. Today she is moored at Pier 45, Fisherman's Wharf, San Francisco and holds the distinction of being classified as a living museum on the National Register of Historic Places in the United States and is listed on maps as an Historic Landmark. The Museum's website states - 'the *O'Brien* transports you back .... to when sailors braved the harshest of high seas and threat of enemy attack.' Launched in the June of 1943 she made seven WW2 voyages between England and Australia, plus others from Ireland to South America. During the D-Day landings the *SS Jeremiah O'Brien* made eleven crossings of the English Channel carrying supplies and personnel.

After the War the *Jeremiah*, as she was affectionately known, was mothballed and laid up at Suisun Bay to the north of San Francisco. Thirty years on it was decided to save her from the scrapyard and it took volunteer crew members hundreds of hours to see her cleaned of the preservative she was smeared with and in 1979 she was sailed into dry-dock in San Francisco to undergo a full restoration. There are many unique things about this gallant lady of the sea, but the one real standout feature is that she is the only ship ever to have steamed her way out of mothball status. This lucky Liberty Ship was the recipient of much largesse and countless hours of work to return her to certifiable seaworthy status. The *Jeremiah* has been described as '.. a steaming memorial to the seamen of the U.S. Merchant Marine who served on Liberty ships in World War II, to their Navy gun crews, and to the civilian men and women who built the largest single class of ships in history.'

On May 23 1994 en route to Europe for D-Day celebrations she stopped off in New York where Robert T. Young was presented with a copy of a memorial plaque, the original of which is now on the Bridge of the *SS Jeremiah O'Brien*. It reads in part -

'This is to certify that the name Robert T. Young has been inscribed forever into history aboard the World War II Liberty Ship, S.S. Jeremiah O'Brien. Your name will be seen and honoured by millions of visitors from around the world for generations to come. Your contribution has helped preserve this historic vessel as a tribute to the spirit of freedom.'

Signed Rear-Admiral T.J. Patterson, Chairman, Normandy '94 Committee and Robert E Blake, Chairman, National Liberty Ship Memorial.'

What a very proud moment that would have been for Robert and indeed for his entire family which by then included daughter Madge Hazel Young born March 1942, and son David Tyrrell Young born February 1945 in Portland, Maine.

V.E. Day marked the end of the war in Europe and the end of the South Portland S.B. Corporation and once again Robert was transferred back to New York's Technical Department before being assigned to the Todd Repair Yards, Hoboken, New Jersey. About this same time the ABS was expanding overseas, and Robert was called upon to proceed to Buenos Aires, Argentina. The family boarded the *S.S. Del Norte* of the Delta Shipping Line and sailed south to a country in political limbo where Juan and Evita Peron were clinging onto rule. Robert was not only responsible for the port of Buenos Aires but the whole of Argentina; which meant a thousand miles of coastline, north and south of the capital, all the way to Tierra Del Fuego. Since it was designated a one man post it was certainly a very busy role. Robert once described it as one of the most interesting periods of his entire life.

There was one particularly interesting project involving the little known trade on the upper reaches of the Parana River, known as the Alta Parana. It surrounds the transport of maté, which is a vegetable tea consumed in large quantities by the gauchos of Argentina and Uruguay. It is transported in self-propelled barges, which have to be shallow draft due to some white water sections along the river. These craft were subject to severe hogging because they have traditionally been constructed with a high length to depth ratio. For the uninitiated, 'Hogging is the stress a ship's hull or keel experiences that causes the center or the keel to bend upward.' As a part of his role, Robert met with a local barge owner who had recently returned to Argentina from Holland where he had purchased a new diesel engine. He approached Robert for advice as to how best to install it. Since these barges were not classed Robert agreed to do it if he could find the time. A window of opportunity presented itself on the 18 October when business shut down for a three-day public holiday to commemorate Peron coming to power. Robert planned to take the Sunderland flying boat from Buenos Aires to Posadas where the barge was moored. They were only half-way into the flight when one engine began sputtering and the pilot announced he was going to land on the river whereupon he climbed out of the cockpit and onto the wing and after some investigation declared it was only a faulty spark plug. The faulty spark plug was duly replaced and then the flying boat took off again and completed its journey without further incident.

Robert conducted a survey of the hull, which revealed it had been subjected to very severe hogging at some stage with consequential buckling of the hull. His recommendation to the owner was to build a new hull to accommodate the new engine and this is what happened. Robert contended that this 'must be one of the very few times where a recommendation to "jack up the smokestack and put a new hull under it" was actually carried out.' Unfortunately, Robert's return to Buenos Aires was delayed for a further three days because of a severe tropical rainstorm, which confined him to his quarters. He described his accommodation as a fourth-rate hotel with a dirt floor in the bedroom. The chambermaid would arrive at bedtime to sprinkle an anti-insect powder around the bedposts and she would announce to him - 'Es para los bichos, Senor' (it is for the bugs, Sir).

Back in Buenos Aires Robert was kept particularly busy, especially in grain export season, when as many as thirty ships could be lined up waiting for a berth to load up. Because of the wait time, many would take advantage of this time to carry out boiler or other surveys, which made Robert's work schedule very crowded indeed. Now given the harbour was more a confluence of two rivers, the Rio Parana Gauzu and the Uruguay, this made it subject to silting as a result of the heavy rainfall. When dredging was inadequate the shallow water gave rise to issues such as ships running aground, or ships running over their own anchors, which resulted in unwarranted hull damage. There was only one dry-dock in Buenos Aires and it was not capable of accommodating anything bigger than a Liberty ship, so Robert was frequently challenged in determining what temporary repairs were sufficient to ensure any ship could make the next available dry-dock on its proposed route.

Life in Argentina for Robert and his family posed personal challenges as well. On one occasion when the family were heading State-side for home leave they decided to take the scenic route. This meant boarding the Trans-Andean Railroad and travelling to Santiago, Chile from where it was an easy matter of taking a ship from either of two ports: San Antonio or Valparaiso. This is Robert's story - 'This train crossed the Andes through a pass which reaches an altitude of almost 14,000 ft. and it was at this point our locomotive had had enough and it quit. After a 10-hour wait, a relief engine appeared. However, it was not altogether unpleasant, as the scenery was magnificent. In spite of the 14,000 foot altitude, Mt. Aconcagua towered another 9,000 above us; at 23,000 ft. it is the highest mountain in the Southern Hemisphere.' This will not be this intrepid family's only brush with calamity while heading home on leave.

After four years in Buenos Aires and having survived one aborted anti-Peron revolution and the death of Eva Peron Robert got his orders to relocate to Antwerp, Belgium. He had been appointed to the post of Principal Surveyor, a very different assignment to South America. Whilst Antwerp was also a very busy port it was also far better equipped, it had several dry-docks with excellent repair facilities. The volume of work was sufficient for four surveyors in addition to Robert. He recalled many interesting jobs while in Antwerp, the largest and most significant of these was the repair survey involving *World Concord*, a large tanker of 80,000 tons, which had broken in two in a raging gale in the Irish Sea. The bow section had been washed onto rocks and had its bottom ripped out. It was later floated on compressed air and towed back to Antwerp. The stern half remained afloat was also towed to

Antwerp. Both halves were placed into the same dry-dock, lined up and re-joined. Robert's initial damage survey report listed in excess of 700 items. *World Concord* was successfully repaired and returned to active service.

After three years in Antwerp Robert was promoted yet again, and this time it would see him take up a post as Principal Surveyor for Great Britain, Ireland and Western Europe. He would now be working out of the London Offices of the ABS. There were many challenges to be faced in an extremely busy port like London, but Robert had his eye on a higher goal; securing British Government recognition and approval for the ABS to assign Load Liners to ABS classed ships which were registered in the United Kingdom and flying the British flag. This had been a long standing frustration within the ABS because other major classification societies had such authority and conversely Lloyds Register was recognised by the US Government to assign Load Lines to US flagged ships. Armed with the knowledge that a considerable number of ABS classed ships were flying the British flag, and recognising that Caltex alone had twelve tankers and was one of the largest single operators in London, Robert approached them for advice. As a consequence of Robert's discussions, Caltex signified that they were more than willing to assist. This not only was a significant victory for the ABS, it cemented Robert's professional status as a negotiator for the ABS. Once this stumbling block was overcome final approval came through in short order.

All up Robert, Virginia and their children Madge and David, spent twelve years in London. Business wise Robert had made a number of good friends across the industry in all his European jurisdictions, particularly with the Greek shipowners who had consistently supported the ABS throughout history. Also, in his time he had seen the London Office grow from a staff of three in 1956 to a payroll of fifty-one by the time Robert left.

It is now time to recount another unfortunate story about home leave. It was the era of the grand passenger liners plying the

In the end 1850-1950

Atlantic; and, being in the shipping business Robert and his fellow Bureau personal patronised ship travel whenever possible. Therefore, when the time rolled around for home leave in 1956, Robert decided to return to the States on the brand new state of the art Italian Line's *S.S. Andrea* Doria, which he described as a beautiful ship. To set the scene for this tale of outstanding good fortune we return to Robert's own words -

'In 1956 we were living in London and due for home leave, so we decided to see a little more of Europe and took the Simplon-Orient Express to Genoa, Italy. Where we boarded the Italian luxury liner Andrea Doria bound for New York. A beautiful ship, excellent accommodations, superb cuisine and good service. The Atlantic Ocean favoured us with fine weather all the way until the last day out of New York, when we ran into fog. The date was July 25, 1956 and we were due to dock say 6 a.m. the following morning. We had our suitcases packed and all ready to go ashore, we were preparing to get into bed at 11:10 p.m. when there was a horrendous crash and the Doria took a serious list to starboard. The children were in an adjoining cabin and all of us were in our nightclothes; we donned our lifejackets and went up on deck to our lifeboat station to begin a long three-hour vigil straining our eyes through the fog hoping for sight of another vessel to come to our rescue.'

'It was not until later that we learned that the M.V. Stockholm, a passenger liner belonging to the Swedish American Line had collided with us, penetrating the Doria's hull on the starboard side for about 50% of the breadth. The list steadily increased, making our vigil, more and more uncomfortable, as we could neither stand nor lie down without holding on to something. The list to starboard made it impossible to launch the port lifeboats as they were of the gravity type. Shortly after 2:00 a.m. we spotted a welcome sight, creeping out of the fog, her name emblazoned on the side of her bridge in bright lights - Ile de France. As long as we live we shall never forget that stirring scene. She initiated rescue operations immediately by lowering all her lifeboats. It was not too long thereafter that with great relief; I saw Virginia and the children safely into a lifeboat. We worked all night to get everyone off the ship and by 6:00 a.m. everyone had been rescued. When I left the ship at that time the list had increased to about 85 degrees and it was possible to step from the edge of the promenade deck directly into the lifeboat where normally that deck would be forty feet above the waterline. I arrived on the Ile de France and it is hard to describe my feelings when I was met by Virginia and the family as I did not know to which of the rescue ships they had been taken. The Doria sank within three hours after the last lifeboat left her.'

'The Ile de France was outward bound for Europe with a full passenger list when she came to our rescue; she now had to return to New York to disembark the rescued passengers. As most of us were in nightwear the Captain came on the intercom and asked all his passengers and crew members to donate whatever clothes they could spare and their generosity was overwhelming, However, I had to make do with a pair of trousers donated by a French steward which were at least three sizes too small for me and no one could produce a pair of shoes to fit my outsized feet. Virginia and Madge fared not too badly but David who was then ten years old could find nothing to fit him and had to make do with a blanket. So we arrived in New York with clothing donated by passengers on the Ile de France. The next day we were most grateful to receive a suitcase of clothes from Tufts classmate, Stan Hyde, courtesy of J.C. Penny. This saga will go down in history as one of the greatest rescues at sea; 1700 people were taken off the Doria in three and a half hours. It would not have been possible without the presence of the Ile de France. It was also greatly aided by the fact that the fog which had caused the collision reversed its role and gave us a dead calm sea.'

In the weeks, months and years that followed, Robert with his marine expertise and first-hand experiences, was invited to do a number of television and newspaper interviews. The Sinking of the *Andrea Doria* made headlines around the world. Several books have also been written and depending on the nationality of the author the version of events seems to take a slightly different slant. One publication entitled - 'Saved!' written by William Hoffer begins with a synopsis, which I think says it all. 'Most people never have to face the ultimate test of courage. Yet in each of us lies the question 'What if?'

This is a synopsis of Hoffer's version of events as the perils of that encounter at sea unfolded. 'At 11:10 pm on Wednesday,

In the end 1850-1950

July 25, 1956, in the dense fog off Nantucket Island, 1,706 human beings were forced to answer the question. For at that moment the beautiful Italian passenger liner Andrea Doria was hit broadside by the Swedish liner Stockholm, whose reinforced hull was constructed to withstand the Scandinavian ice floes. The Andrea Doria was mortally wounded - a gaping hole in her side.' The aftermath of the collision and the behaviour of the crew on both ships have filled countless pages down the decades. On the 60 year Anniversary the Boston Globe printed a further account of the *Andrea Doria* story, and in an interview with Madge Young Nickerson she reminisced about that fateful night when she stood alongside her father on the deck of the *Andrea Doria* in the early evening listening to the fog horns and not realising what would soon unfold. She did recall her father's sense of foreboding at the time; fully appreciating what a dangerous situation fog presents, especially when it comes in waves. For this reason, he declared he had always disliked fog at sea.

Previously, that evening, as the *Doria* 'emerged from the haze .. Robert was shocked to see a cargo ship cutting sharply across the wake of the Andrea Doria. Much too close for comfort.' In an interview with Hoffer, Robert explained he tried hard to hide his anxiety from his family; but, his educated ear could tell the ship had not slowed, that she was still making her top speed of at least twenty-knots which was twice as fast as he deemed safe in the conditions. His training also told him that a ship is more 'tender', as Robert puts it, at the end of a voyage when its fuel and freshwater tanks are almost empty. This can make a ship top-heavy and difficult to stabilise should she take a list. Considering he was on vacation he decided to dismiss his thoughts and leave the safety of the *Andrea Doria* in the hands of Captain Calamai and his crew. It was the last night of the crossing; some passengers had decided to party on while others, like the Youngs, had retired a little earlier. Hoffer says - 'In a short time, some would see clearly how the mystical workings of chance would order lives. Others would never know.'

In an instant all frivolity and slumber gave way to an almighty bang as the blade like bow of the *Stockholm* virtually sliced into the Upper Deck of the *Andrea Doria* about one third distance along the hull. Amid splintered timbers, mangled metal and flying furniture there were bodies and cabins left broken and in ruins. On board the *Stockholm*, Chief Officer Kallback ordered the door of the collapsed crew cabins to be prized open to free the trapped sailors. Then, Chief Engineer Assargren gave orders for the pumps to be manned in order to evacuate the freshwater to right their vessel otherwise it could be lost. These quick actions did save the *Stockholm* and her passengers and crew. There was no quick action taken in relation to assisting the *Andrea Doria*: quite the contrary. Indeed, many of the Stockholm passengers would recount to Hoffer how terribly frustrating it was for them listening helplessly as the screams and cries coming out of the dark and the fog knowing that the Captain and crew of the *Stockholm* were doing nothing to help.

There was at least one miracle that night. In the aftermath of the collision, a young girl awoke to find herself staring up at the night sky. She was still lying on her mattress in her yellow Chinese print pyjamas with her arm hanging useless by her side. She cried out for her mother in Spanish but there was no answer. Now, as luck would have it, her cries were heard by the one and only Spanish speaking sailor on board the *Stockholm* and without regard for his personal safety and in the pitch dark he pushed aside debris and scrambled on in the direction of the cries in order to reach that young girl. After assessing her situation as best he could and realising her predicament, he decided to carry her to safety.

When they finally arrived at the ship's hospital the Chief Purser, Curt Dawe, was already there. When he enquired regarding her name, she replied: 'Linda Morgan'. The Purser knew immediately there was no person by that name on the *Stockholm* passenger manifest. She then suggested it could be Linda Cianfarra as perhaps she was listed under her stepfather's name. It was only when Linda enquired if it was the *Andrea Doria* that those on the *Stockholm* realised what had happened. It would be quite some time before all the pieces of the jigsaw that was Linda Morgan's story could be rightly put together. In short the *Stockholm* had sliced into the *Andrea Doria* at the position of her family's cabin and in the process had killed her stepfather, severely trapped her mother and encased Linda and her mattress in a coil of twisted metal. Then, as the *Stockholm* retreated it had taken Linda and her mattress onto the Swedish liner.

What happened next is best left to Robert's own words: 'One of the greatest sea rescues in history then took place, taking over 1700 passengers off the *Doria* within a period of four hours. This would never have been done without the aid of the S.S. Ile de France and her lifeboats.' Spoken like a true Marine Engineer, calmly relating the bare facts of the horror of that fateful night. However, these words were written some years after the event, so rest assured the reality of their predicament at the time would have had his senses heightened, as he feared for the life of his beloved Virginia and his children.

Once the call went out, numerous vessels braved the conditions that evening to sail to the aid of the *Andrea Doria*. Several Coast Guard cutters were dispatched including the *Yakutet* from Portland, the *Acushnet* from Portsmouth, *Evergreen* from Boston, the *Hornbeam* from Woods Hole, *Lagare* from New Bedford, the *Tamaroa* from New York and *The Campbell* was diverted from an Atlantic training cruise. Sixteen miles from the crash site, Captain Joseph A Boyd of the 6600-ton United Fruit Company freighter, *Cape Ann*, en route from Bremerhaven, Germany to New York steered towards the distress call. Other vessels reported in: the *Robert E. Hopkins*, a 16,000-ton tanker of the Tidewater Oil Company, the Danish freighter *Laura Maersk*, the Honduran tanker *Manaqui* and US Navy destroyer escort *Edward H. Allen*. There was also a US Navy transport ship, the *USNS Pvt. William H. Thomas*, en route from Leghorn, Italy to New York that had changed course and was already heading for the collision site when a wireless message was received from US Navy Headquarters advising the Master, Captain John S. Shea, that he had been placed in charge of rescue operations. Later, when Captain Shea was interviewed by Hoffer, he openly admitted that he held grave concerns. The *Andrea Doria* dwarfed his vessel and his intelligence was that those vessels which were already heading out collectively were still too small to accommodate the 1700 passengers. He told Hoffer all he could do was stare into the fog and pray for a miracle.

This brings us to the lauded *Ile de France*. She was far away from the collision site, in fact, at the 'edge of responsibility', and consequently the decision to answer or ignore the call was entirely in the hands and heart of the fifty-three year Master, Baron Raoul de Beaudéan. It was going to be a big decision for him to make. He had nine hundred passengers on board the *Ile de France* expecting to disembark in Le Havre, France on schedule. If he turned around he could be reprimanded if the situation was not a <u>true emergency</u>. To further complicate matters, he was only a substitute Captain, and this was his first voyage in command of this flagship of the French Line. In his later interview with Hoffer, he confessed that 'The *Andrea Doria* .. must have been the large ship he saw ... on the radar as the Ile de France had passed about ten miles south of the Nantucket Lightship.'

De Beaudéan added that the *Doria's* pip seemed to merge with that of the Lightship and he had jokingly said to his Officer on the Bridge at the time: 'He is sinking the lightship!' De Beaudéan went to great lengths to explain to Hoffer that radar at such a distance could give only an approximate reading of the true position of another ship and 'It was inconceivable to him that the beautiful, seaworthy *Andrea Doria* could be in danger, yet no captain issues an SOS without good reason.' 'At 11:54 the Baron made his decision. He would go to the *Andrea Doria*. As the great French Liner moved into a sweeping turn that headed it back to the west, Captain de Beaudean ordered his engine crew to increase speed from the cruising velocity of 22 knots to the maximum 24 knots. He doubled the watch and asked for volunteers to man eleven of the ship's thirty-two lifeboats.'

Throughout the ordeal, Captain Calamai of the *Andrea Doria*, had been uncommunicative, he had conveyed none of the rescue information or plans to his distraught passengers and with the *Doria's* power resources dwindling Calamai decided to send up several flares, but the red light was immediately absorbed by the dense fog and darkness. The *Doria* would have to rely on her signal lights to guide any potential rescue ships. At this point it was all a waiting game, including for Robert, Virginia and the children. Second Officer Badano on board the *Doria* decided to double-check their position. He went into the chartroom with

Cadet Maracci and took another loran fix. [LORAN is short for long range navigation and was a hyperbolic radio navigation system developed in the United States during World War II. It was similar to the UK's Gee system but operated at lower frequencies in order to provide an improved range up to 1,500 miles (2,400 km) with an accuracy of tens of miles.] He was correct the first time: the *Andrea Doria* was nineteen miles west of the Nantucket Lightship and sixty miles south of the coast. He went directly to the radio room and double-checked with the Radio Officer to ensure the co-ordinates he had transmitted in the original SOS were 40° 30', 69° 53'.

Despite Calamai signalling the *Stockholm* for assistance Captain Nordenson made no response. Two hours had passed, Nordenson had secured his own ship, and then at 1:08 a.m. the *Stockholm* lowered two of her powered lifeboats - a pitifully inadequate gesture way too late. Meanwhile, Captain de Beaudéan proceeded with caution. The fog was thick, and was the worst kind, lifting and then setting in again. When he saw pips on his radar he sent a message to the Coast Guard advising 'The situation is critical. Visibility is nil.' The *Ile de France* continued to drift in slowly, finally got a fix on the *Doria* and then manoeuvred to the starboard side. He could now see the extent of her list and was concerned she would capsize or worst still that his lifeboats could get sucked into the gaping hole in her side. At 400 yards he slowed his engines - 160 crew were standing at the ready to man eleven large lifeboats. Captain de Beaudéan told Hoffer he 'could now hear the screams and prayers of' the trapped passengers.' Then 'Hoping to make his presence known to the Andrea Doria, the Baron ordered his powerful outside lights switched on.' What a sight that would have been, but alas the passengers were far from saved!

To say the crew of the *Andrea Doria* behaved improperly is a massive understatement especially when so many of the first-hand accounts are taken into consideration. It was only at this point Calamai finally issued orders for the *Doria's* lifeboats to be lowered and the crew, unbeknown to many of the passengers, abandoned their assigned stations, ripped off the canvas covers and climbed inside themselves. An Alderman from Toronto managed to scramble into one of the *Doria* lifeboats, which he later reported to Hoffer was carrying forty crew and four passengers including himself. The crew motored away while there were still dozens of empty seats. Pandemonium is all that can be said about what was happening above and below deck. Children were tossed onto steel decks and passengers were releasing injured passengers from the wreckage. Except for a mere handful, the crew were nowhere to be seen. Oil had bubbled up from the bilge making floors and stairways treacherously slippery. After Robert Young got his family on deck he went back down to offer help and at one point called for a hydraulic jack to unfurl steel to release a trapped passenger. Six hours had passed, and the Captain and his remaining Officers left in what they thought would be the last lifeboat - it was now 5:30 a.m. July 26, 1956.

'What the captain did not know, as his lifeboat headed for one of the nearby Navy ships, was that not everyone had left the *Andrea Doria*. One passenger, very much alive, had been left behind.' Robert Hudson had slept soundly for the first night in weeks thanks to a narcotic prescribed for his back injury. It was 5:10 a.m. when he stirred to discover the lights in his cabin did not work. He felt around, expecting to feel a mattress, instead he felt steel bulkhead. He reached for his cigarette lighter and as his eyes adjusted to the semi-darkness, he saw a faint amber glow in the corridor. Why was his cabin door wide open? Robert Hudson's cabin was on the starboard side of the ship, and as he sat up and swung his legs over the side of his bed he felt water on the floor. As he made for the door he realised there was oily water inches deep all around him. He called out but there was no reply.

Hoffer's interview with Hudson is nothing short of spine tingling. 'Ghost ship,' Hudson muttered to himself. 'My God! She's going down' was his first thought. He struggled to make sense out of anything he was experiencing as he made his way along the corridor and out on deck. As unbelievable as it seems, it took him an hour to reach the Promenade Deck. This was because he had to feel his way in the dark, deal with the list of the ship, avoid the rubbish floating all around and not fall over given the slippery oil smeared conditions. The sight that eventually greeted him would have been arresting - deck-chairs and other broken furniture littered the low side, passenger items and ship debris was everywhere, and with dangerous oily sludge seeping through his toes and dressed only in his underpants he was now in the open air. Visibility had slightly improved because dawn was edging over the horizon as he cautiously headed for the stern. All of a sudden a wave rushed in and dashed him overboard into the surging swirling cold ocean.

Coughing and spluttering he got his head above the water; he then saw a lifeboat about three hundred yards away. He cried out for help. A flashlight winked, but alas, the lifeboat did not move. He called again. The flashlight blinked again and this time it fixed on him. They saw him. Still they did not move. Then his brain kicked into gear, he remembered his merchant marine training: when a ship is going down a lifeboat must stand off at least three hundred yards to avoid being sucked down in the vortex. All the while, waves were continually dashing his already battered body against the ship. He honestly recalled to Hoffer how he then let out a string of abuse, 'curses as vile as any seaman ever uttered. They rang loudly and clearly across the waters. The sailors in the safety of their lifeboat heard their parentage, courage, and manhood questioned in bitter epithets. But they would not move in.'

He was beginning to tire. With only a net to cling to every wave was threatening to wash him away, the undercurrent pulled at him as the water receded. He was thrown back against the ship time after time. While he knew he was once an excellent swimmer, now he feared his back injury would inhibit his ability to escape the terrible suction. He made eye contact with the lifeboat crew. They did not budge. He cursed them again, he prayed, he begged and as the sun rose higher, he felt himself succumbing to mental exhaustion and decided to just lay back; resigned to his fate as his tears were washed away by the stinging saltwater. He was almost delirious - he was ready to let go and just slip away when for some unexplained reason he saw the oars spring into action and the small boat shoot forward. They covered the three hundred yards in five minutes. It was now 7:30am and as they reached the stern of the *Doria* two sailors reached for Hudson, dragged him aboard fighting the suction and the current. There was no time to waste. Finally, the craft broke free and made a dash for safety. One sailor on the boat gave Hudson his coat. At this point Hudson began to feel his wounds burning from the saltwater, and he had a hot burning sensation up and down his spine. But he was saved!

After giving Hudson his coat the officer from the *Robert E Hopkins* enquired if he was now feeling better. Hudson's reply came - 'I'd feel better if I had that bottle of Scotch I left under my bed.' With a wry smile the Officer replied - 'I don't have any Scotch but I've got some mighty good bourbon in my room.' Hoffer continues the story: 'As the only survivor on the tanker, he was a celebrity. Crewmen outfitted him with clothes. As Hudson sat on the deck, staring at the hulk of the Andrea Doria, he told his story over and over. The Officer from the lifeboat produced a fifth of bourbon. Robert Hudson drank every last drop.'

Once Robert saw Virginia and his children down the ropes and into a lifeboat, he remained at the rail to help others. At this point he was approached by a desperate looking crewman who asked Robert to get a jack because there was a woman trapped below. Initially Robert's requests were not acknowledged by the French speaking crewmember of the lifeboat. Finally, Robert enquired of yet another sailor on a lifeboat, this time he got a positive response from the American on board. Eventually, a jack was secured on the *Doria* and passed to crewmember Rovelli who proceeded below to where Thure Peterson was attempting to free his wife, Martha from the debris on top of her in Cabin 56 on the Upper Deck. Alas, it was now 4.10 am and despite their most valiant efforts Martha Peterson did not survive her harrowing injuries and entombment.

William Hoffer wrote a fitting epilogue to his documentary on the Sinking of the *Andrea Doria*. In it he says - 'Robert Young, the shipping inspector who had an early premonition of danger on the afternoon prior to the collision, is today president and chairman of the board of the American Bureau of Shipping.'

For his heroic work in rescuing the passengers and crew of the *Andrea Doria*, Captain Baron Raoul de Beaudéan was decorated as an Officer de la Legion d'Honour. Unfortunately, Carstens-Johannsen, who was in command of the bridge of the *Stockholm*, continued to sail until 1965. As for the *Andrea Doria*, Giovanni Rovelli, the heroic steward who laboured alongside Dr Thure Peterson in cabin 56 for five anguished hours rightly continued to work as a steward until his retirement in 1970. Osvaldo Magagnini, second in command of the *Andrea Doria* that night, continued to Captain several other Italian Line ships until he retired in 1963. As for Captain Piero Calamai, who was the Master of the *Andrea Doria* on that ill-fated voyage; he immediately retired to his home in Genoa and was described by his family as a father who had lost a son. He avoided discussing the tragedy with his family to his dying day; 'Then, on his deathbed in April 1972, in a final delirium, he cried out to his older daughter, Marina, 'Is it all right? Are the passengers saved?'

The *Stockholm* was repaired and left New York for Gothenburg in December of 1956 and remained in service on the same Trans-Atlantic route until 1960.

As for the *Andrea Doria*, she remains 225 feet beneath the surface of the Atlantic Ocean approximately nineteen miles south of Nantucket Lightship.

As for Robert Young and his family, they eventually went on to enjoy their home leave in the US before sailing back to London where Robert's career went from strength to strength. One of the highlights of 1960 was when he acted as Technical Advisor to the Liberian Government, then in '66 he was nominated Technical Advisor to the International Convention for Safety of Life at Sea being held in London. He was also appointed Chairman Emeritus of the Board of Trustees of Webb Institute of Naval Architecture, Glen Cove, N.Y. Robert presented numerous papers on topics related to the strength and seaworthiness of ships and safety of life at sea. He even wrote a book entitled - 'The Water Transportation Industry'. During the final years of his London posting Robert not only assumed additional responsibility for ABS operations across all of Western Europe, he also accepted an invitation from People-to-People International to lead a delegation of Naval Architects and Marine Engineers on a technical exchange to locations in the United Kingdom, West Germany, Scandinavia and Poland. This is a very prestigious organisation instigated by President Eisenhower.

As has been shown time and time again, the Youngs like to participate and give back to their profession and their communities. Robert Tyrrell Young is another who shares this family value. Throughout his working life he maintained membership of a number of professional associations including The Society of Naval Architects & Marine Engineers of which he is not only a Past President but served as a Member of the Executive, Finance, Budget and Endowment Committees. He was a Fellow of both The Royal Institute of Naval Architects and The Institute of Marine Engineers of the United Kingdom, and a Life Member of The American Welding Society. He is a Past Chairman of the Welding Research Council of the U.S.A. Robert also served on various Committees with SNAME - The Society of Naval Architects and Marine Engineers - during the 70s and from 1977-79 he served as President of SNAME. In 1979 he was made an Honorary Member of the Society.

Meanwhile, back in 1968, after thirty years of service with the ABS, Robert found himself back in New York where it all began. He was promoted to the position of Vice-President, Research & Development. 1971 he was appointed President and Chairman of the Board, and upon receiving this appointment Robert T. Young is quoted as saying - 'It is, of course, a great honour for me to be elected Chairman and President. When I joined the organisation 33 years ago, as a young man not long out of college, I certainly never dreamed that I would spend more than half my life working for the Bureau and would one day become its principal officer. Following in Mr. Neilson's capable footsteps will be a challenging task; during his tenure, the Bureau has taken remarkable strides forward, and we are all keenly aware of the debt which we owe him. I hope that, with the help of everyone connected with the Bureau, I will continue Mr. Neilson's good work.' Robert continued as Chairman and President of ABS until his retirement in 1979.

This is an excerpt from Robert Tyrrell Young's retirement speech:

> 'I have had a very rewarding life and career, having visited 93 different countries, to 88 of which Virginia accompanied me.
>
> She and I were fortunate in having been able to make two photographic safaris to East Africa. They were both memorable experiences that anyone who loves nature and wildlife should not miss.
>
> Such success as I may have had I attribute to two things: the advice and full support of my dear wife, Virginia, and the fine education that I received at Tufts.'

Recognition, acknowledgement and appreciation for the outstanding contribution made by this Robert Young is unending. In 1992 The Webb Institute awarded him an Honorary Doctor of Science Degree.

Robert Tyrrell Young died on the 28 August 1996.

This particular voyage through the lives of this Young Family has come to an end, we have reached port and it's time to tie up. We have journeyed far and to all points of the compass. We can't help but marvel at the endurance and grit of those brave mariners of yesterday. Several of their fellow travellers have amazed us with their tales of those harrowing days in Arctic waters where death and destruction were constant companions, where survival was a minute by minute challenge and where brazen choices were made in order to once again smell the sweet heather of home and feel the warmth of their own hearth. Alas, all too often success here came down to the roll of a dice.

Those journeys taken by vanguard Arctic whalers like Robert Young [1723-1797] and his son Alexander [1750-1817] set the future direction and fortune for this family for generations to come and enabled others to sail through unchartered waters to new frontiers. Armed with a clear head and a sound education, many seized opportunities and many more moved with the times, stepping out of their comfort zones and embracing technology on a global scale. Along the way their names and deeds have been linked to many of the major institutions, events and people benchmarking history in their Scottish homeland and on several continents. Ambition was plentiful, success was always their goal - failure was never entertained.

Conclusion

Threads, Loose Ends and Dispelling Myths

Logic will get you from A to B.
Imagination will take you everywhere.

Albert Einstein

Threads .....

When I began this journey of revelation, I had several goals in mind. One was to expose this family's inter- and intra- generational maritime legacy, whilst along the way hoping to clarify how the concept of 'Nature & Nurture' might have influenced this family's unique involvement with maritime pursuits. As time went by, it became clear to me that it was no accident that so many of these Young descendants had the sea and all things maritime weaving in and out of their lives. Time and time again I found examples of where they chose marital and business partners whose family histories and community credibility in seafaring and commerce would have shored up their own family's heritage. When all is said and done there is little doubt these behaviours had become intrinsic - a natural way of being.

Along with the many stories of heroism and hard work there have been countless instances where this family's shared values of Honesty, Integrity, Leadership, Devoutness and Camaraderie have shone through. I am pleased to say, that almost three centuries on, these qualities have prevailed and remain a characteristic to be found in many of the current generation. Some would argue this is Nature but from my own life experience, and as a self-confessed Empiricist, I would assert these are values predominantly influenced by environment and taken on via osmosis as individuals resolved to embrace the examples of those closest to them – their family.

Further evidence to substantiate such a general view was discovered in a study undertaken recently, based on a set of identical triplets: three boys separated at birth. Their story is compelling and as it unfolds consideration of the question of 'Nature & Nurture' is unavoidable. Their lives pre and post their eventual meeting when the lads were 19 years of age, later became the subject of a Documentary presented at Sundance Film Festival in 2018. It is entitled 'Three Identical Strangers' and was the work of Pulitzer-prize winning Journalist, Lawrence Wright and film-maker Tim Wardle. In compiling their evidence, they consulted with various professionals whose academic work had been focused on this area of the Humanities. Put simply, what their film highlighted and what these three lads' stories exemplified, is that outcomes in life can be extremely varied, despite common genetics.

Loose Ends .....

The telling of this story of the Youngs was undertaken to give an accurate sociological insight into the lives of some of the proven ancestors. The starting point was chosen simply because conjecture surrounds records prior to Circa 1650, making them less reliable. Whilst the research to date has disclosed this family sat on the periphery of some notable individuals, this alone has been construed by some as an indication of their own social status and for those passionate researchers who dream of finding some tangible link to the rich or famous, this instantly becomes the 'holy grail'. From that point some felt comfortable with making a loose connection, some even took a quantum leap, and what began as an unfounded assumption becomes a new reality.

Conclusion

In the case of those researching the surname of Young it is quite enticing and teasing when British Heraldic and Peerage registers offer no less than twenty-eight entries for the name Young or Younge. However, enthusiasm wanes a little when it is realised only five of these refer to Scottish families. Paradoxically, this narrowing of the field once more offers encouragement when it is found four of these families have Crests sharing a common basis: i.e. they have at their core 'three piles' with three overlaying annulets. For those unfamiliar with these matters - piles look like the pointed end of a sword and generally signify military leadership or significant deeds, and annulets are rings or closed circles, a symbol from Roman times which relates to continuity or wholeness. This commonality could be construed to signify some connection in genealogy but, is that a fair assumption? And, where is the proof?

Remaining with the theme of Crests for a moment, each of the five Scottish Crests sharing this core show wide variation in respect of the other embellishments included. For instance - The *Young of Leny* crest is distinguished by adding a dexter arm [the Scottish lion's arm with paw spread] holding a lance. The *Young of Edinburgh* crest has a large chief which is a band significant of prudence and wisdom or success in command of a war. The *Young of Eastfield* crest has a six point star plus a dexter hand/paw holding a pen. The *Young of Auld Bar* crest shows a lion rising out of a wreath where a lion is generally symbolic of the deathless courage of a valiant warrior.

Finally, this brings us to the Crest favoured by many in connection with this family – that of *Young of Rosebank*. It has the previously mentioned base consisting of the three piles and annulets and is topped by an anchor emerging out of the sea, surmounted by a dove with an olive branch in its beak. Interestingly, an anchor on a coat of arms may symbolise a family's association with the sea, or alternatively, it can represent salvation and hope. The dove and olive branch are predictably related to peace. The *Young of Rosebank* crest also differentiates itself by bearing the inscription 'Sperando Spiro' which is Latin and when loosely translated becomes: 'Breathing Hope'.

Now, from this point the plot thickens slightly!

For those in possession of memorabilia belonging to Alexander Young [1750-1817] they have long known he had a seal on his watch fob. This seal was basically rectangular in shape with hex ends. It had an oval at the bottom containing Alexander's initials in italics. This oval was topped by an anchor sitting on waves and atop that anchor is a bird. Across the top he too included the Latin words 'SPERANDO SPIRO'. Does this guarantee his connection to any of the above families - absolutely not!

Time to put these matters of Latin Mottos and Crests into perspective ...

From the earliest days of education in Scotland, Latin was a set subject but only for the heirs of wealthy landowners. Since the titled upper class males were those leading armies into battle, slogans and mottos were popularised in times of war and used as a rallying cry to action - for example 'A Deo et rege' was 'For God and King'. It follows that if any family or person decided to adopt a motto the selection of a Latin phrase was a mark of their education and status. Centuries before Alexander's time, these slogans became quite commonplace, almost fashionable one could assert. Whilst 'Sperando Spiro' does not exist on the list of most commonly cited Latin phrases, 'optima sperando spiro' does. It translates to - 'by hoping for the best things, I stay alive'. Placing this information into the context of the social order for this family, it is easy to see why someone who possessed ambition would choose to elevate his status by: firstly, having a seal made, and secondly, to likewise select an <u>appropriate but not exclusive</u> embellishment.

There is no doubt that Alexander Young Snr was aspirational, and the previous dissection of his Will gives a clear indication of the business success and the financial status he achieved. This would most assuredly have elevated him to a status where a seal would be absolutely appropriate and would have ensured that his son Alexander carried on the tradition. Or did the seal belong to the father?

Were either of these men aware of another family with the surname of Young associated with the sea? Most assuredly, because there were several so employed, living in England and Scotland. Official Scottish Records list seafaring Scots with the surname of Young linked to the major ports of Leith, Edinburgh,

Dundee, Montrose and Aberdeen. Were they in this time frame directly related to any of these families? Highly unlikely. Was there a covenant or embargo on the use of any motto or embellishment on a seal? Definitely not. So, by extrapolation, this left Alexander Snr and Jnr entirely free to nominate a design and phrase of their own choosing. Was he aware of the *Young of Rosebank* family? Quite possibly.

Dispelling Myths ....

For those who are still holding fast to the ideal of *Young of Rosebank* – here are the facts you will need to consider in making such a final judgement call.

Sir Thomas Young is the man listed in Heraldic Records as the person who adopted the crest for *Young of Rosebank*. Thomas was the youngest son of Walter Young [1610-1685], a Merchant in Edinburgh, and Isobell Wightman [1616-]. They were married in Edinburgh in 1636. Walter Young's lineage runs to his father Robert Young [1589-] and mother Jonet Liddell [C1590 -], then to grand-father Robert Young [1543-]. Sir Thomas [1647-1712] was at one time a Baillie in Edinburgh and also Theasurer [Treasurer] in Edinburgh. His <u>only surviving son</u>, Thomas, entered the Army and served as Ensign in Sir James Wood's Regiment, the 21st Royal Scots Fusiliers, and later as Colonel in the Foot Guards. Thomas Jnr. became heir to his father in 1713 and died at the Abbey of Holyrood in May 1721. The Peerage records list no further male heirs.

Another publication entitled *'History of Edinburgh from its Foundation to the Present Time In Nine Books'* et al. holds transcriptions for the parishes of Canongate, St. Cuthbert, and other parishes in Edinburgh. There is one particular transcript of a tombstone from Old Church Gray-Friars which reads - 'Here lieth Walter Young Merchant in Edinburgh, and Isobel Wightman his Spouse, with several of their Children; As also Marjory Ker his second Spouse. He died 20 March 1685, being the 74th Year of his Age. Here lyeth also Mary Kirland [sic],

Spouse to Thomas Young, late Town Thesaurer of Edinburgh (afterward Bailie of Edinburgh, now Sir Thomas Young of Rosebank) and Son of the said Walter Young, with several of their Children. She died the 20th February 1686, being the 29th Year of her Age.'

In the course of researching any possible *Young of Rosebank* connection, I happened upon yet another burial inscription from Gray-Friars which was wholly in Latin. The translation reads - 'To the pious Memory of Mr Michael Young, doctor of Physick; of Mr Robert Young, a faithful Preacher of the Gospel. The former died in the Month of January 1677, and the latter in that of October 1675; and to the Memory of their most beloved sister, Mary Young, who exchanged Life for Death in February 1679, Thomas Kinkaid Chirurgeon and Apothecary at Edinburgh, surviving Husband to the said Mary, caused this Monument to be set up. At Length here lyes the said Thomas Kinkaid of Auchinreoch, who practised Surgery and Pharmacy in this City for the Space of forty five Years, with equal Skill and Success. Good in his Life, prudent and honest in his Actions, Ingenuous, and without Guile in his Words; which occasioned his being beloved by all good Men; whereby he acquired Wealth, Fame, Honour and Friends: And having left seven children by one Wife, with fifteen Grandchildren he died much lamented, on February the 18th, in the Year of our Lord 1691, and of his Age the 72.'

These individuals are linked to a Scottish family bearing the name of Young of Auchenskeoch, a seventeenth century tower house in Dumfriesshire. This family also owned a cotton plantation by the name of Rosebank on the island of Tobago during the 1700s. Robert Young of Auchenskeoch was the son of Lieutenant Alexander Young of that ilk and brother to William Young. Robert Young has been variously described as a West India Merchant. The original grantee of Rosebank Plantation was the aforementioned William Young who held other plantation leases at the same time and whose wife Harriot Herries subsequently sold Rosebank Plantation and its slaves in 1798. It is recorded she came into possession of Rosebank upon the death of William's brother Robert in 1787 as per Robert's Will and codicil drawn up in Brugge, Belgium and proved at Granada that year.

Conclusion

Heraldic records further show Thomas Young Snr did not receive his knighthood until 1672 and this is also the year when the Rosebank Crest and motto were first registered. Our Young family have no known connection to this family other than to say they share the same surname and were also residents of Edinburgh in a similar time period. It is proved that our Alexander Young [1750-1817] was the son of another Robert Young [1723-1797] and Janet Lundie [1731-1794, and if current research holds true his lineage can be traced confidently backwards through John Young [1680-1732] and Margaret Dick [1686-1743], then to David Young [1650-1706] and Margaret Thomson [1651-1709], especially when it is proven the full names of these ancestors, both male and female, are included across descendant families for several generations.

Preliminary research is being pursued which tentatively takes this Young family even further back in time: to a George Young [1616-1664] cited as son of John Young [1597-1648] and Agnes Paton [C1597-], that John, father, is probably the son of George Young [1568-] and Helene Rankene [1570-], and that George is the thought to be the son of John Young [1540-1596/7] and Elizabeth Esele/Eisele [C1542-]. Lastly, it is highly probable that John's parents will be proved to be Duncan Young [C1514-] and Sara Scrymgeour [C1516-] who married in Canongate Church in Edinburgh, 12 February 1539. Given that all these parental records are being further researched along with the full sibling groups in each of these families, no evidence has yet emerged connecting any individual or family member to anyone associated with either Sir Thomas Young or *Young of Rosebank*.

www.ingramcontent.com/pod-product-compliance
Lightning Source LLC
Chambersburg PA
CBHW051615020526
44118CB00034BB/1025